The Art of Handmade Paper and Collage

Transforming the Ordinary into the Extraordinary

FIBER STUDIO PRESS

An Imprint of
Martingale & Company

Cheryl Stevenson

Untitled collage, 14" x 12". (Collection of Kerry and Chris Smith)

Title page: Untitled collage, 30" x 30". (Collection of Louise and Lloyd Olson)

Back cover: "Stormy Sunset," 28" x 24". Handmade paper, embossing, and resists. (Collection of Nancy Nelson)

Credits

Editor-in-Chief
Kerry I. Smith

Technical Editor
Melissa A. Lowe

Managing Editor
Judy Petry

Copy Editor
Tina Cook

Design Director
Cheryl Stevenson

Cover Designer
David Chrisman

Text Designer
Kay Green

Design Assistant
Marijane E. Figg

Illustrator
Laurel Strand

Photographer
Brent Kane

The Art of Handmade Paper and Collage:
Transforming the Ordinary
into the Extraordinary
© 1998 by Cheryl Stevenson

Martingale & Company
PO Box 118
Bothell, WA 98041-0118 USA

Printed in Hong Kong
01 02 01 00 99 98   6 5 4 3 2 1

Library of Congress Cataloging-in-Publication Data
Stevenson, Cheryl
    The art of handmade paper and collage : transforming the ordinary into the extraordinary / Cheryl Stevenson.
      p. cm.
    Includes bibliographical references.
    ISBN 1-56477-156-3
    1. Paper, Handmade. 2. Papermaking. 3. Collage. I. Title.
TS1124.5.S74   1998
676'.22—DC21
                         97-44459
                             CIP

FIBER
STUDIO
PRESS

MISSION STATEMENT
We are dedicated to providing quality products and service by working together to inspire creativity and to enrich the lives we touch.

ACKNOWLEDGMENTS

Special thanks to Kerry Smith for encouraging me to write this book, and to the rest of the staff at Martingale & Company for cheering me along as my work progressed. My thanks to Tina Cook and Melissa Lowe for the polish and clarity their editing added, and to Kay Green and the rest of the production staff who labored over this book with love. A special thank-you to Brent Kane, whose skill as a photographer brought this material to life.

Thanks to all the artists who take the step to publish and share their work—my work has been shaped by every author whose work I've read. Some of those who have influenced the work in this book most directly are Velda Newman and Laura Reinstatler, with their love of and extraordinary work with flowers, and Gail Valentine and Paula Nadelstern, with their love of and work with kaleidoscope images.

Thanks also to the staff at Cottages at Hedgebrook, where my time as a writer-in-residence provided me with the encouragement I needed to keep writing.

DEDICATION

This book is dedicated to my husband, Barry, whose unfailing love and support provide a place for me to bloom; to my mother and father, for their belief in me; and to Mary Dent, who helped me find my way home.

"Floral Study III," 28" x 28". Handmade paper and watercolor dyes, embossed vase. (Private collection)

Contents

"In the Garden,"
34" x 10".
(Collection of Trish Carey)

C. Stevenson

Introduction

When I was young, I was surrounded by creative, imaginative people. The most influential was my mother, who worked hard to nurture her children's imagination and creativity. When I was seven years old, she showed me how to add curved lines to my still awkward tree trunks to make them look round. I remember my sense of awe that a few simple lines could change things so much.

Thanks to my mother, grandmother, and an elderly neighbor, I learned to sew and cook and draw and paint and "do crafts," to knit and crochet, and to love the intricacies of embroidery. As a teenager, I dreamed of having my own shop where I would sell every art or craft material imaginable, with a place for everyone to take classes, and a place for me to paint.

In my twenties, I explored a variety of crafts and art media. I worked as a professional seamstress. I made dolls of all sizes and varieties. I drew and painted. I completed intricate embroidered pictures. I explored appliqué, completing many wall hangings and a few quilts. Looking back, I

can see that a central theme of my explorations was a love of texture, color, and layers.

Gradually, I became more and more fascinated with translating images from photos into other media, such as embroidery and appliqué. My first large-scale project was a quilt commissioned in 1976. A coworker showed me a calendar based on J.R.R. Tolkein's The Lord of the Rings. The calendar art was the work of the Brothers Hildebrandt. She asked me to design a quilt based on the books and calendar art. Intrigued by the challenge, and completely unsure where it would take me, I said yes.

No material or method was out of bounds in my attempt to translate the colors and textures of the calendar into fabric. I still remember the thrill of finding just the right fabric for the sky and the weird olive fake fur for the Ents. I painted and sewed back and forth over white fake fur to simulate an explosion in one panel. I applied gold rivets and jewels to simulate a dragon's treasure trove for another panel. Sewing through an aluminum pie plate to make armor was not good for my sewing machine, but it

Éowyn fights the Nazgûl Lord

worked! A panel that was not included in the final quilt is shown on the facing page.

Several years later, I was commissioned to make a quilt for the maternity ward at Northwest Hospital in Seattle, Washington. The theme was "Children Around the World," and I based my design on a series of UNICEF cards. I went off in my usual direction, painting children in national dress on muslin and embellishing the costumes with all sorts of things to make them dimensional. The women who commissioned the quilt were quite surprised with the result; it didn't look like a traditional pieced quilt. Fortunately, though, they liked it.

Looking back, I can see that the projects I completed during this period really were collages. However, it wasn't until I took a university class in my thirties that I was introduced formally to the "art" concept of collage and began to explore the medium of paper. These early collages, like the diptych "Sunflowers" at right, focused on magazine pictures.

Later, I got to know an artist whose collages featured a wide variety of materials, including the handmade and specialty papers available at many art stores. I loved the richness these papers added to her collages, but at the time, I had very little money for extras like handmade paper. After viewing a television program on making paper using simple tools and recycled materials, I set out to see if I could make my own specialty papers.

I made my first papermaking mould by stapling an old organdy curtain around a wooden picture frame I found at a thrift shop. What a thrill to see that first piece of paper form! Soon, I had sheets of paper drying everywhere. By experimenting, I found that I could produce an incredible variety of paper using a wide range of recycled materials. This led to using bits and scraps of materials that were inexpensive or free—puzzle pieces; stamps; discarded wrapping paper; snippets of yarn, fabric, and threads; discontinued wallpaper books; dried flowers. I was hooked!

Two early handmade-paper collages featuring embossing and sewing

"Sunflowers," 48" x 36". (Collection of Harvey and Henrietta Senecal)

In the classes I teach, I am always surprised and pleased that other people experience some of the same feelings of delight that I do. It is a thrill to see the unique and wonderful directions each student's work takes and the pleasure it provides them.

I wrote this book so that other people would have a guidebook while exploring all that handmade paper and collage have to offer. I wanted to share the techniques and ideas I had developed from my experimentation and play.

Whatever your level of training or experience as an artist, if you are regularly up to your elbows in art materials in a way you love, you'll never stop learning. With handmade paper and collage, you can explore a wide range of materials and methods, experimenting with anything that catches your attention. With this in mind, I designed the processes and projects in this book as a kind of playground, one that will also help you to develop your own ideas and creativity.

USING THIS BOOK

The Art of Handmade Paper and Collage is organized into three parts: papermaking, collage, and projects.

Papermaking

People have been making paper for centuries, but the very first papermaker was the humble wasp. The female wasp chews pieces of plants or dead wood, reducing these fragments to fibers and mixing them with saliva. When the wasp spits this mixture onto the nest, it hardens into a cardboardlike material. The papermaking process isn't much different. Plant materials are broken down into fibers, usually with the addition of chemicals, then reformed as paper. There are many places where this process is still done by hand, and there are many interesting books on the subject.

"Dogwood Blossoms" (above), 18" x 30". Embossed and painted paper, wallpaper, and stamp. (Collection of Lois LaShell)

Early handmade-paper collage featuring embossed paper

Wasp's nest detail

Rather than start from scratch, I prefer to recycle existing paper. The idea of making paper from recycled materials is not new. In Europe, for instance, papermakers used to buy old cotton garments and rags to make into paper.

I gather discarded paper in much the same way. I change it back to fibers by tearing it into pieces, soaking it, and putting it through a blender. Then I remove these fibers from the water in one of several different ways and make them into paper again. My handmade paper has a very different look and feel from the paper I began with.

The papermaking process described in this book requires little skill to begin and provides great satisfaction. Once you know the basics, you'll be able to produce an amazing variety of paper; the process invites playfulness and experimentation. The paper you make in this first section can be used in the projects that follow, so take a few minutes to review them, then select materials to recycle with a project in mind. What if you want to begin directly with one of the projects? Many wonderful handmade and specialty papers are available at art or craft stores or through the catalogs listed in the back of this book, and they can be substituted for the handmade paper called for in the projects.

Collage

Like papermaking, collage has been around for a long time. Although it is now recognized as an art form, making collages is a part of everyday life as well. Did you make valentines as a child, gluing together paper shapes and lace doilies? The artist Henri Matisse used this same technique, cutting shapes from paper and gluing them down, as studies for his paintings. Have you ever put together memorabilia in a scrap book or a frame, organizing the pieces to look good together? Many art collages include these same elements.

Collage is a friendly process with simple and enjoyable tasks—collecting materials, layering and arranging them in a pleasing way, and gluing them in place. Yet this simple process can take you in directions limited only by what you collect. Collecting materials will change forever the way you look at everything around you and give new life to many bits and pieces destined for the trash. My students tell me (and I would agree) that the more materials you

have to choose from in creating a collage, the more satisfying the process. You might want to skim "Collage Basics" (pages 44–51), then begin looking for materials.

Projects

The reason I've included the projects in this book is simple. I love to do them.

I started out many years ago creating greeting cards. I loved the small scale of these collages, and I could work on many at once. As I gained confidence and began spending more time on the composition of each collage, I began to work on a bigger scale. I call these larger pieces Found-Materials collages, and they can absorb me for hours and days and sometimes weeks. I like to have several in progress at once.

My Kaleidoscope collages take the process a step further. I make color photocopies of a Found-Materials collage, then cut them apart to reassemble in a kaleidoscope pattern, magnifying the richness and intricacy of the original piece.

The last project reflects my enduring fascination with flowers. This paper-sculpture project will give you a chance to see how truly versatile handmade paper is and to begin designing your own flowers in paper.

One last thing before you begin. Have you ever turned the car down an intriguing side road for the sheer pleasure of finding out where it will take you? My hope is that using *The Art of Handmade Paper and Collage* will be like taking that side road for you. Although the processes and projects in this book provide you with detailed instructions, where you go each time will be a surprise.

Handmade-paper flower
with machine stitching

PART ONE

The Art of Papermaking

"Texture Study II," 32" x 18". Embossed, glue resist, overdyed, and bleached. (Collection of Nancy and Dennis Nelson)

When I make paper, I become completely absorbed in the process. It's hard for me to hurry. The feel of the materials under my hands and the possibilities of each sheet can seduce me into spending hours making paper.

I'm lucky to live where I can leave my papermaking materials set up for days at a time, but I've been just as productive in a corner of the kitchen or garage. If you can't leave your papermaking equipment set up for a few days, plan to make paper when you have at least two to three hours. After you become adept at the papermaking process, you'll be able to make a great many sheets of paper in that time. If you change the color and texture of the paper bath as you go, you can dramatically increase the variety of paper produced in one session.

To make paper, you need some simple equipment and supplies. It's nice to work near a water source, such as a sink or garden hose, but you can get around this by making trips back and forth to get water.

This chapter guides you through the equipment, materials, and steps for making paper. If you enjoy it, I encourage you to investigate the many excellent books devoted to papermaking. For more information, see page 94.

"Texture Study I," 18" x 32". Embossed, watercolor dye, crayon resist, and coffee overdye. (Collection of Nancy and Dennis Nelson)

PAPERMAKING
BASICS

The basic equipment, materials, and processes are simple. Once you get started, you can recycle, color, collage, cast, and create! You are limited only by your imagination.

EQUIPMENT

Plastic Containers

You need a number of containers for soaking scraps of paper and storing paper pulp. I like to use yogurt, cottage cheese, and ice cream containers. I have several old ice cream pails and large yogurt containers that I use constantly. Do not reuse these for food preparation or storage.

Plastic Drop Cloth

Papermaking can be a wet and messy process. Cover your work area with a plastic drop cloth if it isn't waterproof. I've made paper in many settings, some of them carpeted, and have had no major problems, but a little care in setting things up goes a long way.

Purchase a heavy plastic drop cloth from a hardware store and cut it to size. It will last a long time.

Blender

You must have a blender specifically for papermaking. While papermaking is fun for you and good for our environment, you don't want to ingest the chemicals and dyes used to bleach and color the paper you recycle. *Do not* use the same blender for papermaking and food preparation.

Purchase an inexpensive blender, look for an old blender at garage sales and thrift stores, or ask your friends. Many people have old blenders they never use and would be happy to send them to your house!

Always follow the manufacturer's instructions for using your blender. The instructions in this book are meant to make the work of reducing paper to pulp as easy as possible on your blender's motor. If you are careful, your blender will last for many years.

Plastic Tub

You need a plastic tub or pan to hold the paper bath. The tub must be at least 8" to 10" deep so you can place a screen under the paper pulp. Be sure it is 8" to 10" longer on each side than the largest screen you want to use. This leaves room for your hands as you immerse the screen and manipulate it. For example, if your mould and deckle is 10" x 12", you'll need a tub that is at least 18" x 20".

Rubber Gloves

You may want to wear rubber gloves so the chemicals in the paper and ink you recycle won't irritate your skin.

Mould and Deckle

You need to buy or make a mould and deckle, which are usually sold as a set, to make sheets of paper. The mould consists of a wooden frame covered with a mesh or screen, much like a screened window. To make a sheet of paper, you place the mould in a tub of water and paper pulp, dipping it beneath the surface. After the mould is completely immersed, you lift it out of the water. The water drains through the mesh, leaving a layer of wet pulp. The paper pulp dries to form a sheet of paper.

The deckle, an open frame, is the same size as the mould. Placed on top of the mould, the deckle forms straight edges on the sheet of paper and keeps the paper pulp from floating off the mould. Using a deckle is optional. With the deckle, the paper is thicker and has a nice clean edge. Without the deckle, the paper is thinner and has a feathery edge.

You can find basic mould and deckle kits at many art-and-craft supply stores, or you can purchase more expensive and better-made equipment from papermaking-supply companies (see "Resources" on page 89). I've included instructions for making a simple mould and deckle. If you plan to make paper frequently, I recommend purchasing a mould and deckle from a papermaking-supply company.

Felts

To form a sheet of paper, you transfer, or couch (pronounced "kooch"), the wet pulp from the mould onto a felt. If you don't want any dye in the felt to transfer to the paper, purchase white or off-white wool or acrylic felt from a craft or fabric store, or order a felt from one of the suppliers listed on page 89. I was given some wonderful brown wool felt, and I like the color it adds to my paper.

Preshrink wool felt before cutting! Cut your preshrunk felt about 1" larger on all sides than your mould.

Although traditional papermaking felts are usually wool, felts can be almost any material that will support the wet paper and allow the water to drain away. I frequently use Handy Wipes. Burlap sheets, bamboo place mats, and towels work well and provide interesting surface texture.

Sponges and Towels

You need one or two cellulose sponges for removing the water from the paper in the couching, or transfer, process. Cellulose sponges are available at grocery stores. You also need several old towels to absorb water as you couch the paper. If you don't have any old towels you can donate to your papermaking supplies, try garage sales and thrift stores.

Waterproof Boards

You need a rigid, waterproof surface, slightly larger than your mould, for couching or transferring the paper pulp onto felt. You can use any flat, waterproof surface. I use the covers of wallpaper books I've taken apart; these usually have a plastic cover and are a nice size. Plexiglas sheets work well, or you can wrap Con-Tact paper around any rigid surface to make it waterproof.

Paper Press

You need a paper press to press out water remaining in the felts and paper. You can make a simple press with four C-clamps, a sheet of 1/4" plywood, and wood sealant. Use C-clamps that have openings at least 4" wide. From the plywood, cut two pieces, each 2" to 3" larger on all sides than your largest mould. Waterproof the surface of the plywood with several coats of wood sealant.

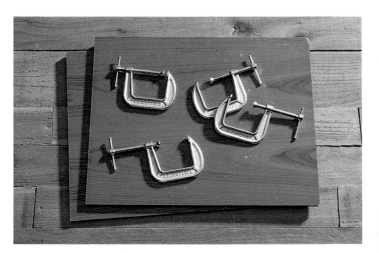

Sieve

When you clean up after papermaking, you'll pour your paper bath through a sieve or strainer to save the pulp. Most hardware stores carry large sieves, and most grocery stores sell food strainers. Do not use a sieve or strainer for food preparation after using it to strain a paper bath.

Making a Mould and Deckle

EQUIPMENT

    4 artist's or needlework stretcher
      bars (8" and 10" bars are good
      sizes to start with)
    Fiberglass screening
    Ruler
    Scissors
    Staple gun

MATERIALS

    Wood glue
    Wood sealant

You can use any basic frame with a mesh of some kind as a mould. I recommend starting with stretcher bars (available at art- or craft-supply stores). If you want just a mold, recycle a wooden picture frame. For a longer-lasting mould, construct the basic frame with 1" x 2" hardwood, corner brackets, and wood glue. For a mould and deckle (I recommend you begin with both), be sure to make or purchase two identical frames.

As mentioned earlier, I've used many different materials—including an organdy curtain—for the mesh. I recommend using fiberglass screening, available at hardware stores, because it is inexpensive and works well. Metal screening rusts over time.

To make a mould:

1 Measure your frame from top to bottom and side to side, including the width or height of the frame bars. Add ½" to 1" to all sides. Cut your fiberglass screen to these measurements. If you are using an embroidery hoop, cut the screen large enough to extend about ½" beyond the hoop.

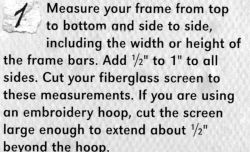

2 Place the screen on a flat surface, then center the frame on the screen. Pull the screen to the frame back and staple, using a heavy-duty staple gun. To keep the screen even, pull the material taut and alternate between sides as you staple. Staple the sides, then the top and bottom. Staple the corners last. To protect the wood, paint the frame with a wood sealant, such as Verathane, following the manufacturer's instructions.

TIP

You can easily make a small mould and deckle like the ones shown on page 15. I use this size to make small test sheets, which help me see quickly how thick the paper pulp is and what color it will be when it is dry.

MATERIALS

Paper

Recycled paper is the basis of all my work. I choose to recycle materials for several reasons. First, recycling is good for the environment, and therefore good for you and me. Also, I like making small batches of paper in a huge range of colors and textures. Because I recycle paper to add color and texture to my paper baths, I don't have to work with additional chemicals and dyes—the paper mills have done that work for me! Finally, the wealth of free materials available for recycling substantially reduces the cost of the paper I make.

In deciding what to recycle, consider the following:

Is the material made from some kind of fiber? Anything that has fiber in it can be recycled. The possibilities are endless. For example, old greeting cards, used stationery and wrapping paper, egg and berry cartons, paper packing materials, fabric scraps, and used computer paper are all part of my palette. Many wallpaper stores will give away discontinued books, and these books are excellent sources for recycling. I recommend you test a few torn pieces first—some vinyl papers don't reduce well. As a rule, look for quality papers designed to last.

Is the dye (color) in the fibers or on the surface? Most (but not all) of the glossy paper you recycle, no matter what color it was originally, will result in paper pulp that is some shade of gray. This is because color has been added to the surface of the paper as part of the printing process, and it disappears when you reduce it to pulp. The ink that was sitting on the surface will form little flecks in the gray pulp. To add color to this kind of paper pulp, you can use a common dye, such as Rit, or a fiber-reactive dye, as mentioned previously.

I prefer to recycle papers colored with fiber-reactive dyes. Colored flyers are good candidates, as is anything in direct contact with food. Green berry cartons, beige egg cartons, and purple box liners make great colored pulp.

There are several easy ways to tell if dye is in the fibers or only on the surface. One is to tear the paper. If you see white, the dye is only on the surface.

Another way to test dyes is to soak a few small pieces of a paper in water overnight. (Discarded yogurt or margarine containers are great for this.) The more color there is in the water the next day, the more color you will lose in the pulping process. But don't reject a paper or color completely. Experiment. A red that loses some of its color can make a nice faded rose.

While I prefer using colored pulp, I do sometimes use commercial dyes when I need really dark paper. I recommend liquid Rit dyes because they are readily available and easy to use. Always wear rubber gloves and follow the manufacturer's recommendations when using any dye. If lightfastness is important, you may want to purchase dyes from a papermaking-supply company, such as Twinrocker Handmade Paper (see page 89).

TIP

Like most fibers, paper pulp dries about a third lighter than when it is wet. If you want a specific color, you may need to experiment a bit. Part of the fun of recycled paper is the surprise you get when your paper dries.

Liquid Starch

Adding liquid starch (sizing) to your paper bath will make your finished paper less absorbent and reduce bleeding of paints and inks. Because I like the way watercolor dyes "feather" on my paper, I prefer not to add liquid starch. If, however, you want to prevent or reduce feathering and bleeding, add liquid starch to the paper bath. Purchase liquid starch from a grocery store.

Dyes

For colored papers, I make pulp from dyed paper (for example, purple apple wrappers), then store the pulp in a container and add it to the paper bath like a dye, as shown above right. Adding a little dark purple pulp to a paper bath made from recycled white copy paper makes a wonderful lavender-colored paper.

Wedding guest book, 9" x 6". Dried carnations and raw silk in paper fiber. (Collection of Tina Cook and Ian Kennedy)

Fabric, Thread, Yarn, Floss, and Ribbon

You can add snippets of any fabric to the paper bath to give your paper texture and interest. Brightly colored fabrics work especially well; the paper fiber covers much of the fabric and softens the color. Add fabric directly to the paper bath as little squares, triangles, or snippets, or embed bits as shown on page 29. If you want to reduce the fabric to fibers, use a blender. Cut or tear your fabric into 1" x 1" or smaller squares before blending. The more loosely woven the fabric, the better the results.

You can also add embroidery thread, sewing thread, string, yarn, and ribbon to your paper bath. Cut these materials into snippets or ½" lengths before using. Do you sew or have friends who sew? Ask them to set aside trimmings and snippets for you.

Other Ideas

Dried flowers, ribbons, sequins... You can add many interesting things to handmade paper. Keep a little "junk" box and experiment with different materials. I do offer a word of caution, however. Add these extras toward the end of a papermaking session rather than at the beginning. A little goes a long way, and if you add materials at the beginning, you may tire of the effect long before you have used all the pulp in your paper bath. On the other hand, once you start adding other materials, you can experiment with many different combinations. I frequently overdye such paper with stunning results.

Detail of dried flowers and raw silk in handmade-paper wedding guest book

HANDMADE
PAPER

TIP

Because of the chemicals used in the manufacture of many papers I recycle, my handmade paper can have an acidic content, which causes the paper to yellow and crumble. If you are worried about your paper disintegrating, you can adjust the pH of your paper bath to neutral or slightly alkaline. Most aquarium stores sell pH testing and adjusting materials.

It sounds impressive, even complicated, but making paper is simple enough that children often learn to do it in school. Prepare to enjoy yourself: papermaking is an inviting and forgiving art. If an air bubble distorts the paper on your screen, or if the paper rips as you couch it, simply throw the pulp back in the blender and start over. You have nothing to lose and everything to gain!

EQUIPMENT

1-cup measure	Plastic containers
Blender	Plastic drop cloth
Cellulose sponge	Plastic tub
Felt	Rubber gloves (optional)
Mould and deckle	Scissors (optional)
Newspaper	Sieve
Old towels	Waterproof boards
Paper press and	
C-clamps	

MATERIALS

Liquid starch (if you want to use inks or watercolors on your finished paper)

Paper and other materials to recycle (see pages 18–20)

PREPARING YOUR MATERIALS AND WORK AREA

1. To prepare paper for your recycled pulp bath, tear it into approximately 1" x 1" squares. You don't need to be exact, but this size is the easiest on the blender motor.

Tearing works better than cutting because the paper separates along fiber lines, which preserves the strength of the fiber. Cutting across the fibers results in weaker paper.

If you are recycling fabric, cut it into approximately ½" x ½" squares. Small pieces are best because long fibers can wrap around the blender blade and make the motor work too hard. Even adding a little bit of fabric to a paper bath creates interesting effects. A 6" x 6" square of fabric provides enough pieces for several batches of paper. I like to use scraps of denim for beautiful texture.

2 Fill a plastic container with water, then soak the squares prepared in step 1 until they are thoroughly wet. You can then use the squares right away, or leave them to soak overnight. I prefer to soak paper for several hours or overnight because the paper begins to break down and provides a smoother pulp (which is easier on the blender motor).

3 Cover your work area with a plastic drop cloth, then assemble your equipment and materials.

4 Fill a plastic container with water, then dampen your felt(s) in it. When the felt is damp, the process of couching, or transferring, the sheet of paper is easier. (If you couch the wet pulp on dry felt, your sheet of paper may wrinkle.) Set the damp felt(s) aside.

5 Place the blender away from the plastic tub and the area where you will couch your paper sheets. Mop up water around the blender to minimize the possibility of electric shock or damage to the motor.

6 Fold 2 old towels in half and lay them near the plastic tub.

TIP
I usually soak different-colored papers in separate containers because most colored paper bleeds a little. If you notice a lot of color in the water, your finished paper will be quite a bit lighter than the original color. If you don't see much color in the water, your finished paper will be close to the original in color.

PREPARING THE PAPER BATH

 Fill the blender two-thirds to three-quarters full of water. If you use less water, the blender will have to work harder to reduce the paper to pulp. Put the lid on the blender. (You may want to wear rubber gloves to protect your hands from chemicals used when the paper was manufactured.)

 From the soaking paper pieces, make a golf-ball-sized wad in the palm of your hand.

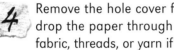 Turn the blender to its lowest setting. It's easier on the motor if the water and blender blade are already moving when the paper pieces are added.

 Remove the hole cover from the blender lid and drop the paper through the hole, adding snippets of fabric, threads, or yarn if you like. Immediately replace the hole cover. As soon as you drop in the wad of paper:
  a) Count to 15, then increase the blender speed to medium.
  b) Count to 15, then increase the blender speed to high.
  c) Count to 15, then decrease the blender speed to medium.
  d) Count to 15 (or 25 if you added fabric or fiber scraps), then decrease the blender speed to low.
  e) Count to 15, then turn the blender off.

Follow this routine for each handful of paper you put in the blender. The slow increase and decrease is better for the motor than running it continuously at one speed.

When adding thread or fabric snippets, use about one-quarter the amount of paper pulp called for in step 2. It's tempting to add more than a small handful of paper, but if you do, you'll make the blender motor work harder. If you hear the motor start to struggle, immediately turn off the blender and remove about half the material and water. Add water to the pulp remaining in the blender and repeat steps a–e. Experience will teach you how much paper or fiber your blender can handle.

 Pour the water and pulp mixture, called "slurry," from the blender into your plastic tub.

Repeat steps 1–5 until the slurry is 2" to 3" below the top of the plastic tub. This is the paper bath. Add liquid starch, if desired.

You can use less slurry, but you must fill the tub at least to the point where the mould and deckle can be completely immersed. I generally stop adding slurry 3" to 4" below the top of the plastic tub, then make a sample piece of paper to measure the thickness of the paper pulp. If I want it thicker, I add slurry. If I want it thinner, I add water.

MAKING PAPER

1 Spread the fingers of one hand slightly. Place your hand in the paper bath and stir back and forth, from side to side. You'll notice that when you stop stirring, the pulp quickly begins to settle toward the bottom. Make sure the slurry is evenly distributed before forming each piece of paper.

2 *If you are using a mould only,* hold it level, grasping each side firmly in one hand. In one continuous motion, dip the front edge of the mould into the paper bath, then level it out under the water.

If you are using a mould and deckle, place the deckle on top of the mould, and hold it firmly against the mould as you maneuver it.

3 In one continuous motion, pull the mould up to the surface of the water, holding it level as shown. If you are working with a deckle, allow the water to drain from the top of the screen before you proceed.

A vacuum will form between the mould and the water. Lift one corner of the mould slightly to release the vacuum. You'll hear a "plop" as the vacuum releases. If you raise the mould without releasing the vacuum, air bubbles will form under the screen and may tear your paper.

As you gain experience, you'll find that you can place the mould in the water (step 2) and bring it up (step 3) without stopping.

4 Tip the screen slightly and drain until the water decreases to drips (a few seconds).

If you don't like the way the paper looks, you can start over by turning the screen upside down and touching the paper to the surface of the water. Shake the screen gently. Don't roll or scrape the pulp from the screen into the tub; this makes lumps in the slurry.

5 Balance two edges of the mould on the edge of the tub as shown below. If you are using a deckle, set it aside. Pick up a damp felt, and smooth out any wrinkles. Carefully place the felt over the mould as shown. Lay the felt down from one end to the other.

Place a waterproof board on top of the felt. Holding the mould and board together on the longest sides, gently flip the whole thing over and set it down on the towel.

6 Using a cellulose sponge, press down on the screen. This removes water from the paper and bonds the fibers firmly together. Move the sponge across the surface of the screen, pressing down to absorb water. After each pressing, squeeze the sponge over a container or over the paper bath. Keep pressing on the screen until water no longer pools on the surface when you press. As you remove the water from the paper, the paper adheres to the felt and releases from the screen.

7 Lift one corner of the mould. With the tips of your fingers, gently flick the screen in one corner. The paper and felt should begin to release from the screen. New moulds require breaking in, so don't be discouraged if you have trouble getting the paper to release. Gently pull on the edge of the felt close to where you are flicking the screen. Moving from right to left, continue to gently flick the back of the screen and pull up the felt until the paper is released. Place the paper and felt aside to dry. You can stack as many felts as you want, then separate them for pressing and drying. If the previous sheet of paper sticks to the top felt, use the edge of a damp sponge to gently tease loose any edges that stick to the felt above.

Like anything new, this process may seem difficult when you first attempt it. It isn't uncommon for the paper to tear or not come off the mould completely when you first start to couch. Keep trying and you'll get the hang of it. Remember, you can put these sheets back in the blender, so nothing is wasted.

8 After making 3 or 4 sheets, check the consistency of the paper pulp in the bath. Add pulp as needed. I often add a different color or kind of pulp at this point. This is where the real fun begins! A good rule of thumb for judging color is that the finished paper color will be about a third lighter than the wet pulp.

PRESSING AND DRYING

1 When you have a stack of paper and felts about 3" high, place the stack between the paper press and attach C-clamps as shown. Tighten the C-clamps as much as possible to force water from the paper. Set the press in a plastic tub or tray to drain. You can leave the paper to drain for up to 24 hours; if you leave it longer, the paper may mold.

2 Remove the press and lay the sheets of paper out to dry. On warm, sunny days, dry sheets of paper outside—be sure to weight the corners so your paper won't blow away. I arrange paper on salvaged window screens. Under the corners of a mould or window screen, place 4 bricks, upside-down mugs, or other objects tall enough to allow air to circulate. Arrange several paper-and-felt sets on a screen to dry. I lay felts side by side, covering the surface of the screen. As one set dries, I remove it and add a new set.

3 When the paper is dry, stretch the felt slightly under one corner, gently pulling on two edges. Peel the paper off the felt.

CLEANING UP

Do not put slurry, or the water left over after straining, down a sink, toilet, or household drain. The tiny fibers are very tough and can ruin your plumbing. Dispose of the water from papermaking by throwing it away outside. That said, there are a number of ways to deal with the remaining slurry and water.

- You can leave the paper bath as it is for a day or two, but it will begin to decompose and smell.
- You can pour the slurry into plastic containers and store the containers in your refrigerator for up to 2 weeks. If the slurry begins to smell, rinse it thoroughly before using.
- If you don't want to store the paper pulp as slurry, pour the paper bath through a sieve into a bucket. Slap the sieve gently against your hand. The pulp will collect in a ball as you slap the sieve. Squeeze the ball to remove any remaining water. If stored at room temperature (about 70°F), the paper pulp will dry in a few days. The dried pulp will keep indefinitely. When you want to make paper again, just soak the pulp in water.

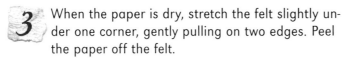

EXPERIMENTING

Now that you've learned how to make paper, experiment! It is impossible to make a mistake; handmade paper is so flexible and forgiving that you will just keep inventing new things to do with it and new ways to make it.

🐜 Embed materials you don't want to put through the blender, such as feathers, bits of fabric and thread, petals, and leaves. When you bring the mould to the surface of the paper bath, let go. It will float on the surface, and the paper pulp will be nice and loose on top of the mesh. Randomly sprinkle or arrange materials on the mesh. Using a turkey baster, gently add paper pulp around the edges of the materials you want to secure.

🐜 Embellish dry paper. Paper is both fragile and extremely strong. You can sew on paper, either by hand or by machine. Use thick paper or carefully iron fusible interfacing to thin paper to make it sturdier. Many of the embellishment techniques that work for fabric also work for paper. I recommend "Complex Cloth" (see page 94) for surface-design and embellishment ideas.

🐜 Mold leftover slurry like clay. You can press it into a cookie cutter, as I did with the hearts shown here. See pages 64–65 for a fun way to use leftover slurry to make paper shapes.

**SURFACE DESIGN
FOR HANDMADE PAPER**

I've developed a number of ways to add color and texture to my handmade paper. In addition to adding materials to the paper bath, I use three techniques—embossing, dyeing, and resists—to pattern dry paper. As you explore these techniques, I encourage you to experiment and improvise.

EMBOSSING

Embossing creates a raised surface. Handmade paper will pick up the form of anything it's pressed against and retain that form indefinitely.

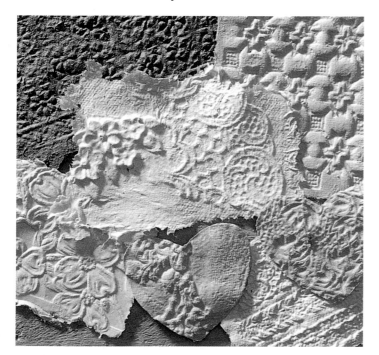

Wet Embossing

You can use almost anything to emboss and form an impression in damp handmade paper—lace, bamboo mats, plastic leaves, netting, and string are just a few examples. I am always looking for interesting surfaces. Try plastic molds and printing blocks. A potter friend made me small clay molds from her collection of Indian printing blocks. My mother, who is also a potter, made me an assortment of molds based on objects I gave her. If you use a new mold, be sure to follow the manufacturer's instructions for cleaning it before use.

TIP

- Handmade paper with embedded materials (like thread or flowers) is not a good candidate for embossing. The embedded materials stick to the surface of the embossed object, making it difficult to release the paper.
- Anything that has a raised surface works as an embossing tool, as long as the item is at least $1/16$" and no more than $3/8$" high. You may enjoy experimenting with higher surfaces, but the paper might fold or break.
- When you're embossing on slick surfaces like ceramic, the paper has a tendency to slip and can tear, so work carefully.

EQUIPMENT

Cheesecloth
Papermaking equipment (see page 22)
Assorted embossing tools: bamboo mats, lace,
    molds, netting, plastic leaves, printing blocks,
    and/or string

MATERIALS

Cooking spray or mold-release spray such as
    AMACO Cotton Press
Paper and materials to recycle (see pages 18–20)

 Lightly coat your embossing items with cooking spray or a mold-release spray and place right side up on damp felt.

 Make a sheet of paper, following the instructions on pages 22–28.

Rest the mould on the side of the plastic tub. Hold the mould with one hand and a cellulose sponge with the other. Drag the sponge slowly across the underside of the screen to remove water and pull the paper fibers together. Repeat, sponging off as much water as you can.

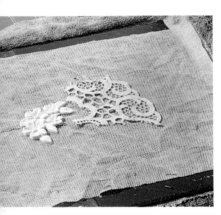

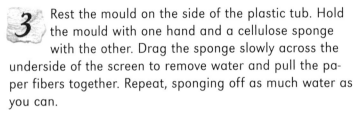

Flip the mould over and place it, paper side down, on your embossing item. Starting in one corner, flick the back of the mould to release the sheet of paper. If your embossing item is larger than the sheet of paper, try lightly rolling up part of one edge while the paper is wet. This will give you something to grip when you remove the paper.

Using the cheesecloth, gently press the wet paper into the surface of the embossing item. Pressing the paper brings out the detail of the embossing design and removes a little more water, and the cheesecloth won't pick up the paper pulp like a sponge would.

6 Allow the paper to dry. Carefully lift one edge of the paper and peel it away. If you can't remove the sheet of paper or if you tear it badly, dip the paper and embossing item in a pail of water and rub to separate. Return the pulp to the blender.

Dry Embossing

You can find embossing stencils at craft and rubber-stamping stores, but I prefer to make my own from illustration board. (To make a matching rubber stamp, cut the embossing design onto an eraser with an X-Acto knife.)

EQUIPMENT

2 squares of illustration board, each 4" x 4"
Book of copyright-free designs (optional—Dover books are great resources)
Drawing or tracing paper
Pencil
Self-healing cutting mat
Tack hammer
X-Acto knife

MATERIALS

Gluestick
Handmade paper (sheets or pieces)

1 Trace or draw a design on paper. Simple shapes less than 2" to 3" in height and width work best.

2 To transfer your design to a square of illustration board, place the paper on the square and trace the design with a pencil or stylus. Press firmly.

3 Place the illustration board on the cutting mat. Cut out the design along the traced line with an X-Acto knife, making small, deep cuts.

4 Remove the cut design from the surrounding illustration board, being careful not to tear the pieces. Set the outer piece aside.

5 Using a gluestick, glue the design in the center of the remaining piece of illustration board. Allow the glue to dry for 24 hours before using.

 6 Place the outer piece set aside in step 4 on top of the embossing board prepared in step 5. The two should fit together snugly. Remove the outer piece.

7 Place the embossing board on a flat surface, right side up. Position a piece of handmade paper on top of the board as shown. Gently place the outer piece on top and push gently to emboss the design onto the paper.

 8 Using a tack hammer, tap the cardboard shape around the edges, going around it until the open board is flush with the paper.

9 Gently remove the open board, then remove the paper. Repeat as desired.

Glue-Gun Embossing

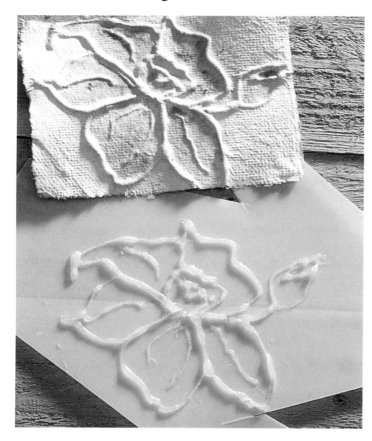

Glue-gun embossing is an easy way to create designs with a lot of detail. I especially like it for making leaf and petal patterns.

EQUIPMENT

Book of copyright-free designs (optional—Dover books are great resources)
Hot glue gun
Illustration board, 1" larger on all sides than your design
Pencil
Scissors

MATERIALS

Cheesecloth
Freezer paper
Handmade paper (sheets or pieces)
Masking tape

 Draw or trace a design on a sheet of freezer paper that is 4" larger than your illustration board.

 Cover the illustration board with the freezer paper, centering the design. Fold the edges to the back and tape in place. If necessary, use scissors to trim excess freezer paper.

3 Trace the design with the hot glue gun. Allow the glue to dry and harden.

4 Place a piece of handmade paper over the design. Dampen the cheesecloth in water. Wad up the cheesecloth and gently press it against the paper to emboss the design.

 Allow the paper to dry, then remove it from the glue design. Repeat as desired.

WATERCOLOR DYEING

There is something magical about the way watercolors move through unsized paper. Rather than sitting on the surface, watercolors move through the layers of fiber unpredictably.

I am often surprised at how well randomly dyed paper complements the subtle color variations in other collage materials. This technique invites experimentation—feel free to improvise.

I use concentrated liquid watercolors to dye my handmade paper. I prefer Dr. Ph. Martin's Hydrus Fine Art Watercolor dyes, available at most art-supply stores. These lightfast, transparent dyes are concentrated and will last a long time. Most brands of watercolor dye have a lightfastness rating—choose those with the highest rating.

EQUIPMENT

Cellulose sponge
Fan
Large tray*
Plastic drop cloth
Small plastic container for water
Tweezers (optional)
Window screen (optional)

MATERIALS

Handmade paper (sheets or pieces)
Watercolor dyes in a variety of colors

*I use a large food-service tray. You could also use a foil-lined cookie sheet, a flat plastic lid for a large container, or a disposable aluminum tray. The tray must be completely flat.

 Assemble your equipment and materials and set up your work area. Cover your work surface with the plastic drop cloth, and fill the container with water.

2 Randomly spread several colors of dye on the tray, adding dye until you have covered one-third to one-half of the tray. I prefer to separate my colors a bit so they won't mix before I start adding paper and water. If the colors mix too much, the paper may end up looking muddy (brown). You may find that you like that look.

3 Lay pieces of handmade paper on the tray, adding paper until you have covered the bottom. Fill the small plastic container with water. Saturate the sponge, then hold it over the papers, slowly squeezing out the water until the papers are completely wet. The water spreads the dye.

For brilliant colors, add dye every 2 to 3 layers. For subtle pastel colors, add water and paper, but not dye. Keep layering paper until the dye stops coming through.

TIP

Watercolor dyeing is great for leftover bits and pieces of handmade paper, paper made with materials such as flowers and fiber, and embossed paper.

4 Continue layering pieces of paper, making sure each piece is saturated with water and color. Press each piece of paper with the sponge so it will soak up the dye. Add water as needed to spread the color.

5 Place the tray of paper in front of the fan. Turn it on, then remove sheets when they are slightly damp or dry.

COFFEE OVERDYEING

I am part of a cooperatively owned and managed gallery in Kirkland, Washington. A fellow gallery artist, Sabah Al-Dhaher, introduced me to the medium of coffee! Sabah uses ink and coffee to create light and shadows in portrayals of landscapes and the human figure.

I use coffee to overdye handmade paper—that is, to dye previously dyed paper—and I've been thrilled with the results. The diluted coffee spreads like a watercolor dye, and the oil in the coffee produces a luminous color.

Experiment with overdyeing your watercolor-dyed paper. Follow the directions on pages 36–37 for using watercolor dyes, substituting a syruplike solution of instant coffee and water for the dyes. Or, for a different color palette, use paper that hasn't been dyed.

CRAYON RESIST

A resist makes the surface to which it is applied resistant to dyes and paints. There are many different types of resists, but my favorite is made with crayons. Normally, a resist is washed out or removed from the material after it has been dyed. However, in the resist recipes that follow, I leave the resist in place. Resists usually block dyes on the surface of the paper, but dyes can pass beneath the resist as well to produce interesting effects.

EQUIPMENT

Cookie sheet or disposable aluminum tray

MATERIALS

Aluminum foil
Crayons (As a safety precaution, use crayons labeled "conforms to ASTM D-4236.")
Freezer paper
Handmade paper (pieces or sheets)
Tweezers

 Line the cookie sheet or tray with aluminum foil.

 Place the sheet or tray on 2 stove burners. Set the heat to low. Lay a sheet of freezer paper large enough to hold the papers to one side of the stove.

3 Peel paper from the top of the crayons. Draw on the aluminum foil. If you prefer clear colors, use few crayons and avoid overlaying and mixing colors.

TIP

You can also use glue as a resist. When I use crayons, I'm adding color to the paper. When I use glue, I'm preventing areas from absorbing color. Glue resists are great for details like leaf veins. Remember, the resist works only on the surface of the paper. I used a glue resist on "Texture Study II" on page 12.

4 Holding them with tweezers, dip sheets or pieces of handmade paper against the melted crayon wax. Place the paper on the freezer paper, crayon side up, to dry.

Experiment with embossed paper. The crayon wax will stick only to the raised surfaces.

5 Once the wax is dry, dye the paper with watercolor dye or coffee.

PART TWO
The Art of Collage

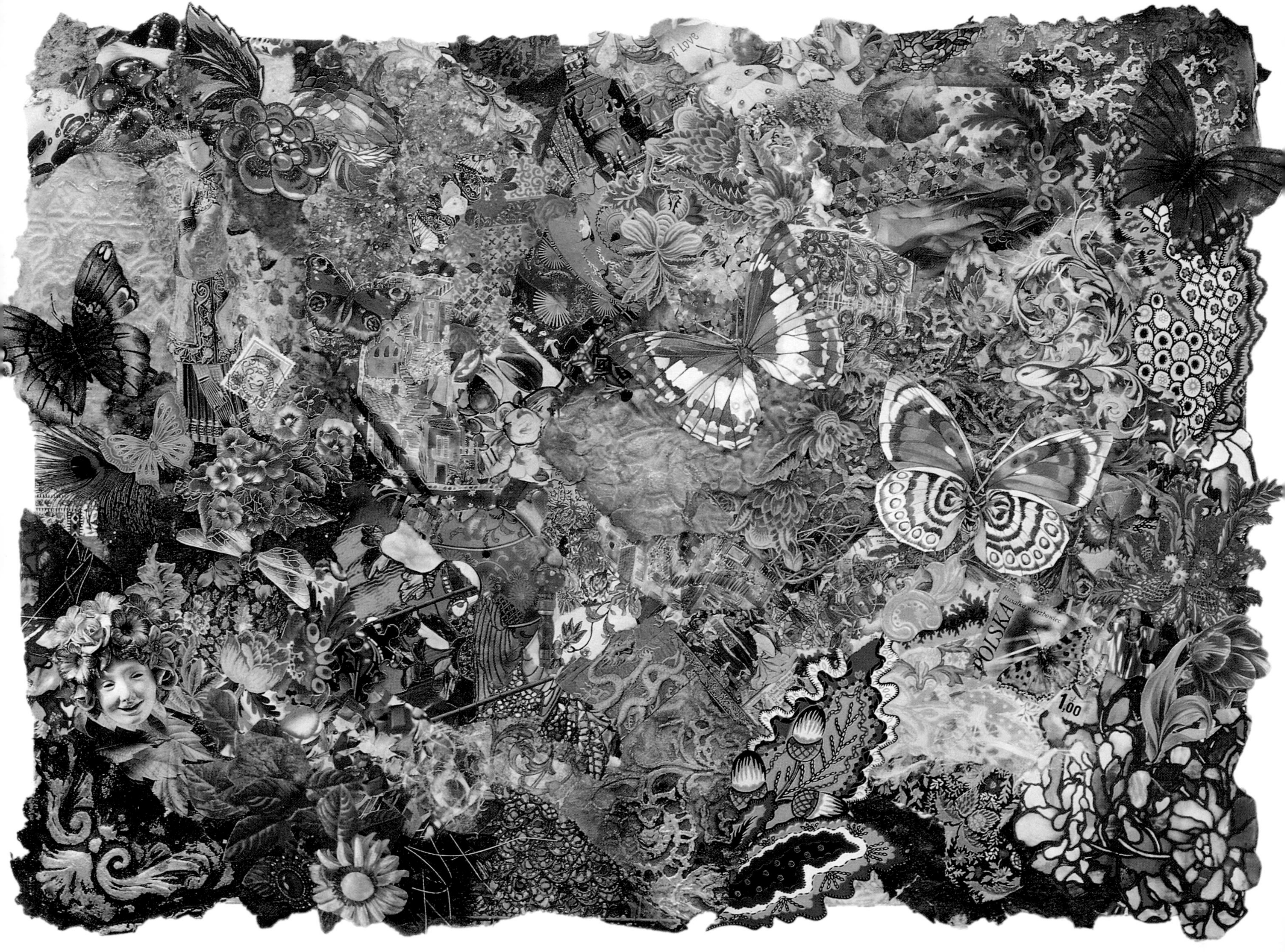
POLSKA
1,00

Recently, walking by a stretch of woods, I realized how much joy I gain from the colors and textures of the trees, undergrowth, rocks, and earth. Landscapes provide so many colors and textures, and odd, exquisite juxtapositions. I love the subtle and unpredictable transitions.

My collages echo the visual complexity I see in nature. Did you know that leaves are not just green, but also red and purple? The tree bark in my woods isn't really brown; it is brown, peach, rust, mauve, and orange. I encourage you to spend some time really looking at nature, at the incredible array and intermingling of colors. Spend a day at the beach. Every color in the rainbow plays across the rocks and stones scattered along the sandy edge of the water.

The same joy I gain from nature, I gain from creating collages, building subtle transitions between the colors, textures, and images of handmade paper, stamps, puzzle pieces, ribbon, wrapping paper, fabric, and magazine pages. An interesting scrap of handmade paper, a bit of wrapping paper, or an intriguing image torn from a magazine will catch my eye, and off I go. I hunt through all my boxes and bags and containers to see what else looks pleasing with that first scrap. I may collect materials for a specific collage for weeks or months or years. Then one day, I feel ready to begin.

Don't feel that you must sit and work until you have a completed collage. I sometimes do work quickly, and you may in the beginning too. Working quickly has its own satisfactions. More often, I work on a collage for awhile, then hang it on a wall to study for a few days. I sit across the room and look for areas that do or don't please my eye. Are there spots where my eye stalls? I take the collage down and work on it a little more, then hang it again. Working this way helps me solve design problems. For example, individual pieces that work beautifully when viewed up close may blend when viewed from a distance. To keep the viewer's eye moving, I increase the contrast in these areas by adding lighter or darker pieces.

There are an unlimited number of directions your collage can take. I experiment constantly and usually work on several collages at the same time. The bibliography on page 94 lists three books that showcase the work of more than a hundred collage artists. It would be safe to say that *every* artist takes a different approach. You can design a collage around a theme by collecting and using images and materials that have to do with a specific subject, such as flowers, children, water, joy, or light. You can design an abstract collage by emphasizing the shape, color, *or* texture of your materials or your use of light. You can emphasize a particular material, such as paper, fabric, found objects, or acrylic paints. The list is endless. This is one art with few rules, and one that welcomes experimentation.

Every collage, no matter how different the approach, shares some basic elements. To collage, you need a background or support for attaching various materials, a collection of materials, and of course, some kind of adhesive to hold it all together. (The word "collage" is from the French word "coller," which means *to glue*.)

Before you jump into the projects, review the basic steps of collage: collecting, sorting, arranging, and gluing. While each is equally appealing, and I often do them simultaneously, you'll have to begin with collecting.

This wrapping paper was the base of the found-materials collage shown on the facing page

"Butterflies in the Garden," 30" x 22". (Collection of Patrice and Thomas Luckey)

COLLAGE BASICS

COLLECTING

I'm not sure if collectors are born or bred, but I think I was born a collector. My mother's house has always been neat and well organized, so I can't blame her. Nevertheless, I came into the world with an extra sense tuned to the fabulous possibility of discards.

When it was time for my older brother to clean his room, he would lean out his bedroom door and yell, "Pack rat!" This was my signal to scurry to his room so I could go through all the potential treasures he was getting ready to toss. Collage artists are pack rats at heart, seeing unlimited possibilities in what everyone else throws away. Really, nothing is off limits! The main criteria is whether or not it strikes your fancy. Collage artists give a second chance to all the beautiful has-beens of our world. Some of the most exquisite art I've seen has been part of a stamp, a puzzle piece, or a snippet of wallpaper or fabric.

Following are some source ideas for collage materials.

- Every time you see gifts opened, ask for pieces of the wrapping paper and ribbons. It doesn't matter if the paper is wrinkled or folded.

- Ask every sewer, needle artist, and craft artist you know to save their snippets, scraps, trimmings, and leftovers for you. Scraps of embroidery thread, fabric, felt, yarn, ribbons, and string are perfect for collaging. Lace can be especially wonderful.

- I've collected thousands of postage stamps during my lifetime, mostly just because I liked the images. Many paper-arts and rubber-stamping stores have a good selection of inexpensive topical postage stamps. For mail-order sources, see "Resources" on page 89.

- Images from greeting cards, postcards, and calendars are excellent. You can tear the images into smaller parts, isolating patches of color or texture.

- Catalogs are among my favorite sources of material. If you offer to recycle your friends' and relatives' catalogs, you will soon have a wealth of images. Museum and gift catalogs are especially good sources.

"Study in Black and White," 18" x 28". (Collection of Melissa and David Lowe)

- Dover produces books of black-and-white and full-color, copyright-free art that you can use in collages.
- Thrift stores, garage sales, and flea markets are great places to find collage materials. Consider jig-saw puzzles, damaged books, odd lots of stationery, intriguing fabric, and yarn and ribbon scraps.
- Most wallpaper, paint, and decorating stores will give away discontinued wallpaper books. The paper is wonderful when recycled, and the patterns provide an excellent source of material for collage.
- You can add dried and/or pressed flowers to hand-made paper and to your collages. Ask friends to pass on their wilting bouquets. You can crush dried petals, and leaves that can't be pressed, and add them to paper. Plant a garden and press your flowers. Contact a local florist and see if you can have their floral trash from time to time, to dry and press.

SORTING

Store the materials you collect so they are easy to sort and use. I generally keep everything of a kind together. I keep stamps in one box, puzzle pieces in another box, fabric and thread snippets in another box, wallpaper pieces in another box—you get the idea. As I work on a collage, I sort through each box for the pieces I want. You can use old shoe boxes or odd containers of any kind for storing your collage materials.

For me, a major part of making a collage is sorting (and sorting and sorting) my materials to find "perfect" pieces. Following are a few tricks I've learned.

- Store each type of material in small-enough quanti-ties to sort through fairly quickly, or you might easily be overwhelmed. Small quantities make going from box to box more like a treasure hunt and less like looking for a needle in a haystack.

Untitled collage, 30" x 30". (Collection of Louise and Lloyd Olson)

It's easier to sort through a box if you have another empty box nearby to toss materials into as you reject them (this time around). Simply pour the materials into their original container when you finish sorting.

Don't be hard on yourself if you spend a lot of time organizing and sorting. A great deal happens subconsciously when you are eyeing all that pattern, texture, and shape. The time spent sorting is an important part of what you will do later. Sorting by color and texture and theme provides a kind of visual training for your eye. The more you do it, the more you will be able to recognize intuitively what might and what might not work for each collage.

Sorting will be important to your collage throughout the process. I do a first round of sorting when I have an idea (or color scheme) in mind. I methodically sort through all my boxes of materials, making a pile of everything that strikes my eye. You can store these piles on shelves as I do, or you can use manila envelopes or a large sheet of illustration board. (The illustration board may later become the base of your collage.) When I get stuck, I go back through my materials. Pieces I rejected earlier may be just what I need.

"Juxtaposition" is a big word, but it is one of my favorites. It means the position of one thing in relationship to another. I have one large drawer under my work table where many of my collage materials mix freely. Time and time again, several pieces have "just happened" to be lying next to or near each other, and I suddenly see that they can be combined in a way I never would have thought of myself. Try mixing your pieces. Just when you think you really understand what will or won't work, you'll see several pieces jumble up, and the unexpected combination of colors, shapes, or textures will be just what you want.

I love using puzzle pieces in my work, but to avoid having several thousand, I choose only pieces that really attract my eye (often these are pieces with a lovely color or a complex design). Out of a 500-piece puzzle, I may save as few as 20 or as many as 50 puzzle pieces, but rarely more.

If you are a sewer or a quilter, sort through your fabric stash regularly. Sometimes a piece of fabric can have just the right mix of colors or the image you have been searching for. For more ideas on using fabric, see pages 62–63.

EQUIPMENT

Binder Clips

I use binder clips, available at stationery and office-supply stores, to hang up collages in progress (once the glue is dry).

Containers

You need jars or plastic containers for rinsing brushes. If you are using paint, plan to have a jar of clean water for brushes used with paint and a separate jar for brushes used with collage medium (glue).

Cutting Mat

A self-healing cutting mat is invaluable for cutting up collage materials. Be sure to use one with your X-Acto knife. Cutting mats are available at art, craft, quilt, and fabric stores.

Paintbrushes

You need paintbrushes in a range of sizes. I recommend having one or two fairly fine brushes for drawing lines, several medium-size brushes for working with watercolor dyes, and several large brushes for applying collage medium and water. Don't spend a lot of money on brushes. Collage medium and some of the other materials can be hard on brushes if you don't clean them quickly and thoroughly, so choose the less-expensive craft variety. If you are careful to completely rinse out your brushes after using them, they should last a long time.

Liquid dish soap is a good brush cleanser. Press the soap into the heal of the brush bristles, then rinse well.

Saucer

You need a saucer or shallow container for presoaking paper materials such as wrapping-paper scraps and magazine images. These must be thoroughly wet to lie flat. Before adding paper, I soak it in a saucer of water for a few moments. If I decide not to use it, I allow the paper to dry and put it back in my box. *Do not soak handmade paper before using it.*

Shallow Tray or Box

Store the materials for a particular collage in a shallow tray or box so you can easily sort them.

Support Board

You need a piece of illustration board, stiff cardboard, or artist's canvas that is a few inches larger on all sides than the collage you want to make. You will use this as a support board or work surface for your collage.

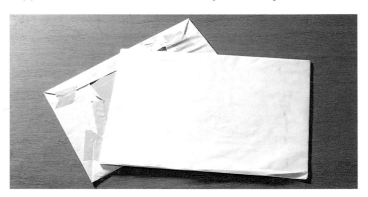

X-Acto Knife and Scissors

You will want to cut out some images and shapes. Make sure you have extra blades on hand for your X-Acto knife, and be sure to change blades often. A dull blade can tear the piece you are working on. A small pair of sharp scissors is handy for other cutting tasks.

MATERIALS

Collage Materials

Nothing is off limits for a collage. You can use stamps; puzzle pieces; wallpaper; fabric; thread, yarn, and embroidery floss; flowers and leaves; ribbon; lace; even greeting card, magazine, and catalog images. For more ideas, see "Collecting" on pages 45–46.

Collage Medium

In collage jargon, "medium" is another word for glue. The medium acts as an adhesive as well as a sealant. There are many types of adhesives and glues, and each collage artist has his or her favorites—mine are Mod-Podge and Liquitex Gel Medium. You may want to experiment with other mediums to determine which you like best. Most craft and art stores carry mediums, and a number of companies listed in "Resources" (page 89) sell them by mail.

I use Mod-Podge for most of my collage work. I like the consistency (like thick cream), the relatively slow drying time (about fifteen minutes), and the ease with which I can dilute it. I also use Liquitex Gel Medium. It's thicker than Mod-Podge, and I find it useful for attaching materials I may not want to cover with medium, such as puzzle pieces, broken bits of tile, or pieces of metal.

Freezer Paper

You need freezer paper for your collage base. As you build a collage, the wax-coated (or slick) side of the freezer paper will hold your materials flat, and you can easily peel the dry collage away from the paper.

Handmade Paper

Embossed, embedded, and textured handmade papers work especially well in collages. Although the emphasis of this book is on recycled materials, please feel free to use the fabulous handmade papers available at most art and stationery stores.

Masking Tape

You need masking tape to attach the freezer paper to your support board. Also, masking tape is great for auditioning materials as you collage. Place a doubled piece of masking tape on the back of the material, position it on your collage, then hang the collage and step across the room to look at the collage.

Watercolors

I use watercolor paints and watercolor pencils, available at craft- or art-supply stores, to color collages.

ARRANGING (AND REARRANGING)

The art of collage is about arranging and rearranging, and most importantly, layering. Layering allows you to shape and develop your work as you go. If part of a composition isn't working, you can tear it away (decollaging) or you can layer other materials over it.

When I am ready to work, I place my background on a support board and my pile of materials around the edges of the background. I begin arranging and rearranging pieces on the background, working until I am satisfied with the placement of each piece. This stage can be fairly simple, as when I'm making a greeting card, or more complex, as when I'm making a large piece like the found-materials collage on page 69.

Take a moment to think about how your collage will be viewed. A composition that is pleasing when viewed close up, while you are working on it, may change completely when viewed from across the room. A greeting card will be viewed at the same distance (or closer) as you are working. A large collage will be viewed from a greater distance. If possible, hang large collages on the wall and examine them from across the room. You may notice areas that disappear or fade together. Try adding a contrasting color or larger element to interrupt the space.

Create a focal point in your collage, such as an especially exciting piece of paper or an intriguing image cut from a greeting card or catalog. This is where your eye begins, where you are drawn into the composition. Most compositions benefit from having one element (or two) dominant.

The point at which I am pleased with an overall composition still varies widely from piece to piece. It is easy to feel that you have just "gone too far." In fact, it has become something of a joke at my house. I'll tell my husband, "It's ruined. I've gone too far!" But when I revisit the collage in a few days, I find a strong work of art. I don't particularly understand this phenomenon, and I've never read about it in any art book. However, every artist I talk with has said he or she also goes through this phase.

It's especially hard, while collaging, to know where or when to stop. It's easy to think you've added one too many elements or experimented just a little too freely. I strongly encourage you to put away your work when you feel like this, *but do not throw it away*. Come back later. At the very least, if you feel you've ruined it, you're free to try absolutely anything. That is often when the fun, and your best work, begins.

GLUING

Most traditional collage artists work directly on a canvas or board of some kind that becomes part of the finished collage. I prefer to work on a surface I can separate from the finished collage. Working this way, I am able to create rough edges around my collage, and I am free to use or mount the finished collage in a variety of ways. I can cut large collages into pieces for greeting cards or framing, or wrap a notebook for a gift. Also, I can use my support boards over and over again.

When you're ready to begin gluing, set up several jars of clean water for rinsing brushes and a small dish of water in which to soak paper images. Wrap freezer paper, coated side up, over your support board, securing the edges of the paper to the back with masking tape. If the board is wider than the freezer paper, use masking tape to seam the pieces. As you build the collage, the materials adhere to the freezer paper and dry flat. When the collage is dry, you can peel it off the freezer paper.

HANDMADE
PAPER COLLAGE

The instructions for this collage are intended as a starting place from which you will develop your own style and technique. Please experiment! I developed much of my technique by accident—through improvisation.

As explained previously, there are many ways to glue collages. In this project, you will use a wet technique, applying the collage medium to the materials with a damp brush. The collage medium seals the surface of the collage as it dries. It also darkens the handmade paper. If you would prefer not to cover the paper with collage medium, brush an acrylic gel medium on the back of each material (or on the edges of the initial pieces) instead. Experiment with the techniques and mediums to determine which you prefer. "Stormy Sunset" on the back cover and "Birth of a Star" at right were made with the wet technique. "Texture Study I" on page 13 was created with the dry technique.

Embossed papers really shine in this kind of collage. You may want to supplement your own papers with handmade and specialty papers from art and craft stores.

EQUIPMENT

Binder clips
Cutting mat
Containers for rinsing brushes
Support board (see page 48), 2" to 3" larger on all sides than your desired finished collage
Assorted paintbrushes for collage medium and watercolor dyes
Plastic drop cloth
Scissors
X-Acto knife

MATERIALS

Collage materials, such as glitter, handmade and embossed papers, lace or net, pressed flowers and leaves, tissue papers in different colors and translucent Japanese papers
Freezer paper
Handmade papers*
Masking tape
Mod-Podge or other collage medium
Watercolor pencils (optional)

*Choose at least 6 pieces of handmade paper, each roughly 8" x 10", or enough smaller pieces to cover your support board, as well as assorted scraps for layering.

"Birth of a Star," 28" x 22".

Assemble your equipment and materials and set up your work area. Cover your work surface with a plastic drop cloth, and fill the containers with water.

 Cover the support board with freezer paper, folding the edges to the back and taping in place. If necessary, use scissors to trim excess freezer paper.

 Choose 4 to 6 pieces of handmade paper as the background or first layer of your collage. Place the papers on your freezer-paper covered board, slightly overlapping each piece.

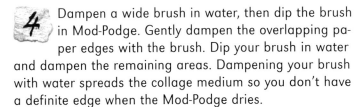 Dampen a wide brush in water, then dip the brush in Mod-Podge. Gently dampen the overlapping paper edges with the brush. Dip your brush in water and dampen the remaining areas. Dampening your brush with water spreads the collage medium so you don't have a definite edge when the Mod-Podge dries.

 Tear small pieces of paper and arrange these over the seams of the first layers. I tear irregular shapes or use scraps, but you can also tear uniform shapes like squares. Plan to work from back to front as you layer collage materials. Try folding, pleating, twisting, or crumpling and flattening the paper to add texture as in "Texture Study I" on page 13.

As you add pieces, create "visual bridges" from one area to another by adding scraps of lace or colored tissue paper. Glitter and pressed flowers or leaves add interest. I like to add translucent Japanese papers because they soften or disguise the seams between papers.

You may want to try using watercolor paints or watercolor pencils to bridge from one color area to another. For example, if blue and green papers are side by side, add a touch of green watercolor paint to the blue where the two colors meet. I often use this technique to transition between colors or to soften the definition between different-colored papers as shown at the top of the facing page. Experiment to find what works best for you.

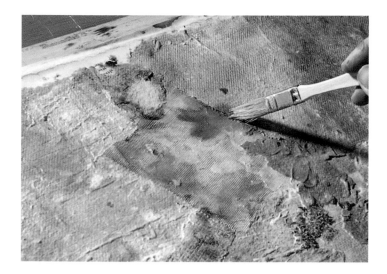

6 Build up layers of your collage until you are pleased with it. I stop when my eyes move smoothly around the collage. This is the uncomfortable part (for some of us), but with experience, you will learn to recognize and feel comfortable with your stopping point.

Bridging

One of the criteria for a "successful" piece of artwork is that the design keeps the viewer's eye moving through the piece. I have developed a technique for achieving this in my collage, a technique I call "bridging" because I connect two areas of a collage with a third element. I use this third element—a puzzle piece, a scrap of paper, or a splash of watercolor dye—to lead the viewer's eye across the edges where two different materials, colors, or textures meet. Look at the photos below. Notice how your eye moves more easily through this area with the addition of the third element.

The following photos show examples of successful bridging:

- Look for materials that combine two or more colors common to the different pieces. Multicolored puzzle pieces work especially well.
- Look for lace, translucent ribbon, or colored net that matches one of the pieces that needs bridging. Semitransparent material softens the contrast between different colors.

- Look for images from which you can cut interior pieces (think of paper snowflakes) so the areas you are bridging will show underneath.

PART THREE

Projects

GREETING CARDS

There is something very appealing about the small artwork of a greeting card. I've made hundreds, but I never tire of these miniature masterpieces.

Layering handmade paper, stamps, bits of ribbon or fabric, and other materials in this small scale is a good way to work on your sense of design and composition. Working on a small scale can be every bit as challenging as working on a large scale, but you don't have to work with as many elements or materials, and tiny elements really shine in this format.

I cut card stock to fit recycled envelopes, so I begin with envelopes. There are a surprising number of ways you can come up with envelopes and card stock:

- Thrift stores often have bags of unused envelopes and stationery. Flea markets and garage sales can also provide great finds.
- Small printing companies sometimes have envelopes and paper left over from printing jobs, and will often let you have them for free or for a small price. Where I live, there is a paper broker who buys up odd lots and discontinued lines of envelopes and paper from printers, then sells them for pennies on the dollar. Look in the phone book to see what is available in your area.
- I once received several thousand envelopes from a greeting-card store. The owner explained that the stores return unpurchased greeting cards to the manufacturer, but they can't return envelopes. Check with local retailers to see if they have similar policies.
- I recycle as much as I can, but sometimes it's more appropriate to buy or make what I need. Office-supply stores, paper-supply stores, rubber-stamp stores, and art stores usually sell packages of blank greeting cards with matching envelopes. Or contact one of the mail-order suppliers listed on page 89. You can also make your own envelopes as described below.

ENVELOPES

EQUIPMENT

Embossing stylus or dull kitchen knife
Heavy dictionary or other weight
Pencil or fine-point marking pen
Piece of lightweight cardboard or template plastic
(This should be large enough to hold the opened and flattened envelope.)
Ruler
Scissors

MATERIALS

Gluestick
Piece of handmade paper, wallpaper, or heavyweight gift wrap
(Your paper must be larger than the used envelope.)
Used envelope (This can be any size you like.)

TIP

Recycle your used envelopes! Colored envelopes—red and green at Christmas, red and pink at Valentine's Day, and yellow and pink at Easter—are a great source for coloring handmade papers for your greeting cards or collages.

TIP

If you have several sheets of similar handmade paper, use one sheet for the envelope and one for the base of your greeting card. I embossed this envelope flap as described on pages 33–34.

Making an Envelope Template

 Carefully pull apart an envelope and flatten it. If it does not flatten well, press it with a cool iron or bend back the paper along the creases.

2 On the piece of cardboard or template plastic, trace around the envelope. Mark the top, bottom, sides, and folds on your template material.

Making an Envelope

1 Place your template on a piece of handmade paper, wallpaper, or heavyweight gift wrap. Trace around it with a pencil or fine-point marking pen.

2 Cut out the envelope shape with a pair of scissors. Cut slightly inside the pencil line so you won't see the line on the finished envelope.

3 Lay the envelope shape right side up. Using a ruler and an embossing stylus or a dull kitchen knife, lightly score the fold lines. Scoring the paper helps ensure a nice, neat fold. If you don't have an embossing stylus or dull kitchen knife handy, you can use a pen that has run out of ink or an opened paper clip—improvise!

4 Fold the envelope along the score lines. Using the gluestick, apply a ½"-wide band of glue along both edges of the lower flap. To keep the strip of glue narrow, use a piece of paper to cover all but about ½" of the flap. Fold the envelope, then place it under a heavy dictionary or other flat weight until the glue dries.

GREETING CARD BASICS

EQUIPMENT

Clear acrylic quilting ruler, 6" x 12", or a regular ruler*

Embossing stylus or dull kitchen knife

Paper cutter or X-Acto knife and self-healing cutting mat

MATERIALS

Card stock, coverweight paper stock, or handmade paper**

Envelopes (see pages 59–60)

*I recommend a clear acrylic ruler, available at fabric and quilt stores, because you can use the grid to line up your card stock for trimming. If you don't have this kind of ruler, you may want to keep a variety of commercial cards handy to use as cutting templates.

**You can find card and cover stock in a variety of colors at stationery, paper-outlet, and print stores. Ideally, the sheet of paper should be at least 1" larger than the desired size of the open card. You'll score and fold the sheet, then trim the sides and bottom after folding. For example, a 4½" x 6½" card measures 9" x 6½" when open. You'll need an 8½" x 11" sheet of paper to make a 4½" x 6½" card.

1 Measure the width and height of the envelope to determine the size to cut your card. I usually cut the card base ½" smaller (width and height) than the envelope. If you plan a simple (thin) collage, such as a fabric-motif collage (see pages 62–63), you can cut the card base ¼" smaller (width and height) than the envelope.

2 Using a ruler and an embossing stylus or dull kitchen knife, lightly score a line across the middle of the paper. Scoring the fold before trimming the sides and bottom helps ensure an evenly trimmed card. Scoring also helps prevent wrinkles along the fold.

3 Fold the paper on the embossed line, then crease by pulling the edge of the ruler across the fold.

4 Trim the paper even on one short side. Measure your desired height from the trimmed edge (for example, 6½"), and trim the opposite side. Measure your desired width from the folded edge (for example, 4½"), and trim the long side.

5 Collage your card, following the instructions for making fabric motifs (pages 62–63), handmade-paper shapes (pages 64–65), or wrapping-paper collages (pages 66–67).

TIP

Don't be surprised if everyone wants to frame your greeting cards. You may want to frame an especially nice one yourself and give it as a gift. Or use color photocopies to quickly make a set of greeting cards. Copy several small collages on a page, trim the photocopy images, then adhere each to a blank card using a gluestick.

FABRIC MOTIFS

I came up with this idea while fraying bits of fabric in the blender. I noticed that the frayed edges were similar to the lacy edges of handmade paper, which led me to experiment with fraying larger pieces of fabric and printed motifs such as flowers and butterflies. The pretty images and frayed edges integrate beautifully with handmade paper.

Choose a fabric with motifs that will fit comfortably on the area you have chosen for the card. Good candidates are images that can be clearly separated from other motifs around them. Stay with shapes that are fairly simple and regular; shapes that you can cut into a square, circle, or oval are good.

EQUIPMENT

Blender
Iron
Polaroid camera (optional)
Scissors
Tweezers (optional)

MATERIALS

Collage materials, such as handmade paper, stamps, and ribbon (If you're using a holiday theme, you might consider scraps of holiday wrapping paper.)
Fabric with printed motifs
Gluestick, rubber cement, or a hot glue gun (The glue gun is the most permanent and won't warp the card stock.)

 Cut several motifs from the fabric, leaving about ¼" around the edges.

 Fill your blender at least ¾ full of water and start the motor. Drop a fabric motif through the lid of the blender.

3 Pulse the blender, turning it on and off about every 5 seconds for 30 seconds. If necessary, free the fabric from the blade. *Unplug the blender before putting your hands in it.* Each time I turn the blender off (and unplug it), I take the fabric out and spread it in my hand to check the edge. Pulsing the fabric 4 to 6 times usually produces a nice frayed edge. Spread the wet frayed edge apart with your fingers so it "feathers." When you're happy with the way the fabric has frayed, repeat the process for each additional fabric motif.

4 Using an iron heated to the cotton setting, iron the motifs dry, pressing out the frayed edge. These motifs can also be used in found-materials collage (pages 68–73).

5 Spend some time arranging (and rearranging) the frayed fabric motif(s) and other collage materials on your card stock (see page 61). You may want to use a Polaroid camera to record each grouping before you dismantle it.

6 Assemble the collage using a gluestick, rubber cement, or a hot glue gun. *Don't use white glue or collage medium; this will warp and wrinkle the card stock or base and the collage.*

If you use a hot glue gun, which I prefer, be sure to examine the card for stray threads of glue when you're finished. I remove these threads with tweezers.

TIP

Sometimes I take handmade paper to the fabric store so I can pick out fabric with motifs in the same color range. A ⅛-yard cut of fabric usually provides many motifs, although some stores require that you buy at least ¼ yard. Plan to make several cards at a time.

HANDMADE PAPER SHAPES

Handmade paper shapes make wonderful holiday cards. I especially like making hearts for Valentine's Day, but you can change the shape to fit the holiday, such as trees, bells, and stars for Christmas. I like to make these shapes at the end of each papermaking session, then I have them handy when I want to create cards.

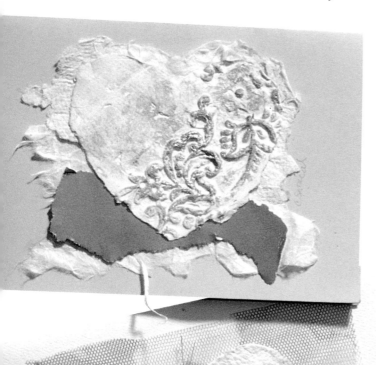

EQUIPMENT

Cookie cutters
Papermaking equipment (see page 22)
Plastic drop cloth
Polaroid camera (optional)
Tweezers (optional)

MATERIALS

Collage materials, such as handmade paper, stamps, lace, and ribbon
Gold craft paint; paper towels (optional)
Gluestick, rubber cement, or a hot glue gun (The glue gun is the most permanent and won't warp the card stock.)
Papermaking equipment

 1 Assemble your equipment and materials and set up your work area. Cover your work surface with a plastic drop cloth.

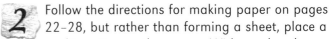 **2** Follow the directions for making paper on pages 22–28, but rather than forming a sheet, place a cookie cutter on the screen. With one hand, press on the cookie cutter to keep pulp from leaking under the edges. With the other hand, scoop paper pulp from the bath into a measuring cup. (If the paper bath has settled a little, you can get more pulp in the cup).

If possible, use a large papermaking mould so that you can balance it on the edges of the tub.

 3 Pour the pulp into the cookie cutter. Fill the cutter several times, allowing the water to drain through the screen. Try to keep the pulp as even as possible. If pouring the pulp produces a dent or hole in the pulp, gently swirl the mould with one hand, maintaining pressure on the cookie cutter with the other hand. Again, allow the water to drain through the mesh.

You can fill a turkey baster with paper pulp and use it to fill in uneven or thin areas. Use gentle pressure. If you press too hard on the bulb, the water and paper pulp will spurt out, making a hole in your shape.

To remove excess water, pick up the mould and gently press a sponge underneath the shape, working from the other side of the screen.

 Repeat steps 1–3, covering the mould with shapes. Space the shapes about ½" apart.

 Place a damp felt over the cookie cutters. Place a waterproof board on top of the felt. Holding the mould and board together, gently flip the whole thing over and set it down.

 Using a cellulose sponge, press down on the screen. Squeeze the sponge over a container or the paper bath.

Try couching or embossing heart shapes onto a lace doily for wonderful texture. Once the shapes are dry, you can paint them if desired. I like to dip a paper towel in gold craft paint, then gently brush the wet paper towel across the embossed heart. The embossed areas pick up the gold.

 Spend some time arranging (and rearranging) the paper shape(s) and other collage materials on your card stock (see page 61). You may want to use a Polaroid camera to record each grouping before you dismantle it.

Assemble the collage using a gluestick, rubber cement, or a hot glue gun. *Don't use white glue or collage medium; this will warp and wrinkle the card base and the collage.*

If you use a hot glue gun, which I prefer, be sure to examine the card for stray threads of glue when you're finished. I remove these threads with tweezers.

TIP

Paper shapes also make wonderful ornaments. Just pierce the top with a needle and make a loop of gold thread. A simple circle makes a great decorating base for a Christmas ornament.

Wrapping-Paper Collage

Gift wrap designs are often so exquisite that it seems a shame to simply throw the paper away, which is why I began recycling wrapping paper in my collages. Christmas stamps and images from Christmas cards and catalogs work nicely in wrapping-paper collages, although I use these sparingly so that the wrapping paper still shows. Experiment with different themes, such as wrapping paper with floral images.

Make a large sheet, about 24" x 36", and work quickly. When you're finished, you can tear or cut the collage into two to four smaller pieces for framing, or twelve to fifteen pieces for greeting cards. This method gives the finished pieces a complexity that you can't get working in a small scale.

Equipment

Clear acrylic quilting ruler, 6" x 12", or a regular ruler

Containers for water

Craft brushes

Plastic drop cloth

Support board (see page 48)

Tweezers (optional)

X-Acto knife and self-healing cutting mat

Materials

Collage materials, such as handmade paper, purchased specialty papers, and tissue paper

Freezer paper

Gluestick, rubber cement, or a hot glue gun (The glue gun is the most permanent and won't warp the card stock.)

Masking tape

Mod-Podge or other collage medium

Wrapping paper

 Assemble your equipment and materials and set up your work area. Cover your work surface with a plastic drop cloth, and fill the containers with water.

 Cover the support board with freezer paper, folding the edges to the back and taping in place. If necessary, use scissors to trim excess freezer paper.

Christmas wrapping-paper collage, 30" x 20".

3 Dip a brush in water, then wet the front and back of a piece of wrapping paper (the brush should have a lot of water in it). Wetting the paper ensures that it will lie flat and helps prevent wrinkles.

4 Using a damp brush, apply Mod-Podge or collage medium to the wrapping paper. Place it in one corner of the support board. Continue adding pieces of paper, working out from the corner, until the board is completely covered.

5 Arrange small pieces of handmade paper, tissue paper, frayed fabric motifs, and other materials on the wrapping paper. Remember that the wrapping paper is the star of the show, so be sure it shows.

6 Allow the collage to dry. When it is completely dry, use an X-Acto knife to remove the freezer paper from the support board. Gently peel the freezer paper from the back of your wrapping-paper collage.

7 Using a ruler or straight edge, either tear (for a rough edge) or trim with an X-Acto knife (for a smooth edge) the collage into pieces for framing or embellishing greeting cards. To tear, hold a ruler firmly against the collage and rip along the edge of the ruler. You may need to experiment with scrap paper to determine the ideal size.

8 Assemble the collage card, using a gluestick, rubber cement, or a hot glue gun. *Don't use white glue or collage medium; this will warp and wrinkle the card base and the collage.*

If you use a hot glue gun, which I prefer, be sure to examine the card for stray threads of glue when you're finished. I remove these threads with tweezers.

TIP

To help you audition different areas of your collage, make viewing and cutting templates. Cut a square or rectangle of the desired size in a piece of illustration board, or use a picture mat. Move the template around the collage, looking for areas to frame or cut out for special cards. Using a marking pen, make a small dot inside each corner of the template. Tear or cut out the areas.

FOUND-MATERIALS
COLLAGE

I've learned two important things from teaching collage. First, the technique is relatively easy and very enjoyable even for those with little artistic experience. Second, the more materials you collect before you begin, the more interesting your collage. Even if you prefer simple designs, you will appreciate having a variety of materials from which to choose. Generally, my student's collages are not as complex as mine, but they still find it easier and more fun to work with a large assortment of materials.

I have piles of material for four or five different wrapping paper collages, and I add to them all the time. If you feel that you don't have enough materials to begin a particular collage, don't give up on the idea. Plan to keep collecting materials until you have what you need.

I like the analogy of a jigsaw puzzle for the process of collage. I've always been soothed by the endless sorting and mesmerized by the emerging shapes that are part of working on a puzzle. This collage technique is a lot like working on a jigsaw puzzle, but much more fun. There is no image to match, only your own idea of what you want to create.

As a child in North Dakota, I spent many long winter days putting together such puzzles. I loved the process of looking for the clues that two pieces belonged together.

What line, what shape, what color moves across both pieces? Ask yourself these questions as you sort materials for your collage.

Wrapping paper is one of my favorite materials for collaging. So much so, in fact, that I've become an avid collector of leftover gift wrap—mine and everyone else's. It's not unusual to find a pile of torn wrapping paper that someone has left in the middle of my desk. Train the people around you to save wrapping paper for you, and you will soon have a wonderful variety!

Detail of wrapping paper used for "The Muses"

"The Muses," 36" x 24".

Quilters have a popular activity called a "quilt challenge." They choose a theme and a particular fabric or fabrics (often "ugly" fabric). Then they see what they can create. I've adapted this idea to wrapping-paper collage. I choose a paper for its interesting use of color, then challenge myself to make the colors work together using the materials at hand.

When I am finished with one of these collages, very little of the paper underneath may remain visible. Even when the paper disappears under other layers, its influence is apparent, for the color and design of the original paper is the basis of the completed collage. Trying too hard to keep the original paper visible can make it difficult to get the overall composition to work. Choose a base sheet that you won't mind covering.

If I started with blank paper, I would never find my way to the color combinations I've used in wrapping-paper collages. Again, experiment with different themes—the possibilities are endless.

EQUIPMENT

Binder clips
Cardboard or illustration board, 1" to 3" larger than the desired finished size of your collage
Containers for rinsing brushes
Paintbrushes for collage medium
Plastic drop cloth
Pushpins
Saucer or shallow dish for soaking materials
Scissors

MATERIALS

Collage materials, such as fabric scraps and motifs, handmade and embossed papers, images from catalogs and magazines, puzzle pieces, and stamps
Freezer paper
Masking tape
Wrapping paper or sheet of wallpaper for collage base*
Mod-Podge or other collage medium**

*To determine the size of the base sheet, you may want to anticipate framing the finished piece. Standard frame-opening sizes are less expensive to frame and mat. The larger your base sheet, the more collage materials you will need.

**Collage medium will darken the handmade paper. If desired, paint an acrylic gel medium on the back of the materials instead of using collage medium.

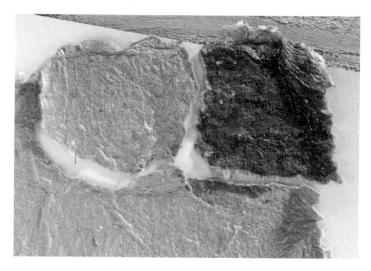

 Assemble your equipment and materials and set up your work area. Cover your work surface with a plastic drop cloth, and fill the containers with water.

 Cover the cardboard or illustration board with freezer paper, folding the edges to the back and taping in place. If necessary, use scissors to trim excess freezer paper.

 Using pushpins and binder clips, hang the sheet of wrapping paper or wallpaper on a wall.

Tearing

When you tear an image from a magazine, calendar, or greeting card, one side of the tear will have a white edge where the inside of the paper is exposed. Sometimes you'll want this white edge along your image, but many times you won't. The secret to controlling the edge is to put your thumbs on either side of where you want to begin your tear. Whichever edge you want clean (not white) is the edge you tear toward you.

Cutting

While sharp scissors can handle most anything with a fairly simple outline, you may want to use an X-Acto knife on a cutting mat to cut out intricate shapes. Here are a few tips:

- Always use a sharp blade.
- When cutting with scissors, move the paper into the scissors as you cut, rather than moving the scissors around the paper. This trick ensures a smooth edge.
- When cutting small details with an X-Acto knife, use short strokes, moving ½" to 1" at a time, to help prevent tearing.

4 Sort your collage materials and select pieces to complement or contrast with the wrapping paper or wallpaper. Pull out anything that catches your eye, whether you think it will work or not. My motto is, "When in doubt, trust your eye." If it is interested, there is something there worth pursuing. Pile these materials next to the surface prepared in step 2.

5 Using a wet brush, dampen the back of the sheet of wrapping paper or wallpaper. When the back is completely wet, turn the paper over and wet the front. Lay the sheet on the freezer paper, carefully smoothing away any wrinkles.

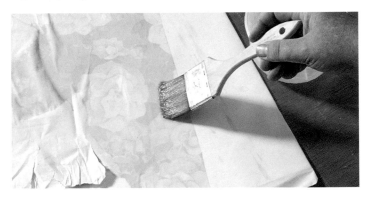

6 Fill a saucer or shallow dish with water, and place it nearby. Use this to dampen paper materials, such as pieces of handmade paper, images from magazines, stamps, and puzzle pieces. Wetting materials ensures that they will lie flat and helps prevent wrinkles.

7 Using a damp brush, apply Mod-Podge or collage medium to the area where you want to begin your collage. Add collage materials, brushing over each piece after adding it to the collage.

You may want to begin by covering areas of the base paper you don't like. I place the materials randomly or use the pattern as a guide, matching the colors of the material to the color and pattern of the base paper.

8 Build up layers of your collage until you're pleased with it. I stop when my eyes move smoothly around the collage. As you add pieces, create visual bridges from one area to another (see page 55).

I find it helpful to work for a half hour or so, then stop. I repeat this process for a week or two until I feel finished. When you're not working on the collage, hang it on the wall as discussed on page 50.

9 Let the finished collage dry thoroughly. Use an X-Acto knife to cut the freezer paper from the board. Gently peel the freezer paper off the back of the collage. Frame the collage as is or cut or tear it into pieces for framing.

KALEIDOSCOPE
COLLAGES

Kaleidoscopes have always fascinated me. When I was young, my father gave me one. When you looked through one end, the scene you were looking at broke up into wonderful slices of color and pattern.

I began making small quilts based on kaleidoscope patterns after reading *Mirror Manipulations* by Gail Valentine. She uses a hinged mirror to identify fabric motifs that would work well for kaleidoscope quilts. While I was working on a small kaleidoscope quilt, I happened to set my mirror down on a color photocopy of a collage. When I noticed the kaleidoscope images, I dropped everything and began to experiment with kaleidoscope collage.

When I discovered the book *Kaleidoscopes and Quilts*, by Paula Nadelstern, I was even more excited. Her kaleidoscope method produces images nearly as complex as those you see in a real kaleidoscope. I experimented with applying her method to collage and was delighted with the results. (If you'd like to learn the technique behind drafting kaleidoscope images, I encourage you to purchase *Kaleidoscopes and Quilts*. It's an outstanding book, even for nonquilters.)

Basically, creating a kaleidoscopic image depends on repeating an image around the center of a circle. This can be done with a variety of different-angle triangles, as long as the sum of the triangles is 360°—for example, you could create a kaleidoscope image using six 60° triangles. You may want to purchase triangle rulers from an art- or craft-supply store or from a fabric or quilting shop. I recommend Sharon Hultgren's Easy Six and Easy Eight rulers, manufactured by EZ International. These are available at fabric and quilt shops.

TIP

Although the kaleidoscope technique is not difficult, you may want to practice. I admit, I am always impatient with such things—I want to get right to work. But in this case, practice does pay off. I recommend using wrapping paper with a repeated pattern or making a few dozen inexpensive black-and-white copies of page 95 and using these for practice.

Untitled quilt, 36" x 36".
(Collection of Louise and Lloyd Olson)

There are two projects in this section. The first project is a design with two simple triangles. The second project is based on Paula Nadelstern's method for creating a complex kaleidoscope image. This book includes templates for the triangles and a copy of one of my collages. *You have permission to photocopy the collage image on page 95 for personal use.*

Kaleidoscope I, 8³/₄" x 8³/₄".

KALEIDOSCOPE I

EQUIPMENT

2"-wide craft brush
Fine-point permanent marking pen
Hinged mirror*
Illustration board or foam-core board,
    10" to 12" square
Pencil
Ruler or straight edge
Self-healing cutting mat
Template plastic
X-Acto knife and blades

MATERIALS

10 color photocopies of page 95 for each kaleido-
    scope (You need 8 photocopies for each collage,
    but it's a good idea to make extras.)
Masking tape
Mod-Podge or other collage medium

*Purchase a hinged mirror from a fabric or quilt shop.

Use the templates on page 90.

1 Using the ruler or straight edge and a pencil, mark the center of the illustration board. Lightly draw a line through the center from left to right, then from top to bottom. Be sure the center is clearly marked.

Use the marking pen to trace templates A and B onto template plastic. Use a ruler or straight edge for accuracy. Hold the pen erect (rather than to the right or left) when tracing.

It's important to trace and cut consistently. If you angle the pen or knife to the left sometimes and to the right others, you may vary the width of each image, which will make it hard to accurately assemble the kaleidoscope. Don't let all this emphasis on precision scare you, just be sure you're consistent.

3 Using an X-Acto knife, cut out the templates. Use a ruler or straight edge to guide your knife.

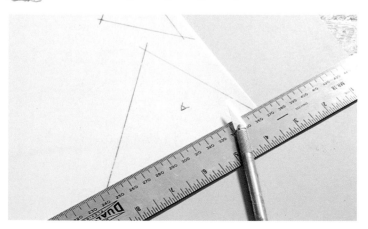

4 Label the templates with the permanent marking pen. Set template B aside.

5 Place the hinged mirror so it fits snugly against template A. Place masking tape across the top of the hinged mirror as shown. (I slip a small piece of tape on the exposed sticky underside of the tape as well so that the tape won't stick to itself when I close the mirror.) When fully open, the mirror should be the same angle as template A. Remove the template.

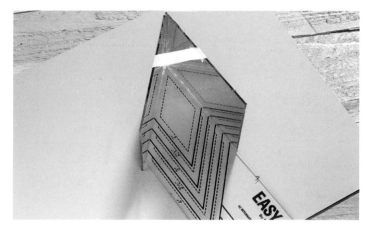

6 Move the mirror around the surface of the photocopy to find areas that interest you. The image you see is not perfectly symmetrical, so the mirror will only give you a general idea of what your center design will look like.

TIP

If you trace the template lines exactly, and cut just inside the lines, the pieces should fit together. You may want to cut plain paper pieces and assemble a test kaleidoscope as described in steps 10–11.

7 When you find an image you like, slide template A into the hinged mirror, then remove the mirror. Using the marking pen, trace a few of the larger design elements onto the template. You'll use these marks to position the template on the other photocopies. Trace around the template.

 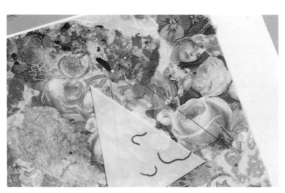

8 Position the template on another photocopy, matching the design elements. Trace around the template. Repeat for the remaining photocopies. For best results, do all your tracing before proceeding to cutting.

9 Place a photocopy on the cutting mat. Using the X-Acto knife, carefully cut inside the traced lines, one side at a time, ending ⅛" beyond each line. Use a ruler or straight edge to guide your knife, placing the edge of the ruler inside the line. Repeat for the remaining copies.

10 Dip the 2"-wide brush in Mod-Podge, then thoroughly paint the area where you'll place the first diamond. Align the tip of a paper diamond with the center mark and smooth in place. Cover the diamond with a light coat of Mod-Podge.

11 Using template B, repeat steps 8–10. Position the triangles as shown.

12 Continue to add diamonds, aligning the center tip and outer edges of each as shown. Don't overlap the diamonds, or you will end up with a gap between the first and last triangles. The very thin white spaces that this alignment introduces echoes the mirror edges of a real kaleidoscope.

KALEIDOSCOPE II

EQUIPMENT

2"-wide craft brush
Fine-point permanent marking pen
Hinged mirror*
Illustration board or foam-core
  board, 18" to 20" square
Ruler or straight edge
Self-healing cutting mat
Template plastic
X-Acto knife and blades

MATERIALS

10 color photocopies of page 95
  for each kaleidoscope (You need
  8 photocopies for each collage,
  but it's a good idea to make
  extras.)
Masking tape
Mod-Podge or other collage
  medium

*Purchase a hinged mirror from a fabric
or quilt shop.

Use the templates on page 91.

1 Using the ruler or straight edge
and a pencil, mark the center of
the illustration board as shown
on page 76.

Kaleidoscope II, 15⅞" x15⅞".

2 Use the marking pen to trace the templates onto template plastic. Use a ruler or straight edge for accuracy. Hold the pen erect (rather than to the right or left) when tracing.

It's important to trace and cut consistently. If you angle the pen or knife to the left sometimes and to the right others, you may vary the width of each image, which will make it hard to accurately assemble the kaleidoscope. Don't let all this emphasis on precision scare you, just be sure you're consistent.

3 Using an X-Acto knife, cut out the templates. Use a ruler or straight edge to guide your knife.

4 Label the templates with the permanent marking pen.

5 Place the hinged mirror so it fits snugly against template A (see page 77). Place masking tape across the top of the hinged mirror. When fully open, the mirror should be the same angle as template A. Remove the template.

6 Move the mirror around the surface of the photocopy to find areas that interest you. The image you see is not perfectly symmetrical, so the mirror will only give you a general idea of what your center design will look like.

7 When you find an image you like, slide template A into the hinged mirror, then remove the mirror. Using the marking pen, trace a few of the larger design elements onto the template. You'll use these marks to position the template on the other photocopies. Trace around the template.

8 Position the template on another photocopy, matching the design elements. Trace around the template. Repeat for the remaining photocopies. For best results, do all your tracing before proceeding to cutting.

9 Place a photocopy on the cutting mat. Using the X-Acto knife, carefully cut inside the traced lines, one side at a time, ending ⅛" beyond each line. Use a ruler or straight edge to guide your knife, placing the edge of the ruler inside the line. Repeat for the remaining photocopies. (See the Tip on page 77.)

10 Dip the 2"-wide brush in Mod-Podge, then paint the area where you will place pieces A–K. Beginning with A, arrange the pieces in a circle around the center point, painting each with Mod-Podge. Align the tip of a paper triangle with the center mark and smooth in place. Cover the triangle with a light coat of Mod-Podge.

11 Arrange pieces B, C, and D around the center (A).

 12 Arrange pieces E, F, and G around the center.

13 Arrange pieces H at the tip of pieces E, F, and G.

14 To finish, place pieces I between the star points.

PAPER-SCULPTURE COLLAGE

I've always been fascinated by the incredible complexity of shape, color, form, and texture in flowers. In a way, flower arrangements themselves are visual collages, as are gardens.

Several years ago, I took a class from Velda Newman, author of *Velda Newman: A Painter's Approach to Quilt Design*. From Velda, I learned how to use acrylic washes and bleach on fabric to create realistic textures and colors for plant images. I made several appliquéd quilts based on her techniques and became increasingly interested in translating floral images.

I was also lucky to work with Laura Reinstatler, another well-known quilt artist. I watched with fascination as she developed a new method for creating floral imagery in fabric. I recognized that Laura's approach was effectively a collage in fabric, and I used her method as a starting point to experiment with handmade paper.

A flower collage is wonderful, but it does have its challenges. To make a successful collage, you need to spend a lot of time studying fresh flowers and pictures of flowers. Before you begin this collage, ask yourself questions. What is it that tells me this is a gladiola? On as Iris, which petals go up and which bend down?

Another challenge I face with flowers is really "seeing" color. No blossom is simply pink or blue or orange. Petals are translucent, and the way the light passes through them is an important part of their color. If a flower is pale yellow, that color is substantially darker on the shadowy undersides of its petals or in crevices in the flower center. (For more information on color, see page 88.)

I've developed a way of working with handmade paper that gives me the widest range of color and control for flower collages. You can adapt this approach to any other picture collage.

Before you begin, you must find a picture that inspires you. Hang it up where you can look at it several times a day. In order to translate the picture into shapes I can cut out and work with, I really have to understand what is happening in the picture. What is farthest away in the picture? Where does that stem go? What is that mass of color in the background? Is that one blossom, several petals, or a group of blossoms? When I think I can see each separate part of the picture and understand its structure, I enlarge it on a photocopy machine. Using tracing paper, I trace and simplify the shapes so I have a cartoon of the original image. The photos at left show details of a picture I explored in fabric and paper.

A rough "cartoon"

Acrylic wash on fabric, quilted, 24" x 32"

Handmade-paper collage

Once you have a cartoon of the image, you must make paper. The handmade paper should be within a few shades of the desired color. For the apple blossoms, you'll need to make some paper that is white or off-white, some that is rosy pink, a few shades of green, and several shades of brown. You'll also need a sheet of paper in a neutral color for the background.

I prefer to make paper that is lighter than the desired color; it's much easier to enhance or darken a color than to lighten it. You may want to overdye existing colored papers to get more complex color (see pages 36–38). Overdyeing a multicolored paper with green provides rich material for leaves.

EQUIPMENT

Several scraps of illustration board, each at least 4" square
Containers for rinsing brushes
Fine-point, permanent marking pens:
  Black or brown for tracing
  Yellow or yellow-gold for flower centers
Hot glue gun (if not using Mod-Podge or acrylic gel medium for assembly)
Light box (see page 87)
Hand sewing needle
Craft paintbrushes
Small, sharp scissors
Stylus

MATERIALS

Freezer paper
Handmade papers:
  1 sheet, at least 8" x 10", of a neutral color for background
  Assorted sizes and shades of white or off-white, pink, green, and brown
Masking tape
Mod-Podge or other acrylic gel medium (if not using a hot glue gun for assembly)
Template plastic (optional)
Watercolor paints: blue, green, yellow, red, and purple
Yellow embroidery floss

"Apple Blossoms," 16" x 9".
(Collection of Jane Dunnewold)

TIP

I have a tendency to draw dark veins on leaves, but in nature, the colors of the veins vary widely from the rest of the leaf. There are several ways to re-create this effect: glue-gun embossing (see page 35), diluted bleach solution (25% bleach and 75% water), or a resist. Use bleach solution sparingly, as the bleach will disintegrate the paper. To use a resist, go over the veins with collage medium before painting. When the leaf is painted, the veins will be a different color because of the resist. This technique works best with lighter value papers.

---

 1 Assemble your equipment and materials and set up your work area. Cover your work surface with a plastic drop cloth, and fill the containers with water.

 2 Study the picture of the apple blossoms on page 85. Do you know what goes under and what goes over? Can you see where the stem comes from and where it goes?

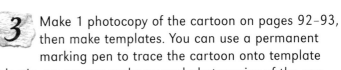 **3** Make 1 photocopy of the cartoon on pages 92–93, then make templates. You can use a permanent marking pen to trace the cartoon onto template plastic, or you can make several photocopies of the cartoon and cut out the shapes.

 4 Group the different templates, such as branches, leaves, buds, stems, and petals, in the order you will layer them. Using the stylus, trace the branches on the brown paper, then cut them out. If desired, you can darken the branches with watercolor paints after cutting.

 5 Place the photocopy on a piece of green paper. Using the stylus, trace leaf shapes and veins.

 6 Cut out the leaves, using a pair of small scissors. To cut sawtooth edges, make cuts in one direction, then make cuts in the other direction. (I prefer to cut out the shapes before I paint them. When you paint a cut shape, dye tends to collect around the edge, giving the shape definition.)

7 Cover the support boards with freezer paper, folding the edges to the back and taping in place. You'll use one board for mixing paint and painting paper and one for the collage.

Cut.

Cut.

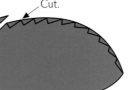

8 Dip a brush in water and dampen the paper you intend to paint.

9 Squeeze a small amount of each color onto the freezer-paper covered board. This is your paint palette. Mix colors, if desired.

10 Place a leaf on the board. Brush watercolor dye across the surface of the leaf. I like to paint all the leaves at once. The cartoon gives you some guidance for painting, but feel free to use your own judgment.

For realistic leaves, you can add small amounts of red, blue, yellow, and purple. Allow the leaves to dry on the board.

11 Referring to steps 5-10, cut and paint flower buds and stems. Since it's easy to get confused when reassembling the flowers, I arrange the pieces for each bud in their own section on the freezer paper and keep the groups separate as I paint.

 12 Position the photocopy of the cartoon and your background paper on a light box. If you don't have a light box, you can make one as shown below.

To assemble your collage, you can use Mod-Podge, a hot glue gun, or acrylic gel medium. Remember that Mod-Podge will substantially darken the collage. If you use a hot glue gun or an acrylic gel medium, you will create visible layers and dimension.

Attach the branch and stems to the background paper, then the leaves. Allow the collage to dry thoroughly before adding the next layer. Continue with the stems, flowers, and buds.

13 In my apple-blossoms collage, I used a permanent marker to draw the flower center. Since then, however, I've found that the following technique works best. Using a yellow or yellow-gold permanent marking pen, draw the center of the flower. Thread a needle with yellow embroidery floss. Stitch a French knot at the end of each line as shown.

Wrap thread around needle. Pull wraps firmly. Hold tension with thumb. French knot

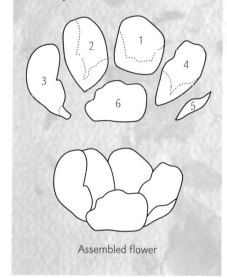

TIP

The numbers show an example of placement order for a flower. As you cut out the pieces, remember to extend by ¼" any lines that lie under another piece, as shown.

Assembled flower

First-stage assembly

Color

Color can fool you. An art instructor told me that every color is in every thing, and if you look at anything long enough, all those colors will emerge. It's hard to explain, but he was right. Study a flower for an hour, and you'll begin to see what he was talking about.

As the final assignment for that class, we had to paint two white eggs on a piece of white silk. We had to retain the feel of a white-on-white painting, and yet use colors. I didn't have a clue how to do this, so I studied those eggs and that silk for an hour. Amazingly, I began to see all this color—mauves, yellows, pinks, browns, and oranges. When the paintings were displayed, you could tell who had really looked. Some of the work was technically perfect, but you could tell the artist had not really looked at the eggs and silk. It was like day and night. Practice "looking" and watch what happens!

Second-stage assembly

Completed assembly

Resources

Art and Collage Materials

Cheap Joe's Art Stuff
374 Industrial Park Drive
Boone, NC 28607
1-800-227-2788
www.artscape.com/cheapjoe
   Cheap Joe's is a good source for
Dr. Ph. Martin's Hydrus Fine Art
Watercolor.

Collage
PO Box 7216
San Francisco, CA 94120-7216

Daniel Smith
PO Box 84268
Seattle, WA 98124-9990
1-800-426-6740

Dick Blick Art Materials
PO Box 1267
Galesburg, IL 61402-1267

Jerry's Artorama, Inc.
PO Box 1105
New Hyde Park, NY 11040
1-800-827-8478

Loose Ends
PO Box 20310
Salem, OR 97307-0310
1-800-390-9979
   Loose Ends is an excellent source for
papers and ribbons. I recommend their
"Fragments" package. It includes pieces
of all the papers and ribbons they sell,
a wonderful range of materials for your
collage stash.

Pearl Paint Company, Inc.
308 Canal Street
New York, NY 10013
   Pearl Paint Company offers inexpensive packets of 50 and 100 stamps.

Sax Arts & Crafts
PO Box 510710
New Berlin, WI 53151
1-800-558-6696
www.artsuplies.com
   Sax Arts & Crafts is a good source
for Mod-Podge, Liquitex paints, and papermaking and embossing materials.

Toybox Rubber Stamps
PO Box 1487
Healdsburg, CA 95448
707-431-1400

Papermaking Kits and Supplies

Gold's Artworks
2100 N Pine
Lumberton, NC 28358
1-800-356-2306

Green Heron Paper
13620 NW Eberly Road
Banks, OR 97106

Lee S. McDonald, Inc.
PO Box 264
Charlestown, MA 02129
617-242-2505

New York Central Art Supply
62 3rd Avenue
New York, NY 10003
1-800-950-6111

Twinrocker Handmade Paper
PO Box 413
Brookston, IN 47923
1-800-757-8946
317-563-3119

Professional Organizations and Journals

National Collage Society
254 W. Streetboro Street
Hudson, OH 44236

Collage Artists of America
Membership Chairperson
4425 Van Noord Avenue
Studio City, CA 91604

Templates

Kaleidoscope I
Templates

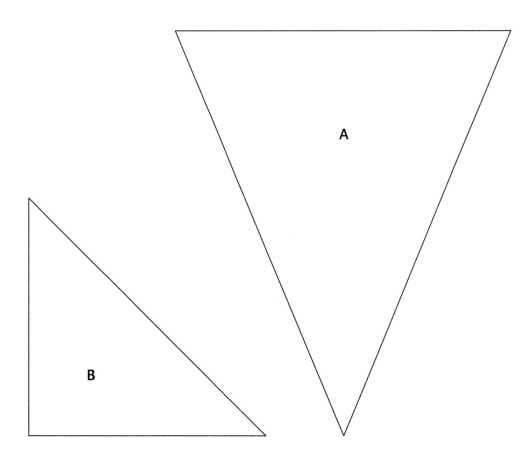

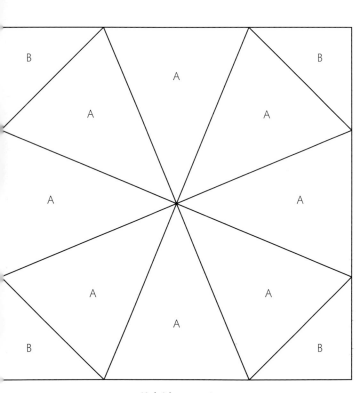

**Kaleidoscope I
Placement Diagram**

Kaleidoscope II
Templates

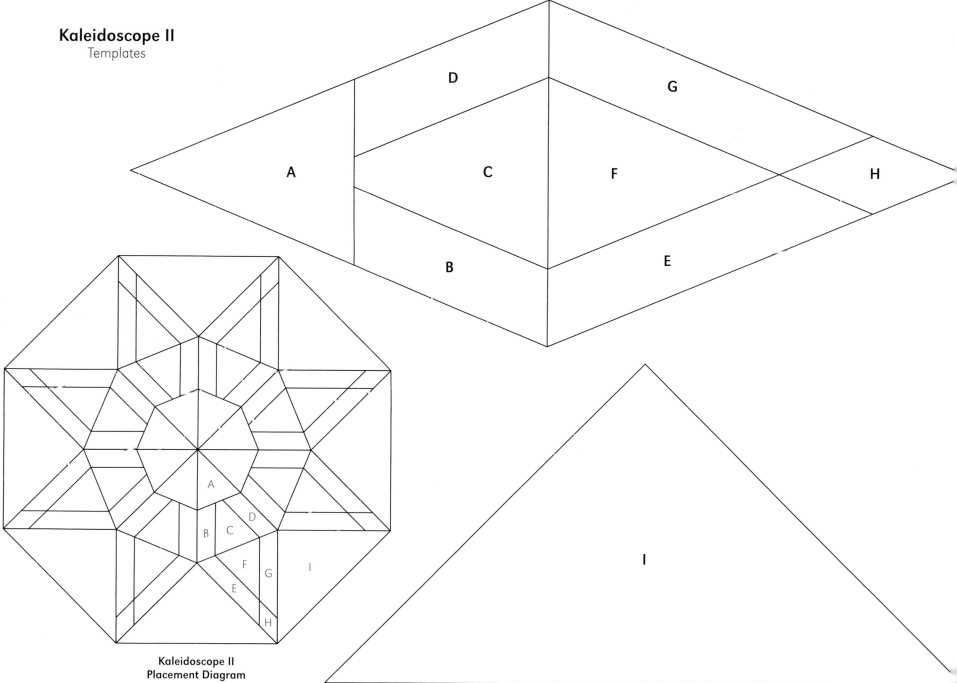

**Kaleidoscope II
Placement Diagram**

Align with lower edge of cartoon on page 93.

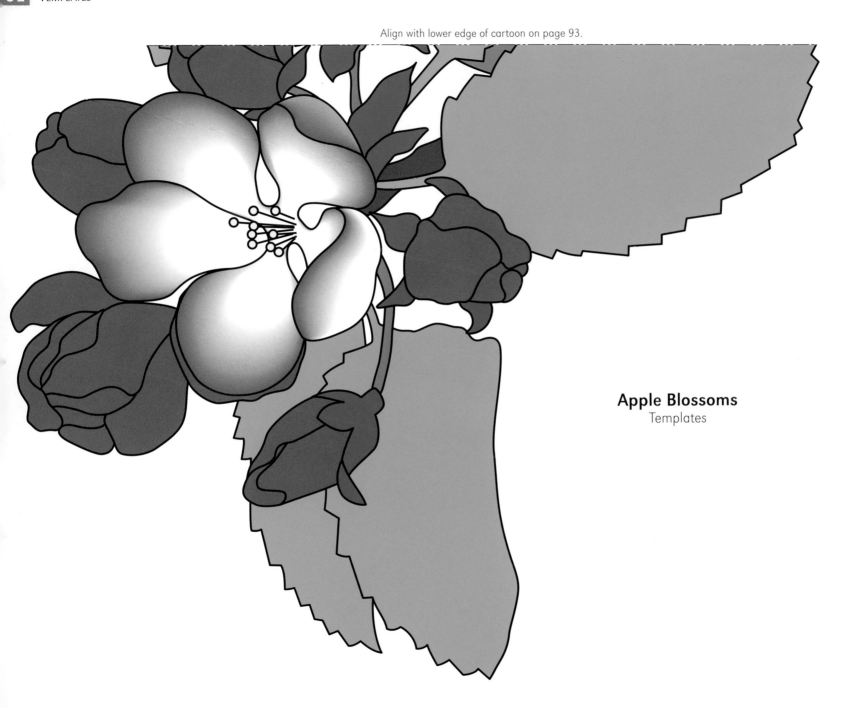

Apple Blossoms
Templates

Apple Blossoms
Templates

Align with upper edge of cartoon on page 92.

Bibliography

"Untitled Collage VIII," 12" x 9".

Atkinson, Jennifer L. *Collage Art: A Step-by Step Guide & Showcase.* Rockport, Mass.: Quarry Books, 1996.

Black, Penny. *Penny Black's the Book of Cards and Collages.* New York: Simon & Schuster, 1993.

Brommer, Gerald. *Collage Techniques: A Guide for Artists and Illustrators.* New York: Watson-Guptill, 1994.

Dunnewold, Jane. *Complex Cloth: A Comprehensive Guide to Surface Design.* Bothell, Wash.: Fiber Studio Press, 1996.

Leland, Nita, and Virginia Lee Williams. *Creative Collage Techniques.* Cincinnati: North Light Books, 1994.

McKechnie, Christine. *Paper Collage: Painted Pictures.* Tunbridge Wells, Kent, England: Search Press, 1995.

Nadelstern, Paula. *Kaleidoscopes & Quilts.* Lafayette, Calif.: C&T Publishing, 1996.

Newman, Velda with Christine Barnes. *Velda Newman: A Painter's Approach to Quilt Design.* Bothell, Wash.: Fiber Studio Press, 1995.

Valentine, Gail. *Mirror Manipulations.* Bothell, Wash.: That Patchwork Place, 1996.

Watson, David. *Creative Handmade Paper: How to Make Paper from Recycled and Natural Materials.* Tunbridge Wells, Kent, England: Search Press, 1991.

"Floral Study II," 12" x 10". (Collection of Harvey and Henrietta Senecal) You have permission to photocopy this collage image for personal use. ➤

SELECTED TITLES FROM FIBER STUDIO PRESS AND THAT PATCHWORK PLACE

FIBER STUDIO PRESS

Complex Cloth: A Comprehensive Guide to Surface Design • Jane Dunnewold
Erika Carter: Personal Imagery in Art Quilts • Erika Carter
Inspiration Odyssey: A Journey of Self-Expression in Quilts • Diana Swim Wessel
The Nature of Design • Joan Colvin
Thread Magic: The Enchanted World of Ellen Anne Eddy • Ellen Anne Eddy
Velda Newman: A Painter's Approach to Quilt Design • Velda Newman
    with Christine Barnes

Bargello Quilts • Marge Edie
Blockbender Quilts • Margaret J. Miller
Color: The Quilter's Guide • Christine Barnes
Colourwash Quilts • Deirdre Amsden
Freedom in Design • Mia Rozmyn
Hand-Dyed Fabric Made Easy • Adriene Buffington
Machine Needlelace and Other Embellishment Techniques • Judy Simmons
Quilted Sea Tapestries • Ginny Eckley
Watercolor Impressions • Pat Magaret & Donna Slusser
Watercolor Quilts • Pat Magaret & Donna Slusser

Many titles are available at your local quilt shop or
where fine books are sold. For more information,
write for a free color catalog to Martingale & Company,
PO Box 118, Bothell, Washington 98041-0118 USA.

U.S. and Canada, call 1-800-426-3126 for the name
and location of the quilt shop nearest you.
Int'l: 1-425-483-3313 Fax: 1-425-486-7596
E-mail: info@patchwork.com
Web: www.patchwork.com

5137

THE ILLUSTRATED ENCYCLOPEDIA OF
ANCIENT
ROME

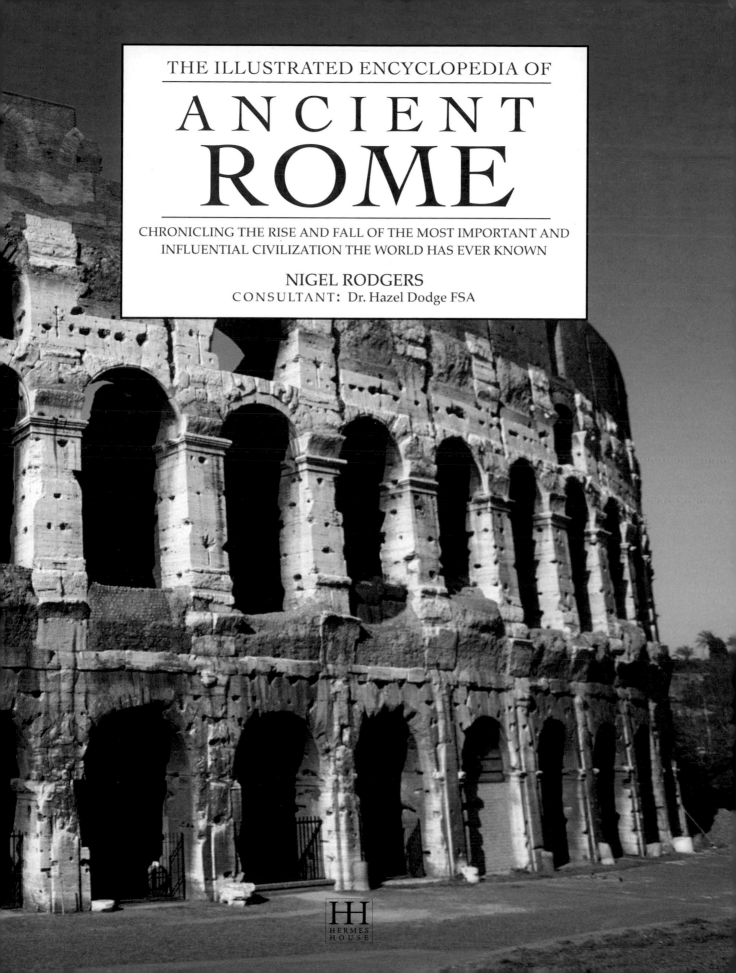

THE ILLUSTRATED ENCYCLOPEDIA OF

ANCIENT ROME

CHRONICLING THE RISE AND FALL OF THE MOST IMPORTANT AND
INFLUENTIAL CIVILIZATION THE WORLD HAS EVER KNOWN

NIGEL RODGERS
CONSULTANT: Dr. Hazel Dodge FSA

HERMES
HOUSE

CONTENTS

INTRODUCTION

Above: Now restored, Trajan's Column in Rome still proclaims his many victories.

Below: Hadrian's Wall, begun AD122, is the most dramatic surviving Roman military fortification, running 76 miles (122km) across northern England.

For many, Rome is the empire. No other city has given its name to an empire and a civilization. Snaking across the north English moors, Hadrian's Wall demonstrates still both the power of the Roman empire and the skills of the Roman soldiers who built it. Thousands of miles south, the well-preserved ruins of Lepcis Magna in Libya display Roman wealth and sophistication at its most flamboyant. But Lepcis is only one of hundreds of cities in an empire that by AD200 stretched from Morocco to Ukraine, from Jordan to Scotland. While other empires may have surpassed Rome's in overall area, the Roman empire remains among the most awesome, both for its longevity – it lasted for more than 600 years – and for its tremendous post-humous influence.

The Romans deserve their fame. If brutal as imperial conquerors and rulers – to discourage future revolts – they were uniquely generous in giving citizenship to their subjects. Free of racial prejudice, they extended this privilege ever wider until in AD212 almost all free people in the empire gained Roman citizenship. (By then even slaves were being better treated.) Long before, Rome had become the greatest cosmopolis yet seen, home to senators, philosophers, merchants and even emperors who often came from Spain, Syria, the Balkans or Libya. Across the great empire, which for 250 years enjoyed the Pax Romana (Roman peace), Roman law prevailed. Revised over centuries, this combined pragmatism and idealism and forms the basis of many modern countries' legal systems. Similarly Latin, the Romans' language, underlies Spanish, French, Italian and Portuguese and is the root of half the words in English.

THE POWER OF THE LEGIONS

The Roman empire was gained by swords, not laws. By 268BC Rome's tough citizen army had established its rule over Italy. In the wars with Carthage that followed, Roman *virtus* (courage, toughness) defeated Hannibal, who annihilated Roman legions in battle after battle but failed to capture Rome itself. Victory in the west led to the conquest of the Greek east. By 30BC the whole Mediterranean world was for the first (and last) time united under Rome by Augustus, the first emperor (27BC–AD14). Augustus made the Roman army – grouped into legions behind eagle standards, ruthlessly trained and disciplined – into a professional permanent force. For centuries it usually defeated all enemies, whether rough northern tribes or rich eastern monarchies. There was to be nothing comparable in Europe for over 1,000 years. In the long periods of peace, legionaries built the roads, bridges and forts that underpinned the power of Rome.

GRAECO–ROMAN FUSION

If Rome conquered Greece militarily, Greece is often considered Rome's cultural conqueror. But Rome, despite its great debt to Greece, fused Greek and Roman culture to create the western classical norm, which was revived in the Renaissance and continues to inspire even in the present day. This fusion is most obvious in architecture. Using concrete, Roman architects erected vaults, arches and domes in ways the Greeks had never dared. The Pantheon in Rome – built AD118–24, its dome's diameter unmatched for 1,700 years – is a triumph of Roman engineering although its perfect proportions derive from Greek mathematical ideals. The Romans built to last, too. Outside Nimes in southern France the noble arches of the aqueduct Pont du Gard, begun c.20BC, still cross the river Gardon.

While Roman philosophers essentially just restated Greek thinking, Latin writers, if following Greek models, revealed novel sensibilities. A new pity for the conquered appears in Virgil, Augustus' poet laureate; unfettered bawdiness marks Petronius, author of *Satyricon*; the subtle intensity of Tacitus has inspired many later historians; while Latin poets can reveal feelings for wild nature unknown again before the Romantic movement.

LIFE UNDER THE EMPIRE

The eruption of Vesuvius in AD79, so catastrophic at the time, preserved at Pompeii an urban time capsule revealing Roman life near the empire's zenith. We can glimpse Romans at dinner parties, shops, baths, temples – to foreign deities such as Egyptian Isis, for Romans were tolerant religiously – and gladiatorial games, the uniquely Roman entertainment that fascinates filmmakers and disgusts moralists. In the great games in the Colosseum in Rome itself, thousands of animals and humans might be slaughtered in a day, but games in smaller arenas could involve no deaths at all, trained gladiators being expensive. Roman games, like their

baths, forums, villas, roads and literacy, spread to the empire's furthest regions. Even on Hadrian's Wall, Roman soldiers had elaborate bath-houses.

While the 'Fall of Rome' in the 5th century AD remains an endlessly fascinating topic, only the western half of the empire actually collapsed – the eastern half lasted another millennium. Even today the Catholic Church, still centred in Rome and perpetuating some Roman customs, represents in a spiritualized form the enduring power of Rome, the Eternal City.

Above: The Forum Romanum was the heart of ancient Rome. Beyond the triple Arch of the emperor Septimius Severus (ruled AD193–211) stands the plain rectilinear Curia (Senate House).

Below: Gladiatorial games, the most famous Roman form of entertainment, inspired fine artworks around the empire, such as this mosaic of a 'Thracian' swordsman.

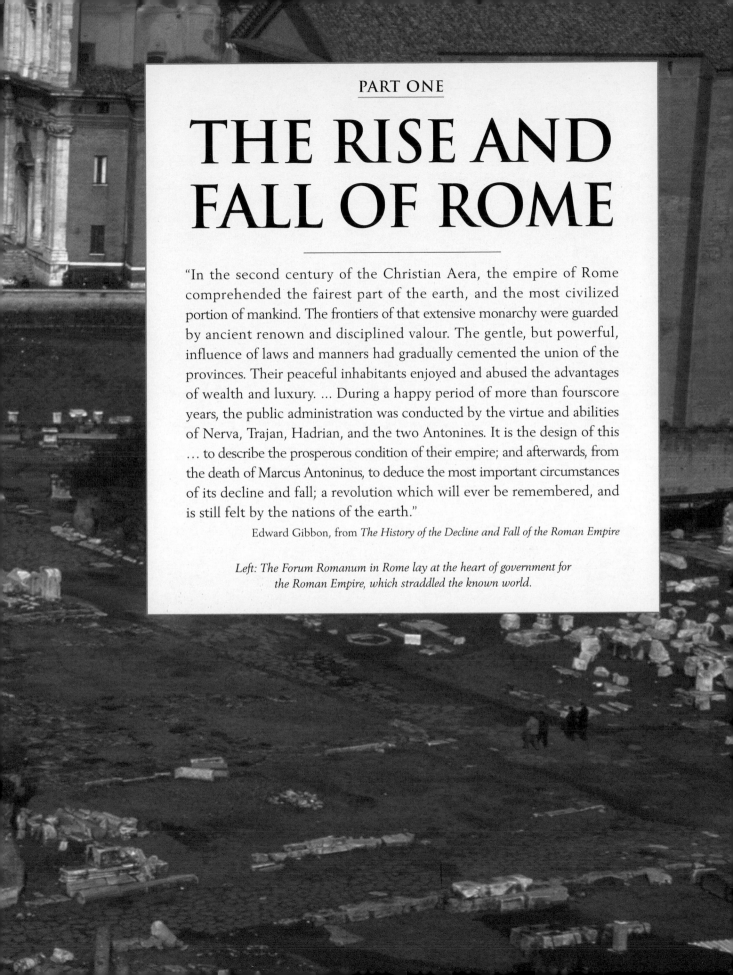

PART ONE

THE RISE AND FALL OF ROME

"In the second century of the Christian Aera, the empire of Rome comprehended the fairest part of the earth, and the most civilized portion of mankind. The frontiers of that extensive monarchy were guarded by ancient renown and disciplined valour. The gentle, but powerful, influence of laws and manners had gradually cemented the union of the provinces. Their peaceful inhabitants enjoyed and abused the advantages of wealth and luxury. ... During a happy period of more than fourscore years, the public administration was conducted by the virtue and abilities of Nerva, Trajan, Hadrian, and the two Antonines. It is the design of this ... to describe the prosperous condition of their empire; and afterwards, from the death of Marcus Antoninus, to deduce the most important circumstances of its decline and fall; a revolution which will ever be remembered, and is still felt by the nations of the earth."

Edward Gibbon, from *The History of the Decline and Fall of the Roman Empire*

Left: The Forum Romanum in Rome lay at the heart of government for the Roman Empire, which straddled the known world.

THE ARCHETYPAL EMPIRE

Above: Rome's influence was as much cultural as political. The Deir, a temple-tomb at Petra, Jordan, was built in the 1st century AD in Roman-influenced style before Rome annexed Petra itself in AD106.

Below: The ceremonial Via Sacra (Sacred Way) runs through the Forum Romanum, which itself was the centre of Roman life. The Arch of Titus is visible in the background.

Rome remains the archetypal empire, the object of admiration, fascination and at times of repulsion. How a small settlement of farmers grew into an empire that ruled so much of the then known world is one of the greatest tales in history. The ruins left by Roman might – aqueducts, bridges, basilicas, arches, baths and temples, many still standing, a few still in use 2,000 years on – have cast a spell on subsequent generations. Rome's empire was not only large – it stretched from Scotland to Egypt – but it lasted a very long time. For six centuries, Rome was mistress of the Mediterranean and western Europe, its sphere of influence reaching even further. If Rome could fall, observers have wondered, how secure is our civilization? Greater than Rome's physical legacy, however, has been its influence on culture and institutions.

This book is written in the Roman (or Latin) alphabet. Nearly two-thirds of the words in the English language derive directly or indirectly from Latin, the Roman language. Spanish, French, Portuguese and Italian are Romance languages, direct descendants of Latin, originally the language of central Italy. The Senate, the upper house in countries like the United States and Ireland, is the Roman name for a Roman institution. The emblem of the United States and many now-vanished empires is an eagle, modelled on that of Jupiter, Rome's chief deity. The American motto, *E Pluribus Unum*, and the British motto, *Fidis Defensor*, are in Latin, the study of which was long considered essential for anybody with pretensions to education, and which is still useful for law and medicine.

Much of the world's law is derived from the legal codes of imperial Rome. The ideal of a world guided by common laws and international institutions, whether political, judicial or economic, owes much to Roman attempts, however imperfect, to create an empire based on law as much as force. The United States, the United Nations and the European Union – all implicitly reflect the influence of Roman universalism.

IMPERIALISM – HARD AND SOFT

Rome did not acquire or keep its empire by noble ideals or fine words. It was, first and last, a nation of soldiers. The triumphal arches the Romans erected around their empire celebrated bloody military victories. For a triumph, a general had to have killed at least 5,000 (sometimes 10,000) of the enemy. Our word emperor comes from *imperator*, victorious commander-in-chief, for emperors were above all the supreme generals of Rome.

As any of the peoples who revolted against Rome could attest, the Romans could be methodically brutal in their reprisals. Tacitus, greatest if gloomiest of Roman historians, has one Briton defeated by Rome's might say, "You made a desert and you called it peace." As Rome

Map labels:

ATLANTIC OCEAN
BRITANNIA INFERIOR
BRITANNIA SUPERIOR
GERMANIA INFERIOR
GERMANIA SUPERIOR
LUGDUNENSIS
BELGICA
RAETIA
AQUITANIA
NORICUM
PANNONIA INFERIOR
PANNONIA SUPERIOR
DACIA
BOSPORUS
CASPIAN SEA
ALPES GRAIAE ET POENINAE
NARBONENSIS
ALPES COTTIAE
MOESIA SUPERIOR
MOESIA INFERIOR
BLACK SEA
ITALIA
LUSITANIA
TARRACONENSIS
ALPES MARITIMAE
CORSICA
DALMATIA
THRACIA
BITHYNIA AND PONTUS
ARMENIA
CAPPADOCIA
BAETICA
SARDINIA
MACEDONIA
ASIA
GALATIA
MESOPOTAMIA
CILICIA
MAURETANIA TINGITANA
MAURETANIA CAESARIENSIS
SICILIA
EPIRUS
ACHAEA
LYCIA ET PAMPHYLIA
SYRIA COELE
NUMIDIA
CYPRUS
SYRIA PHOENICE
MEDITERRANEAN SEA
AFRICA PROCONSULARIS
CRETA ET CYRENE
SYRIA PALAESTINA
ARABIA
AEGYPTUS

acquired its empire, it grew fantastically rich. By the 1st century AD, when Roman power was nearing its height, probably one person in three in the city of Rome was a slave. The whole Mediterranean world had to pay for the luxury and power of the conquerors, with money, goods and slaves. But if a few peoples rose in revolt, many others cooperated in what became a pan-imperial venture.

If Rome benefited from its empire – and empires are run, in the first instance, for the benefit of their rulers – then the advantages did not run all one way. As the empire matured, none of the privileges of being Roman was denied to former subject peoples. Rome was unique among ancient states in being ready to extend its citizenship to others. Under the empire, prosperity spread out in ripples, thanks to the benign aspects of Roman government. If people in the provinces paid taxes to Rome, these were often lighter than the taxes previously paid to their own rulers. In AD14, at the end of

his life, the first emperor Augustus was touched by a spontaneous demonstration. The passengers and crew of a ship just arrived from Alexandria put on garlands and burnt incense to him, saying they owed him their lives and liberty to sail the seas. These Alexandrians, from a great trading city but not Roman citizens, knew that their freedom and prosperity depended on the *Pax Romana*, the Roman peace that Augustus established and that his successors long maintained.

PAX ROMANA: THE ROMAN PEACE

It is easy to forget the benefits of external peace and internal security when they have become the accustomed way of life. Until well into the 19th century, however, most cities in continental Europe, like cities across Asia, were walled to protect them from attacks. What Rome gave the war-torn ancient world was unprecedented peace, security and stability for more than two centuries after Augustus reunited the empire in

Above: The empire in AD200, centred still on the Mediterranean, but now stretching from the Middle East to Scotland.

Below: The arch at Timgad, Algeria, commemorates Trajan, the city's founder. Cities were built across the empire with the full range of civic amenities: baths, theatres, amphitheatres, forums and triumphal arches.

Above: Rome's impact on Western culture has at times been almost overpowering. Pennsylvania Railroad Station in New York (built 1906–10, now demolished), simply recreated the interior of the huge baths of Caracalla in Rome, built 1700 years before.

Below: The Jefferson Memorial, Washington DC, repeats the form of the Pantheon in Rome of 1700 years earlier. This was a political and architectural homage, the young Republic saluting the ancient one.

30BC. Even the walls surrounding Rome were allowed to decay. Many cities across the empire also dispensed with walls, except for ceremonial perimeters. The Roman peace was upheld by a small army of some 300,000 men, perhaps half of one per cent of the population. The army itself was often occupied in building the network of *c.*50,000 miles (80,000km) of roads that stretched across the empire.

The Mediterranean Sea was cleared of pirates to become a marine highway dotted with seaside villas, a state of affairs not to recur until the 19th century. Land communications were better across Europe and western Asia under the Romans than at any other time until the coming of canals and railways. Lighthouses, from the great *pharos* of Alexandria in Egypt to many smaller examples, guided ships. With Rome's enduring peace, and its relatively light taxation, came novel prosperity. As city ruins show, some desert regions in north Africa and western Asia enjoyed under Roman rule a prosperity never to be repeated, while it took a millennium for most cities in western Europe to regain Roman levels of population and wealth.

MULTIRACIAL, MULTIFAITH

Much can be said against an empire that relied so heavily on slavery and a culture in which the chief entertainment of many citizens was watching men or animals fight one another, at times to death. But one accusation cannot be levelled against Rome: that of racism. When the Romans talked of "barbarians", the term simply denoted cultural and social backwardness and brutishness. The inhabitants of previously barbaric provinces, such as Gaul (France), North Africa and Spain, could and did become Romans, some eventually entering the Roman Senate – to the disgust of conservative senators. Several such "provincials" became emperors later in the empire. Racial background had no effect on a person's career. The emperor who presided over Rome's millennial jubilee in AD248 was called Philip the Arab because he came from Arabia Nabataea, now Jordan. Whole dynasties of emperors came from Libya, Spain and Syria. Rome extended the benefits of its empire ever wider, until finally in AD212 almost everyone except slaves acquired full Roman citizenship. Even slaves were being better treated by then, but slavery in a society with no colour bar was very different from that in 19th-century America. Many slaves were freed; a few prospered.

Romans, like most polytheists, were religiously tolerant. The myriad faiths of the empire were not suppressed but regulated, some being incorporated into the Roman pantheon. As long as subjects offered incense to the emperor – a political and not a religious gesture, as few educated Romans literally believed in the emperor's divinity – people had freedom of worship. The Roman suppression of Druidism in Britain, like the crushing of Jewish revolts in Judaea and later their intermittent persecutions of Christians, was political. The Druids potentially threatened Roman rule in Britain; the Jews had violently rejected Roman rule in Judaea and surrounding lands; and the Christians appeared to be disloyal.

Roman culture was so much influenced by the Greek that we often talk of "Graeco-Roman culture". This became effectively the cultural standard, even when influenced by local cultures – Roman civilization in Britain, for instance, was not identical to that in Syria. In the countryside especially, older beliefs and customs persisted beneath a Roman veneer. But it was possible to travel, unarmed, from Britain or Spain to Syria using one currency and speaking only two languages: Latin in the west and Balkans, Greek elsewhere. The traveller would have found that almost every city in the empire had its public baths, forum (market and meeting place), theatres, basilicas (halls), public games as well as students of Greek and Latin poetry and rhetoric. Rome conquered culturally as well as politically. Gauls, Spaniards, Africans and Britons adopted the Roman way of life as it seemed better than the alternatives. At the very least, this adoption helped the ambitious to rise.

ROME'S ENDURING LEGACY

The fall of the Roman empire in the west is irresistibly fascinating and rouses endless debate as to its causes. More significant is that the potent *idea* of the Roman empire did not expire in AD476. The Holy Roman Empire, created when Charlemagne was crowned by the Pope in Rome in AD800, attempted with some success to revive the empire, and it lasted for a millennium. Then Napoleon founded his short-lived empire, complete with eagles, triumphal arches and opportunities for other peoples to join the imperial regime. Perhaps, however, in the end the greatest heir of Rome was spiritual rather than military.

Within living memory, the Roman Catholic Church held all services in Latin, and the Pope still lives in Rome, in a line dating back almost 2000 years to St Peter, the first pope. As Eusebius, the "first Christian historian" (AD263–339), pointed out, it needed the peace and unity established by Augustus for Christianity to spread and establish itself. The Catholic

Church, with its hierarchy and its universalist ambitions, is the most obvious inheritor of ancient Rome.

Rome's greatest legacy is probably its universality, this longing to include all humanity within its realm. Rome's great poet Virgil voiced novel feelings for all human suffering. Rome's wars of conquest were often brutal, but the Roman peace atoned for this in the end. In the west especially, Roman culture went deep. Virgil's poetry was known to ordinary soldiers on Hadrian's Wall as evidence attests, not just to an elite.

> *"You created one homeland*
> *for the differing peoples*
> *Those without justice*
> *benefited from your rule;*
> *By allowing the vanquished*
> *to share in your own laws*
> *You made a city*
> *out of what was once the world."*

The words of the poet Namatianus, written around AD420, are poignant, as, only a few years earlier, the Goths had sacked Rome. His poem summarizes Rome's claim to be the universal city of humanity. To Rome as much as to Greece the world owes what has become Western civilization. The world without Rome would be unimaginably different. Arguably, it would be much the poorer.

Above: The Pantheon in Rome is among Rome's finest, best-preserved of temples, and its great dome has proved lastingly influential. It was built by the emperor Hadrian in AD118–28, but here it is shown as it was in the 18th century, with small towers.

Below: The Roman poet Virgil, flanked by two of the muses, was a protégé of the emperor Augustus. Virgil's greatest poem, the Aeneid, *became imperial Rome's epic, but it is an epic marked by concern for all humanity, not just the victors.*

TIMELINE

The history of Rome in its varying forms – as a tiny primitive kingdom, as an ever-growing republic, as a world-ruling empire and finally as the ghost or legend of that empire – stretches back to the early Iron Age. Its actual history really ends only in the 19th century, when the last Holy Roman Emperor abdicated and Napoleon Bonaparte crowned himself Emperor of the French in an obvious attempt to resurrect Rome's claims to universal empire.

The Romans themselves dated all events *ab urbe condita*, from the (mythical) foundation of the City by Romulus in 753BC – an event they saw, not without some reason, as being of world-transforming significance. Only in the 5th century AD did the present Christian calendar supersede the old Roman system.

Early dates down to at least 350BC remain very uncertain, but the broad sweep of Roman history remains quite unmistakeable and remarkable: the rise and ultimate fall of a mighty empire, whose memories lived on so potently that later rulers tried to resuscitate its titles and grandeurs.

Note: Very early dates, up to 350BC, are approximate.

753–451BC

753 Legendary founding of city by (mythical) brothers Romulus and Remus; Romulus reigns as sole king to 717, regarded by later Romans as actual founder of Rome.

***c*.650** The Etruscan kings (possibly Etruscan outcasts) arrive in Rome.

***c*.590** Solon reforms the Athenian constitution, making it semi-democratic.

578–535 Reign of Servius Tullius; forms the first Assembly, the *comitia centuriata*, on kinship lines.

534–509 Reign of Tarquinius Superbus, the last of the kings; building of first temple on Capitoline Hill.

509 Expulsion of Tarquin and end of Etruscan cultural predominance in Rome. Formation of Republic; kings replaced by elected officials, praetors and then consuls; first treaty with Carthage.

496 Rome defeats Latins at Battle of Lake Regillus; makes equal treaty of alliance with Latins.

494–440 Struggle of the Orders. Patricians (the 100 nobles supposedly chosen by Romulus) versus plebeians (everybody else).

493 First tribunes appointed to defend plebeian interests.

480 Greeks led by Athens defeat Persian invaders at Salamis; beginning of the classical age in Greece.

474 Battle of Cumae: Greeks defeat Etruscans and Carthaginians at sea; beginnings of Etruscan decline.

471 Creation of new Assembly of the Plebs, which elects tribunes annually.

450–300BC

450 Twelve Tables of the Law published; the first written laws help plebeians.

449 Tribunes increased to ten and their sacrosanctity legally guaranteed.

440 *Lex Cannuleia* establishes equality between plebs and patricians; institution of censors.

431–404 Peloponnesian War between Athens and Sparta; Athens defeated.

425 Fidenae (city) taken from Veii.

421 First plebeian quaestor.

405–396 Long siege and capture of Veii, the key to southern Etruria.

***c*.400** Celts (Gauls) invade northern Italy.

***c*.390** Sack of Rome by invading Gauls.

386 Rome grants citizens of Caere *hospitium publicum*, privileged status.

***c*.378** Building of Servian wall.

367 One consul must always be plebeian.

343–341 First war against Samnites, highland people.

338 Defeat of the Latins; Latin League dissolved; Roman power extends into Campania.

336–323 Alexander the Great of Macedon overwhelms Greek states and conquers Persian empire before dying in Babylon. His empire is divided between his generals, the Diadochi (successors).

329 Terracina becomes a Roman colony.

327–304 Second Samnite War.

321 Romans defeated by Samnites at Caudine Forks.

312 Censorship of Appius Claudius; building of first Roman road, the Via Appia to Capua, and Aqua Appia, Rome's first aqueduct.

299–200BC

298–290 Third Samnite War.

295 Samnites defeated at Sentium.

287 *Lex Hortensia*: plebiscites (votes of the people) become law.

280–275 War with King Pyrrhus of Epirus.

275 Romans defeat Pyrrhus.

264–241 First Punic War.

260 Romans build their first fleet.

259 Roman victory at sea at Mylae.

256–255 Regulus invades Africa, but is defeated.

249 Romans defeated at Drapana.

241 Final Roman victory off the Aègates Islands; Sicily the first Roman province.

238 Sardinia and Corsica annexed.

223 Successful Roman campaigns in Cisalpine Gaul lead to first colonies there.

220 Censorship of Flaminius; builds Via Flaminia to Rimini and Circus Flaminius.

219 Hannibal besieges and takes Saguntum in Spain.

218–202 Second Punic War.

218–217 Hannibal crosses Alps; his army defeats Romans at Ticinus and later at Trebbia.

216 Roman defeat at Cannae; Hannibal forms alliance with Philip V of Macedonia; some allies abandon Rome.

214–205 First Macedonian War.

213–211 Siege of Syracuse.

211–206 Scipio campaigns in Spain.

209 Scipio captures Cartagena.

207 Hasdrubal leads army into Italy.

203 Scipio invades Africa, wins Battle of the Great Plains.

202 Scipio defeats Hannibal at Zama. End of Carthaginian overseas power.

199–100BC

200–196 Second Macedonian War.

197–179 Gracchus ends wars in Spain; Spain organized into two provinces.

197 Philip V of Macedon defeated.

196 Flaminius declares "freedom of the Greeks" at Isthmia, near Corinth.

194 Romans evacuate Greece.

191 Cisalpine Gaul (northern Italy) conquered by Rome.

190 Seleucid king Antiochus III of Syria defeated at Magnesia; Seleucids expelled from Asia Minor.

184 Censorship of Cato the Elder.

179 Aemilian bridge, first stone bridge over Tiber, built.

168 Perseus of Macedonia defeated at Pydna; Macedonia becomes Roman dependency.

167 Direct taxation of Roman citizens abolished; sack of Epirus, 150,000 Greeks enslaved; Jewish revolt led by Maccabeus against Antiochus IV; Polybius arrives in Rome as hostage.

149–146 Third Punic War; Africa (northern Tunisia) becomes Roman province.

146 Corinth and Carthage sacked, Achaea and Macedonia Roman provinces.

141 Parthians capture Babylon: final decline of Seleucid empire.

135–132 First Sicilian Slave War.

133 Tiberius Gracchus killed; kingdom of Pergamum (western Asia Minor) left to Rome by last king.

107–100 Marius consul six times; reforms army, defeats Cimbri and Teutones and Jugurtha of Numidia (Algeria).

103–100 Second Sicilian Slave War.

99–1BC

91 Beginning of Social War.

90 *Lex Julia*: full citizenship for Italians.

89–85 First war against Mithradates.

87 Marius seizes power in Rome.

86 Sulla sacks Athens.

82 Sulla becomes dictator; second Mithradatic War.

80 Sulla resigns dictatorship.

73–71 Slave revolt of Spartacus.

70 Consulship of Pompey and Crassus.

67 Pompey eliminates pirates.

66 Pompey given eastern command.

63 Consulship of Cicero.

60 First Triumvirate: Pompey, Crassus and Caesar.

59 Caesar consul for the first time.

58–51 Caesar's Gallic Wars.

55–54 Caesar "invades" Britain.

53 Crassus killed at Carrhae.

49 Caesar crosses the Rubicon.

48 Pompey defeated at Pharsalus; Caesar meets Cleopatra, and they become lovers.

44 Caesar assassinated.

43 Second Triumvirate: Antony, Octavian and Lepidus. Murder of Cicero.

42 Republicans defeated at Philippi: empire divided.

36 Octavian defeats Sextus Pompeius.

31 Battle of Actium.

30 Suicides of Antony and Cleopatra; Egypt annexed by Octavian; Roman empire reunited.

27 Octavian assumes title *Augustus*.

16–9 Annexations of Alpine and Balkan regions under Tiberius; Drusus reaches the Elbe.

12 Death of Agrippa.

AD1–49

4 Death of Gaius forces Augustus to recall Tiberius from exile in Rhodes.

6 Judaea becomes Roman province after death of Herod the Great (in 4BC); start of the Great Pannonian revolt (lasting until AD9), which distracts Tiberius from planned campaigns in Germany.

8 Poet Ovid exiled to Tomis on Black Sea.

9 Disastrous loss of three legions in Germany under Varus; frontier withdrawn to Rhine.

14 Death of Augustus; Tiberius succeeds as emperor; Germanicus quashes Rhine legions' mutiny and campaigns into Germany to avenge Varus' defeat.

19 Death of Germanicus, the designated heir, in Syria.

27 Tiberius retires to villa on Capri, fuelling rumours of his depravities there; Sejanus acts as his sole minister in Rome.

30 or 33 Crucifixion of Jesus.

31 Execution of Sejanus for conspiracy.

37 Death of Tiberius; accession of Gaius Caligula; birth of Nero.

41 Assassination of Caligula; Claudius succeeds him as emperor. Annexation of Mauretania (Algeria/Morocco) as two imperial provinces.

42 Abortive rebellion of Scribonus, governor of Dalmatia.

43 Invasion of Britain, which becomes a province. Claudius increasingly relies on freedmen, who form the nucleus of imperial civil service.

46 Thrace becomes province.

49 Claudius marries his niece Agrippina; Seneca becomes Nero's tutor.

AD50–99

51 Caratacus, British prince, defeated and captured.

54 Death of Claudius; accession of Nero; Seneca and Burrus chief ministers.

59 Murder of Agrippina, Nero's overpowering mother.

60–1 Revolt of Boudicca and the Iceni in Britain; sack of London, Colchester and St Albans.

62 Death of Burrus and end of Seneca's influence; Nero increasingly extravagant

63–6 Settlement of Armenia and eastern frontier by Corbulo.

64 Great Fire of Rome; Nero persecutes Christians as scapegoats. Begins building the Domus Aurea (Golden Palace).

66–70 First Jewish War; Vespasian and Titus suppress Jewish revolt.

68 Suicide of Nero; accession of Galba.

68–9 Year of the Four Emperors: Galba, then Vitellius proclaimed emperor, then Otho, who commits suicide, leaving Vespasian sole emperor.

70 Capture and sack of Jerusalem.

79 Death of Vespasian; accession of Titus; destruction of Pompeii and Herculaneum by Vesuvius.

80 Inauguration of Colosseum at Rome.

81 Death of Titus; accession of Domitian.

85–92 Dacians check Domitian's campaigns and force subsidy payment.

88 Start of construction of *limes*, patrolled frontiers, along the line of the Neckar to cut off the Rhine-Danube re-entrant angle.

96 Assassination of Domitian; Nerva proclaimed emperor by Senate.

98 Death of Nerva; accession of Trajan.

AD100–199

101–6 Trajan's campaigns lead to new province of Dacia (Romania).

106 Annexation of Arabia Petraea (Jordan).

111–14 Construction of Trajan's column and forum at Rome; they are dedicated in 112–13.

113–17 War with Parthians. Conquest of Armenia, Assyria and Mesopotamia (Iraq).

115–17 Jewish revolt in Cyprus, Cyrene and Egypt.

117 Death of Trajan; accession of Hadrian.

118–28 Building of Pantheon, Rome.

121–2 Hadrian visits Britain; starts building of Hadrian's Wall.

131–5 Jewish revolt under Bar Kochba defeated; Jerusalem left a ruin.

138 Death of Hadrian; accession of Antoninus Pius.

142 Building of Antonine Wall across Scotland; Hadrian's Wall abandoned.

150–63 Revolt in northern Britain and abandonment of Antonine Wall.

161 Death of Antoninus; accession of Marcus Aurelius and Lucius Verus.

162–6 Parthian War. Ctesiphon and Seleucia sacked; plague brought back.

167 Marcomanni and Quadi, Germanic tribes, raid across Danube and reach Italy.

168–80 Wars of Marcus Aurelius.

180 Death of Marcus; accession of Commodus; peace with the Germans.

192 Commodus murdered; civil war.

193 Septimius Severus emperor in Rome.

195–9 Severus' Parthian campaigns.

AD200–299

211 Severus dies in York; leaves empire to sons Caracalla and Geta. Caracalla murders Geta.

212 *Constitutio Antoniniana*: Roman citizenship for all free men in empire.

217 Assassination of Caracalla, briefly succeeded by Macrinus.

218 Accession of Elagabalus.

222 Assassination of Elagabalus; accession of Alexander Severus; effective rule of Julia Mamaea, his mother.

235 Assassination of Alexander Severus; anarchy for almost 50 years – at least 30 emperors.

241 Shapur I (to 272), new Persian king, determined to revive old Persian empire.

251 Emperor Decius killed by Goths; plague ravages empire; persecution of Christians.

253–60 Valerian and Gallienus become co-emperors; Persian invasions.

260 "Gallic empire" formed. Valerian captured by Persians; sole reign of Gallienus; army reorganized, administrative capital moved to Milan.

268 Zenobia, Queen of Palmyra, breaks away with eastern provinces and Egypt.

270 Accession of Aurelian.

273 Zenobia defeated by Aurelian.

284 Accession of Diocletian; joint rule with Maximian as Augusti in 286.

286–96 Breakaway British "empire" under Carausius and Allectus.

293 Constantius I and Galerius appointed Caesars in new tetrarchy.

297–8 Persian War brings new Roman gains in east (now Kurdistan).

AD300–399

303–11 Last persecution of Christians.

305 Diocletian and Maximian retire.

306 Death of Constantius; his son Constantine I acclaimed emperor by troops but recognized only as Caesar of western provinces by other rulers.

312 Maxentius defeated at Milvian Bridge; Constantine sole ruler in west.

313 Edict of Milan: religious tolerance.

324 Constantine becomes sole emperor.

324–30 Foundation of Constantinople as New Rome.

325 Church Council of Nicaea presided over by Constantine.

337 Death of Constantine; empire split between his three sons: Constantine II (d. 340), Constantius II (d. 361) and Constans (d. 350).

355 Julian appointed Caesar in west.

361–3 Sole reign of Julian, pagan restoration; killed on Persian campaign.

364 Valens and Valentinian I joint emperors.

375 Valentinian dies of stroke.

378 Valens killed by invading Goths at battle of Adrianople; Goths occupy Roman territory south of Danube.

379 Theodosius I becomes emperor; accepts the Goths as federates.

382 Removal of Altar of Victory from Senate House; campaign against pagans.

394 Battle of the Cold River; Theodosius defeats rivals Argobast and Eugenius.

395 On his death, Theodosius divides empire between sons: Honorius emperor in west, Arcadius in east. Stilicho effective ruler in west.

AD400–535

404 Western imperial court moved from Milan to Ravenna, secure behind marshes.

406 German invaders cross frozen Rhine and sack Trier, the Gallic capital.

410 Last troops withdrawn from Britain; Visigoths under Alaric sack Rome; Alaric dies; Goths later settle in southwest Gaul.

421 Constantine III becomes effective ruler of western empire.

425 Valentinian III emperor in west; mother Galla Placidia at first is real ruler.

434 Attila becomes king of the Huns.

439 Vandals capture Carthage.

446 "Groans of the Britons": traditional last appeal by Romanized Britons for imperial help.

451 Battle of Châlons: Huns defeated by joint forces of Visigoths and Romans under Aetius.

452 Attila's invasion of Italy halted by Pope Leo I.

454 Murder of Aetius.

455 Death of Valentinian III; Vandals sack Rome.

476 Last emperor Romulus Augustulus deposed by mercenary chief Odoacer, who takes power himself. End of the western empire; imperial insignia sent to Constantinople.

493 Theodoric, king of Ostrogoths, becomes ruler of Italy.

527 Accession of Justinian I as emperor in Constantinople.

533 Belisarius, Byzantine general, reconquers North Africa from Vandals.

535 Belisarius begins reconquest of Italy.

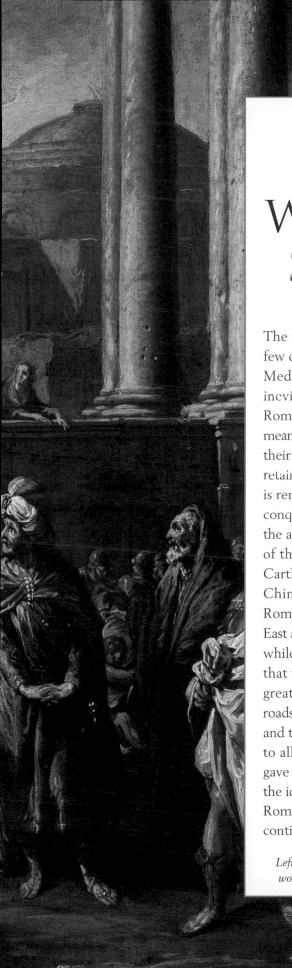

ROME: THE WORLD'S FIRST SUPERPOWER

The rise of Rome, from the mythically simple beginnings of a few dwellings above the river Tiber to dominion over the whole Mediterranean world, was seen by Romans themselves as inevitable and divinely ordained. The qualities on which the Romans prided themselves – piety, fidelity and above all *virtus*, meaning courage, ability, strength and excellence – were what made their empire possible, indeed invincible. So long as its citizens retained them, Rome would remain mistress of the world. What is remarkable about Rome is that, almost without exception, it conquered all other powers, making it the sole superpower of the ancient Mediterranean world. This was a region where many of the great civilizations of antiquity – Egyptian, Babylonian, Carthaginian, Etruscan, Greek – converged, with only distant China ever rivalling Rome in stability, power and longevity. Rome was the heir of these ancient civilizations of the Middle East and Mediterranean, absorbing and propagating their cultures, while adding its own distinctive elements to make a civilization that was unique. When Rome finally fell, it not only left us its great architectural and engineering feats – aqueducts, arches, roads – but also the corpus of Roman law, the Catholic Church, and the idea of a universal empire that could extend its benefits to all under its sway, irrespective of racial background. Rome gave a huge area many centuries of peace, but it implanted also the ideal of a universal, basically benevolent state. This has made Rome an unrivalled cultural as well as political superpower, that continues to inspire and influence the world long after its fall.

Left: As Rome became the most wealthy and powerful city in the ancient world, it drew in foreigners as craftsmen, teachers, traders – and slaves.

CHAPTER I

AN EMPIRE OF FORCE AND LAW

Rome did not acquire its empire in a few dazzling victories, but piecemeal, sometimes unintentionally, if very rarely peacefully. Rome's growth from a small settlement on the Tiber into a great empire was largely due to its military prowess and ruthless aggressiveness. Military service was a central part of life for Roman citizens. Adaptable, superbly disciplined and incredibly tough, the Roman army made Rome an imperial power. This gradual and methodical process took many hundreds of years. While such an approach may have lacked glamour, it certainly created an empire that proved very long-lived.

If most Romans experienced army life, many were also lawyers. Roman respect for the law and legality, although there was no written constitution, long safeguarded the civilian basis of politics. For a surprisingly long time, the Roman army did not intervene in civilian affairs. Its generals, no matter how great their victories, had to relinquish their commands as they entered the city, becoming ordinary citizens again and liable to prosecution for any misconduct. Even the emperor did not claim to be above the law and wore a toga (civilian dress), not armour. Rome also freely extended its citizenship to ever more cities, one of the main secrets of its success as an imperial power.

Left: This detail from the Arch of Constantine in Rome shows Emperor Constantine addressing his army – the sometimes rebellious basis of Rome's imperial might.

LEGENDARY BEGINNINGS
753–509BC

Above: Controlling the lowest crossing of the river Tiber, Rome was poised to dominate the valley of central Italy's largest river when it gained the power to do so. For long periods, however, the Tiber was as much a boundary as a route for expansion inland.

According to legend Rome was founded in 753BC by Romulus and Remus, twin princes of Alba Longa, supposedly itself founded four centuries earlier by Aeneas, a Trojan prince. The twins, his distant descendants, were abandoned as babies on the orders of Amulius, who had usurped their kingdom and ordered their deaths. Miraculously, a she-wolf appeared from a wood to suckle them, and they were brought up by Faustinus, a kindly shepherd, on the Palatine Hill. When they grew up, they killed the usurper and together founded a new city: Rome. But they soon quarrelled, Romulus killing Remus for jumping over his ploughed boundary line. Romulus then populated Rome by inviting outlaws and homeless men to join him, and by abducting the young women of his neighbours in the famous "Rape of the Sabine Women". When the Sabine men marched back in force to reclaim their women, the latter, by now used to being Roman wives, intervened to prevent a battle and the two peoples intermarried. Romulus later ascended into heaven in a thunderstorm, becoming divine. From such violent, mythic beginnings sprang the Eternal City, Rome.

Right: According to legend, the twins Romulus and Remus, distant descendants of the Trojan prince Aeneas, were suckled by a she-wolf after they had been abandoned as babies. In 753BC they founded the city of Rome, which bears Romulus' name.

THE EARLY SETTLEMENTS

Archaeology tells us that by the mid-8th century BC an unimpressive settlement existed on the Palatine Hill. The first Romans were actually Latin farmers or shepherds, the Latins being a subgroup of the Italian peoples, living in separate villages of small huts on the Palatine and the Esquiline Hills. Beneath and between these hills were marshy valleys. Despite later Roman propaganda to the contrary, this was not a particularly healthy or fertile spot, but an island had two advantages. In the midst of the fast-flowing river Tiber, it offered the first practical crossing upriver from the sea 16 miles (25km) distant, while the hills provided good defensive positions.

The settlements remained extremely primitive until the arrival – once again enshrined in myth – of the Etruscan Kings, who are traditionally said to have ruled Rome from 616 to 509BC. Certainly, at about this time Rome came under the sway of the Etruscans. They were a civilized people who dominated Italy from Bologna to the Bay of Naples. Rome's strategic position on the Tiber meant the Etruscans, approaching the height of their power, inevitably wanted control over it. In close contact with the Greek cities to the south, whose art influenced but did not overwhelm their art, the Etruscans were a cheerful, even hedonistic, race, fond of the arts, women, banquets and athletics – or so their surviving bronzes and tomb paintings suggest. We still cannot fully read their language, even though, like the Roman alphabet, it uses a version of the Greek alphabet, but the Etruscans did not write very much.

A NEW CITY

It is probably true to say that the kings made Rome a city rather than a mere huddle of villages. The *Forum Romanum*, the market/meeting place, heart of the city and later of the empire, was established on drained marshland and paved, as was the *Forum Boarium* (cattle market) close to the river.

Tarquinius Priscus, the "good Tarquin", who ruled between *c*.616 and 579BC, held the first census. Citizens were organized into three tribes, each having ten *curiae*, or wards. From these 30 wards the kings chose 300 patricians, or heads of extended families, to sit in the advisory council known as the Senate. The first Assembly, the *comitia curiata*, is also thought to have emerged about this time, although its powers are unknown.

Priscus' successor, King Servius Tullius, reorganized the state, dividing Romans into five classes according to their wealth. Each class was subdivided into centuries, each century being roughly equal in wealth. All citizens were liable for army service, apart from those in the last and poorest class, who could not afford to arm themselves. A legion, or levy, had 6,000 infantry and 300 cavalry, the cavalry being provided by the richest century. In the newly appointed *comitia centuriata*, or Assembly by Hundreds, each century voted as a single block, with the richest (but smallest) century voting first. The vote was decided as soon as an absolute majority of centuries was reached, which inevitably gave the rich centuries the most influence and the poorest (and biggest) centuries the least. Rome never operated on the principle of "one man one vote".

At this time Rome acquired Ostia at the mouth of the Tiber as well as its first wooden bridge across the river. The period culminated in the construction of the first temple to Jupiter, king of the gods, on the Capitoline Hill. Originally simply constructed, the temple was later rebuilt ever more splendidly, and became *the* symbol of Roman power.

Above: The first Romans lived in simple huts, as shown in this mosaic of life on the Tiber.

THE FOUNDING OF THE REPUBLIC

Around 509BC, the kings were suddenly and finally expelled, and the word Etruscan, like the word king, became an insult among Romans. According to legend, the last Etruscan king, Tarquinius Superbus, meaning "the proud", so angered the Roman nobles that they drove him out and declared a Republic, which they dominated through the Senate. From now on, the state was to be run by annually elected officials A new regime based on puritanical, patriotic *virtus*, or courage, was established that would serve Rome well through its coming struggles.

Below: This landscape is typical of the often wild mountains of central Italy east of Rome.

THE CONQUEST OF ITALY
501–266BC

After the expulsion of the Etruscan kings Rome became less wealthy and powerful. The other cities of Latium, which were similar in language (Latin) and culture to Rome, turned against her. Surrounded by enemies, especially the Samnites to the east and the Volscians to the south, Rome was forced to ally itself with them on equal terms – although it was never to accept equality with any city for long.

THE RISE OF THE PLEBEIANS

Inside Rome, the advent of the Republic caused an economic slump. This triggered a lengthy conflict, which was known as the Conflict of the Orders or classes, between the people (plebeians) and the patricians, the old heads of the family who traced their descent from the original Senate members and who still monopolized power. In 494BC the plebeians – who included some moderately rich citizens and many independent farmers or artisans – threatened to secede from the state and leave Rome. These people formed the core of the army, so it was a very serious threat. After several attempts, the plebeians' threat worked and they acquired two tribunes of the people, special officials to defend their interests. Later, in 449BC, their number was increased to ten and they were given special status, regarded as sacrosanct or defended by the gods.

In 471BC the tribunes summoned a special Assembly of the Plebs to run alongside existing councils. At this time, only patricians could interpret the unwritten laws. Only in 450BC were laws written down on 12 tables of stone for everyone to see. These tables, often masterpieces of legal precision, became the foundation of Roman justice. In 421BC the first plebeian quaestors were elected, and from 367BC one of the two consuls (the top magistrates who led the armies) had to be a plebeian. The patricians tried to transfer some of the consul's powers to a new official, the quaestor, but from 337BC there was also a plebeian praetor. Finally, in 287BC a law, the Lex Hortensia (Roman laws were named after their proposer), declared that plebiscites, votes of the plebeian Assembly, could become law. This completed a social revolution without bloodshed – albeit with much dispute – and is an example of the Roman genius for pragmatism.

EXPANSION AND INVASION

Throughout this domestic turmoil, Rome steadily expanded its influence and territory. To the north, just across the Tiber, stood the wealthy Etruscan city of Veii, controlling a network of roads. Rome became involved in an intermittent 40-year war with this great rival. It ended only after Camillus, made emergency ruler, forced the army to campaign continuously – without even stopping for the harvest – and used a drainage tunnel to capture Veii in

Above: Rome alternately fought and treated with its often powerful Etruscan neighbours. This fresco from the 3rd century BC shows a treaty being agreed.

Below: The Via Appia, the first great Roman road, was built to connect Rome with Capua in 312BC and was later extended to Brindisi.

Left: Paestum was one of the first Greek cities in southern Italy to be conquered by Rome in the 4th century BC. Its magnificent temple of Ceres, with massive Doric columns, is one of the best-preserved of the early Greek temples and dates from c.500BC.

396BC. This was a very important conquest. Overnight, it almost doubled Rome's territory, and the way to Etruria (Tuscany/Umbria) was opened.

A few years later, however, Rome faced acute danger. A horde of Gauls, barbarous Celts, swept through Italy in 390BC. Rome sent the whole of its army – some 15,000 men – to face them, but the Gauls, twice that number and better fighters, destroyed it almost completely. The city lay defenceless and most Romans fled, apart from a garrison on Capitoline Hill and some elderly senators who, as Livy related, "went home to await the enemy, fearless". A general massacre ensued and Rome was burnt to the ground.

MASTERING PENINSULAR ITALY

After this disaster many were tempted to abandon Rome, but Camillus rallied them to rebuild the city. In 378BC the Servian wall was constructed. It was 12ft (3.6m) thick and 24ft (7.5m) high and enclosed 1,000 acres (427 ha) – then a huge area. Rome would not fall to barbarians again for 800 years. Troubles with Rome's Latin allies followed, however. After peaceful methods of dealing with them failed, a four-year period of dogged fighting ensued before the Romans gained final victory in 338BC. The Latin League was dissolved, with each city being linked to Rome while retaining internal autonomy. Many were given citizenship, without voting rights (*civitas sine suffragio*). This halfway status satisfied the Latin cities and was a stroke of political genius. Another series of wars against the Samnites lasted nearly 40 years, with Rome suffering a major defeat in 321BC. But again Rome rallied, the Latin cities remained loyal and the first great Roman road, the Via Appia, was constructed to supply the army in the south. The war ended in 290BC with Rome undisputed mistress of central Italy.

Rome now came into contact with the Greek cities of southern Italy. A dispute with the largest, Tarento, led to war in 280BC. The Tarentines hired King Pyrrhus of Epirus, a renowned Greek mercenary leader. Pyrrhus' army included war elephants, the first seen in Italy, and he defeated the Romans twice, marching right into Latium. But Rome adapted its infantry tactics to cope with the elephants and crack Greek spearmen. By 272BC Pyrrhus had left Italy, and Tarento and the other Greek cities accepted Roman alliance. Throughout peninsular Italy, Rome was supreme.

Above: After the Gauls sacked Rome in 390BC, the Romans built the great Servian Wall some 24ft (7.5m) high. When it was completed in 378BC, the wall made the city all but impregnable to later attacks.

THE GROWTH OF EMPIRE
264–133 BC

Above: The Carthaginians regularly used elephants, the "tanks of ancient warfare", in battle. The Roman legionaries soon learnt how to counter them, however, and they did not much affect the Punic wars.

Below: Lake Trasimene in Umbria was the scene of one of Rome's great defeats by Hannibal's armies in 217BC. The Carthaginians trapped the Romans by the lakeside and drove them into the water.

Facing each other across the Messina straits, Rome and Carthage had friendly treaties dating back to 509BC. But tensions soon developed between these two great powers of the western Mediterranean. Founded in *c.*800BC by Phoenician (Lebanese) traders, Carthage had extended its power along the African coast to Tangier and into Spain, founding Malaga and Cadiz. It also had control of most of Sicily. Larger and far richer than Rome, Carthage was ruled by a mercantile oligarchy whose faults showed up Rome's virtues. It relied on mercenary armies whom it often did not pay, led by Carthaginian generals whom it failed to support in success but always punished in defeat. However, as a city of merchants it had an excellent navy, while Rome, a land power, had no navy at all.

The clash came in 264BC when Messina appealed for Roman help against Carthage. Unusually, the Senate let the Assembly decide the issue. The Roman people voted for war and the first of three Punic Wars (the Roman name for Carthaginians) began. Lacking a fleet,

Rome decided to build one, copying a captured Carthaginian ship, but adding a new weapon: the *corvus*, or raven, a bridge fitted with spikes that crashed down and stuck on to enemy vessels. This allowed Roman soldiers to board the enemy ship and fight as if on land. With this weapon a sea battle was won off Mylae in 259BC, but the war turned against Rome when it sent an army to Africa under Regulus. After initial victories, he was crushingly defeated in 255BC and a relief fleet was lost in a storm. At immense cost the Romans built another fleet, and finally in 241BC routed the Carthaginians off the Agate Islands. In its defeat, Carthage was forced to abandon Sicily, which became the first Roman *provincia*, or imperial possession, apart from the great city of Syracuse. This became Rome's first client kingdom or protectorate. Rome had won by tenacity, adaptability and the loyalty of the Italian allies, who supplied Rome's armies with fresh recruits to replace those killed in battle.

A WAR OF ATTRITION
Carthage, plunged into chaos by a revolt of its unpaid mercenaries, stood by as Rome annexed Sardinia and Corsica, the former long a Punic possession. However, Hamilcar Barca, a Carthaginian general, carved out new territory in Spain, where he recruited a better army financed by Spain's silver mines. His son Hannibal took command in 221BC, determined to strike directly at Italy, the source of Rome's vast military manpower. In 218BC Hannibal marched his army, including 37 elephants, over the Alps in a snowstorm. Hannibal's skills, combined with Roman amateurishness, led to a series of Carthaginian victories, leaving Rome almost defenceless after the third annihilating defeat at Cannae in 216BC. Amazingly, only a few allied cities –

Capua, Tarento, Syracuse – changed sides, and Hannibal could not capture Rome itself, although he rode around its walls. With cool courage, the Senate then sent an army to Spain to strike at Hannibal's base. After some initial defeats, Cornelius Scipio landed in 210BC, and in 206 ousted the Carthaginians. Spain now became a Roman possession, divided into two provinces. Meanwhile, in Italy, the Romans had adopted the "scorched earth" policy of Fabius *Cunctator*, the Delayer. This denied Hannibal all resources, but also devastated Italian farms and caused massive homelessness. The war of attrition ended in 204BC when Scipio landed in Africa, and Carthage, which had seldom reinforced Hannibal, recalled its general. At the battle of Zama in 202BC Hannibal was defeated by Scipio, and Carthage accepted a humiliating peace.

ROME AND THE EAST

The Second Punic War was the most momentous in Rome's history. It determined that Rome would rule the western Mediterranean and be arbiter in the east. Rome had already been drawn east, for Philip V of Macedonia (northern Greece) had allied with Carthage in 214BC, when Rome seemed doomed. This First Macedonian War petered out in 205BC but five years later, fearing that Philip was growing too powerful, Rome intervened more decisively, defeating him in 197BC. The Roman general Flaminius then promised "the liberty of the Greeks", meaning self-rule, to the feuding southern Greek cities. Antiochus III, the Seleucid (Hellenistic) king (one of Alexander the Great's successors), was decisively defeated in 190BC when he tried to intervene in Greece, his pan-Asian empire reduced to a Syrian rump. Rome then established a free port at Delos, which soon became the commercial centre of the eastern Mediterranean, thronged with Italian merchants, and a centre of the booming slave trade. Rome defeated Macedonia again in 168BC when it tried to reassert itself, finally

making all Macedonia a province in 146BC along with Greece itself. When the last ruler of Pergamum, another wealthy Hellenistic kingdom in Asia Minor, died in 133BC, he bequeathed it to Rome.

A NEW IMPERIALISM

The sack of Corinth, Greece's richest port, in 146BC, revealed a new brutality and rapacity in Roman imperialism. Although the Senate enjoyed prestige and power both at home and abroad, it did not always act wisely. The final destruction of Carthage in the Third Punic War was partly due to Cato the Censor, a reactionary who ended every speech with "Carthage must be destroyed!" But it was also due to Rome's increasingly aggressive imperialism. Vast fortunes were being made by Roman nobles who returned from military triumphs, or even from provincial governorships, with huge amounts of booty, including slaves. In 167BC, for example, the destruction of Epirus alone brought in 150,000 slaves. Very often these captives were better educated than their masters and helped introduce Greek culture to Roman society. However, the gains of war came at a cost. The stability of the Republic was threatened by the plight of tens of thousands of impoverished Romans, forced off the land during the Punic Wars and now unemployed in Rome.

Above: The meeting of the Roman general Scipio and his opponent Hannibal just before the Battle of Zama in 202BC is one of the most famous encounters in history. Scipio crushed Hannibal's army the following day.

Below: By the 2nd century BC Rome was developing its own distinctive architecture, shown here in the Temple of Portunus. Although influenced by Greek precursors, its layout was uniquely Roman.

VICTORY ABROAD, DISCORD AT HOME: 133–61BC

The problems of small farmers, the backbone of Rome's citizen army, became acute in the 130sBC. During the Second Punic War, many had been forced to abandon their farms. Unable to regain them when they came home, the farmers sold out to larger landowners and many migrated to Rome in search of work. But Rome had no industry and soon many farmers fell into the poorest class, thereby becoming ineligible for military service. This hardly worried the Roman oligarchy, itself growing ever richer.

AGRARIAN REFORM

In 133BC Tiberius Gracchus was elected tribune. A member of the aristocracy but schooled in Greek philosophy, Tiberius proposed that *ager publicus*, public land, often gained by conquest but which the rich had grabbed, should be redistributed to the poor in small lots. Such a proposal was half-expected, but what alarmed the Senate was that Tiberius proposed his reform directly to the Assembly, without taking it through the Senate, employing the *Lex Hortensia* to start a land commission. He then flouted custom by trying to have himself re-elected tribune. Tiberius also issued a challenge to the Senate's power over foreign policy. It was this, perhaps even more than his land reforms, that so enraged conservative senators, who mobilized their supporters and had Tiberius and 300 of his followers clubbed to death. Blood had been shed in Roman politics for the first time in nearly four centuries.

Ten years later Gaius, the more radical younger brother of Tiberius, re-enacted the agrarian reforms and proposed establishing colonies of landless citizens at recently conquered Carthage while subsidizing grain for the poor. To pay for this, he auctioned the rights to collect taxes in the new province of Asia to the knights (equestrians), to whom he also transferred control of the criminal law courts from the Senate. This boosted the knightly, or equestrian, order, the second richest class, which in turn increasingly challenged the Senate's powers. Gaius, too, paid for his reforms with his life. He failed to be elected for a third time as tribune and was killed as the Senate issued a *senatus consultum ultimum*, or Senate's final decree. From now on the Senate would be divided between the optimates, in reality reactionaries, and the *populares*, nobles and others who took the people's side or more often utilized popular support for their own ends. The struggle between these two factions in the end wrecked the Republic.

MARIUS AND SULLA

Rome's growing military weakness was starkly exposed by defeats in Mauretania (western North Africa), whose king Jugurtha proved invincible until the election of Gaius Marius as consul. Marius did not come from the nobility, and his frequent re-election as consul – seven times in all – revealed the new powers of the Assembly. Realizing that the legions badly needed recruits from proletarians, the landless citizens, Marius abolished all property qualifications for the army, while making it semi-professional with proper equipment. He encouraged legionaries to look to their generals, not the Senate, for rewards after service. This tie between general and army was fatally to undermine the Republic.

At first, Marius seemed the Republic's saviour. With his revitalized army he crushed the Cimbri and Teutones – barbarians who had overwhelmed two Roman armies – at Aix-en-Provence and in the Po valley in 102–1BC. The Senate then had to accept proposals that Marius'

Above: Vital in transporting troops and goods, the Romans invested time, effort and money in developing a good road system. This is a view of the Via Appia to the south of Rome.

Below: A great soldier and military reformer, Marius was also very much a man of the people, often re-elected consul against the Senate's wishes. As a politician, however, he proved disastrously inept.

Left: The Aegean island of Delos benefited from the Roman conquest, which made it a free port. Soon it was the most thriving port in the Mediterranean and a centre of the booming slave trade, until it was sacked by Mithradates' Greek allies in 88BC.

POMPEY AND CRASSUS

Spartacus, a gladiator, started a slave revolt at Capua in 73BC that spread throughout southern Italy. Crassus, notorious for his wealth, organized an army to suppress it, helped in the last stages by Pompey, once Sulla's youngest lieutenant. With their armies backing them, the two men became consuls in 70BC, and undid Sulla's measures, restoring the courts to the knights and reducing the Senate's powers. The problem of pirates threatening Rome's corn supply then became pressing, but Pompey, given overall command by the *Lex Gabinia* in 67BC, swept the Mediterranean clear of pirates in three months. His command was extended over the whole east, which he reorganized from the Caspian to the Red Sea. Returning home in 62BC, he disbanded his army but was annoyed at being denied his expected triumph by the Senate. He then formed the First Triumvirate, or Gang of Three, with Crassus and Julius Caesar, a rising *popularis* leader. From this moment, the days of the Republic were numbered.

veterans be given lands in Gaul, Greece and Africa as rewards when Marius marched south with some troops. In 90BC the Italian allies, who had been promised but had never received full citizenship, rose in revolt across Italy. The ensuing war was chiefly won by the *Lex Julia*, granting all free men south of the Po Roman citizenship. The war left more farmers uprooted and more ex-soldiers looking for rewards.

Lucius Cornelius Sulla, one of Marius' ablest generals but a die-hard optimate, went east in 86BC to defeat Mithradates, king of Pontus, who had invaded Greece. Meanwhile Marius, elected consul for the last time, massacred opponents with his troops before dying in January 87BC. The *populares'* triumph was brief. In 82BC Sulla returned from the east without disbanding his army and, after a battle outside Rome, revived the ancient office of dictator. He used it to proscribe (eliminate) thousands of opponents, rewriting the constitution to make it impossible for anyone to challenge the restored powers of the Senate. The guarantor of this regime was his own army, and when he retired in late 80BC, his reactionary settlement unravelled.

Above: Mithradates VI Eupator, King of Pontus (115–63BC), was one of Rome's most determined enemies in the east. His attempts to expand his Black Sea empire into Greece led to his defeat by Sulla and Lucullus, and he took his own life in 63BC.

THE END OF THE REPUBLIC
60–30BC

Above: Julius Caesar, dictator.

Below: Rich but defenceless, Egypt fell to Rome in 30BC.

Julius Caesar was the third man in the secret but powerful triumvirate formed with Pompey and Crassus. Although a patrician, he supported the *popularis* faction, and was therefore hated by many in the Senate. However, he had made himself loved by the people through putting on lavish games, and had gained a reasonable military reputation in Spain. With the support of the other triumvirs he easily won election as consul in 59BC.

Once in office, Caesar quickly passed two land reform measures, giving Pompey's veterans their lands. He also revised taxes in the east, giving Crassus what he wanted for his own supporters, the tax-collecting knights. With Pompey and Crassus' support, his next step was to procure for himself proconsular command in the two important Gallic provinces (southern France and northern Italy) with their large armies, rather than the trivial command over "the woods and forests of Italy" that the Senate had decreed. Caesar pushed these measures through the Senate and Assembly ruthlessly and often illegally. It is reported that he once beat up his fellow consul Bibulus when the latter tried to oppose him. The support his fellow triumvirs had given him revealed the existence of their covert alliance, and Pompey married Julia, Caesar's daughter. Such political marriages were very common at the time.

THE END OF THE TRIUMVIRATE

In 58BC Caesar went north to take up his proconsular command and begin the lengthy conquest of Gaul, gaining for Rome one of its most important provinces. Meanwhile, the other two triumvirs were supposedly guarding his interests in Rome. The triumvirate was formally renewed in 56BC at Lucca. Crassus took up command in the east, keen for military glory to rival that of his fellow triumvirs. Disaster followed at Carrhae in 53BC. Crassus' legions were destroyed by the Parthians in the desert, and Crassus died with them. This left Pompey and Caesar in open and deepening rivalry, with the Senate backing Pompey as a lesser evil. In 49BC Caesar started civil war by crossing the Rubicon into Italy. Moving swiftly, he seized Rome, was appointed dictator by the people – in theory an emergency post – and followed Pompey and his other enemies to Greece, where he defeated them at Pharsalus in 48BC. Pompey, fleeing to Egypt, a nominally independent kingdom, was murdered upon arrival. Caesar, after encountering and being seduced by Cleopatra, then pursued and defeated the Republicans in Africa and Spain, celebrating a grand triumph in Rome while passing through.

CAESAR'S DICTATORSHIP

Once back in Rome, Julius Caesar embarked on a series of reforms including a general cancellation of debt and the founding of new colonies in Spain, Gaul, Greece and Africa for his soldiers and the city's unemployed. He also reformed the calendar, began building the huge Basilica Julia, brought citizens from outside Italy into the Senate, started draining the Pontine marshes and reformed the currency – all this in a few months.

Early in 44BC Julius Caesar assumed perpetual dictatorship, revealing that his monopoly of power was not temporary, but permanent, like a king's. Like a king, too, was the way his image appeared on coins and statues. But this was anathema to all true Republicans. On the Ides (15th) of March 44BC, just before he left Rome for an eastern campaign, Julius Caesar was stabbed to death by a group led by Brutus, reputedly a descendant of the man who had driven out the last king in 509BC.

THE SECOND TRIUMVIRATE

Caesar's assassins, about 60 senators, had nothing realistic to put in his place, except more civil war. In the complex manoeuvrings that followed, Caesar's fellow consul, Mark Antony, formed the Second Triumvirate with young Octavian Caesar, the dictator's adopted son, and

Lepidus, another Caesarean. Savagely proscribing many Republicans in Rome, they pursued the conspirators to Greece and defeated them at Philippi in 42BC. There followed a division of the empire, with Octavian ultimately taking control of all the west, and Antony controlling the east. Antony soon became enamoured of Cleopatra, the beautiful, intelligent queen of Egypt and the last Ptolemy ruler. Although officially married to Octavia, sister of his co-triumvir, Antony soon shunned her in favour of Cleopatra, and Octavia returned to Rome, humiliated.

Antony's military fame was tarnished by his failed campaign against the Parthians in 36BC. Meanwhile, Octavian was completing the basilica of the now deified Julius and establishing his own reputation as a patriotic Roman. The final showdown at the naval battle of Actium in north-west Greece in 31BC was an anticlimax, with many of Antony's supporters deserting. Pursued to Egypt, Antony and Cleopatra committed suicide, depriving Octavian of the joy of exhibiting them in his triumph, but not of the kingdom of Egypt, which he annexed personally. Two years later, Octavian returned to Rome to begin the immense task of the restoration of the Roman world after almost a century of civil war.

Above: The Battle of Actium in 31BC was the final stage in the long civil wars. Octavian's victory meant that the Roman world could at last be reunited and at peace after decades of civil wars. It also marked the completion of Rome's conquest of the Mediterranean world.

Below: The head of Julius Caesar on this silver denarius, a novel honour, shows the victor's laurel crown granted him by the Senate – which he wore all the time to disguise his growing baldness.

PEACE RESTORED: THE FIRST EMPERORS: 30BC–AD68

Above: Augustus, his family and friends are shown on the Ara Pacis, *or Altar of Peace, in Rome, in traditional Roman attitudes, symbolizing the restoration of "the Republic".*

Victorious after the long civil wars, Octavian finally returned to Rome in 29BC. His aim was to found a peaceful, effective but constitutional government, which the Republic in its last decades had failed to supply. The whole empire had suffered from the exactions of rival generals and was exhausted. As a cost-cutting exercise, he disbanded half his huge army, settling the soldiers in colonies around the empire. From now on, there would be a regular army of only 28–30 legions, or around 150,000 men, backed by equal numbers of auxiliary troops stationed in camps along the frontiers. To symbolize peace and to give the city room to grow, Octavian let most of the old Servian walls decay. Respecting Republican laws, he kept no troops in Italy – now extended to include the Po valley – but he retained nine cohorts of special Praetorian guards. Unlike Caesar, he seldom had a bodyguard in Rome. But he used his friends and colleagues, notably Agrippa, his general and son-in-law, and Maecenas, his cultural minister.

OCTAVIAN TO AUGUSTUS

In 27BC Octavian formally resigned his offices and announced "the transfer of the state to the Senate's and people's free disposal". He received them back with thanks, along with the title Augustus, meaning revered, auspicious, augmenting. He was elected consul and gave the Senate new powers as a high court and took part in its debates, becoming *princeps senatus*, leader of the Senate. Its functions became administrative, not political, in his disguised revolution. Augustus termed himself *princeps*, or first citizen, avoiding appearing royal or imperial. He gave up always being consul in 23BC after a serious illness. In its place, the Senate offered him tribunician power, making his person sacrosanct, and *maius imperium*, power over all the provinces. His *auctoritas*, personal prestige and authority, were key to his success, along with his old-fashioned probity, or *virtus*.

But the basis of Augustus' power was military, for he was also *imperator*, commander-in-chief. He used the army to expand the empire, annexing north-west Spain and the Danubian lands from the Alps to the Black Sea. Egypt also came under his control, while in the east he made a peaceful settlement with

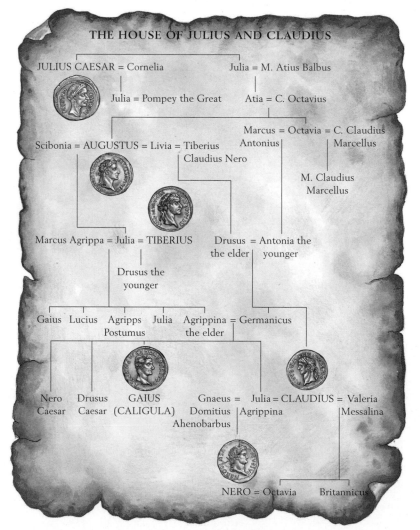

THE HOUSE OF JULIUS AND CLAUDIUS

JULIUS CAESAR = Cornelia

Julia = M. Atius Balbus

Julia = Pompey the Great

Atia = C. Octavius

Scibonia = AUGUSTUS = Livia = Tiberius Claudius Nero

Marcus Antonius = Octavia = C. Claudius Marcellus

M. Claudius Marcellus

Marcus Agrippa = Julia = TIBERIUS

Drusus the elder = Antonia the younger

Drusus the younger

Gaius   Lucius   Agripps Postumus   Julia

Agrippina the elder = Germanicus

Nero Caesar   Drusus Caesar   GAIUS (CALIGULA)

Gnaeus = Julia = CLAUDIUS = Valeria Domitius Agrippina Messalina Ahenobarbus

NERO = Octavia   Britannicus

the Parthians in 20BC. It was only in Germany that his expansionist policy was defeated when Varus was annihilated with three legions in AD9. This defeat plunged him into despair. His grandsons, his intended heirs, had both died and he had unwillingly adopted his stepson Tiberius of the proud Claudian family. None of the Julio-Claudian dynasty would ever repeat Augustus' golden age.

THE HEIRS OF AUGUSTUS

Tiberius, an excellent general, was an embittered man of 53 by the time he came to power in AD14. He continued Augustus' policies but lacked his *auctoritas* and charm. Instead, he relied on Sejanus, prefect of the Praetorian guard, as first minister, especially after Tiberius retired to Capri in AD26. There he was rumoured to indulge in fantastic sexual perversities. Probably untrue, such stories illustrate his unpopularity. Sejanus started treason trials that killed many in the imperial family before being executed for treason in AD31.

Tiberius' successor was his 24-year-old great-nephew Gaius, called Caligula after the little boots (a version of *caligae*, military boots) that he wore as a child. Very popular at first, Caligula abolished treason trials and proved as generous as Tiberius had been mean. But a serious illness six months into his reign seems to have driven him mad. He began a reign of terror, executing the Praetorian prefect Macro and many senators. His behaviour became increasingly eccentric – he joked he would make his horse consul. After he built a temple to himself as co-equal with Jupiter, he was assassinated in AD41.

While the Senate debated, a guard discovered a 50-year-old man hiding behind a curtain: this was Claudius, Caligula's uncle, passed over in the succession because of his bad stammer. But Claudius had a shrewd brain. Hailed by the Praetorians as emperor – he wisely offered them a bribe – his reign followed Augustan precedents, except for his conquest of Britain in AD43, which won

him military laurels. Claudius relied on freedmen as civil servants and began to centralize the government. But his personal life was less happy. His wife Messalina, notoriously promiscuous, was arraigned for treason in AD48. Claudius then married his niece, Agrippina, who probably poisoned him to make way for her son Nero.

Nero was only 17 when he succeeded his stepfather in AD54. At first guided by the philosopher Seneca and the Praetorian prefect Burrus, he ruled well, apart from murdering Britannicus, Claudius' son. He had artistic interests if not talents, and made a public performance as a singer in AD64. By then, with his mother murdered, Burrus dead and Seneca forced to commit suicide, Nero had become a tyrant to rival Caligula. The fire that destroyed half of Rome in AD64 was blamed on him by the people, although he scapegoated the Christians and had many of them burnt. He used the opportunity to build his Golden House, grandest of all the imperial palaces, but he also issued intelligent building regulations afterwards. Fatally, Nero neglected the army, and it was army rebellions that ended his rule in AD68. Abandoned even by his slaves, he committed suicide on 9 June AD68. The line of the Julio-Claudians died with him and civil war flared once again across the Roman world.

Above: The Pont du Gard, supplying Roman Nimes in southern France, is among the grandest surviving aqueducts and a monument to the blessings of the long Augustan peace. Beginning in 30BC, this period saw unprecedented prosperity spread around the empire, especially in the west.

Below: This fresco from the Domus Aurea, the huge palace Nero built in the centre of Rome, illustrates the myth of the birth of Adonis – and also the high quality of Roman frescoes at the time.

THE FLAVIANS AND "THE FIVE GOOD EMPERORS": AD69–180

Above: Scenes from Trajan's Column in the Forum in Rome illustrate his victories in the Dacian wars and also provide us with detailed examples of Rome's army at its zenith.

Below: In AD124 the emperor Hadrian ordered the completion of the vast Temple of Olympian Zeus in Athens, started 650 years before. Hadrian favoured Athens in many ways, eventually becoming its archon (mayor).

Vespasian, emperor AD69–79, emerged victorious from the civil wars of AD68–9. A member of the Flavian family, his father was of equestrian not senatorial rank, but Vespasian proved a far better ruler than many Julio-Claudians. On reaching Rome in October AD70, he found that the state was almost bankrupt. To fill the coffers, he increased taxation and so earned a reputation for meanness – he even taxed the disposal of urine. Vespasian restored the frontiers and strengthened the eastern defences. He recruited from among non-Italians both for the Senate and the administration and made no pretence about the monarchical nature of his regime – only his sons could succeed him. He kept the consulate, still much coveted by senators, almost completely in the Flavian family.

Titus, who succeeded in AD79, had to deal with the Vesuvian eruption. Catastrophic and costly, it was fortunate for posterity, as it preserved Pompeii and Herculaneum almost intact. Charming and lavishly generous, Titus was generally popular and he completed the immense Flavian amphitheatre, or Colosseum, in AD80. But he died suddenly in AD81 and his younger brother Domitian, emperor AD81–96, succeeded him.

In some ways Domitian was an effective ruler, at least outside Rome. He extended the frontiers in south-west Germany and perhaps wisely curtailed Agricola's attempted conquest of Scotland. But at home he assumed a despotic manner, building a huge palace to rival Nero's. Becoming increasingly paranoid, he started a reign of terror that eventually led to his assassination in AD96.

THE ZENITH OF ROME

Domitian's successor, the elderly senator Nerva, realized that the army resented his accession and adopted Trajan, governor of upper Germany, as his son and heir. Trajan's reign (AD98–117) saw the empire at its peak geographically and perhaps economically. He was called *optimus princeps*, best of emperors, by the Senate. His building programme rivalled Augustus', while his care for the poor and sick showed a new imperial compassion. But Trajan was primarily a great soldier. Between AD101–6 he crushed the aggressive kingdom of the Dacians, finally annexing their land (Romania) and settling it with colonists. He then turned east, first annexing Arabia Petraea (Jordan), before dealing with Parthia, the old enemy in the east. Initial successes saw Roman armies reach the Gulf – their furthest advance. Mesopotamia (Iraq) and Armenia were added to the empire in AD115–17 but then abandoned.

Hadrian, Trajan's (probably) designated successor, spent much of his reign outside Rome, travelling round the empire. He visited Britain in AD122, building a

Left: Hadrian was the most peripatetic of emperors, traversing the empire from Egypt to Britain. Outside Rome at Tivoli, he also created the most spacious and luxurious of imperial palaces, with pools, colonnades and even temples – often replicas of what he had seen on his extensive travels.

Below: "Five Good Emperors" of the Adoptive and Antonine dynasties ruled Rome at its zenith in the 2nd century AD, adoption solving the problems of succession.

76-mile (122-km) long wall, to keep northern barbarian Britains out of the Romanized south. Hadrian admired Greek culture, and in Rome he built the Pantheon, one of the finest of all Roman temples. His successor, Antoninus Pius (emperor AD138–61), was an elderly senator who never left Italy. Under him the empire slept in a prosperous calm.

THE FIRST CRISIS

Ironically, under Marcus Aurelius, AD161–80, one of the last great pagan philosophers, Rome was engaged in a series of conflicts. The army was so weakened by the plague of AD166 that invading Germans were able to cross the Alps, while another band almost reached Athens. In a long series of wars, Marcus went on the counter-offensive, intending to annex what is now the Czech Republic and Slovakia. At the same time, he let some Germans settle inside the empire. He was still campaigning on the Danube when he died in AD180. He left the throne to his son Commodus: it was to prove a disastrous choice.

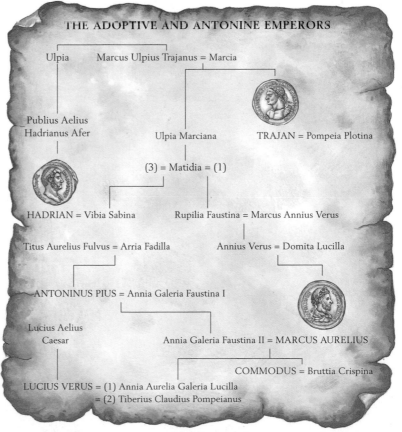

THE ADOPTIVE AND ANTONINE EMPERORS

Ulpia   Marcus Ulpius Trajanus = Marcia

Publius Aelius Hadrianus Afer

Ulpia Marciana   TRAJAN = Pompeia Plotina

(3) = Matidia = (1)

HADRIAN = Vibia Sabina   Rupilia Faustina = Marcus Annius Verus

Titus Aurelius Fulvus = Arria Fadilla   Annius Verus = Domita Lucilla

ANTONINUS PIUS = Annia Galeria Faustina I

Lucius Aelius Caesar   Annia Galeria Faustina II = MARCUS AURELIUS

COMMODUS = Bruttia Crispina

LUCIUS VERUS = (1) Annia Aurelia Galeria Lucilla
= (2) Tiberius Claudius Pompeianus

CRISIS AND CATASTROPHE
AD180–284

Above: Under the debauched and incompetent Commodus, here shown dressed as the hero Hercules, the Golden Age ended in renewed civil wars.

Below: Septimius Severus, who came from Libya, founded a new dynasty that, through its Syrian connections, lasted for 40 years and produced a remarkable range of emperors.

Aged only 18, Commodus was the first emperor to inherit the throne from his father since Titus. Although Marcus Aurelius had groomed his son for his imperial role, Commodus soon shunned onerous public duties, ruling through all-powerful favourites. After an assassination attempt in AD182, he was reluctant to appear in public at all, preferring to spend his time in his palaces or country villas, where he indulged in sexual debauchery. When the last favourite, Cleander, had been sacrificed over a grain shortage in AD190, Commodus returned to Rome, where he ordered the deaths of many prominent citizens. His assassination in January AD193 caused fresh civil wars.

When Septimius Severus, commander of the Danubian legions, reached Rome in April AD193 two earlier claimants had been killed already. It took him four more years of wars before he defeated his rivals in the east and west and began reforging the monarchy. The first emperor of African origin (he came from Libya), Severus was essentially a soldier. He increased the army's size and improved its pay and conditions of service. He ruled as an autocrat, stationing a legion outside Rome and killing 29 senators. But as a general he was brilliant, leading an attack on Parthia in AD197, which captured the capital Ctesiphon (Baghdad). He died in AD211 in York after a northern campaign. On his deathbed, he reportedly told his two sons Caracalla and Geta to "pay the soldiers and ignore the rest".

Although Severus had told his sons to work together, Caracalla soon murdered Geta. Caracalla's reign, AD211–17, is notable for his law of AD212 which gave Roman citizenship to all free males in the empire. This law was probably passed for its taxation potential, as Roman citizens paid death duties, but nevertheless it was a significant move in the widening of Roman privileges. He also constructed the most grandiose baths in Rome.

Assassinated in AD217, Caracalla left no heirs, but the Syrian branch of the Severan family produced a 14-year-old boy, Elagabalus, whose reign (AD218–22) is notorious for his sexual promiscuity. This promiscuity was supposedly in honour of the Syrian sun god Baal, whose orgiastic worship Elagabalus introduced to Rome. His marriage to a Vestal Virgin impressed neither Senate nor people. Aware of the dangers, his grandmother Julia Maesa turned to another grandson, Alexander Severus, who became emperor at the age of 14 after Elagabalus' murder by the army.

Alexander reigned for 13 years – reigned rather than ruled, for real power lay with his mother, Julia Mammaea. She enlisted the Senate's support, but he failed to win the army's loyalty. An unconvincing general, he and his mother were murdered in AD235.

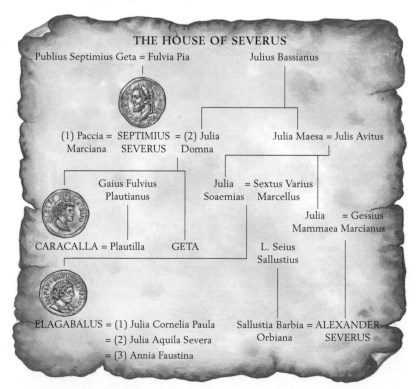

THE HOUSE OF SEVERUS

Publius Septimius Geta = Fulvia Pia   Julius Bassianus

(1) Paccia = SEPTIMIUS = (2) Julia   Julia Maesa = Julis Avitus
Marciana   SEVERUS   Domna

Gaius Fulvius   Julia = Sextus Varius
Plautianus   Soaemias   Marcellus

Julia = Gessius
Mammaea   Marcianus

CARACALLA = Plautilla   GETA   L. Seius
Sallustius

ELAGABALUS = (1) Julia Cornelia Paula   Sallustia Barbia = ALEXANDER
= (2) Julia Aquila Severa   Orbiana   SEVERUS
= (3) Annia Faustina

THE 30 EMPERORS

In the 50 years of chaos that followed, at least 30 emperors, perhaps more, were proclaimed by armies around the empire. Assassination became the norm, as different armies – from the Danube, Syria and the Rhineland – fought each other, rather than the enemy. Barbarians responded with massive invasions, which worsened the economic and financial collapse. For a time, the whole concept of one empire looked doomed: the western provinces broke away to form the Gallic Empire from AD260 to 274, while the eastern provinces were overrun by a resurgent Persian empire under a new dynasty, the Sassanids. Rome's revival owed much to emperors from Illyria (the Balkans), who proved more energetically patriotic than the Romans themselves.

In AD248 the emperor Philip the Arab celebrated Rome's millennium, but there was little to celebrate. (Philip himself was murdered the following year.) The Goths, formidable horsemen from Sweden, crossed the Danube and ravaged the Balkans, Asia Minor and Greece. Plagues swept the empire, while the Persians, under Shapur I, invaded the eastern provinces and took Antioch, the great eastern trading metropolis.

Valerian, who became emperor in AD253, was captured in AD260 by the Persians, ending his life in humiliating captivity. However, his son and co-emperor, Gallienus, reorganized the army into a far more mobile and effective force. He annihilated a Gothic force in the Balkans in AD268, but was murdered shortly after. Gallienus' work was continued first by Claudius II, who again defeated the Goths before dying of the plague, and then by Aurelian, emperor AD270–5, who crushed two German invasions of Italy. Aware that Rome itself was threatened, Aurelian hastily erected the city walls that still bear his name. In AD272 he recaptured the eastern provinces seized by Zenobia, queen of the oasis trading city of Palmyra. Two years later he defeated the last of the separatist Gallic emperors, Tetricus, reuniting Gaul with the empire. However, in AD270 he had to abandon Dacia as it was too exposed to invasion.

Aurelian promoted the worship of the Unconquered Sun, a semi-monotheistic deity to which he built a huge temple in Rome. He tried to restore the economy by issuing a new coinage. Inflation had reached terrifying levels – 1,000 per cent in the 17 years before AD275 – and the currency was almost worthless. This had led to payment in kind by the passing armies exacted from the peasants through whose lands they marched, or from the equally oppressed cities they were meant to be defending. Figures are lacking, but the economy and population of the empire shrank sharply during the chaos. However Egypt and North Africa did relatively well because they suffered few barbarian incursions. Emperor Aurelian was assassinated in AD275 but, although the empire half-relapsed into civil war, enough of his work remained for Diocletian, a soldier from Illyria, to use it as a base for reorganizing the government when he became emperor in AD284.

Above: The emperor Septimius Severus, here shown with his family, was the first Roman ruler to come from Africa, a part of the empire he favoured with lavish building projects and by advancing the frontier far into the Sahara.

Below: This bas-relief from Bishapur, Iran, shows the Persian king Shapur I humiliating the Roman emperor Valerian, who had been ignominiously captured in AD260.

RECONSTRUCTION AND REVIVAL: AD285–363

Above: The tetrarchs, the four rulers of the Roman empire, are here shown embracing each other in unshakeable amity. This system worked only while its founder, Diocletian, remained the senior emperor. Afterwards, the empire reverted to civil wars.

With Diocletian (reigned 284–305AD) the ravaged Roman world entered a period of relative stability and even revival. But in the long term this was at the cost of personal liberty, as the emperors strove to create a quasi-totalitarian state to counter the chaos of the preceding age. Diocletian, a soldier, became emperor in a bloody coup. He thought the problem of defending different frontiers would be helped by having more than one emperor. In AD286, he invited a comrade, Maximian, to become joint emperor and rule the western half of the empire. Both men took the title Augustus. In AD293 he added two junior emperors, with the title Caesar: Constantius I to rule under Maximian in the west and Galerius in the east. The Caesars became the official heirs to the Augusti and each emperor established his own court: Constantius at Trier; Maximian at Milan; Galerius at Thessalonica and Diocletian at Nicomedia in Asia Minor. Rome, still the capital in theory, was ignored.

Each new capital was richly adorned with palaces and basilicas, and anyone approaching the emperor had to prostrate himself. This deification of the emperor was designed to overawe subjects and keep them in their place The three sub-empires were not separate domains. They were all governed by the same laws and obeyed Diocletian, the senior Augustus. This system is called the Tetrarchy (from the Greek for four rulers) and at first it worked well.

LIFE UNDER THE TETRARCHY

In AD296, Galerius suffered a defeat on the troubled eastern frontier, but gained new lands the next year along the Upper Tigris. At the same time, Constantius invaded Britain, returning it to the empire after ten years of isolation. Such victories were helped by the tetrarchs' military reorganization. Each ruler had a mobile field force, the *comitatenses*, armoured cavalry who waged war. The other, larger, section of the army were the *limitanei*, permanent frontier troops who manned the much-strengthened border fortresses. German mercenaries became a regular part of the Roman army, and its manpower was increased to about 600,000 – twice its size under Augustus.

Such huge armies and courts cost money, and the tax burden became overwhelming. Diocletian tried to make reforms, issuing a new coinage in AD294,

Right: The dynasty of Constantine, who divided the empire between his three surviving sons from his marriage to Fausta, ruled the Roman world for nearly 30 years, although fratricidal strife rather than brotherly unity was the norm. Only Julian, Constantius II's half-brother, proved an able ruler.

THE HEIRS OF CONSTANTINE

Fausta (2) = CONSTANTINE I

CONSTANTINE II — CONSTANTIUS II — CONSTANS I — Constantina = Constantius Gallus

VALENTINIAN I

GRATIAN = Constantia

JULIAN THE APOSTATE = Helena

to re-establish people's faith in the currency ruined by constant inflation, but there were not enough new coins to have much impact. Then in AD301 he issued his Edict of Maximum Prices, to try to fix a maximum price for goods and services. This did not work either, for goods simply vanished from the shops and inflation continued. But he had more success in making taxes regular, with annual revisions, and introduced new assessment methods.

In AD303 Diocletian launched the last and greatest persecution of the Christians. Their numbers had increased steadily in the 3rd century AD, until about 8 per cent of the population was Christian. Diocletian, like many in the empire, felt that the Christians' rejection of Roman gods was treasonous to an emperor who styled himself "companion of Jupiter". First the Christian clergy, then the laity had to sacrifice to the gods or face imprisonment and even death. Tired of his rule, Diocletian then made the unusual decision to retire, abdicating in AD305 to grow cabbages in his palace at Split. He made Maximian retire too. Constantius then became Augustus in the west and Galerius in the east. According to the terms of the Tetrarchy, the idea was that the two Augusti would abdicate in turn, to be succeeded by their Caesars.

THE CONVERSION OF EUROPE

When Constantius I died in AD306, his son Constantine I was declared Augustus by the troops in Britain. In AD312 Constantine defeated Maxentius, son of Maximian, and 12 years later overthrew Licinius, Augustus of the east, thereby reuniting the whole empire. Reputedly, before defeating Maxentius, Constantine had had a vision of the cross. In AD313 in the Edict of Milan, he and Licinius granted religious freedom to all faiths, including Christians. By AD325 he was actively presiding over the crucial Council of Nicaea (Iznik), and by the time of his death in AD337 he had come to see himself as the thirteenth apostle.

In AD324 Constantine had established the city of New Rome, or Constantinople (Istanbul), as his new capital. The former Greek city of Byzantium, superbly sited on the river Bosphorus, became almost impregnable behind its double walls. Constantine continued Diocletian's policies, dividing the empire between his three sons at his death, when he was finally baptized a Christian. Of the sons, Constantius II emerged the victor of 15 years of civil war, but he was no general. Faced by barbarian invasions and usurpers, in AD355 he appointed his half-cousin Julian, known only as a scholar, as his Caesar in the west.

Julian proved almost a military genius, repelling German invasions in a series of brilliant campaigns. He also tried to lighten the burden of taxation on the wretched peasantry. Growing jealous of his success, Constantius tried to recall him, but Julian was declared Augustus by his troops in AD360. Civil war was averted by Constantius' death, and Julian, revealing himself a pagan, ordered the old temples be reopened. However, his reign was too short for this to have any effect, for he was killed on a Persian campaign in AD363. Both the house of Constantine and the pagan reaction died with him.

Above: These fragments of a colossal statue of the emperor Constantine illustrate how the later emperors liked to depict themselves: semi-divine absolute monarchs – very different from the modest image Augustus had displayed.

Below: The massive fortress-palace on the Adriatic at Split (Spalato), to which Diocletian retired to die in his bed, survives almost intact.

THE FALL OF THE WEST
AD364–476

Above: From the mid-3rd century AD onwards, Roman fortifications became vastly more massive and imposing. Behind the huge walls of fortresses such as this at Portchester on the English coast, Romans now passively awaited barbarian attacks.

After his death in AD363, Julian was succeeded briefly by Jovian, and then by Valentinian I, who for military reasons divided the empire, with his brother Valens taking the east. Both men were fine soldiers and Christians, but while Valentinian was religiously tolerant, his brother fiercely persecuted pagans and non-conformists. Valentinian proved the last really effective emperor in the west, repelling and avenging German invasions until he died in AD375, leaving his young and incompetent son Gratian as his heir. Meanwhile, far-distant events were leading towards catastrophe.

In AD378, in a defeat by the Goths at Adrianople (Idirne), Valens and most of the finest Roman troops were killed. Gratian then appointed a Spanish officer, Theodosius, as Augustus in the east, who let the Goths settle *en masse* with their own rulers within the empire. In theory, they supplied men for the Roman army but in practice they proved uncontrollable. Theodosius defeated rebel emperor Magnus Maximus in Gaul, reuniting the empire, but he was called "the Great" chiefly for his ardent Christianity. In AD392 he banned all forms of pagan worship, as intolerance became official.

Theodosius, last emperor of a united empire, died in AD395, leaving the empire to his incompetent sons: Arcadius in the east, who died in AD408, and Honorius, who lived to AD423, in the west. But the real ruler of the west was Stilicho, of German descent. In December AD406 the Rhine froze solid; Vandals and other Germans poured across it and spread into Gaul and Spain. The Rhine garrisons that should have repelled them had been withdrawn to face a usurper from Britain. The Rhine frontier was never restored and Britain, too, was soon abandoned. But there were more pressing problems in Italy. Stilicho was murdered by Honorius in AD408, and in AD410 Alaric, the Visigoth king, sacked the city of Rome.

Although the Visigoths were relatively restrained in their conquest – they were Christians, respecting churches and nuns – the world was profoundly shaken. For

Right: The imperial dynasty founded by Valentinian I saw a further acceptance of the division of the empire into east and west. Disaster occurred when his brother Valens, the eastern emperor, was killed at the battle of Adrianople. Theodosius I founded another imperial dynasty but one dependent on Gothic support.

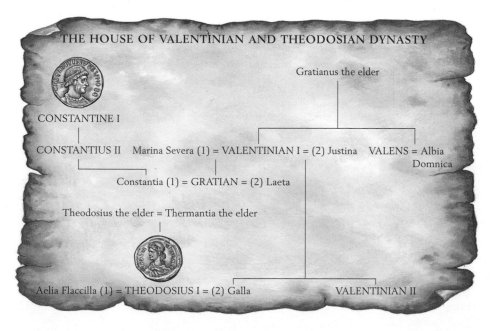

THE HOUSE OF VALENTINIAN AND THEODOSIAN DYNASTY

Gratianus the elder

CONSTANTINE I

CONSTANTIUS II   Marina Severa (1) = VALENTINIAN I = (2) Justina   VALENS = Albia Domnica

Constantia (1) = GRATIAN = (2) Laeta

Theodosius the elder = Thermantia the elder

Aelia Flaccilla (1) = THEODOSIUS I = (2) Galla   VALENTINIAN II

the first time in 800 years, Rome had fallen to the barbarians. Alaric stayed only three days, leaving with much booty and Galla Placidia, the emperor's half-sister. Alaric died soon after, and the Visigoths moved into southern Gaul. Constantius, a general, then took command and forced the Goths to return Placidia. After suppressing other rebels in Gaul, he married Placidia, against her will, and was proclaimed co-emperor in AD421. Constantius III died late that year and his son, Valentinian III, became emperor in AD425. Under his mother Placidia's control, Valentinian reigned for 30 years, and the empire continued to disintegrate.

HUNS AND VANDALS

The best efforts of Aetius, another Roman general, could not prevent the Vandals establishing themselves in North Africa. Gaiseric, the Vandal king, captured Carthage, the second city of the western empire, in AD439 and built a pirate fleet to terrorize the whole Mediterranean region. But Aetius' attention had been drawn north by an even worse threat.

The Huns, frighteningly effective horsemen, had built an empire from the Volga to the Baltic. Their greatest king, Attila, known in history as "the scourge of God" (*flagellum dei*), ravaged the eastern empire's European provinces in

the AD440s and then turned west. Attila retreated after a day's bloody fighting at Châlons-sur-Marne in AD451. This was the one defeat of his life. The next year he headed towards a defenceless Rome. Pope Leo I met him unarmed and the two talked in Attila's tent. What they said is not known, but the Huns turned back across the Alps. Two years later, Attila died and his empire collapsed.

After Aetius' death in AD454, Rome was once more leaderless, and the Vandals viciously sacked Rome. Increasingly, it was German chieftains who made and unmade emperors. Finally, in AD476, Romulus Augustulus, the last emperor of the west, was deposed by the German Odoacer, who declared himself king of Italy. The empire had ended in the west.

Above: The Hunnish king Attila, "the scourge of God", became known as the most terrifying of the barbarian invaders of the 5th century AD, renowned for his savagery. He was not the most effective invader, however, for he did not sack Rome and his empire died with him.

BYZANTIUM SURVIVES

If the Roman empire collapsed in the west, it flourished in the east. Thanks partly to Constantinople's superb defensive position, the east Roman or Byzantine empire (the name comes from the original Greek city) lived on for another thousand years. Although invasions had stripped it of its outlying provinces by the 7th century AD, it remained wealthy and civilized, wholly Greek in language and deeply Christian in its religion. A Russian ruler married one of the last Byzantine princesses, assuming the title Czar, or Caesar.

CHAPTER II

GREAT ROMANS

The Romans of the early Republic were shadowy figures of whom not much is known. A typical example was Cincinnatus. He was working on his farm when called on to become dictator and save the city in 458BC. Wiping the sweat from his brow and putting on his toga, he went off to be emergency ruler and defeat the most threatening enemies. That done, he returned to his plough.

Such self-effacing patriotism could not survive Rome's rise to world power from the 3rd century BC. The influx of wealth and contacts with the sophisticated Greeks gave Romans, too, the desire and opportunity to excel as individuals, to shine on the stage of politics or the arts, to become famous generals, politicians, philosophers or poets. The poet Horace, writing in the 1st century BC, was as much concerned with his posthumous literary fame as Julius Caesar was with his prestige and power when he was alive. Almost inevitably, the only Romans we know much about today came from the political or intellectual elite. We have almost no written records of other Romans to flesh out what archaeology tells us of their lives. What writings have survived, however, are enough to reveal much about the inhabitants of the world's first global city. Soldiers and statesmen, writers and thinkers, and powerful women, all come alive in the pages of historians such as Tacitus and Suetonius, which are at times as racy and bizarre as today's gossip columns.

Left: Julius Caesar, the most famous Roman of them all, receiving tributes from ambassadors of client states.

GREAT ROMAN GENERALS

While military service was a customary, indeed often inescapable, part of life for most Romans in the Republic, a few commanders stand out, either for saving the state or for transforming the armies. Some went on to intervene in civilian life, usually with disastrous consequences.

PUBLIUS CORNELIUS SCIPIO AFRICANUS (235–183BC)

Scipio was only 25 years old when given command of the Roman armies in Spain. Facing an invincible Hannibal in Italy, the Republic had decided to attack Hannibal's base, but the first Roman army sent to Spain was defeated and both commanders killed. They were soon avenged. Scipio captured Cartagena, the Carthaginian headquarters, in 209BC. The next year, he defeated Hasdrubal, Hannibal's brother, by using light troops as a screen for the heavier legionaries. Soon all of Spain went over to Rome, while Hasdrubal was later defeated in Italy. Consul in 205BC, Scipio then led an army to Africa and defeated Hannibal at the Battle of Zama in 202BC, overcoming Hannibal's war elephants by ordering his legionaries to open ranks and let the maddened animals pass between them.

Scipio made two significant military reforms. First, his armies in Spain adopted the short Spanish stabbing sword. Devastatingly effective, it became the standard weapon of Roman legionaries. Second, he reformed the maniple, of which there were 30 to each legion, at times allowing them to act in three separate lines. More than a mere soldier, Scipio was among the first Romans to appreciate Greek culture and to learn the language properly. Partly because of this, he was subject to persecution by Roman traditionalists such as Cato the Censor. In 190BC, accused of misappropriating booty from the Syrian campaign, he finally withdrew from public life altogether.

GAIUS MARIUS (158–87BC)

A great soldier but a disastrous politician, Marius came from an equestrian family. He made his fortune as a *publicanus* (tax-collector), and he was a tribune of the plebs in 119BC, and praetor in 116BC. He was appointed commander of the armies in Africa in the wars against King Jugurtha. Brilliantly successful, Marius became consul in 107BC, finished the war in 105BC and was made consul again the next year.

Marius was given sweeping powers, which he used to reorganize the army, introducing the cohort of six centuries (500–600 men), and giving each legion its silver eagle, which soon became an emblem of tremendous importance. He made the *pilum*, the throwing spear, break at its neck, to render an enemy's shield useless. Marius abolished the last property qualifications so making the army more attractive to the poor, who now, however, had to carry all their equipment – hence their nickname "Marius' mules". These soldiers looked to their general, not the Senate, for reward. Marius used his remodelled army to crush barbarian invaders.

Returning to Rome, Marius got entangled in the struggles between the *populares*, whom he supported, and the conservative optimates, and fled from Rome when Sulla marched on it. He finally returned to Rome – totally illegally – at the head of an army in late 88BC. Becoming consul for the seventh time, he slaughtered his opponents before dying in 87BC.

Above: Scipio Africanus, who defeated the Carthaginians first in Spain then in Africa, was typical of many great generals of the Republic in the jealousy and attacks his feats roused back in Rome. These finally forced him into premature retirement.

Right: Marius reorganized the army, giving each legion its silver, later gilded, eagle, which became the focus of intense loyalty.

Although Marius had shown that military competence did not lead to a successful political career, his political success was nevertheless unprecedented at this time. Despite the rules of the constitution, he had been consul seven times, five of them consecutively.

LUCIUS CORNELIUS SULLA (138–79BC)

An optimate, or senatorial reactionary, Sulla came from an old but impoverished patrician family. Appointed general by the Senate for the war against Mithradates of Pontus in 88BC, he used his army to march on Rome and expel the *populares* – the first military intervention in Roman history. He marched on Rome again in 82BC with a devoted army of 100,000 men. The proscriptions that followed became notorious. Sulla executed 40 senators, 1,600 equestrians (knights) and many other citizens, giving their lands to his veterans. To enact his revolutionary programme, Sulla became perpetual dictator.

He passed measures that robbed tribunes of their power, removed courts from the knights' control and issued new treason laws. All this was done to boost the powers of the Senate, which he expanded to 600 men. Behaving in many ways like a monarch – Sulla inaugurated a huge building programme, repaving the forum and rebuilding the Temple of Capitoline Jupiter – he suddenly resigned all power in 80BC and retired, dying a year later. His settlement at once began to collapse, his career serving as both a warning and an example to later Romans.

MARCUS AGRIPPA (63–12BC)

Augustus' greatest general and later his son-in-law, Agrippa came from a modest background but from 44BC he was Octavian's closest companion and his indispensable military adviser. He was responsible for building and commanding the fleet that defeated Sextus Pompeius at Naulochus in 36BC, and for defeating Antony's much larger fleet at Actium in 31BC. He did this by using Liburnian galleys, which were smaller and much more manoeuvrable than the giant quinqueremes in Antony's fleet.

In 33BC Agrippa accepted an aedileship – although he had already held the consulship, the top post. In effect, he became Rome's first water commissioner: he erected the first public baths, supervised the extension and rebuilding of the *cloaca maxima*, the ancient drain of Rome, and built an artificial reservoir, or *stagnum*. Later he built a network of roads across Gaul. After Marcellus' death, Agrippa married Julia, Augustus' only daughter, and their two sons Gaius and Lucius became Augustus' official heirs. Agrippa died on 20 March 12BC, one of the finest generals and ministers who had helped transform the Republic into the Principate.

Above: Sulla, the dictator.

Below: The capture of Reggio, a Greek city in Italy, as depicted by a medieval artist.

Above: A 3rd-century AD arch in Rome traditionally attributed to Drusus' victories.

Below: Germanicus.

NERO DRUSUS (40–9BC)

The younger son of Livia and the stepson of Augustus, Drusus was the descendant of some of the proudest patricians in Rome and, like his older brother Tiberius, he was a formidable general. He first won military fame campaigning in Illyria. After the death of Agrippa in 12BC, although still in his early twenties, he was entrusted with the steadily advancing conquest of Germany. Drusus crossed the Rhine and invaded northern Germany, conquering territory up to the Elbe, which was designated as the new frontier. It is said he longed for the *spolia optima*, the highest military honours awarded to those who had killed an enemy commander in person, and so rode round the battlefields in search of a German chieftain to be his victim. This was probably slanderous, but he was certainly ambitious.

In 9BC Drusus' ambitions were curtailed by his early death in a riding accident. His death deprived the Julio-Claudian dynasty of a good general who was less morose and suspicious than his elder brother. It also deprived those senators still hoping for a republican restoration, for Drusus, according to Tacitus, was believed to be a secret republican. He had married Antonia, the daughter of Mark Antony and niece of Augustus, and they had two sons: Germanicus, who became a popular general, and the bookish Claudius, who later became emperor.

GERMANICUS (15BC–AD19)

The charming and popular son of Drusus and great-nephew of Augustus, Germanicus grew up partly among soldiers. Unlike his infirm brother Claudius, he was marked out early both as a general and as the successor to his father's reputed republican sympathies. By the time Tiberius became emperor in AD14, Germanicus had been appointed by Augustus as commander-in-chief of the Rhine forces, and Tiberius had had to adopt him as his son and heir.

At eight legions, the Rhine command was much the biggest in the army. Many of the legionaries had mutinied, and Germanicus restored order only with great difficulty and at peril to his own life. He led his armies into Germany, where Varus had lost his life and three legions in AD9. Germanicus buried some of the bones of the dead legionaries and defeated the German leader, Arminius, in a minor victory. However, Tiberius had no intention of resuming a forward policy, and in AD16 Germanicus was recalled. Tacitus has him say, "I achieved more by diplomacy than by war…as for the Cherusci and other savage tribes, Rome's vengeance has been asserted and we can leave them to quarrel among themselves." This proved true. In May AD17 Germanicus celebrated a triumph in Rome, then became consul with Tiberius before being sent to sort out problems in the east. On the way he visited Egypt, thereby arousing Tiberius' wrath, for senators were barred from Egypt without imperial permission. In Syria he soon quarrelled with the new governor, Gnaeus Piso.

When Germanicus died at Antioch in October AD19, it was rumoured that Piso had poisoned him. Whether scapegoat or villain, Piso was tried for murder and he committed suicide soon after. Germanicus left three children by his wife Agrippina, Augustus' granddaughter, of whom one survived to become emperor: Caligula, the vile antithesis of his charming, urbane father.

GAIUS JULIUS AGRICOLA
(AD40–93)

One of Rome's finest generals, Agricola was fortunate in having the historian Tacitus as a son-in-law to laud his life and career. Born in AD40 at Forum Iulii (Fréjus), Agricola's father was a senator and his mother a cultured woman who sent him to Greek schools in Marseilles. He first served as a military tribune in Britain under Suetonius Paulinus (AD58–61). As quaestor to Salvius Titianus, governor of Asia, he was shocked by the "mutual covering up of malpractice" among officials. After holding office in Rome, he returned to Britain as a commander. Governorship of Aquitania (south-west France) was followed by consulship under Vespasian.

When he became governor of Britain (AD77–83), Agricola, under orders from Rome, decided to complete the conquest of Britain. He first subdued North Wales before overawing the Brigantes in AD79 by sending two military columns on either side of the Pennines. He continued north into central Scotland, reaching the Tay. In AD82 he turned south-west, conquering that corner of Scotland and glimpsing Ireland, which he optimistically thought could be conquered by a single legion. In AD83 he continued north along the eastern edge of the Highlands, building forts as he went. Finally, in AD84 he met

the gathered Caledonian clans at Mons Graupius, perhaps near Inverness, defeating but not annihilating their forces. He then ordered the building of a major legionary fortress (for more than 5,000 men) at Inchtuthil above the Tay. But the emperor Domitian, suddenly needing troops for the Danube, recalled a legion and the conquest had to be abandoned. "Britain was completely conquered and immediately let go", was Tacitus' bitter comment, but the Highlands would have proved very difficult to conquer and hold.

Agricola was also a great peacetime administrator. He built over 1,300 miles (2,200km) of roads and 60 forts, repressed abuses, notably in the tax-collecting system, was lenient towards minor offences but hard on major ones, and encouraged the Romanization of Britain. According to Tacitus, he "encouraged individuals and communities to build temples, fora and houses... He had leading Britons' sons educated in the liberal arts... The result was that people who had rejected Latin now sought to be fluent and eloquent in it." Such eloquence was a vital Roman civic skill and spurred the development of a true Romano-British aristocracy. Agricola had no further important commands under the increasingly paranoid emperor Domitian, but at least he kept his life.

Above: The great popularity of the general Germanicus at the time of his sudden death in AD19 led to many arches being raised in his posthumous honour across the empire, such as this one at Pompeii in southern Italy.

Below: One of the greatest generals and governors of the Principate, Agricola conquered almost all Britain but suffered Domitian's jealousy. This Renaissance portrait, if more imaginative than accurate, testifies to his fame.

JULIUS CAESAR
101–44BC

Above: This silver denarius with the head of Caesar – then a novelty in Republican Rome – dates from 44BC, the year of his assassination.

Below: The Forum and, bottom right, the Basilica Julia, which became Rome's chief law court and was perhaps Caesar's most imposing monument, although it was actually completed after his death by his heir Augustus.

Julius Caesar is probably the most famous Roman of all. Due to his early death, he achieved little as a ruler compared with his successor Augustus, yet he deserves his fame, for he was one of Rome's greatest generals and most far-sighted politicians. As a man, he was charming, urbane and often unscrupulous. As a politician, he was the first emperor in all but name. His career demonstrated that only monarchy – whether king, dictator or emperor – could save Rome from chaos. The charisma of his name, Caesar, was such that all his successors called themselves by it, even when totally unrelated to him. This practice continued long after the empire had ended and well beyond its reaches: in Germany up to 1918 (Kaiser is German for emperor) and in Russia (Czar also means emperor).

Gaius Julius Caesar was born on 13 July 101BC. Although a patrician, he was not from the highest Roman nobility. His marriage to Cornelia, daughter of Lucius Cornelius Cinna, linked him with the Marian *popularis* party, making him a wanted man under Sulla's dictatorship, so he withdrew to Asia. Returning to Rome after Sulla's death, he began his political career relatively slowly, supporting the repeal of Sulla's measures. He became quaestor in 68BC and aedile in 65BC, when he gave unusually lavish public games, both alarming the Senate and becoming heavily indebted to Crassus, Rome's richest man. He was now the leading *popularis*. In 63BC he became *pontifex maximus*, the chief priest of Rome, a prestigious post without many priestly duties. After becoming praetor in 62BC, and propraetor (governor) in Spain, he became a consul in 59BC, despite fierce senatorial opposition.

CONQUEROR OF GAUL
Caesar's election as consul was partly due to the support of Crassus and Pompey. Together the three men formed the First Triumvirate, initially a secret pact, always unofficial and essentially illegal. But Caesar's acts helpful to Pompey and Crassus revealed the existence of the triumvirate, so Caesar married his daughter Julia to Pompey to cement the alliance. Caesar often behaved unconstitutionally, forcing his conservative colleague Bibulus to resign. Caesar then got himself extended proconsular command in the "two Gauls".

The Roman provinces of Transalpine and Cisalpine Gaul (southern France and northern Italy) provided good recruiting grounds and opportunities for glory in Gaul itself, a huge area inhabited by warring Celtic tribes. After a victory over the Helvetii in 58BC, Caesar went on to defeat tribe after tribe. Although some

senators objected, the people loved his victories. No Roman had set foot in Germany before. Nor had they in Britain, Caesar's next target. His first invasion fleet in 55BC was damaged by tides, but he returned the next year with a larger force of five legions ferried by 800 ships. This force impressed the Britons, and Britain was claimed as a conquest. A huge final revolt in Gaul was suppressed in 52–51BC. The human cost was immense – over half of all Gauls of military age were killed – but Rome had reached northern Europe. And Caesar had created an effective army, loyal only to him.

The triumvirate had been renewed in 56BC, but the deaths of Julia in 54BC and Crassus in 53BC undermined it. Pompey, jealous of Caesar, refused to let him stand for consul *in absentia* and gain immunity from prosecution. Caesar had either to accept political and even personal oblivion, or start civil war. On 10 January 49BC Caesar reluctantly marched his army across the Rubicon, the frontier of Italy. Civil war had restarted.

THE MAN AND THE DICTATOR
If slow to start war, Caesar was extremely fast to wage it. After an Asian blitzkrieg he uttered three infamous words "*Veni, vidi, vici*" (I came, I saw, I conquered). However, he spent the winter of 48–47BC besieged in Egypt, where he made Cleopatra his lover and installed her as queen.

As dictator in Rome he initiated a vast range of reforms. He overhauled the calendar, he cancelled interest on debts, and started construction of a basilica and forum. He ordered the draining of the Pontine Marshes and cutting of the Corinth Canal, but neither was accomplished. Around 80,000 landless Roman civilians and as many veterans were settled in 40 colonies around the empire. He issued a new coinage with his head on it and gave lavish games. The Senate was expanded to 900 with non-Italians from Gaul and Spain. A huge new library for Greek and Latin literature was planned. While he was preparing for a war with Parthia,

60 senators, led by Marcus Brutus and Cassius, stabbed him to death outside the Theatre of Pompey on 15 March 44BC.

Caesar had wrongly assumed everyone was won over by his generosity. One of the conspirators, Decimus Brutus, was named in his will and scheduled to be consul. But Caesar's growing personality cult was an outrage to republican sentiment; he had gone about with a large bodyguard, and when offered a regal diadem had not refused it convincingly. Caesar paid for his misjudgement with a life he may not have been too keen to prolong; he suffered from epilepsy and his health was worsening. Rome paid for it with another two rounds of civil war.

Caesar was tall, well built with dark eyes. Somewhat vain, he was delighted when the Senate voted that he could always wear a victor's laurel crown, as he was going bald. He was a noted womanizer but because of a youthful homosexual episode, he was throughout his life unable to escape being taunted with accusations of effeminacy. He was among Rome's best orators and a fine historian. A patron of the arts, he was perhaps the closest Rome produced to a "Renaissance man". His career has been an inspiration and a warning for many later rulers.

Above: Among Caesar's many projects for Rome was his new forum and a temple to Venus Genetrix, the goddess from whom the Julian dynasty claimed descent.

Below: This bronze statue at Aosta in northern Italy shows Caesar as the assured and triumphant general – a role he played to perfection.

POMPEY: CAESAR'S RIVAL
106–48 BC

Above: Pompey the Great. Undoubtedly a brilliant general and fine imperial administrator, in Roman politics Pompey often showed himself as being unable to decide between saving or overthrowing the Republic.

Below: Pompey was totally defeated by Caesar's numerically inferior armies at the Battle of Pharsalus. He fled to Egypt, only to be killed upon landing.

Caesar's greatest rival and one of Rome's finest generals, Pompey ended his career as the last defender of the Republic. Yet his own ambitions were fundamentally not so different from Caesar's. If he had won the civil war, he too could have ended up dictator, although he showed little of Caesar's statesmanlike vision.

Gnaius Pompeius Magnus, Pompey "the Great", was born in 106BC to a noble family on the Adriatic coast. He joined the reactionary general Sulla in 83BC and helped defeat the Marian faction in Rome, killing thousands of civilians. For this Sulla reluctantly granted Pompey a triumph, although he dubbed him *"adulescentulus carnifex"* (little teenage murderer). Given command against Spanish rebels in 77BC, Pompey defeated them, returning to Italy in time to deliver the final blow to Spartacus' slave uprising. Crassus then united with him to demand the consulship in 70BC. As consuls, the two men undid most of Sulla's reforms, restoring the tribunes' powers and reducing the Senate's control of the law courts, winning popular support if senatorial distrust.

When pirates began threatening Rome's corn supply in 67BC, Pompey was given command of 120,000 soldiers and 500 ships. He divided the Mediterranean into twelve zones and within three months had solved the problem. The *Lex Manilia* gave him similar powers over the east, where a war against Mithradates of Pontus had dragged on. Pompey, taking over Rome's armies in Asia, led them to a series of sensational victories: Mithradates committed suicide and Pompey united his kingdom of Pontus with the province of Bithynia. He then marched east as far as the Caucasus, deposing or installing kings, making them client states of Rome and founding 40 new cities. Turning south, he deposed the

last Seleucid king and annexed Syria. Continuing into Judaea, he entered Jerusalem and even the Temple, to Jewish dismay. But he confirmed the Maccabee dynasty on the Judaean throne, again as client kings. His settlement of the east was so well judged that it effectively lasted 120 years and boosted Roman imperial revenues by 40 per cent. In 62BC he returned to Italy, laden with glory and booty, with his victorious army behind him.

His return was feared, for he had been expected to emulate Sulla and march on Rome. Instead, he disbanded his armies and entered Rome as a civilian, expecting a triumph of suitable splendour and, even more important, land for his veterans. The Senate procrastinated for a year on the former and refused the latter. This proved fatal. Rebuffed, Pompey formed the First Triumvirate with his rivals, Crassus and Julius Caesar, marrying Caesar's daughter Julia to cement the alliance. As consul, Caesar gave Pompey's men their land, but his conquests of Gaul made Pompey jealous. During Caesar's absence, Pompey was effectively master of Rome, becoming sole consul in 52BC.

All he did with his power was to build Rome's first stone theatre, dedicated in 55BC, and side increasingly with the Senate, now dominated by Cato the Younger, a reactionary. When civil war broke out in January 49BC, Pompey reluctantly accepted command from the Senate. He retreated to Greece in the face of Caesar's superior forces, but at Dyracchium (Durazzo) he surrounded and nearly captured Caesar's army. However, in August 48BC he was decisively defeated at Pharsalus and, fleeing to Egypt, was killed as he stepped ashore. Pompey, a proud soldier if often uncertain of his course in Roman politics, might have preferred this end to being ignominiously pardoned by Caesar.

MARK ANTONY
83–30BC

Mark Antony (Marcus Antonius) was Julius Caesar's trusted follower, Octavian's rival, then his ally and finally his enemy. Lord of half the empire and greatest living Roman general, he was hailed as a god in Greek cities and achieved fame as the lover of Cleopatra, queen of Egypt.

Born in 83BC, Mark Antony started his career as an officer in Egypt in the 60s BC. From 54–50BC, he served under Caesar, becoming one of his most trusted officers. On the fateful Ides of March of 44BC, Antony was consul with Caesar and after Caesar's assassination, effectively became Rome's ruler. He used his position and rhetorical skills to drive the assassins from Rome but was outmanoeuvred by Octavian. Antony was too good a general to beat, however, and they came to terms. The Second Triumvirate was formed by Antony, Octavian and Lepidus, a necessary but powerless third. After the triumvirate had beaten the conspirators, Antony took the eastern half of the empire and Octavian most of the west.

From the start, relations were strained. Antony had greater prestige and larger forces but Octavian had Italy and Caesar's name. Antony married Octavian's sister, Octavia, and the triumvirate was renewed in 37BC. But it was obvious that Antony was entangled with a far more alluring woman, Cleopatra VII, queen of Egypt.

Cleopatra, Greek by culture and descent, was an intelligent woman and a shrewd ruler. Her wealth as much as her person initially attracted Antony, and he ostentatiously accepted her aid, ignoring Octavia whom he sent back to Rome. Deeply offended by this snub, Octavian began planning war and in 32BC read out what he said was Antony's will. In a ceremony in Alexandria, Antony gave many sub-kingdoms to Cleopatra's children by Caesar and himself, although confirming Pompey's eastern settlement.

Worse still, when Antony went north in 31BC for the showdown with Octavian, he took not only his Roman army and navy, but also Cleopatra, confirming his image of being under her thumb. In the stand-off between the two armies, Antony's men began deserting and the sea battle was an anticlimax. Both Antony and Cleopatra fled to Egypt, where they committed suicide when Octavian arrived in 30BC. If unsuccessful as rulers, Antony and Cleopatra became immortal as great lovers, not a fate that the great Roman general would have relished. Mark Antony's life ended in tragic failure. If he had triumphed, then an empire less narrowly Roman might have evolved.

Above: This statue in Vienna shows Antony as a debauched drunkard. In fact, he was a highly competent general.

Below: The banquets of Antony and Cleopatra, where pearls were dissolved in wine, were noted for decadence and luxury.

THE HISTORIANS' VIEW

The Romans recognized the power of history – that an imperial nation needs an inspiring, unifying myth, which history alone can provide. Among the fathers of Western history, Roman historians believed an individual's actions counted and that writing history had a moral purpose. As Tacitus, the greatest Roman historian, wrote, "Virtues should not be silently ignored, while the perpetrators of wrong actions… should be threatened with disgrace before posterity."

JULIUS CAESAR (101–44BC)

Caesar called his histories of the Gallic wars and civil wars *Commentaries* rather than full-scale histories. Although they had an obvious political purpose, the histories remain very readable. Written in the third person in a plain, concise style that only rarely becomes monotonous, they tell the gripping tale of Caesar's remarkable campaigns, with interesting geographical and cultural discussions about the Gauls, a people to whom he was not unsympathetic. He also related and praised his men's deeds as well as his own. The civil war commentary, which was not wholly written by Caesar, was more openly a defence of his actions in precipitating civil conflict.

SALLUST (86–34BC)

An active supporter of Caesar in his youth, Sallust took to writing history after being forced out of politics. He developed a terse, epigrammatic style inspired by Thucydides, the greatest Greek historian, but unfortunately most of his works, relating the history of the Republic down to 76BC, are lost.

Sallust was concerned with virtue and he repeatedly attacked the corruptions of his age, especially those of the luxury-loving aristocracy. Sallust himself had been a radical tribune of the plebs, although he later became a highly corrupt provincial governor.

LIVY (59BC–AD17)

At the age of 30, Livy began writing his life's work: a detailed history of Rome. Made up of 142 books, running from Aeneas' (legendary) arrival in Italy to the death of Drusus in 9BC, only 35 books survive intact, with fragments of others.

Essentially a conservative patriot, Livy retained a belief in Rome's grand destiny that won him both Augustus' approval and lasting popularity. He was the historian Rome had been waiting for. His style varied from the majestic to the vivid, while his imaginative sympathy for Rome's opponents makes him a humane writer. He, too, believed that history must instruct and elevate as much as inform.

Although not consciously dishonest, at times Livy attributed words and feelings to his characters that he had no way of knowing were true. Due to his own lack of military experience and partly, perhaps, to his imperfect Greek, he also made several military mistakes. For example, in describing the battle of Zama between Hannibal and Scipio in 202BC, he

Above: This bust of Caesar is unusually unflattering – unlike his two lively histories.

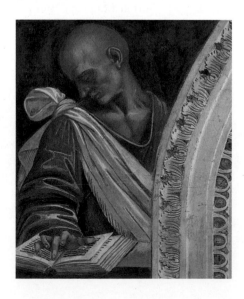

Below: Sallust turned historian only after leaving politics. His terse style recalls that of the ancient Greeks he so admired.

Above: The emperor Augustus approved of Livy's history of Rome's rise.

misinterpreted the Greek historian Polybius' description of Hannibal's third line as Italians, when they were in fact Hannibal's crack veterans from his Italian campaigns, held in reserve. But apart from this, and a tendency to accept legends of Rome's beginnings uncritically, he combined epic grandeur of language and lively description with the conscientious research of a true historian.

TACITUS (AD55–C.116)

Often considered the greatest Roman historian, Tacitus is admired and emulated by many subsequent writers for his style as much as his content. He came from northern Italy, where his father had been a tax-collector. He rose swiftly under the Flavians, entering the Senate under Vespasian and becoming consul in AD97 under Nerva. He wrote most of his histories under Trajan, his major works being the *Germania*, the *Agricola*, about his father-in-law, the *Histories* dealing with the Flavians and the *Annals* of the Julio-Claudians from AD14–64. Much of the last survives and forms a crushing, if unfair, indictment, especially of Tiberius, who slowly emerges as the brutal monster he always secretly was. Other characters – Sejanus, Claudius, Messalina, Nero – are also scathingly depicted. The action alternates between the imperial court at Rome and military camps on the frontiers and is filled with scenes of heroism or of villainy – with no mention of the provinces, which, for the most part, were growing peacefully richer. Tacitus was only interested in the grand themes of a period he saw as "rich in catastrophe, terrifying in its battles, rotten with mutinies". He carefully assessed all available sources before writing, but he was very biased, seeing Tiberius merely as Domitian's forerunner. His *Agricola*, by contrast, is a near eulogy focusing on Agricola's governorship of Britain, and ignoring almost everything else. His *Germania* paints the Germans as noble savages, in contrast to corrupt Romans. Master of the devastating postscript and

ironic put down, his style is intense and subtle, making him one of the great masters of Latin prose. His own gloomy fatalism stemmed from a nostalgic Republicanism coupled with an awareness that the empire had come to stay.

SUETONIUS (C.AD69–C.140)

The raciest and perhaps least serious of the major Roman historians, Suetonius is invaluable to posterity as he had access to imperial records that have since been lost. From an equestrian family, he rose in the imperial service, briefly becoming one of the emperor Hadrian's secretaries before his dismissal in AD119, reputedly for a scandal involving the emperor's wife. He spent the rest of his life writing. His two surviving works are *The Lives of Famous Men* and *The Lives of the Twelve Caesars*, the latter covering the Caesars from Julius to Domitian. He focused on highly entertaining, if not always reliable, accounts of each emperor's personal eccentricities, especially their habits in the bedroom or dining room, after dealing with the political events of the reign. He tended to highlight the former; for example detailing Caligula's remarkable antics in Rome while almost ignoring Claudius' conquest of Britain.

Above: One of the high points of Tacitus' Annals *describes the return of Germanicus' ashes, carried ashore at Brindisi by his widow Agrippina. Tacitus implied Tiberius had had his nephew murdered – almost certainly unjustly. But he hated Tiberius and blackened his reputation.*

Below: Suetonius took a racily biographical approach to history in his Lives of the Twelve Caesars. *He knew about court life, having been Hadrian's secretary.*

ROMAN PHILOSOPHERS
THE GREAT THINKERS

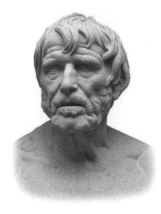

Above: Man of the world as much as philosopher, Seneca tried to apply Stoicism's noble tenets to real life – a doomed attempt that finally contributed to his death.

Below: Epictetus, shown in this medieval illustration talking to the emperor Hadrian, was one of the last and greatest Stoics.

In no area was Rome more indebted to Greece than in philosophy. This was perhaps inevitable, as philosophy was for long considered only a "footnote to Plato", the greatest Greek thinker. From the 2nd century BC on, many educated Romans studied philosophy in Athens, while the major schools of Greek philosophy, Epicureanism, Platonism and Stoicism, found imaginative adherents in Rome. They wrote in Greek as often as in Latin.

LUCRETIUS (C.96–55BC)
One of Rome's greatest poets as well as philosophers, Lucretius turned the dry, austere philosophy of Epicurus (341–271BC) into a lyrical, impassioned plea for a life free of political ambition and superstitious fears of death in *De Rerum Natura* (On the Nature of Things). Epicureans believed in avoiding political engagements, instead cultivating friendship in private communities. Radically, they admitted slaves and women as members, giving rise to ill-founded gossip. Far from indulging in orgies, they actually lived in sober modesty. The gods, according to Epicurus, exist but are unconcerned with human affairs, and human beings have free will. Lucretius writes with an intensity and richness of language, especially in his opening passage, "Delight of men and gods, life-giving Venus", which contradicts his supposed cool detachment. Epicureanism, although attracting the poet Horace, defied Roman belief in public service too deeply to spread far. Lucretius was Rome's great Epicurean poet but contributed little new in philosophy himself.

SENECA (4BC–AD65)
Although not an original thinker, Seneca, who also wrote plays, popularized Stoicism so successfully that his writings are still read today. Founded by Zeno (335–263BC), Stoicism taught universal brotherhood in harmony with a divine, rationally ordered universe. Seneca tried to live, and certainly died, according to his beliefs. Tutor, and also minister for five years, to the emperor Nero, Seneca was implicated in a conspiracy against Nero and forced to commit suicide, which he did with dignity and stoical courage. The essence of his teachings can be found in his letters to friends: "I was glad to hear that you live on friendly terms with your slaves, for so an intelligent, well-educated person like yourself should… Remember: the man you call your slave is of the same species and breathes, lives and dies under the same sky as you. You can imagine him as a free man, he can imagine you a slave… My advice in short: Treat your inferiors as you wish to be treated by your superiors." (*Epistulae Morales*, Moral Letters)

EPICTETUS (c.AD55–135)

As a slave, Epictetus was made lame by his master's abuse. He endured this without complaint, seeing the body as a mere "casing". Freed on Nero's death, in AD89 he was expelled from Rome and settled in Greece. He spent the rest of his life teaching an austere, yet compassionate philosophy. He attacked those who offered quick, easy cures for the human condition, believing that only those with the spiritual strength to cope with their own animal nature and with others' distressed souls and possessing the "counsel of God", could become true philosophers. He urged his followers to trust in divine providence through every misfortune, as he had. His ideas deeply influenced Marcus Aurelius.

MARCUS AURELIUS (AD121–80)

Plato's dream of an empire ruled by a philosopher-king seemed about to come true when Marcus Aurelius became emperor in AD161. Tragically, however, his reign was spent mostly in battles. His *Meditations*, written in Greek while on campaign, are the private records of a troubled man, who used philosophy to help him "as a man, as a Roman and as an emperor". They are also the last Stoic writings, but tinged with Platonism. "Say to yourself every morning: 'Today I shall encounter the officious, the graceless, the arrogant, the treacherous, the envious, the selfish. All this has affected them because they do not recognize the difference between good and evil.'" Marcus Aurelius had an absolute trust in divine providence and saw the universe as one great natural order whose laws men must accept and seek to understand.

PLOTINUS (c.AD204–70)

After studying philosophy in Alexandria, Plotinus settled in Rome, where he became a protégé of Gallienus, emperor from AD253. His writings, collected in the *Enneads*, were the most radically mystical since Plato's and today he is considered the founder of Neoplatonism.

Plotinus compared the universe to a huge fountain of light. An endlessly flowing source, the First Principle, the *monos*, or the One, descends radiantly like the light of the sun through ever lower levels of being until it reaches the very lowest, that of matter, at which point the cosmic dance moves back up towards the One. All human beings are capable of, indeed long for, reunion with the One, which Plotinus called "the flight of the One to the One" and claimed to have achieved three times. This can be experienced through inward contemplation rather than religious rites. Unlike the Stoics, Plotinus ignored completely the external world falling into ruin around him. Neoplatonism later influenced medieval, Renaissance and even Romantic thinkers.

Above: Philosophy continued to interest Rome's richer youths, here shown in debate with a philosopher on a 4th-century AD marble carving.

Above: Plotinus.

ROME'S ENEMIES

As Rome's empire grew, it faced formidable opponents, both civilized and barbarian, who at times inflicted crushing defeats on its armies. But, until the empire finally collapsed in the west in the 5th century AD, Roman discipline, resilience and adaptability always won through and overcame earlier reversals.

HANNIBAL BARCA (247–183BC)

The Romans had no greater enemy than Hannibal, the Carthaginian general who came closer than anyone else to conquering them. While the First Punic War had been fought overseas in Sicily and North Africa, the Second was mostly fought in Italy, devastating the peninsula. The Romans called it "Hannibal's war".

Hannibal was the son of Hamilcar Barca, a Carthaginian general who established an empire in Spain to compensate for the loss of Sicily after the First Punic War. It is said that he made his young son swear enmity to Rome on the altar of Moloch, the chief Punic god, in Carthage. In 221BC, Hannibal took over the Punic army and attacked Rome's ally, Saguntum. Wrong-footing the Romans, who were themselves planning a Spanish expedition, he then marched through southern Gaul and crossed the Alps in late 218BC, braving snowstorms that killed most of his elephants. Emerging into Cisalpine Gaul, he defeated the Romans at Trebbia in December and the next spring routed Flaminius' army at Lake Trasimene. His third, most devastating victory against much superior forces came at Cannae in 216BC. He won this by his tactical genius and professional army, which feigned a retreat in the centre before outflanking the Romans.

After Cannae, some large cities – Capua, Tarento, Syracuse – joined Hannibal, but the majority of Rome's Italian allies remained loyal and the Romans refused to despair. The Senate reappointed Fabius Maximus as dictator, and he waged a war of attrition. Hannibal had no siege engines to attack the walls of Rome, even though they were manned only by boys and old men, and Carthage would not send enough reinforcements. When his brother Hasdrubal finally reached Italy with an army in 207BC, he was defeated separately and his head thrown into Hannibal's camp.

Hannibal maintained his mercenary army's loyalty for another four years with great skill and in increasingly hostile country, before being recalled to Africa. At Zama in 202BC he encountered Scipio, conqueror of Spain, and was beaten in open battle. Hannibal guided Carthage through the dark days after defeat, but his proposed reforms aroused fierce opposition and he went into exile, first in Syria, then in Bithynia, where he finally committed suicide to avoid capture by Roman agents.

He was undoubtedly one of the very greatest generals of the ancient world, resourceful, tenacious and indomitable, with a smattering of Greek culture, like many nobles in Carthage.

Above: Monument at the site of the battle of Cannae, where Hannibal's troops defeated the Roman army in 216BC.

Below: Hannibal led a multi-racial army over the Alps, with Spanish, African and Celtic contingents, along with his elephants, only a few of which, however, survived the passage. Here he rides a small north African forest elephant, a breed now extinct.

Left: Antony met Cleopatra aboard her gilded barque on the river Cnidus, and, according to tradition, at once fell in love with her. But initially her wealth – Egypt was the richest kingdom in the east – probably attracted him even more than her person. The Meeting of Antony and Cleopatra, *1883, Lawrence Alma-Tadema.*

CLEOPATRA, QUEEN OF EGYPT (69–30BC)

Cleopatra VII, last of the Ptolemies, was portrayed to Romans as an oriental *femme fatale* who had lured the great Roman general Mark Antony to his downfall. In fact Cleopatra was Greek in language, culture and background, and she relied more on her intelligence and charm to captivate Caesar and then Antony than on her physical beauty. She wanted to acquire and then keep the throne of Egypt, and used Egypt's wealth to buy the support of Roman armies.

Cleopatra won Caesar's support against her brother Ptolemy XIII, supposedly her co-monarch, when he landed at Alexandria in 47BC. Legend says that Cleopatra was delivered wrapped in a carpet to Caesar's headquarters and they began an affair. Later, she had a son, Caesarion, by him. This liaison so enraged Ptolemy's supporters that they besieged the lovers in the palace. Part of the great library was burnt in the ensuing fighting, which led to Caesar installing her as sole monarch and a client of Rome. Cleopatra followed Caesar to Rome in 45BC, but returned to Egypt after his death.

When Antony met her, he was tempted as much by her wealth as her beauty, but he became her lover, the pair indulging in a life of sensual pleasure in Egypt, much to the delighted horror of opinion in Rome. After Antony had publicly snubbed his wife, the sister of his rival Octavian, he donated some provinces to his and Cleopatra's three children. Octavian's propagandists used this as evidence that Antony wanted to hand over the empire to Cleopatra – clearly not the act of a true Roman.

This famous love affair did not seem to affect Antony's plans for Rome's eastern frontier, but his political judgement was clouded. Instead of leaving Cleopatra behind when he assembled his troops for the final showdown, Antony let her come with him, leading many of his men to desert. The doomed pair escaped from Actium for a last winter of love, but Octavian followed. Cleopatra cheated him of his final victory by committing suicide, traditionally from an asp's bite, before she could be captured. Although Cleopatra may have affronted Octavian's puritanical patriotism, she presented little military threat to Rome.

Above: Antony and Cleopatra, the famous lovers, as played by Richard Burton and Elizabeth Taylor. The Roman soldier's and Egyptian queen's political views may have coincided also, for Cleopatra was determined to defend Egyptian independence while Antony perhaps envisaged a loose Roman hegemony over the east, not annexation.

London, already the trading centre of Britain. They burnt it, together with Verulamium (St Albans), reportedly killing 70,000 Romanized citizens. Then, somewhere in the Midlands, the now huge British force met the Romans under Paulinus with 10,000 men. The Britons were so confident of victory that they brought their wives and children along to enjoy the spectacle. But Roman discipline won the day; the drunken, half-naked Britons fell before the steadily stabbing Roman short swords, and the fugitives became entangled in their own wagons. The legionaries killed every child, woman and even ox they found. According to Tacitus, Boudicca committed suicide soon after. Her revolt had accomplished nothing, except encouraging the Romans to reform their administration in the island and get rid of the *publicani*.

Above: Boudicca, queen of the Iceni, in her chariot. Her revolt against Roman extortions – which included the rape of her own daughters – threatened Rome's hold of Britain, but the Britons were too chaotic to overcome Roman discipline.

Below: This coin struck by Zenobia of Palmyra as empress of the east in 270AD does not do justice to the famed beauty of this descendant of Cleopatra. Like her ancestor, Zenobia was beaten by Rome in the end.

BOUDICCA, QUEEN OF THE ICENI (DIED AD61)

The Iceni, a warlike tribe of Britons, occupied what is now Norfolk. Their king, Prasutagus, had accepted Roman rule, effectively becoming a client king. On his death, Prasutagus left his kingdom equally to his daughters and to the Romans. The imperial procurator, Catus Decianus, however, expropriated all Iceni lands and allowed Roman *publicani* – taxfarmers – into the kingdom. According to Tacitus, when Prasutagus' widow Boudicca objected, she was flogged and her daughters were raped. Her outraged subjects then revolted and marched on Camulodunum (Colchester), traditionally led by their redoubtable queen. "In appearance she was very tall and most terrifying, with a fierce glance and harsh voice; a great mass of tawny hair fell to her hips", wrote Cassius Dio more than a century later. Camulodunum had no walls and the governor, Suetonius Paulinus, was far away in Anglesey with the main Roman forces. After sacking Camulodunum, the Iceni, along with other Britons, almost annihilated the depleted Ninth Legion sent against them and marched on

ZENOBIA, QUEEN OF PALMYRA (REIGNED AD267–71)

In the prolonged crises of the mid-3rd century AD, Rome's eastern provinces were invaded by the Persians, who overran Syria, Mesopotamia and Asia Minor, taking the emperor Valerian captive in AD260. The Persians were repulsed not by Valerian's son, the emperor Gallienus, but by Odenathus, king of the wealthy oasis trading city of Palmyra, officially part of Roman Syria. Odenathus, controlling heavy cavalry and mounted archers, now became the semi-independent "Governor of the East". When he died in AD267, perhaps murdered, his widow, Zenobia, a gifted and beautiful woman who loved hunting and drinking, succeeded him. But she was not content with junior status. She annexed Egypt and much of Asia Minor, and in AD270 declared herself Augusta and her son, Vaballathus, Augustus. For a moment it seemed that Rome's whole eastern empire was lost. But the emperor Aurelian marched east and routed the Palmyrene armies, first outside Antioch and then near Palmyra, capturing Zenobia as she was fleeing towards Persia.

Traditionally, she was taken back to Rome, where she walked in golden chains in Aurelian's triumph, before being allowed to retire to a villa at Tivoli. Palmrya itself never recovered its old glory.

ATTILA THE HUN (C. AD406–453)

The *flagellum dei*, or "scourge of God", Attila has gone down in history as a ferociously bloodthirsty savage. The Huns, exceptionally skilled horsemen, had exploded across the Eurasian steppes in the 4th century AD. Their empire then stretched from the Urals to the Danube. Attila started by extorting money from the Eastern empire. In AD448 he reacted to a cut in this subsidy by ravaging the Balkans, defeating armies sent against him. In AD450, aware that he could not capture Constantinople, secure behind its new walls, he turned west with 70,000 horsemen, herding the terrified Germans before him. He crossed the Rhine in AD451 and ransacked Gaul. The Roman general Aetius hastened north and, with the help of the Visigoths, fulfilling their duties as federates, met the Huns at Châlons-sur-Marne. The battle, which cost the Visigothic king Theodoric his life, lasted all day, but at the end the Huns withdrew. It was the only defeat in Attila's life. Attila returned to winter quarters on the Pannonian plains. Here, in a city of tents, he lived in an odd mixture of squalor and luxury. His captives brought a veneer of Graeco-Roman civilization along with plunder of the empire. Attila himself, reputedly even

Left: The great temple of Baal in Palmyra displayed the sophistication and wealth of the city that challenged Rome in the east.

dirtier than most of his people but with diplomatic abilities, enjoyed receiving Roman dignitaries, although the pleasure was probably one-sided. Next year Attila turned south and crossed the Alps, sacking Milan and Aquileia, whose fleeing inhabitants founded Venice as a refuge. Aetius had no troops to repel him now. Instead, Pope Leo I rode north and met the Huns. What the Pope said to Attila is unknown but possibly he reminded him of the fate of the last man to sack Rome. Attila turned back and died a year later from a burst blood vessel after celebrating his marriage to his latest wife, a young Frankish princess. Within a few years the Hunnish empire vanished and the Huns passed into history and legend.

Below: Attila, advancing on Rome in AD452, reached and besieged Perugia in central Italy. No Roman forces could be found to oppose him, but Pope Leo I rode out to meet him and persuaded the Hunnish king to turn back, so saving Rome for that year.

CICERO
THE PEACEFUL ROMAN

Rome's greatest orator, lawyer and political thinker, Cicero was exceptional among the generals, consuls and warlords of the late Republic in never having been a soldier. He was, however, a fluent writer on subjects from astronomy to philosophy. Although his suppression of Catiline's conspiracy led to many citizens' arguably illegal deaths, he was a civilian and man of peace in an age of civil wars and naked military ambition. As his 800 surviving letters reveal, he was a man of genuine goodwill and optimism – over-optimism, as it turned out. Cicero attempted to apply Greek philosophy's ethical findings to Roman politics and human behaviour in general. Through Cicero's writings, much of Greek culture was transmitted to western Europe.

Marcus Tullius Cicero was born in 106BC in the small town of Arpinum, 60 miles (100km) south of Rome to a family of knights. None of his ancestors had held office in Rome, so his rise to the consulship made him a

Right: Cicero, a novus homo, *or self-made man, remains one of the greatest of all Roman writers and politicians, despite most unusually having no military career.*

novus homo, a "new"or self-made man. He depended on his skills as a lawyer and orator but luckily won the friendship and support of Atticus, a rich banker. Cicero started his legal career by appearing in court against one of Sulla's freedmen in 81BC, risking the dictator's wrath. Wisely, he withdrew to Athens to continue his study of philosophy. He accepted the ethical precepts of Stoicism that all human beings had a spark of the divine in them.

Returning to Rome after Sulla's death, Cicero was elected a quaestor in 75BC. The Sicilians, finding him honest, asked him to prosecute Verres, an ex-governor of the island, for extortion in 70BC. Cicero's speeches were so devastatingly effective, driving Verres into exile, that the grateful Sicilians showered presents on him. He distributed these to needy citizens. Cicero became a praetor in 66BC, dealing with legal cases "fairly and honestly", as Plutarch put it. He also advised Pompey, then assuming his high command. Finally, in 63BC he was elected consul, the highest office.

Cicero owed his meteoric rise, unsupported by any great noble house, chiefly to his mastery of rhetoric – dramatic, impassioned public speaking, a key art of ancient civilization. Brilliant at ridiculing opponents, he used wit, irony and innuendo to overwhelm and seduce listeners. He also embodied the aspirations of the rising commercial equestrian class. Realizing that the senatorial class was too narrow, Cicero envisaged a *concordia ordinum*, a concord of the classes between senate and knights, which he later widened to a *consensus omnium bonorum*, a consensus of all good men. He regarded himself as a saviour of the Republic by his swift if brutal suppression of the conspiracy by the disgruntled patrician Catiline, who tried to overthrow the state in October 63BC.

Unfortunately, Cicero failed to win over the one man with the military power to support his *concordia*. Pompey returned in triumph from his eastern conquests to be snubbed by the Senate. On meeting him, Cicero talked only of his own achievements, annoying Pompey. In 58BC Cicero was forced into retirement, accused of acting illegally over the Catiline affair. Although recalled by Pompey, his political influence never fully recovered and he had to write the co-triumvir Caesar a grovelling letter promising he would not attack him again.

THE WRITER

Cicero's enforced leisure gave him time to write. His letters, mostly to Atticus his banker friend, reveal an urbane and cultured upper-class Roman, fond of dinner parties and literary discussions. His letter describing the visit of Caesar to his villa near Puteoli is a masterpiece. "What a guest! Two thousand troops in all... The villa was sealed off. But it went off all right. He was in a good mood and all the talk at table was of literature. Political subjects were avoided altogether. But once is definitely enough".

Cicero was also a family man. His son Marcus was clearly a problem, getting through a vast allowance in Athens. Cicero reserved his greatest love for his daughter Tullia, whose death in childbirth desolated him. He tried to console himself with a belief in the immortality of the soul, but was not totally convinced.

Cicero wrote copiously on philosophy and politics – not original stuff, "only the exact words are mine". *The Laws*, *The Offices* and *The Republic* deal with politics and the constitution, while *De Finibus* (The Highest Ends) summarizes much of Greek philosophy.

After Caesar's death in 44BC, in which he had no part, Cicero persuaded the Senate to appoint young Octavian to lead an army against Mark Antony. This was a mistake. Octavian, forming the Second Triumvirate, added Cicero's name to the list of those to be proscribed (killed), realizing that Cicero represented the Republic's last best hope. Cicero had set out on a journey to join the conspirators in Greece when Octavian's men overtook him and cut his throat. His severed head and hands were later exhibited in the Forum.

Below: Cicero's humane and liberal views had a profound influence on later western writers, as this illuminated medieval manuscript attests.

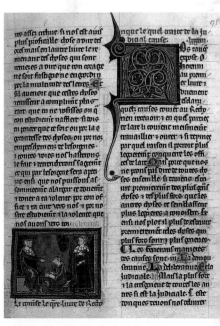

CHAPTER III

THE EMPERORS

Monarchs in all but name, the emperors of Rome are among history's most remarkable, often most colourful rulers, their unofficial position in control of a supposed republic giving them intoxicatingly unlimited powers. Originally reserved solely for the Julio-Claudians, one of the great families of the Roman nobility, the imperial throne gradually became the prize of other men. First there were the Flavians, from small Italian towns, then men born outside Italy, notably the Antonines, in the 2nd century AD. Finally, in the 3rd century AD, almost any halfway successful soldier might hope – or fear – to be chosen as emperor by his armies.

Sometimes Roman emperors were model rulers: among these imperial paragons Augustus, first and longest-lived, ranks high, as do Trajan, Hadrian and Marcus Aurelius. Balancing them are paranoids and near-maniacs, such as Caligula; playboy-buffoons, such as Nero; and the debauched – Commodus and the almost indescribable Elagabalus. Most emperors fall, like most human beings, into a category neither good nor bad. So Claudius, Vespasian and Domitian (initially but not later), Septimius, Diocletian and Valentinian I all proved humanly fallible. Undoubtedly, they worked hard if increasingly ineffectually at their task of governing the empire as they saw fit. In the end, the task grew almost unbearably onerous, becoming more a burden than a prize.

Left: A general of the 3rd century AD commanding his troops. The emperors remained above all army commanders, military prestige being vital.

EMPERORS OF ROME

Julio-Claudian emperors
Augustus 27BC–AD14
Tiberius AD14–37
Gaius (Caligula) AD37–41
Claudius AD41–54
Nero AD54–68

Year of the four emperors
Galba AD68–9
Otho AD69
Vitellius AD69
(Vespasian AD69–79)

Flavian emperors
Vespasian AD69–79
Titus AD79–81
Domitian AD81–96

Adoptive and Antonine emperors
Nerva AD96–8
Trajan AD98–117
Hadrian AD117–38
Antoninus Pius AD138–61
Marcus Aurelius AD161–80
  and Lucius Verus AD161–9
Commodus AD180–92

Above: Vespasian.

Above: Titus.

Above: Domitian.

Above: Trajan.

Above: Hadrian.

Above: Marcus Aurelius.

Civil war
Pertinax AD193
Didius Julianus AD193

Severan emperors
Septimius Severus AD193–211
Caracalla AD211–17 and Geta AD211
Macrinus AD217–18
Elagabalus AD218–22
Alexander Severus AD222–35

Emperors of the age of chaos
Maximinus Thrax AD235–8
Gordian I AD238
Gordian II AD238
Pupienus and Balbinus AD238
Gordian III AD238–44
Philip the Arab AD244–9
Decius AD249–51

Above: Augustus.

Above: Claudius.

Above: Gaius Caligula.

Above: Tiberius.

Above: Nero.

Trebonianus Gallus AD251–3
Aemilius Aemilianus AD253
Valerian AD253–60
Gallienus AD253–68
Claudius II "Gothicus" AD268–70
Quintillus AD270
Aurelian AD270–5
Tacitus AD275–6
Probus AD276–82
Carus AD282–3
Numerian AD283–4
Carinus AD283–5

"Gallic" emperors
Postumus AD260–9
Laelianus AD269
Marius AD269
Victorinus AD268–71
Tetricus AD271–4

The tetrarchs and their successors
Diocletian AD284–305
Maximian AD286–305 and AD307–8
Constantius I AD305–6
Galerius AD305–11
Severus II AD306–7
Maxentius AD306–12
Maximinus Daia AD310–13
Licinius AD308–24

Above: Septimius Severus.

Above: Caracalla.   *Above: Elagabalus.*

Emperors of the house of Constantine
Constantine I AD306–37
Constantine II AD337–40
Constans AD337–50
Constantius II AD337–61
Julian AD361–3

Jovian AD363–4

Valentinian I (east) AD364–75
  and Valens (west) AD364–75
Gratian AD367–83
Valentinian II AD375–92
Magnus Maximus (usurper) AD383–8
Eugenius (usurper) AD392–4

Theodosian emperors
Theodosius I AD379–95
Arcadius (east) AD395–408
Honorius (west) AD395–423
Constantius III AD421
Theodosius II (east) AD408–50
Valentinian III (west) AD425–55

Last Western emperors
Marjorian AD457–61
Anthemius AD467–72
Romulus Augustulus AD475–6
Julius Nepos AD473–80

Eastern emperors
Marcian AD450–57
Leo I AD457–74
Zeno AD474–91
Anastasius AD491–518
Justin I AD518–27
Justinian AD527–65
Justin II AD565–78
Maurice AD582–602
Heraclius I AD610–41

With the advent of Heraclius, it became customary to talk of Byzantine rather than east Roman emperors, as the empire itself finally ceased to be Latin-speaking, even in the army.

Above: Diocletian.

Above: Constantine I.

Above: Julian.

Above: Theodosius I.

Above: Justinian I.

AUGUSTUS: THE FIRST ROMAN EMPEROR

The transition from ruthless battle leader to revered "father of his country" was one of the greatest achievements of Octavian, who became Augustus, first and greatest Roman emperor. In 44BC, the 18-year-old heir and adopted son of Julius Caesar, just assassinated, had only the lustre of Caesar's name as backing. Cicero, the leading senator, gave him an army command against Mark Antony. But Octavian soon changed sides to form the Second Triumvirate with Antony, gaining mastery of the western part of the empire and, after defeating Antony at Actium in 31BC, rulership of the whole Roman world, just as Julius Caesar had.

In January 27BC, Octavian resigned all his powers, to receive them back, as pre-arranged, from a grateful Senate along with the title *Augustus* (literally revered). We call him the first Roman emperor, but to his contemporaries he took pains to seem no more than *princeps*, first citizen of the Republic. He disguised his power so carefully that his claim to have "restored the Republic" seemed almost credible. Typical of his apparent modesty was his home: an average-sized house formerly belonging to the orator Hortensius. It was located on the Palatine Hill, the traditional aristocratic area. His 45-year reign laid the foundations of a regime that lasted almost 250 years. This – revolution, disguised as a conservative restoration – was typically Roman.

Octavian was very unlike his great-uncle Caesar. Aware that Republican feeling was strong and wanting senatorial support, Octavian cultivated an image of traditional Roman *virtus*, which roughly translates as courage, virtue and probity. He needed the senators' and equestrians' help to run the empire – he had no proper civil service, merely a few secretaries. The 27BC settlement gave him proconsular power in provinces with large armies, such as Gaul (France) and Syria, run by legates appointed by him. Senators governed peaceful, unarmed provinces like Greece. The administration was thus depoliticized, but Augustus retained control of the army, and the title *imperator*, effectively commander-in-chief, from which comes the word emperor. His own military reputation was mixed: he relied heavily on capable generals such as Agrippa, but he retained the crucial loyalty of the armies. They swore loyalty to him, not the Senate, and remained remarkably loyal to his successors.

At first Augustus was consul almost every year, until illness in 23BC made him rethink his position. From then on he had "perpetual tribunician power", which allowed him to convene the Assembly and Senate and propose or veto laws. In 19BC he gained *imperium maius* (supreme power) giving him overall control in the provinces. His settlement was so effective that he faced only one feeble conspiracy. In 2BC he was declared *pater patriae*, father of his country, by the Senate.

Above: Although he had won power by the sword, Augustus stressed the civilian aspects of his regime by wearing a toga.

Below: A temple to Augustus was built after his death in Istria – he was not worshipped in Italy while he lived.

THE AGE OF AUGUSTUS

Contemporary writers saw the Augustan era as a golden age in almost every sense – politically, economically and also culturally. Augustus fostered the empire's economic recovery by restoring and ensuring peace. Guided by his cultural minister, Maecenas, he took a direct interest in cultural affairs, and Virgil's epic account of Rome's origins, the *Aeneid*, was a fruit of the age. A great building programme was inaugurated in Rome, completing Caesar's projects such as the vast Basilica Julia. In *Res Gestae*, his list of accomplishments, Augustus claimed to have restored or built 82 temples in one year, including one to Mars, the war god, and one to Apollo, the Greek god of poetry and science. Agrippa, his general, started Rome's first large public baths. Augustus boasted that he had found Rome a city of brick but left it a city of marble.

At heart, Augustus was a social conservative. He wanted to restore the traditional Roman virtues of piety and fidelity, or so propagandists proclaimed. He also wanted to raise the falling Roman birth rate. In the *Lex Julia* of 18BC, he made adultery a crime, penalized celibacy and childless marriages and gave tax breaks to families with three or more children. He banished even his own daughter, Julia, for adultery and the poet Ovid for general licentiousness. He also revived the sacred "secular" games and other old religious festivals.

THE MAN BEHIND THE IMAGE

Augustus was slim, rather short, but well proportioned, "unusually handsome and exceedingly graceful", according to Suetonius, with curly golden hair. Although his health was poor, he nevertheless lived to the age of 77. Ruthless in his youth, he later mellowed. He was a modest gambler and a sociable family man, enjoying dinner with friends. Surviving letters to Gaius, his grandson, calling him "my dearest little donkey", reveal paternal affection. His last years were unhappy, however. Not only did family problems distress him, but the Varus disaster in Germany in AD9, in which three legions were destroyed, shook him badly. He advised Tiberius, whom he had adopted reluctantly in AD4, to expand the empire no further. After his death in AD14 – almost certainly from natural causes – he was given a splendid funeral and declared a god by the Senate. He became the paradigm against which all later emperors would be measured.

FAMILY PROBLEMS

As emperor, Augustus inevitably involved his family in dynastic politics. In 36BC he married Livia Drusilla, who ignored his frequent infidelities and acted as a moderating influence on him. He had only one child, Julia, by his first marriage. Keen to pass on power to a direct descendant, he married Julia to his nephew Marcellus. When Marcellus died in 23BC, Julia, still only 16, was made to marry Agrippa, 24 years her senior. Their five children included two sons, Gaius and Lucius, whom Augustus adopted as his sons. But when Agrippa died in 12BC, Augustus turned to Tiberius, his gloomy stepson who was forced to divorce his wife, Vipsania, whom he loved, and marry Julia, whom he loathed, to be a guardian to the young princes. Disgusted, Tiberius withdrew from public life and Julia began a series of affairs which led to her exile. The premature deaths of the two young princes – Lucius in AD2, Gaius in AD4 – forced Augustus to recall Tiberius to favour. The resulting Julio-Claudian dynasty lasted until AD68.

Left: This cameo gemstone shows Augustus and the goddess Roma. Augustus was often worshipped in association with the goddess of Rome in the provinces but never in the city of Rome itself. After his death he was officially deified by the Senate.

Below: Augustus as the triumphant Roman imperator, *or commander-in-chief. In fact, he was not a brilliant general and in later years never led his armies in person, relying on his very capable generals.*

ORGANIZERS OF EMPIRE

Although the lives and reigns of some emperors were relatively undramatic, they played such vital roles in organizing or restoring the empire, expanding or stabilizing its frontiers and widening its citizenship, that they stand out as truly exceptional emperors. Two of the most notable were Claudius and Hadrian.

Left: On the assassination of Caligula, gangly, stammering Claudius was declared emperor by the Praetorian guard.

Below: The emperor Claudius is shown here in the guise of the god Jupiter – an implausible role for such a physically unimpressive and ungainly man, but one that became increasingly expected of all the emperors.

CLAUDIUS (REIGNED AD41–54)

Already 50 when the Praetorian guard declared him emperor on 24 January AD41, Claudius' appointment was an event that probably surprised him as much as everyone else. Tall, gangly, with a stammer and a tendency to dribble, Claudius had been kept in the background until his nephew, the new emperor Caligula, half-jokingly made him consul in AD37. After the assassination of Caligula, however, Claudius was the only Julio-Claudian available as next emperor.

Claudius was intelligent if bookish – he had written histories of the Carthaginians and Etruscans, which are now lost – and initially at least he had good intentions. He abolished treason trials and set about restoring public order, which had been shaken by Caligula's excesses, trying to work with rather than against the Senate. However, he had no military experience – a big disadvantage for a ruler whose power ultimately depended on the army, although his brother, the general Germanicus, was fondly remembered by soldiers. One of his first acts was to order the invasion of Britain, which Julius Caesar had attempted and of which both Augustus and Caligula had talked. This proved remarkably successful. Part of southern Britain was overrun in AD43, and Claudius hastened north to celebrate its conquest. Conquests of Mauretania (north Algeria/Morocco) and Thrace in the Balkans made him the most expansionist emperor since Augustus and popular with the army and the people.

To please the volatile populace further, Claudius built an entirely new harbour near Ostia, with breakwaters and a lighthouse, greatly facilitating Rome's troubled grain supply. He also completed two aqueducts that had been started by Caligula. What displeased many in the Senate was his liberal policy of making "Gauls" – Roman citizens from Gaul, sometimes of Gallic ancestry but always Romanized – senators, and extending Roman citizenship widely. (Claudius himself was born in Lyons.) The Senate also criticized his reliance on Greek-speaking freedmen: Pallas looked after finance, Narcissus foreign affairs and Callistus the law. At first, Claudius kept his secretaries under control as they built up departments that foreshadowed the bureaucracy of the 2nd century AD. His love life was unhappy, however. His third wife, Messalina, on whom he doted, was 30 years younger than him and notoriously adulterous. She finally plotted to make one of her lovers emperor and was executed for treason in AD48. In his later years, in declining health, Claudius was ruled by his last wife, Agrippina, who probably poisoned him. Hostile historians have depicted him as hopelessly in thrall to his wives and freedmen, but provincials and later emperors like Vespasian remembered him as an unusually effective ruler.

HADRIAN (REIGNED AD117–38)

Perhaps Rome's greatest emperor devoted to peace rather than war, Hadrian is best known for his wall across northern England, but this is only one aspect of a many-faceted man. A distant relative of the emperor Trajan, whose niece Sabina he married, Hadrian was born in Spain in AD76. He distinguished himself in Trajan's Dacian campaigns and was governor of the key province of Syria during Trajan's eastern wars (AD114–17). When Trajan died, he was proclaimed, on rather debatable grounds, as his chosen heir.

Widespread Jewish revolts and Parthian counter-attacks led Hadrian to abandon all conquests east of the Euphrates, although he retained Dacia (Romania) and Arabia Nabatea (Jordan). He adopted a general defensive policy, personally overseeing the strengthening of the frontier defences in his journeys around the empire – he spent over half his reign outside Italy. On his British visit in AD122, he ordered the building of a stone wall 76 miles (122km) long and 20ft (6m) high, manned by 15,000 troops to keep the barbarians out of Romanized Britain. He also constructed less durable fortifications in Germany and Syria.

He built lavishly, reconstructing the Pantheon, Rome's finest temple, building his huge mausoleum (now the Castel Sant'Angelo) and a luxurious villa complex at Tivoli that included 160 acres (64ha) of gardens and pavilions. In Athens he added a new quarter to the old city, being such a passionate philhellene (lover of Greece) that he was nicknamed Greekling. Initiated into the Eleusinian mysteries, the most important in Greece, Hadrian became archon (mayor) of Athens, which he made head of a new Panhellenic League. He also ordered the completion of the immense temple of the Olympian Zeus, started by Pisistratus more than six centuries earlier.

Sexually Hadrian "ran to excess in the gratification of his desires", according to the 4th-century AD *Augustan Histories*, most notoriously in his passion for the beautiful young boy Antinous, who drowned mysteriously in the Nile. Hadrian thereupon founded a city in his lover's memory, Antinouopolis.

Hadrian got on badly with the Senate from the start, executing four senior senators early in his reign for alleged treason, and he was too obviously cultured to please the Roman populace. But he was a superb administrator and legal reformer. His jurist, Salvius Julianus, drew up a "Perpetual Edict", which codified previously unwritten laws. Hadrian also extended Nerva's and Trajan's policy of poor relief. Despite these achievements, he remained unpopular with the Senate, although there were no conspiracies against him while he was away on his long travels. The empire probably reached its economic peak during his reign, in which the eastern provinces finally recovered their political self-confidence and economic strength.

Above: Hadrian was one of the wisest and most conscientious, as well as cultured, emperors.

Below: Hadrian's most lasting achievement in northern Europe was the wall he built across northern England.

BEST OF EMPERORS

Traditionally, the reigns of the "Five Good Emperors" from Nerva to Marcus Aurelius (AD96–180) encompassed Rome's golden age. The differing fortunes of Trajan and Marcus Aurelius, the two great emperors at each end of the epoch, however, indicate that the empire was indeed passing through its zenith.

TRAJAN (AD98–117)

Born in Spain in AD53, Marcus Ulpianus Traianus was the first non-Italian emperor, although his family were Romans of senatorial rank. He was adopted as the son and heir of the emperor Nerva in AD97 as the elderly senator was so unpopular with the army. Trajan already had a distinguished military and civil record and proved an inspired choice. Affable and handsome, he was equally at ease with the Senate, people and army, but it was military matters that occupied him first.

In AD101 Trajan attacked Dacia (Romania), forcing Decebalus, the king of Dacia, to accept a humiliating peace. But Trajan renewed the war, and by AD106 he had captured the Dacian capital. Decebalus committed suicide. Huge quantities of Dacian gold were taken to Rome, along with Decebalus' head on a pole. Dacia became a Roman province, its lands settled by Romans, its gold mines protected by forts. In AD106 Trajan annexed Arabia Nabatea (Jordan).

With an improved and bigger army, Trajan turned to Parthia. Twin armies swept down the Tigris and Euphrates in AD115 to take the capital Ctesiphon (Baghdad). Trajan marched on to the Gulf, the only emperor to do so. Back home, the Senate voted him perpetual triumphs – a unique but empty honour. But he failed to take Hatra, a key city, revolts flared behind him and the Parthians counter-attacked. In AD117, his conquests across the Euphrates already abandoned, Trajan died of a stroke in Asia Minor.

THE GREAT BUILDER

Trajan was also a great peacetime ruler. He created special funds for helping poor children and built on a massive scale. Some projects were utilitarian, such as the new harbour at Ostia, and some were ornamental, such as his column, whose frieze relates his Dacian wars. Others, including his huge forum, his two libraries and his baths, were both. His correspondence with Pliny the Younger, governor of Bithynia, reveals Trajan's humane good sense. Although reputedly fond of boys and wine (as well as hunting and war), Trajan was never seen as drunk or promiscuous and there were few who disputed his right to the title *optimus princeps*, best of emperors, granted him by the Senate.

MARCUS AURELIUS (AD161–80)

Brought up by Stoic philosophers, high-minded, ascetic and self-sacrificing, Marcus Aurelius seemed destined to become Rome's true philosopher–king. But tragically his reign was filled with almost continuous warfare, and he spent much of it fighting. Born in Spain in AD121 to an aristocratic Roman family, Marcus was chosen as Hadrian's sole heir when he was only six. Antoninus Pius, the next (elderly) emperor, adopted him in AD138. Marcus became consul at the age of 18 and then Caesar (junior emperor). Lucius Verus, nine years younger, was his adoptive brother. When he became emperor in AD161, Marcus persuaded the Senate to make Verus co-Augustus alongside him.

Almost immediately, Parthia invaded Armenia. Lucius Verus went east and the Parthians were repelled – mostly by the governor of Syria, Avidius Cassius, Verus preferring the fleshpots of Antioch – and Ctesiphon and Seleucia-on-the-Tigris were sacked in AD165. The total destruction of the latter, a Hellenistic city, was thought to have aroused divine wrath, manifest in a terrible plague that the

Above: Trajan was the most popular of all emperors.

Below: Trajan's Column in Rome celebrates and records his Dacian victories.

Above: Marcus Aurelius, a philosopher by inclination, spent his reign in endless warfare.

Meanwhile, the Germans had rallied and Marcus had to continue his gruelling Danubian campaigns, spending each winter in camp, finding time between campaigns to administer the empire and write his famous *Meditations*. He decided to annex the whole area up to the Carpathians, forming a continuous new frontier that might prove more defensible. But his health, never strong, was now failing – he probably had cancer – and he died in camp near Vienna in March AD180. Commodus, his worthless heir, quickly abandoned his father's campaign and high ideals.

Below: The world-weariness of the philosopher–emperor Marcus Aurelius can be glimpsed even in these panels celebrating his (incomplete) triumph against the Marcomanni. The contrast with the unalloyed martial vigour of Trajan's celebratory column is very obvious.

victorious troops brought back with them. This ravaged the empire, weakened the army and overshadowed Verus' triumph.

An unexpected German invasion across the Danube, which reached Aquileia in north-east Italy in AD168, triggered a financial and military crisis. Marcus armed gladiators and slaves and went north with Verus. Lucius Verus' sudden death in AD169 did not affect operations, in which Marcus showed himself a very competent general despite having no earlier military experience.

THE DANUBIAN WARS

For five years, Marcus struggled with the Marcomanni and Quadi, Germanic tribes in the modern Czech Republic and Slovakia. He had almost defeated them, campaigning through bitter winters – one battle was fought on the frozen Danube itself – when a revolt by Avidius Cassius in Syria distracted him. Avidius had been misled by a rumour of Marcus' death into making a bid for the empire, in which the empress Faustina was perhaps involved. Avidius was murdered by troops loyal to Marcus before civil war could develop, so Marcus merely toured the east with his 14-year-old son Commodus before returning to Rome for a belated triumph in AD176. The column later erected by Commodus to mark this victory echoes Trajan's, but its overall atmosphere is sombre, rather than jubilant. Marcus rides his chariot with a weary, resigned air.

EVIL EMPERORS

Above: Nero, the would-be artist and actual playboy, became one of Rome's most notoriously debauched and despotic emperors.

Below: The antics of Caligula introduced a capricious madness to the Principate that very nearly destroyed it.

The fact that the emperor's powers could appear unlimited encouraged some emperors – usually those who had inherited the throne young – to become power-mad or paranoid, or both, and to behave in ways that were capricious or despotic, if not arguably insane. Others, later in the empire, were simply brutal thugs, despite having undoubted military talent. All met violent ends.

CALIGULA (AD37–41)

When Augustus' great-grandson Gaius Caligula (literally "little military boots", a nickname he got from the boots he wore as a child) succeeded Tiberius in March AD37, Rome was jubilant. Aged 24 and son of the much-loved general Germanicus, Caligula promised to end the terror of Tiberius' later years. His reign started auspiciously: he recalled all exiles, burnt the police files and even made his uncle Claudius, embarrassingly clumsy, fellow consul.

That autumn, however, he became seriously ill, and when he recovered, his behaviour had changed completely. The illness could have unbalanced his mind, as Suetonius believed; alternatively, it could have brought out a latent paranoia and brutality. What appeared first was a reckless extravagance. He gave extremely spectacular games, at times appearing as a gladiator himself, and lavished attention on his favourite racehorse, Incitatus, who lived luxuriously in a marble stall. Caligula declared that he would make Incitatus a senator, even consul – only half a joke, for his relations with the Senate were deteriorating and in AD39 he dismissed both consuls for treachery. That summer he built a useless bridge of boats 2 miles (3km) long across the Bay of Naples and drove a chariot across it – a gesture typical of his extravagance, and perhaps indicative of growing insanity.

Spindly and prematurely bald, Caligula was insanely jealous of men with a good head of hair. Dressing in effeminate, gaudy silks, he generally did not impress people physically. Although he had had a military childhood, he felt his lack of military glory. In September AD39 he visited the Rhine legions before turning back abruptly, seemingly panic-stricken at being on the German side. He also talked of invading Britain, but when his army reached the Channel, he ordered the legionaries to collect seashells. After celebrating this "victory" over Neptune the sea god, he returned to Rome determined to be worshipped as a god himself. He built a temple to himself and forced senators to become its priests. Some historians suggest that in this he was emulating eastern monarchs, who were worshipped in their own lifetimes. Some emperors indeed were, but not in Rome. Finally, disgusted by such caprices, Caligula's courtiers and officers conspired to kill him on 24 January AD41 as he was leaving the games.

NERO (AD54–68)

Just 17 years old when he succeeded the elderly Claudius in AD54, Nero promised to revive the spirit of Augustus' Principate. At first, guided by the philosopher Seneca, his former tutor, and the Praetorian prefect, Burrus, he seemed to rule well. Trajan later referred approvingly to Nero's first fine *quinquennium* (five years), although he may have been thinking only of Nero's building projects. Despite two family murders – the first in AD54 of his step-brother, Britannicus, the second of his mother, Agrippina, in AD59 – the new regime appeared to run smoothly enough.

In fact, Nero spent much of his time engaged with dramatic pursuits. For these he had a real passion if not talent, vastly admiring Greek culture, at least in its more histrionic aspects. At first Nero performed only before select private audiences, as a noble Roman forfeited all dignity by performing in public. He later alienated the upper classes by appearing on stage, first in half-Greek Naples in AD64, where he made his debut as a singer, and later in Rome itself.

After the death of Burrus in AD62, Seneca retired from court, aware that his influence over Nero was fading. Nero was free to give full vent to his passions, including satisfying his bisexual appetites and penchant for the rough trade. He had a boy, Sporus, castrated and then married him in a mock wedding ceremony. He abused married women and freeborn boys equally (slaves being thought "fair game"). Falling for Poppaea, wife of his crony (and later briefly emperor) Otho, he divorced and executed Octavia, Claudius' daughter, but then viciously kicked Poppaea to death in a rage. This last action lost him much popular support.

Nero's discovery of the senatorial Piso conspiracy against him in AD65 led to savage reprisals. When fire ravaged Rome in AD64, Nero was reputed – wrongly – to have started it and then "fiddled" or sung over the flames. In fact, his fireproof rebuilding regulations were very sensible but his new palace, the Domus Aureus (Golden House) appeared intolerably lavish and vast, sprawling over central Rome. To divert his unpopularity, Nero ordered the first recorded persecution of Christians. Most Romans had no fondness for this new sect but they grew disgusted when they saw Christians being coated with pitch and ignited as human torches in the circus to please the emperor.

Nero loved the glamorous absolutism of Hellenistic monarchies, but Rome was not ready for this. To pursue his artistic vocation, he went to Greece in AD66 and participated in the Olympic Games. He fell out of his chariot, but was declared the winner of every prize, the logic being that if he had not fallen out, he would certainly have won! By the time he returned, reluctantly, to Rome in late AD67, he faced revolts. Some collapsed of their own accord, but Nero dithered fatally, finally being declared a public enemy by the Senate. He committed suicide on 8 June AD68, crying, "What an artist dies in me!" Despite a few good ideas, such as cutting the Corinth Canal and restoring "liberty" (self-government) to the Greek cities, he had no concern or understanding of the army and left a half-bankrupt empire in the grip of civil war.

Above: Nero was popularly – but wrongly - supposed to have fiddled while Rome burned during the fire of Rome in AD64.

Below: After the great fire of Rome in AD64, Nero tried to make the newly recognized sect of the Christians into scapegoats. His plan backfired when their sufferings in the arena roused Roman pity.

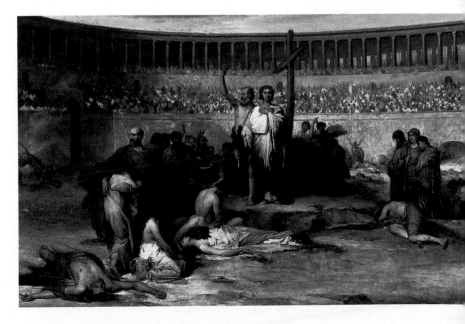

Above: Domitian, the grim, sometimes paranoid, emperor.

Below: Commodus posed as his favourite hero Hercules in the last years of his reign.

DOMITIAN (REIGNED AD81–96)

Depending on the observer, Domitian was an emperor whose reputation varied greatly. To the Senate and its supporters, including Tacitus, and also to many equestrians, he was an increasingly paranoid autocrat and priggish despot. To the army and to many people in the provinces, he was a conscientious and efficient emperor, albeit lacking the charm of his brother Titus, who had died after a reign of only two years. Although 30 years old when he succeeded Titus, Domitian had had little experience of office. He soon showed that he was a conscientious judge, if one of a marked puritanism. He forbade the castration of boys (for sexual purposes), and he punished homosexuality among senators. He also condemned to death four of the six supposedly chaste Vestal Virgins for having lovers, some incestuously. (One was buried alive in the traditional manner.) This was perfectly legal – as *pontifex maximus*, such cases were his responsibility – but the emperor's conservative rigour shook many in easy-going imperial Rome. What hurt the Senate far more was the way he openly treated them as mere subjects and demanded to be addressed as *dominus*, or lord. He assumed the title of Perpetual Censor in AD85 and summoned all his officials to the palace, rather than meeting them in the *Curia* (Senate House) or Forum. He rebuilt the imperial palace on the Palatine Hill in a style reminiscent of a Hellenistic monarchy – and Nero – where he entertained lavishly. Although he enforced a public puritanism, he kept many concubines himself, whom he personally depilated.

Aware of the need to keep his soldiers' loyalty, Domitian increased their pay by a third, and, lacking a military record, embarked on a perhaps unnecessary war in AD83 against the Chatti, taking the honorary title Germanicus for a modest victory. According to Tacitus (a biased source), only Domitian's jealousy prevented Agricola from completing his conquest of northern Britain in AD84. In fact, Domitian needed Agricola's troops to quell an uprising in the Danube region. Coupled with a senatorial conspiracy in AD87, this revolt made Domitian increasingly paranoid.

In AD93, fuelled by informers' reports that reached him in his palace – whose mirror-like walls allowed him to watch everybody – he began a reign of terror that spared none. Finally, his closest attendants turned against him, encouraged even by the empress, Domitia. He was murdered in the imperial palace on 18 September AD96. However, the army and Praetorians mourned him.

COMMODUS (REIGNED AD180–92)

Whatever the truth of the rumours that Marcus Aurelius was not the real father of Commodus and that the empress Faustina had slept with a gladiator, Commodus was certainly very unlike his industrious, disciplined and ascetic predecessor. Yet Marcus raised Commodus, his sole surviving son, as a future emperor, making him joint ruler in AD177.

Upon his accession in March AD180, Commodus abandoned Marcus' forward policy in central Europe. Back in Rome he soon showed his distaste for the tedium of government by handing over power to a series of favourites, usually his lovers. He later often had them executed to defuse outbursts of popular unrest. He meanwhile amused himself with his immense seraglio – allegedly containing 300 girls and 300 boys – mostly in luxurious villas outside Rome.

A botched assassination attempt in AD182, probably instigated by his elder sister Lucilla, fuelled his paranoia about the Senate, and he became more openly tyrannical. His chief favourite after AD185 was Cleander, a former slave from Phrygia (Asia Minor) who openly sold offices; in one year he sold the consulate 25 times, enriching himself with the proceeds. A severe shortage of grain in AD190 led to his downfall, when Commodus sacrificed him to the angry mob. In his last years, Commodus emerged from his seclusion to participate in gladiatorial contests – something that deeply shocked many Romans – and was frequently portrayed as the divine hero Hercules, complete with lion skin and club. He also demanded worship as a living god.

Physically, Commodus was "of a striking appearance, with a shapely, manly body and a handsome face", according to Herodian, but the *Augustan Histories* describe him as having a drunkard's dullness of expression. After a serious fire damaged the city in AD191, Commodus decided to refound Rome as Colonia Commodiana (Colony of Commodus) on 1 January AD193. Such rampant megalomania led to a conspiracy among his closest courtiers. Eclectus, the imperial chamberlain, Quintus Laetus, the Praetorian prefect, and his favourite concubine, Marcia, together planned his assassination on 31 December AD192. Marcia gave him poison but he vomited it up, so a gladiator had to strangle him to death. The Senate then damned Commodus as "more cruel than Domitian, more foul than Nero", but four years later Septimius Severus deified him as part of his campaign to adopt himself retrospectively into the Antonine dynasty.

ELAGABALUS
(REIGNED AD218–22)

Born in Syria in AD204, Elagabalus was perhaps the most bizarre of all Rome's emperors. As a child he assumed the hereditary high priesthood of the Semitic sun god, taking its name, Elagabal. He was proclaimed emperor as Marcus Aurelius Antoninus Pius in May AD218 by a lover of his grandmother, Julia Maesa, sister-in-law of the former emperor Caracalla, who was still revered by the army. Elagabalus did not reach

Rome until AD219, which he entered in company of a divine black stone that the Syrians claimed had fallen from heaven, walking backwards before its chariot, which was drawn by white horses. He installed this meteorite in a new temple on the Capitol and made it the supreme god of Rome, even above Jupiter. This was not a popular move, and the new god's often orgiastic worship, rumoured to include secret human sacrifice, principally of small children, alienated the city further, as did Elagabalus' marriage to one of the sacred Vestal Virgins. Elagabalus' almost pathological sex life perhaps indicates transexuality, for he used to prostitute himself to men in cheap bordellos and asked his doctors to cut an artificial vagina into his body. Such bizarreness completed his unpopularity. Only the semi-competent government of his mother and grandmother, and the prospect of his very different cousin Alexander Severus as successor, delayed his assassination until 11 March AD222.

Above: The temple of Jupiter Heliopolitanus in Baalbek in the province of Syria, from where the later Severans came.

Below: Elagabalus was only 14 when he came to the throne, but already depraved.

SAVIOURS OF THE EMPIRE

Above: Under Gallienus, the empire seemed to touch rock bottom. Then, largely due to his new ideas, it began its long, slow recovery, although he himself was soon murdered.

Below: The walls with which Aurelian hastily encircled Rome in the 270s incorporated existing older buildings such as the Claudian aqueduct.

With the murder of Alexander in AD235, the empire began to glide into chaos. Rival emperors formed separatist realms while, amid endless civil war, barbarian invaders penetrated deep into the empire. Most emperors were army men, acclaimed by greedy legionaries, then casually murdered. But a few, whose efforts helped save the empire in its darkest hours, stand out and deserve to be remembered as restorers of Rome.

GALLIENUS (AD253–68)

Although his reign saw chunks of the empire break away, Gallienus is now seen to have laid the foundations for its subsequent recovery and to have been a patron of the arts. On becoming co-emperor with his father, Valerian, in AD253, he took over the west while his father took the east. Valerian had initial successes against the Persian invaders in Syria, but he ended his life as a Persian captive. Gallienus was unable to revenge this because of barbarian invasions over the Danube. He repelled these but had to accept Postumus' separatist empire in Gaul and Spain. However, Gallienus rescinded his father's anti-Christian edicts and was a patron of the Neoplatonist philosopher Plotinus. He also encouraged a new style in sculpture that revived Augustan classicism, besides being a poet himself. His significant reforms, however, were military. He banned senators from army command and made Milan, closer to the threatened frontiers, capital in all but name, leaving Rome increasingly a ceremonial city. Finally, he created the empire's first armed reserve, a mobile force of crack troops called the *comitatus* (retinue). He also minted new coins to pay them in place of the debased currency. With this new model army, he crushed the Goths in AD268 at Nis in Serbia, killing 50,000, although he was assassinated soon after by his own troops.

AURELIAN (AD270–75)

Commander of Gallienus' new cavalry wing, and possibly involved in the plot against him, Aurelian was one of the Illyrian emperors, tough capable soldiers from the Romanized Balkans who helped save the empire. After turning back another German invasion in AD271, he decided to refortify Rome, three centuries after Augustus had removed most of the Servian walls. The new Aurelianic walls, still standing, ran for 12 miles (19km) and were rushed up, often incorporating older structures. After a victorious campaign against Zenobia of Palmyra in the east, he defeated the Gallic separatists at Châlons in AD274, reuniting the empire in just four years. Aurelian celebrated by building a huge temple in Rome to *Sol Invictus* (the Unconquered Sun), decorating it with booty from Palmyra's temples. Solar monotheism was popular with the army and he presumably hoped the new cult would help unify the empire. The next year, preparing to fight Persia, he was murdered by his secretary for unknown reasons and was mourned by both the army and the Senate.

DIOCLETIAN (AD284–305)

Diocletian was one of the greatest of Rome's later emperors, recasting the empire in a bureaucratic, half-oriental mode that essentially lasted three centuries, an achievement for a man who remained, beneath his imperial splendour, a simple Illyrian soldier. Diocletian realized that the empire's crucial weakness lay in the fickle way the armies made and deposed emperors, and the lack of any principles for the succession. In AD286 he made his fellow soldier, Maximian, co-Augustus. They divided the empire, Diocletian taking the east, and both began campaigning energetically, if not always successfully. In AD293 Diocletian adopted Galerius as Caesar, his junior emperor and heir. Maximian did the same with Constantius I in the west. A Caesar was to succeed his Augustus in this Tetrarchy, or quadruple rulership. Each tetrarch adorned his administrative capital – Trier and Milan in the west, Thessalonica and Nicomedia (north Turkey) in the east – with palaces, basilicas and monuments. Each court's elaborate rituals were based on Persian models, elevating the emperor to semi-divine status to help guard against assassination. A two-tier administrative system was adopted. Provincial governors lost their military powers and their provinces were split and then grouped into 12 dioceses, or super-provinces. The army was expanded and reorganized along Gallienus' lines, with fixed frontier troops and *Palatini*, mobile forces directly under the emperor. The new system was successful; the Persians were defeated and the frontier extended further east in AD297, while Britain was restored to the empire by Constantius.

FINANCIAL REFORMS

This extra government came at a huge cost. Diocletian tried to make the tax burden more predictable and equitable, but was unable to check inflation. His notorious Edict of Maximum Prices in AD301, which fixed prices and wages, merely meant that goods disappeared from the markets, although workers were increasingly tied to their jobs like serfs. Nor was Diocletian's religious policy successful. Persecution of Christians, who were seen as unpatriotic blasphemers, even traitors, for their refusal to worship the gods of Rome, began in AD298 and became more savage in AD303. In the west, Maximian and Constantius hardly persecuted them, but in the more Christianized east, several thousands were martyred from AD303 to AD311 and many more abjured their faith. But in one area Diocletian was outstandingly successful: he died peacefully. In AD305, worn out, he abdicated – the first Roman emperor to do so – and retired to his vast fortified palace at Split in Dalmatia. He emerged only once, in AD308, to try to restore peace among his quarrelling successors, for the principles governing succession in the Tetrarchy did not work at all as intended. He died perhaps disappointed at the way his scheme was unravelling, but at least he died in his bed. His basic reforms underpinned the whole later empire.

Above: Under Diocletian, the empire entered a new, less chaotic phase marked by increasing bureaucratization and official attempts to control all aspects of life.

Below: Not least of Diocletian's achievements was being able to retire peacefully to his specially built palace at Split on the Adriatic, although his plans for the succession soon fell apart.

Above: Constantius Chlorus, the father of Constantine the Great, was an effective ruler in his own right, regaining Britain for the empire and ruling it and Gaul wisely for many years as a Caesar, or junior emperor. He showed religious tolerance.

Right: Constantius received an enthusiastic welcome from Londoners after his troops reached the city in time to prevent its sack by the usurper Allectus' Frankish mercenaries.

CONSTANTIUS I, CAESAR (AD293–305), AUGUSTUS (AD305–06)

Constantius I, nicknamed "Chlorus", or pale – possibly from the leukemia that finally killed him – is often seen merely as the father of Constantine the Great. In fact, he was a successful ruler in his own right, most notably in his restoration of Britain to the empire. The Augustus Maximian's Praetorian prefect, he was made his heir and Caesar (junior emperor) in AD293, and made Trier his capital. He married Maximian's daughter Theodora, putting aside Helena, the mother of Constantine, who may not have been his legal wife. His first major task was to remove the separatist British empire of Carausius. He drove Carausius from Boulogne in AD293 and then invaded Britain in AD296. His troops reached London in time to stop Frankish mercenaries sacking it, which so pleased Londoners that they struck a medal hailing Constantius as the "restorer of light". A restoration of the whole province followed, ushering in a prosperous half century. Nine years later, Constantius, now a full Augustus, returned to Britain and led a campaign to crush the Picts, before returning to York to die of illness in July AD306. Constantius was notably tolerant in religious matters, ignoring the great persecution of Christians started by Galerius and Diocletian. He was a worshipper of *Sol Invictus* (the Unconquered Sun), a form of solar monotheism popular in the army at the time.

JULIAN "THE APOSTATE" (AD 361–3)

As a 24-year-old philosophy student in Athens, Julian had no political or military experience, being noted only for his inky fingers and his unfashionable beard, when his distant cousin Constantius II summoned him to rule the west as a Caesar in AD355. Julian had grown up partly in a remote castle in Cappadocia, where he studied the Greek classics and recoiled from the machinations of the court. Because the court was also avowedly Christian, Julian began to see all Christians as corrupt and murderous. Constantius, surviving son of Constantine – his two brothers had been murdered – could not deal both with a Gaul overrun by Germans and with the eastern frontier.

To great surprise, Julian proved very successful as a general, repelling the Alamanni at Strasbourg in AD357 and marching across the Rhine, emulating Julius Caesar. Julian also reformed the administration, reducing some of the crushing taxes on civilians. Jealous, Constantius tried to recall him in AD360, but Julian's troops proclaimed him Augustus. Civil war was averted by Constantius II's death in AD361, when Julian became sole emperor. He now declared himself a pagan; he had long secretly worshipped the old gods. Although he never persecuted Christians, he forbade them to teach, hoping to reverse the rising Christian tide by excluding them from Greek culture, still overwhelmingly important for anyone with pretensions to learning. Julian himself wrote some philosophy and even a satire. Early in AD363 he invaded Persia with a huge army. He reached, but could not capture, its walled capital Ctesiphon (Baghdad). He then turned back for some reason and was killed, probably by a Christian in his army, on the retreat. His pagan restoration, like his several attempts at administrative reform, died with him, but religiously and militarily he had gained a few years more for Rome and her gods.

Above: The emperor Julian, bearded like ancient Greek philosophers, whose attempted pagan restoration died with him.

VALENTINIAN I
(AD364–75)

A man of the people, Valentinian was another Danubian soldier. He had risen through the ranks to become one of Julian's senior commanders, although the two had not got on well. Tall, fair-haired and blue-eyed, he had a commanding presence and a vigorous personality. Decently educated, he became perhaps the last great emperor in the west.

After the brief reign of the emperor Jovian, who died of natural causes, Valentinian was unanimously acclaimed emperor by the army and civil service in Constantinople. At once dividing the empire, he generously gave his younger brother Valens the east, which was by then much the richer half. He himself moved to Milan, and began to campaign vigorously against Germans who had crossed the Rhine. Driving them back, he marched up the Neckar valley and won a victory in the Black Forest. Then he moved north to Trier, which became once again the capital of the whole western empire. This proved fortunate for Britain, suffering barbarian attacks. Valentinian sent Count Theodosius north in AD368 to restore order. Following an illness in AD367, Valentinian had raised his 8-year-old son Gratian to the throne with him. This was not an inspired choice. Gratian proved an ineffectual emperor, chiefly interested in religion. Valentinian was generally noted for being a poor judge of men, and for having a violent temper. The latter proved fatal. In AD375 he was in Pannonia to repel German invaders. Angered by the insolence of some German envoys, he died of a stroke. Valentinian was also noted for two things seldom associated with late-Roman emperors: a genuine compassion for the poor, whom he tried to help by extending the system of public health in Rome; and, despite his Christian faith, a religious tolerance that was becoming increasingly rare. Meanwhile, his brother Valens in the east was persecuting pagans, and also the Christian majority who did not agree with his version of Christianity, which denied the divinity of Christ. Valens led Rome's forces to a catastrophic defeat at the hands of the Goths at Adrianople in AD378, a defeat from which the empire never fully recovered.

Below: The base of the Egyptian obelisk in the hippodrome in Constantinople, the new eastern capital, shows the emperor Theodosius I receiving the submission of barbarian tribes. Theodosius spent most of his reign (AD379–95) fighting his numerous Roman rivals, but he was the last emperor to rule the whole empire.

CONSTANTINE THE GREAT

Above: Founder of the city of Constantinople and the first Christian Roman emperor, Constantine regarded himself as the "thirteenth apostle".

Below: Constantine was almost the last emperor to adorn Rome with edifices such as baths, a basilica and this triple arch.

Now famed for being the first Christian Roman emperor and for founding Constantinople as the "New Rome", later the capital of the eastern or Byzantine half of the empire, Constantine was, above all, a supremely competent general and a ruthlessly ambitious politician.

Like many other Roman emperors, Constantine's background was that of a soldier. Born *c.*AD276, his father was Constantius I, "Chlorus" (pale), one of Diocletian's junior emperors. Rumours that his mother was a prostitute can probably be dismissed, although Helena was not the saintly Romano-British noblewoman of legend. Constantine was serving with Diocletian's army when his father became Augustus in May AD305. Hastening across the empire, he joined Constantius in Britain.

On Constantius' death at York in AD306, his troops hailed his son as Augustus – prematurely, for at first he was only accepted as Caesar of the west and Constantine initially established his

Above: Emperor Constantine converted to Christianity late in life, yet his role as the founder of the Byzantine civilization is indisputable. Along with his mother Helena, he is still revered by Greek Orthodox Christians as a saint.

capital at Trier in Gaul. In the ensuing struggles, Constantine was victorious over Maxentius, ruler of Italy, at the Battle of the Milvian Bridge in AD312. He attributed his victory to a dream in which Christ had appeared telling him to mark his soldiers' shields with a cross (or so the story goes). Henceforth, Constantine's soldiers always fought under the cross – at least according to Eusebius, an almost contemporary Christian writer anxious to portray Constantine as a true Christian.

In AD313 Constantine, now Augustus of the west, declared religious tolerance for Christians and pagans alike, although he was already moving towards Christianity. In AD324, when he became sole ruler of the empire, he forbade public sacrifices and ritual prostitution and looted pagan temples to finance his church-building programme, which included the first basilica of St Peter's in Rome. He also presided over the Council of Nicaea (Iznik) in AD325, in vain trying to promote religious unity before finally agreeing to persecute those declared heretics by the Council.

Although Constantine's conversion was almost certainly genuine – he saw himself as the "thirteenth apostle" – religious conviction was also much reinforced by political convenience: the Church's highly effective social organization impressed him, as did the prospect of despoiling pagan temple treasures.

DIOCLETIAN'S HEIR

A revolutionary in religion, Constantine continued with Diocletian's army reforms and further elaborated court ritual, wearing a bejewelled diadem and, allegedly, in later years a wig. If personal vanity was a failing, so was paranoia, for he had his son Crispus by his first wife executed for adultery in AD326. Rumours that the current empress Faustina had intrigued against her stepson – either to advance her own sons or because Crispus had rejected her advances – seemed borne out by her suicide soon after, when the emperor's mother, Helena, convinced Constantine of Faustina's guilt. (In the new, ever more elaborate "Byzantine" court, eunuchs played an increasingly vital role as major officials. They appealed to absolutist rulers because they could never found rival dynasties themselves.)

Constantine minted the first *solidus* coin, which, at 72 to the pound (454g) of gold, provided a stable gold currency for many centuries, although inflation continued. Otherwise, his financial policies burdened civilians even more heavily. A new tax, the *chrysagryon*, payable in gold or silver, was levied every four years on citizens. It was so onerous that fathers allegedly sold their daughters to pay it, but money was needed for the huge court, army and building programme. Constantine completed Maxentius' gigantic Basilica Nova in Rome and constructed his own arch – plundering other arches for its decoration. He also built the Baths of Constantine, the ancient city's last grand building, and a palace for the pope. But Constantine did not find Rome, with its proudly pagan memories, sympathetic.

CONSTANTINOPLE

Byzantium had been a small Greek city for almost 1,100 years when it was chosen as Constantine's new capital in AD324. Easy to defend and superbly sited between Europe and Asia, this New Rome, or Constantinople (Istanbul), became a great city. It was later given a Roman-style Senate and its citizens received handouts of free grain and circuses. Constantine liberally adorned his new capital with artworks taken from Greek cities and built new palaces, fora and churches, as well as temples dedicated to Jupiter, Juno and Minerva, echoing those of Rome.

The Byzantine civilization was a fusion of Greek, Roman and the emerging Christian tradition. For this achievement alone, Constantine deserves the title "Great". When he died in May AD337, he was buried in the Church of the Holy Apostles in Constantinople. However, the Senate in Rome deified a ruler who had not resigned the old pagan title of *pontifex maximus*, higher priest, held by every emperor since Augustus. Such a contradiction demonstrates Constantine stood halfway between the old pagan empire of Rome and the deeply Christian Byzantine empire that replaced it and which lasted another eleven centuries.

Above: One of Constantine's greatest feats was the founding of Constantinople. For over a millennium it was one of the greatest cities on earth.

Below: Constantine was a fine general. This ivory shows him triumphing over his enemies.

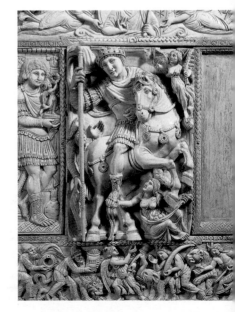

WOMEN BEHIND THE THRONE

Although women in Rome could never hold office or vote, by the late Republic they could own, manage and inherit property. They also joined men at dinner parties and shared Rome's political and cultural life. If their men were of high status, women could also aspire to become powers behind the throne, even occasionally becoming effective rulers.

LIVIA DRUSILLA (59BC–AD29)

In 38BC Livia Drusilla became Augustus' third wife, having divorced her first husband, Tiberius Claudius, by whom she had had two sons: Tiberius and Drusus. As she and Augustus had no children, Augustus adopted first his nephew Marcellus, then his grandsons Gaius and Lucius as his heirs, and only last, when the others had died, Livia's son Tiberius. Because of this, she was suspected of procuring their deaths, although this may be unjust – mortality rates were high at the time – and is certainly unprovable. We do know that Livia gave Augustus invaluable support and stability. The clemency he showed to his (few) enemies in later life was said to stem from her advice. She also tolerated his frequent infidelities, even when he left for Gaul in 16BC accompanied by Terentia, his then mistress. When Tiberius succeeded Augustus in AD14, Livia was rumoured to have poisoned him and his last surviving grandson, Agrippa Postumus. But it is probable that Agrippa, excluded from the succession for psychopathic tendencies, was killed by Tiberius. Livia died at the age of 88, a Julio-Claudian matriarch.

JULIA AGRIPPINA

A sister of Caligula and great-grand-daughter of Augustus, Julia Agrippina had married Domitius Ahenobarbus, a great-nephew of Augustus, which made their son Nero doubly descended from the first emperor. Once divorced from Domitius, Agrippina married her uncle, Claudius, in AD49, who had had his third wife, Messalina, executed for plotting against him.

Agrippina plotted to have Nero succeed in place of Britannicus, Claudius' son by Messalina. In AD51 Nero became *princeps iuventutis* (leader of youth), with Seneca, his tutor, and Burrus, one of Agrippina's protégés, head of the Praetorian guard. All was ready for Nero's succession when Agrippina (probably) had Claudius poisoned in October AD54. Britannicus was executed and she hoped to rule through the 17-year-old Nero. At first he showed her respect, but in AD55 she was expelled from the palace and exiled. In AD59 Nero tried to murder her by having a specially built ship sink under her. However, she swam to shore and it took a freed man of Nero's called Anicetus to finish her off. So perished "the best of mothers", as Nero had once called her.

JULIA MAMMAEA

When Alexander Severus succeeded his assassinated cousin, the depraved Elagabalus, to become emperor in AD222, he was only 14 years old and under the sway of his mother, the Syrian princess Julia Mammaea. He never managed to

Above: Mother of the emperor Nero and last wife of the ageing Claudius, Agrippina aspired to rule through both. But although she (probably) murdered Claudius, her son soon tired of her and had her killed in turn.

Below: Livia, wife of Augustus and mother of Tiberius, had great influence if not power while her husband lived. But after Augustus' death during the grape harvest, Tiberius increasingly ignored her.

escape her maternal domination, but at first Julia ruled very effectively. She reversed all Elegabalus' scandalous policies, chose 16 distinguished senators as advisers and relied heavily on the famous lawyer Ulpian, also from Syria, whom she made commander of the Praetorians. However, Ulpian proved unable to control the Praetorians, and was finally murdered by them in AD228.

Meanwhile, Julia had become madly jealous of her son's wife, Barbia Orbiana, whom Alexander had married in AD225, and whose father he had made Caesar or co-ruler. Julia had her daughter-in-law thrown out of the palace and her father executed. Being still dominated by his mother, Alexander accepted this, but Julia could not control foreign attacks. After an inconclusive expedition to repel a Persian invasion in AD232, mother and son went north to deal with a German attack. Alexander so alienated the Rhine legions by his military feebleness and his meanness about their pay that they chose the giant Maximinus as emperor in AD235. Troops sent to kill Alexander found him clinging to his mother in a tent. Mother and son were butchered together, so ending the Severan dynasty.

GALLA PLACIDIA (AD392–50)
Daughter of Theodosius I the Great, grand-daughter of Valentinian I and half-sister of the emperor Honorius (one of the feeblest emperors), Placidia herself was a far stronger character than her half-brother. However, her efforts to preserve the empire foundered partly on her own likes and dislikes. Abducted by the invading Visigoths in AD410, she was carried off to Gaul and forcibly married to the Visigoth king, Ataulf. She owed her return to Italy to Constantius III, a general who took control of the western empire in AD413 and forced the Visigoths to settle around Toulouse. In AD417 he married Placidia against her wishes. However, his death in late AD421 left their infant son the official emperor: Valentinian III (AD425–55).

After a brief interregnum, troops from Constantinople helped Placidia to gain control of Ravenna, the new imperial capital, and she began ruling through her son, Valentinian, trying to maintain imperial power amid the gathering chaos. She had to rely, however, on the armies of the general Aetius, a highly effective soldier whom she for some reason came to loathe. She embroiled him in a dispute with Boniface, governor of North Africa, that had terrible consequences. Boniface enlisted the support of the Vandals, a German tribe who had settled in southern Spain. This was disastrous, for after their entry into Africa in AD429 they were never dislodged. In AD439 they captured Carthage, cutting off Rome's grain supply. Aetius proved more successful in Europe, defeating the Huns in AD451 at Châlons. By then Placidia was dead. She did not live to see the end of her dynasty, for Valentinian proved fatally incompetent. Jealous of Aetius, he had him murdered before being killed himself by two of Aetius' officers in AD455, leaving no heirs. Shortly afterwards, the Vandals landed near Rome and sacked it, carrying off Valentinian's widow and thousands of Romans. The empire soon ceased to exist.

Above: The ruins of Baalbek (Heliopolis) in Syria, the home province of Julia Mammaea, who in reality governed the empire for 13 years during the reign of her ineffectual young son, Alexander Severus.

Above: Daughter of emperor Theodosius, Galla Placidia was far more determined than her half-brother, the emperor Honorius, but she was too often swayed by her personal feelings to pursue effective imperial policies and actually hastened the empire's fall.

CHAPTER IV

GOVERNING THE EMPIRE

Seeing Rome for the first time in 166BC, the Greek historian Polybius was struck by the apparent excellence of its government, thinking it combined the best aspects of democracy in its Assembly of the people, of aristocracy, embodied in the Senate, and monarchy, in its elected officials or consuls. This seemingly perfect system of checks and balances made Rome's status as ruler of the Mediterranean world look well deserved.

But during the Republic and Principate, Rome never had a written constitution. Real power lay in the informal network of alliances and *clientalia*, the web of dependants that each Roman noble needed for a political career. The Senate, dominated by the interests of its noble elite, failed to cope with the problems of governing an expanding empire. This led to the Republic's downfall and its replacement by the emperors. Under imperial rule, the Senate became increasingly ceremonial and the Assembly disappeared, while the provinces rivalled Rome in power and privilege, if never in prestige. By the 4th century AD, the Roman empire had become an absolute monarchy, albeit one where the emperor (at least in theory) obeyed the laws. The full codification of laws by Justinian in the 6th century AD meant that the Roman legacy transmitted to the Middle Ages was more autocratic than democratic, an inspiration more to rulers than the ruled.

Left: At the very heart of Roman life and of the whole empire lay the Forum Romanum, adorned with monuments such as the triple triumphal arch erected by Septimius Severus.

A SELF-GOVERNING CONFEDERACY

Above: The Maison Carrée at Nîmes, France, one of the finest temples of the Augustan era, testifies to the prosperous sophistication of such colonies founded by Rome but growing into confidently self-governing cities that contributed to the empire's strength.

Below: Ostia's port became Rome's greatest harbour, supplying the voracious capital. The city itself, at the mouth of the Tiber, had been Rome's first colony, the forerunner of many hundreds planted around the Mediterranean and Europe.

Rome ruled its growing empire with the minimum of government by co-opting the aristocracies of other cities, first in Italy then around the Mediterranean, into ruling on Rome's behalf. In essence, the empire became a confederation of internally self-governing cities. Defence and foreign affairs were transferred to Rome's control, however. Unlike other ancient cities with empires, notably Athens, Rome was generous in granting citizenship to other towns in Italy. As its empire spread to the less urbanized parts of Europe, it planted colonies of Roman citizens or made existing cities into Roman colonies, so that the empire ended up as an agglomerate of more than 1,000 cities. (New cities without this status, were founded as well.) Urbanization helped spread Roman culture around the empire.

In 381BC the Romans seized Tusculum, a Latin city, and part of the Latin League of cities around Rome. All its citizens were granted Roman citizenship, which they happily accepted, later supplying many consuls. But there were limits to granting full citizenship, if existing Roman citizens were not to be outnumbered. Another type of citizenship, *civitas sine suffragio*, came with all rights except the franchise, and was imposed on cities of the Latin League after their defeat in 338BC. These cities retained internal autonomy, electing their own magistrates, who often got full citizenship. They had to supply troops to Rome when required, serving under their own officers. If they settled in Rome, they became Roman citizens. This halfway house to full citizenship long satisfied the Latin cities.

Rome now began founding colonies of self-governing settlements, both Latin colonies of mixed Latins and Romans, such as Calvi near Capua, and wholly Roman ones, such as Ostia in *c.*350BC. Between 343 and 264BC, about 60,000 colonists received allotments of land in some 40 colonies throughout Italy, from Cremona to Brindisi. Peoples of Italy not thought worthy of Latin citizenship, such as the rough Samnites, were made *socii*, allies, bound to Rome by bilateral treaties. They lost control of their foreign policy and had to supply troops but retained autonomy. The effectiveness of this system was revealed in the cities' loyalty during the Punic wars, when Rome looked doomed. A century later, Italians pressed for full citizenship. The war of the Allies, the Social War, gained full citizenship for all Latins and Italians in 89BC.

COLONIES OVERSEAS

Among the more radical proposals of Gaius Gracchus was the founding of a colony overseas for some of Rome's landless citizens on the site of Carthage, destroyed 23 years earlier. This proposal came to nothing, as did a similar idea for overseas colonies by Saturninus, a Marian tribune, in 102BC. Only under Caesar was the planting of colonies of Romans resumed, mostly for retired legionaries, but his plans included settling 80,000 unemployed Romans abroad. Arles, Tarragona, Fréjus, plus Carthage and

Corinth rising from their ruins, were among his foundations. Under Augustus, who had even more veterans to settle, colonies of ex-legionaries were founded at Turin, Avignon, Nîmes, Cologne and Zaragossa, among others. All have flourished ever since, showing that Augustus and his legates, like Caesar before him, had a good eye for cities. These colonies were self-governing cities with Roman rights, and include Timgad in Algeria, founded by Trajan for his veterans, and Camulodunum (Colchester), founded by Claudius as capital of Britain.

In the east, an old Hellenistic city such as Tarsus might win Roman rights for some (including St Paul), but it was in the west that Roman colonization really bore fruit. Places like Vienne and Lyons acquired Roman rights and grew into fine cities, with theatres, baths and forums. A grade lower were *municipia* with Latin rights, whose magistrates became full Roman citizens. Below them were *civitates*, urban settlements. The tendency was to upgrade any city that proved worthy. London started as a mere *civitas*, but became a *colonia* and the provincial capital.

Above: The Temple of the Spirit of the Colony at Timgad in Algeria, a colony for veteran legionaries founded by the emperor Trajan.

THE OLIGARCHICAL REPUBLIC

The three-fold constitution that Polybius so admired – the people, gathered in the *comitia*, or Assembly; the Senate, or Council of Elders, composed of older nobles; and the magistrates themselves, annual officials elected by the *comitia* – had existed in that form since only 287BC, although parts of it may have predated the expulsion of the kings in 509BC. Certainly the Senate itself went back at least to the 6th century BC.

In theory, the people, as constituted in the *comitia*, or Assembly, were sovereign and had unlimited powers. In practice, they met only when summoned by magistrates and could vote, without discussion, only on measures put before them. These restrictions meant that Rome was never a democracy in the sense that many Greek cities were in the classical age (480–322BC). This did not seem to concern the people, for they usually had little desire to guide the state. Their main interest was to be protected from any unjust or arbitrary actions by magistrates and nobles and to gain redress for their economic and legal grievances. Later in the Republic, when Rome had an empire to exploit, they also expected entertainment in the form of free, or very cheap, public games and grain – the so-called *panem et circenses* (bread and circuses). This aspect of Roman life survived the end of the Republic and was transplanted to Constantinople in AD330.

The *comitia centuriata*, or Assembly, was traditionally created by the kings, and continued into the Principate. Its origins were military (the kings wanted to establish an army based on heavy infantry), and it was structured corresponding to army divisions. The citizenry was divided into five classes and each class was subdivided into varying numbers of centuries, except the lowest or poorest class, which was exempt from military service. From the start, the Assembly was heavily weighted in favour of the richer citizens, for the more affluent centuries outnumbered the poorer ones in voting power, if not in numbers. As voting on every proposal started with the richer centuries and ended when an overall majority of centuries had voted, the poorest often did not vote at all. This was a long way from a one-man, one-vote democracy.

The Conflict of the Orders, or Class War, which lasted intermittently from 494 to 287BC, was about this democratic deficit and also economic problems. In the 5th century BC Rome suffered economically, partly due to the reduction in trade at the end of the monarchy, partly because of land shortages and partly because endless wars made it difficult for

Above: This bronze dating from the 5th century BC supposedly portrays Brutus, one of the nobles who helped – according to legend – to expel the last Etruscan king, Tarquin.

Right: The Romans were intensely conscious of their ancestors. They kept their busts in their houses and at times they would parade solemnly with them in public. This statue dates from the 1st century BC.

the citizen-soldier, often fighting during the summer, to tend his farm properly. Many poorer citizens grew so heavily indebted that they became serfs, or *nexi*, of their creditors. Because of problems of this sort they threatened to secede – traditionally five times; the first in 494BC, when they gained new tribunes of the people, magistrates outside the senate-dominated run of offices who could veto measures on their behalf. The writing down of the Twelve Tables of the Law in 450BC was meant to help, but it took a range of measures, culminating in the *Lex Hortensia* of 287BC, by which the decrees of the *concilium plebis*, Council of the People, were to be binding on the whole state, for the conflict finally to be settled.

This did not mean that Rome had become in any way democratic, however, for richer citizens generally dominated the *concilium plebis* too, while the eminent plebeians who had, by law, been elected as one of the two consuls since 367BC, formed the so-called plebeian nobility. Further, the tribunes, once the people's defenders and leaders, were now increasingly co-opted into the Senate, first just to listen to debates but finally to initiate them. The tribunes, who were normally among the richer and therefore often the more ambitious of plebeians, thus joined the plebeian nobility, allied to the Senate rather than opposed to it, and the tribunate increasingly became just one office among others. If former tribunes began entering the Senate themselves, this reduced their effectiveness as champions of the poor, but it made for a welcome amity and unity in a state facing horrendous external threats. Under the emperors, the people finally lost their right to choose magistrates in AD14, and the *comitia* became a mere rubber stamp on the Senate's and emperor's decisions. But the informal powers of the people of Rome long remained a major force in Roman politics. Their approval, most vocally expressed in the amphitheatre or circus, was courted for as long as Rome remained the real capital.

THE MAGISTRATES

With Sulla's reforms in 82BC the *cursus honorum*, or ladder of office, was finalized, but before that the Roman system was oddly informal. The highest magistrates were always the two consuls, elected annually by the Assembly. They each had equal powers and could veto the other's, but this rarely happened. No one could (legally) be consul in successive years. In theory, no one under the age of 42 could become consul, but this check on youthful ambition was unsuccessful. Beneath the consuls were the praetors, whose numbers were steadily increased to eight under Sulla and under Caesar to 16. One praetor supervised the administration of justice, while another praetor dealt with foreigners. Propraetors, like the proconsuls, governed provinces after their year's office. To assist consuls there were quaestors, the most junior rank on the *cursus honorum*, and there were also two censors, elected every five years, who took a census of every citizen's wealth, including senators', demoting or promoting citizens. There were also four aediles who looked after the city's policing.

As the astute, if notably reactionary, senator Cato the Censor (234–149BC) justly observed, the Roman Republic was "not made by any one man, but by many; not in a single lifetime but over many centuries". Considering the overlapping of duties and powers, the Roman Republic worked remarkably well until its last century. But what made it work and lay behind the often fleeting powers of the magistrates and the often inchoate desires of the Assembly was the immense and enduring prestige of the Senate.

Below: Aulus Metellus, an orator of the late Republic (c.90BC), here declaims with a gesture typical of Roman public speaking. Rhetoric was always vital to Roman public life, essential not only for aspiring politicians but also lawyers and ordinary citizens.

ROME'S RULING CLASSES

Under the emperors, Rome was administered by its two upper classes, the Senate and the equestrians (knights). Although the Senate was older and more distinguished, equestrians came to play an increasingly crucial role in the state. The Roman people lost all political power.

THE SENATE

Unlike the senior house of modern republics, the Senate in Rome was not the upper house, for there was no lower house, only the Assembly. Nor was the Senate directly elected. However, as it consisted of men who had once been magistrates – elected by the Assembly – there was a democratic element in it

under the Republic. Traditionally, the city's founder, Romulus, chose 100 senior heads of important families as a royal council or Senate. Roman conservatism ensured that this ancient body survived not only the end of the Republic but even the passing of the emperors themselves. The Senate was still debating in the 6th century AD under the Ostrogoths.

The Senate of the early Republic was composed of 300 *patres familias*, or heads of households. They were joined by other prominent men, known as *patricii*, to form a proud nobility of about 1,000 families. From the 4th century BC, plebeian (new) nobles entered the Senate, intermarrying with the older nobility.

Magistrates in the Republic entered the Senate after a year in office as quaestor, the lowest rank. Unless the censors decided to the contrary, they held their seats for life. The Senate's formal powers – to preselect who could stand as magistrates, to approve measures before they went to the Assembly, to advise and consult – made it powerful enough, but this was eclipsed by its informal *auctoritas* (prestige, authority). The Senate expounded its views in a *senatus consultum*, the report of a debate. This had no legal authority, but magistrates normally accepted it. A late development was the *senatus consultum ultimum*, a decree to end all debate.

The Senate guided the Republic effectively through the Punic and later wars. When Hannibal camped outside Rome in 213BC, the Senate's *sang froid* helped save Rome. At that time its members were still recruited from an almost closed circle of *c*.2,000 men. Although they disagreed at times, they did not form destructively divisive factions. But by the time of the reformist Gracchi brothers (133–121BC), the consensus was breaking down and disputes led to violence and murder. From then on, the Senate's control of the state began to

Below: The Curia (Senate House) seen through the ruins of the Temple of Saturn in the Forum Romanum. The present structure, surprisingly small, dates from the 4th century AD, and was rebuilt after a fire.

weaken. The coups and counter-coups of the 80s BC revealed that the Senate no longer controlled the generals. Despite Sulla's attempts to limit the latter's powers, the Senate lost control of Rome.

THE SENATE AND THE EMPERORS

Augustus tried to restore the Senate's dignity in running the empire. He held real power, but the Senate retained, and sometimes gained, important duties, including presiding over law courts and choosing governors for about a third of the provinces. Senators also continued to be appointed legates – meaning they held power delegated from the emperor – as governors of "imperial" provinces such as Gaul and as generals of legions. By AD100 almost half the Senate was composed of provincials – citizens born outside Italy – and most consuls were not Italian born.

Senate-respecting rulers such as Trajan were balanced by despots such as Caligula or Domitian. Hadrian, a humane emperor, soured his relations with the Senate because he executed several members. The Senate sustained a nostalgia for Republican government long after this was remotely practicable. Augustus was punctilious in attending senatorial debates, but few of the later emperors paid it such attention. They were often too busy to do so.

SENATORIAL ORDER

To become a senator was to attain the highest honours in the state, except that of emperor. To win entry into the Senate, its members had to have a fortune in property (not cash) of one million sesterces. Many had far more. In practice, Senate membership in the Principate was mainly hereditary. The son of a senator started his career at the age of 20 as a military tribune and could enter the Senate as a quaestor at the age of 25 if chosen by the *princeps*. He then worked his way up the *cursus honorum* until, if he was lucky, becoming consul at the age of 43. Under the empire, a consul did not hold his office for a whole year but retired to let another fill the post. None of the offices carried a salary, but the governorship of a major province such as Africa did (one million sesterces a year), making it a coveted post.

Senators formed a class above normal Romans. They wore a special toga, which had a broad purple stripe, had the best seats at the theatre reserved for them and were often promised by a new emperor that their members would not be summarily arrested and executed. Until Diocletian, senatorial estates in Italy were free of tax, and even later senators retained many privileges, remaining immensely wealthy.

Above: The ancient Rostra (literally, ships' prows), from which magistrates made speeches in the Forum, Rome.

Below: Roman senators taking part in a procession for a consul's assumption of office c.270AD. Although by that date the Senate had lost almost all its political powers, it nevertheless retained immense prestige and wealth.

Above: While the equestrians as an order failed to maintain their distinctive status in the later empire, senators such as this 5th-century noble retained their importance and their regular meetings in the Senate House well into the 6th century.

Below: Head of a priest of Aphrodite, dating to the 1st century BC. Many of these local cults flourished under the Roman Empire, sometimes attracting the attention of senators from Rome.

THE EQUESTRIANS

Immediately beneath senators in prestige and dignity, and sometimes individually richer, were the equestrians, or knights. Originally, they had supplied the cavalry for the armies of the early Republic, being those relatively few citizens rich enough to equip themselves as horsemen. By 200BC they had lost this role to auxiliary cavalry. Excluded entirely from the *cursus honorum* of the senatorial nobility, they turned instead to making money. The big advantage they had over senators was that they were not barred from all forms of business. As the empire expanded south and east in the 3rd and 2nd centuries BC, literally golden opportunities arose for equestrians in banking, commerce, tax-collecting and bidding for the many government contracts – building bridges and harbours, supplying armies – that were farmed out. Most profitable of all was tax-farming. When the radical tribune Gaius Gracchus, presumably heedless of longer-term consequences, granted the equestrians the tax-collecting contracts for the Asian provinces in 122BC, he was rewarding his immediate political allies. But he also vastly boosted a powerful new class of businessmen who soon began to challenge the Senate's monopoly of office and power, and generally supported the *popularis* reformist party. Sulla, a keen *optimate*, or senatorial reactionary, proscribed (killed) 1,600 equestrians – compared to only 40 senators – when he tried to re-establish senatorial supremacy, but even he was forced to recruit from equestrian ranks for his much-enlarged Senate. Equestrians and their tax-collecting agents, the *publicani*, were among those massacred by angry Greeks in Delos and the cities of the Aegean in 88BC at the instigation of Mithradates.

Caesar made frequent use of equestrians, using them both to fill the Senate and as administrators, some of them being non-Italian multi-millionaires such as Lucius Balbus of Cadiz. By then, equestrians were numerous – there were 500 men of equestrian status in both Padua and Cadiz in Augustus' time. They provided a perfect source of enterprising, often enthusiastic men to run the empire under the Principate, for they had no senatorial-type nostalgia for the days of the Republic. Augustus employed equestrians widely, either as procurators or financial secretaries in charge of the finances of imperial provinces who could control the senatorial legate, or else as governors of those provinces such as Egypt where he wanted to exclude the Senate. In Rome he revived the annual mounted processions of equestrians that took place on 15 July, when up to 5,000 of them would ride past on their ceremonial horses. Tiberius' chief minister Sejanus was an equestrian – but he overstepped the mark, for

CURSUS HONORUM

Originally very flexible, this official career ladder or succession of magistracies was codified by the *Lex Villia Annalis* of 180BC and confirmed a century later by Sulla. After an initial ten years' military service and his 30th birthday, a well-connected Roman could hope to be elected one of the 20 quaestors, whose duties were chiefly financial. A quaestor automatically became a member of the Senate and might then hope to become an aedile. By the age of 38 he might be elected praetor and only at the age of 43 (39 before Sulla's reforms in 81BC) could he stand for the consulship. After being consul, he could become a governor of a province as a proconsul or perhaps a censor, one of two magistrates elected every five years to conduct a census of the Roman people, classifying them according to wealth and conduct. No office could in theory be held until at least two years had elapsed since his previous term of office. The aim, which failed disastrously in the end, was to stop men such as Marius, Pompey or Caesar becoming too powerful.

Tiberius, proudly conscious of his descent from the great Claudian family, struck Sejanus down.

To rank as an equestrian required a fortune of 300,000 sesterces, less than a third of a senator's. Equestrians could be recognized by the narrow purple stripes on their togas; they wore a special gold ring and had the second best seats in the theatres. To belong to the equestrian order did not require residence in Rome, unlike the Senate, and many in fact lived outside the city, either in Italy or in the provinces, often respected members and patrons of the local city magistracy. The sons of equestrians, though not automatically admitted to the order, in practice usually were, first serving as army officers, often in unglamorous posts such as remote frontier forts, then in civilian posts such as customs, finance and general administration. The leading treasury officials under the Principate were most often equestrians, as were the very highest posts in the empire: the prefectures of the corn supply, the *annona*; of the fleet; of the *vigiles*, the night watchmen/firemen; and last and most powerful, the Praetorian prefect, head of the Praetorian guard. Salaries for these posts were considerable, coming in grades of 60,000, 100,000 and 200,000 sesterces. Freedmen and centurions were sometimes given equestrian status and could hope to rise meritocratically. Hadrian (AD117–38) made extensive use of such new equestrians. Unlike senators, however, they had no *curia* (Senate house) as a focus for their class, and their name and status did not survive the end of the empire.

Below: Typical of the new business opportunities for the equestrians, who were allowed to take part in commerce, was the free port at Delos in Greece, which became the busiest entrepôt in the late Republic. Reputedly, Delos could handle the sale of up to 40,000 slaves a day.

THE SECRET WORKINGS OF ROMAN POLITICS

The oligarchic reality of the Republic, which negated its seemingly democratic constitution, depended on the huge web of patronage called *clientalia*. This was an informal, but openly acknowledged, system by which each noble commanded the loyalties of hundreds, or even thousands, of retainers bound to him in reciprocal relationship. This enabled the nobility to manipulate the Assembly, which otherwise could have shown signs of democratic independence. The tenacious network survived the end of the Republic, although it was the emperors who became its ultimate beneficiaries.

Below: Most of public life, not just political, but also social and legal, took place in the Forum Romanum. Here too the networks of clients and patrons could be renewed, cemented or extended.

As early as the 5th century BC, possibly even under the kings, *clientalia* was an important part of Roman life. At its simplest, it was a personal relationship of mutual obligation between the *patronus*, the patron, who was generally a great aristocrat or patrician, and his *clientes*, or dependants, humble and usually impoverished plebeians. In the Republic's later years, such clients came to include freedmen, usually former slaves of the *patronus*, who formed an increasingly numerous group. But unless these freedmen became Roman citizens – and so able to vote – they were second-class *clientes*. Only a full Roman citizen could expect to receive the *sportula*, regular little presents in cash or kind that a client expected from his patron.

The patron would look after his clients in many aspects of life – if they went to law, needed to borrow money, needed advice in general or a guardian for their children. In return, a client gave his patron political support, both by voting for him and his allies in the Assembly and also by augmenting his personal following. The patron saw himself as a *paterfamilias* in relation to his clients, as head of an extended family, and their relationship had the same sort of highly charged feelings of *pietas* (piety) and *fides* (faithfulness) expected in a family.

For the ordinary Roman in a city grown impersonally vast, being a client offered certain advantages besides the obvious financial and legal help a great man could give. It gave a client a feeling of belonging and participating in the affairs of one of the great families who ran the growing empire. By 200BC the major noble families were organizing their bands of *clientes* on a professional basis, mobilizing them in great blocks to vote as required, and to cajole and threaten other voters when required. Tiberius and

Gaius Gracchus were murdered by clients of the optimate senators, not by the senators themselves. The system continued in an apolitical way even after Tiberius had removed the Assembly's last political powers of electing magistrates.

The concept of *clientalia* spilt over into Rome's dealings with its allies and subjects. When Quintus Flaminius declared "freedom" for the Greek cities in 196BC, the sort of relationship he saw between the Greeks and Rome was not total independence but the symbiotic client–patron relationship that worked so well in Rome. The Greeks did not see it this way, having known real freedom, and it took brutal repression by Rome before they accepted the new status quo. But later, when Rome extended its power east to less liberty-addicted kingdoms in western Asia, this informal, essentially personal, system worked well.

MILITARY *CLIENTALIA*
The army was for a long time outside the client system, as of all political life – armies were not allowed into Italy and weapons could not be carried openly in Rome. But from the time of Marius' reforms in 106–102BC, soldiers, now recruited even from the poorest classes, began looking to their generals for rewards for their loyalty in exactly the same way that civilian clients did. The results proved disastrous for the Republic. Caesar's army also formed part of his *clientalia*, as, in a different way, did all his supporters, most of them definitely new men – equestrians or men from the Italian municipal aristocracies or people from even further afield.

Octavian went even further. Preparing for the war with Antony, the climax of his struggle for supremacy, in 32BC, Octavian pressed all the leading men throughout Italy – not just the senators and equestrians in Rome but the local aristocracy of the *municipia* – to swear an oath to him. *"Tota Italia in mea verba iuravit"* (All Italy swore an oath of loyalty to me) he later recorded in the *Res Augustae*, which list his accomplishments. Having sworn such an oath, these men, the ruling classes in the widest sense, became in effect his clients, bound to him by ties of reciprocal fealty. When soldiers swore loyalty to the *princeps* as their supreme commander – although Octavian was never much of a general – the armies, too, effectively became his clients. This personal tie underpinned the Principate throughout its existence; many civilian client–patron relationships had long been hereditary. For the Principate as much as the Republic, therefore, *clientalia* acted as a sort of invisible glue.

Above: As princeps, *or the leading citizen of the state, Augustus was the greatest patron of them all – a role he extended into military life, also binding the army to him.*

Below: Life in the insulae, *the often cramped apartment blocks where most Romans lived, could be grim. Being the client of a rich patron offered a small chance of improvement or at least some support.*

THE PRINCIPATE
A MONARCHY IN DISGUISE

Above: The arrival of Vespasian in Rome in AD69 marked the advent of the second dynasty of emperors: the Flavians. Shorter-lived than the Julio-Claudians, this era ended when Domitian, the last of the Flavians, was assassinated in AD96.

Below: The dramatic public murder of Julius Caesar in 44BC was a stark warning to later emperors to exercise their (unofficial) power with greater discretion and tact. Many failed to do so – and paid the inevitable price.

In February 44BC Caesar, victor of the civil war, had himself created perpetual dictator. Partly because of this latest, most blatant, addition to his powers, he was assassinated soon after. Octavian, later Augustus, was wiser, disguising the absolutist foundations of his new regime so carefully that the Senate could go along with his restoration of the Republic – meaning a stable constitutional government, not rule by the "Senate and People of Rome". Gradually the emperor appeared more and more as an autocrat, whose power depended on force. In the turmoil of the 3rd century AD, the trappings of absolutism finally emerged until, under Diocletian and Constantine, the emperor became a superhuman being, surrounded by genuflecting courtiers.

"If Caesar with all his genius could not find a way out [of the crisis], who can possibly do so?" Gaius Matius, one of Caesar's followers, asked Cicero in a letter soon after Caesar's assassination. It took two more rounds of civil wars before Augustus found an answer. His Second Settlement of 23BC meant that he no longer monopolized the consulate, but let other members of the Senate hold this much-desired office. In fact, it became customary for the first consul of the year to make way for a second. Augustus did his utmost to restore the forms of the Republic – he was ostentatiously first among equals, the *princeps* – and to breathe new if restricted life into its institutions. He offered the senatorial nobility careers running the empire, army and Rome itself. Although Augustus' own household, along with his public behaviour, was notably modest – in reality his wealth, like his power, was vast.

Augustus' successors lacked the tact, patience and *auctoritas* to dissemble so successfully. Tiberius, the next emperor and in many ways deeply traditional, unwittingly revealed the real nature of the Principate by making Sejanus his effective prime minister, although Sejanus was a knight, not a senator, disqualified for high office. Tiberius withdrew to Capri for the last decade of his life and ruled through secretaries, demonstrating again the monarchical reality of power. Tiberius was, however, a morose recluse. The real problems lay elsewhere.

HELLENISTIC GOD–KING OR ROMAN MAGISTRATE?

What often tempted Augustus' heirs was the glamour of the newly conquered Hellenistic monarchies (Alexander the Great's successors) in the eastern Mediterranean. In these empires, it was usual for kings to be hailed as gods while still alive – more agreeable to impatient young princes than waiting until after death. Also, there was no tedious rigmarole of recruiting officials mainly from the ranks of worthy senators and knights. If charming freedmen (ex-slaves), such as Pallas or Narcissus under Claudius, seemed to be the right choice, they could run government departments.

Above: Marcus Aurelius, sacrificing before the Capitoline Temple in Rome. The emperor was also pontifex maximus, *highest priest.*

Germanicus, Tiberius' heir, discovered in AD19 that people in the east were still enthusiastic about worshipping a Roman general as a god if he let them. Germanicus did not, but his son Caligula, his head turned by seemingly unlimited prospects of power if not by illness, did, forcing senators to become priests of his own cult. This was unacceptable and Caligula paid for it in AD41. So, too, did Nero, whose paranoia after the senatorial conspiracy of Piso led to a vicious spiral of reprisals and further conspiracies. Nero succumbed in other ways to the lure of Hellenistic god-kingship. His Domus Aureus, or Golden House, built after the great fire of AD64, was a palace of truly imperial size, eating up acres of prime land in central Rome, with a colossal statue of Nero as sun god just outside it.

The palace was half-demolished after his death. In its place symbolically rose the Flavian Amphitheatre, or Colosseum, an amphitheatre for the people, started by Vespasian. Under Vespasian (reigned AD69–79), solidly Roman in his virtues if honest about his dynastic intentions, the constitutional forms were partly revived. But Vespasian passed on power to his sons, first the charming but short-lived Titus, then his second son, Domitian (reigned AD81–96). Domitian soon revealed himself as a paranoid autocrat, who demanded to be addressed as Lord and God. A vast Flavian palace arose on the Palatine, from which he issued orders. Domitian, inevitably, was assassinated.

Under the "Five Good Emperors" (AD96–180) the Principate seemed to have reached some sort of stability with the Senate. Yet the trend towards absolutism continued. Amid the chaos of the 3rd century, the need for effective rule drowned all forms of opposition until the emperor appeared as he really was: a supreme autocrat.

Below: Trajan was an immensely popular emperor – with the army, the Senate, people in Rome and in the provinces. This detail from a triumphal arch in Benevento, southern Italy, commemorates his services to commerce.

REPUBLICAN EXTORTION, IMPERIAL PROBITY

The Roman talent for pragmatism was revealed in governing its huge empire. Through a system of trial and error – at the provinces' expense – the Roman Republic found efficient ways of governing its provinces without a large bureaucracy. But by AD300 the empire was being governed on an almost uniform basis by the central government. By then, the skeletal secretariat of the Republic had been replaced by the top-heavy bureaucracy of the Tetrarchy.

Below: The theatre of Pergamum, the kingdom bequeathed to Rome by its last king in 133BC, which became Rome's first province in Asia.

Above: The fortifications of Syracuse, the greatest Greek city in Sicily, date back to 380BC. When Rome finally captured Syracuse in 211BC, it completed its conquest of the island, making it its first true province.

Rome, gaining control of Sicily after the First Punic War in 241BC, faced a new problem. Sicily was large, wealthy and urbanized – mostly by Greek cities but with Punic strongholds in the west, plus rustic Sicel peoples inland. Instead of founding colonies with Roman or Latin rights, as in Italy, Rome created its first *provincia* – literally, sphere of command – appointing former consuls or praetors as governors, with the minimum of staff. Syracuse, the island's largest city, an independent client state until 211BC, offered in its *decuma*, or 10 per cent tax on grain production, a model for revenue-raising. But although many governors corruptly enriched themselves, they also found themselves managing local finances and handing out justice. Sicilian cities, like most cities later in the east, kept much autonomy, being administered by local elected officials later called decurions. These local oligarchs allied with Rome, while Sicily proved an invaluable granary for Rome's hungry citizens. In Spain, too, acquired in 197BC, cities like Cadiz remained client states. A 5 per cent tax on grain output and the development of its silver mines later made Spain into a valuable province, while its tough peoples supplied auxiliary forces. In Italy the Po valley was dominated by warlike Gauls, threateningly close to Rome itself, but offered potentially fine farmland. Another approach led to the founding of such Roman or Latin colonies as Parma and Bologna. By 150BC the Gauls and Ligurians were being driven back into the Alps. By 78BC the area was almost part of Italy in fact if not law; the poet Catullus was born there.

Rome's conquest in the 2nd century BC of the eastern Mediterranean, richer and more civilized than Italy, led to no radical changes in provincial policy. Corrupt governors faced only a small chance of prosecution after their term in office, even if they had flagrantly abused provincials. Cicero's famous lawsuit against Verres, infamous governor of Sicily, was a rare exception. In another speech to the Senate, Cicero pointed out, "Words cannot say how deeply we are hated by foreigners because of the foul behaviour of the men sent out in recent years to govern them." Cicero himself tried to govern Cilicia justly and warned his brother Quintus, on becoming governor of Asia, of the problems caused by well-connected *publicani*, tax-farmers. The burden of Roman taxes, if levied justly, was often no greater than when independent – in the case of Macedonia it was less. But the rapacity of the *publicani* could so enrage provincials – in Greece and Asia Minor in the 80s BC or a century later in Judaea – that they led to anti-Roman uprisings.

PROVINCES UNDER THE EMPIRE

Augustus, who had won the war against Antony as a champion of Italy, could not appear over-generous to provincials. But he still managed to transform provincial administration, usually abolishing the *publicani*. Instead, he levied the *tributum soli*, or land tax. Cisalpine Gaul became part of Italy, and the rest of the provinces

Above: The temple of Apollo at Corinth, the Greek city sacked by Roman legionaries in 146BC but later reborn as the capital of the province of Achaea. Such a fate was typical of many Greek cities.

were divided into two groups. Provinces such as Sicily, Africa or Asia were directly under the Senate's jurisdiction, governed by proconsuls, while other regions, such as Gaul and Spain, were part of the *princeps'* giant province, governed by his legates – normally senators, sometimes knights. The founding of cities – whether as colonies of veterans or *civitates*, county towns – made administration easier.

Even in senatorial provinces, good emperors kept a careful eye on governors, as letters between Pliny the Younger, governor of Bithynia, and Trajan show. "Can you send out a land surveyor? A lot of money could be regained...if accurate surveys were made" asked Pliny. Trajan replied, "I regret not. I need all available surveyors here in Rome. Find a reliable one in your own province", and "What is to be done about the unfinished theatre at Nicaea can best be considered and decided by yourself on the spot." But if disaster struck, as when 12 cities in Asia were destroyed in AD17 by an earthquake, even the parsimonious Tiberius promised ten million sesterces in aid and a five-year remission of all taxes, along with a senatorial commission to help in reconstruction.

Below: These Roman soldiers of the 1st century AD came from Gaul, by then a half-Romanized province.

TAXATION

Above: A cloth merchant displays a piece of fabric, seen on a sarcophagus from Trier in the 4th century AD. The steady growth of textile industries in Gaul and other provinces shows that economic activity was not yet crippled by taxes.

Below: This early 6th-century mosaic from Ravenna was made under Gothic rule. By then, maritime trade had shrunk dramatically, although for centuries maritime taxes had been a major source of revenue for Rome.

"It is a statesman's duty not to impose the *tributum soli* on the people", Cicero declared, voicing the sentiments of the Roman people. The *tributum soli* (property tax) had been the main tax on Roman citizens supposedly levied only in emergencies, and the 3rd century BC had seen one emergency after another. But by the time generals were returning with their booty from a ransacked Greece after the Battle of Pydna, the need for it had passed, and in 167BC it was abolished. Taxes remained controversial throughout the Republic, became less so under the Principate and then, under the later emperors, grew into a crushing burden.

Originally, both Romans and their Latin associates contributed to the Roman state through fighting for it, providing their own arms and armour. Indirect taxes such as customs duties paid for minimal peacetime government, with the *tributum soli* raised in wartime. When the acquisition of Sicily in 241BC allowed the Romans the luxury of taxing subject foreigners, they copied the efficient Syracusan 10 per cent tithe on farm produce. In the wealthier provinces of the east Mediterranean, major problems arose.

PUBLICANI – HATED PROFESSION

In 146BC Achaea (South Greece) and Macedonia were formed into provinces, and 13 years later the last king of Pergamum left his wealthy realm in Asia Minor to Rome. The Republic proved incapable of administering, especially of taxing, these new provinces fairly or honestly. Gaius Gracchus' short-sighted assigning of the tax concessions to the equestrians allowed a ruthless type of tax-collector to emerge: the *publicani*, or tax-farmers (the "publicans" of the New Testament), who could, in effect, levy whatever taxes they liked. The Greek cities supported Mithradates of Pontus in 88BC because of these extortions. Some Romans such as Cicero realized this. Writing to his brother Quintus as the new governor of Asia, Cicero admitted that, "however sympathetic and conscientious you may be in everything, there is one immense obstacle – the *publicani*". After Sulla had driven Mithradates out of Greece in 85BC, he fined the Greek cities five years' back taxes – a sum they could pay only by resorting to Italian money-lenders charging interest at exorbitant rates of 50 per cent or more.

IMPERIAL HONESTY

Julius Caesar and Augustus recognized and tried to remedy this abysmal situation. Augustus could not at first completely abolish the *publicani*, but he regulated them closely. Italy and Rome were exempt from the chief direct tax of the empire, the *tributum soli*, a flat-rate percentage tax on supposed land values, but all parts paid the 1 per cent sales tax, the *centesima rerum venalium*, and customs duties, the *portorium*, levied at 2–2½ per cent and tolls at varying levels in ports. Figures from AD90 from the Red Sea port of Coptos, a terminus for the trade with India, show that a sailor paid tolls of 5 drachmae and a captain 8 – but a prostitute paid 108 drachmae.

A 5 per cent death duty was paid by every Roman citizen, which was one reason why the emperor Caracalla in AD212 granted citizenship to most free people in the empire. Another significant tax was the 5 per cent tax on sales of slaves, again levied throughout the empire. In Egypt, Syria and other parts of the east, Rome also continued to levy the *tributum capitis*, or poll tax, based on censuses that Augustus organized. The emperor Vespasian, restoring the general finances, notoriously put a novel tax on urine collection.

Augustus and his successors had other important sources of income, which supplied the *aerarium militare*, the imperial military treasury. One was from Egypt, long considered separate from the empire, a major source of wheat and other products such as linen and papyrus. Many mines also became imperial possessions, some of the very few large-scale industrial operations in the Roman world. The silver mines near Cartagena in Spain employed 40,000 miners, many of them slaves. The *princeps* had a huge *patrimonium*, or private estate, acquired from legacies or confiscations.

All these together supplied enough, in good times, to pay for the army, the slim civil service and entertaining the Roman populace, without, at first, oppressing the provincials. But it left no surplus for bad times.

THE BURDENSOME LATER EMPIRE

Septimius Severus (AD193–211) raised army numbers to *c.*400,000 men and increased its pay, and under the tetrarchs numbers topped 500,000. There were now four courts to support, and the tax burden increased on a shrinking economy. Ignorant of economics, emperors debased the coinage, hitting the administration worst of all with raging inflation that made soldiers' pay worthless. Gallienus (AD253–68) had to issue a new coinage for his crack troops. Other emperors resorted to the *annona militaris*, military supplies, seizing goods directly.

Diocletian undertook a reform of the whole tax system, not completed until after his death. Realizing that the *annona* (the successor to the *tributum*, the tax on land holdings) and the *capitatio*, the poll tax payable in cash, were grotesquely regressive, hitting the poorest hardest, he established a new system: the *capitatio-iugatio*. This was based on the ancient *iugerum*, a plot measuring 60 x 40 yd (55 x 37m). Land and labour were combined to provide a tax unit that varied according to soil quality and use as vineyard, pasture or cornfield. Five *iugera* of vineyards were worth 20 *iugera* of grain land or 60 of rough pasture. Every five, then every 15, years, a general census, the *indictio*, fixed the tax units, and every year a revised budget and tax demand were issued. Italy lost its tax exemption almost completely. Diocletian aimed to make the burden of taxation not lighter but fairer and more predictable, with some success. Taxes from customs dues and sales continued. He also attempted to stamp out corruption among tax officials and fix maximum prices with an edict in AD301. Under his successors, taxes grew ever heavier until tax collectors were feared and hated more than the barbarians.

Above: A tax-collector from the Rhineland, then under Roman rule, counts his money.

Below: Entrance to the Horrea Epagathiana, a 2nd-century AD warehouse in Ostia. Customs duties at 2½ per cent contributed greatly to imperial revenues.

CHAPTER V

ROME AND THE LAW

The Romans prided themselves on the excellence of their laws, with some reason, seeing law as a field in which they were superior to the Greeks. In its imposing entirety, Roman law is one of Rome's great glories and legacies. However, it did not emerge fully formed, but evolved slowly, from custom and experience, and reached its final form only with the codification of laws by the east Roman emperor Justinian (reigned AD527–65) after the collapse of the empire in the west.

Originally, Roman laws were not at all democratic or concerned with concepts of liberty and justice, but were as pragmatic as the Romans themselves. As early as the 5th century BC, the Romans showed a hard-headed grasp of the day-to-day relations of one citizen to another. For long there was no distinct profession of lawyer and judge, separate from that of law-maker, as today. Cicero was a brilliant barrister, magistrate *and* politician. Under the Principate and later empire, the emperor himself frequently judged cases. Paradoxically, as life in the later empire became increasingly brutal and the imperial administration more despotic, the law became more humane. It was revised and amended by a series of outstanding jurists, influenced by Greek philosophical ideas. Roman law increasingly fused the practical and the idealistic. Its universality, clarity and relative humanity have inspired later jurists and legislators from the Middle Ages to today.

Left: The immense Basilica Nova in Rome became one of the great law courts of the later empire.

LAW IN THE EARLY REPUBLIC
THE TWELVE TABLES OF THE LAW

Above: The altar on this coin, struck at Lyons, the Gallic capital, was for the combined worship of Augustus and Rome itself. The emperor found himself forced to judge more and more law cases, despite the many other demands on his time.

Below: Traditionally, the ten men charged with drawing up the Twelve Tables of the Law in 451BC visited Athens for inspiration, although such a long journey seems improbable for the time.

In the Republic's early decades, there were no written laws. This greatly favoured the patricians, who monopolized the offices of both the *magistrati* and *pontifices*, the priesthood that presided over many law cases, meaning that they alone could interpret laws. *Magistratus* meant both an official and a judge, for the Romans for a very long time made no distinction between judicial law – both criminal and civil – and constitutional laws. *Lex*, a constitutional law, expressed the will of the people (stated by the Assembly, but guided by the Senate), and could be applied to widely differing purposes, such as redistributing land, declaring war or appointing a commander. But a magistrate could also, on his own initiative, issue edicts that had legislative effect. Sitting on a *tribunal* that was literally a platform, the consuls and lesser magistrates were the heirs to the kings, as the emperors were later heirs to the consuls, and heard criminal or civil cases brought before them by plaintiffs. Law,

therefore, in some ways predated actual legislation, being an emanation of Roman *imperium* – authority or power that was thought of as semi-divine in origin.

However, there was nothing mystical about the Twelve Tables. These were drawn up by the decemvirs, a commission of ten patricians who wrote down all Rome's laws on twelve stone tablets in 451BC to placate the plebeians. The laws of the Tables, couched in plain, exact language, remained the basis of Roman law for many centuries, and were learnt by generations of schoolboys. For Livy they were still "the source of entire public and private law". Although possibly influenced by the Greek example of writing down laws, the Twelve Tables' subject matter, as well as their language, is very Roman, a mixture of general principles and minutely detailed private and public law. Among the laws was the *ius provocationis*, the citizen's right to appeal to the Assembly against any magistrate's judgement involving a capital penalty or exile. Later this mutated into "appealing unto Caesar". But this protection was of limited use, as magistrates could still in certain circumstances have a criminal summarily executed without any trial.

Many other laws dealt with the facts of rural life, referring to trees cut down or animals that wandered off – most Romans were still small farmers – but all laws were administered by urban officials. The Twelve Tables generally confirmed the far-reaching paternal power of the father, the *paterfamilias*, over all his children. No matter how mature or important they might be in civil life – even if they had become consuls – sons could not make wills or take part in any legal transaction as long as their fathers were alive. In theory, a father's powers extended to killing his children, although this was

Above: Statues line the great Via Appia to Capua, built by Claudius Appius, who wrote a handbook of legal procedure in 326BC.

rarely exercised. Infanticide (the exposure of children who were unwanted because they were deformed or simply superfluous), on the other hand, was common, especially with baby girls. But women, or at least a *materfamilias*, or wife, did have some rights: for example, on reaching the age of 25 a woman regained the right to manage her own property.

LAW REFORMS

Such stark spelling out of the laws did not help to defuse social tensions, as the decemvirs had hoped, for the plebeians could now see for themselves the iniquities of many existing laws. To redress this, about 30 laws were passed as *leges*, statutes named after their proposer, over the next four centuries, on matters ranging from inheritance to citizenship, sometimes revoking or amending earlier laws considered unjust. A good example of such old laws was that of the *nexus*, in which a debtor who did not repay his debts risked becoming a *nexus*, or serf – effectively a slave – of his creditors. This law was abolished by the *Lex Poetelia* of 326BC. In 304BC Claudius Appius, a former consul and one of the great radical patricians of Roman history, published a handbook of the correct forms of legal procedure. As the law had until then remained a patrician monopoly, this was another democratizing step.

An even more important decision was made by Titus Corunianus, the *pontifex maximus* in 253BC. The supreme priest (the law was long seen as a manifestation of sacred power) now admitted students to his legal consultations. The priestly monopoly of legal knowledge had already been broken 50 years before by the publishing of judicial procedures, and there was now a need to train others to deal with the expanding number of law cases. These *iurisprudentes*, or lay jurists, were not professional lawyers, but were other citizens, sometimes ex-consuls such as Manius Manilius. Manilius published a book, *Venalium Vendendorum Leges* (Terms of Business for the Sale of Marketable Goods), which attempted to codify and clarify the laws. Attending court cases, the *iurisprudentes* acquired a broad knowledge of the law, which they could use to advise praetors and other magistrates. Their revisions, enlargements and interpretations of the original Twelve Tables, plus their legal formulation of many customary laws that had not been committed to stone, greatly enhanced Roman law. Later they would sit on the *quaestiones*, the special law courts.

Around the same time, in 242BC, a new office of praetor was created, the *praetor peregrinus*, or praetor to deal with legal cases in which at least one of the parties was not a Roman citizen but either a foreigner or subject of Rome. This praetor helped formulate the *ius gentium*, or law of foreign nations, dealing with other nationalities. This was very timely, for Rome had already begun to deal with foreigners who lived not just outside Rome but outside Italy.

Below: One of the strengths of Roman law, from the Twelve Tables of 451BC onwards, was its attention to minute practical detail, which allowed even poorer citizens, such as this woman grocer from Ostia, to practise their trade freely and relatively peacefully.

HOW THE LAWS WORKED IN TIMES OF CRISIS

Above: The law De Baccanalis *was passed in 186BC to control deteriorating public morality, banning the orgiastic worship of the wine god Bacchus. Later on, the worship of Bacchus, as of many other new foreign gods, was safely regulated.*

The events of the century after the start of the Second Punic War in 218BC, when Rome attained Mediterranean predominance and ever-growing wealth for the aristocratic few, saw huge changes in Roman society. The concentration of masses of usually impoverished citizens in Rome – mostly former farmers who had returned from years of fighting abroad to find their land had been occupied by richer neighbours or had gone to waste – led to a dramatic increase in crime, often violent crime. At first, the authorities simply reacted savagely. Hoping to make an example of those they caught, they appointed *tresviri capitales*, triumvirs to deal with capital offences. Such offences included, however, not only the obvious crimes of murder, arson and theft but even the mere carrying of arms with alleged criminal intent or the possession of poisons. If the accused was caught red-handed or confessed his guilt, he would normally be summarily executed. If he pleaded innocence, he would be tried before a praetor or his deputy, or by a triumvir. In both cases, a *consilium*, or advisory commission of jurors, discussed the case and gave advice. In any case, there were no long-term prisons in the Republic and there was a deep repugnance to having armed officers inside the city itself.

As the political situation became more troubled, extraordinary judicial courts (*quaestiones extraordinariae*) were set up to deal with especially egregious cases of corruption, mass crimes, misgovernment and conspiracies against the state. A consul or praetor would preside over these special courts. Finally, from the middle of the 2nd century BC, *quaestiones perpetuae*, or permanent criminal courts, were established to deal with specific offences such as abuse of office by magistrates or conspiracies against the state. The *Lex Sempronia Iudicaria* of 122BC allowed the *equites*, the richer middle class or knights, to sit on the juries, a move made essential because of their rapid growth in number. Although the knights lost control of the courts under Sulla, who restored the Senate's monopoly of them, they were soon reinstated by Pompey and Crassus in 70BC. However, the composition of the juries of the courts remained contentious down to the end of the Republic. Crimes examined by the *quaestiones* included *peculatus*, embezzlement of public funds; *maiestas*, high treason; *de falsis*, forgery of wills and counterfeit coining; *iniuriis*, or violent crimes against the person, and *repetundae*, extortion in the provinces.

THE COURTS

In the courts of the late Republic, which continued under the early Principate, the presiding magistrate would first decide whether a case was worth proceeding with; all prosecutions were still brought by private individuals. He came to his decision after consulting with the members of his *consilium*, the jurors. Jurors for each case were chosen by lot (to avoid corruption or undue influence) to form a panel of up to 75 jurymen, but both prosecution and accused had the right to object to individual jurors, who might be

Right: Marcus Tullius Cicero (106–43BC), orator, writer, statesman and the greatest lawyer of Republican Rome, rose to fame for his attacks on the corrupt governor Verres. His eloquence and rhetoric have given his legal speeches the status of literature.

their personal enemies. During the trials the jurors did nothing but listen, leaving the often vituperative courtroom drama to the accused and to the individual prosecutor. Private citizens had either to prosecute and prove their case, or hire somebody else as their advocate, as the Sicilians famously did with Cicero in 70BC. Cicero, who was both a brilliant barrister and a magistrate, a politician and a senator, made Verres lastingly notorious by his speeches against him, accusing him of every kind of crime, from conniving with pirates to stripping the island of so many statues that it damaged the tourist trade. (Verres went into exile rather than face conviction.) Few cases were as colourful as his, however.

In fact, the procedures actually gave some advantages to the accused. Not only was he entitled to several advocates, but he was allowed 50 per cent more time to speak than the prosecution. The jury finally voted in secret on the accused's alleged guilt or innocence. If found guilty, the penalty fixed by the law was ordered by the magistrate. If it were only a matter of a fine, the jurors might meet again to decide the exact amount. Death was the supposed penalty for many offences, but in practice only slaves and people of the lower orders were normally executed. Generally, other citizens were permitted to escape into exile. As life in Rome was widely believed to be the only life worth living, exile seemed punishment enough.

The jury system of the *quaestiones* normally ensured a reasonably fair and balanced dealing with most criminal cases. But these criminal cases were often time-consuming and laborious and could drag on for years and years. Under the Principate, therefore, the *cognitio extra ordinem* of the imperial law court grew in importance. This was an extraordinary criminal procedure without a jury. By the 2nd century AD, jury courts had begun to fade away. Augustus, at first unwilling to involve himself in judicial affairs, increasingly found himself called

on to give judgement in courts, something that a legalistic-minded emperor like Claudius later positively welcomed. In reality, of course, the *princeps* could judge any case, for even in imperial times there were no professional judges; the supreme civil official was also the supreme judge (*iudex*). Through his tribunician power, the *princeps* could also have laws passed, and his decrees were anyway treated as law. The emperor's concern with law continued, indeed intensified, under the later emperors, culminating at last in the emperor Justinian's great code.

Above: A lictor, or ceremonial official, who preceded consuls, is shown carrying the fasces. *This was a bundle of rods with an axe head at one end, symbolizing the powers of capital and corporal punishment that such magistrates wielded.*

THE GREAT IMPERIAL CODIFICATIONS

Above: Roman law was not automatically enforced on the provinces. But its superior appeal as the law of Rome meant, as these inscriptions of AD209 from Africa show, that most provinces soon adopted it.

Below: Roman public buildings included great basilicas, where judgements were heard. Their form and plan was adopted by early Christian builders, as at this basilica on the Via Nomentana, Rome.

As the empire grew and more and more subjects became full citizens and fully subject to Roman law, legislation inevitably became more complicated. The need to harmonize accumulated laws variously derived from the Twelve Tables, from magistrates' and emperors' edicts and from the numerous *leges* (statutory laws) became pressing.

THE FIRST CODIFICATIONS

As early as the 1st century BC, Mucius Scaevola, consul in 95BC, produced a handbook on civil law that was long regarded as the standard work. But it was not until the 2nd century AD, under the great organizing emperor Hadrian, that determined attempts were made to codify the law. Hadrian initiated a series of codifications that continued into the 6th century AD.

Iuventius Celsus, who had been consul for the second time in AD129 under Hadrian, wrote 39 books of *digesta* (classified legal decisions). In them, he pronounced numerous celebrated legal definitions and pithy maxims, such as the famous formula *impossibilium nulla obligatio* (*Digesta*, 50), "there can be no legal requirement to do the impossible". Salvius Julianus, who became consul in AD149, collected and revised the edicts that successive praetors had declared during their year in office in his *Edictum Perpetuum*, or everlasting edict, which was the first real codification of Roman law. From that time on, imperial edicts could be recognized as permanently valid legally. His publication helped spread a wider understanding of the legal safeguards protecting the inhabitants of the empire and also revealed a growing humanitarian concern for the empire's subjects – at least on paper.

Slaves now had more legal protection, which circumscribed their owners' rights to treat them completely as chattels. This was partly because they were becoming scarcer and therefore more valuable, but it also marked a change in attitudes. Although both pagan and Christian thinkers abhorred slavery, their views did not reflect a general revulsion, and on economic grounds slavery appeared indispensable. One of Salvius' pupils, Gaius, continued Salvius' work in his *Institutes*, while under Marcus Aurelius (reigned AD161–80), Cervidius Scaevola continued the task of interpreting and codifying the corpus of Roman law. The new basilicas, such as that of Maxentius in Rome, now served as courts where the emperor gave judgement.

Despite the growing political and military troubles of the 3rd century AD, the work of codifying and moderating the laws was carried further. Aemilianus Papinianus, the prefect of the Praetorian guard for ten years (AD203–213) under the militaristic Severans, became famed for his great compendia of the legal decisions that comprised the laws, the *quaestiones* and *responsa* (investigations and findings). Under the emperor Alexander Severus, Domitius Ulpian was a noted lawyer and writer, and adviser to Julia Mammaea. As the emperor's mother was effectively the regent, Ulpian also became Praetorian prefect. His huge works, which endeavoured to cover the full gamut of the laws, are extremely clear and reveal his easy and lucid mastery of very complicated material.

Other distinguished lawyers of the age were Herennius Modestinus, who was prefect of the Vigiles (watchmen) from AD226 to AD244, and Paulus, whose copious writings include the *Sententia* (opinions). Many of these writers either came from the eastern, Greek part of the empire or were deeply influenced by Greek philosophical concepts. Their philanthropic and, in some ways, democratic beliefs modified ancient Roman concerns which had centred on private property and the sanctity of contracts. Paradoxically, just as these high-minded men were writing, the empire was collapsing into a bloody chaos that made all such idealism seem useless.

THE IMPERIAL DIGESTS

Although the empire in the west finally collapsed in the 5th century AD, urban life continued unchecked in the richer and more civilized east. Here, the school of Beirut (in the Lebanon) had emerged as the leading centre of Roman law studies – mostly in Latin – and provided the lawyers who helped draw up the two final grand digests of Roman law. Building on the achievements of Ulpian and other jurists, this led to the Theodosian Code of AD438, issued under the eastern emperor Theodosius II. Accepted in both parts of the empire, this combined humane and enlightened ideals with savagely repressive measures, repeating ineffective laws passed many times before. The majesty of the law was no longer so respected by people in real life.

In the 6th century AD, the eastern empire enjoyed what seemed a golden age under Justinian I (reigned AD527–65). He reconquered half the western empire and enriched Byzantium with numerous palaces and churches, most notably the cathedral of Hagia Sophia. But perhaps his greatest achievement was his enduring *Digest of Roman Law*. Justinian appointed a committee of 16 lawyers to summarize and amalgamate the whole of Roman law. Over 11 years, from AD528, the lawyers compressed three million lines of older laws into a mere 150,000 lines. This gave the Byzantine world its laws for the next millennium, and profoundly influenced law in the then barbarous west. When medieval western Europe rebuilt itself as a civilization, its rulers looked to this great compilation. The jurists who emerged from Europe's oldest university – the University of Bologna – from 1100 onwards, revived and expanded this *Codex* of Roman law. Although it tended to elevate governmental efficiency above individual rights, its comprehensive clarity proved very attractive to successive states, some of them democratic. Under the Napoleonic empire (1803–14), it became the law of almost all continental Europe and, later, of many parts of Latin America.

Above: The Emperor Napoleon's famous legal Code was consciously modelled on Roman law. It forms the basis of much continental European law to this day.

Below: The eastern emperor Justinian I reconquered half the west and built many fine churches, but his greatest achievement was his final codification of Roman law.

POLICE AND SECRET POLICE

For a long time, the Romans lacked two aspects of civil life that seem essential to modern eyes: a professional local or national police force, with some form of central criminal detective agency, and, perhaps even more notably, a prison service to incarcerate criminals for long-term punishment.

KEEPING ORDER
Under the Republic, from 367BC, policing the (still quite small) city was a task for the four aediles – two plebeian, two patrician – who were elected each year and who maintained public order. Later, the *praetor urbanus* helped deal with the growth in crime. This patchy attempt to deal with crime was common, not just in the ancient world, but right up to the 19th century. (Britain had no proper police force until well into the 19th century and used to

deport those criminals it did not execute, as did the Russians.) In Rome, under the generally light government of the early Principate, minimalist policing worked reasonably well at first, with troops from the Praetorian guard always available as a back-up force. From the time of the Severans (AD193–233), however, secret police, who had already appeared under tyrannical rulers such as Domitian and Commodus, multiplied. The later empire effectively became a police state, whose horrors were limited only by its corruption and incompetence.

In the city of Rome itself, whose population must have passed the million mark in the 1st century AD, some sort of police force was clearly necessary, as Augustus realized. Due to the almost total lack of street lighting – Antioch was the one large city in the empire that had some sort of crude street lights – Rome became a dangerous place at dusk, although the rich went out with their own bodyguards, not over-concerned about what happened to lesser citizens. Augustus created two new forms of police; the *cohortes urbanae* and the *vigiles*.

The *cohortes urbanae*, or city cohorts, who comprised first three, then four, cohorts of 500 men, were commanded by a senator, the prefect of the city. The only armed force left directly under the Senate's control, it kept order of a sort in public places. More effective at night were the *vigiles*, or night watchmen/firemen, seven brigades of 1,000 men (one for each two of the city's 14 wards), initially recruited from freedmen, who patrolled the streets at night. They seem, however, to have been more concerned with fighting fire than crime, for they carried buckets and pumps with them, but on their regular patrols through the city they must have also acted as some sort of deterrent to crime. But, despite this, we can assume that Rome remained dangerous at night.

Above: The increasingly suspicious emperor Tiberius centralized the crack Praetorian guard in a special camp in Rome, where they were controlled by Sejanus, who was for long the emperor's most trusted confidant and minister.

Right: Although theoretically part of the regular army, the Praetorians were in reality treated quite differently. Paid more and retiring earlier, they lived in Rome and often, like this guard, were not obliged to wear full armour.

Backing up these unimpressive forces were the formidable cohorts of the Praetorians, the special guard recruited only from Roman citizens of Italy until the reign of Septimius Severus (AD193–211), paid twice the usual rate and under the command of the Praetorian prefect, the highest post an equestrian could hope to reach. Augustus stationed its nine cohorts around Italy, but under Tiberius they were centralized by Sejanus into a large camp in the north-east of Rome. These were the imperial guard, however, not used for day-to-day policing but to suppress popular riots or conspiracies. Although the *Pax Romana* established by Augustus meant an end to large-scale brigandage, there were still plenty of robbers around, even in the mountains of Italy, and at times small-scale military operations were needed to suppress them. Elsewhere in the empire, the army was occasionally called in to deal with major uprisings: from the Sicilian slave revolts of 135BC, when 70,000 slaves united under their "king" Antiochus to defy the Romans for three years, to the revolt of the Bagaudae (literally, brigands) who, from the 3rd century AD on, terrorized central Gaul, setting up their own courts. In between such uprisings, decurions, the local magistrates of the cities around the empire, dealt adequately with local crime on a smaller scale, acting as judges.

THE POLICE STATE

Like all military dictatorships, the emperors made use of *delatores*, spies or informers, who discovered or invented conspiracies, and *speculatores*, special mounted intelligence officers of the Praetorian guard – regular officials, unlike the *delatores* – who sometimes travelled around the empire. But the wiser emperors did not rely too much on such doubtful sources. Despite this, Trajan – *optimus princeps*, or the best of emperors, in the Senate's view – started a new form of intelligence service, the *frumentarii*. This grew rapidly under Septimius

Severus, augmented by similar officials, who set up the sinister office of the *agentes in rebus*, literally those active in public affairs; the *stationarii*, or place-holders, and *collectiones*, or tax-collectors. These special police were usually soldiers, indicating the militarization of society under the Severans. According to the early 20th-century historian M.I. Rostovtzeff, they did not "care a straw for the people", but hunted down those who had defaulted on their taxes or gone into hiding to escape government extortions.

Diocletian's bureaucratic reforms encouraged a huge growth in the number of these officials. Later, in the 360s, the emperor Julian introduced measures to try to reduce their numbers. Such agents were solely concerned with protecting the government and lining their own pockets, not with dealing with normal crime or helping the people, whose well-being and safety held no interest for them. Bribery was the normal means by which most subjects of the later empire dealt with such imperial officials.

Above: Trajan created a new form of intelligence officer, the frumentarii, *who thrived under later, less benign emperors.*

Below: The arch of Septimius Severus, the militaristic emperor in whose reign the secret police multiplied.

PUNISHMENT

Above: This mosaic of the 3rd century AD shows gladiators battling. Due to the inevitably high mortality rate of this, perhaps the most brutal spectator sport ever devised, many criminals were condemned to be gladiators.

Below: The Romans' formidable organizing powers are exposed in the underground network of passages that kept the Colosseum in Rome working smoothly in the long games that filled so many days.

Two things characterize Roman attitudes to punishment. First, there was no real equality before the law, which we tend to take for granted. Second, keeping criminals imprisoned for long periods was impractical, on grounds of expense, and other penalties were the norm.

BREAKING THE LAW

There was a marked division between the way Roman citizens and non-citizens were treated, both under the Republic and under the early Principate. Later, after almost everybody had become a citizen in AD212, an even starker division grew up between the treatment of the upper classes, *honestiores*, and the lower, *inferiores*. Even in the Republic, richer citizens such as senators and knights were better treated than poorer ones.

Roman jails were normally manned by soldiers, and used only in the short term as a place for suspects awaiting trial. Punishments were often gruesome, especially for non-Roman citizens or *inferiores*. In civilian life, Roman citizens, and later the *honestiores*, could not be flogged or crucified, for example, and could "appeal to Caesar", as St Paul did when kept on remand. And while it was widely believed that slaves would tell the truth only if they were severely tortured, citizens were exempt from torture.

Early Rome was essentially a primitive rustic society, and most penalties in the early and middle Republic were draconian, with crude punishments that seem violent to our modern sensibilities. In Rome's deeply conservative culture, such punishments long remained on the books. For example, Vestal Virgins were chosen from high-born Roman maidens around the age of 7 to tend the fire of Vesta, the goddess of the hearth. The girls had to remain virgins for their 30 years of service, by which time they were regarded as being well past marriage. Inevitably, some lapsed and had sexual liaisons. If they were discovered, they faced the potential sentence of being buried alive. Much later, Domitian's revival of this archaic punishment shocked the then more tolerant Romans. Parricide also incurred punishments that reveal the deep religious revulsion that it aroused. The offender was tied up and bundled into a sack with a snake and a cock and then hurled off a rock.

Many penalties, of course, related to civil laws. An article from the Eighth Table of the Law, concerned with penalties, states, "If any man mutilates another's limbs, he must suffer the same, unless he agrees to pay compensation to the injured man." This *Lex Talionis*, the law of an eye for an eye, extended to other crimes, such as arson: arsonists themselves should be burnt alive. The Tables even stipulated the death penalty for any patron – who was almost always a nobleman – who cheated his client, though this was not often enforced. In all these types of cases, it was not the Roman state but individual citizens who brought the actions, the state merely supervising their private pursuit of justice.

EXILE

Although death was a penalty for many offences, it was not always enforced, especially for more important Roman citizens. Instead, exile remained a common and potent penalty. Not only did it end a Roman's political life – for the time being, anyway – but it meant banishment from the one city on earth that really mattered to all true Romans. The incorrigibly metropolitan poet Ovid was exiled to the barbarous remoteness of Tomis on the Black Sea by Augustus in AD8, possibly for involvement in the affairs that led also to the banishment of Augustus' own daughter Julia.

LIONS AND GLADIATORS

Although the image of Christian martyrs being thrown to the lions – tied to a stake in the arena and there chewed to death – remains powerful, Christians in fact made up only a few of the people who were sentenced to this *damnatio ad bestias*, or condemnation to the wild beasts. This form of punishment was anyway not thought particularly entertaining by Romans, the most exacting of audiences.

Many criminals condemned to death ended up in the arena as gladiators, people utterly without rights. From the 2nd century BC on, Rome was developing an insatiable appetite for gladiators, who had a high mortality rate. The games Titus gave for the inauguration of the Colosseum in AD80 required several thousand pairs, some of whom were killed during the day's entertainment. But gladiators were very expensive to train, and combat did not inevitably end in death. Those who survived three years in the games were normally given their wooden sword of freedom.

Special schools of gladiators, with ferocious discipline, were established. One of the most famous of these was at Capua, and it was here that the last great slave revolt broke out in 73BC, organized by the Thracian gladiator Spartacus. Displaying genuine leadership, he united his fellow outcasts and for two years

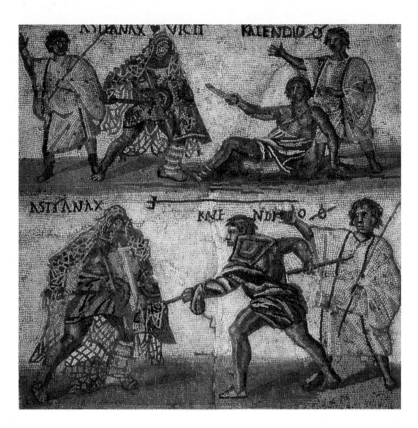

kept the forces of Rome at bay, moving around the mountains of southern Italy until Crassus cornered and killed him in 71BC in Apulia. Along the great Via Appia from Capua to Rome, 7,000 ex-gladiators were then crucified as a ghastly warning to other potential rebels.

CRUCIFIXION

The last, worst and most degrading punishment of Rome's sadistic society was crucifixion. An excruciatingly slow torture (for few had their deaths hastened by a spear like Jesus Christ), crucifixion was adopted by the Romans in the 2nd century BC, probably from the Asian monarchies. Julius Caesar had the pirates who captured him crucified, the normal punishment for such heinous crimes as well as for conspiracy. After the conversion of Constantine and his successors to Christianity in the 4th century AD, crucifixion was discontinued, but this was on religious rather than humanitarian grounds.

Above: Special training schools for gladiators were established in the late Republic to satisfy the insatiable demand of the Roman populace for such brutal thrills.

Below: Crucifixion was a common, if horrifically painful, form of death penalty. It was used for many crimes, from piracy to conspiracy.

CHAPTER VI

FOREIGN POLICY

Although Rome had no foreign office or state department, it certainly had policies towards the non-Roman world. While well-meaning Romans such as Cicero liked to believe that Rome acquired its empire chiefly in wars of self-defence, others must have seen it differently, as they watched the smoke rising from Carthage, Syracuse, Corinth – all cities sacked by Rome.

Yet for a long time Rome, unlike the Persians or the Macedonians under Alexander, initiated few wars of deliberate conquest. From *c*.300BC to Pompey's eastern command in 66BC, Rome's foreign policy was more reactive than pre-emptive. Only when control of foreign policy slipped from the Senate's grasp did clear signs of expansionist imperialism appear, first under Pompey and then under Caesar and his successors. After that, Rome followed an aggressively expansionist policy until it could do so no longer and was forced to go on the defensive in the 2nd century AD.

All other cities had to be subordinated to Rome and were regarded as foreign, even when they were Latin-speaking neighbours. However, the privileges of Roman citizenship were gradually extended to inhabitants of other city-states, first in Italy, then across the Mediterranean world. Ultimately, after the conquest of Egypt in 30BC, there were no foreign powers worthy of the name, except for the Parthians in the east. Instead, there was the Roman world – and the barbarians.

Left: A sculpted head from the ruins of Carthage, the north African city that was for long Rome's deadliest enemy.

EARLY BEGINNINGS
THE CONQUEST OF ITALY

Above: The Via Appia, the first and archetypal Roman road, was designed for the conquest of southern Italy as much as for communication.

Below: This fresco from a 4th-century BC tomb near Paestum, southern Italy, shows warriors armed like the Samnites. The Samnites were Rome's most threatening enemies in the region, taking three wars to subdue.

Although it may sound grandiloquent to talk of the foreign policy of a state whose territory in 500BC was roughly only 10 miles (16km) across, Rome regarded all those beyond its sacred *pomerium*, or city boundary, as foreign. By binding such cities to her in treaties, at times granting them citizenship or alliance, Rome's approach became less "divide and rule" than "conquer and assimilate". Even large, relatively distant cities such as Capua could be incorporated by this incremental method, Rome's most original idea in conquering Italy.

Rome signed a treaty with the cities of the Latin League in 493BC, but she did so only because mountain enemies were threatening farms in the lowlands. These tribes were only ejected from the key Algidus Pass in about 430BC, after a 50-year war. They were overcome by establishing chains of *coloniae* – defensive settlements of farmer–soldiers who received land. At first these were federal Latin colonies, with Romans merely among other settlers, but later Rome began founding her own colonies, which then became civilian settlements too.

Another way of dealing with enemies was assimilation. The Sabines were other menacing neighbours in the hills north-east of Rome, but around 505BC the Sabine nobleman Attus Clausus settled by invitation in Rome, reputedly taking 4,000 followers with him and increasing the city's population. He became a Roman patrician and changed his name to Claudius, founder of the Claudians. Afterwards, the Romans imported the Sabine god Sancus, which symbolized the fusion of the two peoples.

A less malleable threat was Veii. Just 11 miles (18km) north of Rome, this wealthy Etruscan city controlled a network of paved roads and blocked Rome's way north. Wars started in 479BC, until finally the Romans began such a long siege – traditionally, ten years from 406–396BC – that the army had to be paid for the first time. Veii was destroyed, its people killed or enslaved and its patron goddess Juno taken to Rome, thereby symbolizing triumph in a total war. This extermination of a city – along with taking its land for the *ager publicus*, public land – was often repeated.

All such successes seemed to be overthrown by the invasion of the Gauls in *c.*390BC, who sacked the still unwalled city. In despair, some citizens even talked of abandoning their burnt city for Veii until Camillus rallied them. The small city of Caere helped Rome recover and in return received *hospitium publicum*, reciprocal rights with Roman citizens in judicial and financial matters. Rome later extended this formula to other cities. In 378BC Rome fortified itself with the

Samnite League 298 BC

Roman territory 298 BC

Carthaginian possessions *c.* 260 BC

Roman colonies by 272 BC

Under Roman control 270 BC

Annexed by Rome 263 BC

Left: By 265BC Rome controlled the whole of peninsular Italy south of a line from Pisa to Rimini. Besides territories directly part of the Republic and full Roman colonies – strategically planted from Rimini in the north to Brindisi in the south and often linked by roads – there were allied territories, enjoying either Latin or the less prestigious Italian status. All these cities proved a source of vital strength in Rome's forthcoming contest with Carthage, but important long-established Greek cities such as Tarento were sometimes disloyal.

Below: The Etruscans were Rome's most impressive and powerful neighbours. They were wealthy, civilized and had a high level of culture as shown in this life-size terracotta sculpture of a married couple from a 6th-century BC Etruscan tomb.

Servian walls, but it was already expanding again. In 381BC Tusculum, a Latin League city, received full Roman citizenship to keep it loyal to Rome. This novel generosity was later extended to other cities, also usefully boosting the numbers of citizens for military service.

In 343BC Capua, the wealthiest city of fertile Campania, appealed to Rome for help against Samnite raiders. Initially, the war went badly. Roman troops mutinied at having to fight so far from home, and the Latin League, alarmed at Rome's power, joined the Volscians against her. Four years of bitter fighting were required to defeat the Latins by 338BC. Then Rome dissolved the League, treating each city differently. The citizens of Lanuvium, for example, received full Roman rights, as did three other deserving Latin cities. The Volscian city of Antium on the coast, a pirate stronghold, had its ships destroyed – their beaks went to adorn the *Rostra* in Rome – and a Roman colony was planted, which the Volscians were allowed to join. Capua and four other Campanian cities then received Roman citizenship *sine suffragio*, without the vote. The Romans showed themselves fair and pragmatic in these treaties, winning the abiding loyalty of most cities.

RULER BY DEFAULT

Above: Two Greek hoplites (heavy infantrymen) from an Attic vase. Adaptable Roman legionaries repeatedly defeated Greek hoplites massed in the inflexible phalanx, *a major reason for Rome's final total success in the eastern Mediterranean region.*

Below: The Colossus of Rhodes, a giant statue reputedly straddling the harbour entrance, symbolized Rhodes' maritime wealth and power. When its power was wrecked by Rome's expansion, piracy flourished, no longer checked by the Rhodian navy.

There seemed little reason for a major conflict between the Roman Republic, a land power controlling peninsular Italy, and Carthage, a mercantile power based in modern Tunisia, with trade routes extending to southern Spain. Treaties going back to the first days of the Roman Republic were renewed as late as 279BC. But when Rome faced Sicily across the Straits of Messina, it faced new dilemmas. An appeal to Rome by a party in Messina for help against Carthage left the Senate undecided until the Assembly, exercizing its right to declare war, decided for action. The bloody wars made Rome hegemon (ruler) of the Mediterranean.

One reason for supporting Messina was that the Greeks of southern Italy wanted Roman help for Greeks in Sicily, but this counted for little compared with a new aggressive mood in Rome itself. Carthage, too, had been trying to extend its control over all Sicily from its base at Palermo in the west and was determined to control the Straits of Messina. About three times larger than Rome, an immensely wealthy city, with a huge professional fleet and mercenary armies, Carthage was Rome's one significant rival power in the western Mediterranean. As such, Rome was unlikely to ignore it indefinitely.

Victorious after the First Punic War in 242BC, Rome's policy towards Carthage was mixed. Rome helped Carthage suppress a massive revolt by unpaid mercenaries in 239BC, for social order had to be maintained. But it then took advantage of Carthaginian preoccupation to annex Sardinia and Corsica, both in the Carthaginian sphere, in an act of aggression. Marseilles, a Greek city allied to Rome, was worried about growing Carthaginian power in Spain that threatened Ampurias, its colony in Catalonia. (Possibly Hamilcar Barca signed a treaty in 227BC accepting the river Ebro as his northern frontier in Spain.) When Hannibal attacked Saguntum in 219BC, independent if south of the Ebro, Rome decided on war – superfluously, as it turned out, as it was Hannibal who launched the catastrophic Second Punic War.

The final act, the Third Punic War of 146BC, showed Rome at it most odious. Carthage had regained its wealth through agriculture and trade but, lacking a large fleet, posed no threat. However, the Romans, even without reminders from Cato the Censor that *Carthago delenda est* (Carthage must be deleted), had grown greedy. They destroyed Carthage after a long siege, enslaving its citizens. By then, Rome was mistress of the middle sea.

ARBITER OF THE EAST

The eastern Mediterranean around 200BC was dominated by three great Hellenistic kingdoms ruled by descendants of Alexander's generals: the Ptolemies in Egypt, the Antigonids in Macedonia and the Seleucids, whose huge Asian empire centred on Syria. Smaller Hellenistic states included Rhodes, a cultured trading republic, the Aeotolian

Above: Hoplites formation from a Greek amphora from Chigi, Italy. By adopting new tactics, Rome defeated such Greek armies.

Confederacy in Greece and the Attalid kingdom of Pergamum in Asia Minor. For a century these states had been involved in complex alliances and wars that seldom caused serious damage. Upon entering this civilized sphere, Rome proceeded to wreck it through myopic fear, suspicion and greed that together made it look more imperialist than it really was.

Philip V of Macedonia had rashly allied himself with Hannibal in 215BC, angering Rome, although the First Macedonian War involved little fighting. When Philip made a secret treaty with Antiochus III of Syria in 202BC to divide Ptolemaic lands, Rome intervened. Flaminius defeated Philip at Cynoscephalae in 197BC, where Roman legions out-manoeuvred the Macedonian *phalanx*, but he merely reduced Macedonia's size. To the cities of Greece proper, Flaminius promised liberty. This promise was genuine, except that he envisaged a sort of patronage, not the total independence the delighted Greeks assumed. From this misunderstanding came much grief. Meanwhile Antiochus, until then a successful ruler, made a series of clumsy mistakes: he seized the Gallipoli peninsula, although Rome had told him to keep out of Europe; he welcomed Rome's arch-enemy Hannibal to his court in 195BC; and sent a force into Greece in 192BC to support the rebellious Aetolians. Rome, alarmed that he wanted to recreate Alexander's empire, sent armies to defeat Antiochus at Thermopylae and again, massively, at Magnesia in 190BC. Antiochus lost all land west of the Taurus Mountains and paid a huge indemnity. Rome was now arbiter of the east, a point ruthlessly brought home to the next Seleucid, Antiochus IV, when he invaded Egypt in 168BC. The Roman envoy Popilius Laenas drew a circle around the king and told him not to move until he agreed to Rome's terms. Antiochus humbly accepted.

Rome did not fill its hegemonic role well. Many Romans enriched themselves in Greece, while Rome still declined to govern Greece. When the Achaean League rebelled in 146BC, Rome sacked Corinth, Greece's richest city, enslaving its citizens and creating a province. Rome treated its allies scarcely better. Fearing the growing power of Rhodes, it created a free port at Delos that wrecked Rhodes' maritime wealth. With Rhodes in decline, piracy flourished unchecked, also hurting Rome. Attalus III, last king of Pergamum, accepting the inevitable, bequeathed his kingdom to *imperium populi Romani*, the empire of the Roman people, in 133BC.

Below: The Acropolis of Pergamum, the capital of the wealthy Eumenid kingdom in west Asia Minor. Pergamum was long Rome's chief ally in the east, its cavalry helping to defeat the Seleucids at the Battle of Magnesia in 190BC.

DEFENSIBLE FRONTIERS
THE RHINE AND THE DANUBE

Above: Pompey, one the Republic's finest generals, added a whole string of provinces and client states to Rome's eastern empire.

Below: A bend of the River Rhine in Germany. Fast-flowing, the Rhine offered a natural but not inevitable frontier for the empire in northern Europe. It effectively marked Rome's north-western boundary for almost 450 years.

The intermittent expansion of the empire in the middle Republic gave way to rapid, even reckless expansion in the 1st century BC. Between 66 and 63BC, Pompey extended the Roman sphere of influence from the Caucasus to the Red Sea. Caesar conquered the huge area of *Gallia Comata* ("long-haired Gaul") a decade later, and claimed Britain as a client state. Augustus annexed Egypt, the richest kingdom of the Mediterranean, in 30BC. His later wars of conquest added north-west Spain to the empire by 23BC, the Alpine lands by 15BC and most of the Balkans and Danubian territories by 6BC. Later, Tiberius and Drusus conquered as far as the Elbe by AD5, while Roman fleets even nosed into the Baltic. Roman power seemed set on an endless advance. The question was, where would the *termini imperii*, the frontiers of the empire, finally be set, if the empire were not to continue to advance north-east indefinitely? Fixed frontiers, a new concept for Rome, required choosing defensible lines, tactically and strategically.

There was no compelling reason to regard the Rhine or the Danube as definitive frontiers. Despite Caesar's claims in his *De Bello Gallico* about the importance of the Rhine, neither of these two great rivers marked a real cultural or political divide. Augustus, while happy to ignore Britain beyond the seas, decided to conquer Germany between the Rhine and the Elbe, presumably to create a line running roughly from Hamburg through Dresden and Prague to Vienna (none of these cities existed then, of course). This would usefully shorten the frontier, as later emperors realized. Accordingly, a pincer campaign was launched in AD6. Tiberius was to advance north through Bohemia, while other troops moved up the Elbe and others up the Main valley past what is now Frankfurt. But a massive revolt in recently conquered Pannonia recalled Tiberius for three years' bitter campaigning, the worst, according to Tacitus, since the Punic Wars. Then Varus (an army commander) and his three legions were betrayed and massacred by Arminius of the Cherusci in the Teutoburg Forest in AD9. Augustus, now an old man, was shattered by the news and called a halt to all further expansion.

Tiberius followed Augustus' advice to stay within the bounds of the empire to the letter, keeping the Rhine–Danube lines, but this was not very practical. Although both rivers were large, the L-shaped re-entrant angle between their upper reaches was vulnerable to invasion. Claudius, eager for military glory, invaded Britain in AD43, embroiling Rome in a province with a frontier problem in its north that was not settled until Hadrian's visit in AD122. Apart from the suppression of a large-scale revolt by Civilis on the lower Rhine in AD70, Germany was ignored until Vespasian and his sons, especially Domitian, began a

new campaign. Systematic and inglorious, this was mocked by Tacitus, but proved of lasting value. In the Chattan War of AD83–5, Domitian pushed the Rhine frontier east, along the line of the Taunus Mountains, creating a fortified frontier that sheltered the Rhineland behind and projected Roman power deeper into Germany. The frontier then ran south along the Neckar to join the upper Danube. Further additions to extend this new area of Agri Decumates to the Danube at Regensburg came in the 2nd century AD, reducing the Rhine–Danube lines by 150 miles (240km) in total; legions could now move far more swiftly from one frontier to another.

DANUBIAN PROBLEMS

Domitian had been distracted from his German campaign by a Dacian attack in AD85. Well organized, rich (thanks to gold mines) and well protected by their mountainous terrain, the Dacians were a growing threat. After Domitian's campaigns produced a stalemate, it was left to Trajan to deal with Dacia. An initial campaign in AD101 with 13 legions (totalling over 150,000 troops) seemed to have made Dacia an obedient client state, but the settlement, weighted in Rome's favour, failed to last. Trajan prepared for another full-scale invasion by building an immense bridge and road. The final storming of the Dacian capital in AD106 meant Dacia became a province, protected along its northern flank by the Limes Porolissensis, a new fortified frontier along the Carpathians. By creating this great bulwark of a province protruding north-east almost on to the Russian steppes, Trajan divided the tribes on either side of it, so safeguarding the Danubian lands for generations. Beyond them, of course, lay Italy itself, almost unprotected.

The Danube frontier collapsed when the Quadi and Marcomanni (from the modern Czech Republic) poured into Italy in AD166. In a series of campaigns, Marcus Aurelius painstakingly drove

them back. Despite being distracted by a rebellion in Syria in AD175, Marcus won a great final victory over the Marcomanni and Quadi in AD179 and was seemingly about to create two new trans-Danubian provinces, Marcomania and Sarmatia, when he died – and with him died his expansionist plans.

Renewed barbarian pressures in the 3rd century AD saw a general retreat on the northern frontier: Aurelian evacuated Dacia by AD275 and the Agri Decumates were abandoned by c.AD265. In their place came new, heavily fortified capitals near the frontiers, such as Trier and Sirmium, with other massive fortresses that barbarians could bypass but never capture. The whole empire had in some ways become the front line.

Above: Roman troops on the Danube embarking supplies. The Danube became Rome's longest, and ultimately most vulnerable, frontier.

DEFENSIBLE FRONTIERS
ASIA

The best advice for western generals is, "Never invade Russia." For Romans, the advice should have been, "Don't invade Parthia", for it proved fatal to many military reputations. Parthia's huge empire, which stretched from the Syrian frontier to central Asia, was unimpressive militarily. Its kings faced revolts from over-mighty subjects in its Iranian lands, while the Hellenistic cities of Mesopotamia (Iraq) felt little loyalty to it. Its large armies were not professional like the Romans', although their cavalry was well suited to the terrain. Such weakness allowed Rome to invade Parthia at times, but geography – the huge distances, the deserts, the way

the Iranian highlands outflanked the Tigris–Euphrates valley – in the end prevented it ever from holding more than north Mesopotamia. Unfortunately, the precedent of Alexander the Great, who had conquered half of Asia, lured Roman generals east. When the formidable Sassanian dynasty replaced the Parthians in the AD220s, Rome faced worse problems. What had been a quiet frontier became a perilous burden. Yet the frontier between the upper Euphrates and the Tigris fluctuated remarkably little for six centuries.

Rome and Parthia first clashed after Pompey annexed the Syrian rump of the Seleucid empire in 64BC. Crassus, who was

Above: Petra was a wealthy trading city (now in Jordan), and it was annexed under the emperor Trajan.

Right: The Eastern frontier c.AD300. Palmyra's short-lived empire (shaded), did not alter the eastern frontier, but Julian's defeat led to the ceding of Nisibis and half of Roman Mesopotamia to Persia.

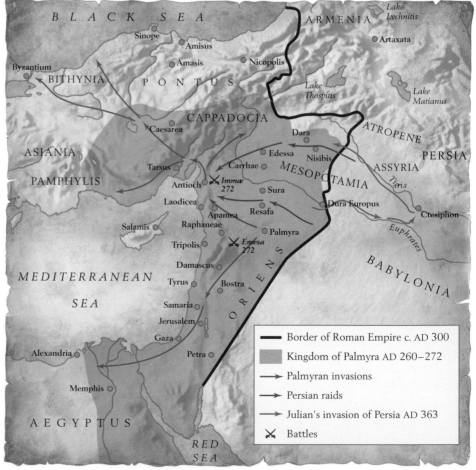

governor of Syria and eager for glory, marched east, to be destroyed with his army by Parthian horse archers in the desert near Carrhae in 53BC. Caesar was preparing an immense invasion of Parthia in 44BC when he was assassinated. Antony, in control of the east after 42BC, decided to attack by the mountain route but failed to capture the key city of Phraapsa in 36BC, when his siege engines were cut off. He had to beat a humiliating retreat harassed by Parthian horsemen. Augustus, after settling other frontiers, was expected to resume the eastward drive but wisely contented himself with a diplomatic triumph in 20BC. This saw the lost legions' eagles (along with a few prisoners) ceremoniously returned and a Roman protégé installed on the Armenian throne. Such client states served as useful buffers between the two powers. For a century, Augustus' successors remained west of the Euphrates, although Vespasian annexed some client states.

Above: The ruins of Dura-Europus, Syria, a vital fortress on the Euphrates, captured and destroyed after a siege by the Persians in C.AD256 and never reoccupied. The defence of the eastern frontier depended heavily on such fortified trading cities.

BETWEEN TWO RIVERS

There was therefore no need for Trajan's grand eastern venture that began in AD114 with the conquest of Armenia. Mesopotamia may have looked similar to Syria – a fertile land, Aramaic-speaking peasants, Greeks in the cities – and there was talk of securing the trade routes east, but it was Alexander's example that really counted. Failure to take Hatra, right in the middle of the new conquests, signalled that the Parthians were not totally defeated and they began to attack the now long-exposed eastern flanks. Even without the many Jewish revolts behind, these new frontiers were indefensible. Hadrian pulled back completely, apart from Nabatea. The status quo was restored, except that Arabia Nabatea was fortified.

In AD165 the Romans retaliated to the Parthian attack by sacking both Ctesiphon (Baghdad), the Parthian capital, and Hellenistic Seleucia-on-the-Tigris, bringing home a crippling plague and almost wrecking Hellenism in Iraq. But the only significant change was to advance the frontier to Dura-Europus, a fortified city on the Euphrates. This left the rest of the frontier as before, between the upper Tigris and Euphrates, stretching from the Black Sea to the Red, with Palmyra as a client state. But there was one possible line that offered Rome a defensive frontier that Septimius Severus saw and seized. In AD197 he captured Ctesiphon but sagely withdrew, annexing only upper Mesopotamia, following the line of the Khabur river as it flowed south into the Euphrates, then east along the escarpment of the Jebel Sinjar to the Tigris north-east of Nisibis. This territory gave Syria, with its wealthy cities, far more protection and also helped Rome to control Armenia, blocking the Parthians' lowland route to it.

This proved a lastingly defensible frontier. Despite the newly aggressive Sassanid Persian dynasty – it claimed all the old Persian empire's lands up to Macedonia – the Romans retained this new province of (upper) Mesopotamia throughout the 3rd-century crises.

CLIENT AND BUFFER STATES

Above: Giant heads c.50BC proclaim the power of the client kings of Commagene.

Below: Pompey entered the Temple in Jerusalem, thereby desecrating it in Jewish eyes.

When Pompey marched through western Asia from the Caucasus to the Red Sea in 66–63BC, annexing and rearranging kingdoms, he recognized many existing smaller kingdoms as client states or allies. The careful use of client or buffer states allied to and to varying degrees under the control of Rome became a characteristic policy of Roman imperialism in the late Republic and early Principate.

Such statelets – most were very small – could supply reinforcements when called for, rather than perpetually requiring costly garrisons themselves. In AD67, Vespasian's legions were reinforced by 15,000 lighter troops from nearby client states for the Jewish war. For Augustus and his heirs, this was an attractive way of defending the empire on the cheap. It resembled the client system in Rome itself and meant, furthermore,

that the states concerned often became half-Romanized, or further Hellenized, before being incorporated into the empire. Armenia was the one significant exception to this trend.

Most client kingdoms lined the indeterminate eastern frontier, beyond which loomed the Parthian empire, Rome's only civilized rival. In northern Europe the various German tribes were, for the most part, too fragmentary or impermanent to be able to create stable kingdoms. Here subsidies and treaties kept these barbarians in check or at each others' throats, but they were not proper client kings.

The major eastern client states, established by Pompey and confirmed by Mark Antony and Augustus, included three vital border crossings: Pontus, on the south coast of the Black Sea, Cappadocia in central Asia Minor, annexed in AD17, and Commagene, controlling the vital passage across the upper Euphrates. This latter was ruled by a dynasty of Hellenized monarchs called Antiochus, whose gigantic heads adorn their hilltop mausoleum at Nemrud Dag. Further south, Arab client kings included Palmyra, rising to wealth, and flourishing Arabia Nabatea (Jordan), with its capital at Petra.

Most important and troublesome was Judaea, later Palestina. Herod I the Great ruled from 37 to 4BC, rebuilding the Temple in Jerusalem and building a second coastal capital at Caesarea Maritima, which became a typical Hellenistic city. He was a tyrannical but effective ruler. After his death, his kingdom was divided between his less competent heirs, until its central portion became a Roman province in AD6. (Its most notorious governor was Pontius Pilate.) It returned briefly to Jewish rule under Cornelius Julius Agrippa, Herod's nephew, and his son Cornelius Agrippa II. As their names suggest, these rulers were half-Romanized.

Another client state was Mauretania (northern Algeria/Morocco), formed partly from the old kingdom of Numidia. Its monarch, Juba, became an exemplary Hellenizing king in his new capital at Caesarea and married one of Cleopatra's daughters. It was annexed by Claudius, who also annexed the client state of Thrace in the eastern Balkans. On the north Black Sea, the Bosphoran kingdom was part-Scythian but had Greek cities on the coast. It remained an important client state to Rome because of the grain trade from the Ukraine.

Vespasian annexed Commagene and other smaller client states in a fit of centralizing enthusiasm in AD69–79 until only the tiny kingdoms of the Caucasus – Iberia in the Caucasus, and Colchis – plus Palmyra and Arabia Nabatea remained. This required the deployment of more troops and the building of more forts to face Parthia directly. Trajan annexed Arabia Nabatea in AD106.

ARMENIA: THE EXCEPTION
On the high plateau between Iran and Asia Minor, Armenia formed a natural buffer state between Rome and Parthia (later Persia). Almost independent, it leaned worryingly towards Parthia, being more Iranian than Hellenic with a feudal aristocracy and few towns. Its key position above Syria and Mesopotamia meant that it could not be ignored. Lucullus was the first Roman to enter Armenia, pursuing Mithradates in 69BC. In 65BC Pompey added Armenia to his clients, but Antony's attempt to win it failed. Yet when Augustus staged a triumph in the east in 20BC that returned the legionary standards lost by Crassus at Carrhae, Parthia (temporarily) recognized Armenia as a Roman protectorate. Nero's fine general Corbulo imposed a compromise in AD63 in which Parthian princes would be the kings of Armenia but invested (crowned) by Rome. In AD66 Nero invested Tiridates as king of Armenia in an extravagant ceremony in Rome. Trajan used the Parthian

replacement of a Roman-approved king in Armenia in AD114 as a pretext for his grand eastern campaign, annexing the kingdom. Hadrian then evacuated it with other eastern conquests. This seesaw continued with minor variations over the next two centuries. When Armenia became the first Christian kingdom – a few years before Constantine's conversion – it became more pro-Roman. It was finally divided between Persia and Rome in AD383, with Persia getting most of it.

Above: Arches of the aqueduct at Caesarea Maritima on the coast of Judaea (Israel) that were restored under Trajan.

Below: One of Herod the Great's proudest feats was the building of a Hellenized city at Caesarea Maritima with a huge Roman-style aqueduct.

RELIANCE ON THE GERMANS
THE *FOEDERATI* AND THEIR DANGERS

Above: Barbarians, such as this captive from Trajan's campaigns, could often be turned by the Romans into useful subordinate foederati.

Below: Stilicho tried to use Visigoths as foederati, *with catastrophic results.*

When Rome was sacked by the Visigoths in AD410, it was by troops formerly in the pay of the Roman emperor: *foederati*, federate or allied troops. Events in the 5th century showed that such allies were often as dangerous to the empire as its open enemies, but they seemed better than no troops at all when it seemed the only way of protecting the empire.

Foederati means those who have made a *foedus* (literally treaty), so it was a term encompassing many types of barbarian. The employment of barbarians as auxiliary troops in small groups had a long history. Julius Caesar used German cavalry in his conquest of Gaul, and Trajan recruited cavalry from the Arabs for his eastern campaigns. Crucially, however, such troops remained firmly under Roman control and were normally as loyal – or disloyal – as any legionaries or other auxiliaries.

Marcus Aurelius faced acute problems after the plague and invasions of AD166–7. His plans included settling numbers of barbarian tribes in Pannonia and Moesia, who would in exchange return devastated land to cultivation and serve as auxiliaries. Later emperors also let barbarians settle in lands they themselves had devastated, hoping that they would supply recruits for the army. Constantine recruited so many barbarians into his elite force, (the *Scholae Palatinae*, who replaced the Praetorians), that he was accused of "barbarizing" the army. However, the barbarians remained under imperial control and sometimes became Romanized officials of high rank, such as Stilicho. Son of a Vandal general who had fought on the Roman side at Adrianople, Stilicho became totally Romanized, marrying Theodosius' niece Serena. He was, however, an exception, for the balance between Roman master and German hireling changed drastically in the late 4th century AD.

ADRIANOPLE AND AFTER

The Huns came from the heart of eastern Asia. They drove the Ostrogoths out of the Ukraine and into the Roman empire in AD376. Some 200,000 Goths, including Visigothic cousins living in Dacia, crossed the Danube, being allowed to settle in depopulated lands in Thrace. Their annihilation of the main Roman army under Valens at Adrianople two years later meant that the Goths now faced no real check on their activities.

The new emperor Theodosius' appeasement of the Goths seemed inevitable. Not everyone was convinced, but Theodosius' Gothic federates proved their worth by fighting at the Battle of the Frigid River in Slovenia in AD394. By the time Theodosius died in AD395, the Goths were settled as *foederati* en masse, under their own leaders *inside* the empire, supposedly loyal to an empire no longer their military superior. The first decade of the 5th century AD revealed the full dangers of such a policy.

While Stilicho intrigued to be guardian of the young emperor Arcadius in the east as well as of Honorius in the west, Alaric, king of the Visigoths, played off one court against the other, escalating his demands for land, money and titles. Escaping Stilicho's pursuit in AD395, he had himself made *magister militum per Illyricum*, general of the army for Illyricum, by Constantinople, gaining access to Roman supply depots in the Balkans. So strengthened, he marched into Italy in AD401, attacking Milan. Defeated by Stilicho the next year, Alaric again escaped. Concentration on the Gothic threat weakened the Rhine frontier, where Suebians, Vandals and Burgundians crossed into Gaul in AD406. Some reached as far as Spain. Meanwhile, the pretender Constantine had landed in Gaul, denuding Britain of its garrison to pursue his imperial claims. Stilicho turned to Alaric, still supposedly a *foederatus*, for help against the barbarian invaders of Gaul and the usurper from Britain.

Alaric demanded 4,000lb (1,814kg) of gold in return for the mere promise of his help. This deal with a barbarian so scandalized many Romans that it led to Stilicho's assassination in August AD408 and an end to the appeasement policy. In response, in October AD408, Alaric crossed the Alps again, marching on Rome. He probably intended not to attack the city directly but to starve it out – it was well defended and the Goths were bad at sieges. On his third attempt, in August AD410, some Romans opened the gates to the Goths. For the first time in 800 years an enemy army possessed Rome.

Alaric stayed in Rome for only three days – the city had no food for his army – and died soon after. Yet the Visigoths, after further disputes, finally did help the imperial government, driving the Suebians and Vandals into westernmost

Iberia. In return, they were granted lands around Toulouse. Finally, at the Battle of Châlons-sur-Marne in AD451, Visigothic *foederati* proved themselves worthy allies by helping to repel the Huns.

Other German *foederati* proved less amenable. The Vandals crossed into Africa in AD429. There, through conquest and extortion, they gained control of the richest provinces in the west – a loss the imperial government tried to disguise by titling them *foederati*. The Vandals went on to seize the great port of Carthage, cutting off Rome's grain supplies.

Above: Marcus Aurelius receiving homage from barbarians AD176, some of whom he enlisted as foederati. *Useful mercenaries, so long as the Romans retained the upper hand, the* foederati *became a threat when the Romans lost control after AD378, and the empire was seriously imperilled.*

AT THE EMPIRE'S EXTREMITIES
EGYPT

When Octavian occupied Egypt after defeating Antony and Cleopatra in 30BC, he decided that this immensely rich, ancient and, to Roman eyes, strange land should become his personal property or private kingdom. This meant that the *princeps* became the heir of the Ptolemies, themselves heirs of nearly three millennia of pharaonic rule. Augustus was depicted and worshipped as a pharaoh. Later emperors at times restored or extended temples, as Trajan did at Philae, although the powers of priests were generally circumscribed. The Romans wanted Egypt as a granary for Rome.

Egypt, with a population of about eight million under the early Principate, was second only to Italy in size. A Praetorian prefect governed the province from Alexandria, and senators were forbidden to visit it without the emperor's express permission. The first prefect, Aelius Gallus, led a campaign deep into the Sudan, making grandiose claims for his conquests. This so angered Augustus that

Gallus was forced to commit suicide. Later prefects were more cautious, and the frontier remained fixed for centuries near Aswan. The bulk of the population, the *fellahin*, or peasants, were tied to their land and governed by a combination of priests and local bureaucrats, as they had been for millennia. Their forced labour continued to supply the wheat and other products – linen, cotton and papyrus, the precursor of paper found only along the Nile's banks – that now went to Rome rather than their own government; but for a long time they posed little problem. Most Egyptians paid the *laographia*, or special poll tax; only the three Greek cities – Alexandria, Ptolemais and Naucratis – were exempt. At first 27,000 troops – three legions plus auxiliaries – were kept to control the country, with a flotilla on the Nile, later reduced to just one legion (needed in turbulent Alexandria), for there was almost no external threat. The native Egyptians still spoke their ancient language, now known as Coptic, and were separate from the two newer populations, the Jews and the Greeks, whose disputes caused the Romans many problems.

Both Jews and Greeks had been in Egypt for some time. The first Jews had been settled by the Persians in the 6th century BC as military colonists around Old Babylon (Cairo), as the Persians were unpopular rulers in Egypt. When Alexander the Great founded Alexandria in 331BC, he invited Jews to settle there. Later, under the Ptolemies, whose empire stretched to the Lebanon, many Jews moved to the metropolis. By the 1st century BC, around 8–10 per cent of the population of Egypt was Jewish. Alexandria must have had a larger Jewish population than any city in Judaea itself. Many Jews prospered in Alexandria and, although they had their own quarters

Above: The temple of Horus at Edfu is the only Egyptian temple to survive almost intact. The Romans continued to support the ancient priesthood to maintain the social status quo.

Below: The annual flooding of the Nile enriched its banks with silt brought down from central Africa, making it the chief granary of the ancient world. Egypt's grain went to feed the Roman populace after its conquest in 30BC.

and kept their religion, some of them were influenced by Hellenism. Most famous of these was the philosopher Philo (*c.*25BC–AD45), whose attempts to reconcile the teachings of the Torah and Plato in works such as *The Contemplative Life* influenced later Christian thinking. Philo also took an active role in politics, leading the embassy of Jewish Alexandrians in AD40 to persuade Caligula not to enforce the worship of his own divinity on Jews. (Jews had been exempted from emperor-worship.) Caligula pronounced that those who could not see he was a god were more to be pitied than hated.

Philo's deputation to Rome was needed because of unceasing disputes and rivalries between Alexandria's Jews and its Greek-speakers, jealous of Jewish privileges. There were further riots between the two groups under Claudius. Under Nero, 50,000 people were killed when the Jews tried to burn down the amphitheatre and the governor had to send in two legions. In AD115 the whole Jewish population rose in revolt, causing immense destruction.

ALEXANDRIA: COSMOPOLIS AND CHRISTIAN CRADLE

With nearly one million inhabitants, Alexandria was almost as large as Rome under Augustus, and was still very much the centre of Greek scientific life. Heron invented the world's first steam engine there in the 1st century AD and Ptolemy drew up a map of the heavens a century later. Its famous library contained 500,000 papyrus rolls, the largest in the world, and its *pharos* (lighthouse), reputedly 400ft (120m) high, was the tallest structure in the world. Alexandria was the centre of trade routes stretching across the Mediterranean and east to India, its markets filled with exotic goods and peoples. Its grand boulevards, such as the Canopic Way lined with porticos, long eclipsed anything to be found in Rome. But it lacked what even the smallest *municipium* had: an elected council and magistrates.

This derived from the extremely autocratic government of the Ptolemies. Augustus continued without a council, which had to wait for Septimius Severus visiting Egypt in AD200–01. When the Alexandrians were not involved in commerce or sectarian strife, their thoughts turned to philosophy or religion. Plotinus, founder of antiquity's last great school of philosophy, was born there in AD204. But Egypt was also one of the most fertile grounds for early Christianity, which appealed both to native Egyptians and to erudite citizens of Alexandria.

The Greek theologian St Clement of Alexandria (*c.*AD150–214) was a bishop of Alexandria (later called Patriarchs). His pupil Origen (AD185–253), one of the first original Christian thinkers, castrated himself to avoid sexual temptation. Many early Christians went to the desert as a solution to this problem, with certain areas becoming almost crowded with hermits. Another Alexandrian bishop St Athanasius (AD295–373) attended the Council of Nicaea in AD325. Constantine accepted his views on the single nature of Christ, which became orthodox Christianity. Religious disputes continued to rack the city nearly as badly as the Greek–Jewish conflicts of earlier times.

Above: The Pharos of Alexandria was one of the Seven Wonders of the Ancient World. Reputedly 400ft (120m) high, it was the prototype of many such structures built by the Romans throughout their empire. This fanciful later picture understates its height.

Below: The bulk of the Egyptian population under the Romans remained fellahin, *or peasants, working the land and paying taxes mostly in kind. Only the advent of Christianity really affected them.*

AT THE EMPIRE'S EXTREMITIES
BRITAIN

Above: The ruins of Vindolanda, one of the many fine stone forts in Hadrian's wall country, built to mark the province's northern limits.

Below: Part of the Mildenhall Treasure, one of the most spectacular examples of Roman art in Britain, dating from the 4th century AD.

Although the English Channel formed one of the best natural frontiers the empire ever had, Britain had tantalized the Romans since Caesar's two brief expeditions of 55 and 54BC. The second, with five legions, had temporarily crushed some Britons, but did not lastingly affect its warring, if artistically gifted, Celtic tribes. Claudius, lacking a military background because of his disabilities, was eager to gain glory in this mysterious and reputedly rich island. Strabo had summed up Britain's exports as "hunting dogs, slaves, gold", but the Romans overestimated Britain's wealth. The cost of its large garrison – up to 30,000 troops – probably exceeded its revenues at first, but recent research suggests Britain contributed much more than was once thought to the empire.

The death in AD41 of Cunobelin (Shakespeare's Cymbeline), who had ruled much of south-east England from Camulodunum (Colchester), led to disputes between his sons, which helped the Romans. The invasion force of AD43 under Aulus Plautius, made up of four legions plus auxiliaries – about 40,000 men – landed at Richborough, moved north to the Thames, crushing all British resistance, then waited until Claudius hurriedly joined them before advancing. Claudius then established Camulodunum as the capital for his new province, and, hailed as *imperator* by his troops, proudly returned home.

Several client kingdoms acknowledged Roman suzerainty: the Iceni in Norfolk, the powerful Brigantes in northern England and the Regni in Sussex. The young general Vespasian led the Second Legion south-west, storming 20 *oppida* or hill forts. Meanwhile, the Ninth Legion moved north to Lincoln, which became a colony in the reign of Nerva (AD96–8). London, St Albans and other towns sprang up in the wake of the army in the AD70s, and the Fosse Way from Lincoln to Exeter marked in effect the first provisional boundary of Roman Britain.

This boundary proved temporary. Caratacus, one of Cunobelin's sons, escaped to rally opposition in Wales and drew the Romans west. Captured in AD51, he was taken in chains to Rome where he marvelled aloud that such a magnificent city should covet his poor land. Traditionally, Claudius, impressed by his courage, spared his life. A new governor, Suetonius Paulinus, decided to eliminate the Druid stronghold at Anglesey in AD58. The Romans rightly saw these priests, who practised human sacrifice, as inspiring British resistance. The revolt of the Iceni under Boudicca in AD60 made Suetonius Paulinus return

in a hurry to crush them, but Roman policies were changed: the *publicani* were removed and a conciliatory attitude was adopted. Soon the burnt towns were rebuilt and British grandees began adopting Roman ways (as the near-palace at Fishbourne suggests), despite a total lack of imperial interest under Nero.

THE NORTHERN FRONTIER

The Brigantes, suddenly turning hostile under Venutius, their new king, were defeated at Stanwick in AD71, and Rome's northward advance resumed. Agricola, governor from AD77 to 83, encouraged the civilizing of lowland Britons, settling them in *civitates*, or towns, rather than hill forts, complete with theatres, forums and baths, and teaching them Latin. The Silures in Wales moved from their hill fortress to a new Roman town at Caerwent. Agricola then turned north to complete the conquest of the still mysterious island. He pushed deep into the Highlands, routing the assembled Caledonians at Mons Graupius (near Inverness), nearly completing the conquest of Britain. He then sent a fleet to circumnavigate the north and started to build a large legionary fortress at Inchtuthill, Tayside. It was never finished, for Agricola was soon recalled by Domitian and his northern forts were then abandoned.

When Hadrian visited Britain in AD122 he found the frontier in flux. True to his retractive instincts, he established a new 76-mile (122km) Tyne–Solway line. Intended to be permanent, it was built in stone in its eastern part, the western part being built initially in turf. In AD139, south Scotland was reoccupied and the turf Antonine Wall (named after emperor Antoninus) was built across the waist of Scotland along the Forth–Clyde line. It was abandoned by AD163, and Hadrian's Wall once again became the northern frontier. The emperor Septimius Severus marched north in AD209 and reached Aberdeen, but on his death in AD211 Scotland was again evacuated.

By AD130, a pattern of military garrisons had been established, with legionary forts at Chester, York and Caerleon and auxiliary troops along the walls and round Wales containing the still barbarous tribes. In lowland Britain urban life developed rapidly, if normally quite modestly. However, the great basilica and forum in London, built under Hadrian, were gigantic in size. The baths at Aquae Sulis (Bath) have an elegant opulence that suggests a sophisticated society, as does the large theatre at Verulamium (St Albans). Mining was developed – far more iron, lead and coal were produced than gold – along with farming and trade. Britain escaped the catastrophes of the 3rd century AD relatively lightly, although most towns now built themselves stone walls. But a new threat was emerging: Saxon raiders along the east coasts who would one day conquer the province.

Above: Housesteads was a typical fort on Hadrian's wall, with a garrison of one cohort of auxiliaries (c.500 men).

Below: A sea-god dominates the centre of a floor mosaic from a Romano—British villa. Such villas flourished up to the mid-4th century AD.

THE POWER
OF ROME

The Romans called their empire *imperium Romanorum*. This translates rather appositely as the power of the Romans. From the Latin word *imperator*, or commander-in-chief, comes our word emperor. For contemporaries, there was no escaping the military fact of Roman power. Certainly, subject peoples who incurred Rome's anger knew that the heavy weight of Rome's military machine could descend on them with exemplary force.

   The Roman army was indisputably the best armed force in the ancient world – at least in those areas it knew – although its navy was of very minor importance. For a period of more than half a millennium, from the defeat of Hannibal in 202BC to Rome's own stunning defeat by the Goths at Adrianople in AD378, Rome was generally undefeated. Individual Roman generals could be outmanoeuvred or outwitted, and at the empire's extremities – in northern Britain, the deep forests of central Germany or the deserts of Asia – Rome's power seemed to reach its limits. But elsewhere, no other army could in the long term resist Roman military might; it was relentless, unflinching and genuinely invincible. Rome's army was not just the first fully professional army on a global scale; for a very long time it was probably the only such force deserving the name. Certainly Europe and the Middle East would not see such a force again until the 17th century at the earliest. In many ways, Rome's example was not to be surpassed until the career of Napoleon Bonaparte, who openly and repeatedly borrowed aspects of Roman power when creating his own militaristic empire with its eagles, arches and client states. Above all, the Romans were remarkably disciplined soldiers. This helped make them and keep them highly effective imperial rulers.

Left: Capturing a city that had not surrendered when summoned, Romans often killed every living thing, even dogs – a brutality calculated to terrify.

CHAPTER VII

THE ROMAN ARMY

The growth of the Roman army, from an unpaid citizens' militia to a world-conquering professional force, made possible the growth of the Roman empire. The Roman army was Rome's greatest institution. The city, surrounded by enemies from the start, survived by taking the offensive. Two factors distinguished the Roman army in its long prime from the mid-4th century BC until after AD200: flexibility and tenacity. As the long, often catastrophic war against Hannibal (218–202BC) showed, panic was a Greek word seldom found in a Roman's vocabulary. In the later Republic, almost constant wars turned a part-time self-defence force into a full-time army. Deficiencies, revealed in wars in Africa, called for radical reforms provided by Marius, who opened the army to the poorest citizens as a career. From 100BC the army became fully professional and under the Principate was paid by the *princeps*. In return, soldiers swore allegiance to the *princeps*. Military and civilian careers long remained intertwined. Young Roman nobles served in the army before starting political careers, retaining vital links between civilian and military life. But from the mid-3rd century AD on, soldiers and civilians were segregated by emperors to prevent revolts. Disarmed, the citizens grew ever more timid, while soldiers became more detached from, and openly contemptuous of, the civilians whose taxes supported them and whose lives they supposedly were protecting.

Left: Officers and soldiers of the Praetorian guard, the elite imperial bodyguard stationed in Rome.

THE PEOPLE'S ARMY

Above: Mars, the god of war, was appositely the god of the early Roman state, forever at war with its neighbours.

Rome, surrounded by land-hungry tribes, was frequently at war. Appropriately, Mars, god of war, was originally its chief god. If its early wars were little more than glorified raids, when the Roman army grew larger it soon distinguished itself from other armies by its tenacity and readiness to innovate, taking what it needed from other people's customs.

Under its first kings, the army of Rome consisted of individual warriors fighting mostly on foot, led by aristocrats. King Servius is credited with having effected a "hoplite revolution" in the mid-6th century BC. He regrouped the citizens into six classes, calculated according to wealth rather than lineage, divided into centuries (of 100 men originally). The last class was exempt from military service, as it could not afford to arm itself, although later its members served as rowers in the usually insignificant navy. In civil life these centuries formed the *comitia centuriata*, the main form of the Assembly. The bulk of the fighting was now done by men of the classes who could equip themselves as armoured infantry. They probably used hoplite armour and arms – round shield, cuirass (body armour), sword and long spear – derived from Greek models. The equestrians, those able to pay for a horse, formed the small cavalry. This Roman version of a hoplite revolution increased the size of the Roman army and survived the fall of the monarchy. Romans were less attached to the hoplite army than Greek or Etruscan cities, whose hoplite armies met for set battles in a *phalanx*, a rigid formation of spearmen. Instead, they seem to have fought more flexibly from early on in a *legio*, or legion.

The word *legio* means levy, the call-up of heavy infantry in 30 centuries, plus 300 cavalry recruited from the richest citizens and *velites*, light troops recruited from the poorest eligible class or the very youngest. By about 300BC, a legion had a total of *c*.4,200 spearmen, commanded by one of the two consuls. Troops paraded and drilled on the Campus Martius just outside the city, for no arms could be carried inside Rome, although the levy took place on the Capitoline Hill. In the mid-5th century BC there was a change in army command. The two consuls, until

Below: The four types of soldier of the early and mid-Republic, of whom the first three fought in the acer triplex *(triple line). The last were poorly armed skirmishers.*

then only the generals, were partly supplanted by six military tribunes, presumably more professional. Such professionalism was needed, for in about 435BC Rome began its first serious long war with its powerful Etruscan neighbour, Veii, which had formidable defences, both natural and man-made. It was not until Camillus took command that Veii was captured. He made the Romans fight continuously – previously they had returned to their farms for the harvest – and introduced pay. By 342BC the Roman army was involved in fighting in Campania, a place that seemed so distant that the troops at first mutinied. By now, however, Rome had established a novel form of fighting that enabled it to survive defeats by technically superior enemies.

THE TRIPLE LINE (*ACER TRIPLEX*)

According to Polybius, the Greek historian brought to Rome as a hostage in 167BC, the Roman army of the middle Republic fought in three lines determined by age and experience. The first line consisted of the youngest soldiers, the *hastati*, literally spearmen. Behind came men in their late 20s or 30s, in the prime of life, called *principes*. In the rear were the veterans, the *triarii*, the third line. All lines wore bronze helmets; the richer ones wore a mail cuirass, others simply had a bronze breastplate. All carried a long semi-cylindrical shield. Roman infantrymen were primarily swordsmen. Their sword was the *gladius hispaniensis*, with a blade less than 2ft (60cm) long, well suited for both cutting and thrusting. The first two ranks carried the *pilum*, a weighty javelin with a wooden shaft about 4ft (120cm) long, surmounted by a 2–3ft (60–90cm) narrow iron shaft with a pyramid-shaped point. This tiny point gave the javelin enough impetus to smash through a shield. Each legionary had two *pila*, with a maximum range of about 100ft (30m).

Each of the three infantry lines was divided into ten *maniples*. Those of the *hastati* and *principes* had about 120–60 men each, while the reserve of *triarii*

made up maniples of 60 men. During battle, the maniples were arranged like a chessboard in a *quincunx*, a five-fold formation, in which the *principes'* maniples guarded the gaps between the units of the *hastati*. In the rear, the *triarii* covered the gaps in the *principes'* lines. In front of the *hastati*, skirmishers engaged the enemy, retreating between the *hastati maniples*, who then threw their javelins and charged the enemy. When exhausted, they retreated between the gaps between the *principes*, who also charged, throwing their javelins. The *triarii* had to fight only in extremis. A saying that things "had come to the *triarii*" meant things were in a terrible state.

The triple line of maniples made for a more flexible, mobile formation than the *phalanx*, which could be easily upset. Triple lines proved their worth, first defeating Samnite cavalry in gruelling wars (343–290BC), then the crack *phalanx* of Pyrrhus of Epirus. Typically, the Romans, then facing war-elephants for the first time, learnt how to open their ranks to let the enraged beasts pass through.

Above: This detail from the Column of Marcus Aurelius in Rome shows well-trained Roman soldiers fighting barbarians on the Danube in the 2nd century AD.

BATTLE HARDENING

King Pyrrhus was astonished less by his defeat at the hands of a non-Greek city, than by the Romans' refusal to accept the rules of war as then understood by Greeks. By the 3rd century BC, these had become relatively civilized. Wars were fought between mercenaries, who were not expected to fight to the last drop of blood. By contrast, the disciplined Romans (whom Pyrrhus acknowledged were "not barbarians"), fought with grim determination both on the battlefield and in the political arena. Rome would tolerate high casualties in its citizen armies, but would accept no compromise treaties with enemies strong enough to recover and possibly challenge her again. Unconditional surrender or total destruction was the choice offered to rival powers. This might be brutal, but it proved devastatingly effective.

When Rome and Carthage went to war in 264BC, Rome had no fleet to combat the Mediterranean's greatest maritime power. Carthage's wealth enabled her to hire huge armies of mercenaries. The Romans, however, set about building a fleet for what proved to be a naval war. Wars at sea were fought by galleys, rowed by oarsmen. The Romans copied a Carthaginian galley that had run aground, training rowing crews – poorer citizens – on land while they built 140 cloned ships. The first naval clash proved a disaster, and the Romans realized that they could not out-manoeuvre the experienced Carthaginians. Instead, they devised the *corvus*, or raven, a boarding ramp with an iron spike that fell and stuck into the enemy's deck, locking the two galleys together. Naval skills became redundant as Roman legionaries charged across and got down to hand-to-hand combat.

At the Battle of Mylae in 260BC, a larger Carthaginian fleet was totally defeated, losing 50 ships including its flagship thanks to this unnautical novelty. The Romans defeated the Carthaginians again in 256BC at Ecnomus. The Romans went on the offensive, landing an army under Regulus in North Africa. However, Regulus was defeated in 255BC and taken prisoner. A relief fleet was sunk by a storm, as were other fleets because the

Below: Only in the First Punic War did the Roman fleet play a crucial role. Thanks to the corvus, *which bound ships together, Rome defeated Carthage repeatedly at sea.*

corvus made galleys top-heavy. Finally, the Romans raised another fleet and won the decisive battle of the Aegates Islands in 242BC. Carthage gave up Sicily and her fleet. Her ruling families, like the Barcas, however, were determined on revenge.

ENDURANCE AND INNOVATION

In Hannibal Barca, Rome encountered a military genius. Hannibal recruited his army from the best fighting nations – Numidian cavalry, Spanish and Celtic infantry. Against such a force, Rome fielded its superior militia. Rome still carried out a fresh mobilization each year, and still appointed amateur generals from that year's consuls. Rome's only obvious strength was the huge supply of recruits from her allied cities – 700,000 men.

Hannibal's three swift victories – at Trebbia, Trasimene and, most devastatingly, at Cannae in 216BC – should have won the war. But they were not cheap victories: Cannae cost Hannibal 5,700 men. The Roman maniples' triple lines helped soldiers to keep fighting even in defeat. So did their discipline. Rome, with its belief in its gods, fought on. Although it might have seemed wiser to keep troops at home, legions were sent to Spain. Fabius Maximus wore Hannibal

down by avoiding open battle and reconquering the south. The long sieges of Capua, Tarento and Syracuse showed Roman inventiveness at its best. Scipio took the offensive in Spain, adopting Hannibal's own tactics (placing heavy legions on the wings with light troops in the centre) to crush the Carthaginians at Ilipa in 206BC. He then defeated Hannibal at Zama in 202BC, where the Romans outfought the Carthaginians, after turning back their elephants.

Above: The scene from the Temple of Neptune in Rome c.100BC shows soldiers of the late Republic equipped with long shields, plumed helmets and, for the officer by the altar, a cuirass. Soon after this time, Roman soldiers stopped providing their own armour.

Below: Roman troops cross water using a bridge of boats.

THE FALL OF THE REPUBLIC

Above: A standard of a cohort, the subdivision of the legion.

Below: Lepidus, Mark Antony and Octavian formed the Second Triumvirate in 43BC.

Success can breed complacency, as Rome discovered in the later 2nd century BC, when it struggled against adversaries who were often less formidable than those it had already overcome. The army's lack of full professional status was one of the main problems. Essentially, most Roman soldiers still expected to return to their farms at the end of a campaign – although these were usually ruined by often long periods of absence. This left many men without property, making them and their sons ineligible for further military service, and so weakening the army. These shortcomings were corrected by Marius' army reforms. In the long term, these proved fatal to the Republic's existence.

Military problems first became apparent in the Third Punic War (149–146BC). Disturbed by Carthage's economic – not military – resurgence, Rome engineered war after Carthage became entangled with its aggressive neighbour Numidia, officially breaking its treaty with Rome. The Roman armies suffered repeated reverses until Scipio Aemilianus (the adopted grandson of Scipio Africanus) took command and stormed Carthage, destroying the city.

Worse followed in Spain, where Iberian tribes fought each other and Rome endlessly. Another revolt against Rome, based in the northern city of Numantia, proved intractable. Untrained Roman armies were defeated until Scipio assembled and trained an army of 60,000 men. Even then, he did not dare face the Numantians in open battle but used siege tactics to capture and destroy their city in 133BC. Such brutality had become a hallmark of Roman imperialism but was now coupled with military semi-competence.

Back in Africa, another challenge to Roman power arose with Jugurtha, a fine general and king of Numidia (northern Algeria). He defeated a Roman army in 110BC, forcing it to "pass under the yoke". He proved so successful at eluding superior Roman armies that treachery was suspected. Roman troops deserted in droves, as their commanders appeared incompetent or corrupt. The arrival of the martinet Quintus Metellus restored discipline and morale, but he failed to catch Jugurtha. Impatient for a successful conclusion, the Roman Assembly chose Marius, a *novus homo*, or "new man", from an equestrian family.

MARIUS AND HIS REFORMS

After serving under Metellus as consul in 107BC, Marius was given the African command the next year. Before leaving Rome, he appealed for volunteers from the propertyless class, the *capite censi*, helping to turn a citizens' militia into a career army that appealed to landless poorer citizens. With a much increased supply of recruits, Marius won victories in Africa that revealed his own military talents. But he failed to corner Jugurtha until treachery led to his capture and final execution in Rome in 104BC.

Meanwhile in the north, two large Germanic peoples, the Cimbri and the Teutones, annihilated twin Roman armies at Arausio (Orange) in 105BC. In the

Left: The Colosseum, Trajan's Column, the Forum, a severed head and streams of blood feature in this depiction of The Massacre of the Triumvirate, *by Antoine Caron, a 16th-century painter.*

worst disaster since Cannae, 80,000 men were reported lost. Marius was again given command by the Assembly and in three years radically restructured the army.

The three lines based on experience and age were abolished. All legionaries now had a *pilum* (javelin) plus the short *gladius* (sword) and had to carry supplies on their backs, hence the new nickname "Marius' mules". The basic sub-unit became the cohort of 480 men, which was divided into six centuries of 80 men each commanded by a centurion, officers who became the backbone of the army. Each legion had its own standard, a gilt eagle, that embodied the legion's *esprit de corps*. The legions themselves became more permanent, and, most importantly, these full-time legionaries started looking to their generals for reward, the Senate having failed to look after its demobilized soldiers.

This new-style army proved far more flexible than its predecessor. Marius used his uniformly equipped cohorts to crush the Teutones in a bloody battle at Aix-en-Provence in 102BC and the next year to rout the Cimbri in northern Italy, reportedly killing 100,000 of them. The most alarming barbarian invasions until the 3rd century AD had been repelled and Marius was (unconstitutionally) re-elected consul yet again.

THE RESULTS OF THE REFORMS

After Marius, no one won supreme power in Rome (as opposed to just becoming consul) without an army to back him. Powerful Roman generals – first Marius, then Sulla, Pompey, Caesar, and finally Antony and Octavian – built up armies that were loyal to them rather than to the state, and could use them for personal reasons. Sulla, once Marius' lieutenant in Africa, led the army he had been assigned for war against Mithradates against Rome itself in 88BC, the first of many such "marches on Rome". From Marius' reforms until the end of the Republic, Rome's armies were used against each other almost as much as against foreign enemies. This wrecked the Republic.

The *military* consequences of Marius' reforms were almost wholly positive, however. The Social War with the Latin allies of 91–87BC had given the allies Roman citizenship and greatly increased the numbers eligible for legionary service. These professional legions made a superb permanent army. Reorganized and supplemented by increasing numbers of specialized auxiliaries – from Balearic slingers to African cavalry – they continued Rome's conquest of the ancient world, successfully defending it until the mid-3rd century AD with only minor changes in their structure.

Below: The eagle-standard introduced by Marius became the focus of loyalty among legionaries. To lose one in battle was a disgrace, and the aquilifer, eagle-bearer, was an important soldier. But loyalty to the legion did not always mean loyalty to the Republic.

LEGIONS AND PRINCIPATE

When Octavian, victorious after the lengthy civil wars, returned to Rome in 29BC, a pressing problem was how to deal with a huge army of nearly 70 legions, plus a large fleet. Such swollen forces were unsustainable by an empire exhausted economically, and unnecessary when Rome faced no major external threats. They also posed a potential future threat to the stability of his regime should they become loyal to a successful and ambitious general. Although Octavian had risen to power by the sword, he did not wish to advertise the fact. Above all, he wanted to ensure the loyalty of the army to himself and later to his family, to avert any recurrence of civil war.

Octavian decided on demobilization, reducing the army's size to only 28 legions (around 150,000 regular soldiers). This meant that he needed to find a way of paying off some 300,000 veterans with grants of land in ways that did not anger too many existing landholders. Augustus, as he was titled from 27BC, did this by founding colonies of veterans, often outside Italy – in Spain, Sicily, Gaul, Greece, Syria and Pisidia (central Turkey). He also established 28 colonies in Italy, some of which became famous in his lifetime. Turin is a good example. His vast wealth allowed him to pay fair prices for land in Italy. The revenues of Egypt flowed directly into the imperial purse and he owned vast tracts of land taken from enemies. In AD6 Augustus set up the *Aerarium militare*, a special military treasury, to meet legionaries' retirement pensions from indirect taxes.

The 28 legions – reduced to 25 after the Teutoburg disaster – were stationed in troubled provinces such as Tarraconensis (northern Spain) and along the frontiers, especially the Rhine and Danube, where permanent fortresses were established, later to develop into towns such as Cologne or Vienna. The Rhine was the early crucial frontier, with eight legions stationed along it, some in double camps such as Xanten. Later, the Danube became the most important. Under the Principate, legions were commanded by legates, who held delegated power (*imperium*) from Augustus. He kept only nine cohorts of the elite Praetorian guard in Italy and stationed only three of them in Rome – a tiny military force for a city of nearly a million inhabitants. Along the frontiers, the lower-paid, more lightly armed auxiliaries, recruited from non-Roman citizens, supplemented the legions.

This frontier deployment meant that there was no central reserve, at least until Septimius Severus (AD193–211) based a legion near Rome. Although criticisms

Above: A legionary of the 1st century BC with his pilum (javelin) and gladius (sword).

Left: Legionaries of the Principate, with curved shields, lorica segmantata armour, short swords and pilum, the javelin with the thin neck.

Right: A Roman centurion as imagined in the Italian Renaissance, with his sword on his left and wearing ornate armour.

have been levelled against Augustus for this lack, in practice it probably made little difference given the length of the frontiers and the slow progress of marching legionaries . The army remained *potentially* on the offensive, ready to move along or across the frontiers. A central reserve under an ambitious commander might also prove a threat to the emperor. Augustus did establish three fleets to keep the Mediterranean free of pirates as well as flotillas on the Rhine, Danube and Nile, but naval power was always secondary to land power.

LOYALTY TO THE *PRINCEPS*

All new recruits swore a *sacramentum*, or oath to the *princeps*, rather than to the Senate. But, unlike Caesar or Pompey, Augustus was not a great general. He owed his earlier victories (over Sextus Pompeius and Antony) principally to Marcus Agrippa, his chief minister and closest ally. After Actium, Augustus campaigned only in northern Spain in 23BC. He fell seriously ill there and seldom again took the field, but troops did not swear allegiance to the general Agrippa. The image of the emperor or of one of his family was carried by an *imaginifer*, a standard-bearer ranking behind only the *aquilifer*, the eagle-bearer. The emperor's name was coupled with that of *Roma Dea* (Rome the goddess) in sacrifices and his image appeared on busts and coins. Such reiterated expressions of loyalty to the *imperator* or Caesar, helped to cement Augustus' settlement, enabling it to survive the antics of Caligula and even, for a surprisingly long time, those of Nero. Nero's almost total neglect of the military was a major cause of his downfall.

Augustus was fortunate that in his stepsons Drusus and especially Tiberius (from AD6 his adopted son) he had extremely competent generals who campaigned steadily on the Rhine and Danube. Their military successes reflected on the *princeps*. Later emperors were less lucky but faced few serious challenges from army commanders until AD68 and the Year of the Four Emperors. Thereafter, dynastic continuity, coupled with generous donations at each emperor's accession, helped to keep the legions loyal. When a general did revolt, like Saturninus in AD89, he was quickly quashed. This contributed to the success both of the Flavians and of the Five Good Emperors – all of the latter being adopted sons. Ironically, when Marcus Aurelius made Commodus (whom he believed to be his actual son) his heir, the dynasty came to an end and the ensuing civil wars, longer and more damaging than in AD68–9, weakened the empire.

Below: The imperial guard as they appear on the base of the Obelisk of Theodosius I, a 4th-century AD emperor, in Constantinople (Istanbul).

ARMY OF THE LATER EMPIRE

During the mid-3rd-century AD crisis, it became obvious that the traditional deployment of the army had become inadequate. Withdrawing legions from one frontier to fight on another left the exposed frontier intolerably vulnerable. The persistent and well-organized Sassanid Persians were more deadly than the earlier Parthians. The Germanic Goths, who first appeared on the Danube delta in AD242, were also formidable. Over the next 30 years they penetrated into the empire's Mediterranean heart, sometimes seizing ships. Athens, far from any frontier, was sacked in AD268 by the Heruli, another tribe that was wandering the empire almost at will.

At least 30 emperors held power between the murder of Alexander Severus in AD235, and AD284, the accession of Diocletian. Only one died a natural death (Claudius Gothicus in AD270). Many more usurpers were acclaimed by mutinous legions throughout the empire. A few, like Postumus in Gaul and Carausius in Britain, formed breakaway empires that lasted years. The lack of a central reserve and the intertwining of civilian and military careers now appeared terrible weaknesses.

Around AD200, Septimius Severus had begun building a reserve in Italy, doubling the Praetorian guard and stationing a legion near Rome. This created a mobile force of around 18,000 men. Later, Gallienus (AD253–68) banned senators from holding senior commands and began building up a mobile cavalry force in northern Italy, drawing on *vexillationes* (detachments). Like his removal of the government to Milan, close to the Alpine passes and the Rhine–Danube frontiers, this concentration of forces around the emperor set a precedent. Gallienus was murdered before he could employ this force to lasting effect, but his successors, Claudius II and Aurelian (AD270–75), used it to defeat the Goths, Palmyrene rebels and the separatist Gallic empire. Aurelian also accelerated the programme of refortifying cities, notably the capital itself. These steps marked the start of a radical change in tactics and strategy that was completed by Constantine.

CRACK TROOPS – AND THE REST

Constantine (AD324–37) continued to make the army more mobile, dividing it into two groups that were distinct in armour, pay, prestige and role. The low-paid *limitanei* were the frontier guards and the elite *comitatenses* were mobile forces grouped around the emperors. The latter were often cavalry: scale-armoured *cataphracts* or *clibanarii* with plate armour. Such horsemen looked imposing but were often ineffectual. Julian had to discipline cavalry units for cowardice during his Persian campaign in AD363 and the indiscipline of Valens' cavalry was partly responsible for his defeat at Adrianople in AD378. Before the widespread adoption of the stirrup – now known not to have occurred much before AD600 – heavy cavalry was of limited use, for lances could not be used in charges. The impact of hitting an opponent would have unseated a stirrupless rider.

Above: Light-armed auxiliary troops, with clubs but no armour, supplement the legionaries on this detail from Trajan's Column in Rome.

Below: The massive walls of Richborough, Rome's chief port of entry to Britain and part of the Saxon Shore defences of the 3rd century AD, show the empire was on the defensive.

FORTIFICATIONS PROGRAMME

To protect the vulnerable cities of the interior, new fortresses or fortified towns – known as *burgi*, a German word – became nodal strong points, usually invulnerable to direct attack by barbarians. At York, old walls were replaced by thick defensive walls capable of carrying pieces of artillery. This huge fortification programme was replicated across the empire. Behind these huge walls, frontier troops could await the arrival of the mobile relief forces. Large landowners began fortifying their villas or farms, so that invaders, even if undefeated in the field, would face starvation outside the walls.

Constantine created *palatini*, imperial Palatine guards, to replace the Praetorians. Many of these were German horsemen. This increasing dependence on Germanic mercenaries is symbolized by the adoption of "dragon standards" – long, wind-sock-style banners – and German war cries. By AD379, when Theodosius became emperor after Adrianople, the Goths had become *foederati*, or allies, with whole tribes enrolled *en masse*. When imperial government divided after Theodosius' death in AD395, the Goths turned against their Roman allies and started the chain of events that led to the sack of Rome in AD410.

The empire in the 4th century AD still had about 60 legions, each now made up of only about 1,000 lightly armed men. The infantry no longer wore much body armour and used darts rather than the *pilum* (javelin). Nonetheless, properly led and trained Roman armies could still defeat their enemies, as victorious campaigns from Galerius' victory over the Persians in AD297 to Valentinian's campaigns against the Germans in the AD360s showed. Often, however, Rome's armies were deployed against each other.

The *limitanei*, stationary frontier troops garrisoning the new forts, were unimpressive. Many were expected to grow their own food, as they were not paid all year round. Nonetheless, some of these frontier troops continued to fight for the western empire right up to the end in the AD470s. In AD534, after the eastern empire had reconquered North Africa, the emperor Justinian ordered the re-establishment of the *limitanei* to defend the long frontiers. But the actual reconquest of the west – Africa, Italy, southern Spain – was carried out by smallish numbers of cavalry. An army of 20,000 men was by then thought large.

How effective the army of the later empire was is debatable, but it was certainly more expensive, and the taxes to pay for it contributed to the alienation of subjects from the imperial government. But as Roman civilians were increasingly loath to fight – there are reports of men of military age mutilating themselves to avoid conscription under Constantine – there seemed little alternative. The continued survival of the eastern empire, and its 6th-century revival, suggests that the late-Roman army could fight effectively at least at times.

Above: York was for long a legionary headquarters and the capital of northern Britain. Two emperors – Septimius Severus and Constantius Chlorus – died in the city, and Constantine I was proclaimed emperor there by his troops.

Below: This scene from the Arch of Galerius in Thessalonica, Greece, commemorates Galerius' victory over the Persians in AD297. Elephants, often used by the Persians, can just be glimpsed in the background.

CHAPTER VIII

INSIDE THE ARMY

As the Roman army became a world-conquering force, it evolved an original system of organization. Based on the legion, this model had the flexibility to overcome much larger, and often technically superior, enemy forces. Above all, it was indomitably aggressive. From the earliest wars of the Republic in the 5th century BC up to the 3rd century AD, its core troops were the legionaries: highly disciplined, well-armoured, heavy infantry-men who could fight in many different ways, from storming fortresses to outfacing charging elephants or even, as marines, fighting onboard ships.

The Roman army was notorious for its tough discipline and rigorous demands. However, for its age it was also oddly meritocratic, and in some ways continued to represent the voice of the Roman people after the Republic had ended. In effect, it spoke, as well as fought, for the people of the whole empire, not just Rome. The legions were often remarkably long-lived – some units lasted more than 300 years. In so doing, they became the unwitting agents of a process of Romanization that transformed western Europe through the towns that sprang up around their camps, or in the peaceful hinterland guarded by them. Many of the bridges, aqueducts and walls around the former provinces were built by legionaries in the long periods of peace that their fighting had established. The Roman army was more than just an army: in some ways it became the heart of Rome itself.

Left: Legionaries, besides being professional soldiers, often also became skilled builders, constructing many forts and roads.

ORGANIZING THE LEGION

Above: A Roman optio, *the second-in-command to a centurion, with his distinctive plumed helmet, worn by a member of the re-enactment group the Ermine St Guard. Officers such as the* optio *and the centurion were the army's backbone, and they received higher pay.*

Below: The symbol of the 20th Roman legion, Valeria Victrix.

Legio means levy, and originally a legion was the levy of all eligible Roman citizens between the ages of 17 and 46, arranged in centuries (literally 100 men). The Roman army of around 500BC numbered around 4,000–6,000 men, hoplite heavy spearmen, like the Greeks. Over the next centuries, however, the legion proper emerged as a new, more adaptable unit that enabled Rome to conquer and hold the Mediterranean world.

By *c.*320BC, the legion of the Republic had been established. According to Polybius and Livy – who do not always agree – a legion had five elements: cavalry, light infantry and three sorts of heavy infantry. The richest citizens made up the cavalry of about 300 men, socially prestigious but too few to affect battles. The all-important heavy infantry, about 4,200 men who could afford their own armour, was divided into three lines. The first line had the youngest soldiers, the *hastati* (literally "armed with a spear", although they carried javelins and swords). Next came the *principes*, men in their prime, and last came the *triarii*, the veterans. Behind the *triarii* were deployed less dependable troops, *rorarii* and *accensi*. All soldiers wore bronze helmets and had a long shield of wood covered with leather. The *hastati* and *principes* were armed with the *pilum*, or javelin, and the *gladius*, or short sword, about 20in (50cm) long. The *triarii* appear to have had longer spears. The *velites* were light infantry too poor to equip themselves with full armour.

All three lines were organized into ten maniples. This, the smallest fighting unit, had two centuries, commanded by the senior centurion. Maniples of the *hastati* and *principes* numbered about 120–60 men each, while the *triarii* made up ten maniples of about 60 men. Each maniple also had about 40 *velites*, or lightly armed troops. In battle, the maniples were arranged in the *triplex acies* (triple battle-order) of a chequerboard formation. The maniples of the *principes* covered the gaps between those of the *hastati*, and their own gaps were covered by those of the *triarii*. The *velites* seem to have been used as skirmishers. Each legion of Roman citizens was augmented by an equal number of allies (about 4,000–5,000 infantry and 900 cavalry), commanded by Roman officers. These were called *alae* (wings) because in battle they were put on the wings of the main legions.

The *triplex acies* proved its virtues by defeating the numerically and technically superior armies of Pyrrhus, the Macedonians and the Seleucids. The flexibility and discipline of the maniples – opening up to let hostile elephants or cavalry through, for example – was very nearly invincible. When the Romans were defeated, notably by Hannibal, it was due to Roman amateurism, for the armies were disbanded after each campaign and had to be recruited afresh. When armies remained in existence for a long time under a great general such as Scipio Africanus, they were superb, as the run of Roman victories from Zama in 202BC to Pydna in 168BC showed.

THE CLASSIC LEGION

Rome's military reputation was dented by defeats in the later 2nd century BC, which culminated in disaster at Arausio (Orange). Twin armies were annihilated by the Cimbri and Teutones in 105BC with the loss of 80,000 men. Such a defeat led Marius, recently emerged as the people's general in the war against Jugurtha, to reorganize the legion radically. He had already abolished the property qualifications. Now he got rid of all distinctions based on class or age: both the *velites* and the cavalry disappeared. All legionaries were identically armed with the *pilum* and *gladius*, and had mail armour and a long shield. The maniples ceased to be the

basic unit, although they remained in existence for a while. Instead, the chief tactical sub-unit became the cohort, ten of which made up a legion.

Each cohort had about 480 men divided into six centuries of 80 men led by a centurion. Later the first cohort was usually double strength, raising a legion's total strength to 5,280 men. *Alae*, no longer allies but cavalry wings recruited from auxiliaries, were specialist, increasingly well-regarded units either 512- or 768-men strong. Ten cohorts were easier to command

than 30 maniples and could be deployed as wanted. The cohort did not command the same loyalty as the century and the legion. Marius introduced the silver (later gilt) *aquila*, or eagle, as each legion's main standard, symbolizing its pride and identity. Legions now became permanent, offering a career to landless citizens who volunteered. These became highly professional soldiers, who looked to their generals for substantial reward after their service. This had huge political as well as military consequences.

Above: The principia, headquarters, at the legionary fort of Lambaesis (Tazoult) in modern-day Algeria.

CENTURIONS AND OFFICERS

Centurions may be seen as the equivalent of sergeant-majors in the modern British army. Yet they were even more important, effectively ranking between a contemporary captain and a major. Beside them, a legion's senatorial officers and commander could appear semi-skilled amateurs.

Centurions needed to be not only excellent soldiers but literate, for they had to read and write orders and could have political or diplomatic roles. A letter of introduction from someone influential helped one become a centurion; in the Roman army, as in the Roman state, personal connections counted for a lot. Former members of the Praetorian guard in Rome and, more rarely, equestrians applied for centurions' posts. But some centurions rose from the ranks of the legion, staying 40 years in the army.

There were 59 centurions in a legion, one for each ordinary century of 80 men in the normal nine cohorts and (from c.50AD on), five for the first cohort of five double centuries. This cohort's centurions, the most senior in the legion, were known as *primi ordines*, of the first rank. In ascending order these were the *hastatus posterior* (a name recalling the extinct *maniples*), the *princeps posterior*, *hastatus*, *princeps* and *primus pilus*. The *primus pilus* was the most important officer in the whole legion. He had to be at least 50 years old and held his post for only a year, after which he might retire, his gratuity of 400,000–600,000 sesterces elevating him to equestrian rank. (A normal legionary received about 3,000 sesterces on retirement under Augustus.) Some went on to

Above: The most vital of officers in the Roman army, a centurion was colourfully, even resplendently, armoured, with crested helmet and medallioned cuirass. Note the vine branch in his right hand – used for beating his men.

Right: This tombstone commemorates the centurion Marcus Caelius of the Eighteenth Legion, who was killed fighting at the age of 53 in the Teutoburg Forest ambush in Germany in AD9.

become prefect of the camp, another very important post, others became *primus pilus* again, adding *bis* or *ter* (second or third) to their title; a few became provincial governors or fleet commanders; one or two even became prefects of the Praetorian guard.

A centurion was distinguishable by his silvered armour, his greaves (shin armour, also worn by legionaries) and his transverse-crested helmet. He wore his sword on his left and his dagger on the right, but still carried a shield. Centurions were responsible for maintaining Roman discipline, using their *vitis* (vine cane) often to ferocious effect on their men. This could make them very unpopular. One centurion was killed by angry legionaries during the mutiny on the Danube in AD14. He was known as *cedo alterum* (Get me another!) due to his habit of beating soldiers until his cane broke. Centurions often took bribes from their men, for granting leave or exempting them from fatigues. But they paid for their privileges in blood, suffering disproportionately high casualties in battle, as they were expected to stand their ground to the end.

Beneath the centurions were the standard-bearers: the *aquilifer* (the eagle-bearer), the *signifer* (the emperor's image-bearer) – who also looked after soldiers' pay and savings – and the *vexillarius*, (legionary standard-bearer). All were important posts, especially the *aquilifer*. When Caesar's troops hesitated before disembarking on the shores of Britain, the *aquilifer* leapt into the water shouting, "Follow me, comrades!" And they did. Like these officers, the *optio*, the second-in-command of each century, was on double pay. Each century also had a *tesserarius*, responsible for the important sentry rota, and a *librarius* (clerk). At legionary headquarters there was a staff of clerks and orderlies, including the *exactores* (exactors of payments) and clerks with special duties such as the *librarii horreorum* (clerk of the granary records).

OTHER OFFICERS

The other officers in a legion, although theoretically senior, were less professional. Each legion had six tribunes, the senior being a *laticlavus*; the broad stripe on his toga indicated he was accepted for the Senate. He would be under 25, having his first military experience for a year or so before returning to civilian life. The other five tribunes, *angusticlavii*, or narrow stripes, came from the equestrian order and were generally older and far more experienced. They had often commanded an auxiliary cohort already. They had general administrative duties and, if competent, might go on to command large *alae* (500 or 1,000 men) of auxiliary cavalry. The commanding officer, the *legatus legionis*, was a senator in his 30s or 40s, appointed by the emperor and serving for three years. He might have had no military experience since serving as tribune long before. He was sometimes also the provincial governor. A legate relied heavily on his *primus pilus* and camp prefect for advice, but, as Varus in the Teutoburg ambush in AD9 showed, amateurish legates could not always be relied on to make sound military judgement in crises.

Above: Disciplined Roman swordmanship – stabbing more often than cutting – was a vital part of repeated Roman successes often against vastly superior numbers of barbarians. Better armour also played a part in Roman victories, although single combat like this was uncommon.

TRAINING AND DISCIPLINE

Above: Re-enactment of combat by Roman legionaries. In full armour, they are using their swords, the short but (in the right hands) lethal gladius.

What most impressed foreign commentators about the Roman army was its exceptional discipline and training. Their battle drills were like war. "It would be fair enough to call their drills bloodless battles and their battles bloody drills" wrote Josephus, the captured Jewish leader who became a Roman citizen in AD67. Training and discipline were what made Roman armies so often victorious, not superiority in arms or numbers. When this combination began to break down in the 4th century AD, the army too began to disintegrate.

Every new recruit swore a *sacramentum* (oath) to his general, by which he abrogated all his civilian rights for his 26 years of service. The oath was renewed every year. From then on, his life was in the army's hands. According to Vegetius, writing on military affairs around AD400, a recruit was taught how to march in step and keep his place in formation. Regular route marches of 20 Roman miles (*c.*30km) in five hours, and of 24 miles (*c.*36 km) in the same time at quick step, helped to get a recruit fit.

Drilled twice a day, he learnt how to vault on to a horse and how to mount and dismount fully armed from either side. He was taught to use his weapons by practising cuts and thrusts against a man-sized wooden stake. Initially, he used a heavy wooden sword and shield to strengthen his muscles. He would then fence with other recruits, the tip of his sword covered, before entire units waged mock battles against each other. The climax of such contests came with the mock-cavalry battles, the *hippaka gymnasia*, which were among the army's grandest spectacles. But above all, he was taught how to fight in formation without panicking, becoming so drilled in such discipline that it became second nature.

Training was not restricted to new recruits or to wartime. Repeated drilling kept the army at the peak of efficiency. The legionary was also taught other skills, including swimming, slinging and pitching camp. From *c.*100BC specialist sub-officers in each legion learnt more technical skills, such as building roads. All these were designed to produce an adaptable, tough, reliable soldier, skilled in swordsmanship and adept at keeping formation under exacting circumstances, and always obedient to military discipline.

Left: A Roman garrison on the River Nile from a 1st-century BC mosaic. Egypt was one of the empire's softest postings.

PUNISHMENTS AND REWARD

Death was the punishment for a wide range of offences: dereliction of guard duty (by falling asleep or going absent without leave), desertion, theft (from a comrade), perjury, homosexual acts with another soldier and cowardice. After a brief trial, the guilty soldier was hit with a staff by the tribune, a cue for the other soldiers to club or stone him to death. If he did not die at once, he was thrown outside the camp and abandoned. If an entire unit was found guilty of cowardice or mutiny, it might be decimated. Every tenth man, chosen by lot, would be bludgeoned to death and the remainder of the unit disgraced, pitching their tents outside the main camp and being fed barley rather than wheat. But there were other, less severe and probably more common types of punishment: reduction in rank, loss of privileges gained over years of service, corporal punishment and discharge with ignominy and no gratuity.

The Roman army did not rule solely by punishment; it offered rewards too. Booty from a successful campaign would be shared among the soldiers – although this obviously dwindled during peacetime – and there were occasional individual donations to worthy soldiers. The army also handed out military decorations such as silver or gold chains and *phalerae* (medallions) of bronze or gold worn on the breastplate. Various *coronae* (crowns) were also awarded: the *corona civica* for personally saving the life of a Roman in battle, the *corona muralis* for the soldier who first scaled an enemy city's wall and the *corona vallaris* for the first to cross the entrenchment of an enemy fort. Under inspired generals, competition for such prizes could be intense and were sometimes shared, as at Cartagena in 210BC. From the time of Vespasian on, legionaries could also expect a donation from a new emperor on his accession.

Above: A modern-day re-enactment of Roman legionaries forming a testudo, *or tortoise shield roof, used when approaching walls. The discipline required to maintain such formations – it was said to be possible to walk on the locked shields – was learnt painfully during long army training.*

Left: A Roman legionary's training centred above all on learning how to use his gladius *(stabbing sword) to devastating effect. He would start with a wooden sword, which he jabbed at a pole, before progressing to a real iron weapon.*

PAY AND CONDITIONS

Above: Emperor Caracalla, who twice raised the soldiers' pay in the 3rd century AD.

Below: The Palestrina mosaic from the late 1st century BC *shows soldiers, perhaps in a scene from a romantic myth.*

Nobody could call the ordinary legionary of the Principate overpaid or pampered. After 26 years' service, he received a gratuity in land (not always where he wanted it) or in cash. This came to 3,000 denarii under Augustus and had only increased to 5,000 under Caracalla 200 years later. For most soldiers, yearly pay was also modest. According to Suetonius, Caesar doubled the pay of rank-and-file legionaries to 225 denarii a year in 49BC at the start of the Civil War, to keep them loyal. Basic pay remained at this rate until Domitian (AD81–96) raised it to 300 denarii. It then stayed unchanged throughout the 2nd century AD, despite steady inflation, until Septimius Severus and then Caracalla raised it twice early in the 3rd century AD. During that century,

rocketing inflation devalued the currency. The government responded by paying soldiers in kind – often letting them seize goods from civilians – or in gold currency, which alone retained its value.

Pay rose less with seniority than with promotion. According to Vegetius, a *tesserarius* received one-and-a-half times a normal legionary's pay, an *optio* twice and so on up the scale to centurions, the most junior of whom received at least five times the basic pay. The elite Praetorians were paid twice the basic rate, auxiliaries only half, although some cavalry *alae* (detachments) probably received at least as much as ordinary legionaries.

Supplementing the legionaries' annual pay were the *donativi*, or largesse, that most emperors gave out after their accession, or after a great – or purported – victory. Caligula, for example, gave all legionaries an extra four gold pieces (100 denarii) after his abortive "invasion" of Britain. Although weaker emperors undoubtedly resorted to bribery – according to Suetonius, Claudius gave the Praetorians who had spared his life 150 gold pieces (3,750 denarii) each – even Augustus left 75 denarii to each soldier in his will.

Out of their meagre pay, legionaries had to buy clothes, food, weapons and tents as well as bribes for the centurion. One of the centurion's chief perks was indeed taking bribes in return for granting leave or exemption from fatigues (chores), a practice that disciplinarians like the emperor Hadrian tried to stamp out. Discontent seems to have been widespread in AD14: Germanicus was almost killed stopping a mutiny among the Rhineland legionaries who had been engaged in campaigns for many years.

For food, Vegetius lists as staples corn, wine, vinegar and salt in plenty at all times. The men mostly ate porridge, bread and beans, supplemented by other vegetables and eggs, with meat on the numerous feast days, plus any obtained by hunting. When campaigning they ate hardtack, long-lasting wholewheat biscuits. Such hardships were made more acceptable by the way many generals, even those from the imperial family such as Tiberius or Julian, shared their troops' hardships while on campaign, sleeping on the ground and eating basic rations.

At first under Augustus, legionaries slept in simple timber huts or even in their leather tents. Soon, however, proper stone fortresses were built, often with amphitheatres just outside and with baths within or nearby. Bathhouses were regarded as absolutely essential, and the remains of a typically impressive one on a basilican plan have been found at Chester. Even more impressive are the baths at Caerleon, the largest military baths in Britain. The amphitheatres, in contrast, normally made of turf and timber in northern Europe, seldom saw full-scale gladiatorial games (since these were too expensive) but were used for festivals and animal displays.

Townships soon sprang up outside the larger camps, where men off duty could go to eat and drink in *tabernae* (taverns), and, of course, to meet women. These settlements (*canabae*) often grew into sizeable towns and a few became *coloniae*. But legionaries, although they often started and supported their own families, were not allowed to marry legally while on service until the reign of Septimius Severus. However, their partners were often recognized by people around them and could inherit a soldier's belongings. Their sons, too, were normally accepted as Roman citizens if they enrolled in the legion. The marriage ban probably stemmed from official reluctance to pay for army widows' maintenance.

MEDICAL TREATMENT

Although the legionary's life was tough, his medical treatment was remarkably good – in fact, the Roman army's medical care was probably superior to that of any army until the 20th century. As all armies used to lose more men to disease than to

enemy action, this was a major advantage. The care the Romans took with their water supply and drains, seeking out good supplies of fresh water and piping it down to the camps, then carrying the sewage to a spot on a river below any watering place, averted many diseases. They also isolated sick, possibly infectious, soldiers and treated them in special hospitals. At Inchtuthil, the northernmost legionary fortress in Scotland, a special *valetudinarium*, or medical wing, has been revealed with spacious wards and double internal walls, presumably for both thermal and acoustic insulation. Doctors (*medici*) were specially trained and became specialists at operations to remove arrowheads and sling-stones from their legionary patients and at cleaning and binding their wounds. Here the Romans continued the medical traditions of the Greeks, which went back to Hippocrates in the 5th century BC. Roman courage must have been needed on the operating table, as there were no anaesthetics.

Above: These soldiers from the 4th century BC are carrying a dead comrade. From the earliest times, the Romans were willing to accept very high casualties in their wars.

Below: The worship of Mithras, the saviour-god of Persian origin, became very popular in the Roman army.

AUXILIARY TROOPS

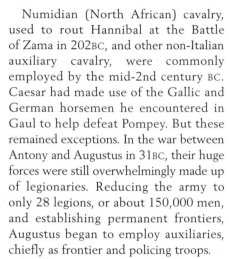

Above: The auxiliaries made up much of the cavalry, which the Romans lacked. Horsemen, lacking stirrups, fought with swords more than spears.

Below: Specialized auxiliary troops such as these archers played an increasingly important role in the Roman army from the 1st century AD onwards. In the east, the Romans often used horse archers from Palmyra.

Legionaries, the army's backbone, were solely heavy infantry . Intended to fight major battles, they were originally recruited exclusively from Roman citizens. During the Republic, legionaries were supplemented by equal numbers of soldiers from the Latin and Italian allies: the auxiliaries. These supplied lighter troops, including much-needed cavalry. With the extension of the full franchise to the allies in 90BC, they no longer provided such troops, seeking the more prestigious and lucrative posts in the legions. However, auxiliaries became increasingly important as Rome began to defend, as opposed to simply expand, its empire. From Augustus' reign onwards, auxiliaries were systematically recruited from non-Roman citizens. One of their big advantages to the government was that their pay was considerably less (an auxiliary infantryman was paid about half a legionary's rate).

Numidian (North African) cavalry, used to rout Hannibal at the Battle of Zama in 202BC, and other non-Italian auxiliary cavalry, were commonly employed by the mid-2nd century BC. Caesar had made use of the Gallic and German horsemen he encountered in Gaul to help defeat Pompey. But these remained exceptions. In the war between Antony and Augustus in 31BC, their huge forces were still overwhelmingly made up of legionaries. Reducing the army to only 28 legions, or about 150,000 men, and establishing permanent frontiers, Augustus began to employ auxiliaries, chiefly as frontier and policing troops.

The Romans employed auxiliaries as specialists to supplement their heavy infantry: Cretan or Syrian archers, slingers from the Balearics and Numidian, Gallic and later Sarmatian cavalry, 3,800 of whom were sent to Britain to repel an invasion. Auxiliaries can clearly be seen on Trajan's Column, which displays the army of the Principate at its peak in the early 2nd century AD. But most auxiliaries were not specialized forces. By Trajan's time they consisted predominantly of infantry equipped, like the legionaries, with mail shirt, cross-braced helmet, sword and javelins. The major difference was that their arms and armour were cheaper and of lesser quality. Reviewing the Sixth Mounted Cohort of Commagenes in Africa, Hadrian commented dismissively that their appearance and condition of their weapons matched their (low) level of pay, but he added that they compensated for their scruffiness by their enthusiasm in military exercises. There was a major exception to the inferiority of auxiliaries in Rome's increasing use of cavalry, especially mounted archers, from eastern cities like Palmyra. Many of these auxiliaries started off as levies supplied by client kings on Rome's eastern frontier. They became more important as the eastern frontier itself became a problem in the 3rd century AD, and by then were paid more than, in some cases much more than, legionaries.

MANNING THE FRONTIERS

Auxiliaries were organized into smaller units than legions. The infantry was grouped into cohorts of 500 or 1,000 men and cavalry into similarly sized *alae* (literally, wings). These smaller sizes made it easier to move them around, although many resented being transferred, and at first auxiliary cohorts were stationed near their land of origin. A cohort of raw recruits from the Lower Rhine, whom Agricola had stationed in south-west Scotland, revolted at being displaced, murdering their officers and then sailing back to Germany. Shipwrecked and captured by pirates, they ended up as slaves back on the Rhineland. Some auxiliaries recruited from Britain served outside the island, presumably to ensure their loyalty. Auxiliary cohorts became ethnically mixed, with recruits from different areas, although they kept their original names.

The organization, discipline and training of auxiliaries mirrored that of the legions, although the command structure was simpler. Centurions were recruited from the ranks and spent their lives with the same unit. These cohorts were commanded by equestrian tribunes starting off their military careers, or else by decurions from the local aristocracy. The commander of an *ala* of cavalry was a *praefectus alae*, quite a senior post. Mixed cohorts, *cohortes equitatae*, containing about 80 per cent infantry and 20 per cent cavalry, were well suited to the low-intensity policing duties that mostly occupied them. Hadrian's Wall, typical of a fortified frontier, was manned entirely by auxiliaries. There were about 12–15,000 of them housed in forts ranging from tiny towers to big 1,000-men cohort camps such as Housesteads.

Military orders were always given in Latin and sacrifices to the emperor were

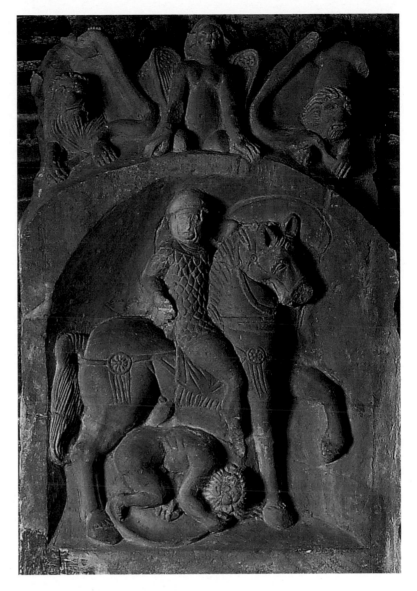

compulsory (hence overtly practising Christians were at first uncommon in the army). After completing 26 years of military service, auxiliaries were rewarded with full Roman citizenship, recorded on a bronze tablet called a *diploma*, and this was a status that their sons inherited. Occasionally an entire cohort received Roman citizenship for outstanding services. Auxiliaries helped spread the Roman way of life. After Caracalla's grant of nearly universal citizenship in AD212, the distinction between auxiliaries and legionaries soon grew blurred.

Above: Memorial to Longinus, a Roman cavalryman of the 1st cohort of Thracians, who died in AD49, aged 40 after 15 years service, and is buried at Colchester. Longinus came from Sardica (modern Sofia) and served a long way from home. The tombstone was found in 1928, but the face was only discovered in 1996.

PITCHING CAMP

Above: Stout stakes with sharpened points lined the palisades of the more heavily fortified camps.

Roman discipline and methodical planning were epitomized by the way that every evening, after marching all day, Roman soldiers constructed elaborate marching camps, always on a rectilinear plan, often for only one night. (These camps left few traces.) Such effort in all conditions required exceptional organization and discipline. Pyrrhus of Epirus realized how formidable his foes were after watching the Romans pitch these camps in 280BC. A century later, Polybius was equally impressed. Such was Roman conservatism that the practice continued throughout the Principate.

One of the best descriptions of the marching camp appears in Pseudo-Hyginus, written in the late 2nd century AD. Every afternoon, towards the end of the day's march, a tribune with centurions would scout ahead to choose the location for that night's camp, ideally a rectangle about 800 yd (731m) long of raised land, clear of trees and with running water nearby. They marked the *praetorium* (the commander's tent) and *principia* (headquarters) with a white flag and then planned the rest of the camp from this centre, using a *groma*, a surveying instrument. The two main streets, the *via principalis* and the *via praetoria*, running through the middle of the camp, were 60ft (18m) wide, lesser ones 50ft (15m) wide. With these streets defined, the lines of the ditch and rampart would be established by spears stuck into the earth at intervals.

Every legionary carried two to three *pila muralia*, palisade stakes about 7ft (2m) long with sharpened points. After they had dug their *fossa* – a trench normally about 3ft (1m) deep and 5ft (1.5m) wide (but deeper and wider if under immediate threat), they planted their stakes in the *agger*, the low rampart formed by the excavated earth, intertwining them so any intruders could

Right: A ditch, rampart and palisade separated the camp from the world outside. A similar arrangement was also used for some frontier installations, here, in a reconstruction of a section of the German frontier, with a watchtower.

not easily remove them. The camp's ramparts, although hard to penetrate and impossible for a unit in formation, did not form defensible barriers but marked it out from its surroundings. Just inside lay the *intervallum*, the space at least 100ft (30m) wide always left empty, to enable the legionaries to deploy within the camp and to bar enemy missiles reaching the tents. All camps were laid out in exactly the same pattern wherever they were. Legionaries camped on either side of the *via praetoria*, the cavalry facing the *via praetoria*, the other auxiliaries and non-Romans being put with the baggage train and cooking tents beyond the *via principalis*. Only the four entrances were more heavily fortified. The legionaries marched out of their allotted gates already armed and in formation.

The *contubernium*, the basic legionary tent, slept eight men. Made of leather, with front and back access, these tents could be rolled up into a sausage shape and carried by mules or ponies. Larger, more elaborate tents were provided for centurions and other officers. That of the general was large enough for administrative and military offices.

Keeping watch was vital. Every evening a guard from the *maniple* or century chosen for the first watch was taken to the tribune's tent and given a *tessera*, a small marked tablet. He surrendered this to a cavalry trooper who made his rounds at fixed hours, collecting the *tesserae* from each guard. If the sentry was absent or asleep, the trooper got witnesses to this. At dawn they reported to the tribune, who checked the *tesserae*. If one sentry had not returned his *tessera*, then he would be tried and cudgelled to death by his comrades, whose lives he had endangered by his inattention. As Polybius dryly commented, "the Roman army's night watches are most punctiliously kept".

Such repeated entrenchments might seem laborious, even wasteful, but they gave the Romans many advantages. By shutting out the possibly alien world and creating a model of Roman order, it helped give soldiers a good night's sleep, protected from surprise night attacks, and left them fresh to face the enemy next day. It also reduced the risk of disease through the properly dug latrines and, not least, impressed possibly hostile observers.

Above: Excavations at Caerleon, the legionary fortress in South Wales, have revealed the network of latrines and waterways at the barracks, a testimony to Roman concerns to keep their army healthy and fighting fit.

ROADS, CANALS AND BRIDGES

The Roman network of roads was both practical and impressive. The empire was united by 53,000 miles (85,000km) of roads from Scotland to Syria. Often built by legionaries, the roads were designed for troop movements, but civilians soon followed. Under many roads across Europe today lie Roman roads. It was not until the 19th century that Europe saw such a comprehensive road system.

The Greeks had built short stretches of paved roads and in the first Persian empire (*c*.539–331BC) the Royal Road linked the Aegean provinces to the capital Susa, 1,500 miles (2,400km) distant. But none approached the audacious scale of Rome's roads. The first road was the Via Appia, dubbed "Queen of Roads", built in 312BC by Claudius Appius the Censor. Running at first 164 miles (264km) from Rome to Capua to supply armies fighting the Samnites, it was later extended to Brindisi, another 234 miles (377km). It had the hallmarks of a classic Roman road: running as straight as practically possible, it crossed marshes on stone bridges and had a gravel top-dressing (replaced in 295BC by paved stones), good foundations and a proper camber to let water drain away, making it usable in all weathers. It was followed by many others, such as the Via Flaminia in 220BC, running across the Apennines to Rimini. Some roads had overt military intentions. The Via Aemilia, built in 189BC and running unblinkingly straight for 150 miles (240km) from Rimini to Piacenza through northern Italy, was intended to overawe Gallic natives and reassure Roman settlers. It did both. Rome's imperialist road-building did not stop with Italy. In 130BC the Via Egnatia was constructed across the top of Greece from Durazzo to Thessalonica and on to Byzantium (Istanbul). It remained a great imperial highway for 1,200 years.

All roads in the Republic, which helped unite and Romanize a very disparate Italy, were built by *publicani*, contractors working to orders from the state, who would inspect the roads on completion. (The same term applied to tax-farmers.) Under Augustus, the road-building programme became more systematic and ever more impressive. He restored many of Italy's roads and built new ones, some high across Alpine passes such as the St Bernard and Mt Genèvre passes, whose bridge and viaducts still impress travellers. In Gaul, important cities such as Lyons became hubs for a network of roads across the province – north to the Channel, north-east to the Rhine, south to Provence. London became the hub of a similar, if smaller, network, as did Antioch in Syria.

Above: The Romans built to last, as this still-surviving, if battered, road across the moors in northern Britain reveals.

Below: The 2nd-century AD road in Petra, the trading city in Jordan. Many roads survive intact in desert areas.

Left: The Roman bridge of Alcantara over the river Tagus in western Spain was built in the early 2nd century AD by Caius Julius Lacer for eleven local towns. It still stands and carries traffic today, which must make it one of the world's oldest functioning bridges.

Along the indeterminate desert frontiers of Arabia Petraea (Jordan), a road built under Trajan acted as a *limes*, a guarded frontier patrolled by cavalry. A similar pattern of patrol roads as *limes* can be seen both in North Africa and in Germany. Along the pan-imperial highways galloped the emperor's emissaries. They changed horses at the imperial posting stations, where they were also fed at the local population's expense. All roads were similarly maintained by corvées of forced labour until the end of the empire. Ironically, Rome's invaders benefited from its excellent paved roads.

CANALS AND BRIDGES

Even for Romans, it was always cheaper to move goods by water than by land. The Mediterranean, with its obligingly many inlets, combined with large rivers – the Rhône, Rhine, Danube, Nile, Tagus – provided a network of waterways. The Rhine and Danube were great military routes with fleets patrolling. The Danube fleet was divided in two, one flotilla operating downriver from the Iron Gates. Rivers were sometimes supplemented by short canals, although there was no canal-building programme. Caesar, like Nero, talked of digging a canal through the rocky mass of the Corinth isthmus, but this vision taxed Roman technology. Traces of Nero's attempt were found when the Corinth Canal was dug in the late 19th century. His builders had stopped when they hit bedrock.

Bridges were not beyond Roman technology and carried Rome's roads across gorges and rivers so successfully that some still stand. The great bridge over the Tagus at Alcantara in Spain was built by the combined efforts of eleven Lusitanian towns in Trajan's reign. Its builder, Caius Julius Lacer, proclaimed in an inscription that his bridge would last forever. In contrast, Caesar threw a timber bridge across the Rhine, then destroyed it, a feat meant to impress Roman audiences as much as Germans. But the most impressive Roman bridge was that built across the Danube at Drobeta by the architect Apollodorus for Trajan's Dacian campaign. With 20 massive stone piers, each 160ft (49m) high, driven into the fast-flowing river over 1000 yds (1000m) wide, and a timber superstructure, it was seen as one of the wonders of the world. Hadrian pulled it down on becoming emperor for reasons of prudence – he said barbarians might cross by it – or through jealousy of Trajan.

Above: Roman soldiers under Trajan (AD98–117) built a remarkable bridge across the Danube, pulled down soon after by Hadrian, and a supporting road along the Iron Gorge's steep cliffs.

FLEETS AND SHIPS

The Mediterranean, which the Romans called both *Mare Internum*, the inner sea, and *Mare Nostrum*, our sea, might appear to be at the centre of the Roman empire. In fact, however, the Romans were never great sailors. Unlike the Greeks, they only turned to controlling the seas when they were forced to. Rome's navy was always markedly inferior in status to its army and the might of the empire was built on land. But in order to conquer and then control their expanding empire, the Romans needed to gain sufficient mastery at sea, having, at the very least, modest permanent fleets – a fact Augustus finally accepted.

Like the other Mediterranean naval powers, the Roman navy consisted of galleys, which were rowed by poorer citizens or allies and very seldom by slaves. By the 3rd century BC these galleys were quinqueremes, with five rows of oars, or triremes, with three rows, arranged in a pattern that is still not entirely clear. Before the development of proper cannon in the 16th century, naval warfare – chiefly ramming and boarding – made galleys the only effective warships in the landlocked waters. However, their large crews of about 300 oarsmen, together with the lack of living space on board, meant that they normally had to be beached at night. Fleets therefore hugged the coasts whenever they could.

The Romans had no navy until their wars against Carthage began in 264BC. As Carthage ruled the western Mediterranean with an efficient navy of galleys mass-produced in its superb double harbours, Rome realized it must build a fleet of its own to fight it. According to Polybius, the Romans modelled their galleys on a stranded Carthaginian ship, quickly building 100 quinqueremes and meanwhile training their oarsmen on tiered benches on land. But their inexperience led initially to defeat, even in harbour. Accepting that they could not match Punic seamanship,

the Romans ingeniously devised the *corvus*, the raven, a boarding ramp fitted with a heavy spike which swivelled on a pole set on the ship's prow. This ramp, about 40ft (12m) long and 4ft (1.2m) wide, was swung over the deck of the enemy ship and dropped on to it, locking the two galleys together. Roman marines – 120 of them to a galley – then swarmed across to overwhelm the Carthaginians.

This tactic won several victories over the startled Carthaginians, beginning with Mylae in 260BC and continuing at Ecnomus in 256BC, where each side mustered over 300 ships according to Polybius. The Romans then grew over-confident, sending huge invasion fleets to Africa to support Regulus' invasion, most of which were sunk in storms. The *corvus* may have made the galleys – always fragile vessels – top-heavy, and the Romans never used it again after finally defeating the Carthaginians in 241BC.

Under the terms of the subsequent treaty Carthage gave up most of her navy, and during the Second Punic War (218–201BC) her ships tried to avoid the now indisputably superior Romans, as did the Macedonian ships. Philip V's 100-strong fleet sailed into the Adriatic in 216BC but fled at the sight of only ten Roman quinqueremes. From the mid-2nd century BC the Romans let their fleet decay, as there seemed to be no naval rivals left. They relied instead on Greek ships to transport their troops, failing to realize the importance of the Rhodian fleet in maintaining freedom of the sea. Rhodes' navy declined after the opening of Delos as a free port in 168BC, and pirates took advantage of this, raiding right up to Ostia and capturing two praetors in 68BC. Pompey was appointed emergency commander under the *Lex Gabinia* to quash them, with a fleet of 200 galleys, which were mostly supplied by Greek cities. With this fleet he swept the seas clean, but in the subsequent civil wars

Below: This Roman pharos *(lighthouse) lies within the ruins of medieval Dover Castle in England. It was one of numerous lighthouses built along the coasts of the empire.*

(49–30BC) fleets multiplied. Sextus Pompeius had a large fleet with which he cut Rome's grain supply until defeated with the aid of Antony's ships at Naulochus in 36BC. The final battle in the civil wars was the naval contest at Actium, in which Antony and Cleopatra's Roman-Egyptian fleet was cornered and defeated by Agrippa, Octavian's general, who traditionally used smaller Liburnian galleys against Antony's quinqueremes.

THE IMPERIAL NAVY

Augustus disbanded most of the huge fleets that victory brought him – some 700 ships – but, needing to safeguard Rome's grain imports, he did not close down the navy. Instead, he set up three small fleets at Misenum in the Bay of Naples, at Ravenna and at Fréjus, using the mainly Greek ships and crews he already had as their core. The fleet at Fréjus shrank to a mere flotilla. There were also river fleets on the Rhine, Danube and Nile and a small fleet on the Black Sea. Later a fleet, the *classis britannica*, was created to patrol the English Channel and southern North Sea. From the mid-3rd century AD this British fleet was used chiefly against the Saxon pirates who were becoming increasingly common. Commanded by prefects under imperial orders, the navy offered a similar career to the army's auxiliaries. After 26 years, sailors received Roman citizenship at the end of their service.

Ships were commanded by *trierarchs*, squadrons by *navarchs*, both names indicating the Greek origins of the fleet.

For a long period, the whole of the Mediterranean was kept peaceful by these measures, essential for the empire's well-being. If it was sometimes swifter to move troops by sea than by land, it was almost always cheaper to transport goods by ship. The 3rd-century AD crisis revealed that these fleets had become inadequate, however, as Goths and other barbarians seized shipping and turned pirate, and they were expanded. Later, the Byzantine empire relied heavily on its navy, but the Byzantine empire was predominantly Greek, and the Greeks always retained a strong maritime tradition.

Above: Navies in the ancient world consisted of galleys such as these biremes. *They had huge crews of up to 300 oarsmen (not usually slaves in either Greece or Rome), essential to propel the ships to ram and board opponents.*

Below: The main port of Rome at Portus, north of Ostia, with the artificial harbours built by Claudius (right) and Trajan (left) to help the import of grain. The canal linked the port with the Tiber, while the pharos *guided shipping into port.*

CHAPTER IX

ARMS AND THE MEN

The Roman army was one of the most effective fighting forces in history, but its weapons were not normally superior to those of its enemies. Most Roman weaponry was simple: a short sword, a javelin, a coat of mail or armour plates, greaves (leg armour), and a rectangular or oval shield. Against often more numerous northern barbarians, the Romans did have some technical advantages: their armour was better, their catapults alarmingly formidable. All these, however, were secondary to Roman discipline and courage. How the Romans used their weapons was what counted; and it was their *virtus*, their courage and ability, that Romans celebrated, not their technological prowess. When necessary, they made other people's weapons, be they catapults, slings or armour, part of their own standard equipment. This Roman adaptability, coupled with ruthless determination and refusal to surrender, were Rome's real secret weapons.

In only two spheres were the Romans true innovators: the maniple and the cohort, tactical formations within the legion that helped them beat Hannibal and the Greeks, and the massive fortifications of the later empire. These constituted the most formidable walls yet seen anywhere in the world. The proof of their effectiveness is shown by the thousand-year survival of Constantinople, whose walls enabled the new Rome to live on when the old Rome fell.

Left: The Romans made good use of catapults and other artillery in siege warfare. Bi-circumvallating the defenders was a popular way of preventing escape and resupply.

ARMOUR

Roman armour in the early Republic (5th century BC) was influenced by Rome's neighbours, the Etruscans, who in turn emulated the Greeks. Etruscans adopted the Greek hoplite method of fighting – heavily armoured spearmen grouped in *phalanxes* – and their armour reflected this. It consisted of greaves (shin armour), a bronze cuirass (breastplate) and a helmet with long cheek guards and high crests. However, as the Romans evolved their own uniquely flexible system of *maniples* and legions after 400BC, they began to develop their own lighter armour, which varied according to the wealth of the Roman concerned, for at that time and for long after, each soldier armed and armoured himself.

The first two lines of heavy infantry in each *maniple* – the *hastati* and *principes* – wore a modest-sized square breastplate called a *pectorale* (breast guard) and one greave for the left leg, the one that was thrust out when fighting. Wealthier legionaries, especially those of the *triarii*, sometimes wore mail shirts, but these could be very heavy, weighing over 30lb (14kg). After the Roman defeat at Lake Trasimene in 218BC, some soldiers who tried to escape by swimming were drowned by the weight of their armour. The legionaries all wore bronze Montefortino-type helmets (named after the place where some were found). These had two tall, feathered plumes 2ft (60cm) high sticking out of them to make the soldiers look taller, long cheek guards and a double chin strap. For defence, the legionaries depended on their long, semi-cylindrical body shields. These were about 4ft (1.2m) long and about 2ft (60cm) wide. Reconstructions show that these shields weighed at least 22lb (10kg). They were made of two sheets of wood glued together, covered with canvas and calf skin. The shields could also be used as weapons to knock the enemy over. The *veles*, light infantry recruited from the poorer citizens, had no armour and so they wore animal skins over their helmets to help their officers recognize them.

From the time of the late Republic (100BC), after Marius' reforms, legionaries were far more uniformly equipped and armoured. The ordinary legionaries wore long mail coats and Montefortino-style helmets, but with horsehair plumes that hung down, and carried long oval shields very similar to the earlier shields. Officers (centurions and tribunes) often wore "muscled" – modelled to the body – cuirasses with greaves over leather tunics, ribbons of rank around their waists – a Greek idea – and elaborate Italo-Corinthian helmets. Some of the armour of this period was of poor quality, probably reflecting the massive demands made on armourers by the fast-growing armies of the civil wars.

By the early 1st century AD, with the Principate firmly established, workshops were set up to mass-produce the body armour the legionaries needed. The standard helmet evolved from the jockey type, which recalled a reversed jockey's cap in the late Republic, to the "Imperial Gallic helmet". Partly inspired by Gallic examples, the latter had an enlarged neck guard and long cheek guards, with a reinforcing strip across the front of the cap to protect the face from a downward cut. With added ear guards, this became the standard Roman infantry helmet over the next two centuries. It was usually made of iron, which was always cheaper than bronze, if less durable. Such a helmet gave a high degree of protection while allowing soldiers to hear and see clearly.

Equally flexible and protective was the *lorica segmentata*, the name given to a type of banded armour developed in the 1st century AD, the first full example of which was excavated at Corbridge. This had bands of soft untempered iron plates forming a corselet, or cuirass, which was buckled on. Such armour was brilliant at

*Above: The higher grades of cavalry (*alae*) wore elaborate helmets to mark their rank. This is a 3rd-century AD cavalry helmet.*

Below: The long, curved shield was standard issue for legionaries in the Principate from the 1st century AD.

ARMOURED HORSEMEN

Cavalry in the Principate came in many forms. Light Numidian horsemen had no armour or saddles, but, at the other extreme, some cavalry would qualify as "heavy" by most standards. Although these heavy horsemen did not have stirrups, they had saddles with four pommels (two of which were at the back corners), which gave them some support when mounted. They wore helmets that covered their ears, with extended cheek and neck guards to protect against sword slashes – lances were generally seldom used. Some wore *lorica hamata*, mail coats, some modest-scale armour weighing perhaps 20lb (9kg). The higher grades of cavalry (*alae*) had elaborate helmets and shields, but their horses wore no armour at all.

absorbing blows and not too heavy – it weighed about 20lb (9kg). This made it lighter than the cheaper, more easily maintained, main alternative, the *lorica hamata*, a mail coat worn by some legionaries and by the auxiliary infantry. The *lorica hamata* was heavy, weighing over 30lb (14kg). In the 1st century AD, the oval shield was replaced by a rectangular curved shield, made of three layers of thin strips of wood, encased in leather and covered with a linen layer, its rim reinforced with bronze. The handgrip in its centre was reinforced by an iron or bronze boss. Auxiliaries normally had a simpler version of the Imperial Gallic helmet and a flat oval shield.

ARMOUR IN THE LATER EMPIRE

The types of armour in the later empire reflect the increasing divergence between the mobile *comitatenses* and elite *Palatini* – and the lowly *limitanei* (frontier guard). The Romans encountered real heavy cavalry, the *cataphracti*, around AD100 when Sarmatian riders appeared on the Danube. They were soon employed as auxiliaries, and in the 3rd century AD the Romans began to imitate them. The typical *cataphract* wore mail weighing at least 60lb (27kg), covering him from hooded head to knee; his horse also wore mail armour. An even more heavily armoured cavalryman wore the *lorica squamata*, scale armour, according to graffiti from Dura-Europus. Such armour looked magnificent when well polished, but must have been uncomfortably hot – *clibanarius* means "oven man". The infantry, meanwhile, demoted from their primary battle-fighting role, wore crude iron *intercisa* helmets and relatively little armour. Apparently this was partly a matter of choice – for they now found it too heavy to march or drill in armour – but it made them less effective.

Above: By the 1st century AD, most legionaries wore a type of armour called the lorica segimentata. *This, with banded soft iron plates, was laced at the back and gave excellent protection, but it was expensive.*

Above: Sword and dagger

ARMS: SWORDS, DAGGERS, BOWS, *PILA* AND SLINGS

The Roman soldiers of the early Republic (509–*c*.350BC) were armed in the prevailing Greco-Etruscan style as hoplites – heavy spearmen with long pikes and swords and small round shields. However, by the 4th century BC the new legions of maniples, the army's smallest fighting units, who were starting to fight in the *quincunx*, or chequerboard pattern, required quite different types of arms.

The basic weapon the Roman legionary now acquired, and which he was to use to create the Roman empire, was the *gladius hispaniensis*, the "Spanish sword". This may have been inspired by Spanish examples, but it was probably being used before Rome had any direct experience of Spain. This sword, which had a blade less than 3ft (1m) long, was wickedly sharp and well suited to both cutting and thrusting. Its long, tapering point of highly tempered steel meant that it could pierce most opponents' armour. Roman swordsmanship was generally much better than that of their adversaries, but the legionaries were also helped by having swords of a quality that only chieftains could afford among most of their enemies.

The *gladius* evolved from the Mainz-type *gladius* to the slightly longer Pompeii type, which could cut as well as thrust. (These swords are named after the places where examples were found.) Roman cavalry, for a long time very secondary in importance, used a longer sword, the *spatha*, which was about 3ft (1m) in length. In the later empire, this longer sword was adopted by most Roman infantrymen, but by then infantry had become very inferior to cavalry. Legionaries wore their swords on their right, probably because their heavy shields on their left would have made it awkward to draw after hurling their other principal weapon. In contrast, centurions, wore their swords on the left, possibly because they carried their shields only some of the time.

Almost equally important to the legionary of Rome's golden age of military might was the *pilum*, the javelin or throwing spear. Each legionary in the first two rows of the earlier legions, the *hastati* and the *principes*, carried two *pila*, which came in two thicknesses according to Polybius. The *pilum* had a thin wooden shaft about 4ft (1.2m) long, with a pyramid-shaped barbed iron head on top of a thin iron neck. When thrown,

Left: A slinger in the Dacian wars, one of the many auxiliary soldiers.

this could often go right through an enemy's shield, but if it did not, the point would stick in the shield and the neck bend, so making the shield useless. An enemy would then have to throw it away, leaving himself exposed to the merciless cutting thrusts of the legionary. (Marius later revised the *pilum* by making it bend even more effectively. It is possible that he was also responsible for adding the weights halfway down the *pilum*'s shaft.)

A *pilum*'s absolute maximum range was about 100ft (30m), although its effective range was only half that. Roman troops painfully acquired the discipline required to wait until the enemy was that close before discharging a devastating volley. The *triarii* were armed with long spears that could be used as pikes until Marius' reforms, when all legionaries received the same equipment. Although primarily intended for throwing, the *pilum* could also be used as a stationary weapon to repel cavalry, when the first row would kneel, bracing the butts of their *pila* on the ground so that they formed a spiked barrier. Behind them, other rows would launch their *pila* at the cavalry, whose horses would not cross such a seemingly solid barrier. Legionaries also had the *pugio*, a dagger about 8in (20cm) long, which was worn on the left hip, but this seems to have been given up in the Principate. Such simple but devastating weapons, when used in the right hands, made the Roman legionary appear almost invincible.

THE AUXILIARIES' WEAPONS

Auxiliary infantrymen of the Principate used much the same weapons as the legionaries, but the other, more specialized, types of auxiliary obviously had different kinds of weapons. Slingers, traditionally recruited from the Balearic islands, used simple slings, as did the club men, both being skirmishing light troops, but they were not significant parts of the army. However, the archers whom Rome employed, at first from Crete but later from many sources including Syria, were at times vital. They normally had composite bows, made of bone and sinew as well as wood, which fired arrows further than simple wooden bows.

The *alae* (literally, wings) of auxiliary cavalry also gained increasing importance. Although they often charged with spears or lances, their impact was small compared to later cavalry charges owing to their lack of stirrups, for which the "horns" of their saddles only partly compensated. This must have hampered the effectiveness of the heavily armoured *cataphracts*. The stirrup is first mentioned only in the *Strategikon*, a military manual written by the East Roman (Byzantine) emperor Maurice (AD582–602). In the later empire, the *limitanei* carried several *mattiobarbului*, lead-weighted darts, which they kept inside their shields, instead of the *pilum*. These smaller missiles would have been particularly useful when defending forts, which was now the chief duty of *limitanei*.

Above: This detail from the Roman triumphal arch in Orange, southern France, shows hand-to-hand fighting with the gladius.

Below: Roman legionaries used many varieties of sword, all based on the gladius hispaniensis, or Spanish stabbing sword. These two examples date from the 1st century AD, near the zenith of Roman power.

ARTILLERY

Above: The onager *(wild ass) was a primitive but highly effective catapult, capable of lobbing large weights surprising distances. It was used mostly in sieges and for defending fortresses, being too immobile for battlefield use.*

Below: This complex late Roman catapult, a ballista fulminalis, *could shoot its bolt or spear up to 300yd (275m). While slow, such catapults could be devastating, terrifying barbarians.*

In the earlier Republic, Rome's armies had little in the way of artillery or catapults. In the epic siege of Veii (406–396BC), the formidably well-fortified Etruscan city, for example, they relied chiefly on surprise to capture the city, eventually digging a tunnel under the walls and crawling up an irrigation channel by night. But in their expansion across the Mediterranean after 264BC, the Romans came across the varied catapults developed by the Greeks (especially by Philip II of Macedon) and learnt how to employ such "artillery", the only kind there was before gunpowder.

The Romans' lack of development in such armaments mirrored the general lack of technological progress in civilian life. Compared to medieval Europe, or even to the Greeks, Roman civilization made few technological innovations. Nonetheless, the Romans adopted earlier discoveries, often to good effect. After the disaster at the Battle of Adrianople in AD378, for example, the Goths were dissuaded from further attacks on the walls of Adrianople by a single bolt fired from a Roman scorpion-type catapult.

WEAPONS OF BOMBARDMENT

There were two basic types of artillery, according to Vitruvius, who was writing in the 1st century BC. The first was the catapult type, among which was the typical *catapulta*, a two-armed torsion catapult firing either bolts or stones. Similar was the *scorpio*, a light, bolt-shooting *ballista*. Both operated on the crossbow principle, with a pair of vertical coil chambers at the front; the bow was drawn back by a windlass and held by a rack and pinion. When the bow was released, the bolt shot along a groove and out through an opening in the front in a flat trajectory. These stationary catapults could fire iron bolts up to 300yd (275m) with some accuracy. In AD363 during the Persian campaign, an officer standing next to Julian was killed by a bolt aimed at the emperor. The Persians used much the same weapons as the Romans.

The *carroballista* was a *scorpio* mounted on a mule-drawn cart; it could be used in the field to fire bolts with large heads up to 1ft (30cm) long, which made a formidable arrow. According to Vegetius – who, writing around AD400, may not be completely accurate – each century of the traditional Roman army had a *carroballista*. Used on the flanks of the legion, they fired barrages over the heads of the legionaries.

The other, much heavier, type of catapult was nicknamed the *onager* (wild ass) because of its kick. This was a slower-firing, lower-tension catapult, based on the principles of a sling rather than a crossbow, but one capable of lobbing huge stones at walls or troops. Josephus records that at the Siege of Jerusalem in AD70, the Tenth Legion had machines that could hurl stones weighing a *talent* (55lb/25kg) about 400yd (360m). Battle stones found at British forts, such as High Rochester, north of Hadrian's Wall, weigh over 100lb (45kg).

THE SECRET WEAPONS THAT ROME IGNORED

As Romans in the 4th century AD knew too well, the empire faced unremitting threats from without and ever-growing manpower shortages within. Although most Roman armies remained better equipped than their barbarian opponents, this did not make up for their lack of numbers. Attempts to cope with the shortage of Roman recruits by recruiting barbarian *foederati* were not only inherently risky but were also leading to the de-Romanization of the army itself. Vegetius, the best-known military writer of the period, advocated a return to the stringent discipline of earlier years, which had underlain Roman triumphs down the centuries, without success.

However, the anonymous writer of *De Rebus Bellicis* (About Wars), who probably lived in the middle of the 4th century AD, had different and more ingenious ideas. He proposed what were in effect a variety of super-weapons with which the Romans might make up for their lack of numbers and their decline in fighting spirit. One such weapon that he proposed was a horse-drawn, arrow-firing catapult that could be swivelled around completely on a four-wheeled cart, and which could be mechanically elevated or lowered to control the trajectory of fire. Another super-weapon he proposed was a mobile armoured shield beneath which attackers could approach a wall – a development of the *testudo*, tortoise formation, of locked shields. He also envisaged a variety of armoured chariots, one with scythed wheels – almost looking back to the scythed chariots once used by Celts and Persians – pulled by armoured horses. At sea, where there was a shortage of oarsmen for the galleys, he cleverly thought of using ox-power to turn a capstan on deck. Through a series of cogs and gears this would have powered two paddle-wheels, one on each side of his novel warship, which he called a *liburna*. Whether or not his schemes, at times anticipating more recent war machines, were at all practical given the technology and resources of the time, nothing came of them.

Only one much later invention really worked: that of *Greek fire*, which was a flame-thrower, using the siphon principles to project a form of liquid fire, highly effective against ships and siege engines. This invention traditionally helped to save Constantinople from Arab attacks at the end of the 7th century AD.

Above: Roman legionaries loading an onager-*type catapult at the siege of Alesia in Gaul in 52* BC, *one of the epic Roman sieges. These cumbersome stone-throwing catapults were normally only used in sieges, or later for defending fortresses.*

Below: Roman legionaries, played by re-enactors, loading a carroballista-*type catapult. A bolt-firing machine on the same principles as the crossbow, this was mobile enough to be used in battle, but its chief role was for attacking or defending forts.*

Special reinforced platforms were built for firing such machines from within forts in the later empire. Technically, the *onager* was a relatively crude machine: its arm was pulled back, tightening the coiled ropes that propelled it, and a sling at the end of its arm was filled with a stone and then released, with a tremendous kick, to be stopped by a padded beam. According to Vegetius, perhaps overstating ancient strengths, each legion had ten *onagri*, one for each cohort, drawn on carriages by oxen. Used *en masse* they were highly effective in siege warfare, either for offence or defence, but they were too immobile to be of much use on the battlefield, unlike the *carroballista*.

SIEGE WARFARE

Above: This detail from Trajan's Column in Rome shows legionaries assaulting walls during the wars in Dacia, a formidably well-defended kingdom.

Below: Legionaries building double wooden walls to bi-circumvallate Alesia, to prevent Gaulish armies from relieving the besieged inside.

The Romans brought to siege-craft their customary determination and aggression. Our word siege comes from the French *siège*, sitting out. In contrast, the Roman word *oppugnatio* means assault, attacking a city relentlessly. In contrast to elaborate Greek siege machinery, the Romans preferred simpler methods. These included bi-circumvallation, building double walls to stop relief getting in. They were also masters of battering rams.

When the Romans attacked the large Greek city of Agrigento (Acragas) in Sicily in 262BC, they built a line of forts around the city, connected these by walls with watchtowers and starved the city into surrender. If an enemy army was in the field, they built a second wall facing outward. They first used bi-circumvallation besieging Lilybaeum in the First Punic War. The greatest bi-circumvallation was at Alesia in 52BC, where Caesar bottled up Vercingetorix and defied a relief Gaulish army.

At ports such as Lilybaeum in Sicily, where complete enclosure was impossible, the Romans tried to close in the harbour with earth, although at Lilybaeum this was washed away by the sea and they captured the city by assault. Syracuse, changing sides after Hannibal's victory at Cannae, presented Rome with its biggest challenge in scientific siege warfare in 213BC. Marcellus, the Roman commander, controlled the sea, but Syracuse harbour was heavily fortified. The Romans made a simultaneous attack by land and sea, using 50 galleys filled with archers, slingers and javelineers. Eight galleys were tied together in pairs and on each a wide ladder was raised. This was the same height as the walls. But the scientist Archimedes, masterminding Syracusan defences, arranged catapults to fire at fixed ranges so that the Romans faced devastating fire. Marcellus tried a night attack to avoid this, but Archimedes designed huge cranes that swung out

from behind the walls and dropped stones on the Roman galleys. Others lowered giant grappling hooks, which pulled the ships up and released them to capsize. Finally the Romans captured Syracuse by stealth. Archimedes was killed in the sack of the city.

Roman tenacity caused many cities to capitulate before the siege started. A story relates how a Roman commander, about to besiege a city, was told by its envoys that they had enough food for ten years. The Roman replied that in that case he would capture the city in the eleventh year. The city surrendered. If it did not surrender, a city faced obliteration. According to the current rules of warfare, once the head of a battering ram touched the enemy's walls or gate, no mercy could be expected and Romans never gave it. From Cartagena in 209BC to Jerusalem in AD70, the Romans systematically killed every living thing in the cities they captured – even dogs – apart from attractive women and children, whom they raped and sold into slavery. Such exemplary terror generally worked. However, Roman commanders preferred to starve a city into submission, because its booty became theirs, whereas in an assault the troops were permitted to sack a city and take what they could.

BATTERING RAMS

The Romans excelled at battering rams, the most basic siege tool. The name comes from its head, a massive iron hammer in the shape of a ram's head. It was fixed to a huge beam in a very strong shed, often on wheels, with a steep-pitched roof covered in hides from animals recently butchered so that their wet skins would repel any fire arrows. Vitruvius and Vegetius describe similar sheds of varying sizes, sometimes called *testudo arietaria*, after the tortoise. This name was also given to formations of men carrying linked shields above their heads. High towers of timber could be rolled forward to protect them by shooting arrows and javelins. If effective against

Mesopotamian mud and Mediterranean stone walls, metal rams were of little use against the timber and turf ramparts of north Europe. Caesar describes a *murus Gallicus* (Gallic wall), stone-faced but its centre filled with soil. Laced with timbers, it was impervious to normal rams. Usually other forms of assault had to be found.

The other great siege tactic was mining a wall. A mine would be dug under a city wall, supported by wooden props that, when ignited, caused the tunnel and the wall above it to collapse. As defenders could hear the tunnellers, they often made counter-mines, causing the attackers' tunnel to collapse. The besieged also mined under the bulky towers of the attackers, causing them to keel over. On the eastern front, especially when the Sassanids replaced the Parthians, there were long and elaborate sieges, as at Dura-Europus in *c*.AD256 and at Amida in AD359. In both cases, these fortified Roman cities fell to the Persians only after long, expensive sieges.

Above: A Renaissance view of a triumph of Julius Caesar shows the spoils and varied war engines used in his conquest of Gaul, including the siege of Alesia in 52BC.

Below: A medieval drawing of a Roman four-wheeled horse-drawn carroballista, *the mobile type of catapult used in battle as well as siege warfare.*

TRIUMPHS AND OVATIONS

On returning to Rome after defeating a (foreign) enemy, a general of the Republic could expect to be awarded the highest accolade, a triumph. According to legend, this celebration dated back to the birth of Rome and Romulus' defeat of Acron, king of the Ceninenses. Wearing a laurel wreath, Romulus led his men singing in triumphant procession to thank Jupiter. The ceremony was influenced by the Etruscans, who added a chariot and other details, including the ceremonial clothes and red-painted face of the *triumphator*, the triumphant general. As the empire grew, the ceremony also grew in splendour. It continued far into the Principate, but by then only members of the imperial family received a full triumph.

The *triumphator* was clad in the *toga picta*, a purple toga edged with gold, over a purple tunic and gilded shoes. He carried an ivory sceptre topped by an eagle, the bird of Jupiter, and an olive branch while wearing a laurel wreath, on his solemn procession to Jupiter's temple to give thanks for his victory. The procession started in the Campus Martius (field of Mars) just outside the *pomerium*, the sacred boundary. At its head were magistrates and senators; next came the horn-blowers, heading a long train of bearers laden with booty. They were followed by models or paintings of captured cities or battles won. Next came priests leading the white sacrificial oxen with gilded horns, with children carrying the *paterae*, golden saucers to catch the oxen's blood. Then came the captives in chains. The *triumphator* brought up the rear in a horse-drawn chariot, with his children beside him and surrounded by crowds of *ludiones*, Etruscan-style dancers. To balance all this, a slave standing behind the *triumphator* whispered in his ear, "Remember, you are mortal." Behind the general came any citizens whom he had

Below: Caesar's final triumph, as depicted in this Renaissance painting. His many victories were celebrated with unparalleled magnificence and splendour.

TRIUMPHAL ARCHES

Among the most distinctive features of the Roman empire were the triumphal arches built to proclaim its victories. The most famous arches are in Rome itself. The Arch of Titus, dedicated in AD81, is among the best preserved; it graphically commemorates Titus' capture of Jerusalem in AD70, and shows the seven-branched candlestick taken from the Temple. Arches, of which many survive, were erected right across the empire, from Jordan to Britain. A vast arch almost 100ft (30m) high and square was erected at Richborough, the chief port of entry to Britain, probably during the AD90s to celebrate Emperor Domitian's supposed conquest of the north of the island. Cased in Cararra marble with gilded bronze statues, it did not long survive Domitian's assassination in AD96.

Above: This Arch of Trajan dominates the ruins of the colony for veterans the emperor founded at Timgad in Africa.

In the Principate, triumphs were reserved for the emperor, and generals had to be content with an *ovatio*, an ovation, in which they sacrificed on the Alban hill and entered Rome on a horse the next day. With this came the grant of *insignia triumphalia*, triumphal ornaments, the right to wear triumphal uniform and a laurel wreath at official ceremonies and have a statue among former triumphators. From Trajan's reign on, all consuls seem to have had the right to such triumphal dress, which must soon have devalued it.

freed from captivity, and last of all his victorious soldiers, wearing olive wreaths and singing verses that alternately honoured and mocked their general.

The procession entered by the Forum Boarium (cattle market) and wound through the Circus Maximus, round the Palatine Hill and up the Sacred Way to the Forum, before ascending the Capitoline Hill. Here the leading captives were taken away and sacrificed with the oxen. However, after Aemilius Paullus' triumph in 167BC, they were normally spared if they had fought bravely. Only those who had broken their word to Rome, like Jugurtha the Numidian king and Vercingetorix the Gallic leader, were executed. Caratacus, the British prince, and Zenobia, Queen of Palmyra, were both spared to live in comfortable obscurity. Cleopatra, however, chose suicide over such ignominy.

Under the Republic, triumphs became more splendid, each successful general proclaiming his – and his family's – glory ever more grandly, despite the efforts of senators to curtail it. Their monuments, statues and, from the mid-3rd century BC, temples all along the triumphal route formed a permanent memorial to their achievements, beautifying the city.

Below: Wearing a special painted toga and clutching a golden sceptre, the triumphant general Scipio Africanus, who had beaten Hannibal, is escorted through the streets of Rome to the Capitoline Hill, where captives were traditionally sacrificed.

PERMANENT FORTIFICATIONS

Above: Reconstruction of a tower and the walls of the legionary camp at Xanten on the Rhine in Germany. This was originally a two-legion camp. The tower, like most built in the Principate, has a wide gate and was not designed for prolonged defence.

By AD150 Rome had surrounded its empire with permanent defences in stone, wood and turf, some still impressive today. But these walls and ramparts were not intended as impregnable defences. Instead, they were built as bases from which troops would march out to fight. Even the grandest wall, Hadrian's Wall across northern England, was intended not as an impermeable barrier but to control movements across the frontier.

The Servian Wall around Rome built in the 370s BC was massive – 10ft (3m) wide and 30ft (9m) high – enough to defy even Hannibal. But after this war, Rome no longer needed such domestic defences, as its frontiers became ever more distant. When the Rhine and Danube became Rome's *de facto* northern Continental frontiers after Augustus, Roman camps along them developed into permanent stone-built fortresses.

These fortresses were generally built on flat ground for convenience, rather than for defence. Each followed a rectilinear plan derived from marching camps. The fortress of the Sixteenth Legion at Neuss on the Lower Rhine is typical: a rectangle 500 by 700yd (450 by 650m) with walls 15ft (4.5m) high and a surrounding ditch. The walls were intended to protect only against surprise attacks. The *principia*, or legionary headquarters, where legionary records and standards were kept, faced the legate's house, the *praetorium*, an imposing edifice built around a courtyard, often with hypocaust underfloor heating in northern Europe. Barrack blocks, where the legionaries slept eight to a room, lined the perimeter, with a large gap between them and the walls to allow troops to form up. With workshops, baths, granaries and a hospital, the legionary camp was almost self-sufficient. The auxiliaries' cohorts had similar, if smaller, forts.

Although still committed to taking the offensive, the Romans came to build extensive lines to control their frontiers. The gap between the upper Rhine and the Danube was covered by the advance under the Flavians and Trajan to a line along the Taunus Mountains and River Neckar, then south-east to the Danube near Regensburg. Shortening the frontier, this was defended not by a stone wall but by timber, later stone, towers. These were connected by *limes*, patrolled frontiers,

Right: Another view of the partially reconstructed tower and walls at Xanten on the Rhine. This shows how towers under the Principate did not protrude and how the walls did not have deep moats in front, being designed merely to break the impact of attack.

Right: The ruins of Aquinicum, a legionary fortress near Budapest on the Danube, overlooked by a modern white building.

defined as much as defended by a narrow wooden palisade, with forts for auxiliary cohorts every few miles. There were almost 100 camps, connected by 1,500 towers, along this new 310-mile (500km) frontier. They signalled to each other using heliographs (sun signals), smoke or fires. Guarding the Rhine from Bonn to the North Sea, forts lined the west bank, with watchtowers between. A similar chain ran down the Danube to the Black Sea, the river serving instead of a palisade.

In North Africa, where the threat came from fast-moving Berber raiders, the long desert frontier was defended by other *limes*. Low, continuous walls, and a series of *fossata*, deep, flat-bottomed ditches or trenches, formed unmanned but continuous barriers inland from the wheat and olive lands of Rome's bread-basket. Although raiding Berbers could cross walls by breaking them down, they were slowed down and forced to return laden with booty through the same gap. There, waiting Roman patrols from nearby forts could cut them off. These barriers made it difficult for the Berbers to raid at will. Such crossing places corresponded to recognized transhumance routes (used by seasonally migrating flocks of sheep) and provided patrolled crossing points to collect customs dues.

HADRIAN'S WALL

The most imposing and monumental of Roman fortifications is Hadrian's Wall. Hadrian ordered its construction during his visit to Britain in AD122, although his original plan was not fully implemented. Running 76 miles (120km) between the Tyne and Solway, the wall was first built partly in turf and timber, only the eastern 45 miles (73km) being built of stone from the beginning. The wall was about 18ft (5.5m) high and 6–8ft (1.9–2.4m) wide, with a ditch that was about 25ft (7.6m) wide and about 10ft (3m) deep,

with another ditch, the *vallum*, behind. This second ditch was to keep civilians out of the military zone and to channel traffic to customs points. Every Roman mile there was a milecastle, with gates opening to the north flank and two turrets between. These were usually tiny – about 14sq ft (1.3sq m) inside – but the milecastles had garrisons of a century. About 15,000 auxiliaries were deployed along or around the wall. Most were not strung out along it but concentrated in camps for 500 or 1,000 men, such as Housesteads, from which they issued forth to deal with intruders. The wall was not a hermetic frontier but controlled traffic and impressed natives. Forts like High Rochester, 30 miles (48km) north, provided advance posts, while strong reinforcements could be summoned from the legionary fortress at York to the south.

Below: The fort at Vindolanda (Bardon Mill) lies south of Hadrian's Wall in Northumberland, with part of the actual wall reconstructed.

Above: Sited on the right (hostile) bank of the Rhine, the massive fortress of Deutz was built by Constantine I in AD310. Huge circular towers and walls 65ft (20m) high were designed to overawe the barbarians as well as repel their actual attacks.

Below: Pevensey Castle on the south coast of England was one of a string of the massive fortresses on what became known as the Saxon Shore, built to provide secure bases for the fleets patrolling against invading Saxon pirates.

GREAT FORTS OF THE LATER EMPIRE

Changes in the Roman army in the later 3rd and early 4th century AD turned it from a fundamentally offensive force to a predominantly defensive one. They also changed its approach to fortification. The Romans finally began to build fortresses that, with their huge towers and complex gatehouses, looked like real castles, rather than barracks surrounded by quite thin walls. Like real castles also, these forts came to control important passes and crossings and were built on easily defended sites. From the mid-4th century AD, they also grew increasingly cramped inside, in stark contrast to the spacious bases of the Principate. Such castles, cripplingly expensive to build, anticipate those of the Middle Ages.

In the AD260s, Gallienus had begun to reorganize the army and Aurelian had given Rome its new wall in AD272–5, but it was only under Diocletian (AD284–305) that the radical shift to a new type of fort-building fully emerged. It can be seen right across the empire – even in parts not controlled by Diocletian, such as Britain, where the admiral of the *classis britannica*, Carausius, had made himself independent in AD286 – so it clearly represented a widespread trend.

THE NEW FORTRESSES

Typically these new fortresses had several common features: they had fewer entrances (often only one) guarded by a complex gatehouse that sometimes had a portcullis. They had massive projecting towers that allowed the archers, or soldiers operating the catapults now sometimes mounted on them, to cover the approaches. Their walls were much thicker and higher than those of earlier forts, sometimes up to 65ft (18m) high and 15ft (4.6m) thick. Finally, their ditches were wider and deeper and their berms (the strip between ditch and wall) wider. Old military camps were often adapted to the new fortress style, typically with fewer buildings inside, suggesting that they housed less forces, and that civilians may have sheltered inside the walls in times of invasion. It is also likely that these empty spaces sometimes sheltered mobile forces, the *comitatenses*, en route through the empire.

Some of the finest surviving examples of these massive new fortresses can be found on the Saxon Shore, the south-east coast of Britain that was fortified from the mid-3rd century AD onwards against

Above: On Constantine I's death, Constantine II and his brothers divided the empire in three.

the new threat from Saxon raiders. Portchester near Portsmouth, the best preserved, dates from the AD280s. Within its giant walls, still rising some 30ft (9m) above the estuary, a medieval church and castle nestle comfortably in opposite corners, with open fields between them. Along the Rhine, similarly huge structures were built to confront the new barbarian threats. The fortress at Deutz on the east (German) bank of the Rhine is typically imposing. Built by Constantine I in AD310 to defend Cologne, its 65ft (20m) walls were punctuated by even taller circular towers. At the other end of the empire, forts such as that at Qasr Bsheir in Jordan, built under Diocletian, were constructed with projecting towers to provide enfilading fire. Like medieval castles, such fortresses must have been defensible for long periods even by very small garrisons and could counter barbarian superiority in the field.

PSYCHOLOGICAL WARFARE

All these massive walls might suggest that Rome's enemies had become markedly more proficient in siege warfare. This was certainly true of the Sassanid Persians, who were far more determined and skilled fighters than the rather shambolic Parthian Arsacid dynasty they replaced. On the eastern frontier, long and complex sieges became common. Those at Dura-Europos and Amida, where the Persians were victorious, and at Nisibis, where they were not, were typical. But the Romans built equally massive fortresses all along their northern frontiers, and very few barbarian tribes, if any, were ever good at proper sieges. But they would have certainly been impressed by these towering walls. So, in a more positive way, would the Roman soldiers inside them, especially as they were normally poorly trained and ill-equipped *limitanei* (frontier guards). Few Germans would have even attempted a siege against such an overwhelming example of Roman military engineering as Deutz. If they could not rush the castle by surprise or capture it by treachery – Rome itself only fell to the Visigoths when someone opened a gate to them – barbarian invaders would bypass them. This gave the Romans time to recover, to bring up forces from the mobile reserves and to stage a counter-attack. If the Romans could no longer overwhelm the barbarians by their unfailingly aggressive spirit, they could attempt to do so by their monumental fortifications.

Below: On the east coast of Kent, Richborough (Rutupiae) was the original Roman chief port of entry for Britain. Its fortifications were massively augmented in the later empire with huge walls, of which large sections still remain.

CITY WALLS

Since Augustus, Rome had been an open city, the Servian walls allowed to decay as they were engulfed by the growing capital. This reflected well-founded Roman confidence in its military prowess, which kept enemies safely distant. Similarly, cities in the provinces seldom needed walls unless on or near frontiers.

There were exceptions to this pacific norm, for older cities often retained their walls. Pompeii, far from any frontier, kept its boundary walls for ceremonial rather than military purposes, until Vesuvius destroyed it in AD79. In Boudicca's revolt in Britain, unwalled Colchester, London and St Albans were all sacked in AD61. So the Romans then built walls for a few towns, mostly those close to barbarous areas. But these walls, like those of the military camps, remained modest perimeters, gateways being more ceremonial than functional. However, further walls were added to London and other British cities after alarming barbarian attacks in AD193.

All this changed radically in the mid-3rd century AD. In the face of massive and repeated barbarian incursions, cities in near panic rushed to surround themselves with walls, using any materials that came to hand, including columns, tombstones and statues. Often these enclosed a far smaller area than before. Autun, for example, an important city in central Gaul, gave itself walls that covered only a third of its original area. Milan, for a time the capital of the western empire, enclosed less than 300 acres (120ha) within its new walls. Cities in the east did not shrink so much. Their walls were often restored, while in Britain the walls of London and York received progressively more massive fortifications but still protected the same areas. In Trier, which became the capital of Gaul and at times of the whole westernmost empire, gigantic walls protected an area of nearly 600 acres (240ha), making the walled city as large as it had ever been. Noteworthy at Trier is the ceremonial but also functional Porta Nigra (black gate), which has survived almost intact. Its two grand semicircular projecting towers rise to four tall floors over 70ft (20m) high and incorporate a portcullis, a device that went back centuries but which had become far more common. Trier remained impregnable until the whole of the Rhine frontier collapsed in AD406.

The walls Aurelian erected around Rome in the AD270s dwarfed those of all other western cities. Built chiefly of brick-faced concrete in great haste, the Aurelianic walls incorporate numerous pre-existing monuments such as the Pyramid of Cestius (a tomb), the walls of the Praetorian camp, the Porta Maggiore, part of Claudius' aqueduct and the small Amphitheatrum Castrense. About 20ft (6m) high and 12ft (3.6m) thick, they had square towers at about every 60yd (55m) with a platform for a catapult on top, while the major gateways had arched entrances flanked by twin semicircular towers. The entire circuit, covering most of Rome as it then was, was nearly

Above: The double walls around Constantinople (Istanbul) built by the emperor Theodosius II in the 5th century AD still stand and have even been reconstructed for a small section. They repulsed attackers for 1,000 years.

Below: The Porta Nigra (black gate) was the entrance, both ceremonial and fortified, to Trier, the capital of Gaul in the later empire. Its towers rise more than 70ft (20m).

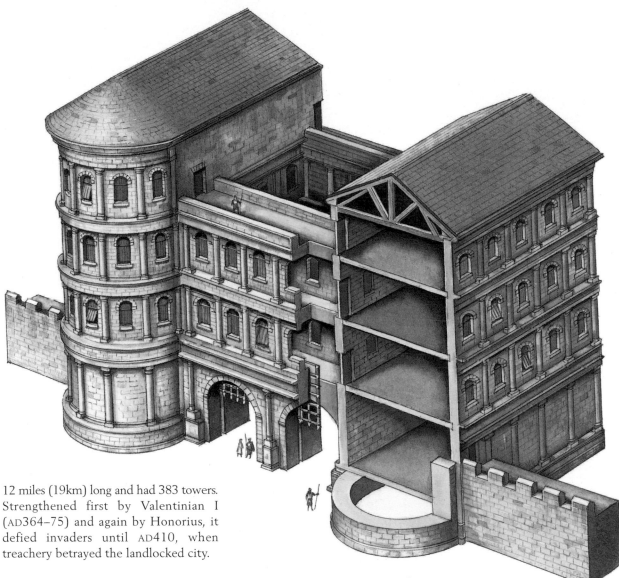

12 miles (19km) long and had 383 towers. Strengthened first by Valentinian I (AD364–75) and again by Honorius, it defied invaders until AD410, when treachery betrayed the landlocked city.

THE WALLS OF CONSTANTINOPLE

By far the grandest, most effective and best-preserved of late Roman city walls are the double (in some places triple) Theodosian walls of Constantinople, now Istanbul, the heart and head of the east Roman empire that metamorphosed into the Greek Byzantine empire. The walls were constructed between AD413 and AD437 in the reign of Theodosius II – a reaction to the sack of Rome. They replaced Constantine's shorter wall, which no longer contained the expanding city. The outer Theodosian walls were 20ft (6m) high with a deep moat in front of them. The inner walls were 40ft (12m) high, with 96 polygonal or square towers. The walls ran for almost 4 miles (6.4km) on the landward side of the peninsula and continued as a single wall right the way round the tip. On the other side of the Golden Horn, the small city of Pera was similarly defended, and a chain could be drawn across the harbour mouth to bar it to enemy ships. The walls defied all invaders – except for traitors – until 1453, when they finally fell to the Turkish besiegers' artillery. This probably makes them the most lastingly and consistently successful defences in history.

Above: The Porta Nigra (black gate) of Trier dates from the 4th century AD. Rising over 70ft (20m) the gate's twin towers incorporated a portcullis. It owes its remarkably good state of preservation to part of it being made into a chapel in the Middle Ages.

CHAPTER X

THE GREAT WARS

More than any other factor it was war that helped to mould Roman society and its empire. Certain wars in particular propelled Rome first to dominance and then to absolute rule of the Mediterranean world: the wars against Carthage, in which Rome almost foundered; the wars in the eastern Mediterranean, which made Rome amazingly rich; and finally, Caesar's conquest of Gaul, which led to the expansion of Roman influence into northern Europe. Caesar's dazzling success was balanced by the more mixed results of Claudius' and Agricola's campaigns in Britain, which helped to link Britain with the Continent. But the unsuccessful wars in Germany left most of that country permanently outside the Roman *imperium* (empire), with momentous long-term consequences both for Germany and for Rome.

Civil wars helped to determine the form of government that Rome would have when ruling its new empire. As the empire matured, Rome reached something like its natural boundaries. From now on, any war would be defensive or, increasingly and catastrophically, internecine. The earlier great wars tend to be well recorded and provided some of the best examples of human conflict for many later generals and rulers. But the instrument of Rome's victories was always its army, unequalled both at marching and at fighting, relentlessly aggressive and willing to suffer almost any level of casualties if it led to final victory.

Left: Of all Rome's opponents, the most formidable was Hannibal, the Carthaginian general who invaded Italy.

MARCHING AND FIGHTING

By the late 2nd century BC, the Roman army had become the world's first large-scale, semi-permanent professional army, a status it maintained with relatively few changes for almost 400 years. In so doing, it developed fixed routines that struck contemporaries as formidably impressive. Flavius Josephus, writing around AD70, repeats the admiring comments made by Polybius over two centuries earlier. The Romans organized their armies for their frequent marches, especially through hostile territory, in the same methodical way that they did everything else. When they engaged in actual combat, their relentless, controlled ferocity, coupled with a readiness to take high casualties if necessary, tended to overwhelm far larger numbers. This combination helped them to win their greatest wars.

When a full-sized Roman army was on the move, according to Josephus, it was preceded by light infantry and cavalry acting as scouts. Then came the vanguard, one legion plus cavalry, the legions drawing lots to decide which should be the vanguard – a prestigious if perilous position. Next came the camp surveyors, ten men detached from each century, followed by the pioneer corps, which had to remove obstacles in the army's path and build any necessary bridges. The general's and officers' baggage train came next, well protected by a strong mounted escort. Equally well protected behind it came the general himself, riding with his bodyguard of select cavalry and infantry. There followed the legionary cavalry, 120 for each legion, and then the mule trains carrying the numerous catapults and siege

Below: The sight of Roman legionaries marching in full armour towards them must have been intimidating to enemies, as these re-enactors demonstrate as they tramp along in formation.

engines. According to Vegetius writing in the 4th century AD each century had its own *carroballista* (a light, bolt-shooting catapult) and each cohort had its own *onager* (a heavy stone-slinging catapult), so this mule train must have been large. Finally came the main body of the legions, all carrying their rations, camp-making tools and armour, marching six abreast. They were preceded by their *aquilifer*, (eagle-bearer) and the trumpeters, and followed by their own baggage trains. A full legion of around 5,500 men must have spread for about a mile. Behind the legionaries marched the auxiliaries, with the rearguard composed of infantry and crack auxiliary cavalry. At the very end came the camp followers: wives, prostitutes, merchants and traders, including slave-dealers who could profit from Roman victory – slavery was the normal fate of any prisoners of war.

Roman armies were not as flamboyant or colourful as many Greek or Parthian forces, especially after Marius' reforms, when the richer soldiers stopped supplying their own armour. However, the well-drilled advance of up to 50,000 men – not such an uncommon number in the late Republic and Principate – must have been intimidatingly impressive.

BATTLE STATIONS

One of the advantages of the Roman *triplex acies* – the triple line of troops – was that troops did not have to fight to victory or to the death, but could be reinforced from the ranks behind. Unlike both the Greek *phalanx* and the Celtic-German mass, which relied on keeping the front ranks fighting until they triumphed by weight of numbers or else broke, this reduced the chances of panic. Iron discipline and rigorous drilling practice made complex manoeuvres second nature, even in the heat of battle. Their long, curved shields also helped to protect their comrades while moving backwards and forwards. But the *triplex acies* in no way softened the rigours of war. Centurions and the *optiones*, their

lieutenants, kept the men fighting, pushing them back into line and threatening cowardice with punishment.

In the Republic, legionaries had advanced shouting, banging their weapons against their shields. But by Caesar's time they kept silent until within almost 50ft (15m) of the enemy, when they yelled and threw their javelins in one broadside. Superb discipline allowed their dense formation to be maintained until the last minute. Then the soldiers fought close up, using the boss on their shields to punch the enemy in the face while they stabbed him with their *gladius*.

The centurions led their men aggressively, but even the generals stayed in close contact with their troops – to oversee fighting and to reward or punish individual soldiers. In close combat, when a gap was made in the enemy's line by killing several soldiers, a bravely determined legionary would fight his way into it. He was in extreme danger until joined by his comrades. But if enough managed to do so, the entire enemy line could start to buckle. Fighting at such close quarters was exhausting, both physically and psychologically, and the forces often used to break off at times, hurling abuse at each other from lines only a few yards apart, before re-engaging. Perseverance and stamina, more than spectacular individual exploits – coordinated so that the legion became one huge stabbing and thrusting machine – dominated and decided most battles. These were qualities Roman legionaries had in abundance.

Above: The Via Appia to the south of Rome. Good roads were a secret of Rome's success in conveying troops quickly to all parts of the empire.

Below: The Roman army marched along its empire's well-paved roads in sandals and boots. Army boots have been found in a number of places, including Vindolanda in Northumberland, England.

THE PUNIC WARS
264–146BC

When Rome blundered into war with Carthage in 264BC, it began an epic contest that would test its foundations. Carthage was a richer, larger and more sophisticated state than Rome. Its string of fortified bases stretched from Cadiz in Spain to Tripoli in Libya, and it was in the process of extending its control of Sicily. Greek observers must have expected it to contain, if not crush, what was still a farmers' republic. But Rome surprised the Greeks by its final victory over Carthage, which made it the dominant power first in the west Mediterranean and soon in the whole inland sea.

WAR AT SEA
The First Punic (Latin for Carthaginian) War was unusual for Rome as it was decided mostly at sea. Recognizing the need to counter Punic naval supremacy, the Romans quickly built fleets and defeated the Carthaginians with the *corvus*, the iron boarding device that let Romans fight as if on land. The *corvus* was a double-edged invention, however, as it made a galley top-heavy and many

Above: Cannae, site of Rome's worst military disaster in 216BC, when Hannibal annihilated a Roman army. But his victory did Hannibal little good in the longer term.

Below: At Cannae, Hannibal destroyed a numerically far superior army by thinning out his centre (blue) and letting it bend like a bow under Roman attack (red). Then his cavalry encircled the legions, driving them into a dense mass unable to wield their swords properly.

HANNIBAL CROSSES THE ALPS
Few feats have captured the popular imagination more than Hannibal's crossing of the Alps. He took the land route to Italy because the Romans controlled the sea and also because no one expected it.

After leaving Spain with an army 40,000 strong and 37 elephants, Hannibal found a Roman army awaiting him in the Rhône delta. To avoid it, he headed north of Avignon before crossing the Rhône. His elephants, however, lured on to rafts, panicked, some upsetting their rafts to wade across, using their trunks as snorkels. He then took a route further north but early snow added to the problems caused by hostile Celts. It took Hannibal 15 days to cross the Alps, and on the way he lost about a third of his army, more of his baggage train and almost all his elephants, but when he arrived in the Po Valley he posed a novel threat to Rome.

fleets sunk. Rome's victory in 241BC was won by normal galleys. This was after Regulus had come to within a day's march of Carthage but was beaten by the Spartan general Xanthippus in 255BC. Regulus was taken prisoner and sacrificed his life for his city, a patriotic act not atypical of Romans at the time.

ROMAN DEFEAT
Regulus may have been no military genius but, in the next war, Cornelius Scipio (later Africanus) was. This was fortunate for Rome, for Hannibal was a fearsome enemy whose daring was shown by his unprecedented choice of route over the Alps, and by his defeats of Roman armies at Ticino and Trebbia in the Po Valley in

VARRO

Roman secondary camp

Roman Cavalry

Legions

Spanish and Celtic Cavalry

Spanish and Gallic Infantry

Roman camp

Heavy Infantry

HANNIBAL

Heavy Infantry

A u f i d i u s

Hannibal's camp

Cannae

218BC. After being ambushed in a mist, 30,000 Romans died. Hannibal, entering Italy on his one surviving elephant, defeated Rome again at Lake Trasimene in 217BC. He ignored the undefended road to Rome, perhaps because he lacked a siege train, but a year later annihilated Rome's biggest army yet – 80,000 men – at Cannae. Here Roman military amateurism was shown at its most inept. Trusting in their numbers, they let their central infantry push back the thin Punic infantry line. As Hannibal intended, this bent rather than broke, enveloping the enemy, while the superior Carthaginian cavalry, routing the Roman horsemen, circled round to attack from the rear. Packed so tightly that they could not fight, some Romans then fled but many more were cut down. Roman losses reputedly approached 70,000 that day.

When Hannibal's peace offers were rejected, the war became one of attrition and, despite the defection of some major cities like Capua, Rome here had the advantage. Hannibal could train his disparate troops, who included Spaniards, Gauls, Numidians, Samnites and other disaffected Italians, into a unified force, but he needed reinforcements, which never came. Meanwhile, Roman reserves of manpower – sources say over 700,000 – were readily available. Provided the Romans followed the unpopular scorched-earth tactics of Fabius Cunctator, their (emergency) dictator, they would win, even if at great cost to Italian agriculture.

SCIPIO IN SPAIN AND AFRICA

In the event, Rome counter-attacked, striking at Hannibal's base in Spain to prevent reinforcements reaching him. Scipio captured Cartagena in 209BC and defeated Hasdrubal's army at Baecula. Scipio finished off Carthaginian power at Ilpica in 206BC. In these battles he emulated Hannibal's encircling tactics to great effect. Despite the Senate's denial of adequate troops, he invaded Africa in 204BC and won over Massinissa of Numidia. With this fine Numidian

cavalry, Scipio finally defeated Hannibal at Zama in 202BC. The final battle between the two generals was a slogging match, Hannibal's many elephants being countered by Roman discipline, and was finally decided by Roman cavalry.

The Third Punic War of 149–146BC was an unequal and unnecessary contest. The Carthaginians, despite economic recovery, presented no military threat to a Rome still paranoid about Hannibal, but war was fomented by the Numidian king, encroaching on Carthaginian territory. It led to the final destruction of Carthage.

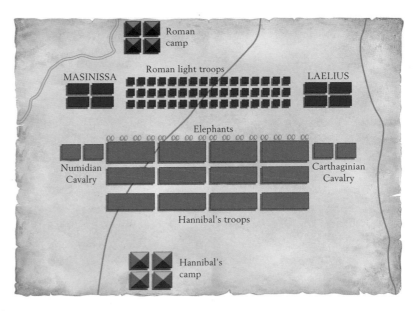

Above: The battle of Zama, which ended the Second Punic War was won chiefly by the discipline of Roman legions after they had repelled Hannibal's elephants.

Below: Hannibal used elephants as tanks. But they were a two-edged weapon, easy for a coolly determined opponent to turn back or avoid, and liable to stampede in blind panic.

Above: Athens, though no longer important politically, also suffered in the wars that marked Rome's conquest of Greece. Later it became the empire's university town.

Below: The theatre on the Acropolis of Pergamum, the capital of the wealthy Attalid kingdom, Rome's chief ally in the Greek world.

CONQUERING THE GREEKS
200–133BC

The eastern Mediterranean world conquered after 200BC appeared to many Romans as wealthy, sophisticated and alluring, but also effete and even dissolute. In a long series of wars, Alexander's generals, the *diaodochi* (successors), had created three powerful Greek-ruled kingdoms: the Antigonids in Macedonia, the Seleucids in Asia Minor, Syria and Mesopotamia, and the Ptolemies in Egypt and Palestine. These dominated the ancient world from the Adriatic to central Asia, but the cities of Greece proper remained independent and feuding. The recurrent wars between the great Hellenistic powers (as the expanded Greek world after Alexander the Great is known) were conducted in a relatively civilized, limited fashion, like those of the 18th century. Their professional but expensive armies relied mainly on spearmen massed into *phalanxes* and armed with sarissas, pikes up to 20ft (6m) long, supplemented by dashing cavalry with plumed helmets, fierce-looking chariots and many elephants. Such military splendours, however, especially the rigid formation of the *phalanx*, could not

compete with the flexible maniples of battle-hardened Roman legions led by generals who had learnt their trade in the rigours of the Punic Wars. The Romans' brutally realistic attitude to war shocked the Greeks, who preferred to resort to diplomacy and negotiations rather than needless battles.

Philip V of Macedonia, a successful if impetuous ruler, unwisely allied himself with Hannibal after Cannae, partly because Rome had annexed nearby south Illyria. This First Macedonian War fizzled out in 205BC but Rome did not forget Philip's action. Urged on by smaller Greek states anxious that Philip's alliance with the Seleucid Antiochus III threatened their independence, Rome sent Flaminius in 200BC to drive the Macedonians from Greece proper. At the battle of Cynoscephalae in 197BC, Flaminius displayed the flexibility pioneered by Scipio Africanus to defeat Philip, his maniples outflanking the clumsy *phalanx* on what was admittedly mountainous ground. Macedonian power in Greece was ended, though Macedonia itself was not destroyed, and Flaminius promised the delighted southern Greek cities liberty. It was to prove a hollow promise, for he meant self-rule as subordinate allies, not full freedom.

KING OF KINGS
Antiochus III was still undefeated, however. A capable and highly ambitious monarch, he appeared to Rome to be recreating Alexander's vast empire, for not only had he reconquered much of central Asia, but he menaced both Egypt and Europe, and was calling himself King of Kings. Even worse, Hannibal, exiled from Carthage, was now a guest at Antiochus' court. In 192BC Antiochus sent a small force into Greece proper to help the Aetolians, disgruntled by the

THE TANKS OF ANTIQUITY

When the Romans first encountered elephants in Pyrrhus' army in 280BC, they were panic-stricken. But they soon learnt to deal with these armoured giants by opening their ranks to let them through, or by repelling them by javelin volleys. In war elephant charges could inflict terrible damage upon infantry that panicked, while their smell drove horses unused to them mad with fear. But elephants were a double-edged weapon, for they in turn were easy to panic and could turn against their own armies. Because of this, mahouts, their riders, carried hammers and chisels to kill them if needed.

The Hellenistic monarchs used Indian elephants, who were more easily trained and came from the elephant stud farm the Seleucids had established in Syria. But Hannibal and other Carthaginians used the North African forest elephant (now extinct), which was ridden like a horse. The Romans occasionally also deployed elephants in their armies, impressing enemies unused to them. However, they chiefly used them for animal and hunting displays, slaughtering them in large numbers in games to amuse the Roman populace.

nominal Roman commander, but Scipio himself was ill on the day of the battle. The key role in the battle was taken by Eumenes of Pergamum, a Hellenistic ally of Rome, whose heavy cavalry routed the Seleucid *cataphracts* and then returned to attack the Seleucid infantry in the rear. The Seleucid chariot and elephant charges had been repulsed earlier by the Roman legions, but the Macedonian *phalanx*, 16,000 strong, stood firm against Roman attacks until their stampeding elephants, panicked by Roman javelins, broke up their ranks. Finally, the Pergamene cavalry was able to surround the remaining Seleucid forces.

This defeat proved decisive. Antiochus had to pay a huge indemnity, withdraw completely from Asia Minor and expel Hannibal. The Seleucids were never again a great Mediterranean power. The Romans, as was their custom at the time, made no new provinces but gave the western Seleucid territories mostly to Eumenes, whose last descendant bequeathed them to Rome in 133BC. However, the Romans were now incontestably masters of the eastern Mediterranean too. Later Roman wars in Greece merely confirmed Roman supremacy, and this was challenged seriously only when Rome itself was divided at the time of Mithradates.

Above: A Roman legionary with a long oval shield and plumed helmet.

Below: Hannibal and his elephants fighting a Roman legion in north Italy, after the school of Raphael.

recent settlement. This roused Roman wrath and they sent an army to defeat it the next year at Thermopylae. Rome followed this up with a naval victory and landed troops in Asia Minor for the final conflict at Magnesia in Asia Minor in 190BC.

For this deciding battle, Antiochus mobilized huge forces of over 70,000 men, including heavy Persian-style *cataphract* cavalry and large numbers of war elephants and chariots. However, the core of his army remained the *phalanx*. This formation, 32-men deep, bristled with spears and was almost invincible to frontal assault. Scipio Africanus was an unofficial adviser to his brother, the

CAESAR'S CONQUEST OF GAUL
58–50BC

Above: The siege of Alesia in 52BC, where the Gallic leader Vercingetorix had retreated, was the final battle in Caesar's conquest of Gaul.

Below: Caesar built a double wooden wall around the fortress at the siege of Alesia, to keep the Gauls in and prevent their relief army of 80,000 men breaking through.

Caesar's proconsular command in 58BC, for the exceptionally long term of five years, included Cisalpine Gaul (the Po valley) and Transalpine Gaul (southern France) with Greek cities at Marseilles and Antibes, a Roman colony at Narbonne and, lining the Rhône valley, various Celtic tribes. The vagueness of this northern frontier allowed Caesar, keen to rival Pompey's eastern conquests, to intervene far beyond his province. The Helvetii trying to migrate to the Atlantic, gave him an excuse. A series of bitter, genocidal wars resulted in all Gaul (France, Belgium, the Rhineland and western Switzerland) being conquered and Romanized. This conquest led to the extension of Roman power northwards and the enrichment of Caesar. In the long term it produced the civilization of France. This makes it among the most significant conquests in history.

The Celtic world Caesar destroyed was underestimated by classical writers because it lacked cities and literacy. But the Gauls were skilled metal workers, producing striking stylized artworks. They were great horsemen and had many types of carriage, while the Veneti in Brittany were fine mariners. The Gauls were also pioneers of the wheeled plough. Above all, they had an acute poetic and religious sense. Most of what we know of Celtic life comes from biased writers such as Caesar; only echoes of Celtic legends survive in Welsh and Irish poetry. However, the Gauls were fatally disunited politically, with about 60 separate states in 58BC. Caesar easily recruited Gallic cavalry to fight their fellow countrymen.

Caesar swiftly crushed the Helvetii at Armecy in 58BC, killing tens of thousands, forcing the survivors back to Switzerland. The next year, he attacked Ariovistus, a German king who had crossed into Gaul. Caesar routed the Germans in Alsace and then turned on the Belgae, living north of the Seine. In 57BC he also crushed the Nervi in Artois before other Belgae had mobilized, a victory that made him arbiter of Gaul. With his command renewed at Lucca in 56BC, Caesar returned to find that the Veneti in Brittany, angered by his proposed invasion of Britain, had revolted. Building a fleet, he defeated them at Quiberon Bay. Early in 55BC he repelled another German invasion even more brutally, building a timber bridge across the Rhine, a feat that stunned opinion in Rome.

Caesar's two "invasions" of Britain in 55BC and 54BC were also intended as propaganda. The first attack was a near disaster: many ships were damaged by tides that Caesar had not anticipated and he himself returned home after only 18 days. The next year he returned with a far larger force of five legions and 2,000 cavalry and forced Cassivellaunus, ruler of the Catuvellauni, the most powerful southern British tribe, to submit after storming his capital. But the conquest proved illusory: the Britons rejected Roman suzerainty as soon as Caesar left. Meanwhile, there was rebellion in Gaul.

● Roman redoubt

Main Gallic

Rabutin

Cavalry camp

ENTRENCHMENT

Ose

ENTRENCHMENT

Infantry camp

Cavalry camp

ALESIA

Cavalry camp

Last *sortie*

VERCINGETORIX

Cavalry camp

Probable position of Caesar during last battle

Brenne

Gallic camp

Infantry camp

Oserain

Left: Caesar's conquest of Gaul was marked by numerous campaigns of lightning rapidity that overwhelmed the far more numerous Gauls before they had time to mobilize. His legions marched from the Rhine – which they bridged – to the Atlantic, on which they sailed, and back with a speed that stunned Romans and Gauls alike. (Only the Britons were unimpressed.) But the conquest of Gaul was only settled by the drawn-out siege of Alesia.

Below: Vercingetorix, last and greatest war leader of the Gauls, shown heroically on horseback. His scorched-earth tactics were less heroic, but they nearly defeated Caesar, whose troops lived off the land and who could not capture Alesia by direct assault.

THE SIEGE OF ALESIA

In 52BC the Gauls united behind a single leader, Vercingetorix of the Arverni in central Gaul. He decided to defeat Caesar by a scorched-earth policy to deny him supplies – the Roman army lived off the land – refusing direct battle. He drew them into central Gaul where Caesar suffered a defeat attacking the fortress of Gerovia, which encouraged other tribes to join the revolt. But Vercingetorix mistakenly retreated behind the walls of Alesia with 90,000 men, thinking it was impregnable. Caesar recognized that it was "on the crown of a hill high enough for blockade to be the only means of capturing it". He built a huge double line of walls, an example of bi-circumvallation, about 14 miles (22km), to starve the Gauls

– who included women and children – into surrender. The 80,000-strong Gallic relief army failed to break through Caesar's lines, fortified by iron-tipped spikes dug into the ground. In desperation, Vercingetorix tried three times to break out before surrendering in late 52BC. This ended the Gallic wars.

The Romans showed no mercy to the Gauls, killing about a third of the Gallic population in the wars. Caesar won by his lightning rapidity and the discipline of his legions. The conquered land was later divided into three provinces (Aquitainia in the south-west, Lugdunensis in the centre and Belgica in the north-east) and assessed for tribute. Ultimately, Gaul would prove the most receptive and fruitful of all Rome's conquests.

THE LAST CIVIL WARS: 49–30BC

Above: A statue of Pompey, showing him posing rather improbably as a god or hero. He was, however, an excellent general and statesmanlike in foreign affairs. But in Roman politics he could never decide which faction to support, a fatal indecisiveness.

Below: Major battle sites of the last civil wars.

Fresh from his conquest of Gaul, in January 49BC Caesar had the best army: experienced, loyal, large – ten legions – and to hand. By contrast, his adversary Pompey's best troops were in Spain and out of practice. Caesar had no wish to start another civil war; memories of the conflict between Marius and Sulla were still fresh in the public mind. His enemies in the Senate tried to divest him of his Gallic command and refused to let him stand for consul *in absentia*. If he returned to Italy as a private citizen he faced immediate prosecution that would end his political career, if not his life. According to Suetonius, as he hesitated on the banks of the river Rubicon marking the borders of Italy, a ghostly figure appeared from the twilight and crossed over. Caesar then moved into Italy with his army – an act of treason – and triggered civil war.

With just one legion, Caesar raced down the east coast to Brindisi but failed to catch Pompey and his other opponents before they left for Greece, where Pompey had huge support. Before turning east, Caesar crushed the Pompeian forces in Spain at Lerida. In 48BC he crossed to Greece, eluding Pompey's numerous ships. Antony joined Caesar three months later with reinforcements, but attempts to blockade Pompey's base at Durrachium (Durazzo) failed disastrously. Pompey out-walled him and he withdrew.

The deciding battle took place in Thessaly on 6 June 48BC at Pharsalus. It was probably the largest battle ever fought between Romans; Pompey had 80,000 troops and was strong in cavalry, but most of his infantry were out of condition. Caesar had fewer men but all were skilled, hardened veterans. The brilliant discipline of Caesar's legionaries, who advanced with their *pila* (javelins) as pikes, countered Pompey's cavalry's initially successful charge. By attacking their flank, the legions drove Pompey's horsemen back. Pompey was killed soon after in Egypt.

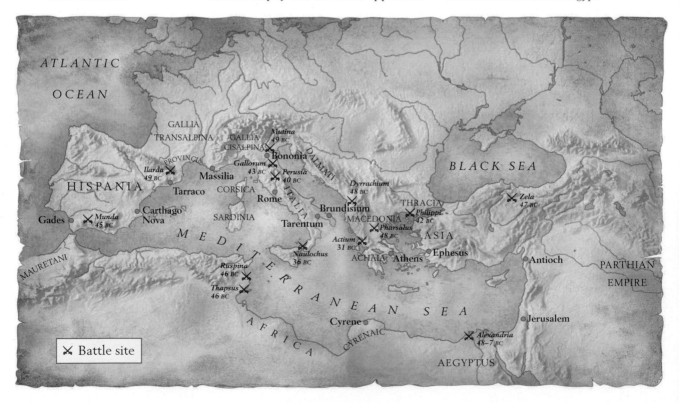

Right: Actium, last battle of the civil wars, was decided at sea when Antony's fleet, trying to escape the blockade, was defeated.

With great speed, Caesar won many other battles around the Mediterranean. But he was less good at establishing peace. After his assassination in 44BC, civil war flared up again between his assassins, led by Brutus and Cassius, and his supporters, Antony and Octavian. The two battles of Philippi in 42BC were won by Antony, who went on to rule the eastern half of the empire and pursue his relationship with Cleopatra. Inevitably, the two dynasts moved towards a renewal of war by 32BC.

ACTIUM: THE LAST BATTLE

Despite Octavian's lurid propaganda campaign, Antony was still popular with his own troops. He also had Cleopatra's wealth, which could give him a fleet, as well as promises of support from many eastern client kings, including Herod the Great. Octavian had the recruiting grounds of Italy, and a very good general in his friend Agrippa. Once again the rivals converged on Greece, Agrippa slipping across the Adriatic in the winter of 31BC, followed by Octavian in the spring. But Antony made a mistake when he took Cleopatra with him to western Greece. His own men began to believe Octavian's propaganda about their general and began to desert. The final battle took place on 2 September 31BC when Antony led his fleet in an attempted breakout Although he had many quinqueremes and more troops, Antony's fleet was defeated by Agrippa's, which used smaller, swifter Liburnian galleys. Antony broke off the battle, following Cleopatra's flight to Egypt. Many of his supporters then surrendered. The following year, Antony and Cleopatra committed suicide when the Caesarean troops entered Alexandria, so ending the last Roman civil war for a century.

Right: At Pharsalus, Caesar's more disciplined but outnumbered troops defeated Pompey's army by flank attacks.

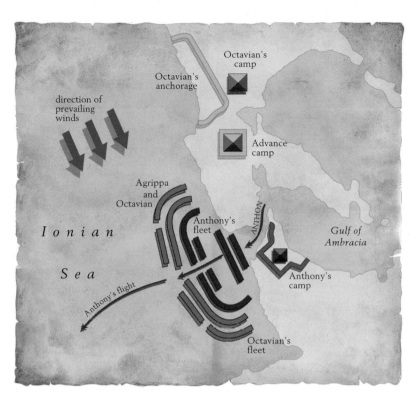

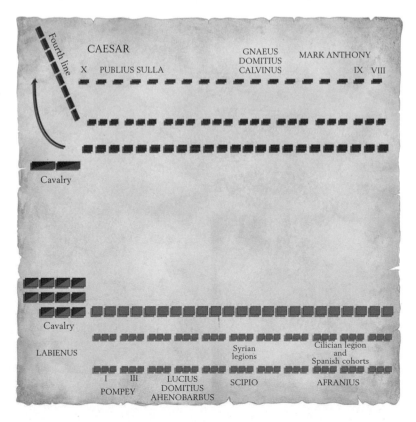

ALONG THE ELBE: 12BC–AD16

Although Caesar had proclaimed the Rhine as the natural, almost inevitable, north-west frontier of the empire, this was not so evident to his successor Augustus. Germanic tribes had already infiltrated west of the river into Gallia Belgica, the north-eastern Gallic province. Further, a German invasion in 17BC by the Sugambri and Isupetes tribes, which had defeated the Romans under Lollius, called for revenge. Augustus, confident after victories in northern Iberia (23BC), the Alpine provinces (16–15BC) and the Balkans (13–9BC), saw no reason to halt the expansion of the empire on this frontier.

Rome's geographical knowledge of northern Europe became more vague the further east it looked, but the tribes between the Elbe and the Rhine did not appear exceptionally formidable. It seemed that Germania could be conquered and pacified as easily as Gaul, a considerably larger, more populous area. A frontier along the Elbe to the Danube would eliminate the awkward upper Rhine–Danube junction, and shorten the whole frontier by almost 300 miles (480km).

There were differences between the two lands, however. If thought barbarous by Greeks and Romans, *Gallia comata* (long-haired Gaul), beyond Rome's old Mediterranean province, had been wealthy and dynamic in its rural way; its fertile land had supported advanced farming. Western Germany, by contrast, had thin soils with heavy, dark forests and many bogs and heaths. Partly because of this, the German tribes were less well developed and less settled than those of Gaul or Britain and their shifting settlements were less easily controlled. But such differences were not then apparent to the Romans.

Accordingly, Augustus ordered an advance to the Elbe, with troops commanded by his stepson Drusus in 12BC, while his other stepson, Tiberius, finally pacified the Pannonian plain. Although Drusus' fleet was wrecked by tides in the Zuyder Zee (his men were saved only by his Frisian allies), in three successive campaigning seasons his armies still advanced up the Main and Lippe valleys towards the Elbe.

Drusus' death in 9BC meant that Tiberius replaced him before retiring in 6BC from public life, in presumed disgust at Augustus' open preference for his grandsons. The German campaigns at first seem to have progressed slowly but steadily, even without Tiberius. Very soon traders and tax-collectors, in the normal pattern, entered the region, which began to be organized and taxed as a province. However, a reaction to the Roman advance led to the formation of a powerful Marcomanni kingdom in Bohemia. To deal with this threat, in AD6 a two-pronged invasion of the area was planned from the Rhine and the Danube. Tiberius, back from voluntary exile in Rhodes, was about to strike north from near Vienna with a huge force of 12 legions when news came of a massive revolt in Pannonia and he turned east. The gruelling war that followed, "the most

Above: The Elbe in north Germany proved a frontier too far for the Romans after the disaster that befell Varus and his legions in AD9.

Below: The "Gemma Augustea" shows Augustus and the goddess Roma receiving Tiberius, who, if charmless, was a very fine general.

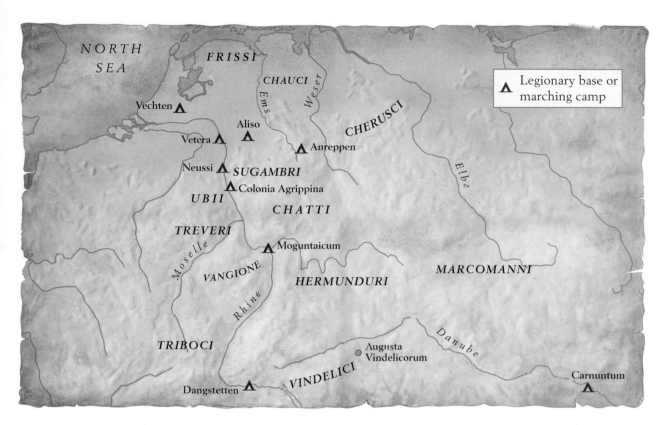

Above: The attempted Roman conquest of Germany.

serious of all our foreign wars since the Punic wars", according to Suetonius, distracted him. Meanwhile, there was disaster in Germany proper.

THE VARUS DISASTER

Quinctilius Varus, who commanded three legions in north-west Germany, was less a soldier than an administrator, although he had suppressed a revolt in Judaea as governor of Syria in 4BC. Hastening in to deal with a revolt by the Cherusci, one of the German tribes, in AD9, his army was ambushed in the Teutoburg Forest near Osnabrück. Varus had been betrayed by the Cherusci king Arminius (Hermann), supposedly a Roman ally. Surrounded by Germans, Varus committed suicide and his three legions were lost. The whole Roman position east of the Rhine began to unravel rapidly. Back in Rome, the aged emperor Augustus was crushed by the news. He ordered special patrols around the city, reputedly banging his head against the wall and crying, "Quinctilius Varus, give me back my legions!"

In fact, the other German tribes did not join the Cherusci (the Marcomanni in particular quarrelled with them) and there was no general attack across the river Rhine. However, Tacitus was right when he referred to the Cherusci king Arminius as "the liberator of Germany", for his revolt marked the end of real Roman attempts to subjugate Germany. Drusus' son, Germanicus, led a series of major punitive raids over the Rhine, in AD15 finding and burying the bones of Varus' legions, and the following year sailing up the river Ems to defeat the Cherusci in a set battle.

However, Tiberius, the new emperor, then recalled Germanicus. Tiberius preferred to rely on diplomacy and bribes to control the German tribes. This was successful, for Arminius was soon killed in a conspiracy by his own people. The frontier then became established on the Rhine, and northern and central Germany remained permanently outside the Roman empire, although influenced by trade and other contacts with it.

Below: The Rhine offered a convenient frontier for the Romans along much of its length but was not impassable.

CONQUEST OF LOWLAND BRITAIN: AD43–70

Above: The bookish emperor Claudius proved remarkably successful as a conqueror, adding lowland Britain to the empire in what appeared a relatively simple campaign. But the island was not at first a great asset to the empire.

Below: The hill fort at Badbury Rings, Dorset, was one of the many oppida, *or fortified British townships, that the Romans stormed in their initial conquest of Britain.*

Paradoxically, one of the most professional of Rome's military campaigns was carried out at the orders of one of its least military emperors, Claudius. This was no coincidence. Aware he lacked the soldiering experience of a Roman aristocrat, Claudius needed to conquer Britain. His predecessor, Caligula, had massed troops on the Channel as if for an invasion but ordered them to throw javelins at the sea, according to Suetonius. But Claudius was serious. The uncomfortable, marginally dangerous journey he made north for the surrender of Colchester (Camulodonum) shows the importance he attached to this campaign.

Ever since Julius Caesar had invaded and misleadingly claimed that he had conquered Britain in 55–54BC, the island had intrigued the Romans. It had a reputation – overrated, it turned out – of being rich in gold, and the south was inhabited by tribes like the Belgae related to those in Gaul. The Gallic connection was a reason for invasion, for the Druids reputedly helped keep alive Gallic hostility to Rome. Another excuse was that Caratacus, an heir of King Cunobelin (Cymbeline), had attacked Verica, who appealed to Rome for help. Prestige was, however, the chief reason for the invasion. It was 40 years since Rome had gained a major new province.

Four legions were mustered under Aulus Plautius, 40,000 men including auxiliaries. Despite a mutiny by troops alarmed at embarking for an unknown land, they landed safely at Richborough, and after two days' bitter fighting defeated the Britons at the Medway. Another victory followed when the Romans crossed the Thames. Plautius, impressed by British resistance, halted the advance until the emperor could arrive with reinforcements, which included some elephants. Then Claudius watched his troops storm Colchester, the Catuvellaunian capital, and declared it the capital of the new province (and six years later, a Roman colony), before returning home to celebrate a triumph.

Plautius continued the swift conquest. Vespasian, commanding the Second Legion, struck south-west, capturing 20 *oppida* (tribal strongholds). Meanwhile, the Fourteenth Legion advanced north-west and the Ninth Legion moved north. Within four years a provisional line was established along the Fosse Way from Lincoln to Exeter. Tribes such as the Iceni and the Brigantes became client kings, shielding the new province. This began to fill with Roman merchants and adventurers. But Caratacus escaped to continue resistance in the Welsh hills.

Plautius' successor, Ostorius Scapula, tried to strengthen the new province by disarming all tribes south of the Fosse and pushing the frontier closer to Wales. Caratacus, defeated in battle, took refuge with Cartimandua, Queen of the Brigantes, who handed him over to the Romans in AD51. Caratacus was paraded through Rome but pardoned by Claudius.

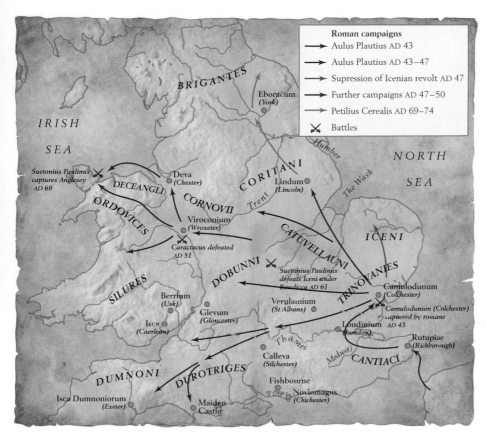

Left: Claudius' invasion of Britain at first restricted itself to the south-east of the island, with a possible provisional frontier along the Fosse Way and a capital at Colchester, although campaigns further west were needed to hunt down Caratacus. But the Romans soon found themselves drawn into Wales to suppress the Druids in AD60, and then Cerialis had to march north to control the large but troubled kingdom of the Brigantes.

The conquest did not, however, go so smoothly as it approached upland Britain. The Brigantes' kingdom was riven by disputes; Cartimandua was driven out by her consort after a disagreement and had to be reinstated by the Romans. Rome's real efforts, under the new governor Suetonius Paulinus, focused on subduing Anglesey, centre of political and religious resistance. The Romans crossed the Menai Straits and overran the island, cutting down the sacred Druidical groves. Then, suddenly, the whole province was endangered by a new revolt.

BOUDICCA'S REVOLT

The last Iceni king, Prasutagus, had made the emperor co-heir with his two daughters. But a venal procurator, Decianus Catus, and his loathed *publicani* seized land and goods. When Boudicca, the widowed queen, was flogged by Romans and her daughters raped, the Iceni rose in revolt. Joined by the Trinovantes, the Britons sacked Colchester and moved on London. Paulinus hurried with a few troops to London. Realizing he could not defend an unwalled city, he withdrew, "undeflected by the prayers and tears of those who begged for his help", in Tacitus' words. The Britons sacked London and St Albans, reportedly killing 70,000 people. Paulinus defeated them near Towcester – according to Tacitus, 80,000 Britons were killed and 400 Romans. Paulinus took a terrible vengeance, even on Britons who had stayed neutral. But before the whole province was devastated, Paulinus was checked by the intervention of Julius Classicianus, the new procurator. Of partly Gallic descent, Classicianus recognized the Britons' real problems and his report led to Paulinus being replaced by the more conciliatory Turpilianus. These two pacified the province so effectively the south never rose again.

Below: Queen Boudicca, who traditionally led her people, the Iceni, in a revolt that nearly ended Roman rule in all Britain.

AGRICOLA'S NORTHERN CAMPAIGNS: AD79–84

Above: Although Agricola marched far up the east coast of Scotland, the Romans did not penetrate the highlands proper, such as Glen Quoich.

Under Agricola, the Romans certainly came closer to conquering all Britain than at any other time. According to Tacitus, Agricola's completion of the conquest was prevented only by the jealousy of the emperor Domitian, who recalled him just as final victory was in sight. *"Perdomita Britannia et statim missa"* (Britain was completely conquered and at once let go), he commented sourly. But Tacitus was Agricola's son-in-law and shared the aristocracy's general hatred of Domitian. Just how feasible such a conquest was remains debatable, and Domitian did have valid reasons for recalling some legions.

When Agricola, who had just been a consul, arrived in Britain as governor, probably in late AD78, he was returning to a province he had fought in as a young man. Taking command of his old Twentieth Legion, then based at Viriconium (Wroxeter), he immediately went on the offensive against the Ordovices of mid-Wales and almost annihilated them. He built forts at Caernarvon and other places in north Wales, but also began "encouraging wild men who lived in scattered settlements… to live in a peaceful manner. Agricola … helped them officially to build temples, *fora* [market places] and private houses… and had the children of important Britons educated in civilized ways", recorded Tacitus. Many Britons now became Romanized, as the numerous buildings of this Flavian period show.

Right: Agricola's campaign, possibly intended to complete the conquest of Britain, started with a two-pronged attack on each flank of the Pennines. Once into what is now southern Scotland, his armies united to push up the east coast, establishing a line of forts centring on the new legionary camp at Inchtuthil. Roman victory in the supposedly decisive battle of Mons Graupius – the site has yet to be determined – in fact did not conclude the conquest. The Caledonians vanished into the highland mists and soon after Agricola himself was recalled, his forts being abandoned a few years later.

Agricola's campaign in Scotland AD 78–84

Battle of Mons Graupius AD 83 (suggested locations)

CALEDONII

Tay

Fort at Inchtuthil abandoned AD 87

Inchtuthil

VENICONES

NORTH SEA

Forth

Agricola advances to the river Tay AD 79

Antonine Wall

DUMNONII

Clyde

SELGOVAE

VOTADINI

Romans control southwest Scotland AD 79

NOVANTAE

Tyne

Hadrian's Wall

In AD79 Agricola sent two large columns of troops up each side of the Pennines, overawing the Brigantes and reaching the Tyne–Solway line. The next year he pressed on to the Forth. Reuniting his armies, he then marched north again, building forts as he went. A provisional line across Scotland, from the Clyde to the Forth, was probably established and he campaigned in south-west Scotland. Looking across to Ireland, he estimated that its conquest would require only one legion – suggesting wild optimism or poor geography on his part. However, north-east Scotland drew him back. In summer AD82 or 83 he moved north with a supporting fleet through increasingly hostile territory with the permission of the new emperor, Domitian. The Ninth Legion was almost destroyed when it became detached from the main army. At Mons Graupius (probably near Inverness), Agricola's army finally met the main Caledonian forces mustered under King Calgacus. According to Tacitus, these northern Britons had about 30,000 men. This was far more than Agricola's forces, which included auxiliaries, among them some Britons. Although the Caledonians had the advantage of the slope and a prepared position, Roman discipline overcame Celtic courage. Reportedly, 10,000 Caledonians were killed for only 360 Romans, although 20,000 Caledonians escaped. These figures may exaggerate the extent of the victory, but Scotland did seem truly conquered.

Agricola ordered the construction of a full-scale legionary camp for the Twentieth Legion at Inchtuthil, the largest of a chain of forts that stretched almost from the Moray Firth to Loch Lomond. A fleet went north to circumnavigate Britain and confirm it really was an island. Agricola was presumably planning another campaign to the extreme north, but Domitian recalled him. Problems on the Danube meant reinforcements were needed. About AD86 Inchtuthil and other forts north of the Clyde–Forth line were dismantled and Rome's advance into Scotland abandoned.

The Highlands were left untamed, indeed untouched, despite Tacitus' claims to the contrary, and the southern uplands were still disputed. From unconquered Scotland would later come many of the tribes that would threaten Roman Britain.

BETWEEN TWO WALLS

The northern frontier remained unsettled until the famous visit of the emperor Hadrian in AD122. Hadrian generally favoured easily defensible frontiers, even if this entailed some withdrawal, and he now chose the line along the Tyne to the Solway for his great wall. At first built partly in turf and timber, it was soon wholly consolidated in stone, requiring the excavation in total of some 2 million tons of rock and soil. It was ultimately the most imposing fortification in the empire. However, this did not mean that the Romans rejected all interests or control north of the wall. Patrols and forts, such as Newstead on the Tweed, were maintained well to the north.

In AD139 under Antoninus Pius, the frontier was advanced to the waist of Scotland again and a new turf wall some 37 miles (59km) long was built. This was the Antonine Wall, about 100 miles (160km) north of the existing line. Hadrian's Wall was not completely abandoned, but some of its gates were removed. However, an uprising led to the abandonment of the Antonine Wall in the early AD150s. It was reoccupied and finally abandoned again and dismantled in AD162. Hadrian's Wall again became the frontier, but due to Rome's civil wars it was overrun in the AD190s, with tribesmen raiding as far as York. To restore order, Septimius Severus visited Britain in person and twice invaded Scotland. But when he died at York in AD211 his sons abandoned his planned conquests. Hadrian's Wall, substantially repaired, once again became the frontier of Roman Britain. Beyond it, the Caledonians began to organize themselves into threatening confederacies that would soon ravage the south.

Above: An emblem of the Twentieth Legion, once commanded by Agricola, which spear-headed his new campaign.

Below: Ruins of a granary at Housesteads on Hadrian's Wall.

TRAJAN'S CAMPAIGNS
THE CONQUEST OF DACIA

Above: Battle scene between the Dacians and the Romans from the Ludovisi Sarcophagus. The wars of AD101–6, which removed a threatening enemy and gained much gold, proved to be Rome's last wholly profitable war of conquest.

Below: A river ferry passes the Iron Gates on the Danube, the great gorge that divides the river. The Romans built a road along the south cliff face.

Trajan (reigned AD98–117) was the last emperor to expand the empire significantly. If his wars in Asia proved a costly failure, his conquest of Dacia was a triumphant success. It led to the removal of a significant threat on the river Danube, a huge gain in booty for the Roman treasury and, despite Roman withdrawal 170 years later, to the enduring creation of the only Latin people in eastern Europe: the Romanians.

Dacia, a mountain-ringed, fertile and gold-rich land, had been a powerful, centralized kingdom under a ruler called Burebista in Caesar's time. Its people were renowned as fighters and skilled metallurgists and engineers, and had developed their own coinage. In AD85 Dacia acquired a brilliant new leader in Decebalus, who called himself High King. He may have had some experience of Roman military life, for he began organizing a powerful army on Roman lines. Twenty years of war followed – they proved among the fiercest Rome ever fought in Europe.

Domitian at once sent an army under Cornelius Fuscus to repel Dacian incursions, but it was humiliatingly defeated. Calling in legions from Britain and elsewhere, the Romans mounted a further campaign that won a victory at Tapae (near Turnu Severin) in AD88. However, the revolt of Antoninus Saturninus, the legate of upper Germany, in January AD89 meant that the troops had to deal with threatened civil war. The result was an uneasy truce. Domitian concentrated on containing the Dacian threat, quelling the tribes in Pannonia and building an earthwork across the Dobrudja, between the Danube and Tomis on the Black Sea, to prevent Dacian raids at this marshy extremity.

Trajan, who became emperor in AD98, was an experienced soldier. He boosted the Roman army's strength to perhaps 400,000 by recruiting two legions, besides doubling the size of the first cohort in each and adding new auxiliary forces. Seeing how Dacian power and pride were continuing to grow he decided to deal

with the Dacians. With other frontiers peaceful, he concentrated 13 legions plus auxiliaries (*c*.130,000 men) on the lower Danube. He crossed the river at the head of this force in AD101.

The wars, vividly recorded on Trajan's Column in Rome, lasted five years. The first led to an inconclusive victory, with Decebalus accepting humiliating terms. Trajan now prepared for a larger invasion by having Apollodorus build his bridge across the Danube and construct a road through the Iron Gates Gorge. Here the river narrowed between cliffs and the armies were able to march all the way along the Danube. The war resumed in AD105 and the final attack in AD106 overwhelmed the Dacian capital of Sarmizegetusa Regia. Decebalus committed suicide. His head later graced Trajan's triumph, along with a huge quantity of gold, the last really significant war spoils in Rome's history.

On the map, the new province – which lengthened the imperial frontiers by some 350 miles (560km) – looked vulnerable. However, on the ground the reality was rather different. By projecting Roman power to the edge of the Eurasian steppe, Trajan made it easier to control the Sarmatian, Carpi and Iazyges tribes on either side. A line of defences along the great mountain wall of the Carpathians, the *limes Porolissensis*, protected the new province with auxiliary-garrisoned forts. These were linked by watchtowers and backed by the Thirteenth Legion stationed at Apulum, reaching a total of 30,000–40,000 men (about the same as Britain). Dacia itself was settled by Romans, and the gold mines, an imperial monopoly, were profitably exploited.

THE PROVINCE ABANDONED

Hadrian is said to have contemplated abandoning the new province completely. This would have been in keeping with his general policy of retrenchment, although jealousy of Trajan's success could also have played a part; his destruction of the amazing Danubian bridge Apollodorus

had built seems pettily negative. But he was dissuaded by the pleas of the colonists themselves – the productive gold mines may have swayed him too – and he evacuated only the Banat plain to the west of the province, which was vulnerable to raids from Sarmatian tribesmen. Over the following century, the whole middle and lower Danubian area, from modern Budapest down to the Black Sea, prospered and became Romanized and increasingly urbanized. It was to provide vital reservoirs of troops – and emperors – in the 3rd century. One of these Illyrian emperors, Aurelian, accepting that Dacia was no longer defensible against new enemies such as the Goths and Gepids, finally evacuated it in AD270, settling its Latin-speaking inhabitants in a new province, Dacia, south of the Danube (approximately northern Serbia). However, some Latin-speaking Dacians must have survived the endless waves of invasion, probably sheltering in the Carpathians to re-emerge centuries later, still speaking their basically Romance language.

Above: The inauguration at Dobrela of the bridge over the Danube, which was built by Apollodorus for Trajan.

Below: Trajan's Column in Rome still proclaims his many victories.

TRAJAN'S CAMPAIGNS: THE EAST

Above: The Parthians relied heavily on horse archers such as this one, about to fire his recurved composite bow.

Below: Trajan's triumphal arch at Benevento, Italy.

Ever since Pompey had marched through Asia in the 60s BC, many Romans had dreamt of eastern conquests. There was widespread admiration for Alexander the Great, who had conquered the Persians *en route* to India. Parthia, the successor to the eastern Persian empire from the Euphrates to central Asia, was a ramshackle, semi-feudal monarchy, which was often unable to control its nobles and which evoked little loyalty from its varied subjects in Mesopotamia (Iraq).

There were more material reasons for invading Parthia and trying to annex at least its richest part, Mesopotamia. The great Hellenistic city of Seleucia-on-the-Tigris (opposite Baghdad) still flourished. In the 1st century AD the city had a population of *c.*600,000, almost as big as Alexandria's. Mesopotamia was very fertile, while its cities' trade with India reputedly surpassed Syria's. The ancient "Fertile Crescent", from the Gulf to the Mediterranean, had often been ruled by one monarch, most recently by the Hellenistic Seleucids. There was no good reason why it should not be again.

Augustus had prudently disappointed Roman expectations that he would revenge the Parthian defeats of Crassus (in 53BC) and Antony (in 36BC). Instead, by a peaceful agreement in 20BC Rome received back the legionary standards lost by Crassus, and Parthia (briefly) recognized Armenia as Rome's client, a diplomatic success that propagandists cried up as a great Roman victory. But the four legions Augustus stationed in Syria, to control that wealthy province and protect the eastern frontier, posed little threat to Parthia, as it realized. The kingdom of Armenia, a pivotal buffer or sometimes client state, caused more problems as it wavered between Rome and Parthia. Nero's fine general Corbulo, by mixed diplomacy and arms, arranged a Roman investiture (crowning) for an Arsacid (Parthian) king of Armenia in AD66, so appeasing both sides.

The Flavians had advanced the frontier east by annexing small client states. Trajan continued this policy, peacefully annexing Arabia Petraea (Jordan) in AD106 with its rich trading city of Petra, and building a military highway through the desert, so rounding off the eastern frontier. Although Antioch, the empire's third largest city, was only 100 miles (160km) from the frontier, the Parthians remained a minor threat. Trajan did not need to launch a war of conquest, but it seems he felt drawn east. Using Parthian interference in Armenia as an excuse, he launched a grand attack on the Parthians from the headquarters he set up at Antioch in late AD113.

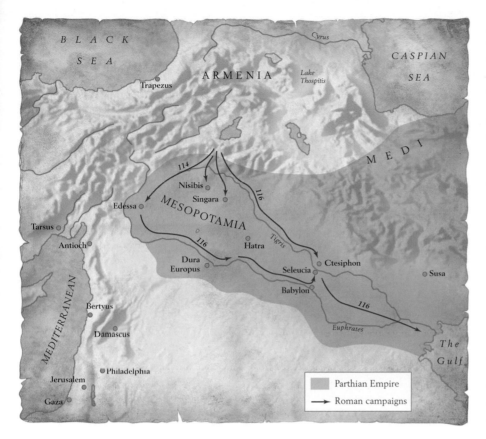

Left: Trajan's conquest of the east started with a successful attack on Armenia in AD114. A massive assault then over-ran all Mesopotamia down to the Gulf. But the Romans' rapid advance left their flanks exposed to counter-attacks while Jewish revolts in the rear threatened Rome's hold of the east. Finally, Trajan's failure to take the key city of Hatra led to the collapse of the invasion even before his death in AD117.

Below: Trajan shown triumphant in military uniform, a captive crouching at the feet of this most genial but expansionist of emperors.

RETREAT FROM THE GULF

Armenia was annexed in AD114 and at first the conquest of Mesopotamia seemed a huge success. Ctesiphon fell and Trajan sat on the Golden Throne of the Parthian kings, hailed by his army as *Parthicus* (conqueror of Parthia). East of the Tigris, a new province of Assyria (approximately Kurdistan) was created, completing the project of detaching what is now Iraq from Iran, and Trajan sailed south down the Tigris to the Gulf. According to Cassius Dio, on seeing the ocean and a ship setting out for India he said, "I would certainly have gone there too had I been younger." But he was 65 and in poor health. He returned via Babylon, already a ruin, to see the room where Alexander had died 400 years earlier. There he received news that all his new conquests were in peril. A wave of Jewish revolts had broken out, while the Parthians were harrying the eastern flanks of the new provinces. Failing to take the city of Hatra in central Mesopotamia, Trajan began recalling his troops. He died of a stroke in AD117 in Cilicia, but his eastern conquests had predeceased him. Hadrian completed the withdrawal and the return to the status quo, except that Armenia was once more in the Roman sphere.

Later campaigns in the reign of Marcus Aurelius between AD162 and 166 were scarcely more successful. Although Seleucia was captured and destroyed, a devastating plague sprang from its ruins. It was left to Septimius Severus to establish a defensible new frontier in AD198 along the lines of the Khabur river and Jebel Singara ridge, making northern Mesopotamia a defensible bulwark. But his victory also proved costly in the longer run, for it so weakened the Parthian empire that it was replaced 30 years later by the far more aggressive Sassanids.

CHAPTER XI

DEFENDING THE EMPIRE

After Trajan's death amid the ruins of his plans for conquering Asia, Hadrian reverted to a generally defensive policy. This was on the whole continued by his successors, despite later minor offensives. A few of these proved successful, like Septimius Severus' annexation of upper Mesopotamia, but most, like Marcus Aurelius' wars on the Danube or Septimius' own Caledonian campaign, failed with the death of their imperial instigator.

A total and official lack of aggressive wars, which had long kept soldiers busy and offered them chances of booty and promotion, posed its own problems. Hadrian addressed these by conducting vigorous exercises, which kept troops on their mettle, and by a huge fortifications programme, of which Hadrian's wall across northern England is only the most famous example. These walls were mostly built by legionaries themselves, so fulfilling the double function of adding to the empire's security while keeping its defenders occupied. But with some 6,000 miles (c.9,600 km) of land frontier, even Rome could not wall them all, and natural frontiers had to be exploited whenever possible. In the shorter term these proved adequate to protect the empire from its external foes, provided that no civil wars distracted the troops, especially when fortifications were supported by colonies of veterans. But certain corners of the empire always posed special problems, which drove even Hadrian to aggressive wars.

Left: Ruins of a milecastle on Hadrian's Wall, England, the most impressively surviving fortified frontier in the empire.

THE DILEMMAS OF DEFENCE

Above: Imperial policy moved decisively on to the defensive under Hadrian, but there was no change in military tactics.

Below: The cardo maximus (High Street) of ancient Gerasa (Jerash), Jordan, one of the many cities that thrived in the 2nd century AD.

For a long time, the Roman empire famously lacked a proper central reserve. The 25 legions Augustus left at his death in AD14 were deliberately dispersed on distant frontiers after inner provinces such as Spain were pacified. They were supplemented by equal numbers of cheaper auxiliaries. The only central force the *princeps* had at his command were the nine Praetorian cohorts, stationed in Italy and in Rome itself. These were crack troops but too few in number (*c.*4,500) to form more than a large bodyguard.

Some military historians have condemned Augustus' policy as a short-sighted economy that left the empire vulnerable to any invasion once the thin perimeter defences of legionary and auxiliary forts had been pierced. Others have condoned it as springing from the Principate's limited finances and the resultingly skimpy army, which had to defend nearly 4,000 miles (6,400km) of

frontier with only 300,000 men. Both have argued over the dilemmas of defence: whether it should be preclusive, making invasion impossible by investing all manpower in a heavily fortified border, or whether it should be a defence in depth. This would rely on a massed central reserve swinging into action against intruders but would leave outer provinces exposed as "marcher" territories. The fate of the later empire, however, which had a strong central reserve and also many troops on the perimeter, yet which was finally overwhelmed, suggests that such arguments miss the point.

There was little purpose in having a strong central force stationed at Milan so long as the main power of the army was its heavy infantry, as it was until the late 3rd century AD. Legions with baggage trains could not march more than 15 miles (24km) a day even on Rome's fine roads. Cologne on the Rhine was 67 marching days from Rome, for example, while the journey from Rome to Antioch took 124 days hard marching.

Nor could Romans make much use of marine internal lines of communications. At the heart of the empire, the Mediterranean scarcely offered speedy alternative transport, and the Roman army avoided sea travel wherever possible as it was too risky. The sea could be too rough for travel even within the normal sailing season of April to October, as ancient navigation skills were limited. It could take 55 days to reach Syria by sea – faster than by land but still slow. Logistics argued against a large central reserve, which could not reach a threatened area in time. Instead, troops were withdrawn from one currently peaceful front to fight on another troubled one. This could cause problems – one reason Agricola could not complete his conquest of northern Britain was because Domitian had recalled some of his troops to fight the Dacians – but

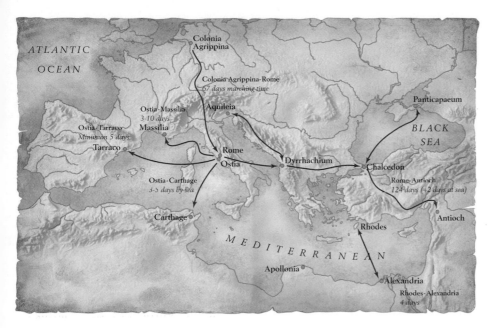

Left: Rome's almost central position in the Mediterranean did not help its military communications as much as might be expected. Moving troops from one frontier to another, whether by land or sea, was generally a slow business – one reason why emperors long dispensed with a central reserve that could not have reached threatened areas in time.

fortunately not more than one frontier was seriously threatened at any one time before the 3rd century AD.

However, the legions of the earlier Principate were *not* usually stationed to hold a fixed perimeter, although auxiliaries might patrol one. Legions were stationed in often indefensible spots so that they could pre-empt, or react to, any attacks before invaders had harmed unprotected lands behind the frontiers. One of Rome's boasts about the *Pax Romana* (Roman peace) was that its citizens had no more need of arms when only a few miles from the frontier than they did in Rome itself. There were, moreover, cogent political reasons for not having a large reserve force, especially one stationed in Italy. Armies were long commanded by legates of senatorial standing – potential rivals for the imperial throne as numerous revolts distracting emperors, from Saturninus in AD89 to Avidius Cassius in AD175, showed. Even without ambitious generals, after the Year of the Four Emperors in AD68–9 the armies grew conscious of their king-making potential. From the 3rd century AD onwards, the soldiers hailed their commanders as emperors with catastrophic frequency.

RESERVE OR BODYGUARD?

Septimius Severus, victor of the civil wars of AD193–7, purged the Praetorian guard, replacing them with his soldiers and stationing a newly created legion, the Second Parthica, near Rome. This created a force of 15,000 men, anticipating a central reserve. In the AD260s, Gallienus created a new reserve at Milan, using mostly cavalry *vexillationes* (detachments) from many legions. By the time this force was established, Gallienus had lost control of much of the empire, while the Danube frontier had collapsed and barbarians were threatening Italy. Milan therefore very nearly *was* the front line. It remained the main western capital after Roman recovery in the 4th century AD. By then, the Tetrarchy had begun a formal division between the *limitanei*, numerous frontier troops, and the *comitatenses*, superior mobile troops. Constantine took this further, concentrating the *comitatenses* and the new elite *palatini* in cities. The central reserve, 150,000 strong, had almost become a gigantic imperial bodyguard.

Below: Septimius Severus (AD193–211), under whom the empire reached its maximum permanent extent, began to create a central reserve by stationing a legion near Rome. But this, even when combined with the purged Praetorian guard, was still little more than a large imperial bodyguard.

NATURAL FRONTIERS
THE RHINE AND UPPER DANUBE

Above: If despotic and paranoid at home, Domitian (AD81–96) pursued a vigorous expansionist policy in south-west Germany.

Below: Hilly and thickly wooded, the Black Forest area remained impenetrable for the Romans until it was finally absorbed into the empire.

The problems that faced all Roman imperial governments in the defences of the two key frontiers, the Rhine and Upper Danube, in the late 1st and 2nd centuries AD, derived from the geography of the region. Not long after it leaves Lake Constance, the river Rhine starts to make a reasonably good frontier. Fast-flowing, it soon enters a deep, almost gorge-like valley, navigable by the Roman patrol flotillas. By Mainz, it has become a formidable river and easily defended. But the Danube, most obviously in its early stretches before the Lech joins it, is not remotely such an effective water barrier.

Both rivers' upper reaches tended to freeze over in winter and shrink alarmingly in summer droughts, so making naval patrols often impossible and barbarian crossings all too easy. Even more worrying, the valley of the river Neckar offers enticing pathways up beyond the Danube's source for possible invaders. The land in the south-west corner of Germany is mountainous and well-wooded – the Black Forest still covers much of it today – and is therefore difficult to patrol. The obvious answer, which meant overturning Augustus' famous deathbed advice *"coercendi intra terminos imperii"* (keep within the frontiers of the empire), was to advance the frontier, to cut off the "re-entrant"

angle between the Rhine and Danube and also, incidentally, to shorten the overall frontier by about 170 miles (270km).

The Flavian emperors Vespasian, Titus and Domitian were the first to have the time, energy and perhaps the vision to attempt this. After the serious revolt by Civilis in AD69–70 in the lower Rhine, when many troops went over to the Gallic separatists, the entire Rhine frontier was systematically reorganized. Vespasian began splitting up the legionary camps to avoid concentrating too many soldiers under one general and rebuilding turf and timber fortifications in stone. He also ordered the annexation of the Black Forest, but left this frontier unsecured at its northern end. It was left to Domitian, the least loved of emperors to date (except perhaps by the army), to advance the frontier permanently and effectively.

Domitian's war of AD83–5 against the Chatti tribes, which was much ridiculed by Tacitus, led to the slow but systematic advancing of the frontier across the river Rhine to a line that exploited natural features, the steep rather than high Taunus Mountains and the river Main. This line linked up with Vespasian's Black Forest forts further south, pushing along the Neckar almost to the headwaters of the Danube, so cutting off half the re-entrant and projecting Roman power into central Germany. The land along the lower Main valley was very fertile, useful for feeding garrisons. Later, the Antonine emperors extended the *limes* – a term that had, by the 2nd century AD, come to mean a fortified line of defence, though originally it meant only a path or a boundary – to the Danube near Regensburg (Castra Regina), which was a legionary fortress. The road connecting the two rivers from Mainz to Regensburg became a major imperial highway, shortening the journey to the Danube by 11 vital days. By finally

closing off this axis of potential invasion, this permitted the romanization of the areas far behind it. Although no real towns grew up within the new province, others lining the Rhine and Danube could now flourish in its shelter.

THE *AGRI DECUMATES*

This territory was known as the *Agri Decumates*, or lands that paid taxes, in contrast to "free Germany" beyond. A part of Upper Germany, the territory remained a militarized zone, but an increasingly prosperous one, defended by the longest and, in some ways, most imposing of all Roman fortifications. These were built mainly – initially entirely – of timber and turf, and included wooden watchtowers – probably with two men in them – every third of a mile (530m). These towers were easily visible to each other down lines cleared of woodland and linked by ditches. Palisades and even hedges were added under Hadrian. The aim was not to interdict movement across the frontier completely – any more than with Hadrian's Wall – but to slow down and hamper any raiders and smugglers.

Auxiliary cohorts stationed every 5 miles (8km) or so backed them up, some of their forts being built in stone. In total, following the bends of rivers or the lines of hills in a way that makes sense on the ground if not on the map, the line covered some 300 miles (480km) with more than 60 forts and 900 signal towers. In fact this created a larger fortification than Hadrian's Wall, but, due to its mainly timber construction, it has left far fewer visible traces. (One or two forts, such as Zugmantel, have been reconstructed.) In the turmoil of the 3rd century AD, the line became increasingly difficult to hold and it was finally abandoned by AD260. The frontier then returned to its former limits under Augustus.

Above: South-west German reconstruction of a watchtower, typical of the hundreds that guarded the Agri Decumates.

Below: The Agri Decumates *reduced the length of the frontier and speeded communications.*

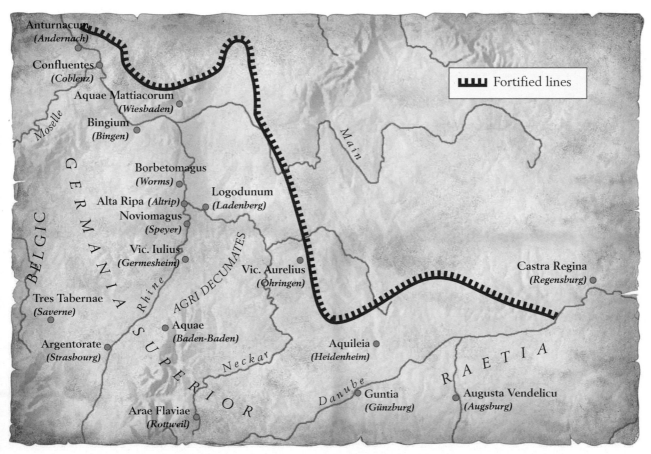

NATURAL FRONTIERS
THE MIDDLE AND LOWER DANUBE

Above: This scene from Trajan's Column in Rome shows Roman soldiers cutting down trees to build fortifications or war machines during the Dacian wars. At times, the army's demands could deforest whole regions.

Augustus had given Rome its longest land frontier – along Europe's longest river – when he occupied all the Danubian lands from the Alps down to the Black Sea. This was for a long time the empire's least developed region. It lacked any real towns or even the rich, if still predominantly agricultural, culture of pre-Roman Gaul and Britain. It was strategically important, however, because it dominated Italy's most accessible passes through the Julian Alps and provided a land route from the eastern empire to the west.

Slowly, the area was organized into provinces. These ran behind the river from Alpine Raetia and Noricum (Switzerland, southern Bavaria/north Austria), through the plains of Pannonia with its large rivers – the Save and Drave as well as the Danube – to Moesia (Bulgaria and northern Serbia). Ultimately, the whole region was to become Rome's prime recruiting ground, providing many great later emperors including Aurelian and Constantine. It was a vital defence against invaders, as

they moved from deepest *barbaricum*, the barbarian world, to the empire. Its final loss foreshadowed the western empire's.

As on the Rhine, Augustus had not originally intended to halt his sweeping conquests on the south or west bank of the river. However, all plans to occupy part of Bohemia (so creating a new line along the Elbe down to the North Sea) had to be aborted after a major revolt in Pannonia and Dalmatia that started in AD6. Coupled with Varus' German disaster in AD9, this marked the end of Augustan expansionism, although the huge Danubian basin remained relatively lightly garrisoned. In the 1st century AD it had only six legions – two of them initially in Dalmatia rather than on the river – compared to the eight on the much shorter Rhine frontier.

Diplomacy (always a major part of Rome's defence), coupled with bribes, kept the various nomadic tribes and peoples of the Pannonian plain divided and harmless; the Iazyges were often paid to keep the menacing Dacians in check.

Right: Rome's long and potentially most dangerous frontier was the Danube, beyond which lay the immensity of the Eurasian steppes, source of endless new invasions. From the early 2nd century AD, this frontier required ever-larger garrisons. Once across its perimeter defences, barbarians could easily penetrate into Italy, as happened in AD166 and on many subsequent occasions.

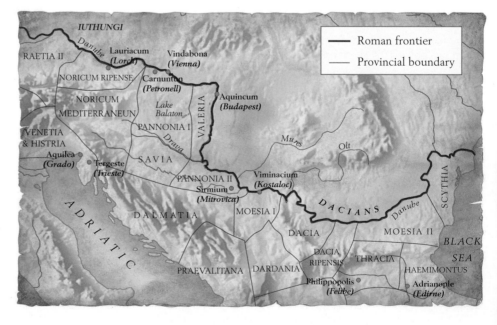

Right: Marcus Aurelius (AD161–80) whose trans-Danubian plans expired with him.

However, when Decebalus, a formidable ruler, became High King of Dacia in *c.*AD85, his country's potential was quickly mobilized. Heavy raids across the Danube into Pannonia generated a quick, if initially unsuccessful, Roman reaction. Domitian's wars with Dacia led to a truce that was more in Dacia's favour than Rome's, due to Saturninus' revolt in AD89. Domitian not only paid Decebalus a subsidy, which was common enough practice, but also lent him engineers to fortify his capital of Sarmizagetusa Regia, which was nothing of the sort. In the following years the Iazyges, a nomadic people, became a problem too, raiding across the Danube and requiring Rome's finally successful attentions. Trajan's great conquest of Dacia in AD101–6 needs, therefore, to be seen in the light of a breakdown of the whole earlier system. Its success can be gauged by the 60 years of prosperous peace that followed. Flotillas – one on either side of the Iron Gates Gorge, which divided the Danube – helped keep the river free of intruders, turning it into a useful waterway as much as an effective barrier.

MARCUS AURELIUS' CAMPAIGNS

The plague that devastated the empire from AD166 after the triumphant Parthian campaign (which itself had drawn off whole legions from the Rhine and Danube), gave the barbarians their chance. The Germanic Marcomanni and Quadi and the Iazyges crossed the lightly defended river and pushed on, bypassing forts, into Italy, attacking Aquileia (near Trieste) in AD167. For the first time in 260 years, barbarians were in Italy. Other barbarians opportunistically pushed through the Balkans to sack Eleusis, on the doorstep of Athens.

Marcus Aurelius, despite the plague and acute financial problems, raised two fresh legions (from gladiators among others), sold even the palace ornaments to pay for them and went north to repel the invaders. His long and hard campaigns along the Danube drove them back over the river. He now decided to copy Trajan, not out of vainglory – he was after all a philosopher – but from necessity. He probably intended to create new provinces of Marcomannia (the Czech Republic) and Sarmatia (Slovakia/Galicia). By advancing the frontiers, Rome would be able to meet the barbarian tide on the far side of the Carpathian and the Sudeten mountains. Whether his great project would have succeeded if the revolt of Avidius Cassius in Syria in AD175 had not distracted him and he himself had not died in AD180 is unclear. What is certain is that the Danube basin in the 3rd century became a key area for barbarian attacks. However, it had also become so deeply Romanized that it was a source of strength as well as weakness, right down to the fall of the western empire in the 5th century.

Below: A model of the key Dacian fortress of Bildaru in the mountains of Transylvania captured by Trajan's men.

NATURAL FRONTIERS
AFRICA, ARABIA, MESOPOTAMIA

Below: The ruins of the triple arch at Lambaesis (Tazoult, Algeria), built by Septimius Severus (AD193–211). The Libyan-born emperor was particularly interested in North Africa, embellishing its cities and advancing the frontiers.

Rome had desert frontiers in Arabia, Mesopotamia and North Africa. In Asia, Rome faced sporadic Arab raiders and its one equal, the Parthian, later Sassanid Persian, empire. In Africa, Rome often faced little – often no – opposition, for the deserts of Libya harboured only nugatory populations of Berber nomads. Egypt was almost impregnable behind its deserts, except from Asia, for upstream the Nubians – as Rome called the Sudanese – were no threat.

Cyrenaica and Tripolitania (Libya) may have needed almost no defence, but Roman Africa, that thin slice of the great continent seldom more than 100 miles (160km) deep, was an increasingly important province. Dry-farming employed a cunning combination of olive trees and wheat fields. It used every drop of moisture through irrigation and, by so holding back the desert, beneficially modified the climate. Africa satisfied much of Rome's demand for olive oil. Josephus described it as "that third part of the world, which feeds the city of Rome for eight months of the year and happily accepts taxation, although only one legion is stationed there".

For the Berbers it was worth raiding. To protect against their attacks, which generally followed the Atlas valleys as they ran down towards Carthage and its intensely fertile hinterland, a series of walls called *clausurae* (closures) were built. Some 15ft (4.5m) high, they closed off the valleys or at least made it extremely difficult for such invaders to return with

much booty. A joint letter from eastern and western emperors (Theodosius II and Honorius), written in AD409, indicates that Africa mattered to both parts of the empire. It also shows that there were *fossata* (ditch works) and *limites* (fortified lines) further south, where fertile land gives way to desert, with watchtowers.

Archaeology has tentatively confirmed this skeletal defence system, which exploited the *chotts* (sand seas, at times full of salt water) and mountains of the Haut Plateaux. Running from east to west, these were the *limes* of Tripoli, the *limes* of Numidia, inland from Carthage, and the *limes* of Mauretania, inland from the Algerian coast. None of these was a solid continuous defence like Hadrian's Wall, because the distances were too immense. Hadrian had ordered the construction of such a line on his visit to Africa in AD128. He realized that nomads and farmers were interdependent: nomads supplied useful extra seasonal labour, farmers repaid them with food-stuffs. The one legion was stationed at Lambaesis, just behind the central *limes*. Later, under Septimius Severus, forts were built much further inland. In Tripolitania Ghadames, some 300 miles (480km) inland, was the most advanced of four forts, built in AD200 and abandoned around AD263. Such forts were intended to control desert routes.

THE EASTERN FRONTIERS

Until Vespasian began annexing them, a screen of client states shielded the Roman provinces from the Arabian desert. But when Trajan took over Arabia Petraea (Jordan) in AD106, the problem of patrolling the edges of the Arabian desert confronted the Romans directly. Trajan built the Via Nova (new road), a military highway from the Gulf of Aqaba north-east past Bostra and Damascus. This was a patrolled *limes* in the old sense of a dividing line with forts built along it, from which cavalry patrolled. The Arabs were more numerous raiders than the Berbers – and in the 7th century AD became

invaders – but did not at this time pose a major threat to the blooming wheat fields of Transjordania. Later, Septimius pushed the frontier 50 miles (80km) east from the Via Nova, but it was further north that he made his major contribution, almost solving the perennial frontier problem with Parthia.

He did this by annexing upper Mesopotamia. Here his new frontier ran along the Khabur river, a small tributary joining the Euphrates 50 miles (80km) north of the key fortress of Dura-Europus, then running along the hills of Jebel Sinjar. These rise to 4,800ft (1,460m) above the desert – high enough to receive 8in (20cm) of rain a year, vital for supplying garrisons. Septimius probably stationed a legion at Singara on this line, and he certainly fortified Nisibis to its rear. His military road ran on to the Tigris at Eski Mosul (old Mosul). Here a walled city 3 miles (4.8km) in circumference was built, the easternmost limit of Rome's might. It would need a change of dynasty in Ctesiphon before such a powerful line would be challenged, and it lasted as long as the empire itself.

Above: The ruins of Dura-Europus on the Euphrates in Syria, once a vital fortress on Rome's eastern frontier. Captured by the Persians c.AD256 after a long siege, it was so badly damaged that it has never been reoccupied.

Below: These laws about the development of Roman lands in Africa are dated AD209.

COLONIES AND SETTLEMENTS
FOR VETERANS

Below: Colonies, originally planned chiefly for legionary veterans, were established right across the empire from the time of Julius Caesar onwards. They acted as a backup to regular legions and, more crucially if less intentionally, helped Romanize the empire. Colonies like Colchester and Cologne later became important cities.

From the mid-Republic, Rome had expanded its power by the planting of colonies in strategically important places, first in peninsular Italy, then in Cisalpine Gaul. Originally, these *coloniae* were always settlements of Roman citizens with a standard Roman city constitution, but later some had only Latin rights, a halfway house to full citizenship that proved very useful in the Principate. All helped knit the empire together.

Gaius Gracchus had first proposed planting a colony for landless Romans outside Italy at Carthage, an idea revived by Saturninus in 102BC for the veterans of Marius' armies for North Africa, southern Gaul and Greece. However, it was Julius Caesar who started founding colonies for his veterans on a massive

scale: in Spain, where the charter of Urso (Colonia Genetiva Julia) survives and where older cities such as Cartagena and Tarragona became full Roman colonies; in Gaul, at Fréjus (Forum Julii) and Arles (Arelate); at Carthage and Corinth (both ruins since 146BC) and in Greece, Syria and even on the Black Sea coast. Many of these had strategic value.

Augustus, who reputedly had 300,000 veterans to find land for after Actium in 31BC, founded about 75 settlements. Twenty-eight were in Italy, such as Turin (Augusta Taurinorum), whose fine gate survives, and Aosta (Augusta Praetoria), facing the Alps. He stressed in the *Res Gestae*, his memoirs, that he paid fair prices for the land. More were scattered across the empire: Mérida and Saragossa

(Caesar-Augusta) in Spain; Nîmes and Avignon in Gaul; Patras and Nicopolis (near Actium, "city of victory") in Greece; and on round the empire, in Africa, Macedonia, Syria, Galatia (north central Turkey) and Pisidia (central/south-west Turkey). Some were built for defence, such as those in Galatia and Pisidia, while others became thriving cities. Tarragona claimed to have a population of 400,000 in the 2nd century AD – which is probably an exaggeration, although it was the capital of the whole Iberian peninsula and a centre of the imperial cult.

All these generally small settlements – usually a couple of thousand veterans, growing perhaps into a city of between 10–15,000 – helped the urbanization and Romanization of the whole empire. Their elderly soldier-citizens could theoretically provide reinforcements to legionary forts and more certainly provided potential recruits for the next generation's legions. As they became permanent, some of the great military bases around the frontiers developed into towns with their outlying *canabae* (settlements). Sometimes, as at Cologne (Colonia Agrippina) in AD51, a colony was founded on the Rhine's west bank to incorporate these. In eastern Algeria, a Trajanic veterans' colony at Timgad (Thamugadi), has remained almost perfectly preserved, its porticoes and arches looking out over a now desiccated but once very fertile landscape.

PROUD TO BE ROMAN

As the colonies became established, they developed a competitive pride in being Roman. Local aristocracies, especially in the west – the long-Hellenized east was rather different – vied to become Roman in clothes, deed and name. Men whose fathers had been Gaulish chieftains began taking Roman triple names and their sons began to think of themselves as Romans. In Vienne (Vienna) on the banks of the Rhône, for example, Strabo reported early in the 1st century AD that "the Allobroges used to be always at war but now they

farm the plains and valleys, living in villages except for their nobles who live in Vienne. That was once a village... but now they have made it into a city." Italians began settling there as early as 70BC, and a century later Claudius could praise it as *ornatissima et valentissima colonia* (an excellent, flourishing colony). Up river on the other side, its rival Lyons (Lugdunum, the "dun" recalling a Celtic origin) had a theatre for 11,000 spectators, an odeon for more select audiences seating 5,000 and a large, centrally heated basilica. Lyons prospered at the centre of Gaul's Roman road network.

Further north, the city of Trier (Augusta Treverorum) became a centre of industry and commerce where the tribe of the Treveri settled and became fully Romanized. A school of sculpture also developed there. The city later became the capital of Gaul, at times of all the west, with a basilica, baths and palaces. In Britain, the tiny but fully self-governing *colonia* of Gloucester (Glevum) was founded under emperor Nerva (AD96–8), joining Lincoln and Colchester in this prized status. More populous was nearby Cirencester (Corinium), which boasted the full range of civic amenities although it was not a *colonia*. Hadrian gave Latin rights to many settlements, whereby all members of their councils as well as their decurions (officials) received Roman citizenship. In this way, Roman civilization and citizenship were spread.

Above: The ruins of the theatre at Bostra, now in Syria, which thrived after Trajan annexed Arabia Petraea, making it the capital.

Below: An evening view of Timgad, Algeria, in what was then a very fertile province.

THE JEWISH REVOLT

Above: Perhaps the most holy of the religious treasures that the Romans brought back from their sack of the Temple in Jerusalem was the seven-branched candlestick, here shown on the Arch of Titus in Rome being paraded in triumph by soldiers.

Below: The bitter siege and total destruction of Jerusalem by Titus in AD70 led to the permanent ruin of the Temple restored by Herod, and so to the last stage in the Jewish Diaspora that had begun centuries earlier.

Uniquely among the disparate peoples of the empire, the Jews refused to accept the Graeco-Roman culture all around them, proudly aware that they had a tradition to rival it. The Romans, despite initial good intentions and a total lack of racist feeling, could not understand a people so different, in their exclusive monotheism, from any of their other subjects. Set between the wealthy provinces of Syria and Egypt, Judaea was too strategically important to be ignored, however. The Jewish Diaspora, which had started some three centuries before following the conquests of Alexander the Great, meant that Jews were already spread across the eastern part of the empire, and there was a Jewish community in Rome by Julius Caesar's time.

Herod the Great, who died in 4BC, had pursued a pro-Roman and Hellenizing policy. His kingdom came under direct Roman rule as a procuratorial province in AD6 because his less than competent successors quarrelled among themselves. Many of their Jewish subjects (Jews were not the only inhabitants of the kingdom, Hellenized Syrians being numerous) objected strongly to the house of Herod but did little, being divided: Samaritans versus Judaeans, reformist Pharisees against Sadducees, with the Zealots as politically active extremists. However, when Rome gradually found itself ruling almost the whole area after the death of Herod Agrippa II in AD44, Jewish resentment was unified against the hated occupier. The troubled province of Judaea, one of the least popular posts for an equestrian governor, does seem to have been unusually badly administered.

A revolt finally broke out in AD66. It was centred on south Judaea and Jerusalem. The governor of Syria, Cestius Gallus, hastening south from Antioch with inadequate forces, was heavily defeated and beat a retreat. Encouraged by his defeat, other Jews now joined the revolt. The emperor Nero, who had become deeply suspicious of military rivals, entrusted the suppression of the revolt to Vespasian, an officer long out of favour but one who had had a good record of storming forts 20 years before in Britain. Vespasian proved a brilliant choice, methodically putting down the rebels, in particular reducing the fortress of Jotapata in Galilee under its Jewish commander, Josephus. By building a huge mound to approach its walls, the three legions involved were able to overwhelm the defenders, especially after Josephus changed sides. At this stage, however, Vespasian was distracted by the Civil War of AD68–9 and went to Alexandria to organize his empire-winning campaign. He left his son Titus to finish suppressing the Jews.

THE SIEGE OF JERUSALEM

By AD70, Titus had closed in on Jerusalem. Heavily fortified and ornamented by Herod the Great, the city was divided into five separately walled parts. It had been well provisioned, but fighting between rival groups of fanatics led to much of their food being burnt. Only at the very last minute did the Jewish factions cease fighting each other. The Old Upper City had Herod's huge palace on its west flank and just northeast of it lay the massively walled Temple Enclosure, with the Second Quarter and the larger New City to its north. Titus had four legions at his disposal, enough men to surround the whole city with a siege wall.

Although the defenders made aggressive sorties to attack the Romans, the final outcome was never in doubt. But at first the Romans' earthworks were undermined by the energetic defenders and collapsed. After rebuilding these and a further 13 days' fierce fighting, the Romans entered the less heavily defended New City and pushed on, breaking through the wall of the Second Quarter to attack the great fortress of Antonia (named after Mark Antony), which immediately adjoined the Temple. This required two new ramps. It fell only when the defenders' tunnels, meant to cause the collapse of these Roman works, actually

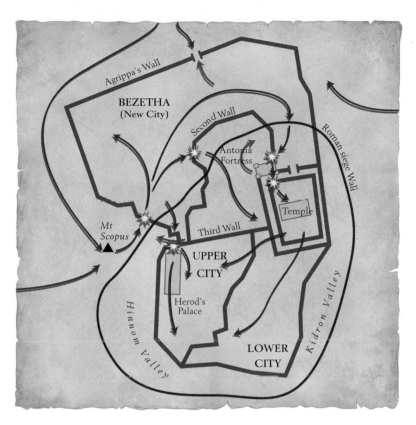

undermined their own walls. A small group of legionaries then scaled the walls and killed the sentries, before sounding their trumpets to tell Titus to start the attack on the fort's inner walls. Weeks of heavy fighting were required to capture the Temple itself, which was burnt to the ground (perhaps accidentally). The loss of this great building, so central to Judaism, disheartened the defenders, but they fought on heroically. The Upper City was the very last to fall. After 18 days of preparation, during which legionaries and auxiliaries raised mounds on the west and east sides respectively, the Romans renewed their assault and finally stormed the area around the palace. The whole city was then pillaged before being systematically set on fire. During the five-month siege, the defenders had become so famished that, according to Josephus, mothers had eaten their own children. Titus ordered that just three towers and part of the wall be left, as poignant reminders of the ruined city.

Below: The Arch of Titus, emperor AD79–81, was built to commemorate his victory in the Jewish war of ten years earlier.

Above: The siege and capture of Jerusalem in AD70 by the Romans under Titus was the crucial engagement of the Jewish revolt. The five-month siege saw the Romans circumvallating the city as usual. They attacked the less well-defended New Town first, before moving upwards and inwards, firing the Temple and finally taking the Upper City, sparing no one in the city.

SIEGE OF MASADA

The last chapter in the bloody Jewish revolt of AD66–73 was the siege of Masada, which required one legion and 4,000 auxiliaries to suppress it. Famous because of its site, Masada is a rock rising some 1,300ft (396m) above a high, arid plateau, surrounded by precipitous cliffs that make it seem impregnable above the great valley of the Dead Sea. Herod the Great had converted it into a fortified palace and place of refuge, but by AD70 it was occupied by just a few hundred extremists, called the Sicarii. The fort was equipped with deep water cisterns and storerooms containing such vast amounts of food that it could not easily be starved out. Flavius Silva, legate of the Tenth Legion, therefore decided on a direct assault. This would make a dramatic statement about Rome's power and the perils of challenging it. It has left the most graphic and complete evidence of Roman siege warfare of any site.

The legionaries built a wall of local stone some 4,700yd (4,300m) long with towers every 30yd (27m) or so to circumvallate the rock, plus eight forts for themselves, inside which they built low-walled cabins. Across the tops of these they put their leather tents, for protection against the blazing midday sun and the bitterly cold night winds of the three-year siege. They then built a huge ramp up the west side of the hill and winched their siege engines up it. Realizing that they could not escape, the Sicarii men committed mass suicide, after killing all their women and children. This finally ended the revolt – at least according to Josephus, the rebel leader turned Roman, who was, however, not an impartial observer.

BAR KOCHBA'S REBELLION

The fall of Masada did not, however, end simmering Jewish discontent with Roman rule across the eastern Mediterranean. Even before Trajan's grand attack on the Parthian empire faltered in AD117, a huge Jewish revolt in Cyrenaica, Cyprus and Egypt had flared up in AD115. More than 200,000 Greek-speaking neighbours of the Jews in these countries were reportedly

Above: An aerial view of one of the camps in the circumvallation at Masada, Israel, where several hundred Jewish zealots defied the Romans under Falvius Silva until AD73. Today, the desert site remains almost perfectly preserved due to its remoteness and aridity.

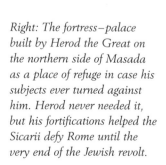

Right: The fortress–palace built by Herod the Great on the northern side of Masada as a place of refuge in case his subjects ever turned against him. Herod never needed it, but his fortifications helped the Sicarii defy Rome until the very end of the Jewish revolt.

ROME AND THE JEWS

Looking at Rome's repeated suppression of Jewish revolts, we might imagine that the Romans were deeply anti-Semitic. Nothing could be less true. As the cases of Herod Agrippa, a close friend of the emperor Claudius, St Paul – a Jewish Roman citizen – and especially of Flavius Josephus demonstrate, the Romans were not racist in any modern sense. Nor were they religiously intolerant like many later Christian persecutors of Jews. In general, the Romans were indifferent to racial and religious differences, despite having a certain distaste for unwashed, drunken Germans. Their crushings of Jewish rebellions were always politically motivated, carried out with their usual brutality so as to discourage others.

The Romans first encountered the Jews in the mid-2nd century BC. They had just revolted against the Seleucid Hellenistic monarchs of Syria, who had tried to enforce the cult of Zeus (Jupiter) at Jerusalem. Out of distrust for the Seleucids, Rome supported this Maccabean revolt and Judaea became independent with Roman approval. The Romans were at first impressed, if puzzled, by the conservatism of Jewish religious beliefs and social customs, and they tried to accommodate them. Jews were generally exempted from emperor worship – such worship was a political rather than religious act – and military service was seldom forced on Jews for the same reason. A few Romans, attracted by its highly ethical message, converted to Judaism in the 1st century AD before the spread of Christianity. However, Jews were by then scattered so widely across the empire – in Syria, Egypt, Asia Minor (Turkey), Cyrenaica (Libya), Cyprus and even Rome itself – that Rome was inevitably drawn into many local Jewish–Gentile quarrels.

killed before the Romans managed to repress it. Yet this was still not quite the end of the Jewish–Roman wars.

Hadrian was among Rome's wisest and most humane emperors. He probably envisaged the empire becoming an equal commonwealth of all its provinces rather than being ruled just for Rome's sake. However, as a passionate philhellene (lover of Greece), he did not understand why any people should not want to participate in the splendours of Graeco-Roman culture. He therefore established a Roman colony at Jerusalem, which he renamed Aelia Capitolina, building a temple to Zeus/Jupiter on the very site of the ruined Temple. This so enraged the Jews still living in Palestine that in AD133 they rose again under Bar Kochba, a talented general, and proclaimed their own state. It took the Romans years of bitter, small-scale fighting to suppress this revolt, after which Jews were banned from Jerusalem. Later, Antoninus Pius (reigned AD138–61) quietly revoked his predecessor's decree and allowed any Jews, who wished to, to return to the now utterly desolate site of Jerusalem.

Above: Storehouses and deep wells inside the fort of Masada. It was so well supplied that the Romans could not hope to starve it quickly into surrender.

Below: Remains of the Jewish fortification at Masada. Behind its walls, Zealots called the Sicarii retreated, thinking they had made themselves impregnable to all attacks.

CHAPTER XII

DECLINE AND FALL

Few historical topics are more fascinating than the decline and fall of world-conquering powers. In Rome's case this took centuries rather than years. The empire had survived a near-total collapse in the 3rd century AD and even the 5th century AD saw only the fall of the western half of the empire – and half of that was recovered by the eastern empire in the 6th century AD. The story is much more complicated than one of inexorable decay.

Although there were a handful of brilliant or exceptional barbarian leaders, notably Attila the Hun and Gaiseric the Vandal, most of the barbarians who overran the empire in the 5th century AD were not especially formidable. Similar tribes had already tried to invade the empire in the preceding centuries and been repulsed, albeit at an often huge cost. This suggests that the fall of the western half of the empire might have been averted by intelligent, consistent and, above all, unified strong government. But the imperial rulers' record in the 5th century AD is one of indecision, feebleness and above all of suicidal disputes, as internecine fighting squandered Rome's remaining strength in civil wars. It was hardly surprising that some, although never all, of the brightest and the best citizens of the western half of the Roman world finally lost faith and hope in their government, turning instead to the City of God to be found only in heaven.

Left: Sacrificing to the pagan gods – a political as well as religious gesture that vexed an increasingly Christian empire.

THE 3RD-CENTURY CRISIS

Above: The reign of the perverted emperor Elagabalus drew Rome further into her 3rd-century AD crisis.

Below: The Emperor Decius addresses his troops. In AD251 he became the first Roman emperor to be killed (by the Goths) in battle, setting an ominous precedent.

In some ways it is remarkable that the Roman Empire survived the 3rd century AD at all. The civil wars, foreign invasions, plagues and other calamities it suffered for more than half a century after 235AD would have been enough to cause the terminal disintegration of most empires. But centripetal patriotism, a loyalty to the idea as much as to the reality of Rome, proved in the end just strong enough to ensure the empire's survival, for a while. It survived, however, in a different form and at a price that grew steadily more crushing, financially, socially and politically.

Cracks in the golden surface of the *Pax Romana*, the Roman peace, had appeared as early as the reign of Marcus Aurelius (AD161–80). The plague – possibly smallpox – which the victorious legions brought back with them from Parthia in AD165, devastated the empire and kept recurring for years. Combined with a series of invasions, primarily but not exclusively along the Danubian frontier – even Egypt suffered a brief attack – followed by the long debauchery of Commodus' reign, this epidemic hit an already somewhat sclerotic empire. The empire's economy had almost certainly started to stagnate by the mid-2nd century AD; by the century's end it was probably contracting.

Far worse, however, were the civil wars that followed Commodus' assassination in AD192. Septimius Severus finally won the civil wars in AD197 but at a terrible cost, both military and economic. Both Severus' and his enemy Albinus' armies had huge casualties in the last campaign. In these wars, trained Roman soldiers were killed fighting each other, a loss the empire could no longer easily make up. Severus, a brutally vindictive man, sacked Lugdunum (Lyons) so thoroughly it never recovered its wealth or status as Gaul's prime city. By comparison with his thuggish son Caracalla, he was an ideal ruler, but the latter's murder brought no improvement for there followed the reign of the manic pervert Elagabalus.

The murder of the last Severan, the ineffectual Alexander, in AD235, is usually taken to mark the end of the Principate and its replacement by mere anarchy. The year AD238 saw the coinage of seven distinct emperors and there were at least 50 claimants to the imperial throne in the half century after AD235. Some of these formed wholly separate states, such as the Gallic, British and Spanish empire of Postumus.

The problem of the succession, always tricky in the crypto-monarchy that was the Principate, became crucial in the ensuing chaos. Of the 27 or so "regular" emperors, 17 were killed by their own troops or officers, two were forced to commit suicide, one died a natural death and the rest were killed in battle. Even outstandingly successful and popular emperors such as Aurelian (AD270–75) were murdered. The custom by which the Senate had sanctioned (even if it did

not always control) the choice of the next emperor became an outmoded farce. Elevation to the imperial purple became effectively a deferred death sentence.

The barbarian peoples outside the empire had long been waiting for an opportunity to renew their raids. Now, with the Romans at each other's throats, they saw and seized it. Tarragona and Athens, both many hundreds of miles from a frontier, were sacked in the AD260s. Once barbarians had penetrated the outer frontier defences, Rome's good roads facilitated their raids, now that there were no longer forces waiting to repel them. The interior cities, with their long-disarmed citizens and no tradition of self-defence, were easy prey. Soldiers had to be called in to build many of the walls for the cities in Gaul, for example.

ECONOMIC CRISIS

This damage to life across the provinces far beyond the traditional frontier zones proved hard to repair. At the same time the increase in the size and cost of the army meant a steep rise in taxes. Septimius Severus had increased Rome's military strength to 400,000 men and raised the army's pay by 50 per cent – perhaps an overdue rise, but Caracalla raised their pay again by another 50 per cent. To pay

for this and subsequent increases, Caracalla debased the coinage, a custom followed by so many of his successors that money became almost worthless. By the mid-3rd century AD, many traders and bankers were refusing to accept Roman coins. The armies resorted to exacting goods and services from the unfortunate civilians they were supposedly protecting.

The economic results were grim but are unquantifiable, for it was an economically ignorant age. It is estimated that at least 15 per cent of all arable land went out of production in the mid-3rd century AD. (Egypt, however, was probably thriving, and archaeological evidence from North Africa also suggests a period of economic prosperity.) But city life, especially in the west, also suffered terribly. The walls Aurelian gave Rome covered most of its existing urban area, but other cities shrank drastically. Within them, the old decurion class of local officials, who had been in many ways the backbone of the empire, began to collapse beneath an increasing burden of taxes. Those rich enough to do so withdrew to self-sufficient country estates; the less wealthy sank back into the urban poor. No matter what the tetrarchs and their heirs attempted, the blow to civic life, especially in the west, was to prove irreparable.

Above: Relatively unharmed by the 3rd-century crisis, North Africa still prospered, building amphitheatres such as this at El Djem, Tunisia.

Below: Philip the Arab (AD244–9) was the emperor who celebrated Rome's millennium in AD248, but it was not a timely celebration. The empire appeared to be collapsing. Barbarians had broken through on almost every frontier, while anarchy spread inside the empire.

THE EASTERN PROBLEM
THE POWER OF THE SASSANIDS

Above: The power of the Sassanids of Persia lay in their cavalry. This cataphract (armoured horseman) charging with his lance formed the backbone of the army, although their lack of stirrups limited their impact.

Below: This citadel, called the Redoubt, overlooks the river Euphrates in Syria at Dura-Europus on the two empires' much-disputed frontier. Both the Romans and the Persians appear to have occupied this citadel at different times.

For nearly two and a half centuries after the battle of Actium, Rome could regard the defence of its eastern frontier along the mid-Euphrates as something of an optional extra. The Arsacid Parthian empire facing it across the upper Euphrates may have been very large (it covered modern Iraq, Iran and parts of south Afghanistan), but it was seldom formidable, except when on the defensive. The Parthian empire's loose semi-feudal structure meant that its sub-kings did not always rally to help their nominal overlord.

Despite this, the Parthians had repelled Roman invaders from Crassus to Trajan, but they never seriously threatened Syria, the Roman province closest to them. Septimius Severus' campaigns in the AD190s again showed up Parthian weakness – he sacked Ctesiphon and annexed upper Mesopotamia, establishing a very defensible frontier province. However, he also unwittingly damaged the prestige of the Arsacid dynasty so badly that it succumbed to Ardashir, a Sassanid prince, in AD224.

The Sassanids came from the province of Persis (Fars). Guardians of Persepolis, Iran's ancient royal city, they were determined to revive the glories of the Achaemenid Persian empire of Darius and Xerxes. This had once extended west as far as the Aegean, so major conflict with Rome seemed inevitable. Early clashes were inconclusive, however. Neither Alexander Severus nor Gordian III were good generals, but their armies, ably officered, managed to avoid defeat, at least according to Roman sources.

The Sassanid army consisted of heavy cavalry – cataphracts, mainly noblemen and their supporters, who charged using lances – supplemented by numerous mounted archers. The Romans commented admiringly on the disciplined skill of these archers, which rivalled that of the legionaries' and was well suited to desert terrain. Persian infantry was of little use, but the Sassanids at times employed Indian elephants to great psychological, if not military, effect. Above all, the Sassanids developed a professional siege corps, something the Parthians had lacked but which was essential for attacking the walled cities of Mesopotamia and Syria. The Sassanids also revived the old Zoroastrian religion, a form of monotheism that stressed martial values and gave their empire a strong ideological basis.

In AD241 Shapur I succeeded to the throne (the Sassanids generally followed the hereditary principle) and began calling himself "King of Kings of Iran and non-Iran", a universalist title to challenge that of Rome. His reign of 32 years outlasted those of 16 Roman emperors. His western offensives began with forcing the new emperor, Philip the Arab, to make a humiliating peace in AD244. His second offensive in AD256 ended with the capture of 37 Roman cities,

Above: The "Arch of Chosroes" stands in the ruins of the audience hall of the Sassanian palace of Ctesiphon, near Baghdad, Iraq.

including Dura-Europus (which fell after an epic siege *c.*AD256) and Antioch, capital of the Roman east. All survivors were carried off into captivity. The emperor Valerian took a huge army of 70,000 men east to repel Shapur but it was hit by plague and cornered in Edessa. Valerian was captured and spent the rest of his life as a prisoner of the Persians, used as a human footstool by Shapur when the Persian king mounted his horse. After his death, Valerian's stuffed body was hung on the walls of a temple. The capture alive of a Roman emperor was an unprecedented humiliation for the empire but one that Gallienus, Valerian's son, was powerless to avenge.

The whole Roman east then seemed about to fall into Shapur's hands, as his forces overran Asia Minor and threatened Egypt. Fortunately for Rome, Shapur snubbed Odenathus, king of Palmyra, while returning to Persia in AD261. This proved a huge mistake. Odenathus accepted a Roman command. Palmyrene cavalry, perhaps the best in the east, now turned against Persia and Persian forces had to retreat for a time.

It would be a mistake to suppose that the Persians were always invincible. They had difficulty maintaining their conquests beyond the Euphrates so far from their Iranian power base. They could also be defeated in open battle, as Galerius, the Caesar of Diocletian, showed. After an initial defeat, Galerius triumphed over the Persian monarch, Narses, in AD298, annexing a useful slice of land beyond the Tigris. The subsequent peace lasted for 40 years.

JULIAN'S DEFEAT

Under Constantine and his successors, the peace unravelled. Constantius II spent much time in the AD340s fighting the Persians before turning west to deal with Roman rivals. The Persians then renewed the offensive, capturing the well-fortified city of Amida in AD359; they had been intending to bypass it until a catapult bolt killed the son of a client king and so forced them to attack. Julian, on becoming sole emperor in AD361, decided to avenge this defeat and crush Persia. After his defeat and death, half of Rome's territories east of the Euphrates were ceded to Persia by the new emperor Jovian in return for safe passage home. Oddly, the peace that followed lasted, with only minor disruptions, for 140 years.

Below: When the Sassanid Persian empire replaced the Parthians in c. *AD226, Rome faced far greater pressure on its eastern frontier. The Persians penetrated deep into Roman territory in the 3rd century AD, but the Romans counter-attacked later, pushing across the upper Tigris. Julian's invasion of AD363, intended to finish off the Persians, ended in defeat with Rome having to cede half Roman (upper) Mesopotamia. From then on the frontier remained relatively stable.*

FOREIGN INVASIONS
FRANKS, GOTHS, ALAMANNI, HUNS

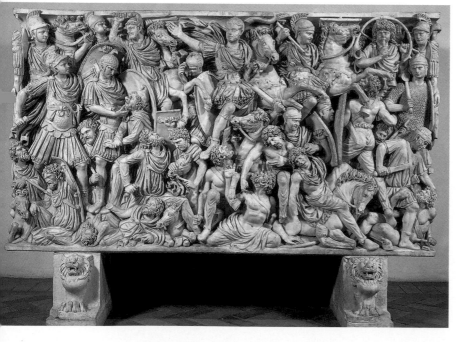

Above: A Visigoth chieftain on horseback leading his men. Not all Visigoths were mounted, but their cavalry was more formidable than that of earlier German tribes.

Below: This sarcophagus from the 3rd century AD shows Romans and Germans fighting hand to hand. By this time, Rome's earlier superb military discipline could no longer automatically be relied upon to win the day.

For more than two centuries the Romans under the Principate had faced generally quite small barbarian tribes who, if at times fierce and tough fighters, were seldom any real match for Roman arms or diplomacy. The latter, along with judicious subsidies or bribes, generally kept most tribes divided against each other or within themselves.

However, centuries of living so close to a far more united and powerful state began to have an effect on the tribes inside Germany. By the 3rd century AD, the older, smaller tribes such as the Chatti and Cherusci had coalesced into two far more potentially threatening groups: the Alamanni in southern Germany, whose name means "all men", and the Franks on the lower Rhine, whose name means "free men". These were loose confederations of similar tribes, rather than unitary kingdoms, but they would combine for the specific purpose of attacking the Roman empire.

THE GOTHS
More formidable were other new peoples who emerged in the 3rd and 4th centuries AD, most notably the Goths. Probably originating in southern Sweden, they migrated slowly south-east (too far east for Rome's knowledge) into the southern Ukraine. The Goths finally burst upon the Roman world in AD245 when they crossed the Danube delta and raided Moesia. Soon they were pushing further south into Thrace (European Turkey and north-east Greece), and in AD251 the emperor Decius went to repel them. He was unsuccessful and became the first emperor to be killed in battle. Emboldened, the Goths renewed their raids over the next 17 years, at times even taking to the sea and ravaging the Mediterranean.

At this stage, most barbarians were after loot and plunder, not lands to occupy. The Goths were crushingly defeated by the emperor Gallienus, at the head of his new cavalry corps, at Nish in Serbia in AD268, losing 50,000 men. Subsequently, the Ostrogoth half of the federation – their name probably means east Goths – retreated to the Ukrainian steppes. There they became formidable horsemen, creating a kingdom stretching from the Don to the Vistula, while their Visigothic cousins established a smaller adjacent kingdom north of the Carpathians. Although it is now known that the Goths did not have stirrups, so useful for heavy horsemen, they were far more effective cavalry than any the Romans had hitherto faced in Europe and posed a threat of a new order. However, for the time being they seemed settled along the north of the Black Sea. The Vandals were a Germanic tribe similar to the Goths, fewer in number but, it later turned out, even more opportunistic under the right leader.

Left: From the mid-3rd century AD on, Rome found itself facing new, much more formidable, groups of barbarian invaders than earlier. Some, such as the Franks and Alamanni in Germany, were coalitions of older tribes, but others, such as the Goths, were totally new peoples. These invaders penetrated frontier defences depleted by Roman civil wars to reach and sack cities as far afield as Tarragona in the west or Athens in the east. The emperor Gallienus' seemingly crushing defeat of the Goths at Nish in AD268 merely checked the invasions.

CHRISTIAN BARBARIANS

A new factor by the late 4th century was that some German peoples – the Visigoths, Ostrogoths and Vandals – had converted to Christianity. Unfortunately for them, it was not orthodox Catholic Christianity but Arianism, a heretical school that denied the divinity of Christ and followed the teachings of Arius, a Libyan cleric. Far from creating a tie with an increasingly Christian Roman empire, their Arianism served to separate Germans, as the one thing worse than a pagan to the Roman Church was a heretic.

One reason why the Franks became the ultimate victors in Gaul, giving their name to the new country, was that Clovis, their first great king, converted to Catholicism in AD496, so making his people acceptable to his Gallo-Roman subjects. Clovis married Clotilda, a Burgundian princess. The Burgundians, too, chose Catholicism and so became permanently embedded in their corner of Gaul, while the Visigoths, Ostrogoths and Vandals, despite conquering Spain, Italy and North Africa respectively in the 5th century, have vanished like smoke.

All the Teutonic invaders, no matter how uncouth and evil-smelling to the Romans, were nothing in comparison to a totally new threat from Asia that emerged in the late 4th century AD. The Huns, originally known to the Chinese – who had built their Great Wall against precisely such terrors – as the Hsiung-nu, entered the outer orbit of the Roman world in about AD370. Ammianus, the great 4th-century historian, described them as, "the most savage and hideous of all races. They have short bull-like necks and their bodies are short and deformed … They are stuck to their saddles, eating, drinking, bartering, even sleeping wrapped round their horse's neck. In fighting they excel by the great speed of their attacks… They are brave in war, faithless at keeping truces, deceitful, quick to anger and insatiably greedy for gold." Directly and indirectly, these savage nomads played a crucial part in the destruction of the western empire, before they vanished from European history, leaving nothing but evil memories, and their name on the Hungarian plains, where they had briefly settled in the 5th century AD.

LOSS AND RECAPTURE OF THE EAST: AD260–72

Above: A triad of gods from Palmyra, the great trading city in the Syrian desert that came to Rome's help in the 3rd century AD and then tried to create its own empire before being crushed.

Below: The wealth and polyglot sophistication of Palmyra were reflected in its flamboyant architecture. Classically Graeco-Roman in form, this was often baroque in spirit, as this ruined monumental arch testified.

Superbly sited in a large oasis between the great cities of Mesopotamia and the ports of Roman Syria, Palmyra had grown wealthy from the most lucrative trade in the ancient world: transporting silks, spices, precious stones and similar luxuries from India and China to Rome. Since the reign of Vespasian, or possibly even earlier, Palmyra had been a Roman dependency. Its exact status was uncertain but it clearly enjoyed enough autonomy to contribute separate cavalry forces to the Roman armies that Trajan and Septimius Severus led against Parthia.

The excellence of Palmyrene cavalry – which included heavy armoured cataphracts and light mounted archers, as well as some camels – seems to have originated from their long-established roles guarding the camel trains that crossed the desert against Arab raiders. The city had a Semitic, mostly Aramaic-speaking population, but its culture was a luxuriant mixture of Roman, Greek and Semitic. Palmyra's exuberantly decorated "baroque" temples and colonnades testified to its great wealth.

Such cultural links, as well as its geographical location on the west side of the Syrian desert, automatically inclined Palmyra to the Roman side in wars with Parthia or Persia. However, the catastrophic defeat and capture of the emperor Valerian in AD260, when all Rome's Asian provinces seemed about to fall into Persian hands, encouraged Septimius Odenathus, leader of the most powerful tribe of Palmyra, to consider changing sides. In AD261 he approached the Persian king Shapor and offered to join him. Shapor, flushed with victory after three successful wars against Rome, rejected the Palmyrene prince. This proved a colossal mistake. Impressive though the Persians' gains were, they were operating in hostile country and their supply lines were perilously extended across northern Mesopotamia and Syria, being particularly vulnerable to any attacks from the south. These attacks Odenathus now delivered.

Within a couple of years, Palmyrene cavalry had driven the Persians out of Syria and the Roman part of Mesopotamia. The emperor Gallienus, distracted by troubles far closer home, made Odenathus *Dux Orientis* (Governor of the East). Under this title, Odenathus became the effective ruler of almost all Syria. In AD266 he even advanced deep into the Persian empire and defeated the Persians outside Ctesiphon. In the following year he turned north and marched into northern Asia Minor to repel a Gothic attack. His domestic position was insecure, however, and he was murdered on his return from this campaign, possibly at the instigation of

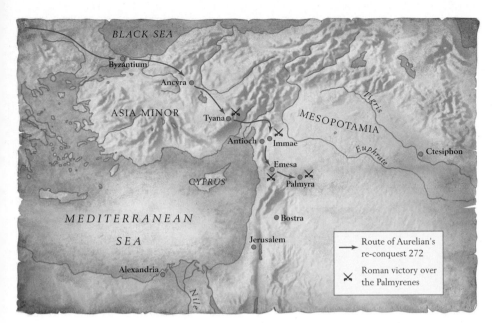

Left: The essential frailty of Palmyrene power was revealed when the emperor Aurelian marched east and crushed the Palmyrene army in a series of battles, culminating in the capture of Palmyra itself. Queen Zenobia was also taken and her rich city sank into ruined obscurity.

Gallienus, who had grown alarmed at the extent of his victories. This was by no means, however, the end of Palmyrene power, for Odenathus' widow, Zenobia, at once took control of the new "empire".

CLEOPATRA'S DESCENDANT

Zenobia claimed descent from Cleopatra, the last Ptolemaic queen of Egypt and Mark Antony's doomed lover. She was certainly as beautiful (she was famed for her long black hair), and as ambitious, although she seems to have been a better military and diplomatic leader, winning over many Arab chieftains and princes to her cause. Palmyra, although a wealthy trading city, did not compare with the huge kingdom of Egypt, so Zenobia needed all the support she could find to continue her city's fine balancing act between the Roman and Persian giants.

Proclaiming herself regent to her young son Vaballathus, Zenobia reasserted Palmyrene control over Syria and Roman Mesopotamia, again winning the acquiescence of Gallienus and then of his successor Claudius II in AD268. However, when she invaded Egypt and Asia Minor in AD270, she openly broke with Rome. Alexandria held out against her and her forces were too thinly spread to control most of the territories they had conquered. In AD272 she had Vaballathus crowned as *imperator* and Augustus, and she herself took the title of Augusta. Aurelian, the new emperor in Rome, would not accept this outright challenge and, after defeating the Goths again on the Danube, he marched east.

Although the Palmyrenes were still superior in cavalry, Aurelian managed to defeat them outside Antioch at Immae. In a second battle at Emesa, Zenobia was again defeated and retreated to Palmyra, hoping that Aurelian's army would be unable to supply itself in the desert. But it was Palmyra that ran short of food and Zenobia decided to escape and seek help from the Persians. Captured just as she was about to cross the Euphrates, she was taken back to Rome where she was paraded in gold chains in Aurelian's triumph the following year, before being allowed to retire to Tivoli. Aurelian spared Palmyra itself, possibly aware of its potential value as an ally, but news of a second revolt reached him in AD273. Quickly returning, he retook the city and punished its massacre of the small Roman garrison left there by sacking it so thoroughly that it soon passed almost completely out of history.

Above: Palmyra was typical in the way it absorbed the Hellenistic culture that had spread across Asia after Alexander and which Rome further encouraged.

THE SPLINTERING EMPIRE

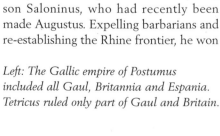

Above: Gallienus, whose reign (254–68AD) saw the empire almost disintegrate.

Rome might have expected to find its conquests ever ready to revolt the moment that central power weakened. In AD68–9, the Year of the Four Emperors, there was indeed a serious rebellion. Civilis, a Batavian (from modern Holland) who was also a Roman citizen and commander of an auxiliary unit of Batavians, roused a revolt along the lower Rhine. He even persuaded some legions to join him before he was suppressed. Yet this was in fact almost the only significant revolt of its kind in Europe. From the time of the reign of Hadrian (AD117–38), the provinces were treated as equal partners in a commonwealth, a trend confirmed when Caracalla (chiefly for financial reasons) granted almost all free men Roman citizenship in AD212. When the empire nearly broke up in the 3rd century AD, it did so because Rome was not providing the protection the provinces expected and needed.

Gaul, the largest and probably most populous of the western provinces, was the leader in this revolt. There had long been a tendency by Rome to downgrade the importance of the Rhine frontier compared to the Danube. By the AD240s there were only four legions along the Rhine, as opposed to 12 on the, admittedly longer, Danube. The legions were also constantly weakened by calls for *vexillationes* (detachments), leaving too few troops to deal with the threat from the new confederacies: the Franks on the Lower Rhine and the Alamanni in southern Germany. Raids across the Rhine began in the AD230s, intensified in the AD250s and led to major invasions. The Franks penetrated through Gaul to sack Tarragona in north-east Spain in AD260, while the Alammani crossed the *Agri Decumates* and the Alps before being defeated near Milan in AD259. Then, in AD260, news of the emperor Valerian's humiliating defeat and capture by the Persians shook the Roman world to its very foundations.

In the circumstances, separatism appeared desirable. Marcus Postumus, a nobleman of Gallic descent and the governor of Lower Germany, was proclaimed emperor by his troops in AD260 after defeating some invaders. Marching on Cologne, he then captured and killed the emperor Gallienus' young son Saloninus, who had recently been made Augustus. Expelling barbarians and re-establishing the Rhine frontier, he won

Left: The Gallic empire of Postumus included all Gaul, Britannia and Espania. Tetricus ruled only part of Gaul and Britain.

Left: The imperial baths of Trier, which probably date from the early 4th century AD. In the late 3rd century AD, the city became the proud capital of the separatist Gallic empire. Later it was the capital of the western Caesars under the Tetrarchy and throughout the 4th century.

recognition by the legions in Britain, Spain and even Raetia, so that the whole western quarter of the empire had seceded. Postumus made it clear that he did not intend to march on Rome, and was left in peace for five years. He then established a separate Senate at Trier, his capital, which he began fortifying and embellishing with an amphitheatre and palaces, while restoring the ravages made by barbarians. The Gallic empire seemed set to survive.

Gallienus recovered Raetia in AD263, but his attack on Postumus two years later in AD265 failed. Surviving Gallienus' murder by a year, Postumus was killed by his own troops in AD269 when he refused to let them sack Mainz after they had defeated another usurper. In the ensuing anarchy, Spain abandoned its Gallic allegiance, as did the south-east of Gaul, but the rest of that province and Britain remained independent until Aurelian led an army against them in AD274. The last Gallic emperor, Tetricus, seems to have reached some kind of understanding with Aurelian. Tetricus' life was spared and he even became governor of Lucania in southern Italy.

A BRITISH EMPIRE

Saxon raids along the coasts of Britain and northern Gaul had led to the expansion of the powerful *classis britannica*, the British fleet, which was based in large fortresses on each side of the Channel. Its admiral, Carausius, quarrelled with the western Augustus, Maximian, in AD286 – he was accused of pocketing Roman goods recovered from Saxon raiders – and declared himself independent. He was a skilful admiral and general, for he got the backing of his troops and maintained his hold on the Channel ports, defeating Maximian in AD289. Carausius then assumed the full panoply of titles, including Caesar, Augustus and *pontifex maximus* (chief priest), and on his coinage presented himself joint ruler with Diocletian and Maximian. Unimpressed, they sent Constantius Chlorus, the western Caesar, to defeat him. Constantius regained the Gallic ports, including Boulogne, in AD293. This led to Carausius' murder by his chamberlain Allectus, who took his place. Four years later, Constantius' invasion forces overwhelmed Allectus with a two-pronged attack and Britain was restored to the empire after ten years' independence.

Below: Roman soldiers from a Gallo-Roman carving. Gaul became so deeply Romanized that the separatist empire of Postumus copied Rome's, complete with Senate and baths. But Gaul returned to the empire by AD274.

THE FIRST RECOVERY
AD260–76

Above: The Porto San Sebastiano, one of the heavily fortified gates in the Aurelianic walls around Rome, was extended by Valentinian I and Honorius.

Below: The largest and most imposing walls in the 3rd century AD very suitably encircled the capital. Built by the emperor Aurelian, they proved effective against direct assault but not blockades.

By AD260, in the wake of the capture of the emperor Valerian by the Persians and the loss of his huge army, the empire seemed doomed to disintegration. Decades of civil wars had alerted the barbarians to its weaknesses, and invasion followed invasion: the Alamanni had finally overrun the *Agri Decumates* by AD260 and threatened southern Gaul and northern Italy; the Franks crossed the Lower Rhine and soon reached Spain; the Goths, Heruli and Gepids poured through Dacia and into Moesia, sacking cities as far apart as Trebizond in AD255 (north-east Turkey) and Athens in AD267, while Saxons raided the coasts of Britain and a German tribe, the Juthungi, ravaged central Italy. On top of all this, the empire had been suffering from plague intermittently for years. The economy, already stagnant if not in decline earlier in the century, now declined still faster, although some untouched areas such as Egypt and North Africa seemed to have remained quietly prosperous. Everywhere

rapid inflation continued, fuelled by successive tamperings with the coinage that gave the government a short-term boost at a crippling long-term cost.

For the first time in centuries, men began openly to despair of the power of the Romans, looking around for alternatives, be they manifestly separatist emperors in Gaul or effectively independent Palmyrene rulers in the east. Yet amazingly, at this darkest hour, a recovery began that within two decades had stabilized most of the frontiers, expelled most of the barbarians and even begun to reform the army, currency and administration. The credit for beginning this turnaround must go to the emperor under whom the empire had seemed lost and who has long been maligned for it: Gallienus.

Gallienus had been co-emperor with his father since AD253, being left in command of the west while Valerian went east in AD254. He had a major success in turning back the Juthungi in

AD259 from their first Italian attack, but the news of his father's defeat triggered a rash of usurpers; traditionally, 20 pretenders arose in his reign. They forced him to spend as much time fighting rivals as barbarians, although he temporarily acknowledged the independence of the Gallic empire under Postumus in AD260. He did so to concentrate on the defence of Italy, where he made Milan his effective capital. Here he assembled a strike force, composed of crack troops, mainly cavalry, recruited from armies on the Danube, in Asia and Africa. He minted a new gold coinage, the *multipla*, to pay this force. This special army seems not to have had a separate base and was probably stationed in cities, themselves now increasingly fortified. An extensive programme of qualitatively different fortifications had already begun, with huge towers and much thicker walls, all intended to endure long sieges. It was to continue throughout the following decades.

Gallienus' chief innovation seems to have been a policy of elastic defence. Replacing the earlier preclusive policy, this essentially meant giving up trying to hold the frontier at every point but instead waiting until the invading enemy could be advantageously attacked with superior forces. The policy bore fruit when Gallienus cornered an army of Goths at Nis in AD268. Unfortunately, although he had tried to secure the throne by forbidding senators from holding command, Gallienus failed to prevent the real threat from his own officers. Aureolus, his cavalry commander, declared himself emperor in AD268 and Gallienus abandoned his Gothic campaign to hurry back. In the subsequent siege of Milan, he was assassinated.

THE ILLYRIAN EMPERORS

Gallienus had come from the Roman nobility, but from now on a new breed of soldier-emperor was to dominate the succession: the Illyrian or Balkan emperors. First of these was Claudius II

"Gothicus", so-called because he defeated the Goths in AD269. His death from plague the next year led to the succession of Aurelian. Aurelian was indisputably a great soldier: he repelled the Vandals, Marcomanni and Juthungi, crushed the Palmyrene revolt and reconquered Gaul, although he had to abandon Dacia. But he had other attributes: he showed unusual clemency to rebels such as Zenobia, queen of Palmyra, and Tetricus, the emperor of Gaul; he built the walls around Rome, which, still standing, perpetuate his name; he was severe towards extortionate officials, one of the banes of every administration, and he built a huge Temple of the Sun in Rome. His death – he was murdered by his private secretary for reasons that are unclear – was much mourned. A series of short-lived Illyrian emperors followed; all were murdered by their troops. Only one, Probus, reigned long enough, from AD276 to 282, to have much impact, again defeating various German invaders before being murdered. Two years after his death, Diocletian found himself emperor and inaugurated what would become a very different regime.

Above: The walls hastily constructed by the emperor Aurelian around Rome in the AD270s were the first walls Rome had needed for 300 years, and they have survived for 1,700 years.

Below: Greatest of the Illyrian emperors was Diocletian who reformed the empire.

THE TETRARCHS' ACHIEVEMENTS: AD284–305

The empire that the Illyrian-born soldier Diocletian gained in AD284 was less immediately imperilled than it had been 20 years earlier, but it was still in a highly precarious state. The military had been expanded but new ways of paying for it had not been found. Inflation continued, with the result that the armies were still being paid – when paid at all – either in kind, by exactions, or in almost worthless coinage. The cost of both bore crushingly on the taxpayers, who were faced with huge, unpredictable demands.

Above all, the problem of the succession, the cause of incessant, empire-wrecking civil war, remained unsolved. Only one emperor had died a natural death in the preceding 70 years. All the rest had been murdered, often by their own armies. Diocletian, however, managed to retire and die in bed, and two subsequent emperors (Constantius Chlorus and Galerius) also died a natural death. Diocletian might have assumed this was due to the Tetrarchy, that system

he had devised with four rulers – two senior Augusti and two junior Caesars, the latter the Augusti's designated heirs. In fact, it was almost entirely due to Diocletian's own *auctoritas*, the respect in which he was held, that led the other emperors to ask him to reassume the throne at their last meeting in November AD308, three years after his retirement. The almost farcical chaos that overtook the rigid tetrarchical system – with numerous emperors emerging or re-emerging – exposed its shortcomings. Chief among these was its total disregard for hereditary sentiment. As Constantine demonstrated when acclaimed by his father's army on the latter's death in York in AD306, this remained very powerful.

In another sphere, the Tetrarchy proved more successful. Diocletian saw that the empire needed more than one *imperator*, or supreme commander. In the almost constant wars, often fought on several fronts, the long absence of the emperor on one front could too easily provoke discontent, even rebellion, on another. This was probably why he made another Illyrian soldier, Maximian, a fellow Augustus – a policy pioneered by Marcus Aurelius – and then appointed junior Caesars. Diocletian also developed the policy (which had originated with Domitian 200 years earlier) of making the emperor appear truly imperial, even divine. This led to elaborate court ceremonies and palace hierarchies. Although a further strain on the taxpayer, these should not be over-stated. Compared to the army, the tetrarchical bureaucracy was still quite small.

Diocletian had mixed success with his financial and economic reforms. He issued his famous Edict of Maximum Prices in AD301, fixing maximum prices for a wide range of goods and services to counter inflation. The attempt failed.

Below: The north wall of Diocletian's Palace at Spalato (Split), Croatia, showing the ornate but massively built Porta Aurea (Golden Gate) built c.AD300. Diocletian's palace-fortress epitomized the spirit of the age, grandiose and yet defensive.

Left: Galerius (Augustus AD305–11) sacrificing to the pagan gods. Galerius instigated the last and worst persecution of the Christians in AD303–11. He thought them both sacrilegious and unpatriotic, but he failed to exterminate Christianity.

However, he had more success with taxation. He based taxes on a hypothetical unit that varied according to the quality of land held. Taxes were now assessed annually by the Praetorian prefect of each province. The *decurions* (officials) of the cities were made responsible for collecting taxes in their province. These were in kind and overwhelmingly agricultural. To ensure that tenant farmers paid them, they were increasingly tied to their land by imperial edicts; other trades were also declared hereditarily binding. Although oppressive, this system was superior to the naked exactions and chaos of the previous century.

MILITARY SUCCESSES

In one sphere, the Tetrarchy was undoubtedly successful: the military. The army was again expanded – to perhaps 500,000 men – with a formal separation of the frontier troops, the *limitanei*, commanded by a *dux* (leader), from the *comitatenses*, the mobile forces under the commands of *comites*, counts, not tied to specific frontiers. These battle troops were no longer under the control of the local governors, whose provinces were much reduced in size if they were increased in number, for a dual system of civilian and military government had by now been established. The aim, successful but superfluous as it turned out, was to prevent provincial governors from revolting.

But army commanders continued to rebel. With these armies, often stationed in camps so heavily fortified that they begin to deserve the name of castles, Diocletian and his colleagues won a series of major campaigns, most notably that of Galerius against the Persians in AD297–8, which gained a new province. At the same time, Constantius was regaining Britain from a usurper. His victory was more typical of the generally defensive victories of a defensive age. It epitomizes the real but limited achievements of the Tetrarchy, principally the sharing of power between several emperors, which led Gibbon to call Diocletian the second founder of the Roman empire. They allowed the empire to continue, in a controlled, rigid but viable manner, for further generations.

Below: This column shows Diocletian embracing his colleague Maximian.

CONSTANTINE
THE LAST GREAT EMPEROR?

Above: One of the new solidi, gold coins issued by Constantine, showing him in idealized perpetual youth – he was noted for his vanity, in his later years wearing a wig. His new coinage proved enduringly successful, however.

Below: A relief from the Arch of Constantine in Rome illustrating his victory at the Battle of the Milvian Bridge in AD312 over his rival Maxentius. He attributed his victory later to a religious dream, but Maxentius was already an unpopular ruler.

The giant head and hands, sole surviving fragments of the titanic figure of Constantine that once dominated the Basilica Nova in Rome, seem to proclaim him one of the greatest emperors. His massive building programmes – at Trier, Rome and especially at Constantinople – reinforce this claim. Certainly, he changed the empire. He left it on the way to becoming Christian; gave it a new capital that became the centre of a new civilization (although he cannot have foreseen this); reformed the army again, if in ways that even contemporaries criticized; and defeated all his enemies, mainly Roman but also foreign – Franks, Sarmatians and Goths – before dying in bed, leaving the empire to his sons. How far he was a truly great ruler remains debatable.

Son of Constantius Chlorus, the Augustus of the west approved by Diocletian, Constantine was acclaimed by his troops at York in AD306. His rise to sole lordship of the empire was by typical rather than glorious means. His attack on Maxentius, ruler of Italy, in AD312 was standard action for an emperor controlling only the western provinces. His subsequent unprovoked attacks on his co-Augustus in the east, Licinius, had little justification except that of final success in AD324. If Constantine was more openly Christian than Licinius, the latter did not persecute Christians as a sect.

Constantine fought effectively against invading barbarians, from the Franks on the Rhine to the Goths on the Danube in his later years. These, along with success in more frequent civil wars, demonstrate military competence. But his military reforms – employing Germans in his crack *palatini* regiments, keeping large forces around him almost as a bodyguard – struck some contemporaries as more concerned to safeguard his power than his people. Quartering troops in towns also caused problems with military discipline. His military record was therefore mixed.

In founding Constantinople as his new capital – intending it less as a replacement for Rome than as a complementary eastern capital – Constantine showed great foresight. The best-defended site in Europe, at the crossroads of several major trade and military routes, Constantinople prospered, the one city in the empire that grew throughout the 4th century AD. According to legend, Constantine traced out its walls guided by a vision. In fact, his wall needed replacing by the Theodosian walls within a century, as the city's population approached three-quarters of a million people.

Constantine enduringly, if unwittingly, reformed the currency. This had been debased many times, so he issued a new coinage, the gold *solidus*, literally solid gold. It became widely accepted for many centuries after his death, a sign of Byzantine economic strength. This high-quality coinage was made possible by his pillaging of pagan temples. Treasures that generations had donated to their gods over the centuries were seized and often

Left: Constantine built his new city of Constantinople (formerly Byzantium, today Istanbul) at a strategic position overlooking the Bosphorus. He would deserve to be remembered as a ruler touched by greatness simply for choosing this superb site for his new capital.

melted down. This was despoilation on a scale comparable with Henry VIII's dissolution of England's monasteries in the 1530s. But the *solidus* was a high-value coin, no good in daily use where inflation continued. Constantine's tax reforms were mixed; his taxes were so onerous that fathers reputedly sold their daughters into prostitution to pay them.

THE FIRST CHRISTIAN EMPEROR?

Constantine's greatest fame is as the first Christian emperor. Certainly, he forged the linkage of empire and Church – in the east until 1453, in the west until the 11th century Investiture Conflict – and ensured that the empire ultimately became Christian. This took time, however. Mass conversions of peasants in Asia Minor were still being carried out 200 years later. Constantine's own religious beliefs remain uncertain. Like his father, he initially worshipped *Sol Invictus*, the Unconquered Sun. After victory at the Milvian Bridge in AD312, he began sporting Christian as well as pagan insignia on his standards, but the Edict of Milan in AD313 granted toleration to *all* faiths, not just

Christianity. Constantine seems to have developed an interest in theological speculation – it was the golden age for it – chatting in bad Greek to bishops at the Council of Nicaea in AD325, although he was thought not to understand abstruse doctrinal points. He favoured the Church by financial measures but did not discriminate against non-Christians – more than 90 per cent of the population – in the army or administration. He continued to use the pagan title *pontifex maximus* (chief priest), did not object to the renovation of temples in old Byzantium and was baptized only on his deathbed. Admittedly this was common at the time, baptism being thought to wash away all existing sins.

Constantine was the last emperor to rule the whole Roman world for a lengthy time (AD324–37). There would be other valiant emperors after him, but none who could be considered great. The empire that he left his successors still looked brilliant, powerful and wealthy. But the extravagances of his court and capital and the rapacity of his tax-collectors, along with his reliance on Germans, augured ill for its longer-term health.

Above: This aqueduct supplying Constantinople with water was begun by Constantine but completed in AD378 by the emperor Valens, whose name it bears. The city had from the start excellent water supplies, as well as huge cisterns to enable it to withstand long sieges.

CONSTANTINE'S HEIRS

It would be fair to say that Constantine's heirs had most of his vices and few of his virtues. The one exception, Julian, ended his reign in military disaster. On Constantine's death in AD337, the army mutinied and murdered many of his family. Constantine II, Constans I and Constantius II, the three surviving sons, divided the empire between them. Constantine was killed in AD340 attacking Constans, who became sole ruler of the European provinces, before being murdered in AD350. Constantius II refused to accept Magnentius, the new western ruler, and finally defeated him in AD353. The empire was now reunited, if exhausted by renewed civil strife.

Constantius was judged stupid and vain by contemporaries. He was certainly fond of showy display: on his triumphant entry into Rome in AD354, he posed immobile in his chariot as though made of ivory and gold. A fanatical Christian, he enforced Arianism (a belief which was later declared heretical) upon the empire and surrounded himself with sycophantic eunuchs. But he still needed a co-emperor and first chose his half-cousin Constantius Gallus in AD351. However, Gallus' highly erratic behaviour, which recalled Caligula's, led to his downfall. Constantius then turned to the sole surviving member of his family, Julian, the son of Constantine's half-brother Julius Constantius, one of the victims of the murders of AD337.

JULIAN

Until then, Julian had led the life of a philosophy student. Unwillingly called from Athens to become Caesar in Gaul in AD355, he astonished everybody by displaying military genius. Julian made

Above: Julian, sole emperor AD361–3, was the last pagan emperor. He was also almost the only later emperor to realize how high taxation was crushing the poorer people in the empire. His tax reforms, like his pagan restoration, however, proved short-lived.

Right: In AD363, Julian's army reached the walls of the Persian capital Ctesiphon, behind which stood its royal palace with its huge arch, but he failed to take it. In the subsequent retreat, Julian lost his life and Rome many of its best troops and half of upper Mesopotamia.

the small city of Paris (Lutetia) his base and recreated a proper army, repelling the barbarians. His greatest victory was at Strasbourg (Argentoratum) in AD357. Against an army of 35,000 Germans, he fielded some 13,000 men. After a long and hard-fought battle, the Romans won, with only 243 losses. Julian then crossed the river Rhine to campaign in Germany and re-established most of the Rhine frontier. He also tried to make the tax-collection system more efficient by stamping out corruption. He sacked some particularly extortionate officials, which boosted his popularity with the populace.

Constantius, now paranoid about his cousin's successes, ordered him to dispatch most of his best troops east in AD360. However, they revolted and acclaimed Julian Augustus: the empire seemed destined for yet another round of civil wars. Constantius turned his armies in the east to the west, but Julian struck first. The city of Aquileia in northeast Italy held out against his troops, but he marched east along the Danube and had reached Sirmium in the Balkans when news came of Constantius' death in late AD361. The empire was united again.

Julian's sole reign lasted only 18 months, but he filled it with activity. He sacked many of the well-paid imperial courtiers and officials. He then revealed his long-standing pagan beliefs, reopening pagan temples while banning Christians from teaching Greek and Roman classics – a major cultural blow. He even tried to encourage the Jews to rebuild the Temple in Jerusalem, as this would confound Christian prophecy. His gaze, however, was focused on the east.

PERSIAN NEMESIS

Julian decided to invade Persia for the usual Roman reasons: popular opinion expected the emperor to emulate Alexander the Great, and Persia appeared an enemy that could finally and profitably be defeated, unlike the drifting swarms of barbarians. An element of official revenge undoubtedly also played its part.

"We must destroy a dangerous nation whose swords are still wet with our brothers' blood!" Julian proclaimed, according to Ammianus. He gathered an army of 65,000 men, supplied by 1,000 boats and 100 galleys. He then sailed and marched down the Euphrates. Although he captured forts and defeated part of the Persian army, the main Persian forces avoided battle, instead adopting a scorched-earth policy to deny the Romans supplies. Julian decided to strike north-east across the Tigris into fresh lands, perhaps aiming to meet reinforcements from Mesopotamia, and the army began its retreat harassed by Persian mounted archers. Hurrying to help part of the army under attack, he left off his armour and received a fatal arrow wound, dying that night. Julian was the last significant non-Christian emperor, the last emperor with a real interest in Graeco-Roman culture, a writer of note and the only later Roman emperor to begin to comprehend the problems of the crushing weight of taxation upon the ordinary taxpayer. His death was a loss in more ways than might be expected.

Above: A coin of Constantine II, the oldest surviving son of Constantine I, whose reign of three years ended in AD340 when he was killed attacking his co-emperor and brother, Constans.

BRITAIN REGAINED AND ABANDONED

Above: The Romans continued to maintain and even expand their chain of fortresses and watchtowers, often on a large scale, all around the coasts of Britain until the very end of Roman rule in c.AD400. This suggests that they valued the province highly.

A realist in military matters, the emperor Septimius Severus nevertheless thought it was worth making the long journey north to Britain and campaigning for two years into Scotland. Britain mattered to Rome. The traditional view that the province required a military garrison disproportionate to its tiny population and wealth has been modified in recent years by archaeological finds. These suggest a far larger population than once thought – perhaps around four million. London, a great trading centre, was certainly the second biggest and richest city north of the Alps, with a population of around 40,000–50,000 at its 2nd-century AD peak. Whatever the exact figures, defending the island was clearly not just a matter of military prestige but also one of retaining a valuable province.

In the mid-3rd century AD, Britain was almost untouched by the waves of invasion that ravaged much of the empire, becoming part of Postumus' Gallic empire. Some Gallo-Romans may have migrated at this time to the relative security Britain offered, bringing their skills and wealth with them. Around this time, Saxon raiders along the shores of the Channel demanded the expansion of the existing *classis britannica*, the British fleet, and the construction of a chain of typically huge forts along the south-east coast. This fleet and the coastal forts formed the basis of the rebellion by the admiral Carausius and his successor Allectus in AD286–96, which for a moment made Britain a separate empire. But Allectus seems to have been an unpopular tyrant and by AD296 the Caesar Constantius Chlorus was poised to regain the province. His invasion met with little opposition; the citizens of London were particularly pleased that his troops reached the city before Allectus' unpaid Frankish mercenaries, who wanted to sack it. On his coins Constantius was hailed as the "restorer of eternal light".

Right: Foundations of a Roman watchtower survive high on the cliffs above Scarborough, Yorkshire, and formed part of the chain of forts and signalling stations constructed along the Saxon Shore of eastern Britain during the 3rd and 4th centuries AD.

Constantius' time in Britain seems to have been fruitful. He recruited British *artifices* (skilled men) to restore the fortifications of Autun, one of Gaul's chief cities. He himself went north, again restored Hadrian's Wall, campaigned far into Scotland and finally died at York in AD306, a city whose walls were much strengthened during his reign.

The 50 years following Constantius' death have been called the golden age of villa life in Roman Britain. Again, recent archaeological evidence suggests that the villas built then were not the provincial half-timbered structures once thought. Some were large, complex and luxurious country houses, almost comparable in scale with those of 18th-century country houses, such as North Leigh in Oxfordshire. Cities now had their defences strengthened, but villas seem to have been unprotected, presumably because they were mostly in the safer, southern half of the province. This British wealth clearly persisted into the AD350s, despite the problems of Magnentius' unsuccessful bid for power, for the emperor Julian sent to Britain for 600 shiploads of wheat to feed his army on the Rhine in AD359.

THE FINAL COLLAPSE

Around AD367 all the barbarians around Roman Britain reputedly conspired to attack it in the same year: Caledonians from the north, Irish raiders from the west and Saxons from the east. Many Roman troops seem to have abandoned their posts, some even joining the barbarian looters who ravaged the whole island. The emperor Valentinian sent Count Theodosius, father of the future emperor, to Britain with some crack troops in AD368. Reaching London, Theodosius was greeted ecstatically by its citizens. From there, he issued proclamations offering amnesties to all troops who had deserted. Reforming the Roman armies in Britain, he systematically cleared the province, rebuilt the walls of many cities and

Left: The Notitia Dignitatum *listed in great detail Roman troop positions and fortresses in Britain and across the whole empire in AD395. This illustration actually dates from 1436 and so shows fortresses in Britain more imaginatively than literally.*

increased the number of coastal watch towers in the north and in Wales. Traditionally, he even marched north into Scotland again, naming the area between the two walls Valentia after the emperor.

However, Theodosius' restoration was Rome's last really effective intervention in Britain. Troops were withdrawn to support usurpers such as Maximus Magnus, who took many soldiers with him in his bid for the throne in AD383. Only 20 years later, many of the remaining troops were withdrawn by Stilicho, the west's effective ruler, and the remainder probably followed the usurper Constantine when he crossed to Gaul in AD407. Left to themselves, the British may have organized some defence, but by the AD430s the province had slipped out of the decaying Roman empire. In AD446 the Romanized Britons allegedly made a last appeal for help to Aetius, the west's great general, but in vain. He was too preoccupied with the Huns. The Saxons may have started settling in large groups along the east coast soon after, while the western areas were ruled by Romano-Celtic princes. This marked Rome's final abandonment of Britain.

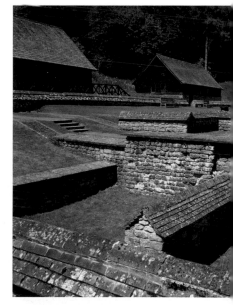

Above: The remains of the Roman villa at Chedworth near Cirencester. Romano-British villas flourished up to the mid-4th century AD, often becoming large, even luxurious complexes of buildings, complete with baths and hypocaust central heating.

THE GOTHIC PROBLEM

Above: An aureus *(gold coin) showing the emperor Valens (AD364–75) who led the army of the east to disastrous defeat by the Goths at Adrianople in 378AD. He was an Arian Christian and persecuted orthodox Christians, pagans and Jews.*

By *c.*AD350, the Ostrogoths had established a huge realm from the Vistula to the Don, centred on the grasslands of the Ukraine well suited to their cavalry. Although not averse to raiding the Roman empire, here they posed little threat. Their Visigothic cousins meanwhile occupied the Dacian region. Both had converted to Christianity. The type that they learnt through a missionary, Ulfilas, was Arianism, which denied the divinity of Christ. However, it was not religion that led to the Goths' next clash with Rome.

Moving west across the steppes of Eurasia, the Huns burst into the world of Germans and Romans around AD373. The Ostrogoths, routed by them, fled west, driving their Visigothic cousins before them. "News spread through the Gothic peoples of a race of men, never before known, risen as if from under the earth and destroying all in their path," recorded Ammianus. The Visigoths,

panicking at tales of Hunnish ferocity, approached the Danube frontier and requested *receptio*, official permission to settle inside the empire. This had been granted to many Germans, often with success. The emperor Valens, senior emperor at the time, agreed provided the Goths surrendered their arms. He hoped that they would supply recruits for the army and farm deserted lands in Thrace. Ammianus described Valens as "overjoyed at the prospect". His joy was short-lived.

The Visigoths began crossing the Danube in late AD376. The river was swollen with rain and many drowned. The survivors were abused by corrupt Roman officials, who sold them dead dogs as food at inflated prices and raped their women. To pay for food, many Visigoths had to sell their children into slavery; the going rate was reputedly one dead dog per child. Meanwhile, Ostrogoths had also crossed the river. Fighting broke out and the Goths turned to pillaging the

Right: The battle of Adrianople in AD378 was a disaster from which the Roman empire never fully recovered, for it let the Goths into the empire en masse. *The army of the emperor Valens, hurrying from Constantinople, blundered upon the Gothic forces led by Fritigern, who had formed a defensive circular* laager *with their wagons in its centre. The battle was decided by the return of the foraging Gothic cavalry who encircled the Romans. Valens himself died in the battle.*

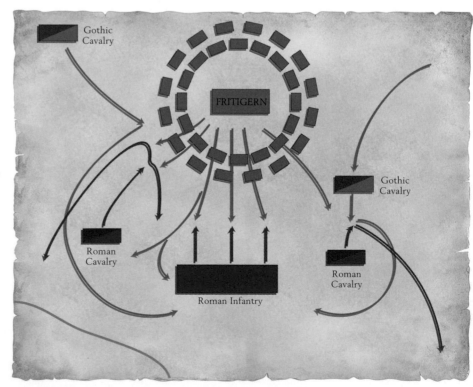

lands. They attempted to take Adrianople but its walls, as usual, defied them. The emperor Valens, deciding to deal with the invasion in person, assembled his armies at Constantinople in summer AD378 and rode north to meet the Goths.

THE BATTLE OF ADRIANOPLE

On a scorching hot day in August AD378 the army of the east, with 60,000 men, approached Adrianople. The Romans, who had been marching all day, were tired and thirsty, but when they saw the Goths ahead, Valens decided to attack at once. He was misled by reports that there were only 10,000 armed Goths ahead and wanted the glory of victory before his co-emperor Gratian joined him.

The Visigoths had formed their wagons into a *laager* (circle). Fritigern, the Visigothic leader, sent out for his cavalry, which was foraging, and for his Ostrogoth allies and their cavalry. Roman skirmishers seem to have begun the battle before Valens intended, for the Roman lines were not fully formed when the Visigoths counter-attacked, driving the skirmishers back into the Romans' main troops. The Gothic cavalry returned and, catching the Roman cavalry in the flank, drove it

from the field. Despite this, the Roman infantry in the centre rallied and, until sunset, the battle raged outside the *laager* like "the waves of the sea", according to Ammianus. However, the Gothic cavalry so tightened its grip on the encircled Romans that the soldiers could no longer wield their weapons effectively. Valens himself fell in the battle and his army fell with him.

Two-thirds of this great army was destroyed, but the Goths were unable to capitalize on their victory. They could not even capture Adrianople, with Valens' treasure and huge supplies within it, and their attack on Constantinople was a complete failure. Even so, two large Roman armies commanded by emperors had been defeated in 15 years. The new emperor Theodosius was forced into a wholesale policy of appeasement. He let the Visigoths settle *en masse* inside the empire in Pannonia and the Ostrogoths in Moesia. Further, he recruited Goths into the army, not just as individuals or small groups, but in whole tribes commanded by their chieftains. While earlier Germans had been Romanized by service in the imperial army, the Roman army now rapidly became barbarized.

Above: Nothing remains of the original walls around Constantinople (Istanbul) built by Constantine I in AD324. Later superseded by the Theodosian walls, they repulsed the Goths.

Below: Theodosius I (AD379–95) presents laurel crowns to the winners of a chariot race in Constantinople. The city shared Rome's urban amusements and also her imperial aspirations.

THE FATAL WINTER

Above: Theodosius I was the last emperor to rule the whole Roman empire.

Below: The interior of the Porta Nigra (Black Gate) at Trier.

In the later 4th century AD, the Rhine frontier looked relatively secure. It had been restored first by Julian and then by Valentinian (AD364–75), who had built or rebuilt many forts along it. He had even crossed the river once more to campaign in Germany, more than 400 years after Julius Caesar first crossed it. Valentinian was the last Roman general ever to do so.

Central to the defence of the frontier was the great fortified capital of Trier (Augusta Trevorum). Trier had replaced Lyons as the first city of Gaul in the 3rd century AD and was progressively fortified and adorned under the emperors Postumus, Constantius Chlorus and Constantine, whose capital it was for six years (AD306–12). A huge basilica, baths, palace and gates – the still-surviving Porta Nigra – and the large area enclosed by its massive walls testify to its wealth. Set about three days' march back from the Rhine frontier in the fertile Moselle valley, the city of Trier had good communications with the Rhine front to the east and with the rest of Gaul behind it. From it, one road ran due west to Reims, another north-east to Coblenz on the Rhine, another south-west.

The lower Rhine below Cologne, where the river often overflowed its banks and so was hard to patrol, was abandoned as a frontier, probably early in the 4th century AD. However, a new *limes* stretched west from Cologne along the line Maastricht–Tongre–Bavay–Tournai–Boulogne. Roman outposts remained as far north as the Rhine's mouth, but this *limes* linked the Rhineland with the Channel and so with Britain. South along the Rhine's banks ran a line of much-strengthened frontier forts, manned with *limitanei*. However, all fortifications were useless without enough soldiers. In AD383 a rebel general in Britain, Magnus Maximus, was proclaimed emperor by his troops. He crossed to Gaul and held court at Trier from where he ruled the westernmost three provinces and was recognized (reluctantly) by Theodosius I. When Magnus marched south into Italy in AD388 to be defeated by Theodosius, he must have taken troops from Gaul and Britain – mobile *comitatenses* rather than stationary *limitanei*. Both were needed in the north.

By AD395, after another round of civil wars, the empire was divided between the sons of Theodosius: the ineffectual Arcadius in the east and the even more incompetent Honorius in the west. Stilicho, a Vandal by birth but deeply Romanized, was to govern the western empire until his murder in AD408, in some ways very effectively, but his attention was focused on the Danube and Italy, to the fatal neglect of the Rhine.

Around AD400, Germany was in turmoil. Suebians, Burgundians, Gepids and Vandals (cousins of the Goths) were

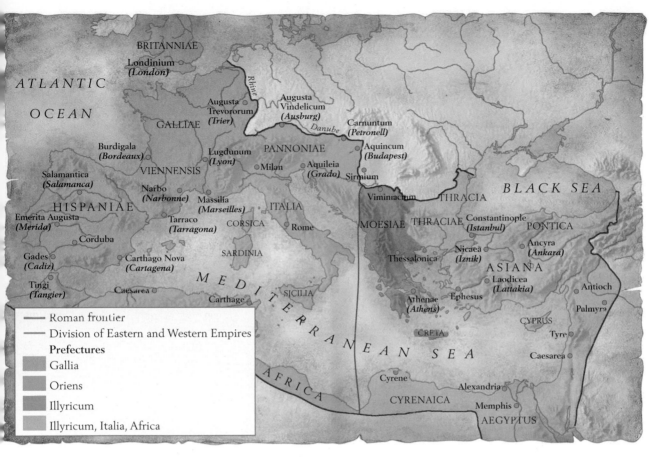

Legend:
- Roman frontier
- Division of Eastern and Western Empires

Prefectures
- Gallia
- Oriens
- Illyricum
- Illyricum, Italia, Africa

Above: The Roman empire c.AD400.

pressing on older-established groupings such as the Franks and Alamanni, all of them alarmed by the advance of the Huns to the east. The winter of AD406–7 was unusually severe and the Rhine froze all the way down to the sea. On the very last day of AD406, a horde, perhaps 300,000 strong, led by the Vandals crossed the river. Trier was sacked so thoroughly it never recovered. (The fact that its great walls could not repulse the barbarians suggests that the city was hardly defended.) Other garrisons cowered uselessly behind their walls, deprived of the *comitatenses* essential to strike back. The barbarians pushed on through the frozen countryside, the Vandals finally crossing the Pyrenees into an almost undefended Spain. With them went the Suebians and the Alans, an Iranian people. The Burgundians turned due south, settling at first around Lake Geneva before expanding to occupy the

land that still bears their name. The Alammani took Alsace, annexing that area for the Germanic world. Meanwhile, further north, in a less rapid but more enduring conquest, the Franks were pushing slowly but irreversibly forward, first to the Somme, then to the Loire. By AD496 they had conquered most of Gaul, giving it a new name: France.

In AD416 the Visigoths, acting now as *foederati* for Rome, temporarily drove the invaders of Spain into the far north-west, but the Vandals were not defeated. By AD429 they had overrun southern Spain (whose name Andalucia recalls their stay) and soon after began their conquest of North Africa, Rome's vital granary. By AD439, they had captured its capital Carthage, the western empire's second city. They had completed a long and profitable journey from their crossing of the frozen Rhine. As a result, the western empire was now doomed.

Above: An ivory diptych (double panel) dated AD406 shows the consul Probus and Honorius, the disastrously ineffectual emperor of the west (AD395–423), in whose reign Rome was sacked by the Goths in AD410.

THE SACK OF ROME

The sack of Rome by the Visigoths in AD410, although a crucial moment in world history, was not as dramatic as many might expect. Pictures of wing-helmeted barbarians brandishing bloody axes over weeping maidens, while palaces, libraries and temples burn in the background, exaggerate. The actual sack, although damaging materially as well as psychologically, was, by the age's standards, restrained, partly because the Visigoths were Christians. In any case, Rome's fall was caused more by the imperial government's miscalculations and vacillations than by Gothic desire to ravage the city. What the Visigoths wanted – and finally got – were titles, land and money for serving as Rome's ultimately surprisingly faithful *foederati* in Gaul. The cause of the sack of Rome lies as much with incompetent Roman government as with rapacious invaders.

Stilicho, who became regent of the western empire for the child-emperor Honorius in AD395, seemed to spend as much time intriguing against his rivals in Constantinople, where he aspired to become regent, as in repelling invaders. However, he was good at the latter. On two occasions he had the Visigoths, led by Alaric, at his mercy after defeating them: in western Greece in AD395 and in northern Italy in AD402. Both times he let them escape, perhaps because his troops were incapable of pursuit or maybe for less honourable motives. Yet although he may have played the Goths off against the eastern government at times, he was no traitor; he was merely trying to use them as Theodosius I had done. This appeasement led to his death, when public opinion turned against him for the loss of Gaul to Vandal, Suebian and other invaders in AD408. His murder was followed by the slaughter of many German mercenaries in the Roman army and the exodus of 30,000 others to join Alaric, gravely weakening the field army.

After extracting titles and money from the eastern empire and pillaging the Balkans, Alaric decided that the west offered richer pickings. The news of the death of Stilicho, which left the empire without a protector, led to three further

Above: An ivory panel of Stilicho (c.AD365–408), the regent of the west for the child-emperor Honorius. Though a competent general, Stilicho's devious negotiations with the Goths finally led to his death and left Rome at their mercy.

Right: Alaric's Visigoths ride into Rome. In fact, Rome's capture and sack was less dramatic but still epochal.

Visigothic invasions of Italy, the first in October, AD408. Bypassing the fortified cities and moving south, the Goths reached Rome and marched on to the port of Ostia. The Aurelianic walls around Rome, which had recently been strengthened and repaired, presented formidable barriers that should have repelled almost any barbarian. However, Rome was a populous inland city: it could be starved into surrender.

The Visigoths themselves also faced starvation, for they had no supply train. The first siege ended inconclusively when Alaric accepted a huge bribe of 5,000lb (2,268kg) of gold, 30,000lb (13,600kg) of silver and 3,000lb (1,360kg) of pepper. The second siege ended when Alaric installed a puppet emperor, Attalus, in Rome, who made him Field Marshal of the West (*magister utriusque militum*). When Attalus failed to please Alaric, the latter marched for a third time on Rome. The Ravenna government may have been pursuing a policy of attrition, hoping that the Goths would starve faster than the citizens of Rome and so be forced to retreat. If so, the strategy failed lamentably. On the night of 24 August AD410, someone – a Roman concerned at the sufferings of starving citizens, a disaffected slave – opened the Salarian Gate and the Goths entered the Eternal City. The unthinkable had happened.

THE AFTERMATH OF THE SACK

The Goths spent a mere three days in Rome, which had no food for their hungry army. Although they did not destroy the great city, they ransacked it and when they rode south they took with them Galla Placidia, the 16-year-old half-sister of the emperor Honorius. The shock of the sack meanwhile travelled round the Roman world. In Bethlehem, St Jerome was stunned, and in Africa St Augustine was moved to write his masterpiece, *The City of God*, to rebut pagan allegations that Rome's fall was due to its desertion of its ancestral deities in favour of Christianity.

The Visigoths reached the Straits of Messina, as Alaric wanted to conquer Africa. However, storms dispersed his fleet and he himself died on the way back through Italy. (Legend says that he was buried under a river briefly diverted for the purpose.) His successor Ataulf led the Visigoths out of Italy into south-west Gaul, where he married Placidia, showering her with Roman booty. Constantius III, who now became co-emperor, refused to accept this situation. Using Rome's monopoly of naval forces, he drove the Goths into Spain, where Ataulf was killed. The next Visigothic king, Vallia, agreed to return Placidia to the Romans and become a *foederatus*, in exchange for receiving lands around Toulouse. In Spain, Vallia campaigned against barbarian invaders while Constantius, capturing the city of Arles, re-established partial Roman control over southern and central Gaul. By AD421, when Constantius died, the Roman empire in the west seemed to have survived the ultimate disaster. However, unnoticed by the court in Ravenna, the Vandals, escaping the Visigoths, had occupied Andalucia by AD422 and were casting their eyes on Africa.

Left: The Mausoleum of Galla Placidia (lived AD388–450) at Ravenna. She was the sister of the emperor Honorius, mother of Valentinian II and effective empress of the west in her later years. Though strong-willed, her rule was nearly as disastrous as her brother's due to her personal vendetta with Aetius, Rome's last great general.

Below: An early 5th-century AD ivory showing Serena, niece of the emperor Theodosius I, who married Stilicho. Although of Vandal ancestry, Stilicho was very much part of the Roman imperial establishment and not remotely "barbarous".

THE FALL OF ROME
HUNS, VANDALS AND AETIUS

As long as the western empire ruled the seas and could control Africa, the coasts of Spain, southern Gaul and Italy itself, it could hope to survive. However, the growing threat from the Huns, excessive preoccupation with Gaul at the expense of Africa and endless palace conspiracies combined to wreck the empire's last hopes of survival. When it finally collapsed, it did so almost unnoticed, having become irrelevant to most people.

The deaths of Constantius III in AD421 and Honorius two years later left Rome leaderless. Galla Placidia, Constantius' widow, managed, with east Roman help, to get her son Valentinian III on to the throne in Ravenna by AD425. Placidia was regent for her son at first. Unfortunately, she loathed Aetius, the Danubian-born soldier who now emerged as Rome's last effective general. Aetius had been a hostage of both the Visigoths and Huns. He got on well with the latter, understanding barbarians better than most Romans, but he was soon caught up in palace intrigues. Boniface, governor of Africa, first quarrelled with Placidia and then was reconciled, receiving the lofty title of *patricius*. Aetius, realizing that Placidia meant to destroy him, raised an army. With it, he fought Boniface in a great battle near Rimini. Although Boniface won, he died of his wounds and Aetius regained control of the government with Hunnish help by AD433. Meanwhile, Africa was being lost.

In AD429, Gaiseric, the Vandal king, led his 80,000 people across the Straits of Gibraltar into Africa. By AD431 he controlled the western African provinces. The recall of Boniface to Italy to fight Aetius allowed the Vandals to consolidate their conquests and they were accepted as *foederati* by Aetius. However, they soon resumed their attacks. By AD439, Gaiseric had captured Carthage, the second city

in the western empire, giving him a fleet and control of the vital grain supply to Rome. The loss of Carthage was disastrous to the empire, but Ravenna agreed by a treaty of AD442 to accept the Vandals. Valentinian even promised to let his 5-year-old daughter marry Gaiseric's son, Huneric. Soon Gaiseric began extending his realm, capturing Sardinia, Corsica and Sicily, while his pirates raided as far as Greece. However, Aetius had his attention focused elsewhere.

In the AD430s Aetius had emerged as the clear arbiter of affairs in Gaul. In AD436 he called in the Huns to control the restless Burgundians – they killed 20,000 of them in battle – while his own troops drove the Visigoths back from Narbonne. In AD446, the despairing Britons even appealed to him for help, without success. By then, other even worse problems were emerging.

Below: This ivory shows Aetius, the last Roman general worthy of the name, presiding as consul over the games in Rome.

Above: Alaric, king of the Huns (AD434–54), was Rome's most ferocious enemy, but he actually harmed the empire less than the cunning Vandal king Gaiseric, who seized Africa and sacked Rome itself in AD455.

THE LAST VICTORY

In AD434 Attila became co-king of the Huns, whose empire stretched from Germany to the Volga. He soon killed his brother and terrorized the eastern empire into paying him tribute. In AD450 a new eastern emperor, Marcian (AD450–57), refused to pay any more. Attila turned for compensation to the weaker west where he had a strange excuse. Valentinian III's sister Honoria had had an affair with her steward. When this was discovered, she was kept in seclusion but smuggled a ring to Attila, asking for help. Seizing this excuse, and demanding half the empire as his dowry, Attila invaded Gaul. Only Paris resisted his 300,000 strong hordes and Attila sacked city after city with horrifying brutality. The Visigoths joined Aetius and, at Châlons sur Marne, their combined forces met Attila. The battle raged all day and left *cadavera vero innumera* (truly numberless corpses). The Romans threatened the Hunnish flank, but it was the Visigoths who bore the brunt and Theodoric, their king, was killed, which makes him an unsung saviour of western civilization. At the day's end, Attila decided to retreat for the only time in his life.

Next year, Attila invaded Italy. Aetius had no troops this time, but Pope Leo I rode north and somehow persuaded Attila to withdraw. Within two years he was dead, his empire disintegrating with him. Aetius, the architect of his defeat, did not live to enjoy it, however, for Valentinian III, in a jealous rage at the general who had outshone him, personally killed him. Early in AD455, two of Aetius' former soldiers killed Valentinian in turn, and the empire began its final decline. Gaiseric now appeared with a huge fleet, taking a leisurely 14 days to sack Rome, removing even the gilded roof tiles from the temples.

Various emperors, mostly puppets of German generals, followed over the next 20 years. Only Marjorian (AD457–61) deserves the title. He made a brave, if unsuccessful, attempt to defeat Gaiseric, before being murdered by Ricimer, the German power behind the throne. Finally, in AD476, the boy emperor mockingly called Romulus Augustulus – in reference to Rome's first king and first emperor – was deposed by another German, Odovacer. The imperial insignia were sent to Constantinople, the fiction being that the empire had been reunited. Few people outside Italy noticed.

Above: The Battle of Châlons sur Marne in AD451, when Aetius repulsed the Huns and their allies under Attila, was the last Roman victory, albeit one gained with Visigothic aid and resulting in little more than a draw. But Gaul was saved from the Huns.

WHY ROME FELL
AND BYZANTIUM SURVIVED

Above: Theodora was allegedly a prostitute before she married the emperor Justinian. She then became one of the greatest empresses, rallying her despairing husband during the "Nike" riots and helping him rule the resurgent empire.

Edward Gibbon, author of *The History of the Decline and Fall of the Roman Empire* (1776), summarized the causes of Rome's fall as the "triumph of barbarism and religion". Gibbon meant that, while barbarians threatened the empire from outside, Christianity undermined it from within, encouraging men to neglect their duties as soldiers to become monks or priests. But his explanation ignores the survival of the more Christianized east Roman (Byzantine) empire for 1,000 years.

Some moralists once saw in the fall of the Rome the "wages of sin" – meaning sexual excesses. Debauchery, according to this theory, so rotted the moral fibre of once upright Romans that they could hardly crawl from their marble baths. They perhaps read Gibbon's description of the teenaged emperor Gordian III whose "22 acknowledged concubines

and... 62,000 volumes attested the variety of his inclinations... it appears that both the one and the other were designed for use rather than ostentation". Gordian (reigned AD238–44) was an ineffectual emperor, but no historian today attributes his failure to his sex life or bibliophilia.

Most later Roman emperors were neither nerveless nor effete. The great soldier–emperors of the 3rd and 4th centuries AD, such as Aurelian, Constantine I or Valentinian I, were energetic, brave generals. Their military efforts were ultimately in vain, however. This has led historians to seek social and economic causes for Rome's fall.

A plausible culprit is malaria. This may have spread as deforestation of mountains led to the formation of more marshes ideal for malaria-bearing mosquitoes. Malaria reduced the overall population,

Right: The Mediterranean world c.AD526 after the final fall of Rome. Of the many barbarian successor states, Theodoric's Ostrogothic kingdom in Italy seemed far the strongest and richest, but it was soon reconquered by the Byzantines (east Romans), who had never accepted the loss of the west. Only the Franks and the still pagan Saxons formed enduring kingdoms.

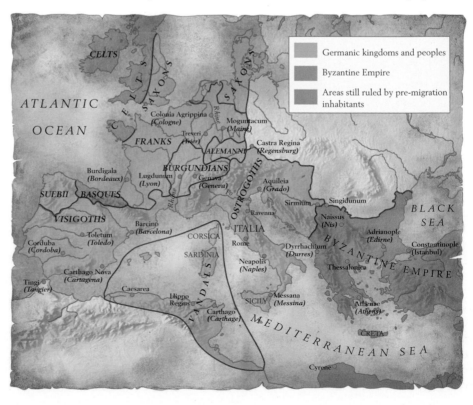

undermining the health of survivors. Similarly, plague, which hit the empire from AD165 on, must have played a part. But recent studies show that climate change did not affect the empire.

Each theory may explain an aspect of Rome's decline but cannot account for the survival of the similarly afflicted eastern empire. This rode out the 5th-century AD cataclysm relatively unharmed, to enjoy a golden age in the 6th century AD. Some historians have given up trying to explain the fall of Rome. Others have minimized the importance of imperial collapse, stressing the continuity of life in western Europe after AD476. Certainly, the German invaders had little new to offer, often perpetuating Roman customs. In Italy under the Ostrogoths c.AD500, the Senate still sat in Rome, aqueducts flowed and races were still run in the circus. Meanwhile, the Catholic Church expanded across western Europe and Latin survived, if mutating into varied forms. The one exception was Britain, where Anglo-Saxons deleted Romano-British culture. The Belgian historian Henri Pirenne argued that the real break between ancient and medieval worlds came in the 7th century AD with the Arab conquest. This divided the Mediterranean world, turning North Africa, Syria and Egypt away from Europe and towards the Islamic east.

For many people the question of why Rome fell remains as intriguing as ever. It is possible to discern major causes. Some were social and economic, a few were psychological and religious (shown by the growth in monasticism). However, political and military factors played an enormous and ultimately fatal part.

THE RICH–POOR DIVIDE

Essentially, Rome's civilization was urban, "a confederacy of cities". Although most of the empire's cities had 10–30,000 inhabitants, and only a handful were much bigger, most cities (outside Egypt) were self-governing. This was partly

because many had old and proud civic traditions, but more because the Principate lacked the governmental machinery for direct rule. Instead, it relied on unpaid officials, the decurions.

These men formed a middle group or class beneath the aristocracy of senators and equestrians. They included former centurions, local officials and landowners. From the 3rd century AD, this group was burdened with onerous tax demands by central governments. Faced with rebellions if they tried to collect the taxes and personal ruin if they did not – for the government made them personally liable – some decurions abandoned urban life altogether and withdrew to the country. Urban life, once so vigorous, decayed.

The plight of the peasants was worse. Most land was cultivated by labourers working as tenants for large landowners. After AD200, facing increasingly heavy taxation, some peasants became outlaws – central Gaul was ruled by the Bagaudae robber league – but most sought the protection of landowners to defend them from rapacious officials. This hurt both imperial revenues and farming. By AD400, up to a third of agricultural land in Africa, the west's most productive region, had gone out of cultivation.

Above: Justinian I (AD527–65), here shown in mosaics at Ravenna flanked by his courtiers, was the greatest east Roman, or Byzantine, emperor. He reconquered half the western empire and ordered the final and permanent codification of Roman law.

Below: The Cathedral of Hagia Sophia (Holy Wisdom) was Justinian's supreme monument in Constantinople (Istanbul), marking a radical development in late Roman architecture. In 2020 Hagia Sophia was rehallowed as a mosque.

Above: Constantine I (AD306-37) was the effective if unwitting founder of the Byzantine empire by choosing Byzantium, so superbly sited, as his new capital, and also by converting to Christianity.

MILITARIZATION, BARBARIZATION

Under the Republic, civilians had usually controlled the military. Citizens were expected to fight for the city but were forbidden to bear arms within the city's sacred *pomerium* (boundary). Augustus upheld this tradition. In Rome he was merely *princeps*, first citizen. The Praetorian guard, although really part of the regular army, was always seen as different. This noble fiction, fraying as early as Domitian, survived until the reign of Septimius Severus (AD193–211). Under the Severans, who posted a legion near Rome, the reality of military power became brutally apparent.

After Gallienus (AD253–68) banned senators from army commands, most civilians lost all experience of – and taste for – military life. The military became a caste apart, recruited no longer from the cities but from less Romanized border peoples such as the Illyrians. Increasingly, these were supplemented by non-Roman auxiliaries. Earlier emperors had employed auxiliaries, but these had been under Roman command. From the time of Constantine, however, Germans came to dominate the best regiments, the *Palatini*. After the disaster at Adrianople in AD378, whole peoples of dubious loyalty, like the Visigoths, were enrolled in the Roman armies. If barbarians never accepted Rome's draconian discipline, soon Roman troops also rejected it. Vegetius, writing *c.*AD400, lamented the decline of the old discipline, which had once made the Roman soldier so effective. Even worse, Roman armies too often fought each other.

CIVIL WARS WITHOUT END

"The Roman world is collapsing... Fighting among ourselves costs us more than fighting our enemies." The lament of St Jerome from Bethlehem in Palestine comes from AD396, just as the western empire began to collapse. Jerome was primarily worried about the Huns then threatening the eastern provinces, but his diagnosis was accurate. Even when the empire was being overrun, pretenders still denuded frontiers of their garrisons.

A crucial weakness of the Roman empire was its lack of an accepted system of succession. Monarchies are normally hereditary. In theory, the empire was not a monarchy, but emperors exploited dynastic feeling where they could, even if they had catastrophic heirs. Diocletian devised an elaborate succession for the Tetrarchy. Unfortunately, he ignored hereditary sentiment among the army and imperial contestants themselves, so that his system, too, failed. Armies continued to proclaim emperors to the end. In AD407, troops in Britain followed the pretender Constantine to Gaul, thereby stripping Britain of its last troops.

The main imperial government behaved no better. The two most capable west Roman generals of the 5th century, Stilicho and Aetius, both fell victim to palace coups. Personal feuds between generals, encouraged by the empress Galla Placidia, led to the loss of Africa to the Vandals. Such court conspiracies were far worse in the west than the east.

Left: The double walls of Constantinople, built by the emperor Theodosius II in the 5th century AD, made a vital contribution to the Byzantine empire's long survival.

Map legend:
- Byzantine Empire 527
- Justinian's reconquests

BYZANTIUM'S STRENGTHS

The most obvious strength of the eastern empire was Constantinople's superb site. Its brilliantly fortified peninsula, coupled with a control of the sea that the Byzantines retained for centuries, made it impregnable to direct attack until the advent of gunpowder. (It fell to the crusaders in 1204 only through treachery.) Any enemy coming from the Danube would find his way blocked by its double walls. Persian and Arab invaders could not reach the European provinces. Its double walls protected not only palaces, libraries and churches, but also warehouses and workshops, for Constantinople became a great manufacturing and trading city, unlike Rome. Its many inhabitants considered themselves Christian Romans – "Romaoi" in Greek, the language they soon came to speak exclusively.

The eastern empire was also far richer than the west. Cities such as Antioch, Alexandria and Smyrna remained great trading centres. With their deep-rooted urban traditions, they survived to profit from the general economic recovery by AD500. The east was fortunate in that the Persian front was quiet at this time. Persia had problems of its own. This let eastern emperors concentrate on their short European frontiers. If Goths and Huns ravaged the Balkans in the 5th century, the rest of the eastern empire avoided direct attack.

In the early 6th century, the emperor Anastasius I (AD491–518), a financial genius, reorganized the army and left a full treasury. Under the rule of Justinian I (AD527–65) a splendid Byzantine culture emerged, embodied in the cathedral of Hagia Sophia (Holy Wisdom), with its radical new design and gold-crusted two-dimensional art. East Roman power reached westward, reconquering Africa and Italy. Byzantium retained outposts in southern Italy until 1071. By shielding Europe from Arab attack for so long, Byzantium helped the survival of western Christian civilization as well as its own.

Above: The Byzantine Empire in the 5th and 6th centuries AD, showing Justinian's reconquest of the richer parts of the west.

Below: St Irene Church in Constantinople (Istanbul).

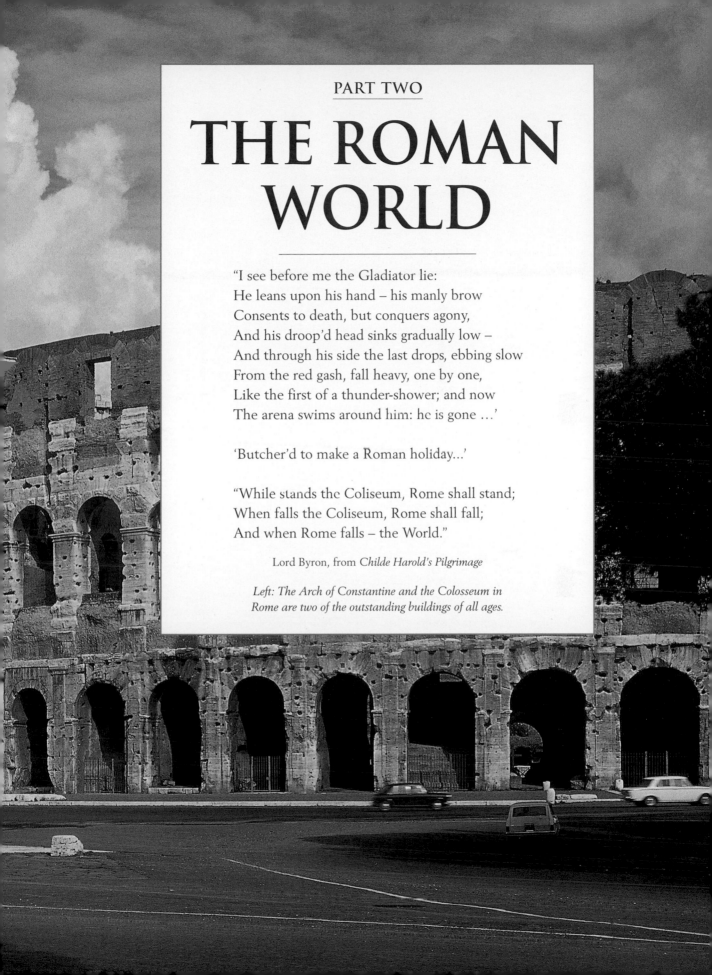

PART TWO

THE ROMAN WORLD

"I see before me the Gladiator lie:
He leans upon his hand – his manly brow
Consents to death, but conquers agony,
And his droop'd head sinks gradually low –
And through his side the last drops, ebbing slow
From the red gash, fall heavy, one by one,
Like the first of a thunder-shower; and now
The arena swims around him: he is gone …'

'Butcher'd to make a Roman holiday...'

"While stands the Coliseum, Rome shall stand;
When falls the Coliseum, Rome shall fall;
And when Rome falls – the World."

Lord Byron, from *Childe Harold's Pilgrimage*

*Left: The Arch of Constantine and the Colosseum in
Rome are two of the outstanding buildings of all ages.*

ROME'S ENDURING LEGACY

Above: This fresco of the Three Graces from the House of Titus Dentatus Panthera in Pompeii of c. AD79 epitomizes the brilliance of Roman art near the empire's zenith.

Below: The Forum Romanum, the ancient heart of the imperial city, was adorned over many centuries with temples and monuments.

The Roman world lies all around us. Even this book is written in the Roman (or Latin) alphabet. Although the Roman empire in the West collapsed more than 1,500 years ago, Rome's fascination and relevance to the modern world are today as strong as ever.

THE CULTURAL DEBT

Western culture is manifestly indebted to Rome and so too is that of Eastern Europe, through the Byzantine civilization which Russia perpetuated and, more indirectly, the Islamic world, conqueror of much of the former Roman world.

Although knowledge of Latin may no longer be common – few people now spice their speeches with Latin quotes – it remains very useful in the legal, medical and scientific worlds. Almost half the words in the English language derive from Latin, while Spanish, French and Italian are all Romance languages, the direct descendants of Latin. Similarly, the legal systems of most Romance-speaking countries, whether in continental Europe or Latin America, remain based on the majestic and logical edifice of Roman law. Symbolically, this was only finally summarized in the 6th century AD in Constantinople (Istanbul), the East Roman capital, after the fall of the Western empire. Rome's world survived the fall of its power.

In a more concrete sense, many of Europe's great cities – London, Paris, Lyons, Cologne, Milan, Seville, Vienna – were originally Roman, for Romans had a genius for choosing the right spot for cities that would thrive, endure and revive even after barbarians sacked them. Similarly, Europe's roads often follow or parallel routes pioneered by Roman road-builders. Roman brilliance as engineers, soldiers and as lawyers has never been disputed, but their literary and architectural achievements have sometimes been overlooked by those obsessed with Greece. Rome was never merely the channel through which Greek culture reached Western and Northern Europe: it provided its own unique input.

Observers looking at the Colosseum in Rome, the aqueduct of the Pont du Gard in France, the ruins of Ephesus in Turkey or of Lepcis Magna in Libya, may be awed by the splendour of Roman cities but they are seeing only the ruins of ruins. Rome's huge edifices were plundered by succeeding generations who saw in them only convenient quarries for marble, stone and brick. This applies even to the Colosseum. Revered as early as *c.* AD700 when Bede wrote of it as the epitome of *Christian* Rome's grandeur, its destruction continued until Pope Benedict XIV declared it a site sacred to Christian martyrs in 1749, so preserving what remained.

Our knowledge of the ancient world, while growing steadily as new archaeological findings supplement older literary sources, remains tantalizingly incomplete.

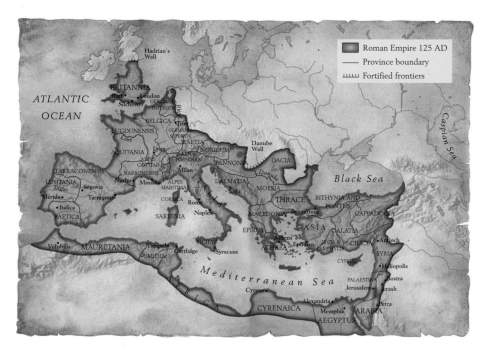

Left: Rome's empire, while centred on the Mediterranean, spread Graeco-Roman civilization far to the north, west and south, founding cities and extending its language, religion and laws in a way that has proved almost indestructible.

For half a millennium the Roman world united the lands of the Mediterranean basin (for the only time in their history) and pushed deep into northern Europe. It was in some ways very different from today's world, with different ideas about gods and the afterlife, the existence of slavery and social hierarchy, and yet it was a world whose inhabitants had many of the same aspirations, anxieties and dislikes as our own. Many aspects of everyday Roman life have been preserved at Pompeii, that urban time capsule buried by a volcano just as the empire neared its zenith. Its stunning wall paintings indicate just how much has been lost.

THE FIRST WORLD CITY

Rome still fascinates as the first cosmopolis, the first truly global city. As its population surged past the one million mark, it drew in philosophers, merchants, slaves and adventurers from across the ancient world, from the borders of Scotland in the north to Iraq in the east. The first to offer the excitement and challenges of a world city, it also pioneered ways of supplying, entertaining and controlling such unprecedented numbers.

Every age, looking back afresh, can find aspects of Rome to admire and emulate, or to abhor and avoid. Some disapprovingly see obese senators, debauched emperors, Christian virgins eaten by lions, gladiators slaughtering each other and slaves toiling beneath the lash. Others glimpse white-colonnaded cities with libraries, theatres and baths, arrow-straight roads spreading prosperity from Britain to the Middle East, broad-minded governors ensuring religious tolerance and many centuries of political stability.

Napoleon Bonaparte modelled his short-lived militaristic empire on Rome's, emulating its eagles, triumphal arches and careers for all, irrespective of national or social backgrounds. In the 20th century, more vicious dictators notoriously copied his worst features. In the 18th century, many liberal Europeans saw in the balanced British political system some of the virtues of *Republican* Rome, which later inspired moderates and extremists in the French Revolution. However, the greatest, most obvious heir to Roman ideals is found in the United States, whose universalism and fusion of peoples echoes that of Rome.

Above: The Library of Celsus in Ephesus, Asia Minor, testifies to that province's exuberant prosperity in the 2nd century AD.

Above: Christian martyrs thrown to the lions – the traditional but usually misleading view of the Roman world. Rome in fact was normally tolerant of almost all religions provided they did not disturb public order.

Below: The arched colonnades of the Theatre of Marcellus, dedicated by Augustus in 13BC in Rome, combine concrete arches and vaults with Greek-style columns to superb decorative effect.

GRAECO-ROMAN FUSION

"*Graecia capta ferum victorem cepit et artes intulit agresti Latio*" ("Greece, the captive, captured its conquerors and introduced the arts into backward Latium"), wrote Horace, one of Rome's greatest poets. He was stressing his own literary contribution while reiterating a point that was already a cliché. From the 3rd century BC, Romans found themselves ruling Greek cities and states more sophisticated and often wealthier than their own.

Although Rome soon siphoned off Greek wealth, it at first had to acknowledge Greek superiority in all intellectual and cultural fields, from technology to philosophy, from poetry to sculpture. Educated Romans became bilingual and knowledge of Greek precursors served to inspire their writers and architects. This produced an astonishingly fruitful Graeco-Roman synthesis.

While Greek writers originated many philosophical or political ideas, these have often come down to us through Roman writers such as Cicero, Seneca and Boethius. Catullus, one of the greatest among love poets, looked back to Sappho, the Greek poetess, when writing his searingly powerful lyric poetry; a generation later Virgil emulated Homer in *The Aeneid*, an epic fitting an imperial people but one touched with a new compassion for the conquered. Both, despite Greek influence, were deeply Latin poets.

This cultural fusion is nowhere more evident than in architecture. In its early days, under Etruscan influence, Roman architecture was colourful but provincial. Under Greek influence, however, it changed and blossomed. Greek architecture was mostly trabeated, using columns and beams to create buildings of sublime but rather static beauty. Roman architecture, by contrast, was arcuated, employing arches, vaults and finally domes to create a dynamic, exuberant and versatile classicism which has been frequently revived and adapted.

The Romans used new types of concrete to erect their monumental buildings. By the 1st century BC they had developed, in the Theatre of Marcellus, a way of building with brick-faced concrete where motifs such as columns, arches and architraves are used mainly for decorative effect. This theatre was built under Augustus (27BC–AD14) who sponsored a classical revival which looked back to classical Athens for its external forms. The solemn elegance this could achieve is still visible in the Maison Carrée at Nîmes, a flourishing Roman colony in Gaul. Perhaps the finest extant Roman building is the Pantheon, where a giant classical portico opens into a huge dome – the biggest in the world before 1800 – that owed absolutely nothing to Greek predecessors. (It owes its rare survival to its conversion into a church in AD608.) There are few Western cities that do not still reveal signs of this Roman classicism.

SLAVES AND CITIZENS

Notoriously, Rome's world was built on slavery – as was that of almost every other ancient culture. Most captives from Rome's successful wars of conquest became slaves, a fate arguably better than human sacrifice. In the 1st century AD almost half of Rome's inhabitants were slaves, but this was exceptional. Across the whole empire, the proportion was about ten per cent. However, Roman slavery was not only often different from that of more recent times – slaves could hold positions of real importance – it was also mitigated by manumission, the formal freeing of slaves by their masters, in which Romans took real pride. Horace was the son of a freedman who had done well enough to buy the future poet a good education; Terence, one of Rome's chief playwrights, started life as a slave; Epictetus, one of the later Stoic philosophers, began life as a slave but ended it by corresponding with the emperor Hadrian. There was no racial prejudice in a modern sense under the Romans, to whom the term "barbarian" implied cultural rather than racial inferiority.

The Romans steadily extended the privileges of their citizenship until in AD212 almost all free inhabitants of the empire were granted Roman citizenship. Such universalism is most unusual historically.

ATHENS, ROME, JERUSALEM…

Rome's was an empire of many different cults and beliefs, adding to, rather than replacing, the original Roman gods, who were themselves given Greek forms and equivalents. Mystery religions such as those of Isis from Egypt and Mithras from Asia won adherents across the empire and the cult of the Unconquered Sun was adopted by some emperors. However, imperial favour finally fell on Christianity, which had earlier been intermittently

persecuted, and it became the religion of the empire. The result was that Jerusalem joined Athens and Rome as one of the triple pillars of the Western world. From Jerusalem came the concept of a single personal god with all that that implies, while from Athens, standing for the whole Hellenic experience, came philosophy, drama and art. Although Greeks and Jews were often intellectual competitors and sometimes even literal opponents – ethnic clashes were common in the streets of the empire's cities – Rome's genius revealed itself in the way it managed to unite and transcend such divisions. Today, Rome lives on in our laws, language, art, architecture and in our religions.

Above: Fructus being served a drink by his slave Myro, in a mosaic of the 3rd century AD from Uthina in North Africa, one of the empire's richest and most Romanized provinces. Much slavery was domestic in scale and nature.

Below: Vault mosaic showing cupids crushing grapes for wine, from Santa Constanza, Rome. This use of pagan motifs in a Christian building of the 4th century AD reveals an early fusion of Christianity and paganism.

TIMELINE

Above: Julius Caesar.

As this timeline of political and cultural events reveals, ancient Rome had a remarkably rich political and cultural history. As Rome's power grew across the Mediterranean, she adopted and adapted other cultures, notably Greece's, disseminating north and west the resulting culture, usually called Graeco-Roman. But Rome was never a mere conduit for Hellenic civilization. This is especially true in architecture and literature. In the late Republic (150–30BC), Greek culture seemed set to overwhelm that of Rome, but already Roman architects were making wholly original use of vaults and arches. Similarly Latin literature evolved its own distinctive voice. There is no exact equivalent in Greek literature of Virgil, ancient Rome's epic poet, nor of Petronius, the racy satirist. Roman women had far more freedom than Greek, if mainly within marriage, and many slaves were freed.

All dates given before 350BC are approximate. The Romans dated all events *ab urbe condita*, from the legendary foundation by Romulus of their city in 753BC. Only in the 5th century AD did the present Christian calendar supersede the old Roman calendar system.

POLITICAL EVENTS: 753–101BC
753 Legendary founding of the city of Rome by Romulus.
c. **650–510** Etruscans dominant in Rome.
509 Expulsion of the last king, Tarquinius Superbus; foundation of the Republic.
496 Rome defeats Latins at the Battle of Lake Regillus.
451 Twelve Tables of the Law published.
405–396 Siege and capture of Veii.
c. **390** Sack of Rome by Gauls.
338 Defeat of the Latin League: Roman power extends into Campania.
312 Censorship of Appius Claudius.
298–290 Third Samnite War.
275 Romans defeat Pyrrhus and conquer southern Italy.
264–241 First Punic War.
241 Sicily becomes first Roman province.
218–202 Second Punic War.
216 Roman army crushed at battle of Cannae by Hannibal.
202 Scipio defeats Hannibal at Zama.
200–196 Second Macedonian War.
190 Seleucid king Antiochus III defeated at Magnesia: Rome arbiter of the east.
167 Sack of Epirus: 150,000 Greeks enslaved.
146 Sack of cities of Carthage and Corinth: Greece, Macedonia and Africa become Roman provinces.
135–132 First Sicilian Slave War.
133 Tiberius Gracchus, tribune, is killed; kingdom of Pergamum left to Rome.

Above: The ruins of Carthage, once Rome's greatest enemy, then a thriving Roman city.

CULTURAL EVENTS: 753–101BC
c. **620** Draining of Roman Forum.
c. **540** *Ambush of Troilus by Achilles* wall painting from Tomb of the Bulls, Tarquinia; traditional date of building of first Curia (Senate House).
510 Building of first Capitoline Temple.
500 Capitoline Wolf bronze; Apollo of Veii.
483 Building of Temple of Castor et Pollux.
c. **390** Wounded Chimaera bronze.
378 Building of Servian Wall.
312 Building of first Roman road, Via Appia, and first aqueduct, Aqua Appia.
300 Bronze bust of "Brutus the Liberator".
275 Eratosthenes in Alexandria works out earth's circumference.
264 First gladiatorial contest in Rome.
254 Birth of Plautus.
239 Birth of poet Ennius at Rudiae.
234 Birth of Cato the Censor.
220 Circus Flaminius built in Rome.
212 Archimedes killed at Syracuse.
204 *Miles Gloriosus* by Plautus staged.
195 Birth of Terence in Africa.
186 Senate issues edict against Bacchic rites.
179 Basilica Aemilia and Pons Aemilius built.
170 Basilica Sempronia built.
169 Death of Ennius.
166–159 Terence's major plays produced.
c. **150** The "First Pompeian Style" of wall painting emerges.
144 Construction of Aqua Marcia.
106 Birth of Cicero.

Above: Painting from the Tomb of the Bulls c. 550BC, a fine example of Etruscan art.

Above: Augustus.

Above: Tiberius.

Above: Caligula.

Above: Claudius.

POLITICAL EVENTS: 100BC–1BC

107–100 Marius consul six times; reforms army; defeats Cimbri and Teutones.

88 Sulla marches on Rome.

82–80 Sulla dictator in Rome.

73–71 Slave revolt of Spartacus crushed by Crassus and Pompey.

66 Pompey given huge command in east.

63 Consulship of Cicero; Pompey captures Jerusalem.

60 First Triumvirate: Caesar, Pompey, Crassus.

59 Caesar consul for the first time.

58–51 Caesar's conquest of Gaul. Death of Crassus at Battle of Carrhae. Start of Civil War.

48 Pompey defeated at Pharsalus: Caesar meets Cleopatra.

44 Caesar becomes perpetual dictator; subsequently assassinated.

42 Republicans defeated at Philippi: the empire is divided, Octavian taking the west and Mark Antony the east.

40–38 Parthians invade Syria.

36 Antony launches major offensive against the Parthians.

31 Battle of Actium: Octavian defeats Antony and Cleopatra.

30 Cleopatra and Antony commit suicide; annexation of Egypt; reunification of empire.

27 "The Republic restored"; Octavian assumes title *Augustus*.

18 Lex Julia: law against adultery.

16–9 Alpine and Balkan areas annexed.

12 Death of Agrippa.

Above: Detail of the Ara Pacis (Altar of Peace), dedicated under Augustus in 9BC.

CULTURAL EVENTS: 100BC–1BC

100 Temple of Neptune in Rome.

96 Birth of Lucretius.

84 Birth of Catullus.

82–79 Building of *Tabularium* (Records Office).

c. **80** Second Pompeian Style of painting develops.

70 Birth of Virgil.

65 Birth of Horace.

60 Cicero published his *Catiline Orations*.

c. **55** Building of Theatre of Pompey.

50s Catullus writing greatest poems.

c. **54** Birth of Propertius.

46 Forum of Caesar and Basilica Julia begun.

44–21 Strabo the geographer active.

c. **45** Cicero *Scipio's Dream*.

43 Birth of Ovid; murder of Cicero.

37 Temple of Mars Ultor in Augustus' Forum, Rome, begun (finished 2BC).

29 Virgil's *Georgics*.

23 Horace's *Odes* books 1–3.

21 Agrippa marries Julia.

20 Prima Porta statue of Augustus.

19 Death of Virgil and Tibullus; publication of *The Aeneid*; building of the Aqua Julia; Start of Maison Carrée and Pont du Gard at Nîmes.

13 Building of Theatre of Marcellus.

9 First edition of Ovid's *Ars Amatoria*; Ara Pacis dedicated.

4 Birth of philosopher and playwright Seneca near Cordova.

Above: The Arch of Septimius Severus in the Forum Romanum, Rome.

Above: Nero.

Above: Domitian.

Above: Trajan.

Above: Hadrian.

Above: Marcus Aurelius.

Above: Septimius Severus.

POLITICAL EVENTS: AD1–199

6 Judaea becomes Roman province.
9 Loss of three legions in Germany under Varus; withdrawal to Rhine frontier.
14 Augustus dies; Tiberius becomes emperor.
30/33 Crucifixion of Jesus.
37 Death of Tiberius; accession of Caligula.
41 Caligula assassinated: accession of Claudius.
43 Invasion of Britain.
54 Death of Claudius; accession of Nero; Seneca and Burrus chief ministers.
62 Burrus dies and end of Seneca's influence; Nero becomes increasingly extravagant.
64 Great Fire of Rome: Nero makes Christians scapegoats and begins rebuilding Rome.
68–9 Suicide of Nero: Year of the Four Emperors.
70 Capture and sack of Jerusalem by Titus.
79 Pompeii and Herculaneum destroyed.
81 Death of Titus; accession of Domitian.
96 Assassination of Domitian; Nerva succeeds.
98 Death of Nerva; accession of Trajan.
101–6 Dacian wars.
113–17 Parthian campaign ends in defeat.
117 Death of Trajan; accession of Hadrian.
121–2 Hadrian visits Britain.
138 Death of Hadrian.
161 Marcus Aurelius, Lucius Verus co-emperors.
165–6 Plague brought back from Parthia by legionaries.
167 Marcomanni and Quadi attack Italy.
180 Death of Marcus on the Danube; accession of Commodus.
192 Assassination of Commodus; civil war.
193 Septimius Severus emperor in Rome.

Above: Human body caught in the eruption of Vesuvius that destroyed Pompeii in AD79.

CULTURAL EVENTS AD1–199

2 Forum of Augustus dedicated.
8 Banishment of Ovid to Black Sea.
18 Death of Ovid.
27 Building of Tiberius' villa at Capri.
c. 40–3 Birth of Martial; Claudius builds new harbour near Ostia and Aqua Claudia.
60 Birth of Juvenal; *De re rustica* by Columella.
64–8 Nero builds the *Domus Aurea*.
65 Deaths of Seneca and Lucan.
66 Suicide of Petronius, author of *Satyricon*.
79 Death of Pliny the Elder.
80 Colosseum dedicated.
82 Arch of Titus; start of construction of Palatine Palace; first of Martial's *Epigrams*.
100 Pliny the Younger's *Panegyrics* on Trajan.
100–10 Tacitus: *Histories and Annals*.
103 Trajan's new inner harbour near Ostia.
110 First of Juvenal's *Satires*.
115 Arch of Trajan at Benevento.
112–14 Dedication of Forum and Column of Trajan; death of Pliny the Younger in Bithynia.
115 Library of Celsus in Ephesus.
120–30s Hadrian builds the Pantheon, Hadrian's Wall, Basilica at London, Villa at Tivoli.
c. 127 Apuleius born in Africa.
131 Hadrian establishes Panhellenion and completes Temple of Zeus in Athens.
140–50s Ptolemy active in Alexandria.
150–60s Galen active as doctor in Rome; Apuleius' *The Golden Ass*.
174–80 *Meditations* of Marcus Aurelius, composed during wars on Danube.
193 Column of Marcus Aurelius completed.

Above: Arches of the Colosseum in Rome, dedicated in AD80 by the emperor Titus.

Above: Elagabalus.

Above: Diocletian.

Above: Constantine I.

Above: Julian.

Above: Justinian I.

POLITICAL EVENTS: AD200–540

211 Severus dies; accession of Caracalla.

212 *Constitutio Antoniniana*: Roman citizenship for all free men.

222 Accession of Alexander Severus.

235 Assassination of Alexander: beginning of the "years of anarchy".

268 Assassination of Gallienus: Zenobia of Palmyra declares independent eastern empire.

270 Accession of Aurelian.

284 Accession of Diocletian: joint rule with Maximian from 286.

303–11 "Great Persecution of Christians".

312 Battle of Milvian Bridge: Constantine defeats Maxentius.

313 Edict of Milan: religious tolerance.

324–30 Foundation of Constantinople.

325 Church Council of Nicaea.

337 Death of Constantine; empire divided.

363 Julian killed on Persian campaign.

378 Battle of Adrianople: Valens killed.

386 Removal of Altar of Victory from Senate House; campaign against pagans.

395 Theodosius I dies, dividing empire between Honorius in west, Arcadius in east.

410 Visigoths under Alaric sack Rome.

439 Vandals capture Carthage.

451 Battle of Châlons: Huns defeated by Romans and Visigoths.

476 Last west Roman emperor, Romulus Augustulus, deposed by mercenary Odoacer.

527 Accession of Justinian I in Constantinople.

535 Belisarius begins (east) Roman reconquest of Italy.

Above: Santo Stefano Rotondo, built AD468–83 to house the remains of St Stephen.

CULTURAL EVENTS AD200–540

203 Arch of Septimius Severus; extensive building at Lepcis Magna.

216 Baths of Caracalla dedicated.

220s Origen teaching in Alexandria.

250–60s Plotinus, Neoplatonist philosopher, teaching in Rome.

270 Death of Plotinus.

270s Building of Temple of the Sun in Rome.

295–300 Building of Basilica and the Kaiserthermem (imperial baths) at Trier.

298 Construction of Baths of Diocletian starts.

305–6 Diocletian's palace at Split, Croatia.

307–12 Basilica Nova built by Maxentius, completed by Constantine.

c. **310** Birth of poet Ausonius at Bordeaux.

313–23 Building of first Christian basilicas in Rome and Piazza Armerina Villa in Sicily.

350s *Pervigilium veneris* (anon); Woodchester "Great Pavement" mosaic depicting Orpheus.

354 Birth of Augustine, Christian philosopher.

361–3 Julian's *Orations* and *Letters Against the Christians*.

380s Ausonius: *Mosella*.

393 Last Olympic games held in Greece.

413–16 Augustine: *The City of God*.

c. **414** Namatianus writes panegyric of Rome.

430 Death of Augustine in Carthage.

c. **450** Mausoleum of Galla Placidia at Ravenna.

c. **520** Boethius: *The Consolation of Philosophy*.

528–39 Justinian's *Digest of Roman Law* compiled at Constantinople.

529 Justinian closes the Academy at Athens.

532–7 Hagia Sophia built in Constantinople.

Above: A charioteer in his quadriga *(four-horse chariot) in Rome c. AD300.*

ROME: THE FIRST WORLD CITY

Rome was the first cosmopolis. By AD100 it had a population of over one million, unmatched by any other city. Greek was spoken almost as commonly in its streets as Latin for educated Romans were bilingual. The resulting Graeco-Roman cultural fusion was most marked in architecture. Greek classical architecture relied on columns and porticoes of stone and marble. The Romans, lacking such good stone, exploited concrete to create vaults, arches and domes. The Pantheon (built *c.* AD124–8) unites a sublime Greek portico with a brilliantly designed concrete Roman dome. The Romans, who never believed that form had to follow function, used classical columns less to support roofs or porticoes than for decorative purposes, humanizing massive, sometimes blank structures. Their columns employed a distinct classical language based ultimately on the human form.

Despite Rome's own vastness, humanity remained the measure and ideal of Roman classical culture. This classical style proved so flexible and inspirational that it influenced Byzantine, Romanesque (Norman), Renaissance, Baroque, Neoclassical and other styles well into the 20th century. Most great Western cities reveal this Roman influence, as the Capitol in Washington, St Paul's Cathedral in London and the Arc de Triomphe in Paris attest. The Romans built lavishly across their empire, founding or refounding cities. Some, since abandoned – Lepcis Magna in Libya, Palmyra in Syria, Pompeii in Italy – now vividly display the wonders of Roman architecture and city life, as does the city of Rome itself.

Left: Rome's influence led to similar buildings across the empire such as the amphitheatre at Nimes, France, c AD80, inspired by the Colosseum.

CHAPTER XIII

BUILDING THE CITY OF ROME

Rome, notoriously, was not built in a day, nor was it built following any clear-cut plan. Instead, its growth from a few huts above the river Tiber into the world's first giant city was often chaotic. The expanding city was short of space within its walls and spread upwards as well as outwards. Caesar, followed by the emperor Augustus and his successors, tried to plan the city along more rational lines. However, Rome, unlike ancient Alexandria or Antioch – or Paris or Washington today – was never a city of great avenues. Rather, it developed as an accumulation of tight-packed buildings and narrow streets punctuated by such immense monuments as the Colosseum or by noble colonnaded open spaces such as the Forum of Trajan.

Frequently ravaged by fires and serious floods, Rome was constantly rebuilt. The population probably peaked in the 2nd century AD, but emperors continued to adorn Rome lavishly until the time of Constantine. He founded a new centre in the East, Constantinople, which finally eclipsed the old metropolis. Rome's subsequent gradual decay – aggravated more by its inhabitants' tendency to use the ancient buildings as quarries than by barbarian attacks – was slowed by the remarkable skills of the Roman engineers who had built so well. Even the ruins of their ruins still impress.

Left: The Forum Romanum today showing, left to right, the Temple of Castor and Pollux, the Arch of Septimius Severus and, far right, the Curia or Senate House.

BUILDING EARLY ROME: 753–200BC

Above: This section of the Servian Wall on the Aventine, constructed after the sack of Rome by the Gauls in 390BC, shows the solidity of early Roman buildings.

Below: The impact of Greek classicism after 300BC, such as the early Doric Temple of Neptune in Paestum (built c.500BC and actually dedicated to Hera), was overwhelming in shaping Roman architecture.

The Romans liked to consider themselves superior to their neighbours of central Italy. However, they were deeply influenced in architecture as in other matters by the Etruscans in their early years, whether or not Etruscan kings ever ruled in Rome. The simple shepherds' huts that supposedly sheltered Romulus and other early Romans were devoutly preserved as late as Augustus' time and still survive today. These gave way to larger buildings as Rome became an urban settlement in the 7th century BC.

EARLY CIVIC STRUCTURES

Central to Roman life was the Forum Romanum (market/meeting place), which was first paved in the late 7th century BC. The digging of the *Cloaca Maxima*, the Great Drain or ditch, allowed the draining of the valley of the later Forum Romanum. When covered over, this became and long remained the world's greatest sewer. The first wooden bridge over the Tiber, the *Pons Sublicius*, was built *c.* 600BC, traditionally by the Etruscan king Ancus Marcius. This was the bridge held by Horatio against the Etruscan forces of Lars Porsena in *c.* 505BC, according to the historian Livy. The location of the city was partly dictated by the fact that it provided the lowest practical crossing point of the Tiber. These solidly practical measures sometimes also had a religious aspect, for the word *pontifex*, bridge-maker, came to mean high priest.

ETRUSCAN INFLUENCE

The Etruscans' distinctive form of temple-building deeply influenced the Romans. The Etruscans were also influenced by the Greeks, but unlike Greek temples, whose columns ran all round the *cella* – the central chamber housing the deity's statue – Etruscan temples had their columns chiefly in front, with only a few on the side and none at the back. Etruscan temples also had a staircase at the front, as the temple stood on a high podium. This meant that they could be approached properly only from the front. This suited Etruscan religious practices, which were always much concerned with divination procedures that required their priests to be exactly positioned.

The temple superstructure was built mostly of mud brick, plus a timber or wattle and daub type of construction that was brightly stuccoed or painted, for the area adjacent to Rome lacked easily available attractive building stone. Yellow-grey volcanic *tufa* was the commonest local material, which was later supplemented by travertine stone. Adorning the temples' roofs were similarly colourful life-size terracotta statues of the gods. (Almost all ancient statues and many buildings, whether Greek, Etruscan or Roman, were vividly painted in a way which might strike modern eyes as garish.)

The greatest temple in Rome was that on the Capitoline Hill to Jupiter Optimus Maximus (Best and Greatest), traditionally built by the last Etruscan king Tarquinius Superbus (the Proud) just before his expulsion in 509BC. Raised on a podium about 13ft (4m) high, the huge edifice, 204ft (62m) long and 175ft (53m) long, was comparable in size to the biggest temples of the Greek world and presumably indicative of the wealth of Rome at the time. Only its podium remains intact. This shows the temple was generally Etruscan in style but that it had three *cellae*, with three rows of columns to the front and a single row of seven columns on either side. The central *cella* contained the cult statue of Jupiter – king of the gods and Rome's supreme deity – flanked by shrines to Juno, his wife, to the left, and Minerva (Athena in Greek), his daughter, on the right. The temple burnt down numerous times and was grandiosely rebuilt by Sulla in *c.* 80BC, actually using columns from the Athenian temple to Olympian Zeus but keeping its overall proportions. All private building on the Capitol was banned in 384BC.

Temples were also built around the Forum Romanum. These included the Temple of Saturn *c.* 498BC, the Temple of Castor and Pollux *c.* 483BC and the Temple of Concord of 366BC. A temple to the Greek healing-god Asculepius, whose worship was introduced in 291BC when a plague threatened, was built on the Tiber island. This was outside the *pomerium* or sacred city boundary, for the god, if essential to avert the plague, remained a foreigner.

Following the expulsion of the kings, Rome may for a time have become poorer but the newly republican city continued to grow, with civic life now more focused on the Forum. At first crowded with *tabernae* (shops or booths), the Forum became and remained the grand ceremonial and civic centre of Rome, especially after the cattle and sheep market was moved to the Forum Boarium and the vegetable market was similarly displaced to the

Forum Holitorium. Porticoes and balconies were added to the remaining shops on two sides of the Forum in 318BC, increasing the square's dignity and providing viewing facilities for the people. Many of the city's greatest buildings were rebuilt around the Forum Romanum: the Curia Hostilia (Senate House), the Rostra (Speakers' Platform) from which magistrates could address the people gathered in the *Comitium* (Assembly) and the *Regia* (the house of the Pontifex Maximus).

THE SERVIAN WALL
Among the most imposing structures of early Rome was the Servian Wall, parts of whose massive tufa masonry survive. This was supposedly first built by the Etruscan King Servius in the 6th century BC but was in fact erected in haste only after the Gauls had sacked the nearly defenceless city in 390BC.

Seven miles (11km) long and about 30ft (20m) high, the wall enclosed an area of 1,000 acres (400 ha) and made the city, if properly defended, almost impregnable. It proved its worth against Hannibal, in the Second Punic War (218–202BC), who failed to capture the city.

Above: The remains of the giant columns of the Temple of Vespasian. It was built at the same time (the AD80s) and in the same style as the Temple of Jupiter was rebuilt, but of this almost nothing remains.

Below: The outlet of the Cloaca Maxima, the Great Drain, dug before 600BC in the Etruscan period.

Above: The austere Tabularium or Records Office dates from Sulla's dictatorship 82–79BC, but it has a Renaissance upper floor.

Below: Dating from c. 120BC, the Temple of Hercules Victor (or Vesta) was one of Rome's first temples to be built in the Greek style and of solid marble.

THE LATER REPUBLIC: 200–31BC

As Rome conquered the Mediterranean, it gained numerous artworks looted from Greek cities, especially after 212BC when Syracuse, the greatest Greek city in the West, was captured. Roman generals soon saw other sophisticated Greek cities in the southern and east Mediterranean.

Rome itself now grew rapidly – its population had probably passed the half-million mark before 100BC – and its upper classes grew richer, developing a taste for Greek art, luxury and ostentation. Some Roman nobles began adorning their houses and, more strikingly, their city with statues and buildings that proclaimed their fame, power and wealth while revealing strong Greek influence.

Stone buildings with Ionic or Corinthian columns, such as the white marble Temple of Vesta (actually dedicated to Hercules Victor) of 120BC or the neighbouring Temple of Portunus, built of local stone, must have seemed shockingly innovative in a city still mostly filled with old-fashioned Etruscan-style mud brick and timber buildings.

A DISTINCTIVE ROMAN STYLE

This Greek influence, which was probably at its peak by *c.* 100BC, never completely dominated all aspects of Roman architecture however. The first basilicas, great covered public meeting places such as the Basilica Aemilia of 179BC by the Forum, were essentially Roman buildings, despite their Greek origin and name. Even the Temple of Portunus differs from Greek models in having narrower proportions and a basically Etruscan plan. Most of its columns are massed in front and its side pillars are engaged – half-buried in the wall – a Roman device, decorative rather than structural, that proved very influential in architecture from the Renaissance on. About the same time, the Romans began to realize the potential of the true arch and vault through using *opus caementicum*, Roman concrete. While none of these was a Roman invention – the arch was known in pharaonic Egypt – Romans were to employ all three to unprecedentedly powerful effect.

Perhaps the most impressive surviving structure of the late Republic comes from Praeneste (Palestrina) just outside Rome. Now thought to date from *c.* 130BC, the remarkable complex of the Temple of Fortuna Primigenia, sited 600ft (196m) above the Latium plain, employs a vaulted substructure to support its upper terraces. Behind them the sanctuary of the oracle, novelly semicircular in shape, is cut deep into the hillside. It is approached by a series of criss-crossing ramps and colonnades up which worshippers would have had to walk in increasingly

breathless awe. The whole complex was built of limestone *opus incertum* and was probably originally covered with white stucco to create a marble-like effect which would have gleamed for miles. Such dramatic exploitation of the site suggests a brilliant if unknown architect.

In Rome itself, less radical buildings remained the norm. Of the many works of Sulla, the *Tabularium* (Records Office) of 78BC overlooking the Forum, is one of the few to survive intact (although Michelangelo added an upper floor in the 16th century). A massive, austerely dignified structure well suited to a dictator, it is built mainly of concrete. Its façade is of stone blocks, however, and has the arched opening flanked by columns which was to become a typical Roman feature.

Pompey's huge 55BC theatre in the Campus Martius, outside the ancient *pomerium* (sacred boundary) was the city's first permanent theatre. Theatres had previously been banned on the grounds that they promoted immorality and plays were performed in temporary wooden structures which were subsequently demolished. Pompey's theatre used concrete to support a stone-faced structure on a series of radial and curving vaults, so making a semi-circle 525ft (160m) in diameter that could seat an estimated 27,000 spectators. More than just a theatre, its spacious colonnaded gardens offered art galleries and new open spaces for the Roman public. Recent excavations have shown that a substantial amount of the substructures still survive.

CAESAR'S GRAND PLANS

Never to be outshone by his defeated rival Pompey, Julius Caesar, in control of Rome from 49BC, drafted plans that would have transformed the city into a true rival of the great Hellenistic capitals such as Alexandria or Antioch in splendour as well as size. According to Suetonius, his projects included a "Temple to Mars, the biggest in the world, to build which he would have had to fill up and pave the lake where a naval mock-fight had been

staged, and an enormous theatre sloping down from the Tarpeian rock on the Capitoline Hill". (This almost suggests Caesar was planning to create a theatre exploiting a natural slope, on the Greek pattern.) He also planned "The finest possible public libraries", one for Latin, one for Greek literature, a new Curia Julia (Senate House) to replace the old one destroyed in a riot in 52BC, and a wholly new Forum and Basilica. He is also on record as apparently planning to change the course of the Tiber, probably to try to alleviate the flooding problem.

Caesar's assassination in 44BC prevented the full realization of such grand visions. (The land alone for the Basilica Julia in the Forum Romanum reputedly cost 100 million sesterces.) However, his heir Octavian later completed his restored Curia and the Forum and Basilica Julia became the first in a series of imperial basilicas and fora. Rebuilt after yet another fire under Diocletian and stripped of its medieval accretions, the Curia Julia still presents a proudly simple symmetry.

Above: The new Curia, planned by Julius Caesar but built by his heir Octavian, still stands, although it was heavily restored c. AD300.

Below: The Temple of Portunus is Greek in its Ionic columns but reveals an Italian design in its high podium and narrow proportions.

AUGUSTUS AND HIS HEIRS:
30BC–AD53

According to Suetonius, Augustus claimed he had "found Rome of brick and left it in marble", boasting that he had restored 82 temples in 28BC alone. Even if this boast is exaggerated, it is certainly true that Augustus transformed the city during the half century that he ruled it after 36BC.

CLASSICAL TRANSFORMATION

This Augustan transformation was classical, even conservative in style, at times looking back to 5th century BC Athens for ideas. What made Augustus' boast possible were the new supplies of marble from quarries at Carrara near Lucca. If not as finely translucent as Greek marble, Carrara marble was abundant and relatively cheap. For his grandest buildings, Augustus also imported coloured marble, setting the seal of approval on the use of coloured marble in public building. However, marble façades covered brick and concrete cores, while most housing, especially the tall

Above: The channels of the Aqua Claudia and Aqua Anio Novus, top right, were carried by the Porta Maggiore, with its rusticated masonry, across two roads. They were completed by Claudius in AD52 to bring water for Rome's growing population.

Below: The Theatre of Marcellus, Rome's largest surviving theatre, dedicated by Augustus in 13BC and named after his first son-in-law, Marcellus.

Left: Known as the first Roman emperor, Augustus took pains to seem no more than princeps *to his contemporaries.*

insulae (apartment blocks), lacked marble even to front their flimsy walls of rubble and mud brick. Rome remained extremely vulnerable to fire.

Augustus' first task was to fulfil the grand projects of his adopted father, Caesar, which had been halted by the renewed civil wars after 44BC.

Among these was Caesar's Forum, designed to supplement the old Forum Romanum, Rome's ancient heart. Augustus completed this with fine colonnaded porticoes on three sides and the Temple of Venus Genetrix, the goddess from whom the Julian dynasty claimed descent, on its fourth. He enlarged and completed the great Basilica Julia (aisled hall) to the south of the Forum Romanum, and rebuilt the Curia (Senate House) on the north-east. This now austere building once had a stucco and marble front. Next to it Augustus also restored the Basilica Aemilia, lavishly decorating it with marble. A century later Pliny called it one of Rome's three most beautiful buildings. Augustus redesigned the whole jumbled Forum Romanum, moving the Rostra (Speakers' Platform) to a position at the west end. He built a second rostra at the east end of the Forum in front of the Temple of the Deified Julius Caesar, which he decorated with the ships' prows of Antony's defeated fleet from the Battle of Actium. At the other end was a temple to the now deified Julius and two arches, the Actian Arch (29BC) and the so-called Parthian Arch (19–18BC). This arrangement essentially shaped the Forum until the empire's end.

Greatest of Augustus' own projects was the Forum of Augustus north of the Forum Julium – the extra forum was needed by Rome's ever-growing population. Started in 37BC to celebrate victory over Caesar's assassins, it was only finished in 2BC. It had some markedly Greek features, notably the caryatids (columns like draped women) copied from the Athenian Erechtheum, supporting porticoes on either side on the upper level. Behind this lay *exedrae* (recesses) housing statues of ancient Roman heroes of the Republic, including legendary heroes like Romulus and Aeneas. The new temple of Mars Ultor (Mars the Avenger) was, by contrast, typically Italian. Resting on a high podium and intended to be seen only from the front, its eight tall columns at the front must have dominated the narrow Forum. Behind rose a huge wall built of tufa, which acted as a firewall and hid a slum area known as the Suburba. Augustus' fame as a peace-bringer was honoured by the sublimely classical Ara Pacis (Altar of Peace), whose reliefs show Augustus, his family and friends in solemn but sociable procession. The last temple of Augustus' reign was the Temple of Concord, which again revealed Athenian influences and was probably part-built by Greek craftsmen. Augustus' own house was relatively modest. It consisted of the old house of Hortensius the Orator with other buildings added, such as the House of Livia. However, its location on the Palatine Hill was imperial: he had the mythical Romulus and the god Apollo as his neighbours.

AUGUSTUS' SUCCESSORS

Agrippa, Augustus' right-hand man, inaugurated Rome's tradition of fine public baths with the Baths of Agrippa in the Campus Martius. If modest compared with later bathing palaces, they already had gardens for gymnastics. He built a new bridge, the Pons Agrippae, improved flood defences against the ever-turbulent Tiber and built new warehouses to store grain.

Nearby he constructed the Pantheon (which was later replaced by Hadrian's more famous temple). To satisfy the city's growing water needs, Agrippa built two new aqueducts, the Aqua Julia in 33BC and the Aqua Virgo in 19BC. He did not neglect basics either, reportedly personally inspecting the Cloaca Maxima in a boat – the Great Drain was big enough for such voyages – and restoring it and other sewers.

By comparison, Augustus' successors built little. Tiberius concentrated the whole Praetorian Guard in Rome and necessitated the building of the large rectilinear camp that henceforth abutted the city to accommodate them. He also built himself a big square palace on the Palatine, the Domus Tiberiana.

Gaius Caligula's brief reign (AD37–41) was dominated by such abortive grandiose schemes as a planned new palace and bridge to the Temple of Jupiter from the Palatine Hill. Claudius looked to essentials, on the other hand. His new aqueducts, the Aqua Claudia and Aqua Anio Novus, entered the city on a monumental double arch, the modern Porta Maggiore, whose rusticated stone inspired Renaissance and Neoclassical architects. He also built the marble gates of the Circus Maximus, but his greatest work lay outside Rome, in the new harbour he created north of Ostia at Portus.

Above: The Forum Romanum looking toward the temple of Julius Caesar. Augustus cleared the by then cluttered Forum and gave it what became its definitive shape.

Below: The remains of the Temple of Mars Ultor (Mars the Avenger), Augustus' greatest temple that crowned the Forum of Augustus.

NERO AND THE FLAVIANS:
AD54–96

Above: The Arch of Titus was dedicated to Domitian in AD81 to commemorate the sack of Jerusalem and the apotheosis of his brother Titus, the previous emperor.

Below: The arches of the Amphitheatrum Flavium or Colosseum, the great arena built by the Flavian dynasty and dedicated in AD80. It remains the biggest amphitheatre ever built.

With the accession to the throne of the 16-year-old Nero in AD54 – an emperor passionate about most things Greek and with genuine artistic interests if not talents – Roman architecture entered what is often called its golden age. It lasted until the death of the emperor Hadrian in AD138, himself another noted philhellene (lover of Greek culture).

BUILDING FOR A GOLDEN AGE

As the empire neared its zenith, architects emerged who could use concrete with daring new confidence on lavish imperial projects. Nero's new public baths were complexes which came to include gymnasia, gardens, libraries, restaurants and art galleries as well as swimming pools. Completed in AD62, they were praised by the poet Martial. (The baths were completely rebuilt in the 3rd century AD by the emperor Severus Alexander, along with a new market and a bridge across the Tiber.) However, Nero's real interest lay in extending and extravagantly rebuilding the imperial palace, which was still modest by the standards of the Hellenistic monarchies he admired.

Nero wanted to link the existing palace on the Palatine Hill with the lavish Gardens of Maecenas – already belonging to the emperors – on the Esquiline Hill about 600yds (660m) away. Around AD64 he began building the *Domus Transitoria* (literally Transit Palace) between them. Surviving fragments give some hints of the palace's lavish polychromatic marble, stucco and gilt decorations and also of its radical new architecture.

EFFECTS OF THE GREAT FIRE

The fire that ravaged Rome in AD64 gave Nero the chance to build on a truly titanic scale. He began constructing his Domus Aurea (Golden Palace) on about 300 acres (120ha) of prime central land. This was laid out like a country estate, with extensive grounds and a lake, "like the sea, was surrounded by buildings that resembled cities, and by a landscaped park with ploughed fields, vineyards, pastures and woods," according to Suetonius. The palace amazed contemporaries with marvels such as a dining-room with a revolving ceiling fitted with pipes for sprinkling guests with perfumes. Architecturally, its octagonal room was revolutionary, for it not only broke with all the earlier conventional rectangular plans but exploited the resulting new spatial effects in ways that proved lastingly influential. The architects' concern with the building's interior was something quite new in the Graeco-Roman world.

Nero also issued sensible new building regulations for the ruined capital after the fire. These stipulated wider, straight streets in place of the previous narrow lanes, the building of porticoes to provide fire-fighting platforms, the use of fire-resistant

building materials and a height limit of 70ft (21m) for *insulae* (apartment blocks). These measures were intended to make Rome a safer, more salubrious city. However, they did nothing for Nero's plunging popularity and his reign ended in civil war.

BUILDING FOR THE PEOPLE
Vespasian, the victorious first Flavian emperor (ruled AD69–79), deliberately repudiated Neronian self-indulgence, building for the benefit of the whole Roman people. The wing of the Domus Aurea on the Palatine was incorporated, often at subterranean levels, into the Palatine palace of Domitian and the Esquiline wing of the palace was used by the Flavians as VIP accommodation. Its lake was drained to provide the site for one of the most famous of all Roman buildings: the Flavian Amphitheatre today known as the Colosseum.

The biggest amphitheatre in the empire, the Colosseum could seat up to 45–55,000 people. A vaulted ellipsoid mass rising 159ft (48.5m) to its upper cornice, the building posed unprecedented structural problems. These were solved by skilled engineering that made extensive use of a honeycomb of concrete barrel vaults, although much of the upper structure was of travertine and tufa masonry. The façade is of travertine blocks with purely decorative arches flanked by columns which rise in four successive tiers.

Vespasian also rebuilt the temple to Jupiter on the Capitol which had been destroyed in the civil wars, completed the temple to the deified emperor Claudius that had been left unfinished by Nero and constructed the Forum Pacis (Forum of Peace), to celebrate the return of peace to the empire and to house some of the spoils of the sack of Jerusalem.

Titus, Vespasian's heir, who inaugurated the Colosseum in AD80 with lavish games lasting 100 days, built new baths. According to a 16th-century sketch (for nothing remains) the modest building pioneered the imperial plan for baths with a central bathing block within a large symmetrical enclosure containing gardens and gymnasia. Built of brick-faced concrete, it offered ordinary Romans free or very cheap baths. Titus' brother Domitian (ruled AD81–96), built a fine marble arch in Titus' memory and constructed a vast palace on the Palatine Hill, the Domus Flavia (Flavian Palace). Approaching Nero's in splendour, it became the emperors' main palace from then on and has given us the word palace (from palatine). The palace was made up of a complex of buildings including state apartments, basilica, baths and private rooms. It exploited the use of vaults and was lavishly decorated with coloured and patterned marbles. Domitian, who had become paranoid and reclusive, was assassinated inside his creation in AD96.

Above: The Palatine Palace seen rising above the Circus Maximus. The greatest creation of the despotic emperor Domitian, it became the chief palace of all subsequent Caesars and gave us our word palace.

Below: Nero's Domus Aurea (Golden Palace) was even more renowned for its lavish decorations than its daring architecture. This typical mythological decorative scene shows the birth of Adonis.

TRAJAN AND HADRIAN:
AD98–138

Above: Built as a mausoleum for the emperor Hadrian and his dynasty, the Castel Sant'Angelo became a fort in the Middle Ages. The Ponte Sant'Angelo leading to it also has Hadrianic foundations.

Below: Among the most remarkable of Trajan's many buildings is his market. This covered complex of shops and offices rises above his Forum, with a vaulted hall at its core.

The building of Rome reached its climax under the emperors Trajan (AD98–117) and Hadrian (AD117–38). As the empire neared its confident zenith, the *spolia* (booty) that Trajan gained from conquering Dacia (Romania) helped to pay for his grand projects. The reigns of Trajan and Hadrian also saw the culmination of the so-called Roman revolution in architecture, in which the use of concrete domes and vaults was fully mastered.

TRAJAN'S ROME
Trajan took advantage of a fire that had destroyed the remains of Nero's Domus Aurea in AD104 to start building his baths on part of its site on the Esquiline Hill. Though not the first *thermae* (imperial baths), they were probably three times bigger than those built by Titus, and were almost certainly designed by Apollodorus of Damascus, who was arguably the greatest Roman architect. The baths were orientated to exploit the heat of the afternoon sun in an early form of solar heating and were built of brick-faced concrete. The great

complex, which included gardens, lecture halls, libraries and other rooms for citizens' varied social activities, was dedicated in AD109.

Trajan spent even more money on his Forum and its adjoining Basilica, which were dedicated in AD113. For his Forum, which measured 220 by 130yds (220 by 120m), he cut away the high ground between the Quirinal and Capitoline hills. Flanked by porticoes with marble columns, with a great equestrian statue of Trajan in the centre and large *exedrae* (semicircular recesses) on either side, the Forum became one of the city's wonders. It also provided another much-needed open space for public life in a city whose population was still growing.

On the north-western side of the Forum and instead of the usual temple, Trajan built the Basilica Ulpia (commemorating his family). The largest such public basilica yet built in Rome, it was 185yds (170m) long, with five aisles and apses at either end. Its interior was richly decorated with a marble frieze and columns of grey Egyptian granite, suitably majestic for a building which often served as a law court. Beyond the basilica rose Trajan's Carrara marble column, 125ft (38m) high with a spiral staircase inside. It is carved with a continuous relief vividly illustrating scenes from the recent Dacian wars. Flanking the column were Trajan's two libraries, one for Latin, one for Greek literature, both damp-proofed to protect their vulnerable scrolls. It has been suggested the higher parts of the column's frieze would have been easily visible from the libraries' upper-floor windows, although they are not today.

Behind such obviously opulent buildings rose another more utilitarian but architecturally more radical structure. Trajan's Market was a covered complex built into the hill and remarkable for its

Left: The Pantheon, the Temple of all the Gods, was Hadrian's great architectural statement. Its diameter of 142ft (43.3m) made it the world's broadest unsupported dome for 1700 years after its consecration in AD128.

Below: Now cleaned so that it looks almost new, Trajan's column is a pillar composed of drums of fine Carrara marble rising 125ft (38m). Originally it had a statue of the emperor on top and held his ashes inside it – a singular honour for the much-loved emperor.

semicircular shape which housed 150 shops and offices. Much of it is still extant, with a great vaulted hall and many booths. The entire market was built of the brick-faced concrete that was now becoming the norm in such complex edifices. Trajan also added a new inner harbour at Portus near Ostia. The hexagonal basin was excavated inland to shelter shipping from the storms that at times made Claudius' older outer harbour unsafe. Its waterfront was lined with warehouses and the basin was connected to the Tiber by a canal.

TEMPLE OF ALL THE GODS

Hadrian, although a more cautious emperor politically (he abandoned Trajan's conquests east of the Euphrates), proved equally radical architecturally. His greatest building was the Pantheon or Temple of all the Gods. Consecrated in AD128, it is often considered the most sublime Roman temple. The temple was revolutionary, for unlike any earlier Roman or Greek temple, the Pantheon was intended to be looked at as much from the inside as the outside. Worshippers stood beneath a perfect hemisphere, its diameter exactly equalling its height, with an *oculus* opening to the heavens above lighting the whole building. The coffered ceiling, which was originally gilded, was cut back in frame after frame, both a structural and a decorative device. The internal columns were, however, purely decorative, for the weight of the dome is carried by the drum's wall, which is supported by eight giant arches inside the brick-faced concrete walls. With a diameter of 142ft (43.2m) it remained the world's broadest unsupported span until the 19th century.

Hadrian also built the Temple of Venus and Roma to a bold, if perhaps not wholly successful, design. Consecrated in AD135, it was modelled closely on classical Greek precedents and was the first temple in the capital to be built to the cult of Roma. The structure was probably built to Hadrian's own designs. It had two *cellae* (inner chambers) which backed on to each other. Like Greek temples, it had columns all round, resting not on a Roman podium but merely on top of steps, which meant that it did not rise clear above its surroundings.

Hadrian also built a mausoleum for himself and his dynasty across the Tiber. This circular building of marble-faced tufa and concrete originally had earth piled high on it but has since become the Castel Sant'Angelo. Hadrian also built the bridge leading to it, the Pons Aelius.

ROME IN THE LATER EMPIRE:
AD138–312

Above: Coin of Marcus Aurelius, emperor AD161–80 who built Rome's second great commemorative column.

Below: The Arch of Constantine, built AD315 by the emperor who started Rome's conversion to Christianity and founded a new capital in the east. His arch, however, is oddly conservative, stealing earlier edifices' decorative figures.

The 60 years following Hadrian's death saw relatively little building in Rome. This was due in part to the exhausting wars that filled most of Marcus Aurelius' reign between AD161–80.

The emperor Antoninus Pius built a temple to the deified Hadrian and another to his wife Faustina (and later his deified self) in AD141 in the Forum Romanum. The temple, now embedded in a later building on the Campus Martius, owes its excellent state of preservation to its conversion into a church, a fate that saved it from being plundered for building materials but which relatively few ancient buildings experienced.

Marcus also began construction of a column commemorating his Danubian wars, which consciously echoed that of Trajan. Completed under his son Commodus, its carvings reveal the sea-change that was beginning to affect Graeco-Roman art. Classical realism had begun to give way to a more stylized portrayal of characters and to much starker and more realistic depictions of war.

With the advent of the new Severan dynasty in AD193 came new ambitions. Septimius Severus added a new wing to the Palatine palace and built more *thermae* (public baths), but these were soon utterly surpassed by those built by his son, Caracalla (ruled AD211–17), the bare ruins of which are still overwhelming today. The *Thermae Antoninianae* or Baths of Caracalla followed Trajan's Baths' layout of a century earlier but on a far larger scale. The whole complex with its gardens and gymnasia was nearly 500yds (460m) square and enclosed an area of almost 50 acres (20ha). Revealing the new priorities of Roman architects, the baths had luxuriously decorated interiors but rather plain exteriors.

EASTERN INFLUENCE
The Severans also built temples, mainly to eastern deities – Caracalla to Serapis, Elagabalus (ruled AD218–22) to Baal and Alexander Severus (ruled AD222–35) to Isis, although this last was essentially a restoration. The influx of Eastern gods reflected the growth of new religions in the population as well as the emperors' own personal preferences. Elagabalus, for example, had been a priest of the cult of Baal in Syria. On a microscopic scale, a detailed map of Rome, known today as the *Forma Urbis Romae* and dated AD205–8, was carved on 151 pieces of marble, under Septimius Severus. The map's few surviving fragments are invaluable for our knowledge of the ancient city.

ROME REWALLED
The catastrophes of the 3rd century AD, when more than 30 rival emperors fought each other in the 50 years after AD235, led to opportunistic barbarian invasions across the empire. This spelt a temporary end to massive but non-essential projects. Rome itself came under threat of barbarian

attack for the first time in almost 400 years. To counter this, new walls were constructed in great haste by the emperor Aurelian (ruled AD270–5), for the Servian walls had long since been allowed to decay. The new walls incorporated existing structures such as the aqueduct of Claudius (now the Porta Maggiore) and the Praetorian Guards' camp. Built of brick-faced concrete, 25ft (7.2m) high with 18 gates and 381 towers, they ran for 12 miles (19.3km) and covered an area of almost 3,500 acres (1,400ha), which was by then the extent of the city. Strengthened by both Maxentius and Valentinian I in the 4th century and Honorius in the early 5th, they protected Rome, often inadequately, up to 1870 when the city was incorporated into a reunited Italy. Aurelian also built a Temple to Sol Invictus (the Unconquered Sun).

ORDER RESTORED

Diocletian, founder of the tetrarchy system of four co-emperors, restored order to the empire during his reign (AD284–305). He rebuilt the Curia (Senate House), together with the two temples of Saturn and Vesta, reorganized the cluttered Forum Romanum and built another set of baths even grander than Caracalla's. Completed in AD305, the huge size of the baths – they measure 785 by 475ft (240 by 144m) – can be judged today by the 16th century church of Santa Maria degli Angeli that Michelangelo built in the *frigidarium* (cold bath). Diocletian and his fellow tetrarchs, however, no longer ruled the empire from Rome, but chose other cities closer to the endangered frontiers as their capitals.

Maxentius (ruled AD306–12) was the last effective emperor to make Rome his capital, although he ruled only part of the Western empire. Appropriately, he adorned the city with its grandest basilica, the Basilica Nova (which was actually completed by Constantine). The basilica's massive structure – rising to 115ft (35m) with a central nave of 260 by 80ft (80 by 25m) flanked by huge *exedrae* – recalls the greatest *thermae*. Maxentius also built a new palace or villa on the Via Appia, complete with a circus and race track.

After Maxentius' defeat, the victorious Constantine built a grand triple arch in AD315, plundering sculptures from earlier monuments for this age saw little new sculpture, and built Rome's last great *thermae* in AD320. Such buildings perpetuated Rome's proudly pagan imperial traditions but Constantine is chiefly noted for his patronage of Christianity.

Above: Ruins of the Basilica Nova, Rome's largest basilica, started by the emperor Maxentius and completed by his victorious rival Constantine after AD312.

Below: Aerial view of the Baths of Caracalla, built AD211–17, which enclosed an area of 50 acres (20ha) with gardens, gymansia and restaurants besides the actual baths themselves.

ROME – THE CHRISTIAN CITY:
AD312–609

Right: The nave of the Basilica of Santa Maria Maggiore, built by Pope Sixtus III in the AD430s, is remarkable for its classicism. Its fine Ionic columns look back almost to Augustan styles.

Below: Santo Stefano Rotondo, built AD468–83, a church whose two concentric rings of columns recall those of pagan mausoleums. This was built as a martyrium to house the relics of Saint Stephen, an early martyr.

The early Christians built little for several reasons: keen expectation of Christ's imminent Second Coming, which made all large-scale building seem rather futile; the relative poverty of many early Christians and, most important, the intermittent but sometimes savage persecution by the authorities that drove them underground. Nonetheless, Christianity gradually became the religion of the empire. This process began with Constantine's famous Edict of Milan of AD313, which granted freedom to all religions. A vast church-building programme began, in Rome as well as in Constantine's new capital on the Bosphorus, which was officially founded in AD330.

FIRST CATHEDRAL OF ST PETER
Constantine gave land and money to Pope Sylvester I across the Tiber in the Vatican where, according to tradition, St Peter had been crucified. Here, the first cathedral of St Peter (it is often called "Old St Peter's" to distinguish it from the present church) was started in AD333. A basilica-style structure, its design owed nothing to pagan temples because it served a very different purpose from housing a god's image in mysterious obscurity. Instead,

the church had to accommodate a congregation or assembly of worshippers – the Latin for church, *ecclesia*, comes from the Greek for assembly. (Christianity was another Eastern religion that had arrived in the capital speaking Greek.)

Architecturally, St Peter's was a simple if large basilica-style building, but with a flat timber-beamed ceiling instead of vaults, supported by a colonnaded nave and with a broad lateral transept. It also had a large courtyard in front with a fountain which was used for ritual washing. The whole building was meant to concentrate the attention of the increasing number of pilgrims on the tomb of the martyred apostle at the far end.

The mausoleum built *c.* AD340 on the outskirts of Rome for Constantine's daughter Constantia and since converted into the church of Santa Constanza, was a circular building. Internally, the wheel-like colonnade of double columns round the centre creates an impression of light and air, while its mosaics show delightful peacocks, vines and other fruitful details, all creating perhaps the most charming architecture of its age. The most resplendent of the 4th-century churches was the Basilica Constantinia, now San Giovanni in Laterano, which Constantine began in AD313. Rome's parish church, it is the seat of the bishop of Rome – the Pope. Built of brick-faced concrete, it originally had seven gold altars and glittering mosaics, but it has been much altered, most notably by Bernini in the 17th century and by a fire in the 19th century.

The city of Rome, usually shunned by Constantine's heirs, now became something of a backwater both politically and architecturally, compared to cities such as Milan and Constantinople, where the imperial courts' presence encouraged building. In any case, the imperial regime was increasingly hostile to Rome's overwhelmingly pagan heritage.

In AD382, the ardently Christian emperor Theodosius I ordered the closure of all the pagan temples and the removal of the statue of the goddess Victory from the Senate House. This step marked the consolidation of Christianity into its new intolerant guise. Most temples were not converted into Christian churches despite their central locations because of their associations with the pagan gods, whom early Christians considered not as charmingly poetic archaic vestiges but as maliciously demonic presences. Only a lucky few survived the thousand-plus years before the Renaissance revived appreciation of Rome's pagan past. The most famous of these was the Pantheon, which was consecrated as a church in AD609, just in time to preserve its glories almost completely.

LONG DECAY
The barbarians who sacked Rome in the 5th century – the relatively restrained Visigoths in AD410 and the far more brutal Vandals in AD456 – merely hastened the decay of the city. Increasingly, Rome's inhabitants and government could no longer afford to maintain their huge inheritance. The long-drawn out war in the middle of the 6th century AD between the invading Byzantines and the Ostrogoths, who had established a kingdom in Italy, saw the aqueducts cut off in one of the many

sieges, an act which Italian historians traditionally regard as the beginning of the Middle Ages in Italy. Hadrian's mausoleum became a castle, for example, as did the Colosseum later. Within the great extent of the Aurelianic walls, large parts of Rome reverted to a rusticity that later charmed northern visitors.

Amid all these disasters, Pope Sixtus III (AD432–40) inaugurated a short-lived classical revival. The noble Ionic columns of the Church of Santa Maria Maggiore support a lintel in an almost Augustan style. Santa Sabina's great Corinthian columns provide another fine example of this surviving or reviving classicism, while Santo Stefano Rotondo (AD468–83), with its concentric rings of columns, again shows classicism flourishing at a remarkably late date.

Even in its long ruin, Rome somehow remained faithful to the classical tradition it had created, for buildings in the Gothic style were to be surprisingly rare in the Eternal City, as if memories of its imperial past discouraged them.

Above: The Mausoleum of Santa Constanza in Rome, built c. AD340, was later converted into a church.

Below: The Church of Santa Sabina in Rome, built AD422–34, reuses grandiose Corinthian columns. It is a well-preserved example of the 5th-century classical revival that ignored all political crises.

CHAPTER XIV

BUILDING TECHNIQUES AND STYLES

Roman buildings often seem to emulate classical Greek models, most notably in their use of classical columns. However, Roman architecture soon developed its own dynamic, versatile and highly practical form of classicism. This employed arches, vaults and domes, all made possible by the Romans' exploitation of concrete. The Romans developed types of *opus caementicum* (concrete) early on, due to a relative lack of attractive, readily accessible stone and also to their desire to build fast. They had abundant tufa, soft volcanic rock of varying densities and, further afield, travertine, a fine but brittle limestone. Only with the opening of marble quarries near Carrara in the 40s BC did relatively cheap white marble reach Rome. Most buildings were concrete structures, brick-faced then covered with marble, stucco or plaster.

Although classical columns or pediments in Roman buildings often had no load-bearing function, they were long thought essential to dignify and humanize buildings. However, in the 3rd century AD fashions changed. Although the exteriors of buildings still had some decoration, they became secondary as architects began concentrating mostly on interiors. As most such decorations have vanished, Roman buildings can look far more austere than they did when originally built.

Left: The bridge at Alcantara, Spain, built under Trajan (AD98–117) and still in use, demonstrates Roman engineering skills at their most inspiring and durable.

BUILDING MATERIALS

Above: Opus incertum, *the first type of facing for Roman concrete, consisted of irregular-shaped small stones placed on a concrete core.*

Above: Opus reticulatum, *the next type of facing for concrete, had small square-faced stones laid diagonally creating a network of interconnecting lozenge-shaped joints.*

Above: Opus testaceum, *the third sort of facing for concrete, had brick or tile facing over a rubble or concrete core.*

Right: The main body of the Pantheon is of brick-faced concrete. The giant portico had 16 grey and red Egyptian granite columns weighing 84 tons each, and the pediment was of white marble.

The earliest building materials used in the city of Rome were mud brick and timber-framing. However, soft volcanic tufa was used for some structures, most notably for the Servian Walls (built *c.* 378BC). Well-suited for the older type of *domus* (one-storied detached house), timber-framed mud brick continued as a common building material in the more jerry-built multi-storey *insulae* (apartment blocks) built from the end of the 3rd century BC. These were built, despite obvious structural weakness, at least until the great fire of AD64. This led to new, although not universally observed, building regulations that encouraged gradual improvements in the quality of *insulae*.

ANCIENT CONCRETE

Using a characteristic trial and error approach, Romans learnt to exploit other materials, especially *opus caementicum*, their own type of concrete. At times this pragmatic approach worked wonders as at Praeneste, whose vaults still stand.

Perhaps inspired by examples from Pompeii, the Romans in the 3rd century BC began building walls using mortar made of lime and *pozzolana* – black volcanic sand first found near Puteoli (Pozzuoli). The walls' cores were filled with smallish stones which produced a solid, cohesive mass when mortar was laid on top. Rome had abundant supplies of limestone which could be burnt to produce lime, essential to lime mortar. Vitruvius, the architect and theorist writing *c.* 30BC, recommended three parts of volcanic sand to one of mortar.

Roman concrete was seldom poured like modern concrete, but was normally laid by hand in roughly horizontal courses between timber frames. These were left in place and mortar added to produce a very strong monolithic whole.

In effect, Roman *opus caementicum* was an artificial stone, vastly cheaper and more malleable than any from a quarry. Initially Roman concrete used for building walls was faced with *opus incertum*, a surface of

irregularly placed, small stones over the concrete core. The Porticus Aemilia, begun in 193BC, used this concrete on a large scale for its rows of barrel-vaults. *Opus reticulatum*, which succeeded this early concrete, had small stones with a square face laid diagonally to create a network of interconnected lozenge-shaped joints. This facing technique was developed in Rome and used to build the Theatre of Pompey. Completed in 55BC, this was Rome's first large permanent theatre. The third and final sort of concrete was *opus testaceum*, that had a brick or tile facing over its rubble and mortar core. By Augustus' reign, the Romans were increasingly using red *pozzolana* which produced a finer, stronger cement. (The Romans never made the mistake, common in the mid-20th century, of leaving bare concrete walls exposed to the elements, where rain could soon disfigure them.)

STANDARDIZED BRICKS

When Augustus boasted that he had found Rome a city of brick and left it a city of marble, he may have been thinking of a city made of mud brick, but fired bricks were becoming more common as building materials. The Theatre of Marcellus – planned by Caesar and completed by Augustus by 13BC – is partly built of a reddish-yellow brick, lightly baked to absorb mortar porously.

Standardized bricks offer builders obvious advantages and Roman bricks came in four main sizes: *bessalis* eight Roman inches square (20cm); *pedalis* one Roman foot square (30cm); *sesquipedalis* 18 Roman inches square (45cm); and *bipedalis* two Roman feet square (60cm). These bricks were often cut into triangles to face walls and into rectangles to face arches. *Bessales* were the bricks most commonly used in the Principate; Domitian's giant Palatine Palace required a lot of *bipedales* for brick facing. *Bessales* were often used for the *pilae* of a hypocaust, and *bipedales* were used to span the distance between *pilae* as well as for bonding courses in concrete

Right: The obelisk in the fountain in the Piazza Navona in Rome (by Bernini, c. 1650) was imported by Domitian for the Temple of Isis he built in the Campus Martius.

walls. Bricks were made along the Tiber valley and transported by barge when possible. Roof tiles, which were hard-baked for waterproofing and darkish red in colour, sometimes had their flanges cut off for use for building purposes. Both tiles and bricks were occasionally stamped with the name of the *figulus* (brick-maker) and with the names of that year's consuls, a common Roman dating method. Travertine stone quarried near Tivoli was also used for structural purposes under the emperors, for example in the Colosseum.

IMPERIAL IMPORTS

Rome imported both finished artworks and building materials on an increasingly large scale. Some victorious nobles in the last century of the Republic used Greek marble to adorn the temples proclaiming their own or their families' genius. Sulla the dictator went further, grabbing giant Corinthian columns from the unfinished Temple of the Olympian Zeus in Athens to rebuild the great Temple of Jupiter on the Capitol in 82BC. (The two gods were by then effectively identical, so the theft was less sacrilegious than it might seem.) Supplementing new supplies of white marble from Carrara, Augustus began importing coloured marbles from the Aegean, Asia Minor and North Africa for his buildings. Coloured marble had been thought decadent before, but there was nothing decadent about Augustus.

Egypt, his greatest conquest, provided another source of building materials and artefacts, notably obelisks. In 10BC Augustus erected Rome's first obelisk, a sundial in the Piazza di Montecitorio. Gaius Caligula imported another, larger, obelisk in a specially constructed ship. In the Piazza Navona today stands an obelisk originally brought to Rome by the emperor Domitian (ruled AD81–96) for the sanctuary of the Egyptian goddess Isis.

Below: Four comparative Roman brick sizes.
A: bessalis, 8 Roman inches square (20cm). B: pedalis, 1 Roman foot square (30cm). C: sesquipedalis, 18 Roman inches square (45cm). D: bipedalis, two Roman feet square (60cm).

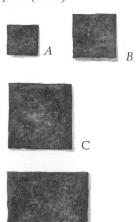

VAULTS, ARCHES, DOMES

Above: The Pantheon's perfect dome remained unsurpassed in span for 1700 years.

Below: In Trajan's Market the Romans made highly practical use of the arch and vault.

The chief characteristic of Roman architecture from a relatively early date was its use of vaults, arches and domes. The buildings so created, especially during Nero's reign (AD54–68) and after, were still often adorned by classically proportioned columns, but they were not usually structurally dependent on such pillars. Instead, vaults, arches and domes transmitted their weight to the supporting walls.

AN ARCHITECTURAL REVOLUTION

This development marked a true revolution in architecture, though one that was unplanned and untheoretical, for Roman architects and builders (there was little difference in practice) discovered the basic principles of engineering through trial and error. A vault is essentially an elongated arch covering a space. Built of brick, concrete, stone or any masonry building material, like an arch it depends on materials supporting each other under pressure.

The simplest vault is a barrel or tunnel vault, the continuation of the semicircular section covered by an arch. A cross- or groin vault is created when two barrel vaults intersect at right angles, producing what looks superficially like a dome. A cloister, domical or pavilion vault derives from the intersection of two barrel vaults, so that it rises from a square or polygonal base to create a dome-like structure. The Tabularium or Records Office (built 82–78BC to Sulla's orders) employs cross-vaults in its lower floors.

ARCHES

A stone or brick arch consists of wedge-shaped blocks (called arch-stones or voussoirs) that stay in place because of the mutual pressure of one stone upon another. These are arranged in a curve to span an opening and to support the often vast weight on top, acting in place of a horizontal lintel (beam).

Stone is normally strong under pressure but weak under tension. This means lintels, lengths of extended stone, cannot span large distances while arches can. Each wedge-shaped voussoir, which is wider at its top than its bottom, cannot fall even if the arch is almost flat, as some are in the Colosseum, for example. However, arches need support until the keystone is in place, so construction of an arch usually requires a timber framework, called centring, to support it while it is being built.

The most distinctive Roman arches are their triumphal arches, which proclaim their engineers' skills as clearly as those of the emperors they commemorate. However, invisible interior arches support many Roman buildings.

TRUE DOMES

A dome is a form of vault, composed of semicircular or segmental sections raised on a circular, elliptical, square or polygonal base. If built on a square base, an intermediate piece needs to be added for the transition between the square and the circle. It took Roman architects a long time to learn to build true domes. Even in the Baths of Caracalla, completed *c.* AD218, the architects were still experimenting.

Central to the dome's development is the extant Octagonal Room in Nero's Domus Aurea (Golden Palace), the grandiose palace he had constructed after the fire of AD64. Little is known about either Severus or Celer, the designer and engineer behind this great (and speedily executed) project. Whether their work represents a revolution or merely an evolution remains debatable, but their ingenuity, amounting almost to genius, in overcoming the problems in the Domus Aurea is indisputable. Standing on eight brick-faced concrete piers, which were originally lavishly covered in marble and stucco, this dome begins as an eight-sided domical vault but becomes a true dome towards the top. It has a wide *oculus* (central opening) to admit light, supplemented by other light wells.

With the Pantheon, built under Hadrian (ruled AD117–38), the problems of building a vast but perfect dome had finally been solved. This was perhaps due to the genius of its probable architect Apollodorus. Both the diameter and the height of its rotunda (cylinder-shaped building) of brick-faced concrete are identical at 140ft (43.2m). Eight piers support eight arches running right through the walls and help to buttress the walls against the outward thrust of the dome. The dome's weight was reduced by coffering (panels sunk in the dome),

Right: The triple Arch of Septimius Severus reveals the Romans as masters of arch-building.

producing an effect which is at once decorative and structural and one which has been much copied in recent centuries. The lightest forms of pumice were used along with concrete in the upper dome to reduce the overall weight.

To reduce the weight of the upper parts of vaults or domes further, *amphorae* (earthenware jars) were later used in the upper parts of some domes, such as the Mausoleum of Constantia (now the Church of Santa Constanza). This allowed windows to be inserted in the dome. The church, though still Roman, points towards Byzantine architecture, whose archetypal achievement would be the dome of the cathedral of Hagia Sophia. The dome of that great cathedral in Constantinople built by the Emperor Justinian in the 6th century AD, seems to sail effortlessly above its square basis, marking both the culmination and the last chapter of Roman architecture.

Above: The barrel or tunnel vault is the simplest form of vault, continuing the semi-circular section of an arch.

Above: The groin vault, very popular with the Romans, is formed by two identical barrel vaults intersecting at 90 degrees.

BUILDING PRACTICES AND TECHNIQUES

The Roman genius at organizing and controlling huge numbers of men was as dramatically demonstrated in the ways they mobilized labour to erect vast public buildings as in their deployment of large standing armies.

MASS MOBILIZATION

There was nothing original about mass mobilization in itself. All pre-industrial societies used huge numbers of labourers for their grand projects, from the Egyptian pyramids up to the 19th century.

What is remarkable about so many of the great imperial edifices, especially in Rome, is the *speed* with which they were erected. Nero's huge Domus Aurea (Golden Palace), for example, was built in only four years after the great fire of AD64. The Colosseum, a far more solidly built and enduring structure, took only a decade (AD70–80) to complete between its conception and its lavish inauguration (although its topmost tier may not have been completed until the reign of Domitian). The immense complex of the Baths of Caracalla apparently took only six years to build in its entirety from AD211. By comparison, some cathedrals in medieval Europe took literally centuries to conceive, design and build.

The Romans usually built fast but they seldom built shoddily, at least for public buildings. Indeed, they built to last. They also built without the aid of any mechanical power – without even the wheelbarrow, as far as we know. The closest they got to any mechanization was the treadmill illustrated in the funerary sculpture of the Haterii family from the late Flavian period (AD69–96). This shows five men turning a great "squirrel cage" at the bottom of a large crane to lift blocks up to a temple building site.

More typical of small-scale Roman building methods is the scene from the 4th-century AD Tomb of Trebius Justus in Ostia. This shows two men on scaffolding laying bricks, two men bringing mortar and bricks up the ladder and another mixing mortar on the ground with a hoe, a sight that must have been common across the empire.

SKILLED LABOUR

Although Roman architects lacked the celebrity status some enjoy today, Vitruvius gave stringent requirements for the (ideal) architect. He was expected to be "literate, a skilled draughtsman and good at geometry, well-versed in history and philosophy, knowledgeable about music, medicine and law, with experience in astronomy". Although not every architect could have had these qualifications, almost all would have been able to draw and make accurate models. We know little about even the most famous Roman architects, such as Rabirius under Domitian and Apollodorus under Trajan.

Unknown master carpenters played an almost equally vital role in making the centring or framework essential in erecting domes, arches and vaults. They had to produce accurate models, for a dome or vault's centring required a continuous surface. This gave the dome its shape

Above: The empire's largest amphitheatre, the Colosseum, took only 10 years to build (AD70–80) but still stands, in parts almost intact.

Below: The tomb of Trebius Justus from the 4th century AD shows a typical small firm of Roman builders at work, perhaps with slaves working alongside free labourers.

while supporting the weight of the *opus caementicum* (concrete) that was laid on it. To reduce the huge amount of wood needed for *centring*, large roof tiles comparable in size to *bessales* or *bipedales* were later sometimes laid across timber scaffolding instead of solid timber planking. When the concrete had set, the timbers could be removed.

A big advantage of *opus caementicum* was that it required far less skilled labour than the masons who cut and laid stone. Even so, many Romans were employed in the building trade – possibly as many as 20,000 during the great imperial projects. The construction of the Baths of Caracalla is thought to have employed about 10,000 men at its peak, including about 700 marble workers and 500 decorators. Many of these would not have been slaves; the millionaire property-developer Crassus (died 53BC), who reputedly owned a team of 500 slave architects and labourers, was the exception rather than the norm.

Most building teams would have been made up of less than a dozen men: the boss, some free labourers and a handful of slaves. Building contractors normally belonged to a guild or trade union, the *collegium fabrum tignuariorum*, which had 1330 members in the 2nd century AD, mostly men of modest means. The *collegium* was divided with almost military precision into 60 *decuriae*, each with its own officials. When someone reputedly suggested a labour-saving device for the building trade to the emperor Vespasian (AD69–79), he rewarded the inventor but rejected his idea, saying he could not deprive the Roman people of work.

SUPPLYING MATERIALS

Such huge projects required prodigious supplies of raw materials. By the end of the 1st century AD, huge amounts of marble, granite and porphyry were being imported into Rome. Exotic imports included Egyptian granite and Aegean coloured marble, but most material came from much closer to Rome. About 100,000 poles would have been needed for the scaffolding alone of the

Baths of Caracalla. Vast quantities of tufa or limestone were excavated; 100,000 cubic metres of material were needed for the Colosseum alone. Much of this was travertine for the façade and load-bearing piers, but a lot of concrete was also used, of which the chief source was the quarries near Tivoli.

As there was no waterway connecting these quarries with Rome, all the stone must have been transported in ox-carts. It has been suggested that one heavily laden cart must, on average, have left the Tivoli quarries every few minutes for 400 years. Sea transport could also have been used to ship stone from limestone quarries on the coast at Terracina. Increasingly under the empire, raw materials were stockpiled in warehouses by the Tiber for use in later projects.

Above: The Tomb of the Haterii, a wealthy family of builders c. AD90, showing a crane being used to lift blocks of stone in a squirrel cage up a construction site. This simple, small-scale machine was typical of Roman technology, which advanced only very modestly. Most teams of builders were quite small, although the total work force employed in the great projects such as the imperial baths must have run to tens of thousands.

ARCHITECTURAL STYLES AND LANGUAGE

Above: The Doric order, left, was the simplest and most rugged sort of column. The Ionic, right, was seen as more graceful and feminine.

For all its innovatory arches, vaults and domes, the Roman architecture of the Republic and Principate (until *c.* AD275) still used the classical language of architecture to dignify and adorn its buildings. Classical details such as the use of columns both inside and outside major public buildings were thought to provide human relevance and scale, especially when statues surmounted pillars or otherwise decorated a building.

THE SIGNIFICANCE OF COLUMNS
Among the most obvious classical features used were columns. These were derived from Greek originals and altered to suit emerging Roman tastes. Roman columns were often employed purely for decoration, in contrast to their use in Greek temples, where they had a load-bearing function, supporting the weight of the lintels. Arcuated Roman architecture generally used arches or vaults rather than columns and lintels. The proportions and decorations of these columns were based on five different "orders" or styles. (Many archaeologists now believe that the Tuscan and Doric orders were not really separate orders for the Romans, although they have become so since the Renaissance.)

The correct proportions for columns were first fully explained by the architect and writer Vitruvius in his book *De Architectura* (On Architecture), written *c.* 35BC and dedicated to the future emperor Augustus. His ideas, enthusiastically rediscovered and reapplied at the Renaissance, have had such an immense influence on Western architecture over the last 600 years that the orders have been called Vitruvian.

THE CLASSICAL ORDERS
Pragmatic and busy Roman architects and engineers did not plan buildings with Vitruvius' book in their pockets, but they scarcely needed to. Examples of classical Greek architecture or buildings influenced by them were all around them and by the mid-2nd century BC many were being built in Rome itself. In Greek cities in southern Italy and especially in Sicily, the conquering Romans could see sublime Greek architecture.

In steadily increasing order of ornateness or luxury, the four major orders were Doric, Ionic, Corinthian and Composite. (The last was a wholly Roman innovation

Left: The Corinthian capitals of the Maison Carrée at Nimes, France. One of the finest and most obviously classical temples of the Augustan period, it looks back to Athenian precursors while using the classical orders in a distinctly Roman manner.

or development.) Roman Doric, the simplest order, differs from Greek Doric in that its column sits on a base, its proportions are more slender and its capital (the decorated head of the column) is simple and angular. The column can be either smooth or fluted. An early example is the Temple at Cori.

Ionic columns have volutes or spiral scrolls at their capitals' corners and are longer and more slender than Doric. An early example is the Temple of Portunus, rebuilt c. 120BC. Corinthian columns have longer proportions and are still more ornate, with two rows of acanthus leaves and other complex decorations. The most luxurious Roman order of all is the Composite, a development of the Corinthian order. Examples appear in the interior of the Baths of Caracalla (AD211–17) and on the Arch of Titus.

According to Vitruvius, the Doric order expressed rugged strength and virility, while the Ionic was graceful and almost feminine. Corinthian columns displayed lavish splendour and Composite columns rejoiced in unabashed luxury and power. In the Colosseum, the decorative columns flanking the arches in the lowest circle are Doric, those in the middle circle are Ionic, those around the top line of arches are Corinthian, while at the very top of the building the Composite order appears.

Besides columns, other key elements in classical architecture include:

pilasters, engaged piers or rectangular columns attached to a wall and only half-emerging from it.

architraves, the horizontal beam resting directly on and linking the capitals of columns.

pediments, the triangular gabled end of a ridged roof.

Right: Roman buildings had an immense influence on later Western architecture, as demonstrated in the Circus of Bath, England, built by John Wood after 1754. It repeats the Colosseum's design, with a development of linked houses with tiers of engaged columns.

entablature, the whole horizontal superstructure carried over a colonnade.

colonnade, a long row of columns at regular intervals normally supporting a covered structure along a street or around a piazza.

exedrae, large, sometimes semicircular recesses often housing statues.

CLASSICAL REVIVALS

Although these classical elements became less important in some great buildings of the later empire (AD284–476), whose exteriors were often relatively austere, they were revived again and again after Rome's fall. These revivals or renascences started with the Carolingian Renaissance of the 8th century AD and continued with the Ottonian Renaissance of the 10th century, until the Italian Renaissance of the 15th century triumphantly and permanently resurrected Rome's classical architectural language in its entirety. This language was to govern most of Western architecture in varying forms until the mid-20th century.

Above: The Corinthian order, left, was used to convey an air of splendour, and the Composite order, right, had an air of opulent luxury.

CHAPTER XV

PUBLIC BUILDINGS

Although most people in the Roman empire lived and worked on the land, city life was considered the only really civilized life, ideally passed in Rome itself. Emperors decorated the imperial city with ever more monuments and buildings – baths, arches, fountains, temples, palaces, libraries, basilicas, fora – until Rome itself became the greatest wonder of the ancient world. The emperor Constantius II, visiting Rome for the first time in AD357, was "thunder-struck" to see "baths built like provinces, the great solid mass of the amphitheatre ... so tall that human sight can scarcely reach its top".

Such majestic buildings were replicated in hundreds of cities around the empire that were built or partly rebuilt in the Roman style by their inhabitants. Urban life, which was mostly lived in the open, focused on the Forum (market/ meeting place). This was a key public space in any Roman city and it was copied across the empire. Life in the open suited a Mediterranean people whose homes were often cramped. However, as Rome became richer, more spacious buildings – most notably the grand imperial baths, along with libraries and basilicas – provided covered, sometimes heated shelter for commercial and legal activities. This was appreciated not only in more northerly cities of the empire such as Lyons, London or Trier but also in Rome itself, where winters can be chilly and wet.

Left: The Forum Romanum in the 19th century. The heart of Rome from very early days, the Forum was replicated in almost every city founded by the Romans across the empire.

THE FORUM ROMANUM

Above: Under Julius Caesar, who ruled Rome for five years after 49BC, the Forum Romanum was extensively replanned, although little was actually built.

Below: To accommodate Rome's swelling population, Augustus constructed a Forum bearing his name just to the north of the Forum Romanum. It was dominated by the Temple of Mars Ultor, three of whose columns still stand.

For the Romans, the word forum meant a meeting place, a public area and a market place. The original Forum Romanum, a marshy area between the Capitoline and Palatine Hills, was drained and paved by the 6th century BC. Long before the expulsion of the kings, traditionally in 509BC, this area became the centre of the city's social and political life.

LIFE IN THE FORUM

On the north-west side of the Forum stood the old Senate House, the Curia Hostilia. In the roughly circular space in front of the Curia the people met in the Comitia (Assembly) to exercise their (strictly limited) powers of voting. From the Rostra, the platform adorned with the prows of galleys captured at the Battle of Antium in 338BC, magistrates and candidates for magistracy orated and harangued the people. So, more rarely, did some of the less autocratic emperors later.

In the Forum Romanum, great nobles met their *clientalia*, supporters or hangers-on. Business (*negotium*) and other deals were made among more general socializing. The custom was that business was conducted in the Forum Romanum in the morning. Meetings for pleasure took place later in the day and elsewhere in the city. Augustus tried to enforce the wearing of the traditional, rather cumbersome formal toga in the Forum, instead of the more casual Greek-style *chiton*, in order to preserve the Forum's special dignity.

Initially, shops or booths (*tabernae*) lined the Forum's north-east and south-west sides, leaving only two sides for public buildings. As Rome grew explosively through the late Republic and early Principate – its population, at least 200,000 in 200BC, more than doubled in the following century before doubling again in the next – other fora became necessary. Rome's emperors provided these with increasing lavishness.

In the early Republic (500–250BC) the Forum Romanum must have still seemed half-rustic with its cattle and vegetable markets. Only a few temples such as those of Saturn or Castor and Pollux added a note of Roman *dignitas* (dignity). This was not inappropriate in what was still predominantly a city of farmer-citizens. (In 458BC, for example, Regulus was called from his plough to save the city in a moment of acute danger but then happily returned to his fields.) However, when the markets were removed in 318BC and porticoes added to the shops, the Forum began to acquire the majesty better suited to the city which was fast becoming the greatest in Italy.

Chief among Rome's new ennobling edifices were the basilicas. These large, aisled buildings were used for both commercial and legal affairs. The Basilica Aemilia, which was built on the north-east side of the Forum and completed by *c.* 170BC, had three aisles and three floors. To the north-west of the Forum, Sulla, dictator from 82 to 79BC, built the grimly

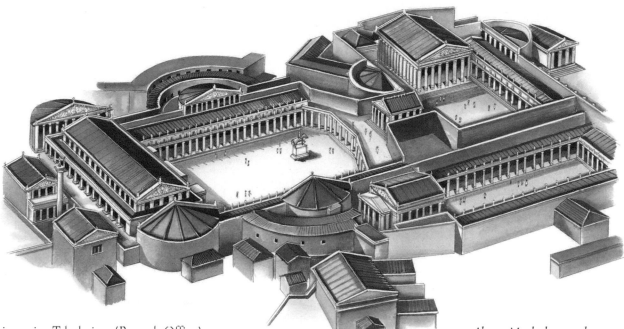

imposing Tabularium (Records Office) on the slopes of the Capitoline, rebuilt the Curia and raised the overall level of the Forum by about 3ft (1m), paving it with marble and tidying up its edges. However, none of these works increased the area of the now overcrowded Forum itself and indeed, they tended to reduce it.

CAESAR AND AUGUSTUS
Julius Caesar's plans for reorganizing the Forum Romanum were typically ambitious and, equally typically, were left unfulfilled at the time of his assassination in 44BC. He ordered the rebuilding of the Curia (Senate House) that had been burnt down again in a riot in 52BC. Henceforth, the Senate House was always known as the Curia Julia. In place of the old Basilica Sempronia, Caesar built a new larger basilica, the Basilica Julia.

Although he settled a reported 80,000 Roman citizens in colonies outside Italy, Caesar realized that radical measures were needed to deal with Rome's growing demand for public space. He therefore spent 100 million sesterces on new land for a brand new centre for Rome: the Forum of Julius Caesar to the north-east of the Forum Romanum. He did not live to see the completion of any of his plans.

Caesar's heir Octavian, later Augustus, had the time, money and authority to fulfil them all and gave the Forum Romanum the shape it retained for most of the rest of the empire. Besides completing the Basilica Julia and the new Curia, Augustus tidied up the whole Forum, which had become encumbered with many monuments over the years, erected by the city's great nobles. He moved the Rostra to the north-west end of the open area of the Forum to provide an axial focus and built a temple to his now deified predecessor at the opposite end. This was dedicated in 29BC, with another rostra in front of it, decorated with prows from his victory over Antony and Cleopatra at Actium.

Beside the new rostra were Augustus' own triumphal arches; the Actian Arch (erected in 29BC) and the Parthian Arch (erected in 19–18BC), which listed all the triumphs celebrated, from Romulus down to the last to be celebrated by a general not of the imperial family, that of Cornelius Balbus in 19BC. When the Basilica Aemilia burnt down after a fire in 14BC, Augustus had it rebuilt in a much more lavish style.

Above: Much the grandest new forum built by any of the emperors was that of Trajan who, flushed with victory over the Dacians and unprecedentedly wealthy, in AD107 ordered the construction of an enormous piazza 220 by 130 yds (200 by 120m), flanked by two semi-circular exedra. There was a resplendent equestrian (mounted) statue of the emperor in the middle of the court. To the right lay the Forum of Augustus and, below it, the smaller Forum of Julius Caesar. Trajan's Column still rises up on the left between what were his two libraries, one for Greek and one for Latin literature.

THE IMPERIAL FORUM

Above: Coin of Augustus, whose officially acknowledged reign started in 27BC but who had already started remodelling Rome by carrying out some of Caesar's grand projects in honour of his adopted and deified father.

Below: The commercial activities that had once taken place in the Forum Romanum found a new home in the covered Markets of Trajan that curved dramatically above Trajan's Forum.

In no other building project did Caesar show himself so boldly radical as in proposing a wholly new forum for Rome, but it was arguably a long overdue decision. The original Forum, while adequate for a relatively small citizen body, was not big enough for the huge numbers who now crowded the imperial city. An Augustan census counted 350,000 male citizens in Rome. Although it is not likely all of them were resident in the city itself and that this number included boys over the age of ten, this was still a huge population. The series of imperial fora that came to supplement (never to displace) the old Forum gave the metropolis vital extra public space, besides allowing emperors and their architects opportunities to shine.

LEGENDARY STANDING
Caesar's Forum had colonnades round three sides. At one end was a temple to the goddess Venus Genetrix, the mother of Aeneas, the legendary ancestor of Romulus and Remus who founded Rome and from whom the Julian family claimed descent. Augustus followed this pattern

for his own Forum just to the north-east. Begun in 37BC, it was only completed in 2BC, an unusually long time for normally speedy Roman builders, as Augustus liked to joke. It was dominated by the Temple of Mars Ultor (Mars the Avenger) which celebrates the victory over Caesar's assassins at Philippi in 42BC.

Inside the temple were statues of Mars, Venus and the deified Caesar, with the standards of the legions lost to the Parthians at Carrhae but restored after the eastern settlement of 19BC. The temple rises abruptly from the Forum's rather narrow space. According to Suetonius, Augustus had wanted to buy more land than he finally did and, perhaps as a result, the Forum is not wholly symmetrical. This was disguised by the flanking porticoes. Massive walls of tufa 115ft (35m) high served as a firebreak and shielded the complex from the crowded *insulae* area of Suburba just beyond. The temple shows Hellenistic classicism in the decorations mingled with Italian architectural traditions. Greek craftsmen probably carved the caryatids (stone female figures supporting an entablature) on the upper floor of the porticoes and the capitals of the columns and pilasters but the plan is very Roman. On each side, semicircular *exedrae* (recesses) housed statues of legendary and historical figures including Romulus and Aeneas and earlier Julians and emphasized the legitimacy of the Augustan settlement. The years of building the Forum also saw the appearance of Virgil's epic poem *The Aeneid*, which gave the new regime the legendary justification which it craved.

No other Julio-Claudian emperor added a forum. However, Vespasian, first of the succeeding Flavians, added the Forum Pacis (Forum of Peace), which was built just to the east between AD71–9. Dominated by its Temple of Peace, it was

meant to emphasize the blessings of peace restored after the horrors of civil war – which were very real, including fighting in Rome itself – and to celebrate the capture of Jerusalem in AD70 by Titus, Vespasian's son.

A rectangle 120 by 150yds (110 by 135m), laid out on the same alignment as Augustus', the forum was occupied mostly by a formal garden which was enclosed on three sides with porticoes whose columns were of red Egyptian granite. The fourth side had a colonnade of large marble columns. The temple façade's six columns were in line with the surrounding columns, so the temple did not dominate the complex. It contained famous trophies such as the Seven-branched Candlestick and Ark of the Covenant from Jerusalem (spoils of war), as well as fine Greek paintings and sculptures. Pliny praised it as one of the three most beautiful buildings in Rome; the others were the Basilica Aemilia and the Forum of Augustus. The short reign of Nerva (AD96–98) saw the completion of the small Forum Transitorium which had been started by Domitian. This linked up the previously disparate series of fora.

TRAJAN'S FORUM

The last and grandest imperial forum was that of Trajan, the greatest imperial builder since Augustus. Flush with gold from his conquest of Dacia, Trajan in AD107 ordered the construction of a vast piazza 220 by 130yds (200 by 120m), flanked by two semicircular *exedrae*. To allow this, the high ground between the Esquiline and Capitoline Hills had to be cut back to a depth of up to 125ft (38m). Inspired by Augustus' Forum and entered through a colonnaded sunken atrium, the Forum had at its centre a huge gilded equestrian statue of Trajan. The upper floors of the colonnades, lined with gigantic marble

Right: This map reveals the intense concentration of public buildings in a relatively small area around the ancient Forum Romanum.

columns, had statues of captive Dacians and horses. The entrance side of the Forum was gently curved. At the far end, instead of a temple, rose the huge Basilica Ulpia with libraries beyond, and beyond that, Trajan's column, which is still intact. The covered complex of booths called Trajan's Markets, which rises up the hill behind in a series of vaulted galleys and halls, also survives.

Above: Despite the many new imperial fora, the Forum Romanum continued to be adorned with new and restored temples including that of the posthumously deified Vespasian. His reign (AD69–79) marked the start of the new Flavian dynasty who proved dramatic builders.

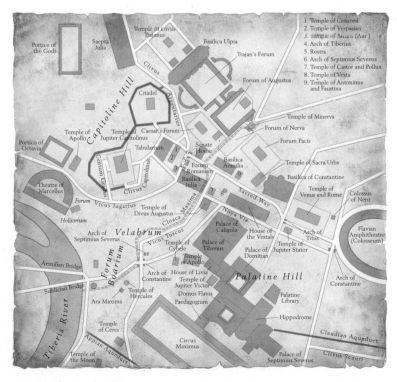

ROME'S BASILICAS AND THE SENATE HOUSE

Above: Constantine I (AD306–37) was the last emperor to erect great buildings in Rome, although he finally founded a new capital on the Bosphorus.

The largest public buildings in Rome, except for the grand imperial baths, were the basilicas. Oblong halls on one or two floors, they sometimes had clerestory lighting and some of the larger basilicas had double colonnades and apses (semicircular recesses) at the end. They were originally used as covered extensions to the forum and later became law courts, exchanges and assembly halls. The word "basilica" may derive from the Greek for royal hall, but the concept was typically adopted and developed by the Romans and later exported across the empire.

A NEW PUBLIC SPACE

The first basilica was built on land bought by Cato the Censor after one of Rome's many fires had destroyed buildings round the north-east of the Forum Romanum *c.* 180BC. This basilica, the Basilica Aemilia, named after Aemilius Lepidus who helped supervise its construction, soon faced another, the Basilica Sempronia which was built in 169BC by Tiberius Sempronius Gracchus, the father of

Below: Some of the ruins of the enormous Basilica Julia. Once one of Rome's grandest basilicas, it was actually built by Augustus and was the place where law courts sat.

the radical Gracchi brothers. Houses belonging to nobles like the Scipios were demolished to make way for it. Both halls were surrounded by porticoes, from which spectators could watch both the Forum's civic life and the gladiatorial games sometimes staged there, and by *tabernae*. Very little remains of them, but they were probably built of local tufa stone. Their function was initially to shelter businessmen and the general public. Only gradually did the proceedings of law courts move inside them, when the halls were subdivided by curtains.

Caesar planned a larger and more splendid basilica, the Basilica Julia, to replace the Sempronia. His plan was executed by Augustus. This basilica was 345ft long by 150ft wide (105 by 46m). It was open on three sides, with a double ambulatory portico and gallery surrounding its central hall, supported mostly on travertine stone piers rather than columns. The arcades of its two main façades were framed between half columns, like the Theatre of Marcellus. The courts of the Centumviri, the "hundred men", and the Chancery Court sat inside the grand building to judge suitably important cases. Augustus also rebuilt the Basilica Aemilia in 14BC after another fire, mainly on pre-existing lines. (It was damaged by yet another fire in 12BC.) It had a long narrow central hall about 295 by 90ft (90 by 27m) with an extra row of columns on its northeast side, which were probably decorative rather than structural. Indisputably decorative were the Doric columns supporting a luxuriant frieze on the side opening on to the Forum. The interior was paved with marble and lavishly decorated.

Trajan's Basilica Ulpia, which commemorated his family name and dominated his new Forum, was even larger and more luxurious, as befit a ruler who expanded Rome's frontiers to their widest extent. Built across the Forum's north side, it measured about 560ft long by 200ft wide (170 by 60m). Its central nave, about 60ft (20m) wide, had two aisles on each side, divided off by giant columns of grey Egyptian granite. It probably had a flat beamed roof with galleries above the inner aisles that would have allowed a view of Trajan's column and a clerestory to provide light. It was dedicated along with his Forum in AD113. Despite its splendour and size, it is thought to have been relatively conservative in style.

Two centuries later, more radical elements in Roman architecture emerged in the huge Basilica Nova (New Basilica). Started by Maxentius, the last emperor actually to rule from Rome (AD306–12), it was finished by Constantine. In place of earlier columnar designs, its huge vaults copied those of the Baths of Caracalla and Diocletian. Also like them, its design concentrated on a very lavish interior at the expense of the plain exterior. Its central nave measured 260 by 80ft (80 by 25m), while its three cross-vaulted bays rose to a giddy 115ft (35m) from eight gigantic marble Corinthian columns. The concrete vaulted ceiling was decorated with painted sunken coffers. Constantine changed the axis of the building by

building another entrance with a staircase. In the apse he placed a gigantic seated marble and gilt statue of himself, staring out over his subjects. Even the surviving fragments – head and hands – still impress, as does all that remains of the basilica, the side vaults.

THE CURIA
Traditionally built by the Etruscan king Tullus Hostilius in the 6th century BC, the original Curia (Senate House) was the Curia Hostilia. Burnt down several times, it was replanned by Caesar in 44BC, completed by Augustus and henceforth called the Curia Julia. A tall gabled building, it was 69ft (21m) high by 88ft (27m) long and 59ft (18m) wide – the exact proportions recommended by Vitruvius – with three oblong windows above a shallow porch. A raised platform opposite the door inside seated the presiding magistrates, and senators sat facing each other on benches. From Augustus' time there were often 1,000 senators, more than the Curia could seat, so younger senators stood at the back. A statue of the winged goddess Victory, presented to the house by Augustus, probably stood by the dais. Diocletian restored the Curia after another fire in AD283.

Above: The Curia was burnt down again in 52BC and replanned by Julius Caesar in what became its final form.

Below: The arches of the Basilica Nova, started by Maxentius but finished and refurbished by Constantine, whose giant statue once dominated the interior.

TEMPLES: THE REPUBLIC AND THE EARLY PRINCIPATE

Above: The remains of the terrace of the temple of Claudius, completed under Vespasian long after his death.

Below: The Temple of Venus Genetrix, the mythical ancestress of the Julians, dominated Caesar's Forum.

As Roman temples evolved in later republican and early imperial Rome, they revealed the intermingling of native Italic traditions, derived ultimately from the Etruscans, with imported Greek styles. By the time of Augustus (30BC–AD14) something of a classical synthesis had been achieved. Although Roman architects continued to develop new ways of building temples, culminating in the Pantheon in the early 2nd century AD, this temple's novel form marked an effective end rather than a beginning to grand temple-building in Rome itself. In the provinces, however, especially in the east, new styles of temple building continued to emerge with often exuberant inventiveness.

The first large temple in Rome, and one that was always deeply revered, was that of Jupiter on the Capitoline Hill.

Traditionally started by the last monarch Tarquinius Superbus before 509BC, it was typically Etruscan in design. It stood on a podium made of tufa blocks about 13ft (4m) high and measured 203ft long by 174ft (62 by 53m), making it comparable in size to the biggest contemporary Greek temples. It had three *cellae* (inner chambers), with Jupiter in the central one flanked by his wife Juno and daughter Minerva. The temple's emphasis is very much on its front, where steps led to a portico of 18 columns, probably of stuccoed wood, with only three on the flanks and none at the rear. (Greek temples had columns all round.) Its overhanging roof was decorated with bright-painted terracotta ornaments and statues, some full-size. Etruscan statues, like the famous Apollo of Veii, could be remarkably fine.

GRAECO-ROMAN FUSION

The early Republic's temples, such as those of Saturn or Castor and Pollux, followed this Etruscan pattern in the 5th and 4th centuries BC, giving the city a colourful if scarcely classical air. However, by 200BC increasing contacts with the Hellenistic world had opened Roman eyes to far more sophisticated styles, while wealth from conquests enabled them to import Greek marble and craftsmen. The resulting temples show Greek detail based on a Roman plan.

The Greek architect Hermodorus built the first all-marble Temple of Jupiter Stator in 146BC. The slightly later Temple of Portunus, which is still almost intact, exemplifies the emerging Graeco-Roman synthesis: classically Greek Ionic columns rest on a raised Roman podium, the approach stairs and portico are at the front and the side pillar is engaged in the wall of the *cella* (inner chamber). This fusion is also apparent at the Temple of Hercules at Cori (*c.* 100BC). Here, the ground-plan

looks Italic, a style closely related to the Etruscans, but the fine Doric columns copy the current fashions of Hellenistic cities such as Pergamum.

Few temples were as wholly Greek in inspiration as the circular Temple of Hercules Victor (formerly called the Temple of Vesta) built soon after 100BC in the Forum Boarium. Made of Pentelic marble from Athens and probably the work of an Athenian architect (the names of most architects in Rome have not survived), its circular form is very Greek, as are the steps wholly surrounding it and the Corinthian capitals. Its construction marks the peak of the Hellenizing influence in Rome. A notable early exception (*c.* 150BC) to this Greek trend was the Temple of Fortuna Primigenia at Praeneste (Palestrina), whose dramatic use of vaulting and circular shapes anticipate the architectural revolution sometimes held to have started two centuries later with Nero's Domus Aurea (AD64–8).

AUGUSTUS' PROGRAMME

Augustus claimed in his autobiographical *Res Gestae* to have restored 82 temples in Rome in 28BC. Augustus' was certainly the biggest temple construction programme ever seen in Rome. His temples reveal his generally classical tastes.

Although generally not large – central Rome was now densely populated and space was at a premium – they were usually magnificently decorated. They were still set on tall podiums, often against a rear wall, with their columns grouped towards the front.

The emperor's grandest temple, that of Mars Ultor in his new Forum, was almost square, backed by a huge, slum-excluding firewall. Its giant Corinthian columns were set on a lofty podium of 17 steps which could only be approached from the front. Augustus' temple to his patron deity Apollo on the Palatine was built of solid Carrara marble between 36BC and 28BC and adorned with famous Greek statues.

The century after Augustus' death in AD14 saw little development in temple-building, as attention was devoted chiefly to secular structures. In his 23-year-long reign, Tiberius did not even manage to complete the temple to the deified Augustus. Caligula finally finished it in the Ionic style. Nero started to build a temple to his deified stepfather Claudius, who had probably been poisoned by Agrippina, Nero's mother and Claudius' last wife. The emperor Vespasian, who admired Claudius, completed it in AD75. The enormous platform of the large structure still survives today.

Above: The Temple of Fortuna Primigenia at Praeneste (c.150BC) was a radically daring building in its use of vaults and circular shapes, anticipating much later styles.

Below: The Temple of Portunus typifies the Graeco-Roman fusion at its finest: classical Greek Ionic columns on an elevated Roman-style podium.

TEMPLES: THE PANTHEON AND AFTER

Often considered not just the most perfect Roman temple but the apogee of Roman architecture, the Pantheon, the temple to all the gods, was the emperor Hadrian's supreme architectural achievement in Rome. Its fame derives in part from its unusually well-preserved state (it was converted into the Church of Santa Maria ad Martyres in AD608) but it is indisputably merited as one of the most sublime of Roman buildings.

STRUCTURE OF THE PANTHEON

Two earlier temples had been built on the same site, one by Agrippa in 27BC and one by Domitian when Agrippa's temple burned down in AD80. Built between AD118–25, the Pantheon is composed of three rather disparate elements: a huge colonnaded porch, a tall middle block, and the rotunda that forms the temple's *cella* and supports its dome. The porch has 16 giant columns of the Composite order. These are made of grey and red Egyptian granite, with bases and capitals of white Carrara or Greek marble. With an

eagle on top of its pediment, the porch originally dominated a colonnaded piazza in front, looking higher than it does now (the surrounding ground has risen, as it has in most of Rome). The intermediary block, like the rotunda, was built of brick-faced concrete covered in marble. The rotunda's diameter and height are exactly the same, 142ft (43.2m), making it larger than any dome built in the next 1800 years. The dome springs 71ft (21.6m) above the floor. This means that a sphere of 142ft (43.2m) diameter would fit exactly inside the temple.

The rotunda rests on an immensely solid travertine and concrete ring 24ft (7.3m) wide and 15ft (4.5m) deep. It has eight load-bearing piers that form the building's framework, between which are curved or rectangular *exedrae* (recesses), each screened by two yellow Numidian marble columns, that may have once housed gods' statues. The piers support eight arches which run through the wall's core from inside out, part of a complex system of relieving arches that buttress the upper walls against the outward thrust of the dome.

The dome itself is built of concrete with an *oculus* (eye) opening 27ft (8.3m) at the top that gently illuminates the whole temple, drawing the eye up past the coffered roof to the sky, abode of the gods, far above. The upper parts of the dome are made of progressively lighter materials, with very light porous pumice stone being used at the top around the oculus. The 140 coffers of progressively diminishing size, arranged in five tiers of 28, also help to reduce the dome's weight while adorning its interior.

Like the roof tiles of the dome, these coffers were probably once gilded. Other interior decorations, surviving at least in part, are slabs of porphyry and dark green marble, while the floor was also paved

Above: The Pantheon's visionary union of portico and dome influenced many later buildings, such as the Church of St Mary in Mostal, Malta.

Below: A partial cutaway of the dome of the Pantheon, revealing the coffering that lightened its weight. Its mathematically perfect proportions help explain its remarkable appeal.

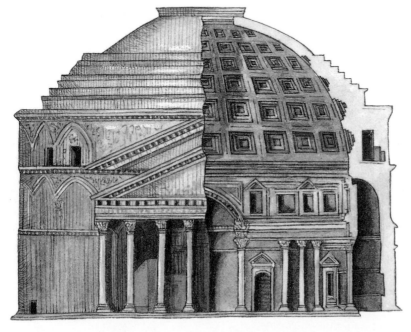

with marble. Only a small section of the original décor has been restored, but the Pantheon has retained more of its original decoration than any other Roman temple and the overall effect is still very lavish. The Pantheon impresses not only as a tremendous feat of engineering but also because it gives us a vivid idea of what a Roman temple may have been like. Its mathematically perfect proportions also elevate the spirit of visitors as they look up into the huge airy dome of this temple to all the gods.

EMPEROR AND ARCHITECT

Hadrian's other great temple, the Temple of Venus and Roma, stands on a high piece of ground between the Colosseum and Vespasian's Forum Pacis. It is also remarkable for a Roman temple for its very Greek design. Instead of standing on the usual Roman podium, it is set, like the Athenian Parthenon, in the centre of a rectangular platform on low steps that encircle it in Greek style. Hadrian was such a notorious philhellene that his enemies dubbed him *Graeculus* (Greekling).

Even more unusually, instead of having a single *cella*, the temple has two, back to back, both with apses, one for each goddess. (Roma Dea was the goddess of Rome itself.) These apses date from a rebuild under Maxentius. The original design had rectangular *cellae* back to back.

The temple was huge, 217ft wide by 348ft long (66 by 136m), with ten columns of grey Egyptian granite on its ends and 20 along its sides. Apollodorus, the brilliant architect of Trajan's great projects, who may also have been involved in designing the Pantheon, criticized the design, which was apparently Hadrian's own. Apollodorus claimed the temple was too wide for its height. Reputedly, the

Right: G.P. Panini's 18th-century painting of the Pantheon's interior. The temple's perfectly proportioned dome rising to an oculus (central opening) makes it among the world's most magical buildings. It is also luckily the best preserved of Rome's temples.

emperor had the architect exiled and then killed in AD129 for such impertinence, which suggests a prickly artistic pride in the emperor. The temple, dedicated in AD135, was rebuilt by Maxentius in the early 4th century AD. After Hadrian, Rome was no longer the one vital centre of great temple-building projects. Other cities across the empire competed with it increasingly and often showed more innovatory flair.

The Temple of Antoninus Pius and Faustina begun in AD141 in the Forum Romanum, which later became a church, was an unexciting rectangle. The Severans built temples to their favourite gods which were notable chiefly for their immense size and restored many older temples.

Before the days of Roman temple building drew to a close, the emperor Aurelian (AD270–5) built a temple to Sol Invictus (the Unconquered Sun), his favourite deity. This was apparently an unusual circular edifice within a large rectangular enclosure, that strongly suggests a Syrian influence.

Above: The Temple of Antoninus Pius and Faustina, Hadrian's successor, is a plain, even dull rectangular structure, preserved by being made into a church.

BUILDING THE THEATRES

Right: The theatre at Sabratha, Libya, is among the best-preserved of all Roman theatres. Its scaenae frons (built-up backcloth) has been reconstructed with 96 marble columns on three storeys.

Below: An actor wears a mask in a 3rd-century AD carving from the theatre at Sabratha, Libya. All actors in Greek and Roman theatres wore such masks.

The Greeks developed the world's very first permanent theatres; stone-built open-air structures where plays could be performed in front of huge audiences. However in their usual way, the Romans adapted the Hellenic model to make something distinctively Roman out of it. Whereas Greek theatres usually exploited natural sites to stunning advantage and retained a religious link with the god Dionysus, in whose worship dramas and comedies were originally staged, by the end of the Republic the Romans increasingly regarded theatre more as an entertainment than as a religious festival.

SUPPLY AND DEMAND

The Roman method of building massive structures raised on concrete vaults dispensed with the need for a suitable slope into which the hemicycle of a Greek theatre could be fitted. This meant Roman theatres could be built wherever there was a demand for them, principally in cities. Despite the huge success of early Roman comic playwrights such as Plautus (254–184BC) and Terence (195–159BC), Roman public taste tended increasingly to prefer mime or pantomime to plays proper. Changes in theatre design included making the theatre completely semicircular and turning the *orchestra* into seating for important officials rather than using it for performers. These changes can be seen clearly at the theatre of Taormina in Sicily. Here, the original Greek structure offered stunning views of Mount Etna behind until the Romans constructed a heavy *scaenae frons* (built-up backcloth). This obscured the view until its partial collapse!

Remarkably, there were no permanent theatres in Rome itself until very near the end of the Republic. Instead, temporary timber structures were built for each set of performances and then demolished.

(These temporary buildings could be grand, nonetheless. According to Pliny, Marcus Scaurus raised a structure in 58BC which, if timber-framed, was covered in glass and marble and could seat 80,000 people.) This lack was due mainly to the Senate's conservative puritanism, for it distrusted the loose morals that were then associated with the stage.

POMPEY'S THEATRE

It was only under the effective domination of the state by Pompey in the 50s BC that the first permanent stone theatre was built in Rome. It was completed in 55BC, just outside the old sacred *pomerium* (city boundary) in the flat Campus Martius. What Pompey built was not just a theatre, but a grand complex, with gardens and porticoes sheltering art galleries and other shops. As a sop to conservative sentiment, he described his theatre as a monumental stairway to the Temple of Venus Victrix (the Victory-bringer) sited at the top of the *cavea* (tiers of stepped seating). The theatre was made of concrete, which permitted the architects to support the seating on a series of radial and curving vaults, rather than having to seek a site on a hillside. Substantial parts of the substructures survive in cellars. Its *cavea* was 525ft (160m) in diameter and could seat about 27,000 spectators.

One of the oldest surviving theatres in Rome is that of Marcellus, which Augustus dedicated to the memory of his son-in-law in 13BC, fulfilling one of Caesar's grand projects. Still mostly extant, although partly converted into a hotel (it has also been a fortress and a palace in its time), it gives a good idea of an early Roman theatre. Built mainly of travertine stone with stone or concrete barrel-vaults, it closed the audience off from the hubbub of city life outside and so rendered the actors' dialogue audible on even the highest levels. There would have been retractable awnings against the sun to protect the spectators. The *scaenae frons* was as high as the *cavea* but seems to have been simple in design. The travertine façade had at least two series of ornamental arches framed by pillars, Doric on the ground floor and Ionic on the first. A third floor may have had Corinthian pillars or have been a simple attic floor. The theatre seated about 11,000 people.

THEATRES IN THE PROVINCES

To see further developments in Roman theatres we need to turn to other cities. At Lyons (Lugdunum), long the chief city of Gaul, a fine theatre was built under Hadrian (ruled AD117–38), enlarging and replacing an earlier building. Here pragmatic Roman architects showed that they were not averse to exploiting hillsides where they could. Next to this large theatre was a much smaller *odeum*, which was originally roofed and used for poetry recitals, lectures and musical performances. At Vienne, across the river Rhône, and even more notably at Orange in Provence, what became the standard type of theatre is still visible. Both theatres have a central *exedra* (recess) matched by two flanking ones in their monumental *scaenae frontes*. The full effect of a Roman theatre is best seen at Sabratha in modern Libya, where the *scaenae frons* has been reconstructed on all its three storeys with 96 marble columns.

Above: Arches flanked by columns from the Theatre of Marcellus. Dedicated by Augustus in 13BC and Rome's largest extant theatre, today part of it is a hotel.

Below: Masks epitomizing tragedy (left) and comedy (right). The Romans preferred the latter but also enjoyed violent melodramatic shows.

AMPHITHEATRES AND THE COLOSSEUM

No type of building is more closely associated today with the Roman empire than the amphitheatre. However, there was no permanent amphitheatre in Rome until the giant Flavian Amphitheatre, or Colosseum, was constructed. Built between AD70 and 80, its top storey may not have been completed until after the emperor Titus' sudden death in AD81.

THE GAMES AND PUBLIC ORDER

Rome's lack of amphitheatres was due less to the Senate's disapproval of gladiatorial activities *per se*, than to well-founded fears of public disorder and as riots had been known to occur after games in other cities. There had been full-scale riots at the Pompeii amphitheatre during games there in AD59, for example. (Pompeii has one of the empire's earliest and best-preserved arenas, dating from the 1st century BC.) Rome, however, was a much more heavily policed city.

Many games in the city took place not in amphitheatres but in the immense Circus Maximus, in theatres or even, in Rome's early days, in the Forum Romanum itself, when gladiatorial combat took place in the context of aristocratic funerals. Conversely, amphitheatres in the provinces such as Britain could seldom afford full gladiatorial fights, so amphitheatres were used instead for sporting contests or for military tattoos. Even so, the grand elliptical shape of amphitheatres, especially of the colossal archetype in Rome itself, remains justifiably linked with gladiatorial games.

A CROWD-PLEASING PROJECT

The emperors Gaius Caligula and Nero had loved gladiatorial games. These had been performed in temporary if lavishly decorated timber structures which were destroyed in the great fire of AD64. (A small stone amphitheatre built by Statilius Taurus, one of Augustus' generals, in 29BC was destroyed in the same fire.)

In a stroke of political genius, Vespasian decided to use the drained lake of Nero's Domus Aurea (Golden Palace) – which was detested less for its ostentation than for the huge area it ate up in the heart of Rome – for a great crowd-pleasing project: Rome's first, and the empire's greatest, permanent amphitheatre. Well-drained, with good clay subsoil for such a heavy building, in the very centre of the city, it was the perfect site. Work began early in Vespasian's reign (AD69–79) and Titus held typically splendid inauguratory games in AD80.

The Colosseum fully deserves its name, given by the historian Bede in the early Middle Ages either because of the colossal gold statue of Nero nearby, or because of its colossal size. A substantial part of the amphitheatre survives today. It was constantly pillaged for building materials over the centuries until Pope Benedict XIV pronounced it sanctified by the blood of martyrs in 1749, safeguarding the remainder. The Colosseum is still the most impressive extant building in Rome and a

Above: Detail of a model of the Colosseum, Rome's largest amphitheatre, built AD70–80, showing the statues that once adorned its arches.

Below: A view of the Colosseum as it appears today from the Via Sacra. Human depredations, not time, have ravaged the huge structure.

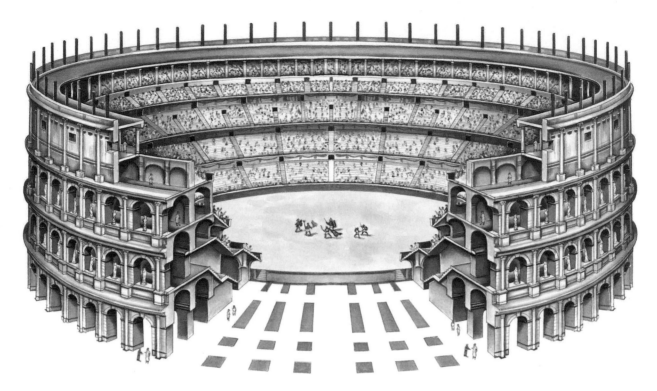

massive testament to the enduring skills of Roman engineers. Its typically elliptical outer shape measures 615 by 510ft (188 by 156m). The arena inside measures 282 by 177ft (86 by 54m) and its outer wall once rose to 171ft (52m), making it the tallest building in the city. It could accommodate an estimated 45–55,000 spectators.

To support the Colosseum's huge *cavea* (stepped seating), a vast ring of concrete 170ft (51m) wide and 40ft (12m) deep was laid. The lower part of about 20ft (6m) was cut into a trench while the upper, equal-sized part was contained inside a huge circle of brick-faced concrete above ground. These foundations supported a framework of loadbearing piers of travertine specially quarried near Tivoli. Between the piers ran radial walls of squared tufa up to the second floor. Almost all the vaults are barrel-vaults made of concrete, but some have brick ribs. About ten million cubic feet (100,000 cubic metres) of travertine were needed to build the façade alone and 300 tons of iron were used just for the nails. The façade has three tiers of low arches

framed respectively by Doric, Ionic and Corinthian columns, all semi-engaged (half columns) and purely decorative. The arches probably once had statues of gods or heroes in them, judging by depictions on coins. The top storey had tall Corinthian pilasters and originally had huge shields of gilded bronze, alternating with large windows, that would have gleamed impressively. Although this storey looks the most solid, it is in fact the lightest-built section.

The Romans erected this gigantic, complex structure with impressive speed, helped by their quasi-military organization of the process. Each material used in the building was handled by different groups of craftsmen, so that travertine could be added to the concrete core in one area while the final marble coatings were being laid in another. The whole structure was so massively built it withstood a lightning strike in AD217 – though it was closed for some years for repairs – and other assaults by recurrent earthquakes and the elements. Only human quarrying has done lasting damage.

Above: A cutaway section of the Colosseum in its prime, revealing the tiers of concrete barrel vaults and arches, suppported on load-bearing walls mostly of travertine stone buttressed by radial walls of tufa stone running between the piers.

Below: To Titus in AD80 fell the honour of inaugurating the amphitheatre that bears his dynasty's name, the Flavian Ampitheatre, with spectacularly lavish games.

Above: The amphitheatre at Arles in southern France is one of the finest extant outside Italy. Probably built in the late 1st century AD, its architect Crispus Reburrus also designed the amphitheatre at Nimes nearby.

Below: The emperor Vespasian (AD69–79), in whose reign the building of the immense Flavian Amphitheatre or Colosseum began.

SEATING BY RANK

The imperial box, richly decorated with coloured marbles, occupied the prime position on the short axis. Elsewhere, seating was allocated according to class or status. Augustus, as part of his attempted restoration of public morality, had tried to stipulate exactly who should sit where while watching performances in theatres, to reduce the opportunities for chatting up girls that Ovid so fondly described, and this seems to have applied in the Colosseum as well.

In the Colosseum, women were relegated to the topmost tiers – where they would have had the worst view but protection from the sun – except for the Vestal Virgins, whose high religious status overrode their lowly sexual status. They joined senators, equestrians (knights) and other dignitaries, often including ambassadors, in the smart seats in the lowest tier. Immediately above them was the first row for the general public, the *maenianum primum*, followed by the *maenianum secundum immum*, the *maenianum secundum summum* and finally the *maenianum secundum in ligneis*, with a gallery around that where ordinary spectators had to stand.

Some tickets were reserved in block-bookings for *collegia* (guilds) or for particular groups such as the citizens of Cadiz, privileges tenaciously preserved down the centuries. Tokens for all types of seats except the very best were given

out free for the games by the emperors on various occasions. This made admission to the games something of a lottery.

All seats were made of marble, another weight carried on the vaulted masonry substructure, except for the topmost tier, where they were made of wood to reduce the weight pressing down on the upper walls. No complete seats survive but fragments found in excavation have been pieced together to give an idea of what seating in the *maenianum secundum immum*, middling rank seats, were like. They were 17in (44cm) high by 21in (61cm) wide. Lower seats may have been more generous in size. Spectators reached their seats by climbing up or down rows of steps half the size of the seats. These led from the points where the inner stairs emerged into the *cavea* (stepped seating) from the myriad stairs and corridors below.

EXITS AND ENTRANCES

There were 76 public entrances, some of whose Roman numbers can still be seen. The emperor's monumental entrance, surmounted by a *quadriga* (four-horse chariot), was in the south, between entrances I (1) and LXXVI (76), a part of the amphitheatre that has been almost completely destroyed. Surviving far better is the next most important entrance, that of the consuls at the other end of the short axis. Renaissance drawings and remnants of stucco show that the vaulted entrance was originally richly decorated with stucco and other ornaments and probably topped by a pediment. The performers reached the arena directly by entrances at the long ends of the axis. The east entrance connected directly via a tunnel with the Ludus Magnus, the main imperial gladiatorial school nearby.

Ordinary spectators would have entered by their relevantly numbered arch and then climbed up stairs that connected the rings of circuit corridors, all of which were plastered and painted, until they reached their particular *vomitorium* (exit ramp) as the Romans punningly called the entrances. To protect the people from the 10ft (3m) drop from the seats into the stairwells, stone balustrades were provided. These were carved with animals such as dogs hunting deer or dolphins or mythological beasts such as sphinxes or griffins. Outside, barriers were erected around the travertine pavements that encircled the arena to control the eager crowds. Surviving stone posts suggest that chains were stretched between them.

ABOVE AND BELOW

The Roman audience was protected from the sun – and sudden rain showers – by a *velarium*, a huge canvas awning that covered the whole of the *cavea* and left only the arena open. Around the top of the amphitheatre are 240 stone brackets. These presumably once supported the rigging masts which held up this giant sunshade. (An alternative would have been long poles, as shown in a painting of Pompeii's amphitheatre, but the Colosseum may have been too vast for this simpler approach.) The whole system was operated by a special team of about 1,000 marines from the fleets at Misenum or Ravenna, who could also have acted as an auxiliary police force if needed. It has been tentatively calculated that the 240 ropes and the canvas would have weighed more than 24 tons.

Beneath the floor of the arena was an even more impressive network of subterranean passages and chambers which accommodated the wild beasts and the human performers before the games. About 246ft long by 144ft wide (75 by 44m) and 20ft (6m) deep, this seeming labyrinth was in fact organized with characteristic Roman efficiency, although later alterations and additions make the original structure hard to discern. It had five parallel corridors down the centre and three elliptical corridors along the sides. Beyond the outermost and narrowest corridor were 32 vaulted chambers which were used to cage the animals. Lifts operated by man-cranked windlasses lifted the animals up in their cages to trapdoors through which they sprang, bedazzled,

into the sunlit arena. The exact dimensions of their cages and the means by which the largest animals – elephants and hippopotami, for example – reached the arena remains under investigation. However, there were at least 30 lifts and many more trapdoors, so beneath the arena's floor a positive machine operated during the games.

The floor itself was probably of wood, although parts may have been made of stone slabs. It was covered with sand during the games to absorb the blood. The floor of the arena was probably not fully flooded to permit the large-scale *naumachiae* (re-enacted sea battles) historians describe and it is likely these took place elsewhere. However, early on there may have been a shallow pool for aquatic displays.

OTHER ARENAS

The Colosseum had few permanently built precursors but many imitators outside Rome, as an amphitheatre became an essential requirement for any self-respecting city. Most follow the same elliptical pattern and some have similar decorations on their exteriors, of arches flanked by columns. The amphitheatre at Verona, which held about 25,000 spectators, is *relatively* much larger than the Colosseum, as Verona was never one of the empire's biggest cities. The amphitheatres at Arles and Nîmes are particularly fine, as are many in Africa such as Thysdrus or Sabratha in Libya.

Above: The amphitheatre of Thysdrus (El Djem) in the fertile province of Africa (Tunisia) was built c. AD238. In its arena Gordian I was proclaimed emperor and later it became a refuge for the local inhabitants. It shows the still overwhelming influence of the Colosseum in Rome.

Below: Amphitheatres were relatively rare in most of the Eastern provinces, but theatres such as this at Pergamum in Asia Minor were sometimes adapted for combats or animal displays.

AQUEDUCTS AND SEWERS

The Romans were proud of their aqueducts and sewers, two essential aspects of civilization. As the geographer Strabo wrote early in the 1st century AD, "The Romans had foresight in matters about which the Greeks hardly cared, such as the construction of roads and aqueducts and of sewers that flush the filth of the city down to the Tiber... Water is brought to the city through aqueducts so copiously that positive rivers flow through the city and its sewers". At the end of the same century Frontinus declared, "Compare if you like the Pyramids or the useless if famous monuments of the Greeks with such a display of essential structures carrying so much water".

IMPERIAL CONFIDENCE

Sextus Julius Frontinus, who assumed the important post of *curator aquarum* (Water Commissioner) in AD96, wrote a book on Rome's water supply *De aquis urbis Romae* (On Rome's Aqueducts), that forms the basis of our knowledge. Classical Athens, among other cities, had piped fresh water to its citizens but Rome, the world's first giant city, needed water on an unprecedented scale, especially for its lavish *thermae* (imperial baths). Rome was also the first city to dig huge sewers to remove its waste waters. The aqueducts' giant arcades testify to something else: Roman confidence in its own power. Such highly visible and easily disrupted (or poisoned) water supplies were only feasible when no enemies closely threatened Rome. Ten major aqueducts built over six centuries finally supplied the city. The cutting of its aqueducts in AD537 during the Byzantine-Gothic wars symbolized the final end of ancient Rome.

PRACTICAL ENGINEERING

Rome's first aqueduct, the Aqua Appia, was built in 312BC by the censor Appius Claudius to supply water for the city's growing population. It had previously been supplied by springs or by the dubious water of the Tiber. Fed by springs near Albano, the aqueduct ran underground for 10 miles (16km); water was only carried above ground on arcades for about 100 yards inside the city. The Romans were far too practical to waste money building grandly arcaded aqueducts except when really needed.

Lead pipes were only used inside the city. For the most part, the aqueducts were stone-lined channels carrying water underground or just above it. As the Romans had no power to pump water uphill they had to ensure that the water always flowed downhill. The gradient of most aqueducts was surprisingly modest: about a 3ft drop per 1000, enough to keep the water flowing steadily.

Further aqueducts followed, at first slowly. The Anio Vetus in 272–269BC, which was almost four times as long as the Aqua Appia, took its water from the river Anio. The Aqua Marcia was started

Above: The Trevi Fountain in Rome is still supplied by the Acqua Vergine (Aqua Virgo), the only Roman aqueduct still functioning.

Below: These arches once carried the Aqua Claudia and the Aqua Anio Novus, the two aqueducts completed by Claudius in AD52.

in 144BC and paid for by booty from the sack of Corinth. It ran for 56 miles (91km) and was famed both for the purity of its waters and for the 6 miles (10km) of its length that ran on arcades, at some stages 95ft (29m) high.

The next two aqueducts were the Aqua Tepula started in 125BC and the Aqua Julia, with a capacity double that of the Tepula, built in 33BC. Both had similar lengths raised on arcades.

The Aqua Tepula was the work of Marcus Agrippa, Augustus' chief minister, who undertook a total restoration of all Rome's waterworks. In 19BC Agrippa also built the Aqua Virgo, the only aqueduct to enter the city from the north and the only one still functioning (as the Acqua Vergine, which supplies the Fontana di Trevi). Agrippa left his team of 240 slaves to Augustus The latter made them public property and set up a permanent commission to oversee water supplies. The office of *procurator aquarum* was created by Claudius.

DEMAND FOR WATER INCREASES

Claudius built two aqueducts, the Aqua Claudia and the Aqua Anio Novus. Both had been started by the capricious emperor Caligula in AD38, partly to supply water for his *naumachiae* (re-enactments of sea-battles). Claudius completed them by AD52. The aqueducts' combined arcade marches for 6 miles (10km) across the Roman campagna before entering the city at what is now the Porta Maggiore.

The last great aqueduct, the Aqua Traiana, was built by Trajan in AD109. It brought good spring water from the hills north of Rome to the west bank (Trastevere), a region of the city that had been undersupplied. However, its elevation meant it could supply all the city's regions, which not every aqueduct could.

By this time the water supply to Rome had increased greatly. Since the building of the Aqua Claudia it had increased perhaps 15-fold to around 200 million gallons per day (900 million litres). This increase was

less a reflection of population growth than of the huge demands of the *thermae*. The aqueducts usually had settling tanks, to allow the sediment picked up en route to fall from the water. Water was also stored in *castella aquae* (reservoirs) or *stagna* (tanks) at the *thermae*.

GREAT SEWERS

Understandably, sewers were less widely lauded than aqueducts – Vitruvius discreetly ignores them. However, since the 6th century BC when the Cloaca Maxima (Great Drain) was dug as a drainage ditch, the Romans had built spacious, durable sewers made of well-crafted masonry.

Most Roman dwellings did not connect with the sewage system, however. This was chiefly because its reliance upon a constant, uninterrupted flow of water to flush it clear made it very expensive. Instead, many poorer Romans used chamber pots or the city's 144 recorded public latrines. Often lavishly decorated, these latrines provided facilities in which citizens could chat while seated in rows above the ever-flowing waters. Meanwhile, ever-flowing fountains flushed street litter into the drains. Down river from Rome, the Tiber cannot have been a salubrious stream.

Above: The Pont du Gard near Nîmes in France forms the most famous part of all Roman aqueducts, partly because it has survived so well. Built by Agrippa between 20–16BC, this arched section rises 160ft (49m) above the river.

Below: The exit of the Cloaca Maxima (Great Drain), an unglamorous but vital aspect of public health. Started in the 6th century BC and restored by Agrippa, it bears testimony to the enduring skills of Roman engineers.

IMPERIAL BATHS

Above: In the 16th century Michelangelo created the vast Church of Santa Maria degli Angeli out of the frigidarium (cold bath), one section of the extant Baths of Diocletian.

Right: The frigidarium of the baths of Diocletian inspired the magnificent waiting room of Union Station, Washington DC. Designed by D.H. Burnham and completed in 1907, it has since been demolished.

The largest and architecturally most adventurous structures in Rome were the *thermae*, the imperial baths, of which 11 were finally built. By far the grandest and best-preserved are the four erected by the emperors Trajan (AD98–117), Caracalla (AD211–17), Diocletian (AD284–305) and Constantine (AD306–37).

BATHS AS A WAY OF LIFE

Roman *thermae* were far more than just baths. Their immense, lavishly decorated complexes – the largest enclosed spaces in the world before the 20th century – included libraries, gardens, art galleries, gymnasia, restaurants, meeting places and bordellos or rooms for sexual dalliance. For many Roman men, long, leisurely baths became a necessity, socially even more than hygienically, and occupied much of the afternoon. From the outset, the *thermae* used concrete vaulting for their construction. This material was ideally suited to such innovative and enormous buildings.

The first public baths appeared in the 2nd century BC. Pompeii had four large and many smaller public baths by the eruption in AD79. All showed the basic division into *frigidarium* (cold bath), *tepidarium* (warm) and *caldarium* (hot), the last heated by hypocausts, the piped hot-air floor and wall heating that became standard in baths throughout the empire.

The first full-scale Roman *thermae* were built by Agrippa in the Campus Martius, probably after 19BC, as they were supplied by the Aqua Virgo aqueduct which was completed that year. Little of Agrippa's original *thermae* remains – they were rebuilt in the 3rd century AD – but they probably had gardens and a gymnasium. For half a century they were the city's only *thermae*. Nero then built baths praised by the poet Martial: "What worse than Nero? What better than Nero's baths?" These were presumably more luxurious but they too were totally rebuilt between 222 and 227AD. Only with the *thermae* of the emperor Titus, inaugurated

in AD80, can we begin to glimpse imperial baths in their full splendour. Even here very little survives and we have to rely on the not necessarily accurate drawings made by the Renaissance architect Palladio. These suggest that the baths, built next to the Colosseum, were symmetrically planned with a terraced rectangular enclosure and the baths themselves placed on the north side, a layout broadly similar to the later, far better preserved baths of Trajan and Caracalla.

THE BATHS OF TRAJAN

Trajan was the most munificent of emperors and the one – after Augustus – with the most money (acquired in his Dacian conquests). He began Rome's first really grand *thermae* in AD104 after fire had damaged much of the Esquiline Wing of Nero's Domus Aurea (Golden Palace). Its wrecked upper floors were completely demolished, leaving only the vaulted ground floor, whose rooms and courtyards were joined together by vaulted roofs to raise the whole area to 154ft (47m) above sea level. The remainder of the hill was then levelled off to create a huge platform 1,115 by 1,083ft (340 by 330m). Almost certainly designed by Apollodorus of Damascus, Trajan's great architect, the *thermae* were three times as big as Titus' baths just south-west of them. They occupied 23 acres (9ha) and were able to accommodate many thousands of bathers at one time.

The *frigidarium* (cold bath), the tallest part of the building, was in the very centre of the baths. This was a large rectangular room with giant monolithic columns of red and grey granite placed in its corners. These seemed to carry the building's soaring roof but were in fact wholly decorative, as the piers behind them really supported the cross-vaulted ceiling. Like the rest of the interior of the baths, the *frigidarium* would have been richly decorated and probably coffered. There were four cold plunge pools. On either side were large colonnaded areas open to the sky and closed off by big

half-domed *exedrae* (recesses) called *palaestrae*, where bathers would exercise before entering the hot rooms. A fraternity of athletes was based there for approximately two centuries.

To the north-east of the baths lay the big *natatio* (swimming pool), open to the sky and flanked by a colonnade. On the other side of the *frigidarium* lay the small *tepidarium* (warm bath), which was maintained at an intermediate temperature to acclimatize bathers to the heat to come.

On the south-west front of the building, carefully sited to capture the heat of the afternoon sun, was the *caldarium*, the (very) hot bath. Its curved bay windows were possibly double-glazed, an example of solar heating. Glass had become more widely available by this time but the row of tall windows along the south side was still startlingly innovatory. The *caldarium* had apses on three sides, each containing a hot plunge pool. The whole vast room, and the similar but smaller hot chambers adjacent, was heated by hypocausts not only in the floor – which might have been almost uncomfortably hot to walk on – but also in the walls and even the ceilings. The heat for both the hypocausts and the hot water came from a series of *praefurniae* (furnaces) beneath, stoked by slaves

Above: One of the great hemicycles of the Baths of Trajan on the Esquiline Hill in Rome, on the north-east side of the baths. Completed in AD109, they surpassed all preceding baths in their grandeur and lavishness.

Below: Mosaic floor decorations such as this were common in the imperial baths.

Above: A fanciful recreation of the Baths of Caracalla by the Victorian painter Lawrence Alma-Tadema captures the atmosphere of luxury, even licentiousness, often associated with the great imperial baths that was much attacked by the early Christians.

1,000 years later sometimes corroborate and sometimes contradict the Marble Plan.) To the enclosure's north-west and north-east ends were other *exedrae*. Each contained a *nymphaeum* (ornamental fountain). The open spaces between the baths and the perimeter buildings were planted out as gardens. The whole complex was made of brick-faced concrete, covered in plain stucco on the outside but lavishly decorated in coloured marble with pillars, pilasters and marble floors throughout the interior.

Water for the baths was supplied partly by Trajan's new aqueduct, the Aqua Traiana, carried in pipes over bridges from its debauchment on the west bank, and partly from the neighbouring reservoir known as the Sette Salle, a two-storeyed building with a capacity of about 1½ million gallons (7 million litres). This was probably supplied by the Aqua Claudia, rather than the Aqua Traiana. The whole complex was inaugurated in AD109 and immediately eclipsed all its predecessors in grandeur and luxury.

THE BATHS OF CARACALLA

Although Rome's population probably did not grow appreciably in the century after Trajan built his *thermae* – in fact, it probably shrank after the great plague of AD164–5 – its citizens' expectations continued to increase, despite mounting problems on the empire's frontiers. To meet these expectations and to boost his own rather shaky popularity, the emperor Caracalla (ruled AD211–17) decided to build a grand new complex of baths to the south of the Forum Romanum.

In the century since Trajan's rule, architecture in Rome itself had not progressed much but in the provinces it had. Caracalla's dynasty, the Severans, came from Africa. This perhaps partly explains the daring size and shape of his *thermae*, dedicated in AD216 and among the most impressive ruins in Rome. Although they follow the general pattern of Trajan's baths, the central block is detached from its surrounding enclosure. This is nearly

who worked in abominably smoke-filled confinement out of sight of the bathers who sweated so contentedly in their magnificent marble halls.

The buildings around the perimeter included two hexagonal half-domed *exedrae*, about 95ft (29m) in diameter, on the south-west and south-east corners. These were probably Latin and Greek libraries respectively, for the Romans tried to cater for the mind as well as the body. Their brick-faced concrete skeletons survive, although most of Trajan's *thermae* have not. (We rely for information about the baths on two written records, the *Forma Urbis Romae* (the Marble Map of Rome) from the Severan period and the unknown medieval architect called the Anonymous Destailleur, whose works

500yds (460m) square and encloses an area of almost 50 acres (20ha). Here water could be stored and the subsidiary amenities now expected of a great *thermae* be provided. The main bath block itself was a simple rectangle 712ft long by 360ft wide (214 by 110m), except for the massive semicircular projecting *caldarium* (hot bath). Its huge circular, elliptical or oblong rooms open logically into each other along two axes that intersect at the great three-bay *frigidarium* in the centre. Its three cross-vaults rose above the level of the adjacent rooms, lighting it by eight lunettes (semicircular openings). Connecting but insulating the *caldarium* and *frigidarium* was the *tepidarium*, a room whose markedly small doors prevented heat entering or escaping from it.

While only four doorways pierced the complex's blank north-east front, the south-west front had a long line of great windows to absorb the sun's rays into the series of hot rooms. Dominating these was the huge circular *caldarium*, a domed hall whose span of 115ft (35m) approached that of the dome of the Pantheon and whose height exceeded it. Beneath each of the eight huge windows that bravely pierced the dome's drum – a feat that no earlier Roman architect had attempted because of the structural problems – was a hot plunge bath.

On the north side of the building was the *natatio* (swimming pool), shielded from the north by a high wall and protected from the sun's rays by the bulk of the *frigidarium*. At either end of the long axis was a *palaestra* (exercise yard) surrounded by terraced porticos. Built of the now standard brick-faced concrete and presenting a blank face to the outer world except on its many-windowed south–western front, the Baths of Caracalla were decorated on the inside with unprecedented lavishness, with multi-coloured marbles and mosaics and a profusion of ornaments. Roman taste may have abandoned the restraint of Augustan classicism but the subtle contrast of differently shaped rooms, the alternation of light and shadow as bathers moved into and out of the sunlight, above all the soaring height of the vaults above, demonstrated a new technical mastery.

THE LAST *THERMAE*

The political chaos of the mid-3rd century precluded much further lavish building apart from the Baths of Decius on the Aventine and the Palace of the Gordians on the Via Praenestina. However, although Rome was no longer the only capital city of the empire, it retained its imperial mystique. Once Diocletian (ruled AD284–305) had restored order and instituted the new Tetrarchy (four-ruler system), he decided to build another massive set of baths as part of his overall renovation of Rome. In AD298 he began building his *thermae*, broadly following Caracalla's design but with greater simplicity and less daring. It was even larger, its central block being 785ft long by 475ft wide (240 by 144m). Its central axis from east to west allowed a view right through the resulting alternation of light and shadow. Again, the *caldarium* was a curved room on the south-west side, with other elliptical or polygonal rooms, but the overall effect was less dramatic. The exterior was rather stark, the interior imperially magnificent.

Constantine I, the last emperor to build significantly in Rome, erected his own *thermae* closer to Rome's centre. Against the rather severely rectilinear plan of Diocletian's baths, this made great use of curves, circles and semicircles, at least according to the drawings made by Palladio in the 16th century. However, it probably still followed the essentially symmetrical pattern pioneered by the Baths of Titus over 200 years before. The imperial *thermae* were prodigious users of fuel as well as water and could not long survive the general collapse of the Western empire in the 5th century. Early Christians generally disapproved of over-lavish baths, with all their sensual connotations, and they were abandoned in the West. In Byzantium, however, *thermae* survived.

Above: Parts of the massive, brick-faced concrete walls of the Baths of Caracalla still stand, but the internal splendour of the building has long since vanished.

Below: The Thermal Baths, as the Antonine Baths in Carthage are known (built AD146–62), which rivalled those of Caracalla in size.

CIRCUSES

Above: A 4th-century AD relief showing the races in full frenzy in the Circus Maximus conveys the heady mixture of glamour and danger that so captivated the Roman populace.

Below: A Roman charioteer on a quadriga (four-horse chariot), a dangerous yet common form of racing chariot, with the outer horses attached to the chariot only by loose reins.

Chariot-racing was immensely popular with Romans from a very early date. By 500BC, races were being held in the Circus Maximus (biggest or grandest circus). This was located in an area in the valley between the Palatine and Aventine Hills connected with the gods that the races originally honoured.

ORIGINS OF THE CIRCUS MAXIMUS

For a long time the Circus Maximus was only a track with temporary wooden stands and a simple central barrier round which chariots raced. Rulers from Julius Caesar onwards added or made improvements to create an increasingly grand, permanent structure and it was entirely redeveloped by the emperor Trajan. Other circuses were smaller and used mainly for ceremonial displays.

In the late 4th century BC, the first wooden *carceres* (starting gates) were built at one end of the Circus Maximus. In 196BC, Lucius Stertinius erected an arch with gilded statues at the entrance. The central eggs for timing races are recorded as having been restored in 179BC, so they must predate this. Real developments started with Julius Caesar (49–44BC). He built the first tier of stone seating with a ditch 10ft (3m) wide in front to protect spectators from wild beasts, for *venationes* (wild beast displays) also took place there.

Augustus created the *pulvinar*, the imperial box, from which emperors could majestically look down on the races. It later connected directly with the grand Domus Flavia (Imperial Palace), completed by Domitian in AD92. Augustus transformed the *spina* (central barrier) by adding a 13th-century BC obelisk brought from Heliopolis, centre of the Egyptian sun-cult.

Augustus' general Agrippa added bronze dolphins as a second lap counter device. Claudius built monumental stone gates but the rest of the Circus, still built of timber, burnt down in the great fire of AD64. Titus added a triumphal entrance arch to celebrate his sack of Jerusalem. Finally, Trajan transformed the structure into a massive monument. Built mostly of brick-faced concrete covered in marble, stone or stucco, the Circus could now seat an estimated 300,000 people, about a quarter of the city's population, making it the largest single structure for public entertainment in the world. (Ancient sources give even higher figures for spectators.)

In Diocletian's reign (AD284–305) the top part of the seating collapsed killing 13,000 spectators. Constantius II erected Rome's tallest obelisk at 112ft (32.5m) in it on his visit in AD357. The site remains but only fragments of the building survive, including the curved end, for it has been plundered for building materials.

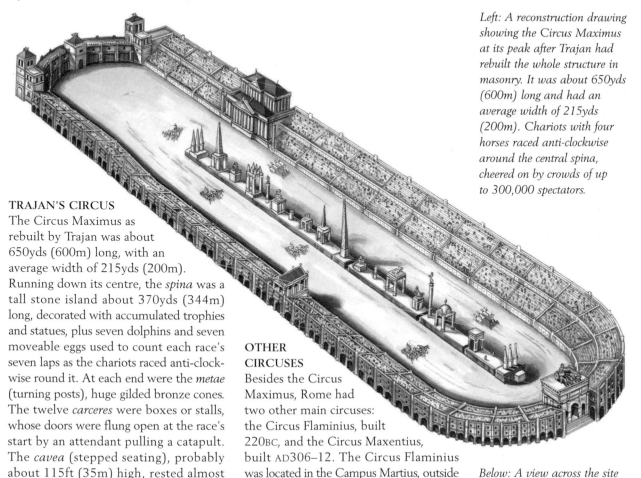

Left: A reconstruction drawing showing the Circus Maximus at its peak after Trajan had rebuilt the whole structure in masonry. It was about 650yds (600m) long and had an average width of 215yds (200m). Chariots with four horses raced anti-clockwise around the central spina, cheered on by crowds of up to 300,000 spectators.

TRAJAN'S CIRCUS

The Circus Maximus as rebuilt by Trajan was about 650yds (600m) long, with an average width of 215yds (200m). Running down its centre, the *spina* was a tall stone island about 370yds (344m) long, decorated with accumulated trophies and statues, plus seven dolphins and seven moveable eggs used to count each race's seven laps as the chariots raced anti-clockwise round it. At each end were the *metae* (turning posts), huge gilded bronze cones. The twelve *carceres* were boxes or stalls, whose doors were flung open at the race's start by an attendant pulling a catapult. The *cavea* (stepped seating), probably about 115ft (35m) high, rested almost completely on vaulted substructures. Externally, it had three storeys, with arcades on the ground floor and engaged (buried) pilasters on the floor above.

The Circus was not used solely for chariot racing. *Venationes* were staged in it – far more people could see wild beast shows there than in the Colosseum – and especially odious criminals, including early Christians, suffered the horrendous fate of *damnatio ad bestias* there: they were tied to a stake and savaged to death by goaded carnivores. In AD204, the emperor Septimius Severus staged special games in which a massive, specially built ship fell apart in a mock *naufragium* (shipwreck) to disgorge 700 wild animals, who then fought each other. At other less sanguinary times, the huge arena filled with stall-holders, fortune-tellers and buskers who turned it into a lively market.

OTHER CIRCUSES

Besides the Circus Maximus, Rome had two other main circuses: the Circus Flaminius, built 220BC, and the Circus Maxentius, built AD306–12. The Circus Flaminius was located in the Campus Martius, outside the city's sacred *pomerium* (boundary), because it was used for games connected with the *dei inferni* (gods of the underworld), as well as for assemblies and displaying booty. In 2BC Augustus flooded it for the display and slaughter of 36 crocodiles, so it clearly had a retaining wall, but it was never monumentalized into a stone structure and was later overshadowed by the Theatres of Pompey and Balbus nearby.

The Circus Maxentius, built outside the city on the Via Appia as part of Maxentius' complex of villa and mausoleum, is large – about 570 by 100 yds (520 x 92m) – but having a low *cavea*, it could accommodate only 15,000 spectators, members of Maxentius' court and hangers-on. It shows interesting architectural developments. The *spina*, for example, is placed off-axis to allow for the crowding of chariots at the start.

Below: A view across the site of the Circus Maximus towards the Imperial Palace built by Domitian on the Palatine Hill. Emperors could enter the Circus directly from their palace.

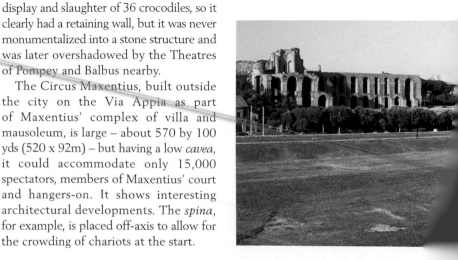

TRIUMPHAL ARCHES

Few monuments are more characteristically Roman than the freestanding monumental triumphal arches that they built, usually to celebrate military or political triumphs. Although the Romans did not invent the arch, they were the first to use it to commemorate such events ceremonially. Cities around the Roman empire and, after the Renaissance, across the world, also built triumphal arches, showing how deeply this monument has caught the Western imagination.

COMMEMORATING VICTORY

In its essence a triumphal arch is a vaulted passageway apparently, but not in reality, supported on pilasters with a decorated frieze (sculpted entablature) and an attic carrying statues, trophies and, in ancient Rome, inscriptions.

The first *fornices*, honorific arches with statues, were built in Rome in the 2nd century BC by nobles commemorating their exploits. These include those of Lucius Stertinius in the Circus Maximus and in the Forum Boarium in 196BC and of Scipio Africanus on the road up to the Capitoline in 190BC. No arches of the Republican period remain, chiefly because Augustus so radically reordered the Forum that few monuments unconnected with his family or faction survived.

Augustus built his Actian Arch, commemorating victory over Mark Antony, next to the temple of his adopted father, the deified Julius Caesar, in 29BC. After his Parthian "victory" of 19BC – actually just a notably successful diplomatic settlement – he either rebuilt it more grandly or built a new arch on the other side of the temple.

In its final form it was, unusually, a triple gateway, the central grand arch flanked by two smaller, attached openings that were not arched but simple flat, pedimented gateways. Above the central arch was a statue of Augustus in a *quadriga* (four-horse chariot). On the sides of the arch, marble inscriptions listed the names of *triumphatores* (generals granted triumphs) from the time of Romulus, Rome's mythical founder, thus linking Augustus with his predecessors. Augustus also built a smaller arch to Gaius and

Above: One of the first triple triumphal arches, the Arch of Tiberius was built in Orange, France to commemorate the defeat of the rebel Julius Sacrovir in AD21. Its large central arch is flanked by Corinthian columns and smaller side arches.

Right: The last great arch in Rome was the triple arch of Constantine built AD315. It looks back to earlier arches, most notably in its plundering of older material. These panels show Marcus Aurelius' head awkwardly reworked to resemble Constantine.

Lucius, his grandsons and intended heirs who both died young. This was probably located on the temple's other side. Arches were built around the Forum for some later victorious generals, all of them descendants of Augustus, such as that of Germanicus in AD16 and of the younger Drusus in AD19. A half-ruined arch to Germanicus survives at Pompeii.

Perhaps the finest arch to survive extant in Rome is that of Titus (ruled AD79–81), the Flavian emperor who was so generous to the Roman people and so merciless to his enemies. Built at the top of the Via Sacra (Sacred Way), it was finished after his death by his brother Domitian. Fine white Pentelic marble from Greece covered its concrete core (it was restored in 1821), but it impresses chiefly through the calm dignity of its lines. Slightly taller than it is wide, its single opening is flanked by massive piers with eight half columns of the Composite order – a favourite in Flavian architecture – standing on a high podium and supporting an architrave and frieze. This depicts Titus' triumphal procession in Rome after sacking the temple in Jerusalem. The eloquent simplicity of the arch marks a peak of Roman classicism. The fine arch to Trajan at Benevento in southern Italy is so similar in design that it could be by the same architect.

The next great arch extant is that of Septimius Severus built in AD203 right over the Via Sacra. A grand triple monument, it is 68ft high by 76ft wide (21m by 23m). It was originally surmounted by a *quadriga* bearing the emperor and his two sons Caracalla and Geta. Besides its size, it is notable for the four great panels depicting Severus' victorious eastern campaign, in which he had won the new province of (northern) Mesopotamia. Rejecting the classical three-dimensional realism that had so long been the rule, the flattened style of its carvings anticipates that of the later empire. By contrast, an austere yet classically proportioned arch erected by Gallienus (ruled AD253–68) survives but is squashed between later buildings on the Esquiline Hill.

THE LAST ARCH

Constantine I was the last of the arch-building emperors in Rome whose work survives. His triple arch, completed in AD315, celebrates his victory over Maxentius. Although it is the biggest in Rome and generally imitates Severus' closely in design, it is hardly the most elegant. Longer than it is wide, it looks rather earth-bound compared to earlier arches. Its finest carvings were lifted from other monuments – of the Flavian, Trajanic and Antonine periods – while the original carvings are poorly modelled. The tradition of carving sculptural reliefs in stone had almost died out in Rome 50 years earlier. Tastes were changing anyway. Newer buildings, such as the Basilica Nova and the Baths of Diocletian relied on coloured marble, stucco and mosaic to embellish their interiors, leaving the exterior relatively austere. Constantine's arch was in fact antiquarian, looking back to an age that had already ended.

Above: The noble dignity of the Arch of Trajan at Benevento, dedicated in AD114, stems from its fine proportions and its Parian marble covering.

Below: The Arc de Triomphe, Paris, is the largest modern arch emulating Rome's arches.

TRIUMPHAL COLUMNS

Commemorative or triumphal columns celebrated great individuals, especially military men. The Romans, like the Greeks or Egyptians, were passionate about perpetuating their fame by the most durable means available, but the idea of erecting marble columns topped by bronze or marble statues seems to have been a wholly Roman one. The practice was revived in the Renaissance and has long continued: one of London's most famous landmarks is Nelson's Column, which dominates Trafalgar Square.

Columns known as *columnae rostratae* were erected from the 3rd century BC. One of the earliest is the Column of Gaius Duilius, a column with ships' prows dating from 260BC. By the 2nd century BC, relatively small columns celebrating successful Republican nobles' exploits were being erected in and around the Forum Romanum. (An ancient pillar, the Maenian Column, originally stood near the old prison to the west of the Curia Hostilia, the first Senate House, but it was a landmark helping officials tell the time of day, not a memorial.) The Forum, however, soon became so cluttered with monuments of various sorts, including statues, arches and columns, that in 158BC the censors ordered that space be cleared to let citizens move around easily.

TRAJAN'S COLUMN

The truly great triumphal columns of Rome were built not in the still half-Republican Forum Romanum but in the grand new complexes of the emperors. Trajan, perhaps the most grandiose of Rome's imperial builders, crowned his resplendent new basilica with a triumphal column rising just beyond its tall roof. This

Left: Trajan's great column soars 131ft (40m) into the sky, the grandest in Rome. In front are the columns of the Basilica Ulpia.

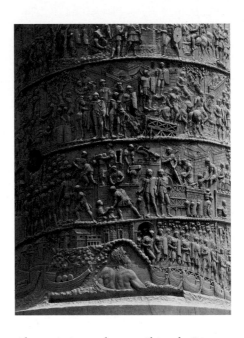

Above: A river god, personifying the River Danube, looks up at the Roman soldiers triumphantly crossing the Danube during Trajan's Dacian campaign.

became the unsurpassed archetype of such monuments. Built in AD112–13, probably by Trajan's famous architect Apollodorus of Damascus, it is truly prodigious. The column is 125ft (38m) high including its base and composed of 19 giant drums of Carrara marble, each weighing about 40 tons. It is both classical, comprising a single gigantic Doric column in form, and radical in its design, with a hollow interior up which a spiral staircase of 185 steps winds to a balcony.

The column is also remarkable for its carvings. These form a continuous frieze which coils around the column like a gigantic illustrated marble scroll about 600ft (180m) long. The carvings depict in amazingly graphic detail the story of Trajan's recent conquest of Dacia (Romania) and give us an impression of the Roman army in its conquering prime.

Scenes of the emperor addressing his troops, of legionaries crossing rivers, marching, building and fighting, and of the wounded being tended, are punctuated halfway up by a figure of the goddess Victory. She is flanked by trophies that form a link with the sculptures at the column's base which show captured barbarian equipment. The columns' higher parts would have been more visible than they are today, as the upper storeys of the adjacent libraries and basilica would have allowed people to view them halfway up. The frieze is one of the finest examples of Roman low relief. Brimming with artistic energy, it had a great influence on carvings around the empire in the following century.

Within this colossal monument to self-glorification was a tomb-chamber for Trajan himself. This was almost certainly not part of the original plan in view of the spiral staircase within the column. Trajan's ashes were laid there after he had died in Tarsus in Asia Minor in AD117 on his way home from his disastrous Parthian war.

The column owes its unusually good state of preservation to Pope Gregory the Great (ruled AD590–604). Reputedly, Gregory was so moved by a relief showing Trajan helping a grieving woman that he prayed to God to release the emperor's soul from hell. According to the story, God agreed, Trajan became the only pagan ruler thus spared and the land around his column was declared sacred.

The gilded bronze statue of the emperor that once topped the column was replaced in 1587 by a statue of St Peter. Restored for Rome's millennial jubilee in 2000, it now gleams with almost pristine freshness.

IMITATING TRAJAN

Trajan's superb column was hard to match but Marcus Aurelius (ruled AD161–80), who fought even longer if less victorious wars on the Danube, had a column erected to him after his death by Commodus, his son. About 100ft (30m) high, it is composed of 28 drums of

marble. It also has an internal staircase and a spiral relief depicting Marcus' wars. The relief's overall tone, however, is very different. In place of Trajanic triumphalism, there is a sense of exhaustion and despair and it is carved in a manner which indicates that the tradition of classical realism was approaching its end. The tradition of self-glorification did not die so easily, however. In Constantinople, the emperors Theodosius I (AD378–95) and Arcadius (AD395–408) both raised similar columns to themselves, of which little survives.

One of the strangest uses for such columns in the now Christian empire was as ostentatiously uncomfortable retreats for saints or hermits, who clambered up, dislodged the pagan statue on top and then squatted between heaven and earth, to be admired by the faithful below. St Simeon Stylites, the Syrian saint (AD387–459) was only the first of many such holy exhibitionists.

Above: The Roman obsession with perpetuating their fame posthumously depended partly on a literate posterity that could read such fine inscriptions as this one, which was dedicated to the deified emperor Titus.

Below: The figures on Marcus Aurelius' column (c. AD180) seem dumpy and exhausted by their years of bitter war on the Danube.

CHURCHES

*Above: The Basilica of Sant'
Apollinare in Classe, near
Ravenna, was begun in
AD490 and finished under
the Byzantines.*

*Below: The simple rectangular
form of the Basilica of Old St
Peter's, Rome, begun c. AD333.*

Poverty, persecution and expectations of
the imminent end of the world meant the
first Christians built little. However, when
Constantine became the first Christian
emperor after AD313, he inaugurated a
vigorous programme of church building
that continued throughout the vicissitudes
of the next two centuries.

A NEW ARCHITECTURE
Christian worship differed radically from
pagan cults. In the latter, the image of the
god was often secluded in a small,
mysteriously dark shrine inside a temple's
cella (inner chamber) and only taken out
on special festivals, with most worshippers
remaining in the outer court. Some old
temples did become churches, as the
Pantheon did in AD608, but its shape and
size were both exceptional. Christian
worship required the presence of the
whole body of the faithful for prayers,

responses and sermons and much larger,
more open buildings were needed.
Architects turned to the great basilicas
that now dominated many cities across
the empire for inspiration. Trajan's grand
but architecturally simple basilica, with
its colonnaded aisles, high beamed roof
and apses at each end well suited for altars,
with lighting provided by clerestories above,
provided a model for many churches in
the 4th and 5th centuries AD.

BUILDING THE BASILICAS
Across the River Tiber on the Campus
Vaticanus, the site of St Peter's
martyrdom in AD64 in the Circus of
Nero, Constantine donated land to Pope
Sylvester I to build Old St Peter's,
the foremost church in Western
Christendom. Started in AD333 (the
present domed church dates only from
the 16th century), it was a simple
rectangular building with a flat, timber-
beamed ceiling supported by colonnaded
naves. The basilica had a broad lateral
transept placed, exceptionally, between
the apse and the nave to allow the
circulation of pilgrims who came to
venerate St Peter's tomb. Above the
tomb, a marble *baldachino* (canopy) with
spiral fluted columns was erected. The
basilica's colonnaded nave and aisles
were used both as the prototypical
covered cemetery – many saints and
popes are buried there, but there had
never been burials within pagan temples
– and as a banqueting and funeral hall.
Outside, a central fountain was provided
for religious ablutions, the only type of
washing that ascetic early Christians
admired. The whole complex was
completed by AD344.

In Rome proper, a grand example
of early basilicas was the Basilica
Constantinia on the Lateran Hill. This is
known today as San Giovanni in Laterano

(St John's in the Lateran). Begun by Constantine in AD313, he gave the basilica and its adjacent land to the pope. Until 1309, when the papacy left Rome for its exile in Avignon, the adjoining Lateran palace was the official papal residence.

Today's basilica retains the original groundplan but has been destroyed by fire twice and rebuilt many times, most notably by Borromini in 1646. The Constantinian church, built of brick-faced concrete, was reputedly very splendid, with seven gold altars, 100 chandeliers and 60 gold candlesticks to illuminate its mosaics. Contrasting with this imperial grandeur is the church of Santa Costanza, built as a mausoleum for Constantine's canonized daughter Constantia in AD340. Its dome is supported by a circular arcade resting on 12 pairs of fine columns, while its barrel-vaulted ceiling has marvellous extant mosaics showing flora and fauna and the grape harvest.

Church-building continued, if more slowly, after Constantine's move east. San Paolo fuori le Mura (St Paul's Outside the Walls), begun in AD385, has columns supported by arches while a giant arch divides its nave from the apse. Unfortunately, the church was drably restored after a fire in 1823. Surviving much better is Santa Maria Maggiore (Great St Mary's). It originated in a dream Pope Liberius had in AD356 in which the Virgin Mary told him to found a church on the spot where snow fell in August. It was actually built under Pope Sixtus III (AD432–40). Its imposing, classical giant Ionic columns line the colonnaded nave. Santa Sabina on the Aventine is another elegant, well-preserved example of this short-lived but remarkable classical revival.

BYZANTINE ARCHITECTURE
Late Roman styles developed into Byzantine mainly outside Rome. At Ravenna, which was the capital of the Western empire from AD402, then of Ostrogothic kings and finally of Byzantine *exarchs* (governors), the empress Galla Placidia constructed a mausoleum for

herself and her brother Honorius in AD425. Its mosaics reveal a joyfully pastoral vision of Christianity. Grander but heavier are the mosaics in the Basilica of Sant'Apollinare in Classe outside Ravenna. Begun in AD490 under the Ostrogoths and finished in AD549 by the Byzantines, it is still a basilica-type church, as most churches in the West were always to be.

However, in the East a new architecture was emerging in the radical designs of the cathedral of Hagia Sophia in Constantinople, built under the emperor Justinian I (ruled AD527–65). A centrally planned church whose 180ft (55m) dome seems to float without visible support – "Marvellous in its grace but terrifying because of its seemingly insecure composition", as the writer Procopius put it – it satisfied Byzantine needs for a cruciform church and must have later inspired Islamic builders. However, its construction marks an effective end to the period of truly Roman architecture.

Above: The mausoleum of Galla Placidia in Ravenna, one of the finest buildings of the 5th century AD in Ravenna, was renowned for its mosaics.

Below: The high point of Byzantine architecture is the cathedral of Hagia Sophia. Its simple, seemingly unsupported dome was hugely influential.

CHAPTER XVI

IMPERIAL PALACES

The English word palace comes from Latin, from *palatium*, the hill that gave its name to the imperial residence on the Palatine Hill. This majestic complex of courtyards, halls, basilica, stadium and private apartments, built by Domitian (AD 81–96), became the palace of all subsequent emperors, some of whom enlarged it. The official wing was called the Domus Flavia (Flavian Palace) and its private section was the Domus Augustana (Palace of Augustus), so the whole building became known as the *palatium* and the word passed into almost all West European languages (*palais, palacio, palazzo, palast*).

The house on the Palatine overlooking the Circus Maximus was not the first great imperial residence, for Nero's Domus Aurea (Golden Palace) had anticipated and in some ways exceeded it in extent and grandeur. Nor was it to be the last word in Roman palace architecture. As the tetrarchs and other rulers of the later empire set up their own administrative capitals – at Trier, Milan, Arles, Thessalonica, Nicomedia and finally Constantinople – they built palaces to match their grand pretensions, complete with baths and circuses. Most remarkable of all was Diocletian's massive retirement home to which he retreated in AD 306: a palace-fortress at Split on the Dalmatian coast. The building of these imperial palaces both incorporated and accelerated some of Rome's greatest achievements in architecture, especially the use of vaults and domes.

Left: The ruins of the imperial palace complex built on the Palatine Hill, as seen from the Circus Maximus.

THE PALACES OF AUGUSTUS AND HIS HEIRS

Above: An aureus (gold coin) of Augustus, first and most successful of emperors, whose own house was deliberately modest and unregal in its size and appearance.

Below: The infant Hercules killing snakes. A fresco from the House of the Vettii at Pompeii, typical of the sort of decorations the earlier imperial palaces would have had.

Augustus, the first and most revered Roman emperor, lived in an almost ostentatiously modest house, not in a palace. On his return to Rome in 29BC after defeating Antony and Cleopatra, Octavian (as he was called until 27BC) did not build himself anything remotely regal.

A HOUSE FOR THE *PRINCEPS*

Republican Rome had never had proper palaces, although Octavian had seen, indeed probably slept in, the palaces of Hellenistic monarchs such as the Ptolemies in Egypt. However, this was not the image he wanted to project in Rome, a city still proud of its Republican traditions. Instead, in line with his attempts to appear only as the *princeps*, the first among (almost) equals of the Roman nobility, he chose to live in the house that had once belonged to the orator Hortensius, a rival of Cicero.

This was a dignified, good-sized but not exceptional *domus* (detached house) on the Palatine Hill, a favoured location for wealthy nobles.

Some nobles in the Republic's later decades had built themselves very large and luxurious houses, on the Palatine among other hilly – and healthier – areas, but usually near the Forum, the heart of Roman life. The house of Aemilus Scaurus on the Palatine, for example, was sold in 53BC for 14,800,000 sesterces, an immense sum. Augustus' house probably still had an old-fashioned atrium, centred on its *compluvium* (pool). This was traditionally where business was conducted, especially where a patron dealt with *clientalia*, his clients or dependants. However, a wealthy noble's *domus* now normally also had extensive *peristyles* (colonnaded courtyards) and proper gardens, that together would have given the space for the social and official activities that even such a modest emperor needed. The best-preserved and halfway comparable villas are at Pompeii and include the House of the Faun or House of the Vettii.

Augustus' *domus* was probably larger than these, with its own libraries. It was right next to the marble temple of Apollo that he had just had built and also near the ancient but carefully preserved hut in which Romulus and Remus had traditionally grown up, so it had a truly imperial location. The so-called House of Livia, which may have belonged to Augustus' wife (who long survived him), was nearby. Later building covered these structures, but they are all visible today.

Tiberius, Augustus' morose successor in AD14, built the Domus Tiberiana before he finally retired to his cliff-top hermitage on Capri in AD27. This was a large rectangular palace 200 by 130yds (180 by 120m) on the north-west side of the Palatine. Built around a vast *peristyle* court with an oval fishpond, it now lies inaccessible beneath 16th-century gardens. Caligula is thought to have harboured grand designs for extending this palace towards the Forum Romanum but was assassinated before anything was built. His successor Claudius was content to live almost as modestly as Augustus.

NERO'S FIRST PALACE

Almost from the start of his reign in AD54, Nero, still only 16 years old, wanted to emulate the Hellenistic monarchies' love of culture and regal splendour. As he shed the early inhibitions imbued in him by his tutor, the philosopher-playwright Seneca, he began to build. Nero decided to connect the Domus Tiberiana and other imperial properties on the Palatine and Oppian Hills with a house inherited from his father by a series of linking buildings across the low saddle of land now crowned by the Arch of Titus. This Domus Transitoria (literally Palace of the Passageway) was destroyed in the great fire of AD64, but some of it has survived to reveal Nero's love of opulent materials, refined if lavish taste and his architects' bold inventiveness.

Traces of his Nymphaeum (Fountain Court) beneath the later Flavian Palace show this was an elongated rectangular building whose open courtyard had ornate shell-shaped fountains along all of one wall. On the other side was a square, raised platform topped by a colonnaded pavilion. Opening off this were suites of rooms – presumably intended for intimate outdoor dinner parties as opposed to the grand public dinners at which emperors often officiated – decorated with marble panellings and vaulted ceilings covered with semi-precious stones, white and gilded stucco and paintings.

Many of the raw materials for this building came from Greece, Asia Minor, Africa and Egypt. Its decorations make very fine examples of what is known (from excavations at Pompeii, buried in AD79) as the Fourth Style, with a few still in the earlier Third Style.

More remarkable architecturally, and still surviving beneath the platform of Hadrian's later Temple to Venus and Roma, is the domed intersection of two barrel-vaulted corridors, supported on four huge piers and probably lit by an *oculus* (central opening). Such a design anticipates many later buildings, most famously the Pantheon. There were marble pools behind screens of columns in two of the arms and the whole area was opulently decorated, partly in coloured marbles, partly in geometric patterns of semi-transparent glass paste. Nero's extravagance on such wholly personal apartments, as opposed to the public buildings on which Augustus had lavished his wealth, was however only just beginning and prefigured the opulence he would eventually create in his Domus Aurea (Golden Palace).

Above: The atrium of the House of Menander at Pompeii. Its murals are very similar to those in the first imperial palaces.

Above: Coin of Nero (ruled AD54–68), the extravagant yet creative emperor.

NERO'S GOLDEN PALACE

Above: The octagonal dining-room lies in the middle of the markedly symmetrical Esquiline Wing, with other rooms radiating off it. Its domed design was strikingly novel.

Below: A gouache copy of a Domus Aurea wall-painting. The style influenced Renaissance artists such as Raphael and 18th-century architects.

The fire that broke out in the Circus Maximus in June AD 64 raged for several days, gutting the Domus Transitoria, Nero's first palace, and three of the city's 14 regions, leaving only four regions untouched. It was one of the greatest of all the recurrent fires in the ancient city's history, but it also provided Nero with an unprecedented opportunity.

While there is no truth in the old stories that he started the fire and then "fiddled while Rome burned" – he was actually at Antium some 30 miles away at the time but hurried back to oversee the fire fighting – Nero could now plan on a scale and with a scope normally reserved for the founders of cities.

Dominating the new Rome was to be Nero's own palace, with immense grounds extending some 300 acres (120ha). He called it the Domus Aurea (Golden Palace). In its design, scale and building techniques, most notably in its use of concrete domes and vaults, it is considered to mark a revolution in Roman architecture.

A BRIEF FLOWERING

Most of the palace had a very brief existence. It was built over or incorporated into later structures such as the Baths of Trajan or the Flavian Amphitheatre by Nero's less extravagant successors. Only some lower rooms survived in the Esquiline wing, which was incorporated into the platform of the Baths of Trajan, to be rediscovered in the Renaissance and influence artists such as Raphael and Giulio Romano, who crawled in to admire and copy them.

These subterranean chambers today appear damp and dark and provide a poor impression of how they must have appeared in their short-lived prime. While the more luxurious types of decoration such as mosaics, marble and stucco veneer have long since vanished, the rooms still have fine wall-paintings with delicate landscapes and architectural motifs. These are mostly executed in the Fourth Style, which is best seen in the well-preserved villas at Pompeii.

The architects of this remarkable complex, which was built in under four years, were Severus and Celer, who had already started, but not completed cutting a canal from Lake Avernus to the Tiber. According to Suetonius, writing about the Domus Aureus early in the 2nd century AD (when it had already mostly vanished), "Its entrance hall was large enough to contain a colossal statue of Nero himself, 120ft high, while its whole area was so great that it had a triple colonnade a mile long. An enormous pool, like the sea, was surrounded by buildings that resembled cities, and by a landscaped park with ploughed fields, vineyards, pastures and woods, where all sorts of domestic and wild animals roamed. Everything in the rest

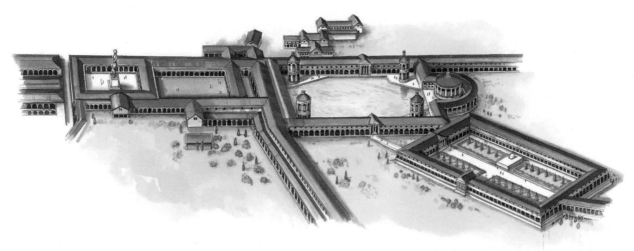

of the palace was inlaid with gold and highlighted with precious stones and mother-of-pearl. The dining-rooms had ceilings with rotating ivory panels which could sprinkle flowers or perfume on guests below. The most remarkable dining-room was circular, its roof rotating day and night like the sky. Sea water or sulphurous water flowed through the baths. When the whole palace had been completed, Nero dedicated it but only remarked, 'At last I can begin to live like a human being.'"

A PALACE IN THE HEART OF A CITY

Nero's walled urban park – about the size of Hyde Park in London, or one third the size of Central Park in New York – was approached from the Forum Romanum along the Via Sacra (Sacred Way), which was straightened and lined with colonnaded porticoes in line with the new regulations for rebuilding all Rome. What angered the Roman people about the new palace was less its ostentatious luxury than the fact that it used so much prime property in the very heart of the city simply for one man's private luxury. A contemporary joke ran, "Rome will become one huge palace, so migrate to Veii [ten miles distant], citizens, until the palace reaches Veii too!" Such open extravagance inside the city contributed to Nero's unpopularity and his downfall within months of the palace's completion in AD68.

Perhaps because the palace was built at breakneck speed – made possible by using brick-faced concrete which was then covered in decorative marble or stucco – the plan of the Domus Aurea is oddly asymmetrical, sometimes even jumbled. The most innovatory of the rooms, which was later incorporated into the platform of the Baths of Trajan, was the octagonal dining-room with rooms radiating off it. The dome had an *oculus* (central opening), while slits let light into the radiating rooms. (This may have been the remarkable dining-room described by Suetonius.) Behind the octagonal room was a jumble of lesser rooms. To the west, at the heart of the palace, was a large pentagonal courtyard which was open to the south and surrounded by a series of major rooms that was flanked by smaller chambers.

As with the rooms opening on to the main courtyard, the architects grouped alternating rectangular rooms, such as the large vaulted dining-room which had screens of columns at both ends, with rooms with apses (semicircular spaces). Of particular note is a barrel-vaulted room off the dining-room, which had a fountain at one end and a mosaic frieze running around the walls made mostly of polychrome glass. The Domus Aurea lived on in public memory as the epitome of extravagant luxury but it also marked a significant development in Roman architecture.

Above: Part of Nero's Domus Aurea, the lavish new palace he built after the Great Fire, with its splendid courts, gardens and colonnades, ate up 300 acres (120ha) of prime urban space in central Rome.

Below: The self-indulgent vanity of this most extravagant of emperors is evident in this bust of Nero.

THE PALATINE: PALACE OF THE EMPERORS

Vespasian, Nero's successor and founder of the Flavian dynasty, chose the Gardens of Sallust as his house with deliberate modesty; his son Titus (ruled AD79–81) occupied the Domus Tiberiana.

Titus' successor Domitian (ruled AD81–96) was commonly remembered as a tyrant – at least by the Senate and the equestrians, though the army loved him. Undoubtedly, he built grandly in a style befitting the absolute monarchy that the Principate was now becoming.

Domitian's greatest achievement was the palace on the Palatine Hill. This became the emperor's residence for the next three centuries. Praised by the poet Martial for its splendour and size, it was dedicated in AD92. Various repairs were made by several emperors and Septimius Severus added bulky extensions to the

eastern and south-western extremities of the palace early in the 3rd century AD. Nonetheless, it remains very much Domitian's monument.

PALACE BUILDINGS

The Domus Aurea had become impractical as an imperial residence for the Flavian dynasty, partly because it was the former palace of the despot Nero and also because, once the Colosseum and Baths of Titus had been built in its park, it was cut off from the main Palatine buildings. Domitian chose Rabirius, a great Roman architect about whose life, typically, nothing is known but who was clearly an inventive genius fond of octagonal and semicircular shapes, to build a completely new palace on the Palatine. The western side of this hill, hallowed by its links with Augustus and Romulus, was already occupied by ancient temples and other venerable buildings, so Rabirius cut a huge terrace in the east ridge which sloped away both south-east and south-west. With the material this produced, he created a flat platform at a higher level to the north.

The palace had two distinct parts: the public audience halls, known as the Domus Flavia, and the private apartments, known as the Domus Augustana. It also had a pleasure garden in the guise of a race track, referred to as a stadium or *hippodromos*, and baths.

There were two main approaches. The official route from the north-east led up the Via Sacra (Sacred Way) and under the arch of Titus into a large paved area, the Area Palatina, which the Domus Flavia overlooked. It was from this approach that the massive bulk of the palace must have looked most imposing. The other route was from the Forum Romanum through a vaulted vestibule. The official wing of the palace, the Domus Flavia, was built on a large platform on

Above: A coloured marble floor from the nymphaeum *of the Domus Transitoria, on the Palatine Hill.*

Below: The courtyard of the nymphaeum *(fountain) in the Domus Flavia, looking towards the basilica from the west side of the main* peristyle.

top of the hill with a colonnade round its edge. Behind this colonnade lay three grand state rooms: the Lararium (Chapel to the Lares or household gods); the Aulia Regia (Throne Room) and an apsed basilica.

The Aulia Regia was the largest state room, measuring 98 by 120ft wide (30 by 37m) and very high. Visitors entering by the official, north-east approach would have seen the emperor majestically enthroned beneath a shallow apse at the far end, ready to receive ambassadors and other dignitaries, including Roman senators. This last group regarded being summoned like mere ambassadors as a grievous insult, for they were accustomed to having the emperor come to the Curia (Senate House) to speak to them. Domitian, moreover, insisted on being addressed as "*dominus et deus*" (lord and god), in keeping with his new splendour. This, too, was bitterly resented.

The walls of the throne room were covered with multi-coloured marble while twelve niches held giant statues in black basalt. Free-standing columns of Phrygian marble on tall plinths supported projecting entablatures. The roof, like those elsewhere in the palace, was probably not vaulted but had timber beams. (Whether or not most rooms in the palace had vaulted concrete or straight timber roofs remains a matter of furious debate.) Alongside the throne room there was another grand hall, the basilica, where the emperor heard law cases. It was divided into three by two rows of columns of Numidian yellow marble, which stood forward about 7ft (2m) from the walls, perhaps to allow those waiting to sit on benches. Soon after its construction, the basilica's outer wall began to show signs of subsidence and needed massive buttressing under Hadrian (ruled AD117–38).

THE *TRICLINIUM*

From the throne room visitors passed into the large *peristyle* courtyard. This had a big octagonal pool with a fountain in its centre. Its pink columns of Cappadocian marble, along with its walls of shining white marble were, according to Suetonius, polished like mirrors to let Domitian see any lurking assassins. (The precaution proved useless, for the emperor, who grew increasingly paranoid, was indeed assassinated in the palace.)

A series of semicircular rooms, perhaps official guest bedrooms, lay on the north side of this court, while on the opposite, west side stood the grand *triclinium*, or banqueting hall, called without undue modesty the *Cenatio Iovis* (Jupiter's dining-room). At the far end, a raised apse held the emperor's dining-table, where privileged guests might join him, while spaces for other dining-couches were marked out on the floor. The floor was paved with coloured marble *opus sectile* of purple and green porphyry from Egypt and Greece, *portasanta* from Chios in the Aegean and *giallo antico* from Numidia. The *triclinium* opened on to the courtyard behind a screen of six huge columns of grey Egyptian granite and had five huge windows on each side.

Above: The ruins of the huge columns in the grand triclinium *(dining-room) of the Domus Flavia that Domitian proudly called "Jupiter's dining-room".*

Below: Some of the surviving coloured marble floors of the Domus Flavia, whose lavishness was noted at the time.

Above: Arches from the heavy Severan additions made to the Domus Flavia in the early 3rd century AD.

Below: Although only the brick-faced concrete core of the Domus Flavia has survived, its arches and vaults still rise imposingly on its hill.

THE DOMUS AUGUSTANA

The south-east section of the palace, the domestic wing called the Domus Augustana, was conceived almost as a separate building. Although it covered about twice the area of the Domus Flavia and had three *peristyles* instead of one, for example, it must have seemed less massive from an external viewpoint, except on the side that faced the Circus Maximus. This architectural understatement was perhaps deliberate, for Domitian wanted to advertise public imperial grandeur rather than lavish personal consumption. The Domus Augustana was, in effect, a private villa on a grand scale. In all probability it was very luxurious, but only its lower part has survived to provide clues to its grandeur.

The Domus Augustana was approached from the Area Palatina through a monumental entrance which gave on to a large rectangular *peristyle*, corresponding to that of the Domus Flavia. This led to another *peristyle* with a sunken pool in its centre, whose walls were decorated in Fourth Style paintings. To the south-west lay a maze of small rooms in many different shapes, heights and sizes. Here Rabirius seems to have given his imagination free rein and, far from the public gaze, his imperial patron may have dallied with his harem of concubines, whom he reputedly depilated personally. The puritanism which Domitian tried to enforce in public, most notoriously by reviving the ancient punishment of burial alive for Vestal Virgins who broke their vows of chastity, did not apply inside the palace. Some of these rooms have niches and two are perfect octagons lined with round-headed niches.

A single staircase led from this suite of rooms down to the lower parts of the palace. The staircase was lit by a light-well, at the bottom of which a pool lined with polychrome glass mosaic would have both reflected and coloured the incoming light. Two other light-wells – again over pools whose waters would have reflected and increased the light – lit the surrounding rooms, which included a fine marble-lined *nymphaeum* (fountain room) and another, more intimate *triclinium* (dining-room). Most of these rooms had concrete vaulted ceilings and many were polygonal in shape, reflecting the contemporary prejudice against rectangular shapes. Services such as latrines were hidden discreetly beneath the staircase.

Throughout the Domus Augustana, as in the Domus Flavia, the decorations seem to have been exceptionally rich, with columns, paving and wall veneers of imported, coloured marbles. The few fragments that survive, such as the *opus sectile* floors of the *triclinium*, were made of differently shaped and coloured marbles and formed geometric patterns or pictures. On the walls, mosaics and wall paintings repeated and reinforced the overall impression of sumptuousness. According to Suetonius, however, Domitian was by no means a great gourmet. He normally ate heavily at midday – which was not the usual Roman custom – and contented himself with an apple and a glass of wine in the evening.

OVERLOOKING THE CIRCUS

A passage led from this second *peristyle* into the *hippodromos* or stadium, a sunken garden about 160 by 700ft (50 by 184m) on the palace's south-eastern flank. Lined by a continuous pillared arcade round its two long sides and curved end, it playfully imitated a real circus with mock *carceres* (starting boxes). Trees and pools adorned this most secluded of imperial gardens, with elaborate semicircular fountains at either end.

On the Domus Augustana's south-western façade, overlooking the valley of the Circus Maximus, Rabirius revealed his genius most clearly, for the towering façade curved gently inward with an inter-columnated screen to produce a truly majestic effect, surpassing in external grandeur anything in the Domus Aurea.

If Nero's architects had begun the Roman revolution in architecture by skilfully employing concrete, Rabirius carried it much further. Incorporated in this façade was a *loggia* or imperial box, which the emperor and his entourage could reach directly from the palace. This innovative convenience was subsequently much copied in the later empire.

Above: The ruins of the lower part of the Domus Flavia, with its elaborate, sunken peristyle, courtyard garden. It was built over earlier structures such as Nero's Domus Transitoria, inadvertently preserving them.

Above: A coin of Domitian (ruled AD81–96), the emperor responsible for building most of the palace on the Palatine.

CHAPTER XVII

HOUSING FOR RICH AND POOR

As Rome grew richer in the late Republic (from *c.*150BC), the gap between rich and poor was reflected in increasingly divergent standards of housing. Originally most Romans lived in modest *domus* (detached houses). But while the rich inhabited ever more elaborate, spacious *domus*, decorated by artworks and with large gardens adorned with fountains and trees, the not so wealthy increasingly found themselves living, at times precariously, in *insulae*.

Insulae (literally islands) – large, many-storeyed apartment buildings that often took up a whole block – have been called the world's first skyscrapers. A few earlier cities, such as Phoenician Tyre, had had very tall buildings, but *insulae* became the first high buildings to house most of a great city's population and the first to reach (and sometimes breach) height limits of up to 70ft (20m). Initially, these blocks of flats were built very quickly and were in constant danger of fire or collapse. Nero's sensible regulations after the great fire of AD64 helped to improve them, and by AD100 not all *insulae* were slums. Both *domus* and *insulae* were eclipsed by the splendours of the great country villas built by emperors, magnates and other wealthy men across the empire. These have survived better than more modest villas, but are not really typical.

Left: A view of the peristyle *courtyard of the Villa di Poppaea, Oplontis, preserved by Vesuvius in AD79. Its size and splendour are typical of the grander villas of Pompeii.*

THE DOMUS: HOUSES OF THE RICH

The early Roman *domus* (house, from which we derive our word domestic) was a simple, one- or two-storeyed building with rooms set around an *atrium*, a central hall open to the sky. An *impluvium* (pool) in its centre caught rainwater. This type of *domus*, called the Italic house, was derived partly from Etruscan originals. Another larger courtyard, the *peristyle*, was increasingly added to the *domus* in the later Republic. Although both courts grew more grandly colonnaded and decorated, a *domus* typically had mere slits for windows. Often wholly windowless rooms opened off the *atrium* to the outer world, for security rather than privacy.

In Rome, up to the First Punic War (264–241BC), although such houses were the commonest form of dwelling, the *domus* of great patricians were far grander than plebeians' houses. As early as 509BC, the traditional date of the founding of the Republic, there were large houses on the Palatine Hill, with several rooms on more than one floor. Although Roman

Above: The interior of a typical Roman house at Herculaneum, showing how the atrium receives light from above and how the impluvium, *a small reflecting pool, catches the rainwater.*

Below: The peristyle *of the House of the Vettii at Pompeii, the house of a wealthy man, showing its recreated gardens surrounded by typical colonnades.*

puritanism, which was strong in the early Republic, long discouraged ostentatious displays of luxury and wealth, houses were nonetheless prized in fashionable areas, preferably close to or in the Forum Romanum, the centre of political life. Bitter rivals among the nobility often had to live side-by-side.

A SOURCE OF DYNASTIC PRIDE

Despite a surprisingly brisk market in Roman property, a *domus* could remain in the same family for generations, sometimes centuries. The patrician Clodius Pulcher, for example, mocked his rival Cicero in 58BC as a *"novus homo"* (literally, new man, one without ancestors in the Senate) for having bought, rather than inherited, his house.

When Cicero was temporarily exiled soon after, his house was pulled down to underline his disgrace. By contrast, when the great general Pompey's house passed into Mark Antony's possession after his fall, his trophies were allowed to remain proudly on its walls. The architect Vitruvius, writing *c.* 35BC, observed that, "Distinguished men, required to fulfil their duty by holding public office, must build lofty vestibules in regal style, with spacious atria and peristyles …also libraries and basilicas comparable with magnificent public buildings, because public meetings and private trials take place inside their houses."

Many nobles' houses, with their revered busts of their ancestors, remained intact up to the great fire of AD64 which destroyed much of central Rome. After this, nobles tended to move further from the centre, as life ceased to focus on the Forum Romanum.

The *domus* was therefore never merely a home; it was also a repository of dynastic pride. In addition, its public rooms provided a place for transacting social and

political, rather than commercial, business. Tacitus, writing more than a century after the Republic had ended, still observed that, "The more impressive a man's wealth, house and clothing, the more his name and *clientela* (supporters) become famous". As the nobility's wealth grew, so did the splendours of their *domus*. According to Pliny, the house of Domitius Lepidus, considered the finest in Rome in 78BC, did not even make it into the top 100 only 35 years later.

A visitor to a typical *domus* of the late Republic or early empire would first enter the *atrium*, which was often a room of majestic height. The water in the central *impluvium* helped to diffuse incoming light and to ventilate the surrounding rooms (although it may also have bred malarial mosquitoes). The surrounding rooms were generally simple bedrooms, offices, store-rooms and *alae*, recesses used to store hallowed masks or the busts of family ancestors.

A curtain or wooden screen separated the *atrium* from the *tablinium* (main reception room/office). Beyond lay the *peristyle*, the colonnaded garden around which other rooms were grouped, including open-fronted *exedrae* and often the *triclinium* (dining-room). Only the grander *domus* had proper bathrooms, as many were not connected to mains water and relied instead on rainwater from the *impluvium* or from public fountains. However, the richest displayed their aquatic wealth with elaborate fountains in huge *peristyles*.

The volcanic eruption at Pompeii in AD79 preserved useful physical evidence for all this. However, the *Forma Urbis Romae* (the Severan Marble Map of Rome) also shows a good number of *domus* in the region of the Esquiline and elsewhere.

DECORATIONS

The walls of a *domus* were often brightly painted and the floors covered in mosaics. Thanks to their usually axial layout, which created a vista from the entrance passage through to the *peristyle*, entering visitors would have been dazzled by strong

Mediterranean sunlight alternating with deep shadow. In summer, a *domus* must have been pleasantly cool and airy. In winter, it might have been dark and chilly, with oil lamps shedding feeble light and the only heat provided by smoky braziers. Hypocaust central heating was uncommon except in bathrooms and among the very rich. Glass for windows was also initially uncommon, as it was relatively expensive before the 1st century AD.

The House of the Faun, built *c.* 120BC, in Pompeii is a well-preserved and exceptionally large house of the late Republic. A truly grand *domus*, larger than the contemporary royal palace of Pergamum in Asia Minor, it has a double *atrium* and remarkable mosaics, most famously one showing Alexander the Great's victory at the Issus in 333BC. The subject indicates that Hellenistic influences – which included the *peristyle* itself – had now fused with Italic traditions to create complex, luxurious houses. However, even in Pompeii, which was less heavily populated than Rome, houses were being subdivided by AD79 and the atrium/peristyle house was becoming confined to the very rich.

Above: The atrium in the House of the Mosaic Atrium at Herculaneum shows both the typically fine black-and-white mosaic floor that gave the house its name and the alternation of light and shade through the axis of the house.

Above: Detail of mosaic of Alexander the Great, from the House of the Faun, Pompeii.

INSULAE: THE FIRST APARTMENTS

Above: Brick-faced concrete was the normal building material used in Rome and, as here, in Ostia for both insulae, *the apartment blocks, and shopping markets.*

Below: While many earlier insulae *were jerry-built, by the 2nd century* AD *solidly constructed apartment blocks with internal courtyards or gardens were becoming common in Ostia, Rome and other cities. They have lasted impressively well.*

By *c.* AD150, as Rome's population peaked at probably more than one million, many of its inhabitants were living in *insulae*. This translates literally as islands, although not all actually occupied a whole block of their own. According to the mid-4th century catalogue, there were 46,600 *insulae* in Rome and only 1,790 *domus*. These blocks of flats rose to five, six, even at times seven storeys. Augustus and later Trajan tried to limit their height to 60 and then to 70 ft, but the reiteration of such regulations suggests that such laws had only a limited effect.

LIFE IN AN *INSULA*

Juvenal, the satirical poet, provides a vivid, unflattering but not impartial portrayal of life in an *insula*. "We live in a city supported mostly by slender props, which is how the bailiff patches cracks in old walls, telling the residents to sleep peacefully under roofs ready to fall down around them. No, no I have to live somewhere where there are no fires or alarms every night ... if the alarm is sounded on the ground floor the last man to be burnt alive will be the one with nothing to shelter him from the rain but the roof tiles."

Some *insula* blocks survive in Rome, but most evidence comes from Ostia, whose remains show that in fact, many apartments on lower floors were very habitable, even comfortable. Some first-floor apartments had running water and large, possibly glazed windows.

Spacious apartments, with separate rooms for dining and sleeping, were inhabited by wealthy citizens, including some equestrians (knights) and even senators, perhaps as friends of the usually aristocratic owner. Often such wealthier tenants paid rent annually and had some security of tenure. In contrast, garrets under the tiles up many flights of stairs must have been cramped, hot in summer, cold in winter, insalubrious without toilets or water and dangerous because of the fires that repeatedly ravaged Rome. Here tenants paid by the week or even day and faced the constant threat of eviction. However, all lived in the same building, the rich beneath the poor, in a pattern repeated in many great cities before the advent of lifts.

Insulae are first recorded surprisingly early – in 218BC an ox climbed two floors up one before falling, according to Livy – but they really developed in the last century of the Republic (from 133BC) as the city's population exploded. At first they were mainly jerry-built, with thin walls of mud-brick and upper floors made mostly of wood. Crassus, notoriously the richest man in mid-1st century BC Rome, made his fortune in property speculation. He would turn up with his gang of fire-fighting slaves when an *insula* caught

fire, commiserate with the bereft owner and buy up the smouldering site cheap for redevelopment at greater density. However, even the high-minded Cicero owned *insulae* which he admitted were unsafe but which brought him the sizeable income of 80,000 sesterces. Rome was less a city of owner-occupiers than one of a few great landlords, with their dependants and friends, and of many harassed, poorer tenants. This hierarchy was typical of Roman society.

TYPICAL *INSULAE*

After the great fire of AD64, new building regulations – which were not universally enforced but which still provide a useful guide – stipulated that *insulae* be built of brick-faced concrete, with balconies or arcades for fire-fighters.

One of the few substantially surviving *insulae* in Rome is on the Via Giulio Romano (named after the Renaissance painter) at the foot of the Capitoline Hill. It is a typical *insula* with shops on the ground floor and residential mezzanines (half floors) above. The first floor proper was occupied by two decent-sized apartments, and its second and third floors by flats with smaller rooms, most with concrete vaults. There are traces of at least two more floors above (the Capitoline Museum now above it precludes further

archaeological investigation), which probably became progressively more cramped. Another *insula* built under Hadrian (ruled AD117–38) has been discovered beneath the Galleria Colonna with shops, some with back rooms, on all four sides on the ground floor. On the west side, facing the ancient Via Lata, was an arcade which reached to the adjoining buildings, obeying Nero's fire regulations. Separate flats occupied its upper floors and were reached by their own staircases. One *insula*, the Felicula built in the 2nd century AD, was so imposing that it became one of the famous sights of Rome, alongside the Colosseum and Trajan's Forum.

However, the best-preserved *insulae* are in Ostia. This city grew into a boom-town after Trajan constructed a new harbour at nearby Portus but was later completely abandoned to the river silt. Here, solid buildings of brick-faced concrete with fine depressed brick arches often faced on to courtyards or communal gardens, with shops on the street side and light-wells on the other. Staircases rose up to apartments above, some of which had balconies and fine wall paintings, as in the House of Diana. This complex of shops and living areas was at least three storeys high, with a communal toilet for nine or ten people. The overall effect is surprisingly modern.

Above: A reconstruction of a typical block of flats in Ostia, probably built soon after AD100. The ground floor would have contained shops with mezzanines above, and the first floor above that could have held spacious, even comfortable apartments.

Below: Ostia boomed after Trajan built a new harbour at Portus, but the Romans always built to last, as the state today of these massive brick-faced piers attests.

TIBERIUS' VILLA AT CAPRI

Above: Tiberius, Augustus' charmless successor, inherited his power but not his tact, and finally withdrew to Capri.

Below: Tiberius chose a markedly inaccessible site 1,000ft (300m) above the sea for his main villa on Capri.

Outside the city of Rome, emperors could build more grandly and freely. Augustus acquired the small island of Capri, which retained some of its original Greek-speaking inhabitants, and built a relatively modest seaside villa there, the Palazzo a Mare. Tiberius (ruled AD14–37) was Augustus' uncontested successor, but his was a hard act to follow.

RETREAT FROM ROME

While Augustus had mellowed into a tactful, deeply revered *pater patriae* (father of his country), Tiberius became embittered by the perceived repeated snub of being passed over in the succession in favour first of Augustus' son-in-law and then of his grandsons. By the time Tiberius assumed power, he was in his fifties. He had a fine military record, great dynastic pride – his family, the Claudii, were grander than the Julii – but also a morose, cynical temperament that gradually emerged from beneath a hypocritical veneer of Republican virtue (or so wrote Tacitus a century later).

Tiberius came to hate living in Rome where his position was awkwardly anomalous: in theory he was *primus inter pares* (first among equals) in a Republic, in practice he was absolute monarch. In AD22, after the death of his only son Drusus, he moved to a villa on the Campanian coast, and in AD27 finally withdrew to Capri. Roman officials now had to go to this relatively inaccessible if beautiful island in the Bay of Naples to consult their emperor. Their journey was made worse by the security precautions that Sejanus, Tiberius' Praetorian Prefect, erected around his master. (Sejanus' own imperial ambitions – he wanted to marry into the imperial family and create his own dynasty – led to his downfall in AD31.)

Tiberius owned 12 properties on Capri, of which by far the most important was the Villa Jovis (Villa of Jupiter), vertiginously sited on the island's eastern promontory 1,000ft (300m) above the Tyrrhenian Sea. It was not a spacious site and, being so high, the water supply was a major problem, but it satisfied the ageing emperor's two main desires for security and privacy. Capri was noted for having few beaches suitable for landing and very high cliffs.

At the heart of the villa was a rectangular courtyard around 100ft (30m) square, probably covered with mosaics and surrounded by colonnades. Beneath it was a network of massive vaulted cisterns that collected every drop of water from Capri's infrequent but heavy rainfall. Built around this were four separate wings at different levels. These were

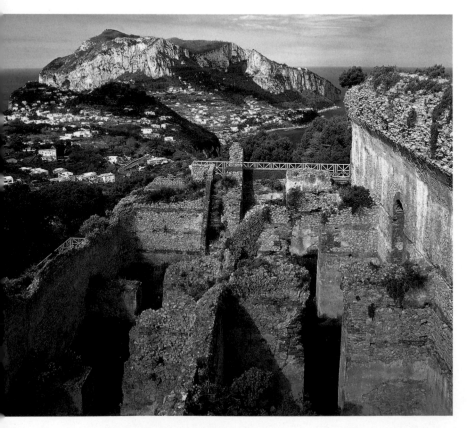

linked by staircases and ramps. At the south-west corner lay the entrance vestibule with the guard house; along the south side was a suite of baths; along the west side, built up against the sheer outer face of the cistern block, were rooms for the courtiers and officials on three floors. On the east was a large semicircular state hall flanked by similar reception rooms and on the north flank, accessible only by a single, well-guarded corridor and almost separate from the rest of the palace, lay the relatively modest quarters of the emperor himself.

Richly decorated, the emperor's quarters opened on to a sheltered loggia below, with steps leading up to a belvedere with stunning views over the Bay of Naples. Here the emperor would walk after his evening meals in the *triclinium* (dining-room), which had coloured marble floors. The unknown architect exploited the site to magnificent effect, allowing the emperor to withdraw from the world to a waterless cliff-top and yet still enjoy his luxurious Roman baths.

UNQUIET SECLUSION

Approaching not on the meandering, tree-lined track that the modern tourist takes, but by a herring-bone brick paved road ascending abruptly from the west, a Roman visitor would have seen the palace rising an impressive 60ft (18m) above the hilly ground. Tiberius seldom welcomed visitors, however, and grew increasingly paranoid in his later years.

Such seclusion fuelled ugly rumours that Suetonius later happily collated and reported as historical facts. Among these was the story of the fisherman who climbed up the cliffs to present the emperor with an exceptional mullet he had caught. This so alarmed the security-mad Tiberius that he ordered his guards to rub the scaly fish in the man's face until he bled. Tiberius also delighted in having victims thrown off the cliffs from his palace, while sailors waited at the bottom with boat hooks to finish off survivors. Although in his seventies, Tiberius, wrote

Suetonius, became sexually depraved in his old age: "Collecting bevies of boys and girls from all over the empire, adepts in unnatural practices, to copulate in front of him in threesomes to stimulate his jaded appetites. Many rooms were filled with obscene pictures … he further had boys and girls dress up as Pan and nymphs to prostitute themselves in front of caves or grottoes".

One man whom Tiberius continued to trust was Thrasyllus, his chief astrologer, for astrology, along with Greek literature and mythology, was one of Tiberius' life-long interests. Symbolically, a light house on Capri that Tiberius used to signal to the mainland was struck by lightning and destroyed shortly before the emperor's death (probably from natural causes) in AD37. News of the reclusive ruler's demise was rapturously received in Rome and his villa at Capri was soon abandoned.

Above: The walkway from the Great Hall in the Villa Jovis, showing construction in concrete with opus incertum facing and brick course.

Below: Part of the massive wall of the substructure of Tiberius' villa, made of reticulate facing with fired brick bands.

HADRIAN'S VILLA AT TIVOLI

Above: Portrait bust of the emperor Hadrian. The most peripatetic, cultured and cosmopolitan of emperors, Hadrian created at Tivoli a villa of unparalleled size and luxury where he could both recall his travels and summon the empire's ruling classes.

Below: Model of the villa-complex at Tivoli, showing the Piazza d'Oro at its centre. The grandest of imperial residences, the villa in many ways witnessed the climax of Roman architecture with its boldly, even astonishingly innovatory, curved shapes.

Hadrian followed Nero in being a great builder and a passionate philhellene (admirer of Greek culture), but similarities end there. While Nero was an increasingly debauched playboy and would-be artist who neglected affairs of state, Hadrian was an excellent soldier and tireless administrator, traversing the empire and founding cities or fortifications from Egypt to Britain, where he built his renowned Wall.

A MUCH FAVOURED SPOT

Although Hadrian was among the finest emperors Rome ever had, paradoxically, he did not much like the city of Rome itself. He got on badly with the Senate, four of whose most senior members were summarily executed at the start of Hadrian's reign on dubious charges of treachery, possibly on his orders. Nor was he popular with the Roman people, who preferred their emperors less openly cultured. (He was contemptuously nicknamed *Graeculus*, "Little Greek", by the upper classes.) However, his reputation with the army, administration (including

the equestrian order) and the provinces – with troubled Palestine perhaps the one exception – remained unshakeable.

The huge villa-palace Hadrian built at Tivoli (Tibur) some 20 miles (32km) east of Rome, where he spent most of his last years, did not rouse the same disapproval as Nero's Golden Palace precisely because it was *outside* the city. The area had long been a favourite beauty spot and the poets Catullus and Horace and the emperor Trajan had owned villas there, but for Hadrian it marked no hermit-like retreat from public life to the *campagna* (countryside). Instead, the highest members of Rome's increasingly cosmopolitan governing class came to his villa-palace both to discuss affairs of state and to be imperially entertained. Tivoli remains the most radical, intriguing and grandiose of Roman villas. Its buildings cover an area of around 300 acres (120ha) and stretch nearly half a mile (800m) along a plateau.

AN ARCHITECTURAL CLIMAX

The period of the villa's probably intermittent construction (*c.* AD118–33) is sometimes considered to mark the climax of the Roman revolution in architecture, when the design of a building's interior came to dictate its overall shape. It certainly shows the keen interest of Roman architects at the time in curvilinear forms, which produced some of the most remarkable of all Roman buildings.

The villa, which was some distance from Rome, had to be big enough to accommodate the emperor's entourage – soldiers, servants, bureaucrats and courtiers – but it also provided Hadrian with the opportunity to recreate, imaginatively rather than exactly, some parts of the empire that had appealed to him. In this he was following Roman precedents but on a much grander scale. The layout, which deliberately juxtaposed conflicting

axes to follow the lie of the ground, was influenced by earlier villas' landscaped gardens. This produced what initially seems a haphazard appearance but one that worked well with, rather than against, the contours of the land. The palace and its gardens were unwalled although guarded, for Hadrian was no recluse.

Construction of the complex probably began around the Republican-era villa owned by the Empress Sabina, Hadrian's unloved wife. A pre-existing grotto with fountain and *cryptoporticus* (basement or subterranean vaulted corridor) was incorporated into the new villa around what became the library court and Hadrian's private suite.

Among the main structures was the *poikile*, a huge *peristyle* courtyard measuring about 250 by 110yds (230 by 100m) with a large pool in its centre. Substantial buttressing with rows of concrete barrel vaults was needed at its west end to produce the required flat area. These vaults then provided rooms for guards or servants. All four sides are lined with colonnades and the two shorter ends are curved like Trajan's Forum, which had been built only a few years before.

It was once thought that the *poikile* was a careful reproduction of the *stoa poikile*, (painted colonnade) in Athens, which gave its name to the Stoic school of philosophers who met there. However, the recently excavated Athenian Stoa does not really resemble it and the complex was more probably an imitation of either Aristotle's Lyceum or Plato's Academy.

The central part of the *poikile* was arranged as a *dromos* (race-track). From the east of this *dromos*, visitors could pass through an apsed library into the Island Villa, the so-called Teatro Marittimo (Maritime theatre) set within a circular moat, crossed by bridges, around which ran a barrel-vaulted passage supported by white Ionic columns. This is perhaps the most original building in the whole highly original palace, without a single straight line in it. Instead, an amazing mixture of convex and concave chambers face on to a

miniature courtyard with a small fountain, whose conch-shaped plan echoes that of the surrounding rooms, which are themselves arranged in four curved groups. Here the emperor could retreat from the state business of the rest of his palace and devote himself to literature (he was a poet) or to other relaxations, soothed by the sound of running waters and by their sparkling in the sunlight which they reflected into the shaded rooms around. A small bath house and latrines were secreted within the building, along with a suite of bedrooms.

PUMPKIN VAULTS

The motif of curve and counter-curve is repeated in the Piazza d'Oro (Golden Square), as the richly decorated *peristyle* court is now known because of the surviving gold-yellow mosaics on the floor of its colonnades. It was entered from the north through an octagonal vestibule with niches on seven of its sides. The whole room was covered by an eight-sided umbrella vault, the famous "pumpkin vaults" supposedly criticized by Trajan's great architect Apollodorus. Opposite, on the south-east side, stands a larger pavilion or *nymphaeum*, that was octagonal with alternately concave and convex sides.

Above: The Maritime Theatre, or Island Villa, offered the busy emperor a retreat from affairs of state.

Below: Floor mosaics retain some of the gold that explains the name Piazza d'Oro.

Above: Caryatids, modelled on Greek originals, line the Canopus, a waterway recalling the canal near Alexandria in Egypt. They are a typical example of Hadrian's highly original, even capricious, eclecticism.

(Second-century AD Roman architecture has sometimes been called baroque because of such complex and dynamic shapes.) The Corinthian columns of this building and courtyard were of white marble and some have been re-erected. In the centre of the *peristyle* was another long pool.

THE IMPERIAL APARTMENTS

The largest group of buildings at Tivoli lay south-west of the Piazza d'Oro. This included the *triclinium* (state dining-room), stadium (or hippodrome) and what were probably the main imperial apartments, which were approached by a single staircase. These combined to form a single, imposing block.

The rooms west of the secluded court have the villa's best views – St Peter's in Rome is now visible from them – and the only hypocaust heating of the villa, suggesting they were inhabited by the emperor himself.

The *triclinium* on the far side of the stadium is half open with three *exedrae*, each with a semicircular garden, while the fourth side has a large ornate fountain whose roar must have soothed diners. Domitian's palace in Rome was the obvious inspiration for this. The *triclinium*'s walls were covered in white Proconnesian marble with remarkably elaborate columns. Beyond were two sets of baths: the Small Baths were probably for the emperor's personal use and their design was again curvilinear to suit the site. The Large Baths are more conventional but have an impressive vaulted *frigidarium* (cold bath) with Ionic columns. To their west is a circular room, the *heliocaminus* or sun room, whose tall windows faced south-west to capture the sun's heat.

MEMENTOES OF TRAVELS

The Canopus/Serapeum complex directly north of the baths most obviously recalls Hadrian's travels in Egypt. The lake, 130yds (119m) long, resembles in miniature the canal from Canopus to Alexandria and is lined with copies of Greek and Egyptian statues, while the

The four convex sides gave on to four remarkably shaped rooms, each of which ended in a semicircular *exedra*. Two of the concave sides open on to small summer rooms with fountains in their centres, while one formed the entrance. On the opposite side, the other wall led into a large semi-circular *nymphaeum* whose dramatically curving back wall was lined with alternately round and square fountain niches. The whole pavilion must have been filled with the sound of jetting waters and lit up by the sunlight reflected off them.

Above: A figure of a river or sea god reclining near the Canopus. One of the numerous Greek statues copied at Tivoli.

semicircular half-domed *nymphaeum* at its end recreates, again in miniature, the Serapeum, the temple to Serapis in Alexandria. A special aqueduct supplied the whole villa. Beyond the Serapeum lay the Academy, a mainly open-air, octagonally shaped building. An exact copy of the Temple of Venus on the Greek island of Cnidos is among the other buildings which adorn the grounds.

STATUES AND PAINTINGS

If the villa Hadrian built at Tivoli was architecturally radical, the sculptures and paintings he chose to decorate it were artistically conservative or nostalgic. The caryatids lining the Canopus look back –

beyond Augustus' own neoclassical use of them for his Forum over a century before – to the 5th century BC originals of the Erechtheum on the Athenian Acropolis. Other statues at Hadrian's villa are also copies of famous Greek originals and some of the mosaics are copies of famous classical Greek artworks. For example, the *Centauromachia* (Battle of the Centaurs) imitates a painting by Zeuxis of almost 500 years earlier.

Such emulation, common among Romans of many classes, was especially marked in Hadrian's reign, which witnessed the movement called the Second Sophistic. This, one of many neoclassical revivals in Rome's history, was a deliberate attempt to recreate the styles, manners and even debates of classical Greece in its 5th-century BC heyday.

The villa at Tivoli shows the resources of the whole empire devoted to realizing the grand vision of a man of exceptional talent and originality – this was probably the emperor himself, who is thought to have quarrelled with and exiled Apollodorus – using the latest techniques of Roman concrete and vaulting. Plundered repeatedly after the collapse of the empire, its marble stolen or burnt to make lime for cement, the Villa has been partially restored in recent decades to recall a few of its former wonders.

Above: The Baths of the Heliocaminus, a circular sun room whose tall south-west-facing windows would have caught the afternoon sun and so helped to heat the chamber.

Below: Intersecting vaulted corridors with skylights. These ran beneath the villa complex and gave access to the rooms built into the substructure where the emperor's many guards and other attendants were quartered.

VILLAS OF THE RICH IN ITALY

Above: Typical of the many opulent villas built on the shores of the Bay of Naples in the 1st centuries BC and AD is the Villa di Poppaea at Oplontis, near Herculaneum. It was preserved for posterity by the eruption of Vesuvius.

Below: This landscape fresco imaginatively but not perhaps unrealistically depicts villas with fine colonnades, porticoes and gardens looking out over the Bay of Naples.

If no other villa approached Hadrian's in lavish inventiveness or size, many wealthy nobles built themselves remarkably fine villas across the empire, most especially in Italy. A villa in the Republic meant a country house, increasingly comfortable perhaps, but still the centre of a working agricultural estate with farm buildings often attached, as they were with Palladio's Renaissance "villas" in the Veneto much later. They were not mere pleasure pavilions, as the writings of Cato and Varro attest. By the 1st century AD, however, elaborate villas were being built solely for the relaxation of wealthy Romans. Seaside villas – for wealthy but not necessarily noble owners – were common around the Bay of Naples, the Roman "Riviera". Such villas often had slender, elongated pillars, broken pediments and elaborate sun terraces and colonnades looking out to sea. These were depicted in the murals in the House of Lucretius Fronto of the mid-1st century AD. These murals are now thought to depict actual houses, if perhaps imaginatively. This Roman love of the seaside was not to recur before 18th-century England invented seabathing and it testifies to the peacefulness of the Mediterranean, the empire's inland sea. The greatest Roman villas in Italy were mostly built further north. These very large , luxurious structures are the exception rather than the rule. Many villas in Italy were much smaller and far less luxurious, but still relatively opulent and well-appointed.

THE VILLA OF PLINY THE YOUNGER

Few villas had such an interesting owner as Pliny the Younger (*c.* AD61–112), the genial man of letters, senator, consul and friend of the emperor Trajan, who ended his career as proconsul (governor) of Bithynia in Asia Minor.

Pliny had two villas which he used as retreats from urban business, one near Rome at Laurentum, the other, larger one in Tuscany at Tifernum. As he confessed in one letter, beautiful surroundings were the first thing Pliny looked for in a villa, although he was also a conscientious landowner, overseeing his mostly tenanted farms. (They brought him in a huge 400,000 sesterces a year.)

Pliny's writings about his villa, with its large glazed windows, heated bath houses, formal gardens filled with statues and topiary, *triclinia* (dining-rooms), libraries and picturesque site, later influenced houses from the Renaissance on, especially in Georgian England. In it, Pliny could enjoy *otium cum dignitate*, the cultured, dignified leisure that was the Roman ideal. His villa was conservative in style, however, for it retained, on an expanded scale, the *atrium/peristyle* plan *"ex more veterum"* (in the old manner) as he expressed it.

More radical architecturally was the so-called Grotte di Catulle (Grottoes of Catullus), although the great poet had nothing to do with the building erected long after his death except for the fact that he, too, had once owned a villa on Lake Garda. The huge villa, built for an unknown but wealthy Roman on the northern tip of the peninsula of Sirmione, which juts into the lake, probably dates from the early 2nd century AD. It exploits concrete in a way which suggests that the architect was aware of recent developments in Rome, which included Domitian's Domus Flavia.

A huge platform was built over massive concrete vaults at the villa's northern end, offering superb views of the lake and mountains. Its plan was severely rectilinear, consisting of a great central block 590ft long and 345ft wide (180 by 105m). Roughly symmetrical, it had rectangular, almost block-like *exedrae* at each end. The rooms were grouped around the vast *peristyle* court, although the *tricilinia* probably looked out over the lake to allow diners to enjoy the views. Roman appreciation of such dramatic natural beauty anticipates that of the Romantics by almost 17 centuries.

A LUXURY SURBURBAN VILLA

Many Roman nobles preferred to build their luxurious villas closer to Rome. Typical of these is the Villa of Sette Bassi, only 6 miles (10km) south of Rome on the Via Latina and therefore almost suburban in location.

The villa seems to be the result of three separate phases of construction, carried out with typically Roman speed between AD140 and 160. In the first phase its plan was conventional enough, with a modest residential section ranged along the south side of a large *peristyle*. This first villa was mostly single-storeyed, with a simple exterior. Not long after its completion, a second wing was added on the west of the entrance *peristyle*. This required the construction of terraces on concrete substructures, a rather more adventurous

project, if on a smaller scale. On the southern side of the new west façade projected a semicircular veranda with a fountain in the centre of a colonnade courtyard. The surface of the supporting terrace was topped by shallow segmental arches on brackets of travertine stone similar to contemporary *maeniana* (balconies) in Trajan's Market in Rome.

In the third and most complex phase of building, a wing was built across the north end of the area west of the older buildings and a huge *cryptoporticus* (underground vaulted corridor) about 1,000ft (300m) long enclosed the whole complex as a formal terraced garden. A massive new north wing, built on terraced vaults, rose at least three storeys, with two immense, tall reception halls with triple windows and gabled roofs. These halls were lit from above in a way developed by later Roman architects.

Buildings of such scale must have been hugely expensive, affordable only to the wealthiest of aristocrats. It is possible that the villa was built by a senator who wanted to keep a safe distance from the imperial court, but this was exactly the sort of lavish suburban villa the debauched emperor Commodus (AD180–92) later expropriated for orgies.

Above: The Grotte di Catulle is a splendid villa of c. AD120 at Sirmione, but it is not connected with Catullus.

Below: The House of Marcus Loreius Tiburtinus at Pompeii. Some of the fine and elaborate decorations that once covered the building still survive.

PIAZZA ARMERINA

In the centre of Sicily, once one of the empire's most fertile provinces, lie the ruins of one of the grandest Roman villas. Now listed as a UNESCO World Heritage Site, the villa dates from the early 4th century AD, a period when the empire had partly recovered from the turmoil of the 3rd century under the iron leadership of Diocletian (ruled AD284–305).

Luxurious and complex, the villa boasts such remarkably fine and extensive mosaics – they cover nearly 400,000sq ft (35,000sq m) – that it was long thought to have belonged to Maximian, Diocletian's co-emperor, who retired to Sicily. It was called the Villa Imperiale.

Today, the imperial connection is doubted and the owner is thought to have been a very wealthy member of the Roman aristocracy. It is thought possible that he had estates in North Africa – the greatest Roman families had estates in many parts of the empire – for the villa's plan suggests African influences. Whoever the owner was, he clearly enjoyed a life unclouded by threats from barbarians, for the villa is rambling and unwalled, unlike Diocletian's compact fortress-palace at Split of slightly earlier origin. It seems that the owner was also unconcerned by the rise of Christianity, for the scenes in the mosaics are sensually and exuberantly pagan, revelling in hunting, mythological and bathing scenes.

LOOKING INWARD

The villa is made up of four connected groups of buildings, probably constructed between AD310 and 330 on the site of a modest 2nd-century AD villa. The overall irregularity of its plan in some ways recalls the planned informality of Hadrian's Tivoli villa, but at Piazza Armerina there is no attempt to relate the buildings to the landscape. This suggests that its owner preferred to look in on his own elaborate decorations rather than out at the natural world beyond.

Piazza Armerina is typical of late Roman buildings in the way that the design of the interiors dominates that of the exteriors. The suite of bath houses, for example, was planned as a series of inter-connected interiors and creates a jumbled effect from outside. However, the overall plan reveals a unity of design which suggests that a single mind may have been behind the entire project.

The villa may have been inhabited as late as AD900 – Sicily was reconquered by the Byzantines in AD535 and remained in their hands for more than 400 years. In the 12th century the whole area was covered by an immense mudslide. This destroyed most of its walls but preserved the mosaics both from the elements and from vandalism. Excavations only began in 1881 and are still continuing. Some of the pillars have been restored and, in a few areas, walls rise high enough to reveal the layout very clearly.

Above: One of the villa's fanciful and colourful mosaics shows a putto *or cupid in the god Neptune's entourage riding a sea monster.*

Below: A huge peristyle, *with a fountain, gardens and paths decorated with mosaics, lay at the heart of the villa.*

Left: Part of the Great Hunt Mosaic in the ambulatory or hall of the villa. These mosaics, which are very well preserved, are Piazza Armerina's crowning glory and rejoice in exuberant scenes of life and death. Here, a lion kills a deer.

Approaching through a monumental triple arch into a horseshoe-shaped entrance courtyard to the west, Roman visitors would have turned right into the main part of the villa. This consisted of an enfilade of rooms: a vestibule gave on to a massive *peristyle* with living quarters around it. Beyond this, approached by a small staircase, lay a transverse corridor about 200ft (63m) long, now known as the Ambulatory of the Great Hunt Scene.

Beyond the walkway was a large hall with an apse at its far end. At the south end lay the private wing with a tiny semicircular *sigma* (courtyard). This had two bedroom suites and a small *triclinium* (dining-room). South of this was another ceremonial wing with a large trilobed *triclinium*. The substantial baths complex projected obliquely to the north-west of the *peristyle*. The nearby latrine was typically elegant, with a brick drain, marble wash basin and lavish mosaics.

GLOWING WITH COLOUR

The greatest glory of the Piazza Armerina lies underfoot in its superb mosaics, which still glow with colour after their centuries under 30ft (0m) of preserving mud.

Probably the work of craftsmen from Africa, they give an extraordinarily vivid picture of life in the later empire, at least as enjoyed by the very rich. The transverse corridor is also more poetically called the Ambulatory of the Great Hunt Scene because it has the finest mosaics. These show figures in imperial-looking capes watching a remarkable scene in which all sorts of animals – leopards, tigers, elephants, ostriches, antelopes and a rhino – are being caught and loaded on to a ship, presumably for transport to Rome to be slaughtered in the games.

West of the main *peristyle* in the *palaestra* (gymnasium), mosaics show detailed and informative scenes of games in the Circus Maximus in Rome. The owner probably sponsored these games in a typical form of aristocratic patronage. A smaller room to the *peristyle*'s south is the aptly named Room of the Ten Girls. Here, colourful mosaics depict girls wearing what may be the world's first bikinis. The mosaics in total are a splendid manifestation of the still vibrant and sensual pagan world, although their rather flattened style points to the emergence of a new, late Roman-early Byzantine art.

Below: The world's first bikinis? These mosaics, in the well-named Room of the Ten Girls, show girls wearing jewellery but not much else, dancing, exercising and swimming in bathing costumes that look surprisingly modern.

DIOCLETIAN'S PALACE AT SPLIT

Above: The steely resolution of Diocletian, who established the tetrarchy and, uniquely among Roman emperors, retired peacefully.

Below: The Golden Gate, the main entrance to Diocletian's fortress-palace, was ornamental and functional. Its statues in niches hint at Syrian influences.

Diocletian (ruled AD284–305) was unique among Roman emperors in retiring peacefully – traditionally to grow cabbages in his garden – before dying in bed six years later. Equally unusual was his retirement home. Far from being a luxurious villa in Italy, it was a massive fort enclosing a palace on the Adriatic coast at Split (Spalato), now in Croatia. Its military plan testifies not just to Diocletian's life in the army – in fact, he was more an administrative reformer than a brilliant soldier – but to the general insecurity of the age.

While Split was far enough from any frontier, barbarians had, within living memory, penetrated even into central Italy, the heart of the empire. Diocletian may not have completely trusted his successors in the tetrarchy, his carefully designed system of four emperors, either.

As it was, his retirement was disturbed only by calls for him to mediate between his quarrelling heirs, which he did only once, in AD308, without success. It is possible the huge walls he constructed helped to deter would-be aggressors. They later sheltered the whole of the small town's population for many centuries and still stand substantially intact today.

DOMESTIC MEETS MILITARY STYLE
Built AD300–6, the palace is halfway between a self-contained, fortified country residence of a type becoming common across the increasingly troubled empire, and a small town. Its overall plan, however, recalls a typical Roman army camp. It is rectangular – 590 by 710ft (180 by 216m) – with square towers in each corner, six further square towers along the walls and

octagonal towers flanking the three land entrances. Two intersecting colonnaded streets divide the palace into four sections. On the seaward side, the wall was surmounted by a gallery of arches flanked by columns, the whole facade unbroken apart from one small postern gate giving access to the quays. That part of the Dalmatian coast is relatively inaccessible by land, and Diocletian must have relied on ships to supply him with the news and other necessaries that were required for his imperial retirement.

The palace's northern parts formed barracks for the imperial guard that Diocletian retained, while the southern two sections, built out on terraces over lower ground, formed the palace's residential and state apartments. These have not yet been fully excavated. The southern end of the street forms the so-called *Peristyle* and is flanked by still impressive arched colonnades with a huge broken-pedimented end wall. To the west of this street lay a small temple and to the east an octagonal mausoleum, that was circular inside. The *Peristyle* led to a circular vestibule, beyond which was a large rectangular hall, presumably a state reception room. This gave on to the corridor flanked by the line of arches overlooking the sea, and was itself flanked by two further state rooms.

Although in retirement, Diocletian maintained much of the almost hieratic splendour with which he had surrounded the throne. The western hall had an apse at one end and was probably a throne room; the eastern hall was probably the *triclinium* (dining-room). Beyond these halls on each side lay domestic suites with bedrooms and bath houses.

THE PALACE'S PRECEDENTS

It has been suggested that the palace's layout derives partly from Diocletian's palace at Antioch – which he had built on the other side of the River Orontes on a site first occupied by the emperor Valerian in AD259 – and partly from the city-palace of Philippopolis in southern

Syria, the birthplace of the emperor Philip the Arab (ruled AD244–9). Diocletian, although born in the Balkans, had spent most of his reign governing the East and would have had the opportunity to see and even to occupy both. The extreme regularity of the plan more obviously recalls the roughly contemporary Baths of Diocletian in Rome.

Architects and craftsmen from Syria and other Eastern provinces were probably employed in building Split. Typical of this Syrian influence are the arcuated lintel – an arched entablature over the centre of a classical façade – and the arcaded columns of the *Peristyle*. The main entrance, the Porta Aurea (Golden Gate), also reveals Eastern influences. Its open arch with horizontal lintel and its decorative front with statues in niches were probably inspired by the Temple of Bacchus at Baalbek, built 150 years before. However, more recent, Western influences are apparent too, such as the circular vestibule and the framing of the seafront gallery's arches between decorative half-columns, a device also employed in the Mausoleum of Maxentius outside Rome and the grand Porta Nigra at Trier.

The palace's thick walls enclose courtyard gardens where the elderly emperor could have strolled and done some gardening. But the monumental architecture, while undoubtedly palatially opulent, is distinctly heavy. The final effect is both impressive and oppressive, rather like Diocletian's imperial regime itself.

Above: An imaginative reconstruction of how the palace looked in its prime, c. AD306. It was mainly supplied by sea.

Below: Diocletian built an elaborate mausoleum for himself that was later turned into a cathedral, while his palace became a town.

VILLAS OF BRITAIN

Above: The larger and more luxurious Roman villas made great use of hypocausts (underfloor) and intramural hot-air heating, as in this villa at Chedworth. This was the first and almost the last form of central heating in Britain until the 20th century.

Below: Cupid rides a dolphin in a fine mid-2nd-century AD floor mosaic from Fishbourne Palace. Built c. AD75, the Sussex villa was palatial in size and luxury if not in name.

Britain, part of the Roman empire for nearly four centuries, soon became far more than a mere frontier province, and today is recognized as having been wealthier and more Romanized than was once thought. Unlike villas nearer the Mediterranean, British villas were not usually built around a *peristyle* but tended to be "winged corridor" types, with wings of rooms added incrementally, almost accidentally and sometimes forming courts. If most Roman villas in Britain (as elsewhere) remained modestly rustic, a few developed into grand houses of a scale and complexity not seen again in Britain until at least the 16th century.

THE PALACE AT FISHBOURNE

The first great villa – in every way atypically grandiose because of its royal and imperial links – is the palace at Fishbourne on the Sussex coast. It may have belonged to the client king Cogidubnus, king of the Regnenses. Alternatively, it could have been the residence of a Roman governor

in the Flavian period (AD69–98). However, almost no evidence survives to link the villa with specific individuals. A substantial villa was built on the site under Nero (AD54–68) with baths, colonnaded garden and mosaic-decorated rooms. These were all luxuries then unique in Britain. Ten years later this was demolished to make way for a truly palatial complex.

Visitors approached from the east through a grand porticoed entrance hall that led into landscaped gardens. The main official buildings lay to the west, with an apsed audience hall for the king/governor. The residential wing lay to the north. The palace interior was richly decorated with mosaics in the black-and-white style of the time, with fine marble and stucco-work on the walls. In the 2nd century further buildings, including a bath house, were added, but in AD296 Fishbourne was abandoned after a fire.

Most villas in Britain in the century after the conquests of AD43–84 remained simple. When Tacitus wrote that his father-in-law Agricola, Britain's most far-sighted governor (*c.* AD77–84), persuaded British nobles to build themselves Roman houses, he meant town houses, northern versions of the *domus*. Rural villas developed slowly, sometimes on top of round Iron Age farmsteads – perhaps owned by important Britons Romanizing themselves in the Agricolan way – into rectangular houses of several rooms fronted by a veranda. These corridor villas were often built of timber, which was then abundant in the British Isles. However, the small, late 1st century Villa of Quinton in Northamptonshire was of rectilinear stone built over a round house. At Brixworth nearby, the villa's development can be traced from Celtic round house through successive stages of Roman construction. These developed from the first rectangular house, built AD70–100, which boasted painted walls, to the grandest 4th-century phase, when a bath house was added. However, the villa remained haphazard in design throughout and was built for use rather than for ostentation.

More impressive is Lullingstone Villa in Kent beside the River Darenth. It was first built (AD80–90) on a terrace cut into the hill on the winged-corridor pattern. In the 2nd century AD, the "deep room" in the centre, once a grain store, was seemingly turned into a shrine, complete with a painting of nymphs adorning a niche and two fine portrait busts. In the 4th century AD, the central room was reconstructed, with an apse and a mausoleum built to the north. A Christian chapel seems to have been built in one chamber, judging by wall paintings bearing the chi-ro Christian symbol, making the villa one of the few Christian sites in Roman Britain. The villa was burnt down and abandoned early in the 5th century AD.

A GOLDEN AGE

In AD306, Constantius Chlorus, Augustus (senior emperor) of the West, died in York. He had just returned from a northern campaign that, while only half successful, had restored Roman prestige throughout an island which a decade before had appeared to be slipping out of the Roman orbit under rebel rulers. The half century that followed has been called the golden age of British villas. While towns built themselves ever thicker walls against possible barbarian attacks, villas in southern Britain expanded to sometimes majestic size, apparently unworried by Saxon raiders. Some fertile areas, such as the Fens, have few villas, indicating probably huge imperial estates that precluded private ownership.

Woodchester Villa in Gloucestershire exemplifies the building of the golden age. Started c. AD100 with a line of buildings on the north side of what became the central courtyard, it was extended southwards around this court in the next 150 years. The villa reached its climax after AD300 with a grand second northern courtyard

and bath houses. It is famed for its Orpheus mosaic. At 2,500sq ft (225sq m) this was the largest and most ornate mosaic in Britain, showing the mythical Greek poet charming the beasts. Other rooms in this and comparable villas were similarly decorated.

Chedworth Villa in a secluded valley near Cirencester was among Roman Britain's finest. Started in the late 2nd century AD as two houses with a bath suite, it developed in the 3rd and 4th centuries into a single building with two parallel wings connected by a veranda. The north range had elaborate bath suites, beyond which was a small temple with an octagonal pool, possibly devoted to the healing god Lenus-Mars (the Romans assimilated local deities whenever they could). Another villa which was occupied over many centuries is Gadebridge Park, Hertfordshire. Originally built of wood c. AD100, it grew into a large house of the winged-corridor type in the 4th century. It had a bath suite with a sizeable swimming pool and towers at either end. It was demolished c. AD350. No Roman villa long survived the collapse of Roman power after AD400.

Above: Mosaic at Lullingstone Villa, early 4th century AD, showing the Rape of Europa.

Below: Among the greatest Romano-British villas was that at Chedworth in Gloucestershire.

CHAPTER XVIII

CITIES OF THE EMPIRE

Rome's empire has been called a "confederation of cities". City to the Romans meant a self-governing polity, with its own *curia* (council) of annually elected magistrates. There were more than 1,000 such cities in the empire by AD200, ranging from metropoli such as Carthage to tiny but proud Gloucester. Some were former city-states of great antiquity like Ephesus, prospering again in the long Roman peace. Other cities, especially in the unurbanized West, were new foundations. Trier in Germany, Paris, Nîmes and Arles in France, London and Bath in Britain are cities founded by Romans and still flourishing. Other cities, such as Timgad in North Africa, blossomed and died with the empire, leaving only ruins as eloquent reminders of former wealth. Corinth and Carthage were refounded to boom under the empire after being deleted under the Republic.

As the empire grew, so did its cities, many building theatres, amphitheatres, baths, basilicas and fora, in expensive competition. At times older local traditions – Punic (African), Syrian, Celtic – influenced the classic Graeco-Roman mould. A few cities were seen as emulating Rome: Carthage was called Rome-in-Africa by its inhabitants, and Trier the Rome-of-the-North. Any survey of the empire's cities must start with the two that suffered the singular fate of being preserved for posterity by the eruption of Vesuvius: Pompeii and Herculaneum.

Left: Aerial view of the ruins of Pompeii with Vesuvius in the background, the volcano that both destroyed the city in its eruption of AD79 and preserved it in ash.

POMPEII AND HERCULANEUM

Above: A view of the atrium of the House of the Faun, Pompeii, a typical atrium-style house of a wealthy citizen just before the eruption of AD79 that has so well preserved it.

Below: A map of Pompeii just before the eruption of AD79, showing the major public buildings and the mainly rectilinear street plan. The grey areas on the map are as yet unexcavated.

The eruption that began about midday on 24 August AD79 was a catastrophe for the people of the small cities who had lived for centuries in the fertile lands under Mount Vesuvius – a mountain no one had ever suspected of being a potential volcano. That vast eruption blew the top off the mountain and killed thousands of people. Not realizing their danger, many had remained in the city until too late, although others escaped. The eruption covered Pompeii in 17ft (5m) of volcanic matter and Herculaneum in very hot ash, dust and stones to a depth of up to 70ft (21m), which hardened to form an excellent preservative.

Much of central Italy was powdered in dust, prompting the ever-generous emperor Titus in Rome to promise all the aid he could. It proved of little use and the cities were never reoccupied. They were forgotten until chance discoveries fuelled passionate if destructive excavations from 1748 on. However, Vesuvius' eruption has proved an immense blessing to posterity, for it has preserved – almost ghoulishly – intact the houses, artefacts and corpses of two prosperous, fashionable towns as the Roman empire neared its zenith. Bread has been left preserved in ovens, meals left ready on tables, scurrilous election

notices for the forthcoming *curia* (council) elections – "Thieves support Vatius for aedile!" – survive on the walls. Inside the houses the bodies of lovers have been found entwined in doomed embrace, while in the streets looters were overwhelmed with their booty. Without that terrible day, our knowledge of ordinary Roman life would be far less vivid.

LIFE BEFORE THE ERUPTION

Pompeii was a city long before it came under Roman rule. First inhabited in the 8th century BC, by 500BC it had acquired solid walls made of local tufa and limestone which ran for 2 miles (3.2km). The urban area of some 165 acres (66ha) was not built over completely at first, for there are signs of orchards or gardens within the walls, but by AD79 Pompeii's population was approaching an estimated 15,000. Greek and Etruscan influences, along with the local Samnites', are apparent in the early city. (In the 6th century BC a temple to Apollo, the archetypally Greek deity, was built, but Etruscans also worshipped Apollo.) By the 3rd century BC, Pompeii was under Roman control but Hellenistic influences still predominated artistically, as is most evident in the city's wall paintings.

In 80BC, the dictator Sulla settled about 5,000 Roman veterans with their families in Pompeii, renaming it Colonia Cornelia Veneria Pompeianorum. Local inhabitants must have been displaced but many important public buildings date from soon after this date. However, a major earthquake struck the city in AD62 and at the time of the eruption in AD79, many of the city's buildings were being rebuilt.

In the last century before its end, the Forum acquired notable temples to most Roman gods, indicating that Pompeii was an official religious centre.

The Villa of the Mysteries
House of Vettii
Vesuvius Gate
House of Faun
Nola Gate
Sarno Gate
Amphitheatre
Herculaneum Gate
House of Sallust
Forum Baths
Temple of Jupiter
The Forum
Palaestra
Nuceria Gate
House of Menander
Temple of Isis
Temple of Apollo
Stabiae Gate
Marine Gate
Macellum
Large Theatre
Basilica
Stabian Baths
Small Theatre (Odeon)

Left: Under the shadow of Vesuvius at dusk, a plaster-of-paris cast captures a Pompeian at the moment of death, caught in the violent pyroclastic flow from the volcano in AD79. The bodies of those who died, overwhelmed by ash and rock, left hollows or "moulds" from which these poignant casts were made.

Below: A street crossing showing the stepping stones in what is now called the Via dell'Abbondanza in Pompeii. The city, if small, had all the amenities of a Roman city, including proper paved streets.

THE TEMPLES OF POMPEII

Approaching from the seaward side, the first temple the visitor saw before entering the Forum would have been the Temple of Venus – the divine mother of Aeneas and so, according to later imperial propaganda, of the Julian dynasty. This rose impressively on the right and was probably built by Sulla's colonists. Typically Italian in form, the temple stood inside a wide precinct on a tall platform with a deep colonnaded front porch.

The Temple of Apollo dates to the 6th century BC and, with the Temple on the Triangular Forum, is the oldest building in Pompeii. It stood on the west side of the Forum at a slight angle, suggesting it was planned to align with an earlier Forum. It was much expanded and decorated under Augustus.

The Temple of Jupiter or the Capitolinum was the grandest of Pompeii's temples, in whose ruins a colossal torso of a seated male figure, presumably the king of the gods, has been found. A temple to the recently deified emperor Vespasian (AD69–79), with a wide colonnaded porch, was under construction on the east of the Forum, while next to it the Lararium, a temple to the Lares, the city's guardian gods and intended to ward off further catastrophes, had just been completed. Another temple, that of Isis, had also been swiftly restored. Built originally *c.* 120BC and dedicated to the popular Egyptian goddess – if one whose cult had been half-Hellenized – this had elaborate exterior stucco decorations covering plain brick walls. Interestingly, its restoration was paid for by Numerius Popidius Celsinus, the son of a freedman (former slave), indicating that upward mobility was not uncommon.

Other buildings in the centre added in the city's last century include the vegetable market, the *macellum*, the meat and fish market, and the vast Eumachia, the guild headquarters of the cloth fullers, named after their rich patroness. A large basilica, built 130–120BC – before the city became a Roman colony – had three aisles and fine Ionic columns. The Forum itself was in the process of being rebuilt more grandly with paving in travertine stone when the volcano woke.

Above: The fine Ionic columns of the city's large basilica, built 130–120BC, before Pompeii became a Roman colony.

Below: Fresco still life of a rabbit and figs from the House of the Stags, Herculaneum.

BATHS, THEATRES, AMPHITHEATRES

Pompeii, though it was only a modest provincial city, had public baths and a stone theatre and amphitheatre well before Rome. It boasted five different public bath houses. The largest, the Stabian Baths, dates back to the 4th century BC and came to cover an area of 40,000sq ft (4,000sq m). It is possible that later the Romans were inspired to build public baths with three rooms at progressively higher temperatures by Pompeian examples.

The Pompeians made extensive use of brick from Augustus' time, notably in the façade of the Central Baths, where half-columns alternate with large windows. A big theatre, built partly in stone and more Greek than Roman in plan, predates Rome's first permanent Theatre of Pompey of 55BC by a century.

Pompeii also had one of the first stone amphitheatres (earlier arenas were wooden). Built in the south-east corner of the city against the city walls, which reduced the need for massive earth banks to support its tiers, it probably catered initially for Sulla's veterans. An inscription dates it to about 70BC. With an estimated capacity of 20,000 spectators, it drew crowds from the surrounding area, sometimes with unpredictable consequences. In AD59, an argument over one gladiator led to a full-scale riot between the citizens of Pompeii and those of neighbouring Nuceria, anticipating more recent problems with football hooligans by almost two millennia. The Roman authorities reacted strongly, however, and the Pompeians were banned from holding any further gladiatorial events for ten years.

VILLAS AND HOUSES

Pompeii is famed for its houses which, if not the largest in the empire, are now among the most interesting because they survive in such quantity. Their design shows increasingly strong Hellenistic influences, revealing the city's links to the Greek East.

Early houses like the House of the Surgeon, built before 200BC, which centred round the *atrium*, gave way to more luxurious houses in which the *peristyle* and gardens gained ever greater importance. The House of the Gilded Cupids, built *c.* 150BC, had a huge *peristyle*, which was effectively a colonnaded garden. The House of the Faun, among the largest in Pompeii, covers about 1 acre (0.4 ha). Decorated throughout in the elegant, rather austere First Style, it progresses from an entrance passage through the *atrium* with bedrooms only on the left, to another bigger *atrium* opening to the right, which has two Ionic columns of tufa. Beyond this lies the room which contains the Alexander the Great mosaic. Perhaps the most famous mosaic in Pompeii, it was copied from a Greek painting. Beyond lies a large garden.

Increasingly, wealthier citizens tended to move out of town. About 400 yards out of Pompeii stands the famous Villa of the Mysteries. Built on an artificial earth platform, it is entered by the *peristyle*. Beyond this is a large *atrium* on the far side of which is a *tablinium* (central room) overlooking the sea. The house, which dates from the 2nd century BC with later alterations, is vast; it has 60 rooms and covers 1.4 acres (0.56 ha). Its famous murals show in dramatic detail scenes of a mystery religion, probably that of the god Dionysus.

A bedroom in a villa at Boscoreale outside Pompeii was decorated with murals showing gardens, fountains and bowls of fruits in frescoes. The murals are expressive of the superb illusionistic skills of the Second Style of the mid-1st century BC. Here too the inspiration was Greek.

By AD79, in luxurious houses like that of Loreius Tiburtinus, which was being extended at the time of the eruption, the *peristyle* had shrunk. The still spacious *atrium* was flanked by two-storeyed buildings, but the *peristyle* simply led into the long formal garden on to which many rooms, including the luxurious *triclinium*, opened. With its pergolas, statues and fountains, the garden was clearly the villa's real focus, from which a view of the mountains could be enjoyed.

HERCULANEUM

Smaller and far less extensively excavated than Pompeii, due to the hard, compacted volcanic material, which buried it, and the busy modern town above it, Roman Herculaneum boasts fine villas overlooking the sea. The Bay of Naples was considered to have some of the finest scenery in Italy, as well as the best climate.

Here the *peristyle* was replacing the *atrium*, as is evident in two adjoining villas built on terraces over the city walls, the House of the Stag and the House of the Mosaic Atrium. In the latter, built in the mid-1st century AD, the traditional pattern was partly followed in the north wing. It had an *atrium* minus its side

rooms and then a large central garden surrounded by rooms on two floors with a *triclinium* at the far end. Two small living rooms flanked a long narrow terrace, in the centre of which were the main reception rooms.

In the House of the Stags the *atrium* is only an entrance lobby with rooms arranged symmetrically around the garden courtyard. The inner *triclinium* faces on to this courtyard. Villas such as these had magnificent decorations. These often took the form of vividly realistic murals such as that of the Tragic Actor and show Graeco-Roman painting at its zenith.

Above: This fresco shows the riot in the amphitheatre between the people of Pompeii and those of nearby Nuceria in AD59. The amphitheatre at Pompeii is the earliest dated example of a permanent amphitheatre.

Below: Pompeii's Forum was dominated by the temple that is thought to have been dedicated to Jupiter, king of the gods. In its ruins was found the colossal torso of a seated male figure.

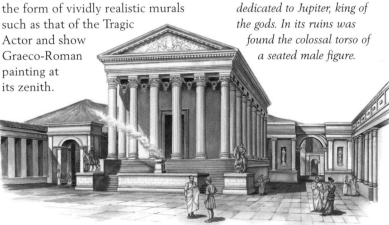

OSTIA AND PORTUS

Above: The ruins of the Baths of the Charioteers, one of 18 such baths in Ostia.

Below: A portico in Ostia decorated c. AD120 in the fashionable black and white style with ships, the symbols of Ostia's then booming trade.

Ostia, situated at the mouth of the Tiber, was one of Rome's first colonies. Founded *c.* 350BC as a base against pirates, its walls covered only five acres (2 ha). Later it became one of the colonies Sulla took for his veterans, expanding its walled area to around 160 acres (64ha). Ostia was early Rome's main port, but its harbour was open to storms and plagued by sandbars, and never ideal because it was a river port and could not cope with big ships. As Rome became crucially dependent on imported grain, Pozzuoli (Puteoli) near Naples became the deep water harbour for Rome. There, goods were transhipped to barges which crawled along the coast to Ostia. The latter was still Rome's outlet to the sea. This was expensive and risky, so in AD42 Claudius, reviving one of Julius Caesar's grand projects, decided to build an artificial harbour on the coast two miles north of Ostia, called Portus.

THE BUILDING OF PORTUS

A gigantic ship with a displacement of 7,400 tons, used by Caligula to transport an obelisk from Egypt, was sunk to provide the base for a large *pharos* (lighthouse). Breakwaters were built to make a harbour 1,200yds (1,100m) across., but storms still wrecked ships sheltering inside the wide harbour – Tacitus records 200 sunk in AD62 alone – and most grain fleets still avoided Ostia in favour of Pozzuoli.

Trajan (ruled AD98–117) solved the problem by excavating an octagonal inner basin about 770yds (700m) across, with a canal link to the Tiber. Flanked by large warehouses, the new quays at Portus had numbered columns corresponding to mooring berths. More than 100 ships could dock in its inner basin at the same time, while the outer harbour was used as a holding area for arriving ships.

Ostia boomed thanks to Portus' new dock and for two centuries the places' fortunes intertwined. Many merchants, chandlers and others associated with Rome's import trade – Rome *exported* nothing except edicts, administrators and refuse – lived in Ostia, although they presumably worked in Portus. Their joint population approached an estimated 100,000 at their 2nd-century peak.

Ostia declined in the 4th century and its buildings were abandoned to the river silt that finally blocked up its harbour. The river silt also, however, preserved Ostia's buildings, to provide evidence of how ordinary Romans lived.

Private houses initially remained mostly simple *domus* (individual house) types, some half-timbered, although they began to unite their porticoes to create colonnades

like those of Eastern cities. The rebuilding of Ostia began under Domitian, and, with Trajan's new docks, Ostia was rapidly transformed into a showcase of contemporary Roman building techniques.

REBUILDING OSTIA

The western quarter was rebuilt first with *insulae* (apartment blocks) in brick-faced concrete. Although not covered in stucco, this was meant to be seen, as arched doorways and balconies broke up its otherwise plain façades. The *insulae* rivalled those of the capital but at a lower density – they seldom rose more than four floors – and are today much better preserved.

The House of Diana is a typical *insula*. Its south and west sides had large windows facing the street but the other sides, which adjoined neighbouring houses, lacked windows. To give them light, the architect put a courtyard in the centre, along with a water cistern for all residents to use, as piped water was a luxury restricted to the first floor at best.

Fronting the streets were *tabernae* – single-roomed shops with a mezzanine above where the shopkeepers often lived. Staircases between the shops led to the upper floors. Many *insulae* looked impressive and some, with inner gardens, were spacious and comfortable.

Even the city's warehouses were imposingly built. The Horra Epagathiania of *c.* AD150 had an arched entrance made of brick but flanked by proper Corinthian columns with pediments.

Among the major public buildings was the Capitolium (Temple to Jupiter, Juno and Minerva). Built on the Forum's north side *c.* AD120–30, it stood at the end of a broad street which led down to the river and was flanked by brick porticoes. Built of brick-faced concrete sumptuously covered in marble, it was raised on a high podium to dominate surrounding buildings and measured about 70ft (22m) tall. A temple to Roma and Augustus, also covered in marble, dates from Tiberius' reign (AD14–37), but Ostia's many temples to more exotic gods reveal foreign influences. The city also had at least 18 public baths, reflecting Roman priorities. Of these, the Forum Baths (*c.* AD150) is the finest, its octagonal west-facing room recalling the sun rooms in Hadrian's Villa at Tivoli.

This surge of building activity faded after AD160. In the 4th century AD, as Ostia's population fell to make more space available for bigger houses, some fine new *domus* were built, such as the House of Cupid and Psyche.

By the 4th century AD Ostia was in decline as Portus supplanted it. Although far smaller, Portus had notable buildings of its own, including the Imperial Palace, which lay on the western quay of the new basin looking out over Claudius' harbour. Built of fine brick-faced concrete with a bath house, it was probably connected with the administration or it may have been the Forum. Portus was to remain Rome's port for centuries.

Above: Ships laden with amphorae (earthenware jars) sailing past the lighthouse at Ostia. This 3rd-century AD relief is rather unusual as it comes from a Christian tomb in the Catacombs of Praetextatus.

Below: The House of Diana in Ostia. A typical insula (apartment block), with large windows facing the street and a light-well and courtyard behind it, it dates from the early 2nd century AD.

CONTRASTING CITIES: CARTHAGE AND TIMGAD

Above: Corinthian capitals of the Antonine Baths, Carthage.

Below: Ruins of the Punic district of ancient Carthage.

Founded by the Phoenicians in 814BC, Carthage swiftly became the most powerful city in the western Mediterranean, with an extensive commercial network, and later Rome's most feared opponent. Hannibal, its great general, devastated Italy in the Second Punic War (218–202BC) and even threatened Rome itself, so Carthage's total destruction by Rome in 146BC was an act of delayed revenge. Yet Carthage's superb site, with fine harbours and fertile hinterland, led Romans such as the reformer Gaius Gracchus in 122BC and later Julius Caesar to propose a colony there. Under Augustus, these plans were realized in 29BC with the foundation of Colonia Julia Concordia Karthago. Three thousand colonists were settled on what became one of the empire's largest cities and the magnificent capital of one of Rome's richest provinces.

ROMAN MEETS PUNIC CULTURE

If the Romans had tried to delete all traces of the Punic city in 146BC, the suburbs of modern Tunis today cover the Roman city very effectively. However, enough has been excavated to show that Augustus' surveyors created a typical grid pattern for the new city.

The old Punic citadel of Byrsa was levelled to make a rectangular platform of about 10 acres (4ha) on which the usual public buildings – forum, basilica, temples – were erected. Local topography meant, however, that the Roman city followed the general alignment of its Punic predecessor, while its inhabitants themselves became a mixture of Roman newcomers and slowly Romanized Punic inhabitants. An altar to the *gens Augusta* (family of Augustus) deliberately recalled the Ara Pacis (Altar of Peace) in Rome. The Capitoline triad was worshipped but local Punic gods were also tolerated and assimilated into the Roman pantheon. Only Moloch with his reputation for human sacrifice was excluded.

Punic Carthage had been renowned for its rectangular outer harbour and an inner, circular harbour reputedly able to shelter and launch 200 galleys. Carthage now became the chief port as well as capital of the Roman province of Africa. As the province became Rome's main source of wheat and olive oil, the harbours were rebuilt for more peaceful traffic. A large amphitheatre was built in the west of the city around the time of Augustus, along with a circus 1,700ft (516m) long, able to seat up to 55,000 people. Only the Circus Maximus in Rome itself was larger. Under Hadrian (ruled AD117–38) a luxurious theatre, decorated in marble, onyx, granite and porphyry, was constructed. Finally, the immense Antonine Baths were built in AD143–62, the largest baths outside Rome itself at the time. With an ingeniously planned ring of interlocking hexagonal *caldaria* (hot baths), these were enormous – 650ft (200m) long, covering 192,000sq ft (17,850sq m) – and richly decorated with mosaics and imported marbles. An aqueduct, substantial parts of which survive, brought water from 35 miles (56km) away, supplying an estimated 7 million gallons (32 million litres) a day to the city.

From Carthage came Apuleius, the novelist of the 2nd century AD and a short-lived dynasty of emperors, the Gordiani (AD238–4). St Augustine, the great theologian, lived there AD370–83 (Carthage was an important centre of early Christianity) and praised its tree-lined avenues and many churches. Despite conquest by the Vandals in the 5th century, the city remained a bastion of Roman culture and provided loyal support to the Byzantine empire after it was restored to the empire in AD535. Carthage only fell to Arab invaders after prolonged sieges in AD698, a fall that marked the end, after seven centuries, of Rome in Africa.

TIMGAD: A VETERANS' COLONY

Almost 200 miles (320km) south-west of Carthage, on a low and then fertile plateau, stand the ruins of a very different city, Timgad (Thamugadi) in modern Algeria. Founded by Trajan in AD100 as a colony for veterans, it was planned exactly like a large legionary camp, forming a square of 1,200 Roman feet (1,165 ft/355m) subdivided into 12 equal blocks, each 100 Roman feet square. The two main streets – the *cardo* and *decumanus* – intersect at the exact centre, where lay the forum with a basilica,

a *curia* (local senate house), temple and public lavatory – this last a building of some elegance, with marble arm rests in the shape of dolphins. Just to the north was the 4,000-seat theatre.

Intended to provide homes for retired legionaries and to help Romanize a still half-wild region, Timgad grew into a town with a population of around 15,000 people by AD200. It spread rather chaotically beyond its original plan as more baths, temples and a library were built. At first its houses were simple if solid single-storey buildings made of local limestone and timber – the mountains nearby were then well wooded – but with continuous colonnades in the Eastern style.

Before the city of Timgad was totally abandoned in the 7th century AD, a small Byzantine fort was built to the south. Most spectacular of the surviving ruins is the triple Arch of Trajan – which was actually built *c.* AD190, and so commemorates the city's famous founder – with pediments above the side arches, at the end of a colonnaded street.

Above: A servant offering a diner wine in a mosaic from Carthage of the early 4th century AD. Carthage soon became second only to Rome in the Western empire in its size and wealth.

Below: The triple Arch of Trajan standing at the end of a colonnaded street in Timgad. It was built about AD190 to commemorate the city's imperial founder.

LEPCIS MAGNA: AN EMPEROR'S BIRTHPLACE

Above: A bust of Septimius Severus (AD146–211), Lepcis' most famous son who became emperor in AD193 and richly adorned the city.

Below: One of the central pavilions of the macellum *(market) in Lepcis. It was built c. 8BC of the fine local limestone as the city grew under the Augustan peace.*

Lepcis Magna in Tripolitania (western Libya) was founded by the Phoenicians or Carthaginians *c.* 600BC. A Punic (Carthaginian) city long before it became part of the Roman empire after 100BC, under the Pax Augusta, the 250-year-long peace established by Augustus in 30BC, it became steadily more prosperous. It was opulently adorned by its greatest native son Septimius Severus, emperor AD193–211. Later totally abandoned, its surviving ruins are among the finest of any Roman city.

Little remains of pre-Roman Lepcis, although many of its inhabitants long spoke Punic as well as Latin. Under Augustus, the Old Forum by the sea was laid out on standard rectangular lines, except in the north-east where an earlier temple survived. The three new temples are typically Italian in style, with high podiums and frontal emphasis. The central temple to the goddess Roma and Augustus was dedicated *c.* AD18. A *macellum* (market) with two central octagonal pavilions was built inside a rectangular courtyard in 8BC, with shops sheltering from the harsh African sun under its porticoes. A private citizen, Annobal Rufus built the theatre in AD1–2, which had an auditorium 300ft (90m) across. Partly resting on a natural slope, it had a splendid *scaenae frons* (stage wall), with three tiers of curving columns (some later rebuilt in marble) and a slot in the floor into which the curtain was lowered before performances.

GROWING PROSPERITY

Under Hadrian, magnificent new baths modelled on those of Trajan in Rome were erected in AD126–7. They made novel use of expensive marbles that were imported from Greece or Asia Minor even in their well-appointed communal lavatories, which could seat 60 people. The baths had the usual *natatio* (swimming pool), *tepidarium* (warm room) and *caldarium* (hot room) sequence, with the addition of *sudatoria* (sweat rooms), ancestors of the Turkish bath. They reveal Lepcis Magna's growing prosperity, as careful dry farming techniques, capturing and conserving every drop of rain, pushed back the desert to give Tripolitania its golden age.

Many public buildings were now opulently remodelled in marble. The Hunting Baths, externally unadorned concrete vaulted structures on the beach, are notable architecturally. They may have been used by wealthy local huntsmen, but the name comes from the hunting scenes painted on the vaults inside. It is thought they might have served as the baths of a guild or as private baths which could be hired by groups. By the 2nd century AD, Lepcis was one of the empire's richest cities, but its best was yet to come.

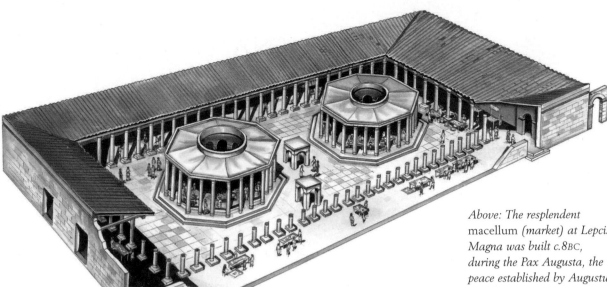

Above: The resplendent macellum (market) at Lepcis Magna was built c.8BC, during the Pax Augusta, the peace established by Augustus, the first emperor. A large colonnaded peristyle measuring 73 by 43m (80 by 47yds) surrounds the market. Two circular market-halls, rather than the usual single hall, stood in the centre, crowded with market stalls. Its size shows Lepcis was already a wealthy city.

Below: The citizens of Lepcis erected a four-sided triumphal arch in gratitude to their emperor Severus for his visit in AD203. It was exuberantly decorated with winged victories holding wreaths.

SEVERAN HEYDAY

Septimius Severus was a senator (of Rome) and commander of the Danubian legions when he launched his bid for the imperial throne in AD193, but he always remained faithful to his home town. Indeed, his family was so obviously Libyan that it is reported that he had to send his sister back home because her marked Lepcis accent made her ridiculous at court. Septimius endowed his native city with a new monumental quarter, including an enclosed harbour, temple, new forum and basilica and a piazza dominated by a huge *nymphaeum* (fountain building) – buildings that would have looked impressive even in Rome.

The harbour was a circular basin about 400yds (365m) in diameter with a lighthouse and warehouses. From the waterfront a colonnaded street about 450yds (411m) long and 70ft (21m) wide, flanked by porticoes, led up to the piazza near the Hadrianic baths. North of this Severus built a new forum, 200 by 330ft (60 by 100m).

On the forum's south-west side was a vast temple to the Severan family. Standing on a double-height podium on a tall flight of steps, it had eight red Egyptian granite columns in front, with columns of green *cipollino* marble with white Pentelic marble capitals on either side. It resembled but

surpassed in grandeur Augustus' Temple of Mars Ultor in Rome. On the other side of the forum rose a huge new basilica, over 100ft (30m) high, with apses at both ends flanked by two pairs of white marble pilasters. The galleries over the double height lateral aisles were supported by Corinthian columns of red Egyptian granite. The timber roof had a span of 62ft (19m). Elaborate coloured marbles were used throughout Severus' projects. The raw materials and the craftsmen were imported; even the unknown architect probably came from the Aegean world.

The Forum was surrounded by a high masonry wall – it became a fortress under the Byzantines – but inside ran an opulent arcaded portico with alternating Medusa and Nereid heads. The *nymphaeum* had a big semicircular fountain basin, which was richly decorated with niches and columns of red granite.

In gratitude for this imperial largesse, the citizens of Lepcis erected a triumphal arch to their emperor for his visit in AD203. Four-sided, it has exuberant decorations, with columns, winged Victories holding wreaths and reliefs showing Severus and his triumphant armies. Lepcis was finally covered by sand as the collapse of Roman farming methods allowed the Sahara to push north to the coast.

ATHENS: A GLORIOUS PAST

Above: Tiers of marble seats in the Theatre of Dionysus in Athens, refurbished and restored under the Romans.

Below: The School of Plato, traditionally the greatest of Greek philosophers, shown in a 1st century AD mosaic.

Athens lost its last political importance after Sulla brutally sacked it in 86BC for supporting Mithradates' war against Rome. However, it retained a unique status in the empire broadly comparable to that of Florence or Venice today, under which it was revered for its past artistic and intellectual glories. Illustrious Romans, from the great orator Cicero in 80BC to the last pagan emperor Julian in AD354, studied in Athens, while emperors endowed it with new buildings or special privileges. Far smaller than Hellenistic cities such as Alexandria, Athens was still recognized as the cultural capital of Greece and its craftsmen's skills were much appreciated in Rome. It even regained its position as the chief centre of philosophy. It did not, however, regain its democracy, for emperors were also making a political point through their buildings, emphasizing Rome's power over Greece. Roman imperial monuments filled up the old *agora* (forum), which had once been the centre of Athenian democratic life. Most Athenians, who had suffered in Rome's civil wars, were too impoverished to object to the wealthy new masters who gave them work.

PROCLAIMING ROMAN POWER

Julius Caesar had provided money for a new *agora* that was built under Augustus and dedicated in 10BC. A rectangular court 270 by 225ft (82 by 69m), it was enclosed by Ionic porticoes and entered by a monumental gateway whose style revived Athenian 5th-century BC classicism. (Augustus chiefly admired Greek classicism for its air of dignity and authority.) Greek cities in the East used brick, stone and mortared rubble rather than Roman concrete. The Temple of Ares (Mars), originally 5th century BC and erected elsewhere in Attica, was moved block by block into the Agora and linked with Augustus' temple of Mars Ultor in Rome.

In 15BC Agrippa, Augustus' chief minister, built an *odeion* (roofed theatre), a lofty rectangular gabled hall to seat about 1,000. Its carved marble ornaments again copied classical examples but its giant scale – its interior was 76ft (23m) high and 82ft (25m) square – was new in Athens. A small circular temple to Rome and Augustus was built on the Acropolis. This was artistically influenced by the nearby classical Erechtheion but politically it proclaimed the power of Rome.

The flamboyantly philhellenic emperor Nero refurbished the old Theatre of Dionysus beneath the Acropolis between AD54 and 61, erecting a Roman-style stage building. This had seen the first performances of most of the great Greek tragedies by Aeschylus, Sophocles and

Euripides. It now also witnessed gladiatorial games. The games themselves apparently became popular with some Athenians after an initial period of disgust. Meanwhile, wealthy young Romans came to Athens to study at one of the competing schools of philosophy: Stoic, Platonist, Epicurean or Cynic.

THE CITY OF HADRIAN

By the early 2nd century AD, Athens had regained a modest prosperity through the export of its fine Pentelic marble and skilled craftsmen. The emperor Hadrian, whose philhellenism ran deep, spent some of his happiest years in the city he first visited in AD124–5.

Hadrian became *archon* (mayor) of Athens and made the city head of his new Panhellenion League (an essentially honorific title). He also completed the temple of Olympian Zeus (Jupiter) whose building was started by the tyrant Peisistratus in the 6th century BC and revived in 174BC by the Seleucid king Antiochus IV. Antiochus' Roman architects, the Cossutius brothers, had opted for the Corinthian order for the 60ft (18m) high columns, but the huge temple had suffered when Sulla removed many columns to Rome. Hadrian dedicated it in AD132, placing a chryselephantine (gold and ivory) statue of Zeus inside the building.

Hadrian also provided a new aqueduct, a library whose plan recalled the Forum Pacis in Rome, a *stoa* (portico) with symmetrical gardens and baths. To commemorate his work, Hadrian erected an arch at the boundary between the original city and the new quarter he had founded in AD131. This was not in the usual triumphant Roman style but linked him to Theseus, Athens' legendary founder. The inscriptions on one side read, "This is the city of Theseus, not Hadrian", and on the other, "This is the city of Hadrian, not Theseus."

In AD143, Herodes Atticus, a wealthy aristocrat, restored the Hellenistic stadium (which was used for the Panathenaic games) in Pentelic marble. The stadium

was also used for gladiatorial games after this restoration. He built a new marble *odeion*, but there was little further construction. Third-century troubles saw Athens sacked in AD256 by marauding barbarians and, like so many cities at this time, it rewalled itself. More damagingly, the Visigoths under Alaric ravaged all Greece in AD398, attacking pagan temples in particular. (The Visigoths were keen, if heretical, Christians, but the remaining temple treasures were the chief attraction.) Despite this, Plato's Academy continued to flourish as the centre of Neoplatonism, the last great philosophical movement of antiquity. Proclus (*c.* AD410–85), who lectured in Athens, was its supreme systematizer. He extended the thinking of its founder, Plotinus, to stress the interconnectedness of all things, arguing that time itself is a circular dance.

However, Christian intolerance was growing. In AD529 the Byzantine emperor Justinian ordered the closure of all the schools of philosophy, so ending a thousand years of intellectual freedom and ancient Athens itself.

Above: The gigantic Temple of Olympian Zeus was completed by Hadrian in AD132, some 650 years after it was started.

Below: The Tower of the Winds, which housed an elaborate monumental clock dating from c. 50BC.

TRIER: THE ROME OF THE NORTH

Above: The now plain interior of the huge Basilica was once decorated with glowing mosaics that surrounded the emperor enthroned in majesty in the apse at the far end.

Below: The Porta Nigra (Black Gate), the northern gateway, rises 100ft (30m) and dates from c. AD300. Its unusually fine state of preservation is due to its conversion into a chapel in the Middle Ages.

Three days' march up the Moselle valley from the Rhine frontier, Trier (Augusta Treverorum) had a superb strategic position. When Postumus proclaimed his separatist Gallic empire in AD260, he made Trier his capital, but in the ensuing civil war and invasions the city was sacked. It recovered, however, to become the leading city in the Western empire in the 4th century AD. Politically, economically and culturally it supplanted Lyons (Lugdunum), which never recovered from being sacked by Septimius Severus in the civil wars of AD195.

ORIGINS OF A CITY

There was no pre-Roman settlement at Trier when Agrippa, Augustus' general, chose the site for a military camp. This attracted the local Celts and a township grew up around it. (The Treveri had been a warlike people, supplying Caesar with cavalry, but had not previously been city dwellers.) Under Claudius (ruled AD43–54) Trier gained the important status of *colonia* and a charter. It developed rapidly thanks to its position on the major trade routes that ran north–south and east–west and to the stone bridge which Claudius had constructed. Its piers still support the modern bridge. Trier became the seat of the procurator (governor) of the province of Gallia Belgica. There are traces of houses with stone foundations and a large rectangular hall from the 1st century AD.

Soon after AD100, the grand St Barbara Baths were constructed. Elaborately decorated, with marble statues in semi-circular niches around an open-air *natatio* (swimming pool), they also had several heated rooms, essential in a city so far north. Along with a stone amphitheatre that could seat up to 20,000 people, private houses were now constructed that boasted fine mosaic floors. The Forum, about 1,300 by 500ft (400 by 150m), was built around this time, as was the *curia* (council room). The monumental northern gateway known as the Porta Nigra (Black Gate – age has weathered it) is an early 4th-century building in a deliberately archaic style. At 100ft (30m) high and 120ft (36m) long, it was intended to impress visitors or invaders with the majesty of Rome, with its many tiered arches flanked by pillars. It may have been left unfinished, which accounts for the rough, even crude quality of its stonework. Its survival is due to its conversion into a chapel in the Middle Ages.

A GOLDEN AGE

In AD293 Constantius Chlorus became Caesar (junior emperor) of the West from Morocco to the Tyne, and Augustus (senior emperor) in AD305. Like the other tetrarchs, he chose a permanent new capital, in his case Trier, and adorned it lavishly. Among his new structures was the Basilica, although it was probably completed by his son Constantine I who held court at Trier from AD306–312. Built of solid red brick, the Basilica is a huge

bare hall, measuring around 95 by 220ft (29 by 67m) and almost 100ft (30m) high. Part of the imperial palace, it was not then a free-standing building. Today it is a completely plain Lutheran church, lit by two rows of round-headed windows, which continue around the apse. The upper windows of the apse are lower and shorter than those in the nave, producing the illusion that the apse is larger than it is. This effect was intended to magnify the power of the emperor who sat enthroned in its mosaic-covered apse. The floor was originally covered in black and white marble and heated by hypocausts, which were themselves veneered in marble. The exterior of the building would not originally have seemed as austere as it does now, because it was probably stuccoed and had two rows of wooden balconies around it.

Equally imposing buildings formed the Kaiserthermen (Imperial Baths) erected after AD293 at the southern end of the palace complex, probably for courtiers' sole use. Their main bathing-block (450 by 400ft/ 137 by 122m) occupied half the rectangular site, facing the large porticoed court and surrounding buildings. They may not have been completed when Constantine finally left Trier in AD316, and only parts were used as baths by later emperors. Other parts were probably used as offices.

A CENTRE OF CULTURE

Trier continued to enjoy imperial favour. Constantine II and later Valentinian I (AD364–75) and his son Gratian (AD375–83) all chose to rule from it. Constantine I had started its polygonal cathedral, the first in northern Europe, which now forms part of Trier Cathedral.

Two massive limestone warehouses were built near the river, each 230ft long by 65ft wide (70 by 120m). About AD300 city walls, 20ft high and 10ft thick (6m by 3m), with 75 towers, were built to enclose an area of 700 acres (280ha).

In the 4th century AD, Trier was a centre of culture as well as power, with its own university. Ausonius, the poet and courtier who tutored the young Gratian,

famously praised the beautiful Moselle valley and its terraced vineyards in his poems. Other intellectually distinguished visitors included St Augustine, St Jerome – both key Church fathers – and Lactantius, a noted Christian orator. Trier deserved its title *Roma Transalpina*, Rome north of the Alps, but it did not survive the calamitous 5th century. Finally abandoned by the imperial court in AD395, it was sacked by German invaders in AD406.

Above: A carving on a tombstone of the 2nd century AD showing a tavern scene (top) and a wine barrel being transported by ox cart (beneath). The Moselle valley was already famed for its wines under the Romans.

EPHESUS: WONDER OF THE WORLD

Above: Artemis (Diana), the great goddess of the Ephesians, portrayed as a fertility goddess with many breasts in this statue of the 2nd century AD. Her huge temple was one of the seven wonders of the world.

Ephesus was a very ancient city dating back to Mycenaean times when the Romans made it the capital of their new province of Asia (western Anatolia) in *c.* 129BC. Like Athens, Ephesus had long been an important intellectual and religious as well as commercial centre. However, unlike Athens, it boomed under the Pax Romana, becoming one of the wealthiest cities in the empire, with a population of perhaps 200,000 people. Large areas of the central city have been excavated and many buildings testify to this long prosperity. While remaining firmly Greek in spirit, Ephesus' architecture was more innovative than Athens', reflecting its citizens' greater wealth and self-confidence.

Up to *c.* 180BC, Ephesus had thrived, sometimes as the Western capital of the vast Seleucid empire, more often as an independent city state. However, Rome's wars – especially its civil wars – half-ruined the Greek cities of Asia Minor and Ephesus only recovered after Augustus had restored peace in 30BC. The city grew rich primarily from trade, as it was never a manufacturing centre. Traders from the East, coming down the Meander valley from Anatolia and points east as far as China, which was then the world's only source of silk, offloaded their valuable cargoes in the port at Ephesus on to ships bound for Rome.

DIANA OF THE EPHESIANS

Ephesus' gigantic temple of Artemis (Diana) – traditionally built with money provided by the wealthy King Croesus of Lydia *c.* 550BC and certainly dating to before 500BC – was another, if smaller, source of wealth and a great source of civic pride. It was among the first Greek temples to use the Ionic order throughout, rather than the Doric or Aeolian orders. Many times restored or rebuilt to the same design after fires (one of them started deliberately), the temple was constructed mostly of marble and considered one of the seven wonders of the ancient world, chiefly because of its size. It measured 374ft by 180ft (114 by 55m). With its huge Ionic columns 65ft (20m) high, it was the largest temple of the classic rectilinear column and lintel type ever constructed. Within its *cella* (central chamber) was a giant statue of Artemis, depicted not as the usual chaste huntress-goddess of Graeco-Roman mythology but as a many-breasted deity, pointing to the Asian origin of her cult at Ephesus.

Around the temple precincts swarmed peddlers of locally made religious trinkets. Theirs was the highly profitable trade that St Paul tried to disrupt on his mission, causing local craftsmen to riot shouting, "Great is Diana (Artemis) of the Ephesians!" After Constantine had made Christianity fashionable, however, Ephesus became an important Christian city and the seat of a bishop.

Left: The Library of Celsus, Ephesus, built c. AD110. It is remarkable for its undulating façade with projecting pavilions topped by curved and triangular pediments.

THE ARKADIANE

Ephesus had reasonably abundant building materials and most of its public buildings in the Roman period were of solid masonry. This applied to the colonnaded street, running 650yds (600m) from the harbour to the theatre – superbly sited at the foot of Mount Pion – called the Arkadiane. Along this 36ft (11m) broad avenue lay most of the important buildings of the Roman era.

The Library of Celsus was among the most striking of the buildings of Ephesus. Dating from about AD110–35, it stands at the bottom of Euretes Street. It was built by the son and grandson of a rich and illustrious citizen, Caius Julius Celsus Polemeanus, who had become a consul in Rome – the highest honour a normal citizen could attain – and who was, most unusually, buried inside the Library beneath its apse. A tall rectangular hall, 55ft wide by 36ft long (16.7 by 10.9m), it had a small central apse with a statue of Celsus. Round three sides ran three rows of recesses to house the books or scrolls. Two orders of columns carried the two tiers of balustraded galleries to give access to the upper bookcases. Its richly carved façade has been re-erected, revealing that pairs of upper columns were staggered over the lower columns and alternated with curved and triangular pediments. This has shown that Ephesian architects could play sparkling new variations on old classical themes. The nearby Temple to Hadrian – which was erected by a private citizen and is therefore relatively small – is remarkable for its Syrian arch where the central span of the façade is arched up into the pediment. Like the colonnaded Arkadiane, this may also have been Syrian-inspired.

The most innovatory buildings of Roman Ephesus were its numerous resplendent baths. Largest of these were the Harbour Baths of the late 1st century

Right: The Temple of Hadrian, built AD130–8, has an ornate frieze across its façade rising up into an arch resting on two Corinthian columns.

AD. In the centre of this bulky complex lay the two *Marmorsualen* (Marble Rooms), opulently decorated marble halls on either side of a *peristyle* court, with the baths themselves in between. The Greek preference for gymnasia with covered running tracks distinguishes these baths from those in the Romanized Western empire. Such very Greek taste for athletics and classical architecture survived until the advent of Christianity in the 4th century.

Above: Detail of a garland from a sarcophagus, probably from the 2nd century AD, when Ephesus was booming under Roman rule. The dynamic exuberance of this relief illustrates the self-confidence and wealth of the city at the time.

VANISHED CITIES OF THE EAST

Above: The Temple of Bel in Palmyra, dedicated in AD32, is Hellenistic in its tall Corinthian columns, but its entrance by a grand side doorway is not at all classical.

Below: Reconstruction of the markedly Graeco-Roman theatre in Palmyra. Here its most famous ruler, Queen Zenobia, reputedly liked to watch Greek dramas after her victories.

Pompey had added western Asia from the Caucasus to the Red Sea to the Roman sphere of influence in the 60s BC, but it was centuries before Rome directly controlled all this area, home of many ancient civilizations. While most cities gained a Hellenistic veneer after Alexander the Great's conquests (334–323BC) – and metropoli like Antioch in Syria or Seleucia-on-the-Tigris were totally new Greek-speaking foundations – the population remained mainly Aramaic-speaking (Semitic). This made for a fertile mixture of styles. Meanwhile, the Pax Romana allowed long-distance trade to flourish even beyond Rome's eastern frontier.

PALMYRA

Located in the Syrian desert, Palmyra, long a semi-independent client state, was well situated to benefit from this peace. The city was an oasis midway between the Euphrates and the Mediterranean ports. Its excellent cavalry – it included heavy armoured cataphracts besides mounted archers – protected caravans carrying the spices and other exotic goods so valued in Rome and it became a major caravan city on the trade routes with the East. (The "protection" may not have been entirely voluntary, but it helped rather than hindered trade.) Visiting Palmyra in AD128, Hadrian granted it the status of "free city", allowing it to set its own taxes and dues. It consequently prospered even more, while moving closer into the Roman orbit. The Palmyrene Tariff is a list of taxes charged for goods coming and going and for the use of the springs.

AN AUDACIOUS QUEEN

When the Persians over-ran Rome's eastern provinces and captured the emperor Valerian in AD260, Odenatheus, ruler of Palmyra, rode to Rome's rescue. His cavalry drove the Persians out of Syria and Anatolia and he won himself the title *Dux Orientis* (Duke of the East), before he was assassinated in AD267. His widow Zenobia, noted alike for her dark-haired beauty and for her audacity, inherited his power.

Zenobia claimed descent from Cleopatra, the last Ptolemaic queen of Egypt, and rivalled her in ambition. The great historian Edward Gibbon, admittedly writing 1,500 years later, called her, "The most lovely as well as the most heroic of her sex…Her large black eyes sparkled with an uncommon fire, tempered by the most attractive sweetness".

Proclaiming her son Augustus and herself Augusta, Zenobia rejected Roman suzerainty and invaded Egypt in AD270. Finally provoked, the emperor Aurelian marched east and crushed her in a series of battles, capturing Palmyra in AD271. After these defeats the city became a

Roman frontier fort – an ignominious fate that, paradoxically, has preserved it well. The most striking aspect of Palmyra today is its long colonnaded streets. The main colonnaded street, dating from the early 2nd century AD and three-quarters of a mile (1.2km) long and 35ft (11m) wide, ran from the Grove Temple in the west to the Temple of Bel, intersecting similarly colonnaded streets.

The great temple of Bel, the city's chief deity of Babylonian origin, was dedicated in AD32. From the outside it appears to follow classical canons fairly closely, with six columns at either end on a low platform, like many Hellenistic temples. However, it is far from classical in layout. It is entered not from the front but through an elaborate doorway at the head of a grand staircase on the west side. Inside are two cult chambers. It was possibly topped by a parapet of crowstepped merlons and its roof, behind its classical pediments, had flat terraces. Parthian influences are also apparent in many of its statues, which are stiffly stylized. However, architecturally Palmyra became more Graeco-Roman in the following centuries, with the construction of an *agora* (forum), a theatre – where Zenobia reputedly watched Greek dramas after her victories – and a bath house.

THE ROSE RED CITY

Almost impregnable in its remote valley among the Edom mountains in the south Jordanian desert, Petra is another city abandoned after a brief period of glory. Described by Strabo early in the 1st century AD as peaceful and well-governed, with caravans converging on it from the south or east, its great days as a trading city were already fading when Trajan annexed it in AD106, but it had once surpassed Palmyra. Debate continues about the exact date of its most famous monuments, the rockcut façades – some scholars date them before the Roman occupation, others after it – but their architecture is remarkably original. Situated in the Siq gorge between towering

mountain, Petra is built of the local reddish sandstone – hence its nickname "the Rose Red City". The visitor today first sees the Khasneh, or Treasury, with a remarkable central kiosk in the middle of its broken pediment. The same design is seen in Petra's most majestic building, the mausoleum called the Deir. Its façade is massive – 150ft long by 125ft high (46 by 38m) – larger than the west front of Westminster Abbey. However, it remains only a façade with a style that deserves the name baroque. Lost completely in its valley after its decline, Petra was only rediscovered in the 19th century.

Above: Façade of the Khasneh or Treasury at Petra, which has a circular kiosk in the middle of its broken pediment, an architectural extravagance typical of a style sometimes called Roman baroque. It was never a treasury, but was later thought to contain treasure by tomb robbers.

NÎMES AND ARLES: CITIES OF ROMAN GAUL

Julius Caesar called Gallia Transalpina *nostra provincia* (our province), because southern Gaul (today Languedoc and Provence) had been Roman since 121BC, and had long been influenced by Greek colonies such as Marseilles and Nice. Narbonne, which gave the province its later name Gallia Narbonensis, was Rome's first colony outside Italy, founded in 118BC. Under Augustus, the province thrived, becoming almost a second Italy and so peaceful it could be governed by a senator without an army. Meanwhile Roman civilization spread up the Rhône valley into central Gaul, transforming the region, with Lyons (Lugdunum) as its central city. Lyons' theatre, odeum, aqueducts and amphitheatre are all well-preserved.

Nîmes (Nemausus) was founded as a legionary veterans' colony in 35BC on the site of an earlier tribal capital and shrine to Nemausus, Gallic god of the local spring. In 16BC Augustus endowed his new city with walls nearly four miles (6.4km) long, enclosing an area of about 500 acres (200ha). These walls, by then as much status symbol as military requirement, were 8ft wide (2.5m) and had 19 towers, of which the highest is the Tour Magne, a 130ft (40m) octagonal tower. A fine gateway has survived with two arches for wheeled traffic and two smaller side arches for pedestrians.

CLASSICISM IN THE PROVINCES

One of the best-preserved and most elegant of all Roman temples is the Maison Carrée (literally square house), which was begun in 19BC and dedicated to Augustus and his *gens* (family) – the imperial cult flourished outside Italy even while Augustus was still alive. Influenced by contemporary buildings in Rome, especially the Temple of Mars Ultor and the Ara Pacis (Altar of Peace), this is a superb example of Augustan classicism transplanted to the provinces, indeed possibly even built by the same craftsmen, with mathematically perfect proportions: its podium, columns and entablature are related in the ratio of 2:5:2. Nîmes' amphitheatre, dating from the late 1st century AD, has survived well. Its creators were clearly inspired by the Colosseum (Flavian Amphitheatre) built shortly before in Rome, as well as by the older Theatre of Marcellus, for they used the now standard motifs: arches framed by pilasters on the ground tier and by engaged columns in the second.

The Romans had realized very early on that Nîmes' spring waters would be inadequate for the growing colony. An aqueduct built by Agrippa or in the later 1st century AD brought water from near Uzès 31 miles (50km) away. Mostly this flowed in a channel buried underground or carried on a low wall, at a gentle 1:3,000 slope, but where the line crosses

Above: The Tour Magne, Nîmes, an octagonal tower 130ft (40m) high above the walls built by Augustus.

Below: Perhaps the most striking section of all aqueducts, the Pont du Gard crosses the gorge of the Gardon River.

Right: The calm elegance of the Maison Carrée at Nîmes shows how successfully Augustan classical ideals were transplanted to southern Gaul.

the gorge of the river Gardon, the most celebrated Roman aqueduct bridge was constructed: the Pont du Gard. Built entirely of squared stone, without clamps or mortar but with some individual stones weighing six tons, it is 295yds (269m) long and carries the water over the valley at a height of 160ft (49m) above the stream. Its proportions are simple yet aesthetically satisfying: four units for the central arch, three for the lateral arches, one for the upper tier of arches and six for the height of the whole structure. Its many projecting bosses were left to support scaffolding when repairs were needed. Inside the city the water flowed into large circular settling tanks from which outlets carried the water throughout the city. At its peak *c*. AD100, Nîmes had a population of possibly 50,000, so a copious water supply was needed.

THE LAST CAPITAL OF ROMAN GAUL

On the banks of the Rhône, which became an important trade route, Arles (Arelate) rivalled Nîmes as a wealthy, increasingly sophisticated city under the Principate (30BC–AD285), but it was also important in the empire's last days. The first legionary colony was founded in 46BC by Caesar after his Gallic conquests. Arles' two outstanding earlier Roman monuments still extant are its amphitheatre and its theatre. The amphitheatre is probably contemporary with that of its rival in Nîmes (AD80–100). The same architect, Crispius Reburrus, is thought to have designed both in the same essentially classic style. The theatre nearby resembles that of Aosta just across the Alps in northern Italy, in that the outer extremes of its *scaenae frons* (stage backdrop) was straight, not curved and its central door stands in a porch at the back of a shallow curved *exedra*, suggesting transalpine links.

The vaulted remains of a double portico lie beneath what must have been the Forum. Arles' town walls, again initially more ornamental than functional, resembled those of some Italian cities. They were strengthened in the 4th century AD when Arles was becoming increasingly important. The site of the first imperially sanctioned Church Council in AD314, Arles became the military headquarters of the westernmost empire after Trier was abandoned in AD395. It was briefly the capital of the pretender Constantine from Britain in AD407–9. Much grander imperial-style baths survive from this period. Arles was one of the last Gallic cities to remain in Roman control as the Western empire finally disintegrated in the AD450s.

Below: Remains of seating substructure at the amphitheatre at Arles dating from the late 1st century AD.

ROMANO-BRITISH CITIES

Above: Unearthed in Southwark in 2002, this plaque is inscribed with the name Londinium and dedicated to the god Mars. It is the oldest evidence of London's Roman name.

Below: This vivid mosaic of a horse is typical of the colourful decorations of the Roman baths at Bath.

Pre-Roman Britain had no cities in the Graeco-Roman sense and few cities apparently survived the Roman withdrawal of *c.* AD407. However, most Roman cities – London, York, Bath, Leicester, Chester, Winchester – later revived to show that the Romans had chosen their sites with typical acumen. Colchester, rather than London, was the Romans' first urban settlement and also their first British colony.

Two very different places, London, the great commercial centre that became the province's capital and Bath, the pleasure town, exemplify the Romano-British city.

LONDON
At the lowest possible crossing point on the Thames, Londinium was the merchants' preferred site and an important port, whether or not there was a Celtic settlement there earlier (the name Lun is Celtic). During Boudicca's revolt in AD60, the Britons killed a reported 70,000 Romanized traders in London and St Albans so it must have already been very populous. Tacitus said that London was "Crowded with traders, a hive of commerce". By *c.* 100AD it had acquired a governor's palace, a military fort on the north-east of the city covering 11 acres (4.45 h), a bridge across the Thames – initially in wood, later rebuilt in stone – and the city had probably become the administrative capital.

London retained its role as capital of Britannia Superior after the province was subdivided *c.* AD200. When Constantius I recovered Britain for the empire in AD296 from the rebel Allectus, London's citizens were so overjoyed by Constantius' troops' timely arrival to rescue them from Allectus' pillaging Frankish mercenaries that they hailed him as "Restorer of the eternal light". In the 4th century AD London received the title *Augusta*, indicating continued high status. Written records are few, however, and subsequent rebuilding has destroyed most of the archaeological remains.

One building was exceptional: London's basilica, beneath modern Gracechurch Street. The largest in the empire north of the Alps, comparable to a cathedral in scale and grandeur, it must have overwhelmed the north side of London's forum. A modest basilica had been erected under Domitian (ruled AD81–96) but when Hadrian visited Britain in AD122 – and ordered his wall built across northern England – it was massively reconstructed. (A coin of his reign has been found in its mortar.) The new building's main hall was around 49ft (192m) long, 115ft wide (35m) and about 89ft (27m) high. With triple aisles, it probably had apses at either end and statues such as the famous bronze bust of the emperor found in the Thames, but none have survived *in situ*. Refurbished in the 3rd century, it was demolished for unknown reasons in the 4th century AD.

Right: The Roman baths at Bath, where hot water bubbles out of the earth. Although other areas of the baths are still roofed, this section is now open to the sky.

One of the few Roman buildings now in the open is the temple to Mithras near the Mansion House. Built *c.* 200AD, it was about 60ft (19m) long, divided into a nave and two aisles by a row of columns, with an apse at one end. Later, other cult images, including Minerva, Serapis and Dionysus were added. These are among the finest found in Britain and make the temple almost a pantheon.

London's walls probably date from the reign of Caracalla (AD211–17) because a coin of his reign has been found in one section. They enclose an area of about 330 acres (132ha). Today, with few changes, these walls, which are about 3 miles (4.8km) long, mark the line and base of the medieval city walls and the boundaries of the City of London, although the street plan has changed. In the 330s AD, a wall reusing masonry and bits of sculpture was built along the Thames for the first time. After Count Theodosius' restoration of authority in Britain in AD367, London's walls were strengthened with projecting polygonal bastions incorporating not just old building materials but even tombs. By then, the city's population must have fallen from its 2nd-century peak of 35–40,000 people.

A ROMAN SPA TOWN

The Celts had worshipped the goddess Sulis at the place where hot waters bubble out of the ground at 125°F (46.5°C). The Romans, identifying her with their Minerva, developed Aquae Sulis ("the waters of Sulis", Bath) as a religious sanctuary and fashionable spa. The spring was given a stone pool to create a head of water. This supplied what became a remarkable bath complex, part of which has recently been restored. At its centre was the Great Bath, a lead-lined swimming-pool with a wooden roof, later under a vault, with other smaller baths with heated water to the west. North of the spring a temple to Sulis/Minerva was built in a colonnaded courtyard. It had four Composite-style columns on a base about 29ft (9m) wide. The gap between the columns was twice their diameter of 2.6ft (0.8m), an unusual ratio that was also found in the Temple of Fortuna Virilis in Rome. The columns supported an entablature containing a relief of a Medusa-like male head in a shield carried by flanking winged Victories. There is a Celtic air to these carvings, in contrast to the distinctly Roman temple itself.

The baths were obviously successful and the complex continued to be extended into the 4th century AD, when the temple may have acquired flanking chapels. All the Roman ruins now lie about 20ft (6m) below street level.

Below: Bust of Hadrian, in whose reign (AD117–38) London gained an immense new basilica.

ROMAN ARTS AND SOCIETY

For centuries, Rome eclipsed all other cities. Its vast population, enriched by the taxes and tribute of the empire, sucked in raw materials, goods and human beings, many of them slaves, both from around the Mediterranean and from further afield. In order to supply Rome, traders explored new routes across the known world, bringing exotic goods back to the city. Fleets of huge ships set sail annually from Egypt, Spain and Africa with vital cargoes of grain and olive oil to feed the city, while agents roamed the empire's fringe to find the wild beasts whose violent deaths would amuse the Roman populace.

The urban life that developed in Rome after 150BC anticipated some aspects of modern city life, with its tall blocks of apartments, mass entertainments, high crime rates and problems with water supply and sewage disposal. However, Rome also offered opportunities that attracted free men to settle there, with its theatres, temples, libraries and lecture rooms and popular entertainments such as the arena or the baths.

Rome was a city of many gods and cults, which were often officially welcomed. Despite the numerous artworks adorning the city – it was joked Rome had more statues than living inhabitants – Roman culture was predominantly literate. A knowledge of both Greek and Latin was essential for any aspiring educated man. Women too could often read and, although barred from public life, played a greater role in Rome than in some comparable cultures. All these splendours were made possible by slavery, but slavery took many forms and lacked any hint of a colour bar. This allowed freed slaves to become citizens and to rise in what was, in some ways, a meritocratic civilization.

Left: Roman pragmatism, shown in the census-taking scribe, is depicted in Greek style on the Altar of Domitius Ahenobarbus, c.100BC.

CHAPTER XIX

LITERATURE

The story of Latin literature begins with two great comic playwrights, Plautus and Terence, and the epic poet Ennius *c.* 200BC. Latin as a language survived the end of the West Roman empire in AD476 and continued to be used up to the 1960s by the Catholic church, which in the early Middle Ages had had a near monopoly on literacy. Latin remained the language of much science and diplomacy until the late 17th century in western Europe – Isaac Newton, a Protestant Englishman, wrote most of his scientific works in Latin.

Considered of central importance in education into the mid-20th century, Latin is still admired for its clarity and brevity and is useful for medicine, natural science and law. Ignoring the fall of Rome, poets carried on writing in Latin through the Middle Ages, and the language enjoyed a classicizing revival during the Renaissance (1400–1600) in western countries.

The great pioneers of Latin literature, especially the writers of its golden age (*c.* 70BC–AD14), were conscious of their debt to Greek literature, with seven brilliant centuries of achievement behind it. Ultimately the Greeks inspired rather than crushed their Roman followers. Roman poets such as Virgil, Horace and Ovid and prose writers such as Cicero created a classical style comparable to that of Greek writers. For the Roman empire was an empire of letters as well as of arms; literacy being relatively widespread. Sadly much Latin literature has perished, hand-copied books and scrolls being few and fragile.

Left: View of Tivoli with Rome in the distance, painted by Gaspard Poussin in the 17th century. Tivoli was a favourite retreat of writers and emperors such as Horace and Hadrian.

THE FIRST ROMAN WRITERS

Above: A portrait of Menander, the Athenian comedian who so influenced Roman playwrights.

Below: The theatre at Pompeii, built in the 2nd century BC, long before Rome had a permanent theatre. Its original plan followed Greek models in having a narrow stage front, but it was later remodelled by the Romans.

Latin literature got off to a flying start with Plautus, a comic genius who knew how to entertain still relatively simple Romans with hilarious slapstick comedies. Terence wrote less rumbustiously and with less success for a possibly more select audience. Enough survives to give us a good idea of both their works, but only fragments remain of the work of their great contemporary, Rome's first epic poet, Ennius. All three adapted Greek originals for Roman audiences.

PLAUTUS c. 254–184BC

Born to poor parents in Umbria, Plautus worked as a stage carpenter among other jobs and only started to write plays in middle age. He then became Rome's most successful adapter of Greek "new comedy". (This was derived from the work of the Athenian Menander, who had lived 100 years before, and of other Greeks whose works have been lost.) Plautus reputedly wrote 130 plays, of which 21 survive. Written in verse, like Greek comedies, they usually involve characters with Greek names in Greek cities. However, Plautus was mainly concerned with getting laughs from his audience, so he sacrificed consistency or subtlety of character for jokes and puns, far easier to accomplish in Latin than Greek.

Plautus often replaced spoken dialogue with songs accompanied by pipe music or with *cantica*, duets or solo arias, producing what might be called Roman comic opera or musical comedy. The result was an earthier, cruder comedy than that of Menander, and proved immensely popular and influential. Shakespeare and Molière, the French 17th-century playwright, were indebted to him in their plays such as *The Comedy of Errors* or *L'Avare*, while comic opera, pantomime and television sitcoms today are Plautus' distant but direct heirs.

Performed at first in makeshift wooden theatres, his comedies were, like the Greeks', usually linked with religious festivals, but as time went by they came to be seen as entertainment. In a typical early play *Aulularia* (*The Pot of Gold*), Euclio, a poor

elderly Athenian, discovers a hoard of gold and becomes obsessively suspicious of his daughter's suitor, who he fears is after it. All ends happily, however, after various alarms. In *Captivi* (*The Prisoners*) an old Greek, Hegio, buys prisoners of war, hoping to exchange one for his captured son. Two such prisoners, master and slave, secretly swap identities. The master is freed to negotiate the return of Hegio's son and the slave is finally revealed as Hegio's other son, kidnapped in childhood. In one of Plautus' most famous plays, *Bacchides* (*The Bacchis Sisters*), a dishonest slave called Chrysalus (Goldfinger) dominates the action, scheming to defraud his master, as he proudly tells the audience. Confusion is increased by two prostitutes who are both called Bacchis. Cunning slaves, desperate young lovers and miserly, jealous old men are among Plautus' stock characters.

TERENCE *c.* 195–159BC

Born in North Africa and brought to Rome as a slave, Terence (Publius Terentius Afer) gained his education, his freedom and his entrée to aristocratic circles through his talents and good looks. Closer to the Greek model than Plautus', Terence's plays are concerned with love affairs and complications arising from ignorance or misunderstandings. Only one play, *Eunuchus* (*The Eunuch*) enjoyed popular success, because he added broad comedy to it. Normally, Terence retained the original Greek irony, translating Attic (Athenian) Greek into elegant, pure Latin that lacked Plautus' verbal exuberance. The resulting plays, six of which survive, found little favour with still unsophisticated Roman audiences but became part of the classical canon. Terence bitterly attacked the gladiators, tight-rope walkers and others who proved more popular than his plays but was himself criticized by literary men for cannibalizing different Greek plays to make his own. Although he died young during a visit to Greece, his influence on later European comedy of manners was huge.

ENNIUS 239–169BC

Called the father of Latin poetry, Ennius was actually born to a Greek family in Calabria. (Southern Italy was then known as Magna Graecia, greater Greece, being deeply Hellenized.) After serving with the Roman army in Sardinia, Ennius came to Rome with Cato the Elder *c.* 204BC and ultimately gained Roman citizenship.

Ennius began writing epic poetry late in life, dying impoverished but confident of posthumous fame, as he claimed to be a reincarnation of Homer, the great Greek poet. Unfortunately, only fragments of his work survive, but they reveal his versatility, for he wrote tragedies, comedies, satires and other works. His greatest work was his *Annals*, a poetic history of Rome from Aeneas' flight from Troy to his own day. The work extended to 20,000 lines, written in the smooth-flowing Homeric hexameter (a verse line of six metrical feet) he introduced from Greek.

Ennius' few surviving lines, which are quoted by later writers such as Virgil, mingle high Greek heroism with Roman alliteration and love of puns. Although later sometimes mocked for clumsiness, Ennius was the first to show that Latin poetry could achieve epic greatness by adopting Greek classical forms.

Above: Scene from a comedy by Plautus, the first and always the most popular Roman playwright. His fame spread around the empire, as this 3rd century AD mosaic from Sousse in Africa shows.

Below: A portrait of Ennius, the first Roman epic poet who came to see himself as a reincarnation of Homer. Ennius also wrote tragedies and comedies for the stage.

AUGUSTUS' POETS LAUREATE

Above: Scene from the Prima Porta statue showing Augustus' diplomatic victory in 19BC when Parthia returned Roman legionary standards, a victory which Horace duly praised as effective poet laureate.

Below: A mosaic shows the poet Virgil writing The Aeneid *between the muses* Clio (history) *and* Melpomene (tragedy). *Virgil's epic became popular across the empire.*

Although neither Virgil nor Horace sought the role, both became, in effect, poets laureate for Augustus. Although very different – Virgil introspective, moody, Horace urbane, if keenly aware of life's sorrows and joys – both wrote supremely classical verse.

VIRGIL 70–19BC

Perhaps the greatest of all Roman poets, Virgil (Publius Vergilius Maro) was born near Mantua, in Cisalpine Gaul, which was by then almost fully Roman. His parents were only modest farmers, but Virgi was well educated and became closely involved in imperial affairs. He lived through civil wars that wrecked the Republic – there were wars in 16 of the 51 years of his life – and lost his farm in the chaos following the Battle of Philippi.

However, it was returned to him after an appeal to Octavian and he died rich, leaving 10 million sesterces. Such experiences deepened the longing for peace which permeates his poetry.

Virgil's first work, *The Eclogues*, written before 37BC, is set in an idealized Arcadia, influenced by Theocritus (310–250BC). It depicts shepherds' lives and loves but also refers to recent troubles, such as farmers' arbitrary evictions. *Eclogue IV* contains a passage in which the Sybil, Rome's oracle, foretells the birth of a divine child who will restore the golden age. *Jam redit et virgo, redeunt Saturnia regna…*("Now the Virgin returns, the reign of Saturn returns …"). Actually praising the Julian family, this was interpreted by Christians as a prediction of the birth of Christ.

Virgil was now given substantial properties by Maecenas, who acted as patron for many poets under Augustus. His next work, *The Georgics*, appeared in 29BC. Its praise of Italian farm life – echoing Hesiod's *Work and Days* of *c.* 700BC – marvellously evokes the beauties of the Italian landscape but is of limited use as a farming manual. Pressed to write an epic about the emperor, Virgil instead responded with *The Aeneid*.

This work relates the legendary adventures of Aeneas, the Trojan prince who fled burning Troy to found Lavinium, Rome's legendary precursor. As the Julians claimed descent from Aeneas, this was subtle flattery. Aeneas is no bloodthirsty hero but an upright man who hates – yet excels at – fighting. His betrayal of Dido, queen of Carthage, appears shabby but he is driven by his destiny to abandon her. (Dido despairingly kills herself.) Virgil, who died before he completed his epic, wanted it destroyed, but after Augustus published it, it became accepted as Virgil's masterpiece, vital to Rome's self-image.

While rivalling Homer's *Iliad* in scope and grandeur, the *Aeneid* takes no delight in war. Instead it stresses Rome's responsibilities as ruler. *Hae tibi erunt artes, pacisque imponere morem/ Parcere subjectis et debellare superbos* ("These shall be your skills: to impose peace, spare the conquered and overthrow the mighty").

The epic starts majestically:
*Arma virumque cano, Trojae qui primus
   abo oris*
"Arms and the man I sing, who, forced
   by fate
And haughty Juno's unrelenting hate
Expelled and exiled, left the shore.
Long labours both by sea and land
   he bore."

(translated by John Dryden)

HORACE 65–8BC

The son of a freedman (ex-slave) who had prospered enough to pay for his education in Athens, Horace (Quintus Horatius Flaccus) fought on the wrong Republican side at the Battle of Philippi in 42BC. Returning unhurt but penniless to Italy, he was introduced to Maecenas' circle by Virgil *c.* 37BC, later becoming a sincere supporter of the Augustan settlement. Maecenas gave him a small farm in the Sabine Hills at Tivoli near Rome. There Horace built a villa which he celebrated in his poems, but he was also a sociable man of the world.

Horace's *Satires* (*c.* 35BC) contain little satire in today's sense but praise Maecenas, a friend as well as patron, and include a tribute to his father, in lively, colloquial Latin. Celebrating peace after Actium (31BC), Horace produced the *Epodes* (lyric poems). Inspired by Archilochus (*c.* 640BC), they deal mostly with love and politics but also praise rural life: *Beatus ille, qui procul negotiis…* ("Happy the man who far from business, ploughs again his ancestral lands").

The poor reception for his first book of *Odes* in 23BC upset him, but they contain his finest poetry. They celebrate the return of spring: *Diffugere nives: redeunt jam gramina campis/Arboribusque comae…*

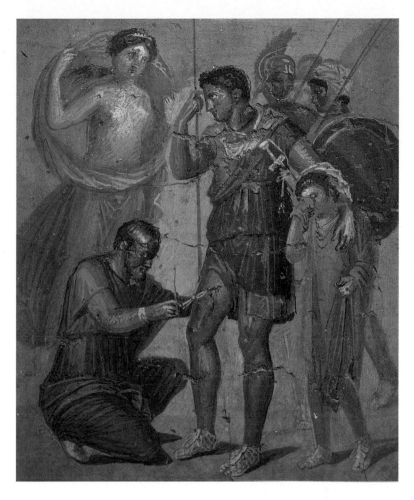

("The snows have fled. The grass returns already to the meadows, and leaves to the trees"); the joys of drinking: *Nunc est bibendum* ("Now's the time to drink!") and the passing of youth: *Ehue fugace, Postume, Postume/Labuntur anni, nec pietas moram…*("Alas, Postumus, Postumus, the years slide swiftly away and piety will not fend off wrinkles, old age or death…"). He ends triumphantly, proclaiming artistic immortality: *Exegi monumentum aere perennius* ("I have created a work longer-lasting than bronze…").

Horace had no successor as poet laureate, but some poems speak as freshly today as ever: *Dum loquimur, fugeret invida/Aetas: carpe diem, quam minimum credula postero.* ("While we talk, hateful time runs on. Seize the fruits of today, never rely on the future.")

Above: A mural from Pompeii showing a wounded Aeneas being tended by a doctor.

Below: Virgil reading The Aeneid *to Augustus, as painted by Ingres, c. 1812.*

CATULLUS AND THE ELEGIAC POETS

Above: The Venus de Milo, one of the most famous portrayals of the goddess of love in antiquity. Venus was a deity of overwhelming importance to the elegiac poets, whose poems deal primarily with affairs of the heart and of lust.

Below: Catullus, the supreme Latin poet of love, fancifully depicted reading a poem, in a painting by Stepan Bakalovich in 1885. In reality, Catullus was passionate but hardly romantic like this.

The last decades of the Republic and first years of the Empire (Principate) saw huge political and social changes in Roman life that inspired the *Neoterici* (New Poets) to experiment radically. Greek models gave Catullus, then Propertius and Tibullus, the means by which to create new, more direct and moving forms of Latin poetry. (The description of these poets' work as Elegiac refers to their hexameter/pentameter metre. It does not mean that they wrote funereally!)

CATULLUS 84–54BC

Born at Verona, Catullus (Gaius Valerius Catullus) was a leader of the *Neoterici*, or New Poets. His father was rich enough to entertain Julius Caesar but Catullus had no interest in politics. He owned a villa on Lake Garda, whose beauties he praised, but spent most of his short life in Rome and most of his energies on literature and love. In Rome he fell in love with Clodia, called Lesbia in his poems, who was probably the sister of Clodius Pulcher – Cicero's enemy – and Catullus'

social superior. Lesbia/Clodia became his obsession, adored then reviled in 25 brilliant, brief poems. For poetic models Catullus looked back to polished Alexandrians such as Callimachus (*c.* 320–240BC) and to Sappho (*c.* 600BC), perhaps the greatest woman poet, who wrote on love's bitter-sweet joys and torments. Catullus' poetry, mingling passion, urbanity and awareness of life's transience, raised colloquial Latin to new heights.

Amemus mea Lesbia atque vivemus /Rumoresque senum severiorum. "Let us live and love my Lesbia, and ignore all old men's censorious talk", begins one poem addressed to her, which continues, "We, when our brief day is done, must sleep in everlasting night". He goes on to urge her in vivid, demotic Latin, *Da mi basia mille, deinde centum /Dein mille altera, dein secunda centum.* "Give me a thousand kisses, then a hundred, then another thousand and a second hundred".

Unlike most Greek poets, Catullus was writing about an individual woman at a time when aristocratic women in Rome were enjoying novel freedom and could appreciate – or reject – such admiration. Clodia seems to have rejected him, so Catullus later wrote angrily, *Odi et amo*, "I hate and I love" and described Lesbia "Giving herself to the sons of Remus", (becoming a common prostitute).

Catullus could also write in other ways. He lyrically mocked Lesbia's dead sparrow, for example: *Lugete, o Veneres Cupidenesque…* "Mourn, you Venuses and Cupids, and all men of true feeling. My lady's sparrow is dead". He also savagely lampooned his contemporaries.

Although what won Catullus contemporary renown were long mythological poems such as *Peleus and Thetis*, he was indisputably one the world's greatest lyric love poets.

PROPERTIUS *c.* 54–16BC

Son of an equestrian (knight) of Perugia, Propertius (Sextus Propertius) probably had a legal training in Rome as a young man. In Rome he became friends with Virgil and Ovid and then with Maecenas, who gave him a house on the fashionable Equiline Hill. Propertius, however, had little interest in political life and refused Maecenas' request to write an epic about Augustus. Instead, his poems concentrate on his love life, especially his relationship with Cynthia.

Cynthia seems to have been either a high-class courtesan or a widow of independent mind and wealth. She used both to torment Propertius – or so his poems imply, depicting him in a grovelling role that was novelly demeaning for a Roman knight. His first book of poems was dedicated to, and about, Cynthia. *Non ego nunc tristes vereor mea Cynthia, Manes/Nec moro extremo debita fata rogo* ... "I don't fear death's sad kingdom, Cynthia, nor resent being doomed to the funeral pyre at the last, as I have a fear that is harder than death itself – that I may no longer be loved by you when I die". Propertius' affair with Cynthia started in *c.* 30BC and lasted about five years, during which time his passion cooled as Cynthia was often unfaithful to him. For solace from love's torment Propertius turned not to nature – he was very metropolitan – but to art. He talked knowledgeably about classical Greek painters such as Apelles and some of his poems apparently describe scenes from extant wall-paintings.

TIBULLUS *c.* 50–19BC

Handsome and wealthy, the son of an equestrian, Tibullus (Albius Tibullus) differed from Propertius in his love for the countryside. His first poems describe an idyllic existence far from city cares. However, Tibullus resembled Propertius in that he too was in thrall to a mistress. Delia – another pseudonym – had little time for such bucolic joys and clearly had the upper hand in their relationship. Her successor in Tibullus' affection was the even more demanding and ominously named Nemesis. Tibullus also fell in love with a boy, Marathus, who spurned him but used him to help pursue a girl. Tibullus dwells masochistically on his suffering in this love triangle. It is uncertain how much of the three extant books in Tibullus' name is really his own poetry.

MAECENAS THE PATRON

The greatest literary patron of the Roman empire under Augustus, Maecenas claimed descent from Etruscan kings. One of the young Octavian's key ministers, he was renowned for discovering promising poets. Virgil and Horace were protégés who repaid his support with great poetry praising the new regime. Maecenas himself reputedly had luxurious, even decadent tastes, as surviving fragments of his own poetry suggest, affronting Augustus' official restoration of Roman *virtus*. Maecenas lost official favour well before his death in 8BC, but his name lives on as the archetypal patron.

Above: The Surrender of Briseis, *from the House of the Tragic Poet at Pompeii. Briseis was a slave girl in* The Iliad *who Achilles, bitterly jealous, had to hand over to Agamemnon. Catullus wrote on the subject with typical bitter-sweet passion.*

Below: A view of Lake Garda in northern Italy, Catullus' birthplace, whose beauties he was the first to praise.

OVID AND LATER SILVER AGE POETS

Above: An amber figurine of Cupid and Psyche from the 1st century AD. Ovid's poetry delighted in such myths.

Below: Ovid's grandest and most celebrated work, the Metamorphoses, *had a huge impact on later artists and writers. This grand depiction of the myth of Cupid and Psyche was painted by the Renaissance artist Raphael (or his studio) in 1518–19.*

With Ovid, Latin poetry finally attained an elegance, lyricism and wit to rival that of any Greek. His unfading popularity down the ages is partly due to these characteristics, partly to his fantastical invention and partly to his sophisticated eroticism – the last finally led to banishment by Augustus. After Ovid, there was a hiatus in Latin poetry, then two poets of the "silver age" emerged, who attempted with mixed success to emulate the poets of the golden age.

OVID 43BC–*c.* AD18

Born to an equestrian Italian family, Ovid (Publius Ovidius Naso) finished his education with the customary grand tour of Greece before settling in Rome. His first book of poems was the very successful *Amores* (*Loves*). He began writing the first book of the first edition *c.* 25BC, publishing the other four books over the next decade. (The surviving edition dates from *c.* 3BC.)

In his early books Ovid parodied the elegiac poets' love sickness but soon Ovid himself emerged as a fervent if light-hearted lover. Addressed to Corinna – who, unlike the lovers of earlier poets, was probably not an actual mistress, but a composite figure – the *Amores* depict amorous adventures among the more openly frivolous Roman upper classes. In the *Amores*, as in subsequent works, Ovid used myths not for deep psychological resonance but decoratively, to describe a woman's legs for example. If Horace tended to treat love as a light-hearted game from which the poet remains wisely detached, Ovid treated love as the only game worth playing. The title of Ovid's *Ars Amatoria* (*The Art of Love*) mimics Horace's *Ars Poetica*.

Ovid's longest and most lastingly famous work was the *Metamorphoses*, 15 books of mythology which are epic in scale and by turn bewitching, moving, erotic or

witty. At the other end of the scale from Virgil's solemn myth-making, its underlying theme – that everything changes form – included serious comments among its erotica, such as *Video meliora, proboque;/Detrioria sequor* ("I see the better way and approve it, but follow the worse") and *Tempus edax rerum* ("Time, the devourer of all things").

OVID'S EXILE AND DEATH

While many Romans laughed with Ovid, one important Roman was not amused: the ageing emperor. Always annoyed by upper-class promiscuity, Augustus particularly disliked his grand-daughter Julia's behaviour, exiling her for immorality suddenly in AD8. Ovid, caught up in the scandal, was exiled to Tomis on the Black Sea, a cold, unciv-ilized, remote area, now in Bulgaria, then Rome's Siberia. Augustus and his successor Tiberius stonily ignored the poet's piteous pleas to be allowed to return, and Ovid died in exile among a people he found barbarous.

In his last decade Ovid wrote *Tristia* (*Melancholia*) and *Epistulae ex Ponto* (*Black Sea Letters*). The lonely tedium of exile is conveyed by lines such as *Gutta cavat lapidem, consumitur anulus usu* ("Dripping water hollows out a stone, a ring is worn away by use"). However, his fame suffered no eclipse. He was revered throughout the Middle Ages and a bowdlerized version of his works called *Ovid Moralisé* (*Ovid the Moralist*) was circulated widely. The first great poet in English, Geoffrey Chaucer (1340–1400) wrote of "Venus' clerk, Ovid, that hath sown wonder-wide the great god of Love's name". Ovid's fame continued to grow during the Renaissance and after, with many translations or adaptations especially of the *Metamorphoses*.

SILVER AGE POETS

After Ovid's death no significant poet emerged for 40 years until Lucan (Marcus Annaeus Lucan; AD39–65). Born in Spain, a nephew of the philosopher Seneca, Lucan was studying Stoic philosophy in Athens when Nero called him to Rome in AD60. For a short while he enjoyed imperial favour, being made a *quaestor* (magistrate), before he became involved in the Piso conspiracy of aristocrats with Republican sentiments against the despotic emperor. It cost him his life.

Lucan's great work was his uncom-pleted epic *Pharsalia*, which deals with Rome's civil wars of the 1st century BC. He begins with an address to his fellow citizens, not the usual invocation of the Muse: *Quis furor, o cives, quae tanta licentia ferri?* ("What was this madness, citizens, this great orgy of slaughter?"). The epic lacks a hero – Julius Caesar is portrayed as villainous and his rival Pompey is not wholly admirable either. Instead it focuses on the internecine bloodshed that wrecked the Republic. Lucan's poem abounds in epigrams, paradoxes and biting wit, with over 100 grand speeches. However, it can be argued that his characters are over-simplifed, his style is sometimes monotonous and that at times Lucan's work degenerates into sentimentality.

Statius (Publius Papinius Statius; AD45–96) was an epic poet who also felt driven to emulate Virgil. His chief work, his *Thebaid*, took him a decade to write. Published in AD92, it dealt with the same Greek legends about Oedipus' curse on Thebes and its traumatic conse-quences that the Athenian dramatist Aeschylus had written about 500 years before. Statius' style is too highly polished and suggests that, like Lucan, he had talent rather than genius. Such legendary heroics were increasingly seen as dated anyway.

Below: Apollo and Daphne, sculpted by Bernini in 1622. The beautiful myth of the transformation of Daphne into a myrtle was wittily retold by Ovid in his Metamorphoses.

GREAT PROSE WRITERS

Above: Marcus Tullius Cicero, the great orator, lawyer, statesman and man of letters. Although seldom an original thinker, Cicero translated major works of Greek philosophy into Latin, summarizing their arguments brilliantly. His superbly readable Letters *inspired generations with their humane and liberal outlook.*

Rome was a nation of orators schooled in the art of high rhetoric. To match this, Roman writers created prose of unsurpassed power, clarity, pithiness and at times majesty. While there were cogent earlier writers such as Cato the Elder (234–149BC), only in the 1st century BC did Latin prose began to achieve its full, formal splendours, as befitted the language of the new rulers of the world.

CICERO 106–43BC

Marcus Tullius Cicero, statesman and lawyer, wrote on many subjects from astronomy to art and education and in so doing almost invented philosophy in Latin. Caesar, Cicero's political opponent and not modest about his own feats, said that Cicero's was "A greater achievement, expanding the boundaries of Rome's culture, than those of its empire".

Much of Cicero's work, including 900 letters, has survived. This is unusual but hardly accidental: it survived because it was admired and copied. To the critic Quintilian (AD30–c. 100) Cicero was "The name not of a man but of eloquence itself". Cicero's philosophy also deeply affected Augustine, the Christian writer.

Cicero made some of the most brilliant political and legal speeches in Roman history, such as that against Verres, the corrupt ex-governor of Sicily in 70BC, which drove Verres into exile. However, his career as a writer really flowered later during his enforced absence from politics when Caesar dominated Rome (49–44BC). Starting with two minor works of political philosophy *De republica* and *De legibus* (*On the State* and *On the Laws*), he went on to produce *The Paradoxes of*

Right: Bust of Seneca, Roman statesman, playwright and philosopher. He was Nero's tutor and adviser before being forced to kill himself.

the Stoics, a rhetorical masterpiece in which he argued both sides of a debate (he had studied in Athens under the Sceptics). In 45BC Cicero outlined a plan to "give my fellow citizens a guide to the noblest form of learning" (philosophy). He wrote twelve books over the next two years most – following Plato – in the form of dialogues covering the main schools of ancient philosophy. *De finibus* (*Concerning Ends*) is typical of his brilliant summary of earlier Greek thinkers, notably the Stoics, and is expressed eloquently and clearly in Latin.

Cicero seldom propounded fixed philosophical viewpoints, nor did he claim to be original in his thinking. Instead, however, he established the rendering of basic Greek philosophical terms into Latin – terms such as *qualitas, moralis, beatitudo* for "quality, moral, happiness" – that remain in use today.

In *Scipio's Dream*, Cicero also outlined current geocentric views on the nature of the universe. His letters reveal more about urbane, cultured upper-class Roman life in the late Republic than any others and are profoundly admired even today for their style and humanity.

SENECA 4BC–AD65

A Stoic philosopher, tutor and then minister to the young Nero, a successful if at times unscrupulous businessman, Seneca (Lucius Annaeus Seneca) was also a noted essayist and Rome's greatest tragic playwright.

Seneca's nine plays all deal with Greek legends and have titles such as *Oedipus, Hercules* and *Medea.* They are "closet tragedies", intended to be read aloud at small, aristocratic gatherings rather than performed in large Roman theatres.

Although Seneca's dramas hardly bear comparison with their prototypes in classical Athens, they proved very influential later, inspiring Shakespeare and other Renaissance dramatists. His *Epistulae Morales* (*Moral Letters*), 124 brief sermons in letter form dealing with subjects from vegetarianism to the humane treatment of slaves, were equally influential. He also wrote longer essays such as *De clementia* (*On Mercy*).

Seneca was eventually forced to kill himself by Nero after he had been implicated in the Piso conspiracy to assassinate the emperor.

PLINY THE ELDER AD23–79

Pliny (Gaius Plinius Secundus) was a successful Roman administrator of the equestrian order as well as a writer of a boundless, indeed reckless, curiosity that finally killed him. Although he also wrote a history of the German wars, the work which has survived is his *Natural History.* This consists of 37 volumes that represent an encyclopaedia of Graeco-Roman knowledge of the universe, humanity, animals, trees, birds and plants, while also covering in detail medicine and the arts. Edward Gibbon later described it as "An immense register of the discoveries, the arts and the errors of mankind", for Pliny sometimes seems credulous to modern eyes. As commander of the fleet at Misenum near Naples during Vesuvius' eruption in AD79, he tried without success to investigate it and to organize relief efforts but was probably asphyxiated on shore by volcanic gases.

PLINY THE YOUNGER AD61–c. 112

The studious nephew of the elder Pliny who wisely stayed behind at Misenum while his uncle sailed off with the fleet, Pliny the Younger (Gaius Plinius Caecilius Secundus) was tutored by Quintilian.

Pliny had a successful senatorial career, and he finally became a consul under Trajan in AD100. He thanked the emperor for this in his *Panegyricus*, which reveals a talent for fulsome flattery. Far livelier are his letters, many of them written for publication, which give a vivid picture of their age from a cultured noble's viewpoint. His letters to Trajan, written when he was the conscientious if somewhat flustered governor of Bithynia (in north Asia Minor) are also revealing. They cover topics from local fire brigades to the proper way to treat alarming new sects such as the Christians. Pliny the Younger probably died in office.

Above: Using mud to cure skin complaints, as recommended by Pliny the Elder, in a book of 1481.

Below: The oldest extant manuscript of Pliny the Younger's Letters, *dating from the early 6th century AD.*

NOVELISTS AND SATIRISTS

Right: The dreamlike, lyrical quality of Apuleius' The Golden Ass *is echoed in this mosaic from Asia Minor of the 3rd century AD. It illustrates the myth of Cupid and Psyche, which forms the core of the book.*

Below: Martial had the whole Flavian dynasty as his patrons, including an unlikely patron in the dour and despotic emperor Domitian (below), chiefly because he only attacked men who had prospered under Nero.

After the heroic age of Roman literature, writers turned increasingly to satire in prose or verse – Juvenal's biting wit effectively created satire in its modern sense – or to novels that were satirical, romantic or both. However, prose fiction was considered a very low literary form.

PETRONIUS (d. AD66)

One of Latin literature's most colourful figures, Petronius (Gaius Petronius Arbiter) was a Roman aristocrat about whom little is known. According to Tacitus, writing decades later, "His days were passed in sleep, his nights in the business and pleasures of life. The reputation that most men win through energy he gained through sloth. Yet as governor of Bithynia and later as consul, he showed himself highly competent". One of Nero's courtiers, Petronius was implicated in the Piso conspiracy and committed suicide – but not before he had recorded all Nero's vices and sent off the list and smashed a precious vase he knew the emperor wanted. His one surviving book – unmentioned by the historian – is his *Satyricon*, a sprawling picaresque novel about some

insatiably bisexual adventurers, devoid of morals if not of intelligence, who wander around the Greek cities of southern Italy. They all have Greek names – Encolpion the cultured but depraved narrator, his faithless boyfriend Giton, Ascyltos his rival – following Roman theatrical custom. The most remarkable figure is that of Trimalchio, the multimillionaire freedman (ex-slave) whose gross vulgarity dominates many passages. Petronius was better at catching "street Latin", everyday language, than any writer since Plautus. He records but does not judge – not even the clause of Trimalchio's will which stipulates that all his legatees eat a bit of his corpse before they can inherit. The novel, of which only Books XV and XVI survive, was long considered obscene.

APULEIUS (b. *c.* AD127)

Born in North Africa and educated at Carthage and Athens, Apuleius (Lucius Apuleius) lectured and travelled extensively. He also wrote the only Latin novel to survive complete, *The Golden Ass*. This relates in eleven books the amorous and comic incidents which lead Lucius, a sorcerer's apprentice, to be transformed into a donkey. The rest of the work recounts his varied adventures and misadventures in this form until his final restoration to human shape by the goddess Isis. The longest of these episodes, which takes up about a fifth of the book, is the tale of Cupid (Greek Eros) and Psyche. Parts of this tale, and even more the closing section's vision of Isis, are described with a true religious intensity which is unusually revealing of the depth of pagan devotion to the gods, especially in such an essentially light-hearted work. Although Apuleius may have derived his tale from the Greek poet Lucian's *Metamorphoses*, he wrote a strange, poetic, beautiful and original form of Latin.

MARTIAL (AD40–c. 104)

Probably the greatest master of the epigram – a short, sometimes very short, poem with a sting in its tail – Martial (Marcus Valerius Martialis) was born in Spain but spent most of his adult life in Rome. Some 1,500 of his poems survive. Probably helped by his compatriot Seneca at first, he came to know people close to the emperor Domitian, in whose reign (AD81–96) he enjoyed his greatest success. Martial can be human, even genial when writing about children or pets, although at other times his work is blatantly pornographic. An early poem, *Liber Spectaculorum* of AD81, celebrated the opening of the Colosseum but he got into his stride with the *Xenia* and *Aphoreta*, which were written between the mid-80s AD and AD97, when he retired to Spain. Martial's dismissive two-liner "On a Critic" is typically pithy: *Versiculos in me narratur scribere Cinna/Non scribit, cuius carmina nemo legit.* ("Cinna is said to write versicles against me. A man whose poems nobody reads cannot be called a writer.")

JUVENAL (c. AD60–c. 130)

The greatest Roman satirist and the first poet to devote himself to satire in our sense, Juvenal (Decimus Junius Juvenalis) came from a well-off family and held local

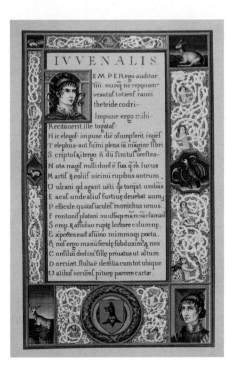

Left: Manuscript from the 15th century with a page of Juvenal's satires. The first great poet who can be considered wholly satirical, Juvenal's devastating honesty proved inspirational to later Western satirists.

magistracies. He then fell foul of the emperor Domitian and may have been banished to Egypt before returning to a life of embittered poverty in Rome. His situation improved later under Hadrian and he ended his life in modest comfort, with a small country estate as well as his Roman residence.

Juvenal's early experiences helped shape the jaundiced view he gives of Roman life in which *probitas laudatur et alget* ("Honesty is praised and starves"). His 16 *Satires* were published in 5 books between AD110 and 130. In the first he declared his *saeva indignatio* (fierce indignation) at Roman corruption and vulgarity, but his prudent intention was to attack mainly those who had flourished under Domitian. He lambasted the aristocracy's bad habits – venality, parsimony, sexual voracity – in his first book. *Satire VI* contains a 700-line-long diatribe against women. Markedly misogynistic, it attacks female vanity and virtue. Later satires attack life in the megalopolis more generally: *duas tantum res anxius optat/panem et circuses* ("The populace longs for just two things: bread and circus games").

Below: Juvenal savaged women for wearing too much jewellery in a way that could be markedly misogynistic, so setting an unfortunate example for some later satirists. This mummy portrait of a woman is from Egypt, c. AD120.

LATE ROMAN WRITERS

The decline of the empire did not see the end of Latin literature, which continued even after Rome's final political collapse in AD476.

AUSONIUS (*c.* AD310–95)

A native of Bordeaux, at whose university he both studied and lectured, Ausonius (Decimus Magnus Ausonius) was a prolific if uneven poet. A summons to the imperial court at Trier to be tutor to the young emperor Gratian led to his meteoric rise: he became governor of Gaul, then Africa and in AD379 consul. After Gratian's murder in AD383, he returned to his native Bordeaux. Letters to his friend St Paulinus of Nola reveal the widening gap between pagans and Christians – Ausonius was basically a pagan. Ausonius' most famous poem, which is lyrical if unoriginal, sings the praise of the beauties of the Moselle valley that he had seen around Trier.

PERVIGILIUM VENERIS (*c.* AD350)

Both the author and date of this beautiful poem are unknown. The title means "Venus' Vigil" and the poem celebrates in 93 haunting, romantic lines the eve of the spring festival of Venus in rural Sicily; the upsurge of new life in flowers, animals and humanity. It has as its refrain *Cras amet quis nunquam amavit…*("Tomorrow let them love who have never loved; and let those who have loved love tomorrow. Spring is new, spring full of song, the springtime of the world is reborn.") Its language forms a link between classical and medieval Latin, while its content makes it a swansong of paganism.

ST AUGUSTINE (AD354–430)

One of the great Church fathers, whose writings are fundamental to both Protestantism and Catholicism, Augustine is also an important figure in both literature and philosophy.

Born in Tagaste, North Africa, his mother was a devout Christian but his father only a reluctant convert. The young Augustine, tormented by sexual urges yet drawn to philosophy, joined the Manicheans, who believed the whole physical world was ruled by the devil. Augustine began teaching in Carthage in AD371 and had a 12-year-long relationship with a woman who bore his son. He only returned to Christianity in AD385 after his move to Rome and a mystical experience in a garden when he heard the voice of God. Intellectually he was influenced both by the teachings of Ambrose, Archbishop of Milan, and by Plotinus, the Neoplatonist whose pagan mysticism Augustine fused with Christianity.

Augustine now began writing the books that make him among the most eloquent of theologians: *Against the Academics, On the Greatness of the Soul, On Free Will* and *Against Faustus the Manichean*. In AD396

Above: The Moselle, whose vineyards and slopes Ausonius praised in his longest and most famous poem, Mosella.

Below: St Augustine grew up in the still-thriving province of Africa, whose splendid town life is revealed by these extensive 3rd-century mosaics from Carthage.

Right: The Wheel of Fortune shown in this 15th-century manuscript was one of Boethius' main ideas, inspired by life and death.

he became bishop of Hippo, an African city. He preached to the local people in lively demotic Latin, while writing a more formal classical Latin for his literary peers. His *Confessions*, his literary masterpiece of *c.* AD400, shows an honest, even agonized self-scrutiny unmatched until the 18th century. "Oh Lord make me chaste but not yet!" is its most famous line.

Augustine aggressively propounded orthodox Catholic beliefs against heretics such as the Donatists – who believed that only sinless priests should serve Mass – and Pelagius, a Romano-Briton who believed in human perfectibility. In *On Grace and Free Will*, he argued that every human was damned to hell unless God through his grace saved us from our sins. This gloomy doctrine suggested damnation for the majority.

Another pivotal work was *The City of God*. This was written after the Visigoths sacked Rome in AD410 to rebut pagan charges that Rome's desertion of its old gods was to blame. Augustine essentially held that the kingdom of God was not of this world, although we ourselves have to live in it. Such beliefs were needed, for Augustine died as the Vandals – barbarians who deserved their infamy – besieged the city of Hippo.

NAMATIANUS (fl. AD404–16)

One of the last important non-Christian Roman poets, Namatianus (Claudius Rutilius Namatianus) came from Toulouse. Despite his paganism, Namatianus became Prefect of Rome under the (Christian) emperor Honorius.

Although he left Rome in AD416 soon after its sack by the Visigoths, Namatianus' parting poem expresses undimmed confidence in Rome's eternal glory. *Exaudi, regina tui pulcherrima mundi/Inter sidereos Roma recepta polos…* ("Listen, most beautiful queen of the world you have made your own. O Rome received into the starry heavens,/Listen, O mother of gods and men.") There were to be no further such pagan panegyrics of the Eternal City.

BOETHIUS (*c.* AD480–526)

Although he was a Christian, Boethius (Amicus Manlius Severinus Boethius) never mentioned Christianity in his work. He came from an old aristocratic family, became consul in AD510 and then chief minister to Theodoric, king of the Ostrogoths, who was ruling Italy remarkably well. Boethius was implicated, probably unjustly, in a conspiracy against the king and sentenced to death. While in prison awaiting execution, he wrote *The Consolation of Philosophy* in a mixture of verse and prose. In this work, the most popular philosophical book in Western Europe for 1,000 years, Boethius drew on Platonist, Neoplatonist and Stoic ideas. He also provided much general intellectual knowledge that proved invaluable in the Middle Ages in a clear, classical Latin. He was the last such writer.

Below: This ancient Roman statue and the Pervigilium Veneris are both sensually beautiful invocations to Venus.

LITERATURE AND LITERACY

Above: A 1st-century AD portrait from Pompeii shows the young Roman magistrate Terentius Nero and his wife. The image of the young couple pensively clutching writing materials reveals that women as well as men could read and write.

Below: Typical writing materials – a wooden tablet with three panels, a bronze inkwell and a stylus – from the 1st century AD. Papyrus, then the best writing material, was too expensive for most people for everyday use.

Literacy was relatively widespread in the cities of the Roman empire, at least in the sense of being able to read and write the odd inscription, if not to read major pieces of literature. Despite the lack of a formal education system, especially beyond the primary level, for all but the children of a small elite – even they relied heavily on private tutors – it seems that many people in towns and cities were at least semi-literate, as the abundant graffiti and marks on potsherds (pottery fragments) or walls testify. These ordinary citizens were, however, only a minority of the empire's inhabitants. At least 80 per cent of the population were peasants.

A certain degree of literacy was essential for advancement in public life and very useful elsewhere, not just in the households of great nobles or in the imperial bureaucracy that very gradually grew out of the emperor's own household.

In the absence of printing technology, literate slaves and later monks painstakingly (and sometimes inaccurately) copied manuscripts. Cheap, convenient writing writing materials were also lacking. The two rival materials papyrus and parchment were both very expensive. (The Chinese are credited with inventing paper which was later adopted by Europe.) Instead, Romans had wax tablets, which were used and reused. While many citizens of the empire may have been literate,

Above: A wall painting from Pompeii shows a young woman, once thought to be the Greek poet Sappho, pausing for thought.

fewer probably had access to much literature. Few would have been able to read the Latin classics regularly or easily, for books or scrolls were very expensive in real terms. While papyrus fragments of Virgil's *Aeneid* found on Hadrian's Wall show that some knowledge of the classical canon was widespread, scrolls or books remained relatively few and much-cherished, lent only with caution even to close friends. Symmachus, the wealthy, cultured late 4th century AD Roman aristocrat, offered a would-be historian of Gaul his copy of Caesar's *Gallic Wars* only as a special favour.

ANCIENT LIBRARIES

Culture in the Graeco-Roman world remained overwhelmingly oral and declamation in public was the commonest means by which new books were published. (Traditionally, even the fully literate read everything aloud, though some historians now doubt this.) Both public and private libraries of any size were so few as to be noteworthy. In Pompeii, so far only one villa, the Villa of

Right: The reconstructed interior of a typical Roman library such as those in Trajan's Forum, with shelves for the papyrus rolls.

the Papyri, has been found to contain a significant number of scrolls. Although carbonized, they are slowly being deciphered. The emperor Gordianus III (AD238–44) reputedly had 60,000 tomes in his own library. This suggests a distinctly cultured emperor and was unusual enough to merit recording at the time.

The greatest library of the ancient world at Alexandria had around 500,000 volumes. Athens also had renowned public libraries. In the 2nd century AD, Rome reputedly had 39 libraries, although few if any of these were lending libraries. (The library behind Trajan's Basilica was divided into Greek and Latin sections.) Unlike public baths, aqueducts or amphitheatres, public libraries were not an automatic or even usual attribute of the typical Roman city. Ultimately, when urban life almost collapsed in the 5th and 6th centuries AD, monastic libraries became the chief repositories of Roman manuscripts. However, most Latin literature did not survive at all.

PAPYRUS v. PARCHMENT

The commonest way of writing in the Roman world before *c.* AD250 was on papyrus, made from the papyrus plant that grows abundantly only on the banks of the Nile. (Tiny amounts grow elsewhere, such as Syracuse, but this did not affect Egypt's monopoly, which also sustained its high price.) Papyrus was manufactured into scrolls up 25ft (8m) long. Unrolling such scrolls while reading was difficult – a slave's help was useful – and they were easily torn. More expensive than even the best paper today, papyrus was also more fragile and less durable.

The Romans did not use clay tablets for literary works, although bureaucratic records on clay tablets survive in some abundance from Egyptian and a few Mesopotamian sites. Parchment, made from animal hides and far tougher than papyrus, was first made in the Hellenistic kingdom of Pergamum (Asia Minor). By the 1st century BC parchment sheets tied together with thongs were being used for commercial records. A century later, parchment was being used for literary texts as a *codex*, initially for cheaper editions. By AD200 this format was starting to replace papyrus scrolls.

The advent of Christianity in the 4th century AD accelerated this process. It was easier to find and read a passage from the Bible from a *codex* than a scroll and codices were also suited to legal documents. (Hence our term codex.) However, papyrus continued to be used until the Arab conquest of the Mediterranean in the 7th century AD finally cut Western Europe off from supplies in Egypt.

Below: A piece of papyrus signed by Cleopatra VII of Egypt, which dates to 33BC, gives tax benefits to the Roman Publius Candius.

CHAPTER XX

THE ARTS

If Roman art was heavily indebted to the Greeks, it soon developed its own characteristics, especially in portraiture and in reliefs commemorating particular historic events. Among opposed artistic currents are those of native *veristic* (realistic) art versus idealised Greek art and metropolitan versus provincial. The art of classical Greece long epitomized perfection to Rome's ruling class (and to many artists) and was much copied. Augustus in particular employed classical art in the service of the state.

Sculpture has generally survived better than painting, in part because of its sheer quantity. In the 4th century AD it was claimed that the city of Rome contained as many statues as it did people. This was an exaggeration – there were perhaps 700,000 Romans – but contemporary surveys record 154 gold or ivory, 22 equestrian and 3,785 bronze statues. Few bronzes survive as valuable metal statues were melted down. Marble statues still intact have lost their paint, giving an unduly marmoreal impression today. Inevitably, these sculptures mostly depict the rich and powerful.

Fortunately for posterity, the eruption of Vesuvius in AD79 preserved the wall paintings of more ordinary houses in Pompeii and Herculaneum. Other murals unearthed from Nero's palace display imperial taste in the mid-1st century AD. Art became flamboyant under the Flavians, then came a Greek revival under Hadrian. By c. AD330, the long tradition of classical realism was giving way to the more stylized art that we call Byzantine.

Left: The arrival of Io in Egypt, a painting from the 1st century AD, shows Roman wall-painting in its prime, almost three-dimensionally realistic but also romantically poetic.

THE ETRUSCANS AND THE EARLY REPUBLIC

Little distinctively Roman art survives from the city's first centuries, when Rome was much influenced by its neighbours, the Etruscans. The latter, it is now accepted, were an indigenous Italian people like the Romans, not newcomers from Asia Minor as ancient legends suggest. In the 6th century BC they established a confederacy of 12 cities across central Italy. Their cultural influence extended south to the Bay of Naples and dominated Rome well after the traditional expulsion of King Tarquinius in 509BC that led to the founding of the Republic.

ETRUSCAN VIVACITY

While the Etruscans were wealthy, Rome itself probably became economically poorer in the 5th century BC. The Etruscans were induced by the Greek vases they imported to copy Greek legends as well as styles, but they did so with novel vigour and colour. Most of their statues were made of brightly painted terracotta (baked earth) rather than the marble and stone which were so abundant in Greece. The Etruscans were also formidable bronze smiths. Roman art was for a time little more than a variant of Etruscan and the artists themselves were probably often Etruscan.

Etruscan vivacity is manifest in the Apollo of Veii, taken from the temple of the Etruscan city that Rome captured in 396BC. Dating from c. 500BC, this life-size terracotta statue shows the god striding forward in a long flowing robe with an enigmatic "archaic" smile. The contrast with the still static *kouroi* (naked male figures) of contemporary Greek archaic art is marked but the Etruscans lacked the idealizing drive that was about to create Greek classical art. Although the Etruscan Apollo is walking, the upper part of his clothed body shows no real sign of movement, suggesting that the sculptor had not studied the nude body as the Greeks did. The statue, whose colours faintly survive, is the grandest of the terracotta statues that adorned the roofs of most

Above: The Apollo of Veii of c. 500BC, a terracotta masterpiece of Etruscan sculpture, shows Greek influence interpreted by Italian craftsmen. The enigmatic archaic smile is typical of statues of the time.

Right: The Wounded Chimaera of Arezzo, c. 380BC. This mythical creature, which bristles with almost electric menace, represents the peak of Etruscan bronze casting.

Etruscan and early Roman temples. A fine sarcophagus, from *c.* 500BC, which depicts the terracotta figures of a couple reclining connubially on top of their coffin, also comes from Veii. Later the Etruscans began to portray individuals more realistically, as in the limestone and stucco Urn of Arnth Velimnas from the Tomb of the Volumni in Perugia of *c.* 150BC. Arnth Velimnas is depicted with a paunch.

Probably the earliest statue in Rome itself is the Capitoline Wolf, a bronze dating from *c.* 500BC whose pointed teeth and jutting ribs still radiate feral savagery. The statue illustrates the myth of Rome's foundation, when a she-wolf suckled the abandoned divine twins Romulus and Remus. It could be the statue referred to by Cicero that was struck by lightning on the Capitoline, although the figures of the twins are Renaissance additions or replacements. Even more aggressive is the Wounded Chimaera from Arezzo of *c.* 380BC, a creature that in myth breathed fire and here bristles with electric menace. Both are superb examples of the early bronze working skills developed in Italy.

Roman artists also created fine busts or statues of prominent men, always a vital art in Rome. Unlike the Greeks, Roman artists normally concentrated on depicting the face, which from the start they portrayed more realistically. The finest surviving such statue from the earlier Republic is the so-called Brutus, once thought to portray the Roman noble who, according to legend, helped to expel the last Etruscan king. The bronze is now thought to date from *c.* 300BC, two centuries later, but it catches the determination, intelligence and dignity of a noble Roman. There is a thin-lipped grimness about the figure which is appropriate to the men who would lead Rome through the long trials of the Punic Wars.

Work such as this shows Greek influence creatively mediated by Italic veristic (realistic) traditions. This would become less possible after Rome's conquest of the rich Hellenistic world led highly skilled Greek artists to flood into the city.

ETRUSCAN TOMB PAINTING

The Etruscans' superb tomb paintings are interesting as little painting has survived from the ancient world outside Egypt. (According to Pliny the Elder, Fabius Pictor (Fabius the Painter) painted superb battle scenes inside the Temple of Salus in *c.* 300BC, but these are now lost.)

The Etruscan *Ambush of Troilus by Achilles* from the Tomb of the Bulls from Tarquinia in southern Tuscany illustrates a scene from Homer's *Iliad*. It reveals Etruscan knowledge of Greek culture and myth as early as 540BC. The technique used is dark silhouettes for most people and distinct outlines for Troilus' horse, the lions and the blocks of the fountain.

Another delightful tomb painting is that from the Tomb of Hunting and Fishing of the same period. It depicts birds and boys climbing rocks and diving.

From the Tomb of Orcus in the 4th century BC comes the profile of a beautiful woman called Velia, crowned with leaves and with her hair hanging loose. Greek classicism is evident here, but again mediated by Etruscan taste. All this is very far from the art trumpeting military or dynastic glories that was to become the Roman norm.

Above: The Ambush of Troilus by Achilles, from Tarquinia, is typical of c. 540BC. It shows the Etruscans' awareness of Greek myths and style but interprets both in their own distinctive manner.

Above: The so-called Brutus, a fine bronze statue from c. 300BC, shows Greek influences in its style but is very Roman in its subject matter: a dignified Roman nobleman of the sort who would soon have to face the threat of Hannibal.

ART IN THE LATER REPUBLIC: 211–31 BC

Above: A fantasy city painted with almost perfect perspective in the bedroom of a villa at Boscoreale near Pompeii in the 1st century BC.

In 211 BC the Roman general Marcellus captured and sacked Syracuse, the great Greek metropolis of the West, bringing home art treasures that bedazzled the Romans. "Before this Rome knew nothing of these exquisite refined things… rather it was full of barbaric weapons and bloody spoils of war", wrote Plutarch 300 years later. He was exaggerating but in the following decades Greek artworks indeed poured into Rome as its armies returned triumphant from the eastern Mediterranean. Corinth fell to Roman arms in 146 BC and the sophisticated kingdom of Pergamum was bequeathed peacefully in 133 BC.

ADAPTING GREEK STYLE

With the artworks came Hellenistic artists whose impact was for a time over-whelming (although the native veristic tradition of portraiture survived only marginally modified). Demand for Greek artworks among Roman nobles became so insatiable that artists began copying them in the often repetitive Neo-Attic style. Unlike their Greek originals, many such copies have survived.

Greek influence from southern Italy appears in the simple, elegant Ionic *volutes* (scrolls) of the Sarcophagus of Lucius Cornelius Scipio *c.* 200 BC. The first relief depicting a Roman historical event is the marble frieze of the monument to Aemilius Paullus at Delphi in Greece, which was erected after his victory at Pydna in 168 BC. It features a specific event from the battle – a bolting riderless horse – in a way that is typically Roman although Greek artists sculpted it. Paullus brought back to Rome the Athenian painter Metrodoros, one among many imported Greek artists.

The famous reliefs in marble from the Temple of Neptune in Rome (once called the Altar of Domitius Ahenobarbus) of *c.* 100 BC mingle Greek and Roman motifs. Three sides depict the usual mythological scenes – the wedding of Amphitrite and Neptune for example – with typical Hellenistic flair, but the fourth shows a mundane scene of Roman census-taking. This is handled more awkwardly as the unknown artist(s) struggled to adapt Greek style to Roman demands for commemorative works. It is possible that this last side was added to an existing altar.

A less happy adaptation of Greek styles was the practice of putting Roman portrait heads on to idealized Greek statues. The so-called Pseudo-athlete, in which the head of an Italian businessman of *c.* 80 BC tops the heroic torso of a Greek athlete, is typical. The middle-aged Roman has

Below: The reliefs from the Temple of Neptune in Rome (formerly called the Altar of Domitius Ahenobarbus) mingle Greek style and Roman subject matter in a way very typical of the time, c. 100 BC.

the head of a clearly older man and a well muscled torso with drapery around the hips. Equally ridiculous was the way some Roman magnates allowed themselves to be portrayed as Hellenistic god-kings in emulation of Alexander the Great. Pompey, hailed as a god on his victorious march through the Hellenistic East (66–62BC), was portrayed with an Alexander-style quiff that sits like a wig above his middle-aged Roman features.

Balancing this uncritical importation of things Greek was the veristic style favoured by more conservative Romans who had no taste for fancy foreign art and who preferred styles that reflected older Republican virtues. Instead, they favoured an almost excessively realistic portraiture style that emphasizes every wrinkle and furrow, such as the "Republican portraits" from the mid-1st century. These portraits may have been taken from the death masks many Romans kept in their homes for the worship of ancestors.

POMPEIIAN ART: THE FIRST STYLES
The small but wealthy cities of Pompeii and Herculaneum in Campania, near Naples, were very open to Greek influences. They have the best preserved Roman mosaics and wall-paintings, although similar paintings have been found in Rome itself. The consecutive decorative styles of wall painting have been labelled the First, Second, Third and Fourth Pompeian styles. The First Pompeian style emerged in the 2nd century BC. Generally simple, it used plaster moulded and painted to look like coloured marble or stone.

The Second Pompeian Style that developed after 80BC was more interesting. It used realistically painted architectural features to create almost three-dimensional effects. The Villa of Oplontis, which belonged to Poppaea, Nero's second wife, boasts a remarkable vista – a colonnade behind a peacock and theatrical mask – that approaches true trompe l'oeil. The bedroom of the villa at Boscoreale has murals that show gardens or fantastic

buildings that never existed except in the unknown artist's imagination. The aptly named Villa of the Mysteries, however, shows rituals from a real Dionysiac mystery cult, with life-size figures that seem to stand or move on painted ledges in real space. This copies Greek *megalography* (large-scale figure painting). In a house on the Esquiline Hill in Rome, wall paintings of *c*. 50BC illustrate scenes from the *Odyssey* that use atmospheric perspective to increase the illusion of distance in the dream-like landscapes.

Mosaics, made by pressing small stones and pieces of glass or marble into a soft mortar bedding, were used widely by the Romans but had been used in the Hellenistic world too. The renowned Alexander Mosaic from the House of the Faun in Pompeii probably copies a Greek painting done by Philoxenos of *c*. 300BC. It may have been imported from Greece in the 1st century BC, but it is more likely that it was the craftsman who was imported. About 17 by 9ft (5.2 by 2.7m), it creates illusory real space to depict the drama of the Battle of Issus (333BC), when Alexander almost captured the Persian king Darius II.

Above: In the Villa at Oplontis near Pompeii, which belonged to the empress Poppaea, the illusionism of the Second Pompeian Style, c. 50BC, is fully manifested, with the pillars receding dramatically into the distance.

Below: A fresco from the Hall of the Mysteries, in the Villa of the Mysteries at Pompeii, showing an initiate to the Dionysian cult weeping.

AUGUSTUS AND THE
CLASSICAL REVIVAL: 31BC–AD64

Above: A cameo showing an ageless Augustus in dignified profile. Such images had strong propaganda purposes, as the medieval emperor Lothair realized when he incorporated it in his crown.

Below: A sacro-idyllic landscape of the type which first emerged in the Third Pompeian Style. Supposedly depicting country shrines, in fact they offered the artists opportunities to create imaginary landscapes of a type not seen again until the Renaissance.

After defeating his rival Mark Antony at Actium in 31BC, Augustus (as Octavian was known after 27BC) declared a policy of *restitutio rei publicae*. This meant a return to stable, constitutional, above all peaceful government. Art, architecture and literature were all enrolled in a highly successful propaganda campaign to proclaim the advent of a golden age after a century of civil strife.

EMBODYING ROMAN *VIRTUS*

Augustus looked back to the art of classical Athens at its 5th century BC peak for an authority, perfection and calm that appealed to him both personally and politically. (He did not of course emulate Athenian democracy, but Rome had never been truly democratic.) The result, which marked the first classical revival, was far more original than most Neo-Attic art had been, for Augustus used Athenian forms for most un-Athenian ends: his portrayal as the supreme embodiment of Roman *virtus*, the archetypal Roman virtue of courage, excellence, piety and strength.

Virtus is very obvious in the statue of the Prima Porta Augustus (so-called after the villa where it was found, which had once belonged to the empress Livia). Possibly a copy of a lost bronze, it dates from *c.* 20BC, and was originally painted with lifelike colours.

A still youthful-looking Augustus is shown, larger than life, as a triumphant *imperator* (emperor/general) in ceremonial armour. On his breastplate, personifications of the sky, Caelus, and of the sun, Sol, at the top are balanced by the figure of Tellus, the earth, reclining at the bottom. Around them are other deities, including Diana and Apollo. Between them Augustus is shown receiving the legionary standards lost at the battle of Carrhae in 53BC from a baggy-trousered Parthian. This refers to a recent diplomatic triumph (20–19BC) and links the mythical and the political. At Augustus' feet a cupid emphasizes the claimed descent of his family, the Julians, from Venus through her son Aeneas, while the dolphin the cupid rides recalls his naval victory at

Actium. The whole statue is therefore loaded with political significance. Augustus' stance is modelled on the nude *Doryphoros* (spear-carrier), a statue by the great Athenian sculptor Polyclitus of *c.* 450BC.

Another, less idealized statue shows Augustus with his toga over his head in the role of a priest (he became Pontifex Maximus, supreme priest, in 12BC). Augustus is, as always depicted as boyishly youthful but here he is also solemnly pious. His features are typically classical – smooth skin, regular features, sharp-edged nose and brow – suggesting calm, benign authority. The same classical dignity pervades the bust of his grand-daughter Agrippina, wife and then widow of Germanicus, the popular general whom Tiberius allegedly harassed. There is a strong facial resemblance to her grandfather in a bust of *c.* AD30.

The Gemma Augusta, a cameo showing the dead and deified Augustus passing power to his successor Tiberius from *c.* AD20, perpetuates this fine classicism. However, later statues of the Julio-Claudians, such as that depicting the ungainly emperor Claudius as Jupiter, are less successful.

Perhaps the greatest achievement of Augustan sculptors was the Ara Pacis Augusti (Altar of Augustan Peace). Constructed between 13 and 9BC and dedicated on the empress Livia's birthday, it is set in a walled enclosure with its main decorations on the outer walls. These are about 34ft long by 38ft wide (10.5 by 11.6m). Their message is that Augustus has restored peace, piety and prosperity and their form is sublimely classical. A sculptural panel on the east side portrays a personification the earth Tellus (or of Italia or Peace), with fruits and babies on her lap to symbolize fertility, flanked by two female figures symbolizing the oceans and rivers. The inspiration came from a Greek 5th-century relief, the Stele of Hegesos. Similarly, the famous frieze of the Panathenaic Procession from the Parthenon in Athens probably inspired the imperial procession on the side walls of the altar. Here Augustus is portrayed as *pater patriae* (father of his country). He takes centre stage without overwhelming his friends and family, including the empress Livia. Small boys, his grandsons, clutch at the grown-ups' hands, adding a homely touch. This reveals the Principate at its height, dignified yet family-minded. Another relief shows Aeneas, renowned for his piety, sacrificing to the *penates*, the household gods that he had brought from Troy.

WALL PAINTINGS

The Second Pompeian Style continued after 31BC. Livia's house on the Palatine is decorated with marvellous murals of gardens, while another house, now beneath the Villa Farnesina, had walls painted with remarkable trompe l'oeil to resemble a picture gallery. Outline paintings, such as one from this villa showing a woman pouring perfume, recall classical Greek art's sublime simplicity.

The succeeding Third Pompeian Style, which emerged at the end of the 1st century BC, was less solidly illusionistic. It treated walls as flat surfaces rather than as windows. Painted columns became slimmer, holding up delicate ornamental pediments. This style also saw the first emergence of "sacro-idyllic landscapes", romanticized misty landscapes centred supposedly on a shrine or temple but in reality rejoicing in vistas dotted with bridges, rocks and shepherds' huts, with mountains in the vague distance. While perhaps influenced by Hellenistic precursors, these are among the finest and earliest of European landscapes.

Above: Official Augustan art looked back to classical Athenian precedents in works such as the Ara Pacis Augusti (the Altar of Peace of Augustus) finished 9BC. Tellus, the personified earth, has fruit and babies on her lap and is flanked by rivers.

Right: The Prima Porta statue of Augustus c. 20BC, a copy of a lost bronze. The ever-youthful emperor is in symbolic armour proclaiming the Parthian victory, while the Cupid at his feet hints at descent from Venus. All is nobly classical.

THE ROMAN ZENITH:
FROM NERO TO TRAJAN AD64–117

Right: A gouache copy of one of the now-faded wall paintings discovered in Nero's Domus Aurea, illustrating the elegant Fourth Pompeian Style which once decorated it. Architectural elements are colourfully mixed with the illusionistic Second Style.

Below: The playboy-emperor and would-be artist Nero, unflatteringly portrayed with curled hair and a double chin although still in his twenties.

In AD64 the great fire that destroyed most of Rome also allowed Nero, now unrestrained by his old tutor Seneca and his first Praetorian Prefect Burrus, to give free rein to his far from classical tastes. Although Nero was deposed four years later and his final successor Vespasian favoured a more popular art, the fifty years following the fire saw Roman art flourish as never before. Hellenistic influences were finally absorbed and the empire's wealth allowed a dynamic, almost baroque yet Roman style to emerge. The eruption of Vesuvius, from the archaeologist's viewpoint, provided a blessed preservative.

The murals of Nero's Domus Aurea (Golden Palace), which were fresh when rediscovered by Renaissance artists – Raphael crawled down into the "grottoes"

to admire them – have sadly faded but still give a good example of the Fourth Pompeian Style. This continues the Third Style but reverts also to more solid, illusionistic architectural elements of the Second Style in a fanciful manner.

THE FOURTH POMPEIAN STYLE

In Pompeii, superb examples of the Fourth style come from the House of the Vettii brothers – probably merchants – which was rebuilt after a major earthquake in AD62. Copies of famous Greek paintings of legends – the death of King Pentheus, the baby Hercules strangling snakes – were incorporated as painted panels within wall decorations. The painting of Achilles and Briseis, a scene from the *Iliad*, in the House of the Tragic Poet is also impressive. Achilles smoulders with half-suppressed wrath as his favourite slave-girl Briseis is led away for King Agamemnon's pleasure. Other Pompeian paintings treat everyday subjects and reveal that local artists could paint diverse subjects with equal skill. This window on to life in antiquity closed in August AD79.

NERO'S SUCCESSORS

Sculpture and relief carvings remained the favoured forms of official art, prominently displayed in cities across the empire. Along with each emperor's coins, they carried the imperial image and official messages, although the effects may not have always been exactly what their imperial propagators envisaged. The statues and coins of Nero (ruled AD54–68) reveal more of his character – part debauched buffoon, part genuine aspiring artist, very seldom competent emperor – than he probably realized, with fleshy double chin and grandiose laurel crowns to proclaim his "victories" in the Olympic Games where he carried off every prize.

The busts and coins of his successor Vespasian, already 60 and a fine general when he gained the throne, are very different. Bald, unbeautiful but earthily humorous – on his deathbed he joked, "I think I must be becoming a god", referring to an emperor's customary posthumous deification – his features are shown in a revived veristic style.

Titus, Vespasian's handsome, young and prodigal son and heir, trumpeted his triumph over the Jews whose revolt he had crushed with flamboyant reliefs on his arch. The nearest figures in the imperial entourage, which include Titus himself in his four-horsed chariot with a winged Victory behind him, stand out in such high relief they are nearly in the round. These contrast with the lesser figures modelled in low relief but all, as usual in imperial art of this period, create the illusion of being in real space.

Under Trajan (ruled AD98–117), perhaps the most popular of emperors, Rome approached its zenith. His great column in Rome, erected in AD113 behind his Basilica, carries a brilliant spiral with some 2,500 figures showing his victory over the Dacians. Its scenes provide vivid (if not always wholly accurate) snapshots of the Roman army in action as it crossed rivers, stormed forts and tended its wounded. Panels from the Arch of Trajan erected at Benevento AD114–17 in southern Italy show the humanitarian ruler distributing food to poor children and presiding over the construction of a new port near Ostia, all facets of a great ruler.

THE PLEBEIAN TRADITION

Not all surviving Roman art is imperial or aristocratic. The Tomb of the Haterii of c. AD100 was commissioned by a non-aristocratic Roman family, who were probably successful builders. Here attention is lavished on details of the building, a family mausoleum under construction. A disregard for perspective and a delight in rich, almost fussy ornamentation shows that this sort of popular art remained blithely unconcerned with the nobility's favoured classical naturalism and idealism.

Above: The native Italian veristic tradition was revived for this bust of Vespasian, the emperor who came from small-town Italy. It shows him as realistically bald and elderly, but wryly humorous.

Below: A scene from the Tomb of the Haterii, probably erected for a family of rich builders c. AD90, shows a taste for rich ornamentation far removed from upper-class ideals of naturalism.

HADRIAN AND THE GREEK REVIVAL: AD117–285

Although the emperor Hadrian displayed architectural radicalism in the Pantheon in Rome and in his villa at Tivoli, he was conservative in his choice of artworks, favouring a return to classical or even earlier Greek styles. This second Classical Revival derived not just from his personal tastes, for the century saw the emergence of what is termed the Second Sophistic. This attempted to revive some aspects of classical Greek life – cities even began debating political issues of the 5th century BC – as Greek provinces finally regained some of their prosperity and self-confidence after the devastation wrought by Rome's conquest and civil strife.

Above: The statue of Marcus Aurelius, the only surviving bronze equestrian statue from antiquity, AD164–6.

Below: Along with the multicoloured mosaics, the 2nd century AD saw very fine black-and-white mosaics, such as this floor at Ostia.

ART AT HADRIAN'S VILLA
At Tivoli, 20 miles (32km) from Rome, Hadrian filled his villa complex with numerous statues, mostly reproductions of famous Greek or Egyptian works, to remind him of his travels. His decorators also created superb mosaics such as that showing a battle between centaurs and

wild beasts based on a Greek work by Zeuxis of *c.* 400BC. On his travels Hadrian fell in love with Antinous, a beautiful youth of royal birth from Bithynia, who accompanied him until he was drowned in the Nile in AD130. To commemorate him, the grief-stricken emperor founded a city on the Nile (besides more enduring foundations such as Hadrianopolis, now Edirne in Turkey) and "set up statues of him, or rather cult images, throughout the entire inhabited world", according to the historian Dio Cassius. Greek artists made statues showing Antinous as Apollo, Bacchus, Hermes and Osiris. If his body is truly Hellenic, he often has a most unclassical pout.

The Baths of Neptune in Ostia at the Tiber's mouth had a fine mosaic floor in black and white. Completed in AD139, it showed mythical sea-creatures – tritons, hippocamps, nereids – circling around the sea-god. The lack of colour brings out the fine draughtsmanship and this style remained popular into the 4th century.

Far to the north a remarkable fresco has been found in Southwark, across the Thames from Roman London, dating from *c.* AD150. It used very expensive pigments – gold leaf and cinnabar – to revive or perpetuate the Third Pompeian Style. Slender pillars supporting delicate pediments provide evidence that Roman wealth and sophistication had reached even this remote province.

One of the greatest of all Roman artworks is the sole surviving Roman equestrian bronze statue of Marcus Aurelius – preserved because it was thought to depict Constantine, the first Christian emperor – which was erected AD164–6. The philosopher-emperor is shown in heavy tunic and cloak as a general, his arm raised as if addressing a crowd, but his features retain a thoughtful, nobly compassionate air.

Above: The debauched megalomania of Commodus, shown dressed as Hercules, is wonderfully conveyed in this decadent bust.

A different, world-weary tone dominates the column of Marcus Aurelius of AD180–92, where the horrors of war are vividly portrayed. In comical contrast, the full-size naked portrait of Lucius Verus reveals the vanity of Marcus' idle co-emperor. The bust of Commodus, Marcus' worthless heir, dressed as Hercules with lionskin and club, is another masterly portrait, revealing the debauched megalomania of the last of the Antonines.

SEVERAN ART

A new art began to emerge with the succeeding dynasty, the Severans (AD193–233). This partly rejected Graeco-Roman classicism for a more stylized art. However, the two approaches long co-existed (as the classical and veristic traditions had for centuries) and often mixed. There is a florid exuberance about the busts of Septimius Severus (first of the dynasty), whose elaborately curled beard and hairstyle sit oddly with the ruthless face of a general who destroyed two rivals to gain the throne. The busts

of the following period are increasingly in the veristic tradition and that of the brutal emperor Caracalla (ruled AD211–17) is almost alarmingly realistic. Most of his successors, such as Maximinus Thrax or Trebonianus Gallus, cultivated this thuggish look as the empire disintegrated into chaos. Only the emperor Gallienus (ruled AD253–68) reverted to a noble, spiritual air. This was well-suited to a ruler who patronized the unworldly philosopher Plotinus and lost much of the empire.

SARCOPHAGI

One art form that developed steadily even in troubled times was the sarcophagus. This reflected the growing trend towards inhumation (burial) rather than cremation from Hadrian's reign on, and provided great opportunities for Attic (Greek) sculptors. In the 2nd century AD, these sarcophagi have fine classical carvings, often of Greek legends unconnected with the deceased's life. Typical is the sarcophagus of AD190 showing the scene from the *Iliad* of the corpse of prince Hector being dragged around the walls of Troy. Others combine myth with personal touches, such as the sarcophagus from AD250 showing a couple reclining together in death on the lid and legendary scenes from Achilles at the court of Lycomedes round the sides.

A rival to the Attic school of sarcophagi sculptors was the Asiatic school. Here too mythological scenes in a classical style decorated the sides of sarcophagi, but columns divide the scenes. A particularly elaborate example is dated *c.* AD180. Now in Melfi Cathedral in southern Italy, although its original occupant was pagan, it has *aediculae* (pavilions) on all four sides with mythological figures in each and a door at one end. The deceased's carved image reclines on top. Such pagan funeral imagery continued well into the Christian empire.

Right: Hadrian's beautiful lover Antinous, who died mysteriously in the Nile, was portrayed in many different poses.

Above: Under the new African dynasty started by Septimius Severus in AD193, new forms of less classical art emerged, often more stylized but not wholly displacing classicism.

ART OF THE LATER EMPIRE:
AD285–535

Above: The grim determination of the four tetrarchs (co-rulers) is graphically revealed in this unusual statue of c. AD305, now built into St Mark's, Venice, but originally from Constantinople.

Below: Constantine I favoured an art that overwhelmed the onlooker in its size and majesty. This head, once part of a huge statue, is 8ft 6in (2.6m) high.

With the advent of Diocletian in AD284, the troubled empire entered a new, more stable but more politically restricted era. Roman art reflected this as earlier trends away from classical idealism and its accompanying naturalism intensified. Instead, there emerged an art that aimed at creating overwhelmingly imposing images of imperial power, turned inward away from a collapsing natural world. This makes later Roman art effectively a bridge to that of the Byzantine and medieval world.

THE STYLE OF POWER

Diocletian and his successors tried to exalt the imperial throne so far above its subjects that none would dare to challenge it. While this aim had limited success politically, it had huge repercussions aesthetically. The statues of the tetrarchs (four co-rulers) embracing in St Mark's, Venice, of c. AD305 reveal the new order's grim determination and also the tetrarchs' astonishing lack of individuality – their features are almost interchangeable. However, the real power of the new style is seen best in the giant head and

hands of Constantine, all that remain of a colossal seated statue of the emperor that once stared down on observers in the Basilica Nova in Rome. The head alone is 8ft 6in (2.6m) high and the whole statue intact would have risen 30ft (9m). The huge eyes gaze out blankly yet all-seeingly on the subjects dwarfed below. The aquiline nose and clean-shaven jaw – Constantine was the first beardless emperor since Trajan – reinforce the feeling of sheer power which emanates from this superb piece of propaganda.

Less startlingly original was the Arch of Constantine. This partly reused Trajanic, Hadrianic and Antonine material but also has some new friezes. On two of these, panels showing Constantine delivering an oration or distributing gifts to the Roman people, the emperor stares out in grandiose isolation while his courtiers, lined up stiffly, gaze adoringly up towards him. The contrast with the classical realism of the two purloined Hadrianic roundels is striking. The change cannot be attributed simply to a decline in craftsmanship but must reflect a preference, emerging even before Constantine became Christian, for an art that was more hieratic and oppressive and less realistic and humanist than earlier official art. Man had ceased to be "the measure of all things", as he had been in classical Greece and Augustan Rome and now humbly genuflected before awesomely distant imperial – or divine – majesty. All the earlier panels are re-worked so that the emperor looks like Constantine. As a result he sometimes has a very small head.

Later imperial monuments such as the base of the Obelisk of Theodosius I in Constantinople (Istanbul) of AD390–3 take yet further this process of magnifying imperial glory while reducing subjects to mere ciphers. The emperor is shown standing behind the imperial pavilion's

railing with a wreath in his hand, while beside and below him his courtiers, reduced to rows of anonymous heads, gaze out full-frontally. (Severe weathering has probably accentuated this impression of impersonality.)

Better preserved is the superb silver dish some 2ft 5in (73.6cm) in diameter made in AD388 which shows Theodosius with his co-emperors Valentinian II and Arcadius, his son, all holding orbs to symbolize power. The co-emperors are portrayed smaller to indicate their lesser power. Theodosius is presenting something to an official, who is shown far smaller, befitting a man of lower status. Such symbolism marks a clean break with naturalistic classicism.

The most beautiful examples of Late Roman/Byzantine imperial art come from Ravenna, reconquered by the Latin-speaking but Eastern emperor Justinian (AD527–65). The mosaics at San Vitale which show him staring out, flanked by clergy and soldiers, are Byzantine in their full-frontal two-dimensionality against a flat gold background, although traces of classicism remain in their individually identifiable features.

Ravenna's mosaics mark the final transition to post-Roman medieval art, for the wars to regain Italy from the Goths wrecked the last of Roman civilization more thoroughly than the Goths could.

CLASSICAL SURVIVALS

Although the now Christian imperial court preferred the new unnaturalistic art for propaganda purposes, many educated pagan Romans long continued to favour some form of classical art. The Symmachus family, one of Rome's grandest noble families, commissioned ivory diptychs (two-leaved panels) in c. AD390. These depict pagan priestesses before a shrine to Bacchus and Jupiter in a style that consciously aimed to revive something of Augustan classicism.

In Britain, where villa life flourished in the first half of the 4th century AD, the superb mosaic, the Woodchester Great Pavement of c. AD350, shows Orpheus charming the beasts amid geometric patterns that recall a carpet. A similar subject is treated more naturalistically in the Littlecote villa near Hungerford of c. AD360. Even more dramatic is the Mildenhall Treasure, a superb silver dish about 2ft (61cm) in diameter that was buried around AD360 for safekeeping. It shows scenes of bacchic revelry with maenads and satyrs that in both spirit and form recall a far earlier art.

In Sicily, the remarkable mosaics depicting hunting and bathing from the Piazza Armerina villa of c. AD310–30 glow with truly pagan vitality, although their style has moved away from classicism to a less naturalistic if still vivid art.

Above: This 6th-century AD mosaic from Sant'Apollinare Nuovo in Ravenna of the Three Magi (Wise Men) is a marvellous example of Byzantine art.

Below: The joyful, exuberant colours of the mosaics of the Piazza Armerina Villa in Sicily show that, even in the early 4th century AD, not all art was concerned with depicting grim power.

FURNITURE

Above: A fresco of the 1st century BC *showing a Roman banquet with the typical small, portable tripod table that was then common. These were usually richly decorated.*

Roman furniture was rather sparse but often also surprisingly elegant and comfortable. It certainly surpassed anything Western Europe was to know again for the next thousand years.

As with so much else, there was a marked Greek or Hellenistic influence on much Roman furniture design. Furniture for all but the poorest was always decorated in some way, for minimalism was never a virtue in Roman eyes. Excavations at Pompeii and Herculaneum have been invaluable for revealing well-preserved examples of furniture from the late Republican and early Imperial periods (100BC–AD79). The styles greatly influenced Neoclassical European furniture of the late 18th and early 19th centuries. However, it is unlikely that Roman furniture design changed radically in the three centuries that followed the eruption of Vesuvius.

TABLES AND SEATING

The Romans seem to have used five different types of table. These were all of Greek origin and made of bronze or marble as much as wood. The tables could be rectangular with three or four legs, or round with three legs. These were often zoomorphic in form, with lions' paws or griffins' legs or even with legs formed with ithyphallic satyrs. Small bronze tripod tables with rims to prevent things falling off – very useful on uneven floors – were particularly popular. So, too, were square stone or marble tables with a single central leg. The latter design was particularly common in courtyards or gardens, where they might be fixed, but most other furniture could be moved around. Portable charcoal braziers, the chief source of heating in private houses around the Mediterranean, were an exception. (Hypocaust central heating remained a very rare, expensive luxury in private houses and was only used in certain parts of the house.) A particularly fine example of a bronze tripod brazier dates from the late 1st century BC. A masterpiece of Roman metalwork, its elaborate sphinxes reveal the brief fashion for things Egyptian following the victory at Actium in 31BC and the annexation of Egypt.

Couches were made mainly of wood. A rectangular frame held the mattress, which was supported by leather straps, webbing or wooden slats to make a firm bed. There seems to have been little difference between the couches used for dining and beds proper – in many houses the two were probably interchangeable. Traces of couches with leather sides and backs that may have had cushions have also been discovered. Headboards sometimes had ornaments in the form of bronze or brass animal heads and could be inlaid with ivory, silver or tortoiseshell. A couch with a relief of bones has been partially restored and is displayed in the Fitzwilliam Museum, Cambridge.

The Romans had many different types of seating. Benches were generally considered poor people's seating and were made of wood or stone. Elaborate chairs, sometimes with arms and back supports, are shown in Roman sculptures and paintings. Heavy, ceremonial chairs with solid sides

Below: A bronze Roman couch or bed probably from the 1st century AD. *It would have had cushions and covers and a mattress of wooden slats and might have been used both for dining and for sleeping.*

were used for official occasions. There is a carving from Trier of what looks like an armchair made of wicker in which a teacher sits instructing his students and a bronze-sheathed wooden chair leg has been found at Pompeii. Stools were widely used. A *sella curulis* (folding stool) with curving crossed legs was used by magistrates on official occasions. They were also used domestically; a relief from Ostia shows a woman seated under a tree on such a stool and Pompeii has produced a fine bronze-legged example. Thrones are usually shown with footstools.

CUPBOARDS AND LAMPS

Roman cupboards, cabinets and chests were generally similar to modern ones. A remarkably fine wooden cupboard cum shrine has been found in Herculaneum. The shrine at the top takes the form of a little temple, with finely carved Corinthian colonnettes (mini-columns) at its corners, and housed the statues of the household gods, the Lares and Penates. The cupboard below contained glassware and ornaments.

Discoveries at Herculaneum have shown that many rooms had wooden shutters or partitions that have normally left no archaeological record. These could be elaborate, folding, multi-panelled affairs with doors in them. External shutters were made of solid wood. It is clear from literature, painting and sculpture that large curtains would also have been used to divide rooms, but none have survived.

LAMPS

Roman houses were lit by lamps which burned olive oil. These ranged from very simple earthenware dishes to elaborate bronze stands. The simplest of these bronze lamp stands was a slender fluted column that rested on three animal paws and was topped by some form of calyx (flower top). Far more complicated were those with four or more arms, shaped either like branches or in the form of *volutes* (scroll-like ornaments). A particularly resplendent example comes

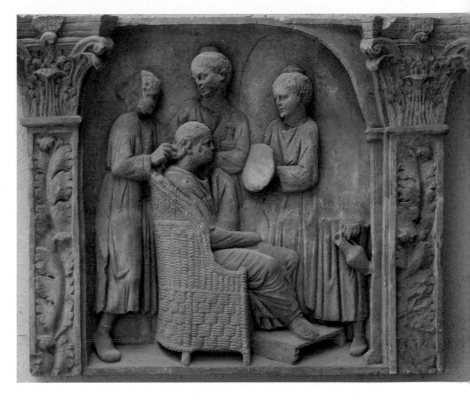

from the House of Diomedes at Pompeii. Dating from just before AD79, the lampstand rests on a platform decorated with a figure of a satyr riding a panther. The feet of the base are shaped like animal's paws.

Above: A woman seated at her toilette in a wicker armchair from near Trier in Gaul, 4th century AD. A servant holds a mirror in front of her.

Above: An elaborate Roman strong box for money and other valuables. Decorated with classical motifs and very fine lion legs, it probably dates from the 4th century AD.

CHAPTER XXI

RELIGION AND MYTHOLOGY

The Romans had many gods and, like most other polytheists, normally accepted those of other peoples. Most Greek gods were identified with Roman ones early on but, as Rome's power spread east, stranger gods found followers in the multiracial city: Cybele from Asia Minor, Isis and Sarapis from Egypt, Mithras from the Persian world. Their cults, which offered initiates mystical experiences and usually promised salvation after death, appealed especially to poorer people in the empire. In contrast, the official religion of the Roman establishment was essentially pragmatic and utilitarian. Worship involved precise rituals to ensure that the gods brought victory in battle or that they saved Rome from plague.

From Augustus' time on, the worship of the emperor, whose *genius* or divinity was linked with Roma Dea, the goddess of Rome, was encouraged. This imperial cult helped to unite the disparate empire and was vigorously enforced in the troubled 3rd century AD. The Jews were exempt because of the antiquity of their religion, but Christians suffered for their refusal to worship the emperor. Christianity's final triumph was due chiefly to its promotion by Constantine after AD312. But, as the Roman empire became Christian, Christianity in turn became imperially Roman.

Left: A scene thought to show the mystery rites of Bacchus (Dionysus) in a mural from the Villa of the Mysteries, Pompeii, c. 60–50BC. Note the goatlike ears of the left-hand figures.

THE CAPITOLINE GODS

The gods of early Rome were not initially anthropomorphic but, after 250BC, under increasing Greek influence, they soon acquired human characteristics. They were given mythical fixed forms like the 12 Greek Olympian gods by the poet Ennius. However, although myth and religion intertwined, religious fervour was not appropriate to the worship of Rome's state gods. Instead, punctilious performance of the rites was all-important.

Rome did not have a separate priestly caste or profession, although there were four priestly colleges by the late Republic. The *pontifices* were pre-eminent, while the *augures* divined the gods' will by observing the flight of birds or animals' entrails. Important Romans performed priestly duties as required, pulling their togas over their heads to indicate sacerdotal functions. The emperors from Augustus on became *pontifex maximus*, supreme priest, a title the Pope inherited.

The sacrifice of animals was central to the gods' worship. The animal entrails were examined for omens, an Etruscan habit which the Romans perpetuated. The best portions of the sacrifice were burnt as offerings to the gods and the priests and worshippers would eat the rest. Offerings of flowers or cakes were acceptable from poorer people and for lesser endeavours.

The temple of a pagan god was its house, not a place where worshippers gathered for collective rites. These rites were normally performed outside the temple. On special occasions the statue of the deity might be paraded through the streets, a custom still performed with Catholic statues on feast days. Jupiter, his wife Juno and his daughter Minerva, who sprang from his head fully grown and fully armed, formed the central Capitoline triad. However, Mars, the war god, was equally important.

JUPITER

The king of the gods, equated with Zeus (though lacking the Greek god's colourful sex life or touchy temper), Jupiter was a sky god associated with thunder, lightning, rainfall and storms. He used to warn men and punished them with his three thunder bolts when required. The first he could discharge as a warning whenever he wanted; the second, also a premonitory bolt, could be hurled with the agreement of the 12 other gods, his *complices*. The last, destroying bolt could only be unleashed by the god with the consent of the *superiores*, the hidden superior gods.

At first the god of a rustic Rome, Jupiter Elicius (Who Brings Forth) was concerned with farming, but as Rome's power grew, so did his. Called Jupiter Imperator (Supreme General), Invictus (Unconquered) and Triumphator, his highest title was Jupiter Optimus Maximus (Best and Greatest).

In his temple on the Capitoline, Jupiter was portrayed majestically, bearded, with an eagle on a sceptre and thunderbolts. Long the supreme god of the Roman

Above: The goddess Minerva, third of the Capitoline triad, from Souedia in Syria. Less obviously Roman than the other two, this patron of doctors and craftsmen was revered for her wisdom and widely worshipped.

Right: Thetis appealing to Jupiter in a painting by Ingres, 1811. The assimilation of such Greek deities into the Roman pantheon happened very early in Rome's history.

state, senators declared war under his aegis and triumphant generals would donate a gold crown and part of their booty to him. The *Ludi Romani*, the chief games, were celebrated in his honour.

The Temple of Jupiter on the Capitoline Hill, which was built under the kings and rebuilt many times, was the grandest in the city of Rome. The rise of the cult of Sol Invictus (Unconquered Sun) eclipsed Jupiter's primacy in the 3rd century, but Diocletian (ruled AD284–305) revived Jupiter's glory, calling himself and his soldiers *Joviani*. Finally, the Christians adopted Jupiter's title of Optimus Maximus for their own god.

JUNO

The consort and sister of Jupiter, equated with the Greek goddess Hera, Juno was the supreme goddess of the Roman state and of very ancient origins. A statue of Juno was taken from the captured Etruscan city of Veii in 394BC and installed in Rome in a form of religious annexation, but she had been worshipped in Rome long before. A temple to her was built on the Esquiline Hill in 735BC.

As Juno Lucetia she was a goddess of light, a moon goddess. Traditionally shown with a peacock and sceptre as *regina coeli*, queen of heaven, her sacred geese on the Capitol warned the Romans of a night attack by the Gauls during their sack of Rome in 390BC. She was also the mother of Mars, although not by Jupiter but by union with a magic flower. Above all, Juno embodied the virtues of Roman matronhood, which were much respected in the Republic. As Juno Lucina she was goddess of childbirth and fertility – the Sabine women prayed to her after their rape by Romulus and his gang. As Juno Pronuba she presided over marriage and as Populonia she encouraged the Romans to multiply. The month of June is named after her.

MINERVA

Although identified with Athene, patron goddess of Athens and daughter of Zeus, Minerva was originally the Etruscan goddess Menrfa or Menarva (associated with an owl) and the least Roman of the Capitoline triad. At first the goddess of commerce, industry and education, she later became a warrior-goddess, depicted with helmet, shield and armour. Later still she also became the patron goddess of doctors, musicians and craftsmen and, in a typical example of Roman assimilation, was equated with the local goddess of Bath's hot springs, Sulis, in Britain. Her festival was celebrated in the Quinquatrus with Mars at the spring equinox.

Above: Mars, the helmeted god of war, was a deity of central importance to the all-conquering Romans.

Below: Apollo, god of music, poetry, medicine and science, shown with his lyre, was a Roman import from Greece who was fully assimilated into the state religion by Augustus.

MARS

The war god Mars was perhaps the most truly Roman of the city's gods and his cult was more important to Rome even than Jupiter's. At first he was a rustic deity living in fields and forests, called Silvanus. Later, Ceres and Liber, deities of wheat and wine, took over these agricultural roles but Mars' chief festival was always celebrated at the Quinquatrus at the spring equinox in the month that bears his name.

Born almost parthenogenetically from Juno's mystical union with a fantastic flower, he was identified with Ares but was a nobler and more dignified figure than the often irascible Greek god. At Rome he had a *sacrarium* (shrine) on the Palatine, where his 12 sacred spears were kept. His grandest temple in Rome was that built by Augustus to him as Mars Ultor, Mars the Avenger, to celebrate victory over Julius Caesar's assassins.

The Romans built temples to him across the empire, in which he was generally portrayed bearded with helmet and armour. Sacrifices were made to him by generals before they set out for battle and after their victory he received his share of booty. On the battlefield he might appear accompanied by Pavor and Pallor (terror and paleness) which he inflicted on Rome's enemies, while his other two companions, Honos and Virtus, filled Roman soldiers with honour and courage. In the Romance languages Tuesday (Martes, Martedi, Mardi) is named after Mars.

APOLLO

The archetypal Greek god of poetry, medicine, music and science, Apollo had no Roman equivalent but was imported into the city in the 5th century BC to ward off plague. The dictator Camillus promised Apollo a tenth of the spoils from the Etruscan city of Veii, which Rome captured in 396BC, for Apollo was honoured also by the Etruscans.

Apollo was the son of Zeus (but not of Jupiter) and the titaness Leto. His twin sister was Artemis/Diana. Born on the island of Delos, Apollo slew the dragon Python at only four days old. Renamed as Delphi, the spot where the slaying took place later became the site of his oracle, the most sacred in the Greek world. Called Phoebus (brilliant), Apollo was a god of light and was later sometimes identified with the sun. Augustus built a fine temple near his house on the Palatine to the god whose lucid virtues he tried to propagate and many more were built across the empire.

DIANA

The goddess of the hunt and of the moon, later equated with Artemis and so Apollo's twin, Diana was the patron goddess of wild beasts. She was also associated with the moon, especially the harvest moon, for she was a fertility goddess. In her great temple at Ephesus in Asia Minor she was shown as many-breasted.

Diana undoubtedly had a savage temper. When Actaeon the hunter chanced upon her bathing with her nymphs, she angrily changed him into a stag and he was then killed by his own dogs. At Rome Diana

Left: Diana the chaste goddess, portrayed as a huntress on a 2nd-century AD mosaic from North Africa. In this guise Diana was virginal and almost amazonian, in contrast to more typically feminine goddesses.

was worshipped as a goddess of childbirth in a temple on the Aventine founded in the 6th century BC. Her greatest shrine was on the shores of Lake Nemi north of Rome, where her priest was traditionally an escaped slave. To win this priesthood he had to kill his predecessor in single combat, after which he had to patrol the lake's forested shores looking out for potential successors.

SATURN

An ancient agricultural god whose name was connected with *satur* (literally: stuffed), Saturn was identified with the Greek god Cronus. Expelled from heaven by Jupiter, Saturn was held to have ruled Italy during its golden age before the invention of iron and war. Saturday is named after Saturn.

Saturn's annual festival, the Saturnalia, which took place between the 17th and 23rd of December, saw an orgy of merriment when all rules were relaxed, the Lord of Misrule governed, masters waited upon their slaves and huge public banquets were eaten in the open. Saturn's temple in the Forum Romanum housed the public treasury and the standards of legions not actually campaigning. It was also a very early shrine of the Republic dating from *c.* 494BC.

VESTA AND THE VESTAL VIRGINS

Vesta was goddess of the domestic hearth and sown fields. She was linked with the Greek goddess Hestia, a notably chaste goddess. In Rome she was served by six patrician girls who were chosen by lot at the age of six. They were required to serve for 30 years from the age of ten in the special Atrium Vestae, the House of the Vestals next to the circular Temple of Vesta in the Forum Romanum. After that time they were free to marry, although few did, as they were considered too old. The Vestal Virgins were, however, much respected. Their main duty was to keep the goddess' sacred flame burning, and their chief restriction was their vow of chastity. Any Vestal Virgin who broke this vow faced whipping to death or burial alive. Apparently only 20 Vestals broke their vows in over a thousand years.

Below: A 3rd-century AD statue of a Vestal Virgin. The Roman goddess of the household hearth, Vesta's temple in the Forum Romanum housed the eternal flame. Her shrine was constantly attended by six Vestal Virgins who lived the life of nuns.

VENUS, VULCAN AND OTHER GODS

The Romans adopted gods and goddesses from many different civilizations. Venus, for example, filled a huge gap in the Roman pantheon, which was notably lacking in amorous or beautiful deities, and Vulcan was identified with the Greek god Hephaestus.

VENUS

Originally a minor Italian nature goddess associated with spring, in the 3rd century BC Venus became identified with Aphrodite, the daughter of Zeus/Jupiter and supremely beautiful Greek goddess of love. Venus had many shrines, including a Greek shrine on Mount Eryx in Sicily and another in Pompeii. Her fame grew when Julius Caesar, claiming divine ancestry for the Julian family, ordered the building of the temple of Venus Genetrix in 46BC.

According to Homer, Aphrodite/Venus was the mother of Aeneas, the Trojan prince. The fragmentary Roman legends that Virgil transformed into the *Aeneid* state that Aeneas had fled burning Troy to found Lavinium, the precursor of Rome. As the Julio-Claudian emperors claimed descent through Aeneas, Venus was linked with Rome's imperial destiny. Hadrian dedicated a huge double temple to Venus and Roma Dea in AD135.

Imperial propaganda did not reduce the allure of the sweet-natured goddess. Born from the sea's foam, she was wafted ashore naked on a shell by gentle zephyrs, to land at Paphos in Cyprus, where the Horae, the attendant hours, were waiting to clothe her and usher her into the presence of the gods. All were overwhelmed by her. Both Mars and Mercury had affairs with her as erotic chaos broke out on Mount Olympus, the gods' home. Finally Juno and Minerva, furiously jealous, competed in a beauty parade with her to see which goddess Paris would pick. The Trojan prince chose Venus and from the other goddesses' undying enmity arose the Trojan war. Aeneas was born of Venus'

Above: Venus by the forge of Vulcan, the blacksmith god to whom the goddess of love was improbably married – although not for long.

Below: The birth of Venus and her passage ashore on a seashell, depicted on a fresco in Pompeii.

affair with the Trojan Anchises, but she herself was no warrior-goddess and relied upon her charms, rather than strength. Doves were sacred to her, as was the evening star, the planet Venus. Lucretius started his great philosophical poem *De rerum natura* (*About the Nature of Things*) with a passionate invocation to Venus: *Aeneadum genetrix, hominum divumque voluptas, alma Venus* ("Mother of Aeneas, delight of gods and men, kindly Venus"). Catullus and other poets constantly invoked her and she remains the most enduringly appealing of all Graeco-Roman deities.

VULCAN

The ugly blacksmith god Vulcan was the polar opposite of the graceful goddess of love. Under the name Volcanus he was an ancient Latin deity, an original protector of Rome and consort of Juno.

After Jupiter displaced him, Vulcan concentrated on working in the hot bowels of the Earth: the Romans placed his divine smithy both inside Mount Etna and on the volcanic Aeolian islands. Vulcan was lamed after being thrown from Mount Olympus for interfering in a quarrel between his parents Jupiter and Juno. Falling into the sea, he was rescued by nymphs and there learnt his metal-working trade, creating a marvellous gold throne that glued Juno to it when she sat down. To obtain her release, the gods had to agree to allow him to marry Venus. Their marriage was not made in heaven, however, for Venus, repelled by the dirty smith, had an affair with Mars. Vulcan angrily threw a metal net over the adulterous couple as they slept, trapping them for the other gods' mirth.

JANUS

One of the very few Roman gods without a Greek counterpart, Janus was an ancient and popular Italic god, his cult traditionally established by Romulus.

Janus was the god of all doorways and public gates through which roads passed. His emblems were his keys and the *virga* (stick) that porters used to drive intruders

Left: Vulcan's forge, a 2nd-century AD mosaic from Dougga in North Africa. The god of all metal workers, clever but unlovely, Vulcan had his forge either beneath Mt Etna in Sicily or in the Aeolian islands just to the north.

away. Janus was most famous for being *Janus bifrons*, two-faced, so that he could see people coming and going. Because he was the god of new beginnings, the first month of the year, January, was named after him, and the first day of each month was sacred to him. In the Forum Romanum his temple had gates that were opened in time of war and – far more rarely – closed in times of peace.

LARES AND PENATES

The domestic gods Lares and Penates, the guardian spirits of the household, were also typically Roman deities. Each Roman house traditionally had one *lar* (the word was originally Etruscan, meaning prince) and two *penates*, whose names derived from *penus*, larder.

The *lar* was invoked on all important family occasions such as marriages and funerals. A bride crossing the threshold of her new household made an offering to the house's *lar*, whose image was always decorated at festival times. There was also a *lar* of the crossroads.

The *penates* oversaw the family supply of food and drink and their altar was the hearth, which they shared with Vesta. On the Ara Pacis, Aeneas is shown sacrificing to the *penates*.

Below: The two-headed god of the crossroads, Janus was unusual in that he was a completely Roman deity. His ancient worship, traditionally started by Romulus, was very popular throughout Italy.

EMPEROR WORSHIP AND THE GODDESS ROMA

Above: Augustus with his toga pulled up over his head to indicate that he is acting as a priest. He took the title Pontifex Maximus (Highest Priest) but never let himself be worshipped as a god in Rome or Italy while he was alive. He was only deified at his death.

Since the reign of Alexander the Great (336–323BC), the Greeks had hailed as gods kings or generals whom they wished to honour or appease. The step from superhuman hero to demi-god or god was a short one in a world filled with gods. When Roman generals succeeded Alexander's successors as arbiters of the eastern Mediterranean, Greeks began treating them, too, as divine, starting with Flaminius in 196BC. Many cities set up altars to the deity Roma Dea, the goddess Rome. Mark Antony, who ruled the East from 42–31BC, was hailed as an avatar of Dionysus/Bacchus in Greek cities in Asia Minor and in Egypt, where he sat enthroned beside Cleopatra dressed as Isis. This did not help his reputation among the Romans, however. Augustus' supporters said that Antony had gone native and lost his Roman *virtus*.

THE IMPERIAL CULT

Augustus dealt pragmatically with the desire of many of his non-Roman subjects to worship him in his turn. He allowed altars or temples to his *genius* (guardian spirit) or *numen* (divinity) to be erected across the provinces. In Aphrodisias in southern Asia Minor, a large *Sebasteion* (temple to Augustus) was built by prominent local individuals and served by priests recruited from local aristocrats. Cities competed with each other to offer the emperor honours and sacred hymns were composed to him at Pergamum. More deliberately, Augustus built a small temple on the Athenian acropolis to Augustus and the goddess Roma combined, underlining Rome's divinely sanctioned power in the heart of Greece.

In Egypt, where Augustus was the heir to the divine pharaohs and Ptolemies, his worship presented no problems. At the other end of the empire in Gaul, a Great Altar to Augustus and Roma was set up at Lyons (Lugdunum), Gaul's largest city. Representatives of the three Gallic provinces came every year to demonstrate their devotion to Rome and the emperor. Many Romanized Gallic nobles happily contributed to such cults, which demonstrated their new status in the empire. At Colchester (Camulodunum) in the new province of Britain, a temple to Claudius the god was established but proved less popular. It was burnt down in Boudicca's revolt of AD60. However, this reaction was uncommon.

In contrast, the Roman nobility, whose support Augustus needed to run the empire, regarded any presumption of divinity by the emperor as an outrage tantamount to tyranny, and he had to tread carefully. During his lifetime, Augustus was still only *princeps* (first citizen). Although he prominently advertised himself as *divi filius*, son of a god, he never allowed anyone to call him a god in Rome or to build a temple to him in Italy.

It was different with the dead, however. Julius Caesar was deified posthumously and a temple was built to him. On his death Augustus was also declared a god by the Senate, his soul soaring into heaven in the form of an eagle released from his burning pyre. Most popular emperors were subsequently deified, although rulers found odious by the Senate – Tiberius, Caligula, Nero, Domitian, Commodus – were denied this honour. Antoninus Pius (ruled AD138–61) had to threaten to abdicate before the Senate would deify Hadrian, a superb ruler but one who had not got on with the Senate. Later Septimius Severus deified the megalomaniac Commodus to link his family with the Antonines.

Wiser emperors – Augustus, Trajan, Marcus Aurelius – accepted these encomia reluctantly, but by the 3rd century emperors were assuming divine attributes

during their lifetime and some, especially those who had inherited the throne, let this worship go their heads. Caligula (ruled AD37–41) was one of the maddest, addressing Jupiter's statue on the Capitoline as an equal. Nero saw himself as an incarnation of the sungod Helios, and Domitian insisted on being called *dominus et deus* (Lord and God). Commodus even wanted to rename Rome after himself. However, most educated people knew that the emperor was not literally divine and throwing incense on the altar to the emperor and Roma required no religious commitment. It was merely indicative of a general patriotic loyalty.

PERSECUTION

Not all the peoples of the empire could accept this, however. The Jews, spread around the Mediterranean even before Titus destroyed the Temple in Jerusalem in AD70, regarded emperor worship as an abomination. The Romans respected the Jewish religion for its antiquity and dignity (although they found it puzzling) and exempted Jews from emperor worship. When Caligula tried to have his statue installed in the Holy of Holies in the temple in Jerusalem, he almost triggered an uprising, but this was an exception.

The Christians, who were recognized as a sect distinct from the Jews by AD64, were not exempted in the same way and so were intermittently persecuted. However, as the correspondence between the emperor Trajan and Pliny the Younger, governor of Bithynia, reveals, the Romans did not usually seek out Christians to persecute. It was only during the crises of the 3rd century AD, when Rome's rulers appealed to every god in heaven to aid the stricken empire, that Christians were harshly persecuted for risking the gods' wrath. Even then, only the most stubborn – or devout – experienced martyrdom.

Above: Base of the Column of Antoninus Pius (AD138–61), showing the apotheosis of Faustina, his wife, and also of himself.

Above: Gold coin showing the head of the deified Claudius. Even the undignified Claudius was worshipped in Britain during his lifetime and became a god after his death.

BACCHUS AND CYBELE

Above: Bacchantes dancing with a whip and cymbals from the House of the Mysteries, Pompeii.

Below: The so-called Temple of Bacchus (Dionysus), the god of wine and ecstasy, at Baalbek, Lebanon.

The official Roman gods were vital to the maintenance of Rome's political fortunes and of family life. However, they lacked the mystical appeal of the new gods and mystery cults from the East which promised immortality to those initiated into their secret rites. The Senate, alarmed that secret devotions might lead adherents to neglect their social and political duties, initially tried to restrict them.

BACCHUS

The Romans had their own cheerful rustic wine god, Liber Pater, whose festival they celebrated in March. However, Bacchus, identified with the Greek Dionysus, the most dangerous god in the Greek pantheon, was very different.

Born to Semele, a Theban princess, son of Jupiter, the young Bacchus overcame the jealous goddess Juno's varied attempts to kill him. (His mother was blasted by lightning and he himself was chopped up by Titans and cooked in a cauldron.)

Resurrected by Jupiter, Bacchus was educated partly by nymphs and led a procession of satyrs, muses and maenads in a chariot drawn by tigers or panthers. He was famed for spreading the cult of wine and his intoxicated festivals.

Bacchus married the abandoned Cretan princess Ariadne on Naxos and drove the mother of King Pentheus of Thebes (who had imprisoned him) so mad that she blindly tore her son to pieces. In classical Greece, Bacchus as Dionysus was recognized as the official god of drama. His spring festival was noted both for the plays staged under his auspices and for the ecstatic excesses of the maenads, his female followers.

Later, Bacchus' cult spread wider and became secretive. In 186BC the Roman Senate ordered the suppression of most altars to the god throughout Italy after the "Bacchanalian incident", details of which remain obscure. The cult, which had entered Rome via the Greek cities of southern Italy, went underground for a time until, wiser than King Pentheus, the Romans accepted Bacchus' worship.

The remarkable murals of the Villa of Mysteries at Pompeii show a woman being whipped and then comforted while a winged *daemon* (spirit) looks on. The murals probably depict an initiation scene from this mysterious cult, which was especially popular with women.

CYBELE, THE *MAGNA MATER*

Few cults less suited to the dignified Roman Republic could be imagined than the orgiastic worship of Cybele, the *Magna Mater* (Great Mother). A Phrygian fertility goddess , she was worshipped on mountain tops and underground. Her son Attis emasculated himself in ecstatic devotion to her in an act her followers repeated in public in gory rituals. All her priests were eunuchs, something no

Roman citizen could be and retain his citizenship. However, in the darkest days of the war against Hannibal, the Romans consulted the Sibylline Books. These predicted that Italy would only be freed if the "Idaean mother of Pessinus" was brought to Rome. The Romans understood this to refer to Cybele and set about bringing her cult to Rome. It arrived in the form of a black stone, possibly a meteorite, in 204BC, just as Hannibal was about to leave Italy.

Installed in 191BC in her own temple on the Palatine, the *Magna Mater* had a special band of eunuch priests (*galli*) to serve her, and her festival, the Megalensia, was held annually from the 5th to 10th April, with religious processions, games and theatrical performances in the Circus Maximus. Although a Roman magistrate presided over the ceremonies, the *galli*, dressed in bright-coloured robes stained with blood from their self-flagellation, offended Roman sensibilities, for Roman citizens were forbidden to be priests. Finally the open-minded emperor Claudius (ruled AD41–54) incorporated her cult into the official Roman pantheon.

THE PYTHAGOREANS

Pythagoras (*c*. 570–500BC) was the great mystic among mathematicians. One of the leading early Greek Presocratic philosophers, traditionally he was the first man to call himself a philosopher.

Little definite is known about Pythagoras' life or teaching, but he reputedly believed in metempsychosis, the transmigration of souls, whereby human souls are reincarnated in animals or plants according to their past lives. He also advocated strict vegetarianism and forbade the eating of beans because they caused the breaking of wind, which he held to contain the human soul.

Pythagoras moved from his native island of Samos to southern Italy, where he established a school at Crotona. There he taught a select few mathematics, astronomy and music. He also taught a secret political programme that allowed

the Pythagoreans to wield real power for some years in several western Greek cities before they were eventually expelled and driven underground.

Under the Romans their beliefs revived. Nigidius Figulus, a praetor in 58BC, was a Neopythagorean as, apparently, was Apollonius of Tyana *c.* AD200. A tiny underground basilica by the Porta Maggiore in Rome, discovered by chance in 1917 and decorated with exquisite mythological scenes about the love and death of the Greek poet Sappho, is probably Neopythagorean. The cult clearly had to remain half-secret, however. One likely member, Statilius Taurus, was condemned in AD53 for practising "magic arts". In fact the Neopythagoreans were the most intellectual of the mystery cults.

Right: A eunuch priest of Cybele, the Great Mother goddess. Her worship was imported into Rome in 204BC.

Above: A 3rd-century AD mosaic showing the triumph of Bacchus over the Indians in his tiger-drawn chariot. The Romans adopted the worship and myths of Dionysus, the Greek god of drama, whom they called Bacchus.

NEW GODS FROM THE EAST

Above: Statue of Tiber, the god of the river. It was found at the sanctuary of Isis and Sarapis in the Campus Martius, where Caligula had built a temple to the two Egyptian deities.

Below: A 2nd-century AD relief from Alexandria in Egypt showing the bearded Sarapis seated between the goddesses Demeter and Venus (Aphrodite). His worship was more usually associated with that of Isis.

For the Romans as for the Greeks, the traditional gods of pharaonic Egypt, such as the jackal-headed Anubis, seemed absurdly zoomorphic, suited only for Egyptian peasants. Nonetheless, the antiquity and mystery of the land impressed Western rulers from Alexander the Great on and two deities emerged from Egypt that spread around the Roman empire as far north-west as Britain: Isis and Sarapis.

ISIS

The greatest goddess of Egypt in Hellenistic and Roman times, Isis was of great antiquity. Originally she had been simply a local goddess of the Delta. According to much-embroidered myth, she was the consort and sister of Osiris and mother of the hawk god Horus. When Set, their evil brother, murdered Osiris, she wandered the earth to find her husband's dismembered body, mourning as she went. The legend reveals that she was originally a fertility goddess connected with the natural cycle of death and rebirth, like Cybele and many other goddesses. Under the Greek-speaking Ptolemies, who ruled Egypt 323–30BC,

she was Hellenized and her role expanded into that of a cosmic saviour. Aspects of her cult then acquired genuine spiritual and ethical elements that Apuleius later voiced most lyrically in his novel *The Golden Ass* of *c.* AD150.

As her worship spread around the Mediterranean from its origins in Alexandria, Isis became known as Stella Maris (Star of the Sea), the divine protector of sailors and fishermen. In Rome, spectacular annual festivals in her honour celebrated the start of the sailing season on 5th March with *navigium Isidis* (the Relapse of the Ship) and its completion in the autumn.

Isis' strongest appeal initially was to women, freedmen and slaves; old-fashioned Romans such as Augustus and Tiberius disapproved of her. The emperor Caligula (ruled AD37–41) was a devotee, however, and encouraged the building of a temple to her and her co-Egyptian deity Sarapis in the Campus Martius in Rome. Pompeii boasted a fine temple of Isis, the earliest one in Italy, as did many other cities across the empire, especially those involved with foreign trade such as Ostia. These temples had heavily Egyptian decorations to stress their exotic appeal, but the cult itself seems to have been uplifting rather than orgiastic. A mural from Herculaneum shows very solemn-looking priests and worshippers conducting ceremonies. In the final section of *The Golden Ass*, Apuleius waxed lyrical about how Isis appeared to him in a dream, saying "I am the first of heavenly beings, mother of the gods, I am Minerva, Venus, Diana...the Universal Mother, mistress of the elements, primeval child of time...queen of the dead, queen also of the immortals".

The worship of Isis continued to grow through the 3rd century and even survived early Christian persecutions; her great temple at Philae in Egypt was only

Right: The worship of Isis, the great goddess of Egypt, was very popular. The rites were dignified if mysterious, as this fresco from Herculaneum shows.

finally closed in the 6th century. Some aspects of her cult, including her blue robe and the title Stella Maris, were taken over by the cult of the Virgin Mary.

SARAPIS

Sarapis was a wholly syncretic deity, invented under the Ptolemies who conflated Osiris, Isis' consort, with the sacred Apis bulls. The resulting god, Osor-apis, or Sarapis, then became identified with the dynasty and with Zeus/Jupiter.

Worshipped in Alexandria as a bearded man, Sarapis was seen by the Greeks as a healing god, similar to Asclepius, the Greek healing god who was introduced to Rome in 291BC. Sick people went to his temple to be cured through divine dreams in a process called incubation.

Meanwhile, and supposedly connected with this but in reality perpetuating a far older cult, Egyptian priests continued to worship Apis at Memphis.

Vespasian (ruled AD69–79) titled himself the new Sarapis when he launched his victorious bid for the imperial throne in Alexandria in AD69. Later Caracalla (ruled AD211–17) built an impressive Serapeum on the Quirinal Hill in Rome.

THE SIBYL

At several desperate moments in its history, the Sibyl and the Sibylline books were of crucial importance to Rome. Traditionally, the Sibyl, a priestess of Apollo from Cumae, a Greek colony near Naples, offered to sell King Tarquin nine books of prophecy in the 6th century BC. King Tarquin refused twice to buy them, baulking at the price. Each time he refused, the priestess threw three of the books into the fire and doubled the price of the remainder. Tarquin eventually capitulated and bought the last three, which were then kept in the Capitol. The books were consulted by the Senate in

emergencies about which foreign gods to import. An outbreak of plague led to the introduction of the worship of Apollo in 431BC. The books were also thought to contain prophecies and some Christians later maintained that they foretold the birth of Christ. They were all lost in the invasions of the 5th century AD.

Right: A wayfarer consults the Sibyl. Originally a priestess of Apollo from Greek Cumae, she became central to Rome's religious practices.

CULT OF THE SUN

The Graeco-Roman pantheon was essentially anthropomorphic and did not deify natural phenomena. However, the Greeks worshipped the sun god Helios just as the Romans worshipped Sol Indiges. Worship of Sol Invictus, the Unconquered Sun, was at times linked to the worship of Mithras.

MITHRAS

Possibly Indo-Iranian in origin, Mithras became an archetypal saviour deity for the Romans, a precursor and rival to Christianity. First appearing in Rome in the 1st century BC, Mithras was usually portrayed in Persian clothes wearing a Phrygian cap (from Asia Minor), killing the bull of cosmic darkness.

There were strong astrological associations to the cult of Mithras. Aion (impersonal time) sometimes appeared as a lion-headed deity beside him on carvings and the evil scorpion was depicted being crushed. Mithras offered his worshippers redemption from the otherwise inexorable fate revealed by astrology.

Mithraism's hierarchy mirrored that of the Roman army, of which most of its adherents were members, and initiation into his worship came in grades. Each congregation was composed of *fratres* (brothers) and *patres* (fathers) – titles the Christians later copied – who promised to support each other.

The final initiation rite may have required the neophyte to lie in a pit while the blood of a freshly sacrificed bull showered down on him but, as with other mystery rites, the exact details of Mithraic rites are unknown. The cult was spread around the empire mainly by the army, but it also appealed to unmilitary types such as merchants of Ostia, where 15 *mithraea* (shrines) have been found, and to the emperor Nero. Ever interested in novelties, Nero appeared dressed as Mithras when investing Tiridates as king of Armenia in a grand ceremony at Rome in AD66. In the 2nd century AD, Hadrian and Commodus were initiated as emperors and so, reputedly, was Julian,

Above: The 3rd-century AD Altar to Mithras in the mithraeum of the Circus Maximus in Rome. Most shrines to this god were underground, like this one. Only the initiated were able to watch the rites whose secrets are now lost.

Right: One of the most attractive aspects of Mithraism was its practice of mutual support, which rivalled Christianity's. Here a mystical banquet sanctifies the solidarity of his worshippers.

the last pagan emperor (ruled AD361–3) who ordered the building of a *mithraeum* in Constantinople, the new capital. There was an underground *mithraeum* in London, whose ruins are almost the only Roman buildings which survive in the open in the city. An obvious limitation to the spread of Mithraism was its restriction to men. Mithras' cult vanished with the fall of the Western empire in the 5th century AD.

THE UNCONQUERED SUN

During the imperial period there was a growing tendency among the intellectual to look for a unifying divine force behind the empire's plethora of deities. This is implied in the dedication of the emperor Hadrian's greatest temple, the Pantheon, to *all* the gods.

Sol Invictus, the Unconquered Sun, was first mentioned in the 2nd century AD and the emperor Septimius Severus added a radiant solar nimbus to his imperial attributes around the same time. His son Caracalla, who extended Roman citizenship to (almost) all free inhabitants of the empire in AD212, unwittingly furthered such syncretic attempts to unite the gods in the *pax deorum*, the harmony of the heavens. (Caracalla was concerned chiefly with extending the death duties which were paid only by Roman citizens.)

The solar cult took a giant step forward in the reign of Elagabalus (ruled AD218–22), the juvenile high priest of the sun god Baal in Emesa. His orgiastic worship of his Syrian deity, aimed at making Baal superior to all Rome's gods and said to involve human sacrifices and mass homosexual orgies, proved too much for Romans. After his assassination his successor Alexander Severus carefully restored the older gods.

Alexander reputedly had images of many saviours in his private chapel, including Orpheus, the legendary poet, Apollonius of Tyana, a recent pagan magus, Abraham and Christ. Yet in the subsequent catastrophic decades, when the empire almost foundered amid endless civil wars, barbarian invasions and

massive economic disruption, people yearned for a simpler, universal god. Among these, Sol Invictus, immediately visible as an object of adoration and the obvious bringer of light to all men, incorruptible and perfectly round, had the strongest appeal. The emperor Aurelian (ruled AD270–5), who regained Gaul and the Eastern provinces for the empire and built Rome's new walls, also built a fine circular temple to Sol Invictus in Rome. With a special new priestly college, Sol Invictus was now made the primary object of official imperial worship in Rome and across the empire and 25th December, the dedication day of the temple, was made a public holiday. Christmas was later deliberately moved to that date.

The tetrarch Constantius Chlorus (ruled AD293–306) also worshipped the Unconquered Sun as did Constantine I in his early years, until the Edict of Milan in AD313, when he and his co-emperor Licinius proclaimed tolerance for all religions. Even in AD324, after his final victory over Licinius, Constantine was still issuing coins bearing images of Sol Invictus and in Constantinople he erected a statue of himself with a crown of solar rays. Although this reflected political caution vis-à-vis his overwhelmingly pagan subjects, it also shows the solar cult was not just an imperial preference.

Above: A reconstruction of a Mithraic temple showing Mithras slaying the bull of cosmic darkness. The most popular saviour god among the legions, Mithras was also worshipped by civilians, but his cult excluded women.

Below: Head of the sun-god Helios or Sol Invictus. The Romans were slow to worship the impersonal sun, but 3rd-century AD crises led Aurelian to institute an official cult of the sun to help unite the empire.

CHRISTIANITY: TRIBULATION TO TRIUMPH

Above: A head of Constantine I hints at the colossal arrogance of the first emperor to actively promote Christianity.

Below: The Apostles Peter and Paul from an early 4th-century AD Roman bas-relief. St Peter's, Rome, was one of the first great basilicas.

In *c.* AD33 Jesus, an obscure but probably heterodox Jewish preacher, was put to death on the reluctant orders of the governor of Judaea, Pontius Pilate. The event had no impact on the Roman empire, although Jesus' followers claimed to have seen him alive soon after and began preaching his resurrection, first to Jewish communities around the Mediterranean and then, under the forceful guidance of Paul of Tarsus, to the wider Greek and Latin-speaking world.

A NEW RELIGION

Initially considered a form of Judaism by the Romans, Christianity was recognized as a distinct sect in AD64 after the great fire of Rome, which the people blamed Nero for starting. The Christians made useful scapegoats for the emperor, who had some rounded up, coated with pitch and set alight. Even Roman audiences found this hard to stomach and such mass persecutions were long the exception. The Christians were not popular, however. Tacitus, writing *c.* AD100, called them "haters of the human race". Like many Romans he misunderstood Christianity's doctrines and saw the eucharist as an orgy involving cannibalism.

Christianity first appealed mainly to women and slaves and so attracted official suspicion. However, letters between Trajan and Pliny the Younger, *c.* AD110, show the emperor restraining would-be persecutors, insisting that Christians be given fair trials and forbidding anonymous letters of accusation. Hadrian restated this approach in AD122.

Although mobs seem to have enjoyed tormenting this helpless minority, Christianity continued to expand and the Christian church's cellular structure proved supportive in a way unmatched by any other cult. Christianity also appealed to intellectuals (such as St Clement) and to the illiterate alike.

What Christians believed did not worry most pagans; it was what they openly refused to accept that caused problems, especially when the empire was in crisis. By refusing even to sacrifice incense to Roma and the imperial *genius* (spirit), Christians were offending the *pax deorum*, the gods' united protection that the empire desperately needed. This led to imperially sponsored persecutions, from the brief attack under Decius (AD251) to the Great Persecution launched by Diocletian and Galerius in AD303.

Not only priests but ordinary believers were now hunted out. Diocletian himself was no fanatic – he had a Christian wife – nor were many of his officials. Transcripts of AD303 show the governor of Egypt urging his Christian prisoners to reconsider their decision the next day. Many Christians did abjure, but Christian

martyrs (witnesses) went to their deaths with impressive confidence in the life to come, finally convincing Galerius and many others that persecution was pointless. In AD311 Galerius rescinded his edicts and asked Christians, too, to pray for the empire.

CONSTANTINE'S CONVERSION

Traditionally Constantine had a dream the night before his victory at the Milvian Bridge in AD312 which led him to put Christian insignia on his army's standards, so guaranteeing him victory. Afterwards, he noticeably failed to climb the Capitol to make the usual offerings to Jupiter.

While the Edict of Milan in AD313 granted toleration to all religions, Constantine attended the Council of Bishops at Arles in AD314 and the more important Council of Nicaea in AD325. At both, he vainly strove to reconcile warring factions, for Christians, upon ceasing to be persecuted themselves, now began persecuting each other.

Further victories confirmed Constantine in his belief that he was protected by the Christian god. However, he continued to employ pagans and for a time himself observed pagan rituals, even permitting the restoration of old temples in Byzantium after he made it his capital.

Such moves were common sense, as perhaps 95 per cent of his court, army and empire were non-Christian. Nonetheless, he tried to restrict public pagan sacrifices and exempted the Christian clergy from onerous public duties where possible.

Constantine also had material reasons for favouring Christianity. The pagan temples whose despoliation he started were filled not just with centuries of great artworks, many covered with gold and ivory, but had also been used as safe deposits by locals in the absence of reliable banks. Constantine's looting of old treasures – comparable in scale perhaps to Henry VIII's dissolution of the monasteries – helped to pay for his huge building programme. This included not only his

many secular works – in Rome and Constantinople – but also vast numbers of churches, including Old St Peter's and St John Lateran in Rome.

When Constantine died in AD337 (he was buried in the Church of the Apostles in Constantinople), his successors continued his Christianizing policies. The notable but brief exception of Julian's two-year reign revived pagan hopes but failed to shake the slowly emerging Christian establishment.

Imperial toleration of paganism, which was always reluctant, vanished in the later 4th century AD. In AD386 the fervently Christian emperor Theodosius I ordered the removal of the statue of the goddess Victory from the Senate House in Rome, despite the impassioned protestations of Symmachus, a pagan, that "So great a mystery could not be approached by one path alone".

With the disasters of the 5th century AD, most Romans in the West turned in despair to Christianity, whose kingdom was not of this world. However, in the East paganism survived in substantial pockets into the 6th century AD.

Above: The disciples pictured in the catacombs of St Callistus in Rome. Christians may have worshipped in the catacombs and were buried there, but they did not live there.

Below: This mosaic from the 5th-century AD Mausoleum of Galla Placidia in Ravenna shows St Lawrence the Martyr as a deacon carrying a cross. Martyrs were much revered.

CHAPTER XXII

SPORT AND GAMES

Games, especially gladiatorial combats and chariot races, are among the most famous, even notorious, aspects of life in ancient Rome. Many Roman cities built amphitheatres. The Colosseum in Rome was the largest such arena in the Roman world, but gladiatorial games were first staged in the Forum Romanum and beast displays in the Circus Maximus, which could accommodate possibly six times as many spectators as the Colosseum.

The games required expensively trained professionals, most of whom were slaves, and did not necessarily involve the killing of the human combatants. Although the chariot races staged in the Circus Maximus in Rome were indisputably expensive and dangerous, the arenas of less well-developed provinces such as Britain may have seen far more sporting contests and military tattoos than gladiator fights.

The Circus and the Colosseum were also the venues for *venationes*, wild beast hunts and games which, along with public executions, were much relished by audiences. Roman theatre, in contrast, saw mimes, dances and the Roman *pantomimus* – an entertainment which often involved real violence – grow in popularity during the empire.

Physical fitness was long thought desirable in Rome, where men were liable for arduous military service in the Republic. Exercise grounds were later laid out in Rome and other cities.

Left: A wild beast hunt in a 4th-century AD mosaic. These venationes *(wild beast hunts) rivalled gladiatorial displays in their popularity.*

GLADIATORIAL COMBATS

Above: A terracotta oil lamp from the 1st century AD, showing gladiators in combat. Gladiatorial combats were popular decorative themes.

Below: A Retiarius (right) and a Secutor (left) depicted on a mosaic from a Roman villa in Negra de Valpolicella, Italy.

Gladiatorial combats were funerary in origin, hence their name *numera* (rewards, sacrifices). The spirits of the dead were thought to appreciate human blood, so captives or slaves were set to fight each other to death at aristocratic funerals.

The first recorded gladiatorial show in Rome was staged in 264BC, when three pairs of gladiators fought to the death in the Forum Boarium (Cattle Market) for the funeral of Marcus Iunius Brutus. Over the next 200 years, Roman nobles competed to put on ever more lavish shows. In 65BC, Julius Caesar displayed 250 pairs of gladiators at funeral games for his father – who had died 20 years before.

This extravagance, which the Senate tried to limit, was an attempt to win votes, for, as Juvenal later noted, *duas tantem res anxius optat, panem et circenses* ("The mob cares only for bread and circuses"). Finally the emperor became the main, often sole, provider of games for Rome's frequent public holidays, while in other cities local magnates continued to provide gorily expensive games involving gladiators and wild animals. Games were often staged as part of ceremonies to do with the imperial cult in the provinces or with triumphs in Rome under the emperors.

At first, gladiators were recruited from among slaves, condemned criminals or war captives. Later, as supplies of these groups dwindled, some free men volunteered for a fixed, usually three- or five-year term. Some slaves were sold off for training as gladiators by owners who wanted to punish them, until Hadrian forbade the practice in the 2nd century AD.

A successful gladiator might hope to earn his *rudis* (wooden sword) of liberty, after three years in the arena and to make enough money from gifts to retire in comfort before he was killed.

SCHOOLS FOR GLADIATORS

Gladiatorial training was always arduous and often brutal. Petronius recorded the oath of obedience that the *tiro* (novice gladiator) swore to his *lanista* (trainer), "We solemnly swear to obey the *lanista* in everything. To endure burning, imprisonment, flogging and even death by the sword". Although discipline was savage, the food was good and accommodation not bad by contemporary standards.

Novice gladiators learned how to fight with wooden swords and wicker shields, feinting at the *palus* (wooden post) before progressing to real but padded weapons in a way that paralleled military training. *Lanistae* were used in the later 2nd century BC to train soldiers and in emergencies, such as the Marcomanni invasions of AD167, gladiators could be enrolled into the army, receiving their freedom in return. As it took several years to train a skilled gladiator, they did not usually fight to the death.

Training schools for gladiators were established across Italy and then the Western parts of the empire. In Rome, about 2,000 gladiators, along with doctors, armourers and trainers, lived in one of four *ludi* (schools), of which the biggest was the Ludus Magnus, located just 60 yards east of the Colosseum. Probably started under Domitian (ruled AD81–96), its construction was completed under Hadrian 30 years later. It was an imposing building of brick-faced concrete with a central courtyard surrounded by porticoes. Occupying much of this courtyard was an arena large enough to accommodate 3,000 spectators, where gladiators practised. The Ludus Magnus was connected with the Colosseum by an underground tunnel.

To the south of the Ludus Magnus and much the same size was the Ludus Matutinus, where *venatores*, wild beast fighters, were trained. These schools were considered so central to Rome's well-being that they were eventually run by the state. The emperors appointed Praetorian Prefects to recruit and supervise the training of new gladiators.

TYPES OF GLADIATOR

By the early imperial period there were a number of different types of gladiator, who were usually identified by their equipment and fighting tactics.

The Samnite or *hoplomachus* was originally a light-armed fighter, who was not necessarily a Samnite but who fought like one. He became progressively more heavily armed and armoured until he was called a *hoplomachus*, like a Greek heavy infantryman. He now wore a large-crested helmet with thigh-length greaves and carried a large rectangular shield and a stabbing sword (the *gladius hispaniensis*), much like a legionary.

The Thracian gladiator emerged in the 2nd century BC when Rome first encountered this warlike part of the Balkans. He was armed with a small round or square shield and two thigh-length greaves and carried a *sica*, a typical curved weapon from the Danube.

The Gaul was at first lightly armed, with a long flat shield and a cut and thrust sword about 2ft (60cm) long. By the end of the Republic he too had gained a helmet and a slashing sword. He then became better known as a *murmillo*, from the Greek fish *murmillon* which adorned his helmet.

The Secutor, the traditional opponent of the net-wielding Retiarius (literally sword man), was among the most recognizable of gladiators, for he had a unique egg-shaped helmet with a metal crest but no brim. He bore the legionary's *scutum* (rectangular shield) and stabbing sword and had a laminated *manicae* (arm-guard).

The Retiarius was armed with a *rete* (net) and trident and had defensive armour only on his left arm and shoulder. He normally fought one of the more heavily-armed gladiators. Technically, the Retiarius was not a gladiator since he did not have a sword.

There are records of women gladiators, who fought each other and wild beasts, but they were less common and in AD200 were banned altogether.

Below: A typically ornate gladiator's bronze helmet from Pompeii, 1st century AD. Gladiators always dressed to impress.

Below: This swordsman, probably a hoplomachos *or* murmillo, *seems to have just finished off a Retiarius, a trident-wielding netman, who is lying beside him.*

THE GREAT GAMES

Above: Gladiatorial combats continued into the 4th century AD, as this mosaic shows. Here a heavily armoured gladiator is shown with a dead Retiarius.

By the time of the late Republic and early empire huge numbers of gladiators were assembled and wounded or killed for special celebrations. For example, the games that marked the inauguration of the Amphitheatrum Flavium, or Colosseum, in AD80, reputedly lasted 100 days.

THE CONDUCT OF THE GAMES

Such games opened with a procession of gladiators, who had had a special dinner (the *libera cena*) in public the night before, although not all may have been feeling hungry. To rousing music from a band in the arena – consisting typically of a water organ, horn blowers and trumpeters – they marched around the arena two abreast in full costume, with purple and gold embroideries if they could afford it. When they reached the *pulvinar* (imperial box), they raised their right hands and cried out, *Ave, Caesar! Morituri te salutant!* ("Hail Caesar, those about to die salute you!")

The gladiators were then paired off by lot. Different types of gladiator were pitted against each other; a nimble Retiarius against a heavier Secutor, for example. Often the *lanista* was present less as a

referee than to goad them on with whips and cries of *Iugula! Verbera!* ("Kill! Strike!"), cries which the crowd echoed. Bets were placed and the fight lasted until one combatant was either badly wounded or surrendered. Then trumpets sounded and the wounded man appealed for *missio* (reprieve). The games' sponsor – in Rome normally the emperor – then turned to the spectators. If they thought the gladiator had fought well, they cried *Mitte* ("Let him go"). If the emperor agreed, he would "press his thumb" – a Latin phrase whose precise meaning is unknown but which is interpreted in Hollywood films as raising his thumb. Otherwise, an attendant dressed as Charon, a figure from the underworld, approached with a mallet to finish off the defeated gladiator, whose corpse was dragged through the Porta Libitina (Gate of Execution) with hooks.

The bloodied sand was then replaced while the victor pranced around the arena receiving gifts from spectators and perhaps the palm of success. More rarely he won the wooden foil of freedom. Graffiti from Pompeii, which had the earliest permanent amphitheatre, record various gladiators' fates: "Pugnax, a Thracian of the Neronian *ludus* with three fights to his credit, victorious; Murrans, a *murmillo* of the Neronian *ludus* with three fights to his credit, killed… Atticus, a Thracian with 14 fights, killed".

STAGED SEA BATTLES

Sea fights with small galleys (*naumachiae*) were also staged. At his triumph in 46BC, Julius Caesar had an artificial lake dug in the Campus Martius (just outside the city) and a battle enacted. These battles were very realistic. Galleys were propelled by slaves who

Below: Terracotta figurines showing two gladiators fighting. Both are similarly armed with swords.

fought ferociously. Augustus had a special *naumachia* or artificial lake dug in Trastevere across the Tiber, with its own aqueduct. Here in 2BC he staged a lavish re-enactment of Athens' great victory over the Persians at Salamis in 480BC.

For the inauguration of the works to drain Lake Fucinus under Claudius, a *naumachia* involving 19,000 men took place on the lake. It almost ended in farce when Claudius returned the traditional gladiators' salute, "Hail Caesar, those about to die salute you!" with the quip, "Or not, as the case may be". This so annoyed the gladiators that they downed swords and had to be coaxed back to fight. Nero used Augustus' *naumachia* for varied nocturnal frolics but after that it seems to have fallen into decay. The Colosseum may have been partly flooded for *naumachiae* later.

Most Romans accepted and some even defended gladiatorial shows. Cicero asserted they taught Roman audiences contempt for pain and death, while Pliny the Younger maintained that watching such massacres, in which even criminals and slaves showed a love of glory, would make Romans courageous.

A few emperors, such as Marcus Aurelius, who openly dealt with his correspondence in the arena rather than watching the games, tried to interest the Roman populace in *lusiones*, mock games without bloodshed, but were unsuccessful. Claudius, who watched the fights eagerly and spared no wounded Retiarius, was more typically Roman. Expense led to the decline of the games after the 3rd century AD.

SPARTACUS THE REBEL

The most famous gladiator of them all, who challenged and threatened to overthrow Roman power, Spartacus took his name from the Greek city of Sparta, although he probably came from Thrace. Trained at the Capua *ludus*, he started his revolt there in 73BC, leading the gladiators out from their barracks, then freeing agricultural slaves to form an army many

thousands strong. Reputedly, Spartacus had once served as a Roman soldier, which explains how he managed to defeat hastily conscripted armies sent against him.

For a time Spartacus controlled much of southern Italy. Finally Crassus, the richest man in Rome, was given command. Decimating his legions (killing one man in ten) to restore order, and with the help of Pompey arriving belatedly from Spain, he cornered and destroyed Spartacus' army in 71BC. Along the Via Appia from Rome to Capua 7,000 rebels were crucified in ghastly but effective warning. There were no more such revolts.

Above: An orchestra, sometimes with a woman playing the water organ, often accompanied the games, as in this mosaic from Zliten, near Lepcis Magna, Africa.

Below: In this 4th-century AD mosaic, found on the Via Appia, just outside Rome, gladiatorial combat is carefully controlled by the lanistae, the trainers. Strict rules governed most combats.

WILD BEAST GAMES

Above: A bestiarius (animal fighter) is thrown into the air by a bull in this 3rd-century AD funerary stone from Africa. Fighting wild beasts could be very dangerous.

Below: A lion fight in the Circus Maximus in Rome in the 1st century AD. The lion on the right seems to have already killed a man, but is about to be speared himself. On the left a lioness leaps to savage an armed man.

Parallel to the gladiators' fights were the *venationes*, the wild beast games, which were if anything an even larger business. The *venatores* (huntsmen) and the *bestiarii* (animal fighters) had their own *ludus*, the Ludus Matutinus (so-called because the beast displays were usually staged in the morning), although they never enjoyed the same prestige as gladiators.

Venationes provided the Roman urban populace with a glimpse of the often dangerous hunting – for wild boar among other animals – that the emperor himself enjoyed in the country proper. However, they became almost as ruinously expensive as the *munera*.

The first *venationes* or hunting displays started innocuously enough: a hundred elephants that had been captured from the Carthaginians in 251BC were forced to perform tricks. However, in the 2nd century BC more violent displays developed. By 99BC, full-scale fights between elephants were being staged in the Circus Maximus. Marcus Scaurus, who reportedly built a luxurious if temporary amphitheatre of marble and glass in 58BC, imported 150 leopards along with a hippopotamus and five crocodiles for his games. Increasingly bloody *venationes* were hosted from then on.

Caesar had 600 lions, 400 other great cats and 20 elephants in his triumphant *venatio*. Titus surpassed this, killing 5,000 animals on one day to inaugurate the Colosseum in AD80. Trajan had 2,246 wild beasts slaughtered in just one of his many *munera*. The poet Martial mentions more innocent circus turns, including teams of panthers obediently drawing chariots and elephants kneeling to trace Latin phrases in the sand with their trunks. The populace wanted blood, however, and to satisfy it the Romans pitted bears against water buffalos, panthers against leopards, lions against tigers and bulls against rhinoceroses. (The latter were normally victorious, tossing great bulls into the air like balls.)

The *venatores*, armed with spears, bows, daggers and firebrands and sometimes assisted by hunting dogs, fought animals in the arena. Trees and shrubs were placed in the arena to create the illusion of a forest in which the *venatores* hunted and killed the doomed animals. The Romans were no more sentimental about killing animals than about killing humans and viewed the *venationes* as a re-affirmation of their dominance over nature.

Criminals were sometimes executed by the *damnatio ad bestias* (thrown unarmed or with rudimentary weapons into the arena to face wild animals or gladiators). War captives were another source of arena fodder. Under Claudius, captive Britons were slaughtered in the arena in AD47. Titus had Jewish captives killed in games after the Jewish War (AD66–70) and Constantine I had Frankish captives thrown into the ring in Trier in AD308 to celebrate his victory over them. At the other extreme, one or two debauched

emperors, including Nero and Commodus, personally took part in the games. Commodus actually performed in the arena, shooting hundreds of ostriches to demonstrate his *virtus* (courage), but Nero forced senators and equestrians to fight (though not kill) in the arena themselves. Young Roman nobles under the empire sometimes stepped into the arena to fight as amateurs to exhibit their *virtus*, but gladiators on the whole never escaped their low status. Although a few became celebrities, no gladiator ever held high office, although some were used as bodyguards or assassins.

CATASTROPHIC EFFECTS
The Romans imported exotic wild beasts from all over the empire and at times from well beyond their frontiers. In the first millennium BC, great cats such as lions, panthers and tigers still roamed freely in western Asia; in 51BC Cicero's brother, who was governor of Cilicia, was asked to supply panthers from Asia. There were hippopotami and crocodiles on the banks of the Nile and elephants and ostriches could be found north of the Sahara. This rich fauna was devastated over the centuries, as a highly efficient system of capturing and transporting them was established to satisfy audiences in Rome and in other great cities around the empire. By the 4th century AD it was becoming increasingly hard to find animals to satisfy the demands of the arena. Almost none of these great animals, with the exception of a few lions in the Rif Mountains of Morocco, are to be found north of the Sahara or west of India today.

Above: A Roman fresco from the amphitheatre of Mérida in Spain showing a venator *(huntsman) facing a lion with only a spear. Animal games were popular in cities all round the empire.*

Below: Arena substructures, possibly a lion pit, in the amphitheatre of Thysdrus (El Djem), Africa, built c. AD230.

AT THE CIRCUS: CHARIOT RACES

Above: Chariot races in the Circus Maximus, Rome, with the spina *in the centre.*

Below: A quadriga *chariot from a 3rd-century* AD *mosaic. Only one man rode a chariot.*

Although they had different origins, the *ludi circenses* (circus games) were the *munera*'s greatest rival attraction. Racing with chariots generally took place in the Circus Maximus (the biggest circus). The arena was well-named since it was truly vast, over 660yds (600m) long and 220yds (200m) wide, sited in a natural hollow between the Aventine and Palatine Hills. Progressively adorned, it was given its final form under Trajan, who turned it into a massive structure with three marble-faced arcades built up on vaults. It is estimated it could seat up to 300,000 people, about a third of the city's population.

THE RUNNING OF THE RACES

All drivers belonged to one of four *factiones* (teams) in the imperial period: the Whites, the Reds, the Blues and the Greens. These were sizeable companies or corporations, each with its own stables and team of trainers, coaches, saddlers, vets, blacksmiths and grooms sited in the Ninth Region of the City near the present Palazzo Farnese.

The *factio* normally supported by the people was the Greens, while the Senate supported the Blues. Huge bets were placed on each team or rider. The number of races held per day was 12 under Augustus, but under Caligula – who was almost literally mad about the games – this was doubled and 24 races a day became the standard. Each lasted 7 laps of 620yds (568m), run anti-clockwise around the central *spina* (masonry rib). This was decorated with seven metallic eggs, seven bronze dolphins and other statues. At each end of the *spina* were the *metae* (turning posts).

Most races were for *quadrigae*, four-horse teams. Two-, three-, six-, eight- and even rarely ten-horse teams (*decemiuges*) were known, but the last was normally reserved for egomaniacs like Nero who drove one while collecting every prize at the Olympic Games in AD67. Only the inner pair of horses actually pulled the chariot. The outer pair were only loosely attached by a *junis* (trace),but they were vital to the chariot's stability. Racing chariots were mere boxes, given a little stability only by their driver's weight.

Charioteers wore short sleeveless tunics and leather helmets, and carried knives to cut themselves free from the leads tied round their waists if there was a collision. As up to 12 *quadrigae* chariots could compete in the circus, collisions were common occurrences.

Before a race started, each of the chariots was placed in one of the *carceres* (starting gates). Above them a magistrate presided over the games. When he gave the signal, by dropping a white napkin into the circus, a trumpet sounded, a spring mechanism opened the gates and the chariots were off. Each charioteer strove to attain the best inner position on the left, but fine judgement was crucial. If his chariot wheel so much as touched the *spina*'s stone kerb, it could shatter, wrecking his own and probably others' chariots in the crash. However, if his chariot swung out too far, it risked losing the advantage of the inner position.

As each lap was completed, one of the eggs on the *spina* was lowered to keep count. The last lap was the most excitingly dangerous of all. The winner was greeted with ecstatic applause and given a victor's palm or gold crown and neck chains. To placate the losers among the spectators – and many poorer Romans gambled madly – donations of money would be thrown to the audience and free meals provided afterwards.

As well as the races, there were exhibitions of trick-riding and other less dangerous gymnastic sports. The Circus Maximus also staged wild beast shows.

FAMOUS CHARIOTEERS

Although almost all charioteers were slaves or ex-slaves – and so scarcely higher in Rome's social hierarchy than gladiators – a few became very famous and very rich, both from gifts they received from magistrates and other rich men and also from the fantastic wages they could command from their *factio* for their loyalty.

Supreme among these star charioteers was Gaius Apuleius Diocles, who competed 4,257 times and won 1,462 victories. He wisely retired in AD150 – with a fortune of 35 million sesterces – to a life of quiet philanthropy at Pozzuoli.

Others in the races' heyday – the later 1st and early 2nd centuries AD – also did extremely well. They were known as *milliari* not because they were millionaires – although they often were – but because they had competed more than 1,000 times in the races. Among these *milliari* were Pompeius Musclosus, who competed 3,559 times, and Scorpus, who completed 2,048 races before he was killed.

Chariot-racing, unlike gladiatorial combat, was not banned by the newly Christian rulers of the empire. Indeed, a hippodrome (circus) in the new capital of Constantinople was built right next to the imperial palace in direct emulation of Rome. The bitter rivalry that existed between the Blues and Greens (the other *factiones* were ultimately subsumed) also continued into the 6th century AD and caused the *Nike* (victory) riots in AD529 that almost drove the emperor Justinian from his throne.

Above: Chariot-racing was popular in the provinces too, as this 2nd century AD mosaic from Lyons, then Gaul's greatest city, shows.

Below: A charioteer from the Circus Maximus, Rome, in the 1st century AD. Horses were occasionally raced individually by jockeys as well as being used to pull chariots.

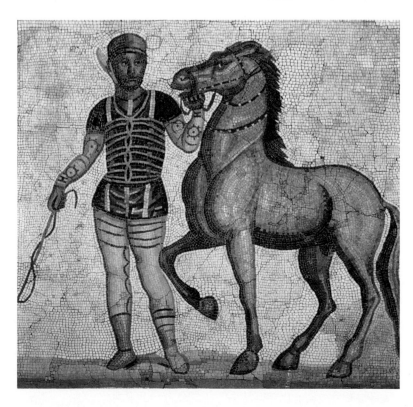

AT THE THEATRE: FARCE, MIME AND PANTOMIME

Above: Two actors wearing masks, from a 1st century AD relief. Roman actors normally wore masks both for comedy and for tragedy.

Below: A 1st-century AD fresco of a tragic actor. This copies a Greek 4th century BC original, revealing Roman links with Greek drama.

Other entertainments the Romans enjoyed were *ludi scaenici* (theatrical performances), performed in the impressive theatres found in almost every city across the empire. These still often splendid buildings give a misleading impression of the importance of theatre, especially of tragedy, to the Romans, however.

In the Roman world, theatre never had the central role that it had in the cities of classical and Hellenistic Greece (500–100BC). This was partly due to the rival attractions of circus and arena which shaped public tastes. Traditional plays without music or dancing were supplemented by musicals accompanied by dancing, spectacular performances, mimes and *pantomimus*. In these lavish displays, spoken dialogue took a distant second place after extravagant special effects.

THE ORIGINS OF ROMAN THEATRE

Roman theatre emerged in the 4th century BC with broad comedy and farce, the *Phlyakes* and the Atellan farces and was performed mainly in southern Italy. The actors wore grotesque masks and padded costumes suiting their stock characters, who had ludicrous names such as Bucco and Maccus (both fools) or Dosennus and Manducus (greedy buffoons). As the play's titles also reveal – *The Pig, The Sow, The Inspector of Morality* – this was unsubtle, rustic humour, with satire directed not at the ruling class – who would have reacted strongly – but at ordinary people.

Rhinthon of Tarento, a Greek city in southern Italy, was one of the most popular playwrights but there was much ad-libbing and many plays were not written down until much later. Farce was the dominant note, forever loved by Italian audiences.

In the 2nd century BC, Plautus and Terence raised the level of comedy. Their plays, concerned with love and its problems, were inspired by the Greek New Comedy, which lacked the satirical bite of Aristophanes and Old Comedy and so was politically acceptable. Only 21 of the 130 comedies attributed to Plautus survive, but his work and that of Terence remained popular with Roman audiences for centuries. However, the Roman comic repertory expanded only slightly later.

Roman poets such as Ennius (239–169BC) also wrote tragedies, but none has survived. However, tragedy was never very popular with Roman audiences. This was partly due to the huge size of many theatres. (The Theatre of Pompey in Rome seated an audience of around 29,000 and the Theatre of Marcellus seated around 14,000.) Such vast structures were not well-suited to plays that required the audience to concentrate carefully on spoken dialogue, no matter how good

their acoustics. It was more importantly due to the fact that Roman audiences were generally less well-educated than those of classical Greece and to their wish to be entertained and amused rather than intellectually taxed. Seneca's melodramatic tragedies, so influential in later European theatre, were probably never performed in public at all but reserved for private readings.

BRUTAL THRILLS

Perhaps the fundamental reason why Roman audiences turned away from even the broadest situation comedy lay in their increasing attraction, even addiction to the brutal thrills provided by the amphitheatre and circus.

However, the Romans resourcefully found other uses for their theatres. These involved dance or balletic performances, mime and pantomime. The last was a truly Roman invention, consisting of masked dancers miming a story, which was often based on, or a burlesque of, myth. The first great *pantomimus* (He Who Mimes Everything) was Pylades in Augustus' reign, an actor of great skill who performed most of the action accompanied by music. His performances were so popular that they literally caused riots.

The earlier Roman stage had no actresses and women's roles had been taken by men, as in Greece. Women now appeared on stage, not wearing heavy masks but elaborately made up to add to their appeal. In some later mimes actresses stripped off completely. This was especially useful for enacting mythical scenes such as the rape of Pasiphae, the Cretan queen who became so enamoured of a bull she had a special wooden cow built in which to receive him. (The resulting child was the half-bull, the Minotaur.)

At times, executions in the plot, such as that of *Laureolus*, were literally carried out on criminals. *Laureolus*, who was crucified, remained very popular with Roman audiences for two centuries, as did the *Death of Hercules*, which involved the immolation of a criminal on a pyre.

There is no evidence that these "plays" were staged in the theatre, although they were certainly staged in the Colosseum in AD80. Some theatres in the Eastern half of the empire, where purpose-built amphitheatres were rare, were adapted to stage gladiatorial combats or wild beast displays, even in Athens itself. The citizens of the supposedly more civilized east seem to have got over their initial revulsion, although the first gladiatorial games performed in Antioch reportedly caused a riot.

Actors were considered scarcely better than charioteers or gladiators socially. It was thought demeaning for a Roman citizen to act at all, such things being better left to half-Greek freedmen.

When Nero performed in public theatres, sometimes taking female roles, he deeply shocked all Roman opinion, not just among the nobility. The Christian emperors finally put an end to such entertainments because of their religious associations, which St Augustine found particularly immoral.

Above: Broadest comedy was what most pleased Roman audiences. Buffoonish comic actors such as this one, with his clown-like mask, from a 1st century AD mosaic at Pompeii, were much loved.

Below: Elaborate masks such as this one, depicted on a floor mosaic, covered the faces of all actors except some women in later productions, who even reputedly sometimes stripped.

GAMES AND EXERCISES

Above: Caracalla built (AD 211–17) enormous public baths that included palaestrae (exercise areas).

Below: Roman aspiration to Greek athleticism is exemplified by this statue of c. 100BC, in which a Roman head is stuck on a Greek body.

The Romans regarded keeping fit as a vital part of a citizen's personal regime, but they never fostered a cult of athletics in the way that the Greeks did. Their lack of enthusiasm for nudity was the inverse of the Greeks' near mania for depicting heroic nudity, from soldiers on funerary monuments to stark naked gods, wearing only a helmet. Combined with the ingrained Roman sense of *dignitas*, this meant that no athlete became a civic hero as had happened so often in Greece. However, *mens sana in corpore sano* ("A healthy body and a healthy mind"), as Juvenal put in one of his less satirical satires, was a Roman motto as much as a Greek ideal.

Although ordinary Roman life involved at least a modicum of daily exercise for everyone, rich Romans, unlike their counterparts in classical Greece, appear to have suffered from some of the diseases of affluence, possibly because they were such very enthusiastic gourmands.

From the later Republic on, Rome was a crowded city notably lacking in public spaces. To counter this, Marcus Agrippa, Augustus' chief minister, built *palaestrae* (exercise grounds or gyms) in the open land of the Campus Martius just west of the old Servian walls where the

Above: Boxing, shown in this 3rd century AD mosaic from Africa, was a popular participatory sport.

very first legions had mustered. Later *palaestrae* were generally attached to the great public baths, so that athletes could bathe after their exercises. At Trajan's Baths, built AD104–9, a corporation or club of athletes was based in the large open-air *palaestra* on the Baths' west side. It flourished for more than 200 years up to the mid-4th century AD. There seems to have been a similar corporation in the Baths of Caracalla, which were built just over a century later.

Wrestling was a popular sport and wrestlers used to smear themselves with *ceroma*, a lotion composed of oil and wax which made the skin more supple. Women also wrestled occasionally, thereby offending the moralistic Juvenal. Dumbbells were popular with men and women as was rolling a metal hoop and running.

BALL GAMES

The Romans had many kinds of ball game. These included the *trigon*, in which three players formed a triangle and tossed the ball back and forth between them; a sort of tennis played with the palm of the hand for a racquet; and the *harpastum*, in which contestants had to catch the sand-filled ball as it flew between players. For all these games except wrestling, a short tunic was worn, for the Romans generally did not like to exercise naked as the Greeks did.

PUBLIC GAMES

None of these simple sports could rival the races or gladiatorial games in popularity, but there were repeated attempts under Nero and Domitian in Rome to enthuse the populace about athletic displays derived from Greek models. This was partly, no doubt, because they were cheaper as well as more edifying to stage than *munera* or *ludi*.

Athletics displays were popular as interval entertainment in the circus, and continued to be important in the Greek part of the Roman empire. Augustus, following the precedents of some earlier philhellenes such as Pompey, founded the Actiaca, games to commemorate his victory at Actium, in which he encouraged young Roman nobles to participate in Greek-style games. He had only fleeting success, however, for the Actiaca is not recorded after AD16 (only two years after the emperor's death).

True to his philhellenism, Nero tried to revive these contests with his Neronia, which were intended to be regular festivals with both athletic and poetic competitions. The senatorial nobility participated in the first but shunned the second, probably because they feared competing directly against the emperor.

It was Domitian (ruled AD81–96), normally considered among the more dourly despotic of emperors, who finally established a cycle of athletic games which endured. In AD86 he set up the *Agon Capitolinus* (Capitoline Games), with prizes for racing on foot, boxing, discus-throwing and javelin-throwing, as well as for eloquence, Latin and Greek poetry and music. He built the Circus Agonalis, now the Piazza Navona, for the sporting

events and an Odeum on Monte Giordano and the Campus Martius for the cultural contests. The poet Martial sang the praises of the winners. The games survived Domitian's assassination and continued into the 4th century AD. This was partly because they recurred only once every four years, but also because they were aimed at relatively small, select audiences. The Odeum could seat no more than about 5,000 people and the stadium only about 15,000. These were small numbers compared to the crowds in the Colosseum and the Circus Maximus.

Unlike theatres and amphitheatres, these games were not widely copied around the Western empire. In Greece itself the Olympic Games continued to be staged, although the Roman nobility chose not to compete. Theodosius banned them by AD393.

Above: Two wrestlers in a gymnasium are shown in this relief from the tomb of Caecilia Metella. Wrestling was a hugely popular sport. Wrestlers would smear themselves all over with ceroma, an oil and wax lotion to make it harder for their opponents to grip them.

Left: A sculpture of a Hellenistic athlete, signed by Agasias of Ephesus and dated to c. 100BC. Such fine imported artworks helped shape Roman attitudes to physical beauty.

CHAPTER XXIII

SCIENCE, TECHNOLOGY AND THE ECONOMY

The Romans, famously pragmatic, were not speculative scientists in the Greek mould, but in the prosperous centuries of the Pax Romana (Roman peace) neither science nor technology stood still. Most scientists were polymaths, interested in many fields. Strabo was a philosopher and historian as well as a famed geographer, while Ptolemy wrote on music and mechanics. Practical matters were not neglected, although they were under-recorded by writers concerned with more prestigious subjects. Water power was exploited more thoroughly, new forms of concrete and glass were developed and ships became far larger. Agriculture, too, made incremental advances and better olive presses were introduced. One revolutionary idea was developed for a tantalizing instant only to be abandoned: Hero's steam engine.

Despite the Romans' complete ignorance of economic theory, there was an immense boom in trade both within and beyond the empire, with new routes reaching as far as India and even China. Massive amounts of wheat and olive oil were shipped across the Mediterranean from Egypt and North Africa. Intercontinental trade on such a massive scale would not recur before the 17th century.

Left: A Roman soldier kills Archimedes, the Greek scientist, during the siege of Syracuse. Fortunately such disasters were exceptional, for Greek science flourished under Roman rule.

STRABO AND GRAECO-ROMAN GEOGRAPHY

Alexander the Great's conquests as far as northwest India (356–323BC) led to a vast expansion of Greek geographical and scientific knowledge. There followed the golden age of Greek science of the following centuries. This knowledge was collated by Alexander's heirs, especially the Ptolemies of Egypt (322–30BC), who used their vast wealth to turn their museum and library at Alexandria into the greatest scholarly and scientific centre of the ancient world.

A NEW GEOGRAPHY

When Roman power spread – around the Mediterranean, east as far as the Caspian and the Gulf, then north towards the Baltic and Britain – so Roman interest in, and need for, such knowledge grew.

Lucullus and Pompey, the Roman generals who in the last decades of the Republic conquered Eastern kingdoms such as Syria and Pontus, inherited these monarchies' cultural assets and pretensions. Lucullus set up a fine library at Rome with the intellectual spoils of his victories and it was to Rome, the new world ruler,

that Greek philosophers and polymaths such as Posidonius (135–50BC) came, teaching rich Roman students and even a few Greeks. Foremost among the Greek students was Strabo.

Strabo (64BC–*c.* AD21) came from the aristocracy of his native town of Amaseia in northern Asia Minor. Rich and well-connected, he made friends with the Roman nobility, spending long periods in Rome whose government and institutions he admired almost uncritically. "Never before has the world enjoyed such perfect peace and prosperity…cities and peoples united in a single empire, under one government," he enthused. He came to see his work as a two-way bridge between Greek culture and learning and Roman government and authority. Roman power would facilitate the extension of Greek knowledge, while Greek thinking and culture would complement and underpin Roman arms.

Strabo's learning was openly derived from the works of his great predecessors, especially Eratosthenes (275–194BC) – an Athenian who settled in Alexandria to become one of the city's brilliant polymaths – and Posidonius. He wrote in Greek, then the language of almost all scientific thought across the Mediterranean. His first work, a history in 47 books, has vanished completely but he went on to write 17 books on geography which he published in 7BC. These have mostly survived. For Strabo, geography encompassed history, folklore and mythology as well as astronomy and geometry. So, when talking about Palestine and the Jews, he briefly mentions Moses; when discussing Tarento, he notes its legendary and its historical links with its mother city, Sparta.

Strabo accepted the then commonly held view that the Earth was a perfect (immobile) sphere, with all the (known) continents, Europe, Asia and Africa,

Above: Inscribed with many languages, the walls of the Bibliotheca Alexandrina rise in a modern recreation of Alexandria's great library.

Below: The flooding of the Nile was among the mysteries that perennially fascinated Graeco-Roman geographers.

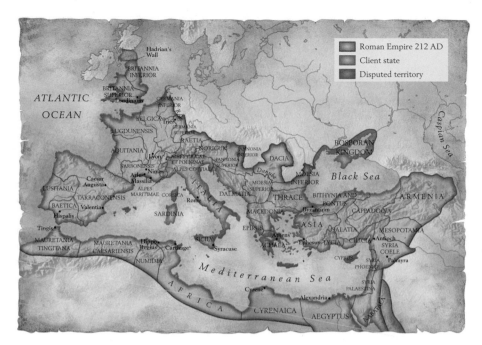

Left: A map of the Roman Empire and its neighbours AD212. As Roman power spread outwards, around the Mediterranean and into northern Europe, Graeco-Roman geographical knowledge grew with it.

forming a single mass surrounded by the encircling waters of Oceanus, a belief as old as Homer. In his first two books he gave reasonably accurate latitudes and longitudes for the cities, oceans and countries he described, ranging from Spain to Assyria (Iraq), from Britain to Ethiopia. He then described each country and people's beliefs and customs.

Strabo seems to have travelled extensively himself, although his description of Armenia suggests that he had a rather credulous acceptance of local beliefs. "Armenia also has huge lakes, one being the Mantiane which, translated, means 'Blue'. It is the largest salt water lake after Lake Mareotis (in Egypt), it is said, extending to Atropatia, and it also has salt works. Another is Arsene, also called Thopitis. It contains soda that cleans and restores clothes, but this ingredient makes the water undrinkable. The Tigris flows through this lake after rising from the mountain country near the Niphates. Because of its swiftness, its current remains unmixed with the lake. Hence its name Tigris, which in Median (Iranian) means arrow."

(*Geography*, Book V.12)

THE ROMAN CONTRIBUTION

Although no later writer under the Roman empire rivalled Strabo in scope and information, he did have successors among writers in Latin, a language still regarded as unsuited for scholarship by many Greek-speakers. For example, Lucius Junius Columella, a Roman of equestrian status from Cadiz who seems to have served as a tribune in the army, wrote a book about geography and agriculture – the two topics were not then distinct – around AD50.

Much the most significant later such writer, however, was Pliny the Elder (AD23–79), an intellectually omnivorous if often undiscriminating writer. In his encyclopaedic works, especially his *Naturalis historia* (*Natural History*) Pliny showed himself the heir of Strabo. He claimed to have recorded 20,000 noteworthy facts about life on earth in its 37 books.

In Books III to VI, Pliny deals with geography and later volumes cover his views on biology and botany. His views, like those of many Latin writers, came to be regarded as almost papally infallible in the Middle Ages.

Below: Roman merchants often ventured beyond the empire's boundaries, but John O'Groats, at Britain's northernmost tip, was Ultima Thule, the furthest land known before the encircling ocean.

ASTRONOMY

Below: The Farnese Atlas, a Roman statue showing the mythical titan who sustained the Earth on his shoulders. Myth and science intermingled in ancient astronomy.

The greatest astronomers of the ancient world were all Greek, although Cicero gave a poetic version in Latin of current cosmogonies in *Scipio's Dream* around 45BC. In the Roman empire Alexandria remained the centre of astronomical science.

Its most brilliant figure was Ptolemy (Claudius Ptolemaus) who wrote in the middle of the 2nd century AD. Ptolemy's work, however, was merely the culmination of a tradition going back six centuries that combined often meticulous observations with daring speculation. Without any form of telescope, all ancient astronomers had to rely solely on what could be discerned of the universe with the naked eye. This inevitably shaped their views.

Greek astronomical theories originated with the early Ionian thinkers of the 6th century BC such as Thales, who predicted the solar eclipse of 585BC, and his reputed pupil Anaximander, but during the classical period (480–320BC) astronomy languished. With the establishment of the great library at Alexandria *c.* 300BC, astronomy was revived as a more systematic science.

About 275BC, one especially daring astronomer, Aristarchus of Samos, had suggested

that, "The fixed stars and the sun stay motionless and the Earth moves in a circle about the sun", but his ideas were almost universally rejected for what were at the time very cogent reasons. (If the Earth rotated around the sun, centrifugal forces would spin everything off the Earth's surface while the "fixed stars" would have to be unbelievably distant to remain fixed in our view of the sky.)

More typical was Eratosthenes who calculated the Earth's circumference with remarkable accuracy (to within 4 per cent) about 225BC. Hipparchus of Nicaea, probably the finest Hellenistic astronomer, invented varied optical aids a century later, drew up star maps and discovered the precession of the equinoxes, while noting a *nova* (new star).

PTOLEMY'S GRAND COMPILATION
Ptolemy inherited, summarized and consolidated these achievements. He wrote books on mathematics, optics – based on his own experiments in refraction and reflection – and geography. However, his great achievement was his *Grand Compilation*, better known by its Arabic name the *Almagest*, which indicates its amalgamated nature.

Developing Hipparchus' system, Ptolemy provided a detailed mathematical theory to describe the movements of the sun and moon and of the five planets known without a telescope: Mercury, Venus, Mars, Jupiter and Saturn. His system, which was based on his own precise astronomical observations, perfected the geocentric theory of the universe, ingeniously detailing the epicycles and regressive motions needed to make the "wandering planets" fit such a system.

Ptolemy also wrote a book on music, *Harmonics*. This describes several musical instruments but is chiefly concerned with mathematically perfect harmony – an idea

first developed by the mystical philosophers Pythagoras and Plato. He believed that such harmony underpinned the universe and linked it with the human soul. One section is headed, "How the interrelations of the planets are to be compared with those of musical notes.".

Such an apparently workable but mystical view of the cosmos proved hugely influential over the next 1,400 years, both in the Christian and Islamic worlds. Shakespeare was still under its sway in 1598 when he wrote the famous passage in *The Merchant of Venice*, which gives perhaps the most lyrical exposition of the geocentric universe. "Look how the floor of heaven is thick inlaid with patines of bright gold/There's not the smallest orb which thou beholdest/but in this motion like an angel sings/still choiring to the young-eyed cherubins./Such harmony is in immortal souls."

A DANGEROUS SCIENCE

Astrology was one of the Romans' many cultural imports from the Hellenistic East The Romans were very superstitious and heeded soothsayers and other diviners, including *haruspices*, who read the future in the entrails of sacrificed animals. Accepted almost universally by intelligent people, astrology was a deadly serious business in the Roman empire.

Astrology's basic premises fitted what was then known of the universe and Ptolemy himself related astrology to his own cosmogony. (The five known planets were increasingly identified with their corresponding gods.)

Augustus and his friend Agrippa, young men in 44BC, consulted the astrologer Theogenes at Apollonia in Greece – he predicted amazing futures for both – while Augustus' gloomy successor Tiberius kept his own astrologer Thrasyllus, who established an observatory at Capri. As astrologers were thought to be able to forecast precisely the hour of an emperor's death, it became a crime under the more paranoid Caesars to consult one on such a sensitive subject.

The despotic Domitian had the astrologer Ascletario put to death to confound his prediction that his corpse would be torn to pieces by wild dogs – in vain, for it was – but he entirely believed astrological predictions of the exact hour and manner of his death in AD96.

Above: The Constellation of Perseus and Andromeda, painted by James Thornhill in 1725. The Greeks and Romans viewed the stars' patterns anthropomorphically.

Below: The Ptolemaic system postulated that the Earth lay immobile at the centre of the universe, with the planets and stars circling it in sometimes very complicated epicycles.

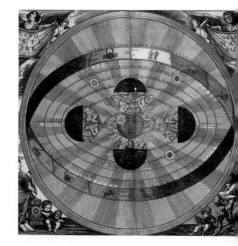

WATER MILLS

Above: A fresco from Alexandria showing oxen turning a mill. Such animal-powered mills were very common but not nearly as powerful as water mills.

Below: The remains of a giant water wheel of the Roman era near Cordoba, Spain. Water power was used in Spanish mines for pumping out water and for sluicing rock faces clean of debris.

Among the most enduringly useful innovations that spread around the Mediterranean under the Pax Romana were water mills. They seem to have originated in western Asia and to have been known, if scarcely used, in Greece by the 4th century BC. Traditionally first seen by the Romans in Armenia during their wars against Mithradates of Pontus (89–66BC), they were taken up only slowly at first, probably because of the abundance of slaves in the late Republic and early empire (*c.* 100BC–100AD). However, as the empire ceased to expand so rapidly, supplies of cheap slaves dwindled and water power was exploited to supplement animal and human muscle power for the first time in Western history. It has been calculated that while a slave-operated mill could grind only 15lbs (7kg) of grain per hour and a mule-powered mill about 60lbs (28kg), a typical water mill could grind 330lbs (150kg) per hour. However, as such technological developments were not thought especially interesting or prestigious, they were seldom mentioned by writers or rulers and we have to rely on archaeological evidence which is only now emerging. Who supplied the finance for the larger projects remains unknown, but the state probably played a major role. Windmills do not appear to have been used by the Romans.

THE USES OF WATER POWER

The Romans used water power not only for grinding corn but also for pumping water, especially out of mines, for sawing wood, raising hammers in iron works and washing out mineral deposits. In Spain, whose mines employed thousands of slaves to produce much of the empire's gold and silver, huge reservoirs were built above the workings at Rio Tinto with sluices at one end. When the reservoirs had been filled via aqueducts, the sluices were suddenly opened and a great surge of water washed over the exposed seams to carry away the soil. Sophisticated water-powered pumps were also used to pump out mines, where flooding was a perennial problem.

One of the largest water mill complexes so far discovered was at Barbegal near Arles in southern Gaul. Supplied by a branch of the main Arles aqueduct, 16 mill wheels were set in pairs down a steep slope which dropped about 80ft (23m). This complex probably dates from around AD200 and was involved in supplying the city with its daily bread. It is thought to have ground about 660lbs (300kg) of flour an hour – enough to supply a large proportion of the population of Arles. Only ruins of this industrial-sized complex remain. At the other end of the empire, a Roman-era mill, its huge wheel repaired many times, still turns slowly but proudly at Hama in Syria. However, most mills of the Roman period have long since vanished, leaving no visible remains.

WATER MILLS IN ROME

The first known water mills in ancient Rome were situated on the slopes of the Janiculum Hill. They were powered by the waters falling from the Aqua Traiana, the aqueduct built by the emperor Trajan early in the 2nd century AD. Probably early in the 3rd century AD, a complex of water mills was built in the standard brick-faced concrete across the aqueduct. Parts of the site have recently been excavated, although much remains concealed under nearby streets.

Two mill races branched off the Aqua Traiana and ran parallel to it before rejoining it. There were either three or four mill wheels in the northern mill race and one larger one in the southern mill race.

Mills like these ground Rome's wheat into flour, a necessity as the *annona* (wheat dole) was from the late 2nd century AD normally distributed in the form of baked bread rather than wheat. This particular mill complex seems to have survived the political catastrophes of the 5th century AD. In AD537, Rome was easily captured by the Byzantine general Belisarius and then besieged by the Ostrogoths under Totila, who were trying to regain the city they had ruled for 40 years. When the Goths cut off the city's water supply by breaking down the aqueducts, they also cut off Rome's supply of bread. Ingeniously, Belisarius circumvented the problem by floating water mills placed in boats at a sheltered spot on the Tiber near the island. (The Tiber itself supplied water, along with the city's wells, to the much-reduced population.) The floating mills managed to grind wheat into flour for the populace, according to the Byzantine historian Procopius, who accompanied Belisarius for a time on his military campaigns.

The use of the aqueducts for powering water mills outlasted that of supplying the baths, institutions of which the Christian clergy, by then dominant in the city, disapproved. Water mills for grinding corn lined the Tiber until the late 19th century.

Above: Roman water wheels at Hama in Syria, still turning slowly but effectively after nearly 2,000 years in use. Water mills were built across the empire wherever there was demand and a suitable river.

Below: The emperor Trajan (AD98–117), whose Aqua Traiana aqueduct came to supply water power for Rome's mills.

STEAM ENGINES

Above: Hero of Alexandria, whose many inventions included the world's first steam engine.

Below: Hero, like most scientific polymaths of the Roman empire, had a very practical side, describing in his Metrica ways of measuring land and cubic capacity and in his Stereometrica ways of measuring volumes.

The scientific curiosity and technological experiment of the Roman empire is exemplified by the career of one of the most remarkable inventors of antiquity, Hero of Alexandria, who lived in the 1st century AD. Hero was another gifted Hellenistic polymath – his mention of the solar eclipse of AD62 reveals that his interests included astronomy – but his chief fame is as the author of *Pneumatica*, which lists his varied inventions. Among these are mechanisms which use steam to produce a rotary motion.

This mechanism, which was almost certainly the world's first steam turbine, was more thermodynamically efficient than the piston engines that powered the early industrial revolution and anticipated the steam turbine of Charles Parsons by 1,800 years. Unlike the British engineer's invention, however, Hero's device remained little more than a toy.

HERO'S INVENTIONS

Hero mentioned more than 80 different devices in his main works, *Treatise on Hydraulics*, *Treatise on Pneumatics* and *Treatise on Mechanics* (the last preserved only in an Arabic translation). In these, he described the fundamentals of hydraulics, pneumatics and mechanics as well as many applications, including drinking fountains, self-trimming lanterns, self-filling wine goblets and temple doors that were opened by heat which caused the metal hinges to expand.

The *Treatise on Mechanics* dealt with utilitarian devices such as cranes, hoists (lifts) and presses, while another book, *Metrica*, outlined geometrical methods of measuring land, weights and cubic capacity, including that of the pyramids.

In *Stereometrica* Hero gave highly practical advice on how to measure the contents of *amphorae* (jars) and ships' cargoes. More fancifully, in *Automatapoetica* Hero described two mechanized puppet theatres which he had constructed. In these, miniaturized versions of *The Bacchae*, along with other classical Greek tragedies, were staged. His book on clocks, sundials and other chronometers, *Dioptra*, has sadly been lost.

The inventions which have made Hero lastingly famous were his steam engines. One simply used escaping steam to make a ball jump in the air. The other, more sophisticated version was the *aelopile*. This consisted of a large sealed metal cauldron beneath a hollow metal sphere. Steam from the cauldron's boiling water was forced into the sphere, from which its only way of escape was via two small hooked pipes attached to the top and between which it could rotate freely. As pressure built up inside the sphere, the steam made the sphere rotate swiftly on its axis. This delighted onlookers but most scholars now think it did no more.

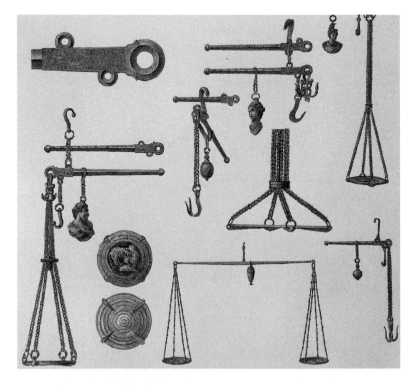

dissections in private.) Following contemporary customs, Galen used these anatomical exhibitions to prove preconceived theories, rather than discover new and possibly disconcerting facts. Nonetheless, he was one of antiquity's greatest anatomists. He was also a true physician, taking a holistic view of medicine and of human health.

Galen's works have survived unusually intact – they now make up about ten per cent of all extant classical Greek literature – and deal with many subjects. One is called *The Ideal Physician is Also a Philosopher*, a title which perhaps reflected his own ambitions. Galen aimed above all to establish medicine as an exact yet humane science. He always stressed the importance of exercise, a balanced diet, general hygiene and baths.

Galen acquired such immense authority in his own lifetime and subsequently that all ensuing ages, until at least the 17th century, followed his advice – often blindly. Oribasius, the personal physician of the emperor Julian 200 years later, when told by his master to "Collect all the main writings of the best physicians", started with Galen's summaries on the uncontentious grounds that Galen was the best doctor of them all.

KNOWN BY REPUTATION

There were no medical boards or recognized qualifications for doctors in the Roman empire. Reputation, therefore, was vitally important to a successful doctor. This in turn depended partly on luck, partly on skill and partly on a good bedside manner. Doctors were urged to be dignified but smart in their appearance and to give poor people free treatment. Greek and Roman doctors had almost no effective drugs, although they used a variety of herbal remedies and may have had opium. They therefore laid great emphasis upon listening to their patients.

Asclepieia, shrines dedicated to Asclepius, the god of medicine, received the sick overnight. Patients would sleep in the sacred precincts and there have healing dreams in which Asclepius might appear and take away their illness. One of the best-preserved of these shrines is at Pergamum. Surgery, in an age without anaesthetics, was only performed when absolutely essential and speed was crucial to avoid death through shock. Medical instruments recovered from Pompeii include probes, catheters, forceps, chisels, scalpels and needles.

Above: A young boy is examined by a doctor in this 1st century BC relief with a Greek inscription.

Below: Building in the Sanctuary of Asclepius, Pergamum, where the sick may have slept, hoping to be cured by the healing god.

PERILS OF URBAN LIFE: PLAGUES, FLOOD AND FIRE

Above: The Tiber, which flows through Rome, was a turbulent, unpredictable river, prone to sudden floods that could sweep across the city.

Below: Plague, graphically personified in this painting by Elie Delaunay of 1869, ravaged Rome repeatedly from AD166 onwards and added to the perils of urban life.

For most people in the world's first cosmopolis, life could be dangerous, unpleasant and short. Public health was probably far better in the empire's smaller towns, but they and the countryside supplied Rome with the stream of immigrants needed to maintain and expand the metropolitan population. Smallpox is the most likely culprit for the plague that ravaged Rome from AD166 for several years and that may have killed 300,000 people (nearly a third of Rome's population). However, epidemics were only the most dramatic of the endemic health problems that dogged the rich and poor inhabitants of ancient Rome.

MALARIA

The worst of these endemic health problems was probably malaria. As Galen dryly commented, doctors practising in Rome had no need to consult the writings of Hippocrates for descriptions of semitertian fever (a stage of malaria among adults), because its symptoms could be observed any day in the city. However, malaria was not recognized as such and the link with the disease-bearing mosquito was unsuspected. Run-off water from the seven hills, overflows from the constantly running public fountains and water-basins and stagnant residue left by the Tiber's frequent floods created ideal breeding grounds for mosquitoes.

Cicero and Livy praised the healthy hills of Rome, where the nobility and later the court lived in spacious houses, in contrast with the low-lying parts of the city, where the large majority of the population lived in often cramped *insulae* (apartment blocks). However, even the rich found it advisable to quit Rome in late summer when malaria was at its most rampant, leaving the poor to their uncertain fates.

No figures are known for Roman malaria deaths, but extrapolation from other parts of Italy similarly afflicted until recently, reveals that mortality rates as high as 60 per cent in the 20–50 age group may have been common.

Malaria would also have increased the mortality rates for pulmonary diseases such as pneumonia, bronchitis and asthma. All are likely to have been as common in Rome as in other cities whose populations approached the million mark before modern medicine.

However, Rome added further unique problems. Although the abundant fresh waters brought in by its aqueducts helped reduce waterborne diseases such as dysentery and typhoid – scourges of metropolitan life until the 20th century – other Roman habits would actually have spread them. People with bowel infections, for example, were urged to bathe their exposed anuses in the public bathwater that other people then bathed in!

Communal as well as private brushes were used instead of paper in public lavatories, another effective way of spreading germs. Further, while the rich few suffered from overeating, many Roman people were chronically malnourished, despite the grain dole. (This was later supplemented by free olive oil, wine and even sometimes pork, but a typical Roman's diet must have left him or her with vitamin deficiencies and this would have further undermined resistance to disease.)

FLOODS AND FIRES

The Tiber provided a useful waterway down to the sea and up into central Italy, but it was a swift, sometimes violent river, prone to dramatic flooding as the snows on the Apennine mountains melted. There were floods nearly every year and major floods in 193BC, when the lower parts of the city were inundated and many buildings collapsed.

As the growing city spread on to the low land in the great bend of the river about the Campus Martius, its inhabitants became yet more vulnerable. In 23BC the Pons Sublicius was swept away – for the second time in 40 years – and for three days the city was better navigated by boat than on foot. Hadrian, among other emperors, tried to improve the embankment walls, but in AD217 floods poured through the Forum Romanum in the heart of the city, sweeping away many startled citizens.

Even worse were the dangers from fire. The *insulae*, blocks of flats up to seven storeys high which housed most of the population, were often jerry-built and prone to collapse (although their construction did improve after the great fire of AD64). Heated by moveable charcoal stoves, lit by smoky oil lamps and built mostly of timber before AD64, they were also extremely flammable. Crassus, one of the late Republic's richest and most powerful men, famously boosted his fortunes by turning up at the site of a fire and buying the still-smouldering site cheap from its stunned owner.

Augustus created a corps of *vigiles*, nightwatchmen/firemen, but they had only limited success. The fire of AD64, which totally destroyed three of Rome's 14 districts, gave rise to Nero's subsequent sensible building regulations. *Insulae* were to have terraces for fire fighting, buildings were to be faced in fired brick and there was to be a minimum distance between them. However even this failed to prevent fire recurring. In AD192 Rome was so devastated by fire that the (half-mad) emperor Commodus proposed to rename the reconstructed city after himself, a project his assassination prevented. The Curia (Senate House) was later destroyed by fire and rebuilt under Diocletian.

Above: The great fire of AD64, here depicted by the 18th-century painter Robert Hubert, was one of the most devastating and also the best documented of the recurrent fires that the inflammable cosmopolis experienced.

TRADE, SHIPS AND NAVIGATION

As Rome grew, it sucked in ever more products from across the globe, establishing new patterns of supply and demand. Although merchant ships had criss-crossed the Mediterranean for millennia, early in the 2nd century AD trade grew to a peak under Roman rule that was not to be reached again for more than a thousand years. This growth is confirmed by the increase in the number of shipwrecks found along major trade routes – such as that past the Aeolian Islands north of Sicily, where many ships bound for Rome sought clearly inadequate shelter from storms – and by the huge numbers of *amphorae* found, the clay jars in which loose liquid substances such as oil, fish paste and wine were transported to Rome.

Below: A woman grocer from Ostia, Rome's great river port, is depicted standing at a trestle table selling fruit and vegetables stored in wicker baskets. The capital city of Rome traded in goods of all sorts.

THE MERCHANT CLASS

Members of the senatorial order, Rome's wealthiest class, were banned by the *lex Claudia* of 218BC from owning sizeable ships – those that could carry more than 300 *amphorae* – for commerce was considered debasing. However, some senators probably traded through proxies. Other classes did so openly, the equestrians (knights) particularly benefiting from the boom in trade during the late Republic. So did the numerous *mercatores, navigatores* and *negotiatores* (merchants, ship owners and businessmen) who were often not Roman citizens but freedmen.

Emperors, anxious to keep the Roman populace supplied with essential wheat and oil, offered incentives to ship owners. Claudius, for example, promised privileges to anyone owning a ship with a capacity of at least 10,000 *modii* (about 70 tons) who used it to supply Rome with wheat for six years. These ranged from citizenship for non-citizens to exemptions from taxes and burdens such as the *lex Poppaea* which penalized childless couples.

However, most merchants preferred to invest their money in land, which offered security and prestige, rather than found mercantile dynasties. In the 2nd century BC, Cato the Elder voiced the opinions of many Romans for a long time to come when he wrote, "The trader I regard as energetic man, bent on making money; but his is a dangerous career, liable to disaster".

Nonetheless, goods flowed in to Rome, and to other cities and between provinces. Wheat for the million mouths of the metropolis came first from Sicily and Sardinia and then from Egypt and Africa; olive oil came from Spain and Africa; gold and silver from Spain and Dacia; ivory from Egypt and Africa; papyrus and linen from Egypt; textiles and jewels from Syria, and from beyond it silk and spices. Wine, honey and marble came from Greece and

Asia Minor; wool, wheat, wine and pottery from Gaul; tin, wool and lead from Britain; copper from Cyprus and wild animals and timber from Mauretania (Morocco). In the earlier empire Italy produced much wine and pottery and always produced fruit and vegetables. Such a list is far from exhaustive.

SHIPS AND SHIPPING

The *pharoi* (lighthouses) the Romans built around their empire as far north as Dover show the importance they attached to shipping, which was preferred to slow, laborious land transport over longer distances. On the few rivers that were truly navigable, such as the Rhône, regular barge services connected cities like Lyons with the coast, but sea trade was far more important.

As piracy had been almost eliminated under the empire, sea travel might appear to have been relatively safe, but in fact perils abounded, despite the astonishing size of some merchant ships.

The ship that was used by Claudius as the base for the lighthouse of his new harbour near Ostia was vast. About 340ft (104m) long and 64ft (20.3m) wide, with six decks and displacing 7,400 tons, it required a crew of 700–800 men. Pliny the Elder recorded that its main mast was so massive it could only be spanned by four men linking arms and it had a ballast of 800 tons of lentils. This may have been the largest vessel built in antiquity – possibly the largest wooden ship ever, specially made to carry an obelisk from Egypt to Rome – but there may have been other large cargo ships of 3,000 tons ferrying wheat or oil. Galleys, which were highly expensive to crew, were seldom used for cargo.

Although remarkably large, these sailing ships remained technically simple. They generally had only one main mast in the centre with one or two sails and smaller masts at the bow and stern. They never evolved the complex rigging and sails of 17th-century warships or merchantmen. They continued to rely on steering-oars and did not develop rudders like ships of the later Middle Ages.

These lumbering monsters were probably never very seaworthy or manoeuvrable, as they were unable to tack easily with their crude sails. St Paul's famous shipwreck on Malta was not that exceptional. Roman navigators also lacked compasses, sextants and other aids, relying instead on landmarks and the stars in the night sky to determine their position. Fortunately both were often visible in the clear Mediterranean.

Above: A mosaic from Sousse, Tunisia of the 3rd century AD shows a cargo of iron being unloaded from a ship. Heavy goods such as this almost always went by sea, sea transport being generally far cheaper than land transport.

Below: Galley-type ships like this wine-barge from Neumagen on the Moselle, from a 3rd-century AD funerary monument, were used on the larger rivers such as the Rhine, Tiber and Moselle. At sea sailing ships were the norm.

PASSAGES TO INDIA

Above: A cloth merchant presents a client with a length of fabric in a relief from a Christian sarcophagus from Trier of the 4th century AD. Textiles were often traded over long distances.

Below: A harbour scene in a fresco from Pompeii gives a vivid impression of the commercial bustle of a Roman port in the 1st century AD.

Trade grew within the empire but did not stop at the empire's limits. In 116BC a sea captain in the service of the Ptolemy rulers of Egypt discovered the sea-route to India from the Red Sea port of Berenice. Using the monsoon winds that blow across the Indian Ocean, he set sail eastwards in July and returned blown by the reverse winds in December. The routes east were outlined in the *Periplus Maris Erythraei*, a handbook for sailors of the 1st century AD. Greek navigators had by then mostly replaced the Arabs who had once monopolized trade with India.

After Egypt passed into Roman control in 30BC, the lucrative trade grew even faster. From India and other parts of Asia, especially Felix Arabia (the Yemen), came spices, nard, incense, unguents, jewels, cotton textiles and ivory; in return went Roman pottery, glassware, gold and silver. This trade could be fantastically profitable. One consignment alone might be worth three million sesterces and a good-sized

ship could carry many consignments. The Greek orator Aelius Aristides (AD117–89) was only slightly exaggerating when he noted that, "Cargoes from India and even from Felix Arabia (the Yemen) can be seen so abundantly as to make one think that in those countries the trees will have been stripped bare and their inhabitants, if they need anything, must come and beg us for a share of their own produce".

Conservative Romans like Seneca muttered about the debilitating effects of such luxury, and Pliny the Elder worried about the adverse economic effect of the outflow of gold and silver to pay for imports – 100 million sesterces a year, he claimed. However, finds of pottery and other artefacts made in the empire along the coasts of western India suggest that Rome's eastbound merchants often exported the empire's products too. The imperial coffers would have profited by the *portorium*, import/export duties levied at 2½ per cent.

THE SILK ROAD

The Indian Ocean was not the only great trade route to the East. Caravans went east across the Syrian desert via the great merchant city of Palmyra – which provided and charged for "protection" and use of its water resources – or down through Mesopotamia, most of which was normally outside Roman control, via the great emporium of Seleucia-on-Tigris, to the Gulf. Spasinochorax at the head of the Gulf seems to have been semi-independent under the Parthian kings, like Palmyra under the Romans. Its great port, which was briefly captured by Trajan in AD116, had regular connections with India and Sri Lanka.

Another route, going entirely by land, struck north across the Iranian plateau to link up with the legendary Silk Road. This is a misleading title, for this was no pan-Asian highway but several different routes taken by camel caravans through central Asia to the western outposts of imperial China. The first Silk Road route was traditionally if unintentionally pioneered by Zhang Qian, an official sent by the Han emperors of China in 135BC to discover and import large horses for the Chinese army. Zhang ultimately succeeded in his mission, although it took him ten years. Traders ventured in his wake, bringing silk west, among other luxury goods, often in stages through the Kushan kingdom in central Asia and via Iran to Syria. Some caravans may have turned south into India, their goods reaching Egypt by sea.

Whatever the route, silk remained an expensive luxury for Romans. Cleopatra VII, last Ptolemy monarch of Egypt and Mark Antony's famous lover, wore silks from China. Such sensual clothing was portrayed as a sign of dangerous decadence by Antony's opponent Octavian, although rich women in Rome soon began wearing silk too. (Sericulture remained a jealously guarded Chinese monopoly until in the 6th century AD, some Byzantine monks under orders from the emperor Justinian managed to smuggle silk worms out of China and inaugurate the Byzantine silk industry.) There were only rare direct contacts between the two distant giants. Chinese envoys arrived in Antioch during the reign of Marcus Aurelius (AD161–80) whom they called Marc-Antun, reputedly mistaking the Syrian metropolis for the imperial capital.

TRADE WITH THE BARBARIANS

Not all trade went east, however. The barbarians to the north traded as well as fought with Rome. Amber had long been imported from the Baltic but Germania – between the Rhine and Vistula rivers – became an increasingly important source of furs, hides, leather, honey and above all, as the empire matured, of slaves. Scythia (the south Russian and Ukrainian steppe) was another important source of hides, furs and honey. It was also for a long time a major exporter of grain,

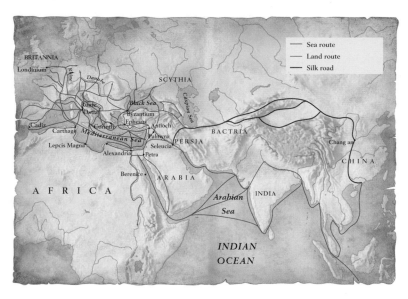

helping to feed the cities of Greece. Unfortunately, the migratory chaos of the 3rd and 4th centuries AD disrupted grain-growing in the area just when Constantine's new capital on the Bosphorus would have welcomed it. The problem was dealt with by diverting wheat from Egypt bound for Rome to feed the city of Constantinople.

To the south, the Sahara Desert formed a barrier nearly as effective as the Atlantic for the Romans, who seldom rode camels. Rome had few contacts with sub-Saharan Africa except in Egypt, but there were some routes across the Sahara, and Africa north of the Sahara was still fertile enough to provide wild animals for the circus.

Above: The famous Silk Road from China across central Asia to the Mediterranean ports was eclipsed in economic importance by the sea routes to India via the Red Sea or the Gulf.

Below: A stele showing ship-building in Ravenna, one of the empire's main naval bases.

FARMING

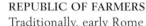

Above: Taking manure to the fields, from a cycle showing the country months in Gaul c. AD200.

Below: Vineyard workers, from a mosaic at Cherchel, Algeria, c. AD100. Wine was produced around the empire.

The great majority of the empire's population (at least 85 per cent at Rome's economic zenith *c.* AD100) always lived and worked on the land. This rural dominance formed the constant background to urban life in the ancient world and farming was always the basis of the Roman economy. Farming, or at least living off the rents and profits from estates, was also considered the most respectable form of existence by the ruling classes.

All senators had to possess land worth at least one million sesterces and most owned far more. Poets such as Virgil and Tibullus praised an idealized rural life that in practice must have been very tough for all but wealthy landowners taking a break from metropolitan cares. However, upper-class Romans were not being entirely hypocritical when they praised country life, for many did take an interest in their estates.

From the 2nd century BC, writers such as Cato the Censor in *De re rustica* (About Rural Matters) gave other landowners advice on how best to profit from their lands in Italy, where *latifundia* (large slave-worked estates) seem to have become common. Cato considered farms as small as 100 jugera (62 acres) as viable but most estates were larger. All such estates strove to be self-sufficient not just in basic foodstuffs but also in carts, tools, harnesses and even in labourers' clothes. The owner should "be inclined to sell and disinclined to buy". Large landowners, however, could afford the outlay of 724 sesterces required for an olive press in Pompeii, for example, while smaller farmers could not.

REPUBLIC OF FARMERS

Traditionally, early Rome was a republic of robust independent farmers, tending perhaps tiny plots but still able to buy their own armour and so rank as Roman legionaries. The influx of slaves and wealth following the Punic and Macedonian Wars of 264–168BC, coupled with the long periods that the Roman soldier-farmer was away from his farm, led large landowners to buy up or simply take over neglected farms, where slaves replaced the doughty Roman peasant.

This view, propagated by the land-reformer Tiberius Gracchus in 133BC among others, painted a dismal picture of an Italy devoured by rapacious great landlords dispossessing little farmers. It is only part of the picture, however. While there certainly were huge new ranches worked by hundreds of slaves, the sort of farm Cato envisaged would have had only about a dozen slaves. Their efforts would have been supplemented by seasonal free labourers working side by side. Another group, the *coloni* (tenant farmers) remained important, as the letters of Pliny the Younger, who made a point of listening to all his tenant farmers' complaints, attest. A few small independent farmers survived alongside their powerful neighbours well into the empire.

Some large estates came to specialize in viticulture, which needed semi-skilled workers; in sheep rearing, which required little labour of any type; and some near Rome in market gardening.

The phenomenal growth of Rome (and other cities) expanded demand, but expanding supply was more difficult. Marginal land in Italy and other well-settled areas could be taken into cultivation but this might make only a marginal difference. Those working such land even in meteorologically good years might consume most of its meagre crop.

In newly conquered Britain parts of the Cambridgeshire fens were drained to grow cereals that were exported to feed the army on the Rhine in the 4th century AD, while in Africa careful planting of olive trees and the collection of every drop of rain allowed agriculture to advance into what had been arid savannah. Southern and central Spain also saw a great expansion of grain and olive cultivation. All these products could also be exported, but Roman wealth created no agricultural revolution. The commonest way to increase farm production was simply to work labourers, whether free or servile, harder.

FARMING TOOLS AND TECHNIQUES

The Romans had good farming tools on a small scale but failed to exploit other technological possibilities. A Roman farmworker would have had excellent axes, spades, sickles, scythes, saws, shears and forks. The multi-purpose vine-dresser's knife, *falx vinotoria*, which was developed from the billhook, has never really been surpassed for its purpose. On a larger scale, the Romans at times used the wheeled plough, which

was Gallic in origin and could turn heavier soils easily, a wheeled threshing-machine with spiked axles called the *plostellum poenicum* and possibly of Carthaginian origin, and two types of reaping machine.

These tools were known and used in Gaul and Britain but they do not seem to have spread round the empire, partly because the Romans remained limited to oxen as draught animals for ploughs and carts. They had failed to develop a form of harness for horses that would allow the animal to draw heavy loads without half-strangling itself. Horses in antiquity therefore only pulled light ceremonial or racing chariots, not carriages, wagons or ploughs.

Farmers normally let some of their arable land lie fallow every other year, to allow it to recover its fertility. This was essential but limited production and illustrates one restriction on Roman power at its most fundamental: it could not easily grow more food.

Above: Oxen being used to plough fields in a mosaic from Cherchel, Algeria, c. AD100. Africa became Rome's chief source of grain and olive oil.

Below: Ploughing with oxen, from a sarcophagus of the 2nd century AD. Oxen were the main draught animals.

CHAPTER XXIV

PEOPLE OF ROME

The citizens of Rome of all social classes often showed a preference for *otium*, leisure, over *negotium*, or business of any sort, whether this was governing the empire or running a shop. The cities built or expanded in the centuries of the Roman peace reflected the belief common at the time that the good life was one spent enjoying the amenities of urban life: the baths, theatre, circus, amphitheatre, forum, libraries and the social rounds of dinner parties for those who could afford them.

Most people in the empire in fact lived not in cities of any size but in the country, yet urban life still set the overall tone. Complementing life in the public sphere, the Romans had a strong sense of family and – at least among those who could afford it – of their ancestors.

The position of Roman women, although they were barred from public life, was better in some ways than in comparable cultures, possibly no worse than it was in Britain before the late 19th century. Slavery, a notorious part of the Roman world, was a far more mixed affair than might be assumed. Many slaves were freed and sometimes prospered in business or other work and their sons were later able to hold public office.

Before the triumph of Christianity, the Romans displayed typically level-headed pragmatism about sex, being at times bawdy, at times romantic.

Left: A frieze on the Ara Pacis (Altar of Peace) dedicated in 9BC, showing Tellus (Earth) or Italy, surrounded by symbols of the fertility and harmony restored by Augustus.

MARRIAGE, DIVORCE AND THE POWER OF THE FATHER

Above: A father reclining at ease among his family, a relief from a child's sarcophagus of the 3rd century AD illustrating a Roman paterfamilias' power at its most benign. The Romans were markedly family-minded, even among the nobility.

Below: A plan of Rome showing the imperial metropolis at its prime c. AD200. Rome was never a city of grand boulevards or avenues but rather a city of densely packed buildings. filled with political and family intrigue.

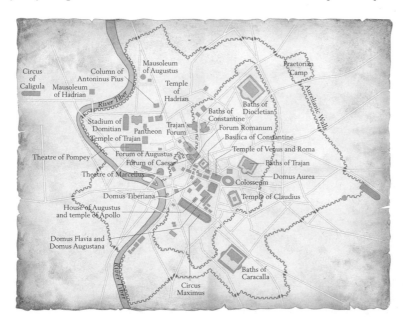

Like the Greeks but unlike the early Jews or the Persians, the Romans were always monogamous. The extended family was central to Roman law and society and especially to the real workings of its informal political system.

Although Roman marriage had as its explicit goal the production and rearing of children, among the great political families of the late Republic and empire political motives often dictated unions. Caesar's daughter Julia was married to the much older Pompey to help seal the First Triumvirate in 60BC; Octavia, Octavian's sister, had to marry Mark Antony in an unsuccessful bid to keep the Second Triumvirate together 20 years later, and Tiberius was forced to divorce his adored first wife Vipsania and marry Augustus' only child Julia instead, in a marriage that proved a most disastrous mismatch. Financial motives also played a major role in most noble marriages. However, this did not mean that all were unhappy. Augustus (when still Octavian) married Livia for love rather than politics (she happily divorced her first husband) and despite his later frequent infidelities, theirs was a happy marriage.

Divorce had become common at least among the nobility by the end of the Republic, although for less exalted people, where personal feelings possibly counted for more, it remained more unusual, although devoid of any stigma. In divorces, children normally remained in their father's custody. However, judging by the feelings expressed on memorials, many ordinary Romans were devoted to their spouses.

THE *PATERFAMILIAS*
The theoretical powers of the father in the early Republic were unbounded. A *paterfamilias* (male head of the household with no living father or grandfather) held *paterpotestas*, powers of life and death over all family members, including his slaves and most of his freedmen. In theory, a father could beat his son although the latter might be middle-aged and hold high office. Family courts dominated by the *paterfamilias* could even hand out death sentences, though these became so rare as to be almost legendary. The *paterfamilias* nonetheless retained the key right to accept – or occasionally reject, if the baby was deformed or of dubious paternity – every newborn child laid at his feet.

Such was the prestige linked to being a *paterfamilias* that senators were hailed as *conscripti patres* (conscripted fathers) and one of the proudest titles held by Caesar and Augustus in turn was *pater patriae* (Father of His Country).

The dependents of a *paterfamilias* could number hundreds for a great household – and later for the *familia Caesaris*, the imperial family, thousands. However, Roman politics in the Republic and the early Principate depended crucially on these extended households for governing

the empire, with slaves or freedmen effectively taking on the role of civil servants. In practice, these vastly extended and powerful dynasties were balanced by more numerous nuclear families, composed just of parents and children. When a *paterfamilias* died – and not many lived long enough to torment their grown-up children for long – his estate had by law to be divided equally among all his surviving children, for primogeniture (in which the first born inherits all) was unknown. Because Roman mortality rates were so high, especially among women giving birth, many people found themselves marrying several times without divorce.

MARRIAGE CUSTOMS

Among the upper classes in Rome, marriages were often arranged for dynastic reasons, but the comedies of Plautus (among others) demonstrate that love was as important for the Romans as for anyone else. Paternal consent was needed, however, for the first informal engagement. This was followed by a banquet at which the man, who was normally about ten years older than the woman, gave his fiancée a large present and the future father-in-law promised a dowry in return.

On the day of the wedding – June was a popular month – the bridegroom arrived early in the morning at the house of the bride with his friends. The matron of honour joined the couple's right hands ceremonially in the *dextrarum iunctio*, an animal was sacrificed and the marriage contract was signed. The groom paid for the reception, which included food, dancing and music. Augustus became alarmed at the increasing extravagance of wedding ceremonies and introduced a sumptuary law to limit the cost of a marriage to 1,000 sesterces. This proved ineffectual.

The bride wore a prescribed hemless tunic-style dress (*tunica recta*) tied at the waist by a woollen girdle (*cingulum herculeum*), with a saffron-coloured cloak over it and an orange veil (*flammeum*). Her hair was dressed in an old-fashioned style, with strands parted using an iron

spearhead. In the wedding procession after the banquet, all the guests escorted the bride to her new home.

The bride herself had three young boys to attend her: one held her left hand, one her right hand and the third carried a torch before her that had been lit at the hearth of her own home. As she approached the bridegroom's house, the torch was thrown away. According to old beliefs, whoever caught the torch was assured a long life.

Upon reaching the bridegroom's house, the bride performed a set of symbolic acts. She smeared the doorposts with oil and then covered them with wool, and ritually touched the hearth fire and water inside the house. She was then helped to prepare for her wedding night by women who had only been married once. Most girls, at least among the nobility, were virgins for their first marriage.

Above: Portrait, possibly of an engaged couple, with a cupid between them, from a fresco in a villa at Stabiae destroyed by Vesuvius in AD79.

Below: Detail of a marriage ceremony from a votive altar of the 3rd century AD, showing a couple formally linking hands.

ROMAN WOMEN

Above: A young woman wearing a wreath of leaves from Herculaneum, c. 10BC.

Women in Rome were barred from playing any role in public life, whether in war or in peace. There were no women consuls, generals, senators or emperors. In this exclusion Rome was in tune with classical Greek precedents but not with the Hellenistic world, where queens such as Cleopatra in Egypt ruled as acknowledged sovereigns. High-ranking women could hope to be powers behind the throne, like Augustus' wife Livia or Nero's mother Agrippina, but they could never assume imperial power in their own right.

In Rome, women were regarded as unfit for that supreme test of Roman *virtus*, military service (which was indisputably arduous). Further, women's voices were thought to lack the carrying power to make themselves easily heard in public places such as the Forum. Oratory was vital to Roman political life even after the end of the Republic.

DOMESTIC POWER

Traditionally women remained always *in manu* (under a man's control), first their father's or guardian's and then their husband's. However, even as early as the 3rd century BC such constrictions were being evaded by marriage contracts that specified the dowry the woman could take back with her if the marriage ended in divorce or death. Divorce could be initiated by either party without formality, although aristocratic marriages with political implications remained more complicated.

Left: Cornelia, mother of the Gracchi brothers, who held the first known literary salon in Rome.

A Roman *matron* (married woman) ran the household, controlling the domestic slaves and holding the keys of the house. By the age of 25 she could normally manage any property that she had inherited independently, which made her better placed than women in early Victorian Britain. When her husband was away, a wife took control of family affairs. Domestic duties, such as looking after the children and the household, traditionally included making clothes for the family even for wealthy women. *Lanam fecit* (she made wool) was a common tribute to a deceased wife. However, by the later Republic women were joining men at dinner, that central event in convivial Roman life, where they acted as hostesses. This was in marked contrast to their seclusion in Greece, as Cornelius Nepos, the first extant Latin biographer, noted. Although girls received less in the way of formal education than their brothers, by the 2nd century BC many upper-class Roman women were literate, as is shown by the life of Cornelia Gracchus.

INCREASING FREEDOM

Cornelia, daughter of the great Scipio Africanus who had defeated Hannibal, was among the first newly independent women (although scarcely liberated in the modern sense). She married Tiberius Cornelius Gracchus and among her progeny were the famous if ill-starred reformers Tiberius and Gaius Gracchus.

Cornelia took control of her six sons' education – a task traditionally reserved for the *paterfamilias* – and selected the finest Greek tutors for them. She was the first woman known to have held a literary salon in Rome where poets, philosophers and politicians gathered. As a widow she was so widely admired that Ptolemy VII, the Hellenistic king of Egypt, asked (unsuccessfully) for her hand

Left: A mother breast-feeding her child in a vivid fresco from Pompeii. The maternal role was inevitably considered women's chief occupation, although aristocratic women in fact had relatively few children by the late Republic.

in marriage. Although she was later content to be known as "the mother of the Gracchi", Cornelia deserves fame in her own right as a pioneer of women's independence. By the 1st century BC, other women were enjoying considerable freedom. The married aristocratic woman, who Catullus addressed as Lesbia and passionately loved, clearly had enough independence to have affairs.

Augustus tried to restrict women's freedom in his restoration of public morality. This re-emphasized gender differences, in deliberate contrast to the perceived immorality of the late Republic and to Cleopatra's "Eastern" court which had allegedly corrupted Anthony. Augustus even banished his daughter Julia and her daughter (also called Julia) for sexual immorality. Here he applied his own laws, for under the *Lex Julia* of 18BC, adultery had become a serious crime, at least for women, who could be banished, lose half their dowry and be prohibited from remarrying. Women now went to the public baths at different times to the men and were restricted to high seats in the

theatre and amphitheatre. (They continued to sit with men in the Circus, however, and Ovid recommended the Circus as a good place for young men and women to meet and flirt.)

WORKING WOMEN

Most women could never be empresses or wives of great politicians, but some still made their way in a male-dominated world. A few managed to be accepted as doctors – there is a funerary inscription in Latin for a female doctor, Asyllia Polla, from Roman Carthage – although later women seem to have been excluded from practising medicine for a time. As no formal medical body existed to regulate doctors, this may have reflected changes in the social climate.

Some women worked as bakers, pharmacists – another then unregulated profession – and shopkeepers, either with or without their husbands. There was only one woman Latin poet of note, Sulpicia, niece of an important politician *c.* 20BC, and almost no opportunities for women to make their voices heard in public life.

Below: A relief showing a woman pharmacist in her shop. Pharmacy, like medicine, was a totally unregulated profession and so one which women could enter and where they could, with luck and industry, prosper.

CHILDREN: EDUCATION AND UPBRINGING

Above: Children play with walnuts in a relief from Ostia of the 2nd century AD, then a thriving harbour city.

Below: Sculpture of a sleeping child. Very high rates of infant mortality meant that few children lived to adulthood.

In the 2nd century BC, Cato the Censor boasted, perhaps untruthfully, that he had taught his sons everything from reading to swimming but, over time, education in richer households passed from the hands of fathers to professionals, slaves and free, as Rome filled with well-educated Greeks. However, Roman education remained generally unsystematic and for girls was almost non-existent beyond a basic level which was normally taught at home.

AN AD HOC EDUCATION SYSTEM

Primary schools, which were mostly private and which only some Romans attended, taught the three basic subjects of reading, writing and arithmetic. Most teaching took place in porticoes or similar public areas such as the great *exedrae* (recesses) of Trajan's Forum.

Teaching was mostly a matter of learning texts by rote, with underpaid teachers beating lessons into boys. Among wealthier families, a *paedagogus*, a slave-tutor who was usually Greek-speaking, took care of the education of boys. Supposedly his pupil's master, he was in reality his slave and accompanied him everywhere.

Relatively few pupils progressed to secondary education where a *grammaticus*, again often a Greek-speaker, taught Latin and especially Greek literature. The poet Virgil was grateful that his parents, who were only moderately prosperous provincial farmers from the Po Valley, had given him a good education in Milan and Rome rather than at the local school full of "centurion's sons with their satchels".

Although emperors such as Trajan established chairs for lecturers paid by the public purse in Rome, there were only sporadic attempts to establish an educational system across the empire. Hadrian, for example, tried to encourage primary schooling in remote parts of the empire by offering tax concessions to school masters willing to teach in the villages of the mining region of Vipasca in Lusitania. Even fewer students went on to higher education, where a *rhetor* taught the vital art of public speaking. The Senate at first actually discouraged the spread of higher education in case it undermined its own monopoly on power.

After being taught by a *grammaticus*, some young Roman nobles went to one of the acknowledged Greek centres of cultural excellence to learn not only rhetoric but philosophy. Athens was long acknowledged as the greatest of these but it always lacked a proper university in the modern or even medieval sense, for private lecturers competed openly for students.

Marseilles' enduring Greek character in the 1st century AD made it a centre of learning. The mother of Agricola, who became a great general, sent him there to complete his education. Later, a few Western cities such as Bordeaux acquired universities, but their prestige never rivalled that of medieval Bologna or Oxford or contemporary Harvard.

THE LANGUAGE OF LEARNING

Latin was the language of most of Italy and later of the Western provinces, but not of every inhabitant of polyglot Rome, let alone of the empire. Greek was also very widely spoken. Almost all cities in the Eastern half of the empire, and most in Sicily and southern Italy, were at least partly Greek-speaking, while until *c.* 50BC Latin literature hardly compared with Greek.

For a long time, the majority of Romans acknowledged, with varying degrees of reluctance, the supremacy of classical Greece in the cultural field, while considering contemporary Greeks their political and social inferiors. So important was a fluent knowledge of Greek to an

educated Roman thought to be that the Roman rhetorician Quintillian (*c.* AD35–100) suggested that upper class boys should learn Greek *before* they learnt Latin. Quintillian, who wrote on education, was given a salary by the emperor Vespasian. As tutor to Domitian's nephews, he soon became the acknowledged head of the teaching profession in Rome, so his views were hardly those of an outsider.

Latin remained, however, the language of the army, the administration and the law. In the 4th century AD, a school teaching law in Latin was actually established in Beirut in a long-Hellenized part of Syria. Although many Greeks must have known a little Latin in order to deal with officials and soldiers, they hardly mentioned it. One exception was Ammianus (*c.* AD330–94), a native of Antioch who learnt Latin to write stirring histories of the Persian wars in the mid-4th century in a style that was modelled on Tacitus and Livy. Apuleius, the Latin-speaking author of *The Golden Ass*, makes his central character a Greek-speaker who (comically) apologizes for his poor Latin.

COMING OF AGE

Between the ages of 14 and 19, usually at the age of 17, the Roman male came of age, putting on a new white *toga virilis* to mark his status as a full citizen. He then went to the *Tabularium* (Records Office) with his family to be officially enrolled, after which a family banquet was held in his honour. High infant mortality meant that many children died long before this age, however. In the Republic, young male citizens were liable for military service.

Above: A 4th-century AD class from Gaul, showing a teacher, flanked by pupils, all in fine, probably wickerwork armchairs, while a late arrival tries to apologize. The students are reading from papyrus scrolls.

Below: A woman baths a child in a mosaic of the 3rd century AD from the House of Theseus in Paphos, Cyprus.

SLAVES AND FREEDMEN

Above: A slave serves wine in a bas-relief of the 2nd century AD in Rome.

Below: A mural from Pompeii showing two young women and a younger girl attended by a slave hairdresser. Rich Roman women usually had many domestic slaves to look after their every need.

The traditional view of the wealth and power of the Roman empire existing only through the sweated efforts of wretched slaves can be very misleading. The truth is more complicated, for the relative status of "slave" and "free" might appear strange to modern eyes.

THE STATUS OF SLAVES

A Roman nobleman might have a Greek-speaking slave as his secretary or clerk, another as a librarian or tutor to his children and another as bailiff or overseer of his land. These were often positions of importance and responsibility and sometimes of real if limited power. As Romans prided themselves on *manumission* – formally freeing worthy slaves – and as other slaves could at times save enough money from doing work on their own to buy their freedom, the number of freedmen, especially in Rome itself, was large. A few,

like the gross Trimalchio – a fictional but half-plausible character from Petronius' novel *Satyricon* (*c.* AD64) – became multi-millionaires. Others, like Narcissus and Pallas, the emperor Claudius' principal secretaries, indeed rose to become some of the most powerful men in the empire, although their influence over the malleable emperor was resented by the Roman aristocracy. Freedmen's sons could hope to rise to be magistrates, while freedmen themselves often became priests in a local cult in the provinces.

Slavery in ancient Rome was therefore radically different from its last manifestations in the Western world, when millions of enslaved Africans remained slaves just because of their colour. Most slaves who flooded into Rome as it conquered the Mediterranean world in the years after 260BC would have looked broadly similar to the Romans themselves, with darkish hair and olive skin. Those from the Eastern cities were often at least as educated and cultured as their Roman masters, sometimes more so. As the empire developed, less sophisticated Germanic tribes from across the Rhine and the Danube became the chief source of slaves and there was no more such cultural enrichment. The Romans always snobbishly disdained everything about the Germans except their fighting qualities (despite Tacitus' seeming praise for the Germans' love of primitive freedom). There are few depictions of black Africans in Roman art, which suggests that the Romans had only a few slaves from sub-Saharan Africa.

Precise figures are lacking, but probably nearly a third of the population of Italy in the 1st century AD were slaves, while at that time about half Rome's own population may have consisted of slaves and freedmen. A proposal in the Senate in the 1st century AD that all slaves should

Left: Making a will: a funerary stele for man and wife from the 1st century AD, showing a slave with a counting tablet on the left. Slaves were sometimes given their freedom by their masters in such wills. This was a strong inducement to good behaviour.

wear a uniform to identify them was rejected when it was realized that this would reveal how numerous they were. Across the whole empire, however, the proportion of slaves to non-slaves was close to 10 per cent. Slavery probably peaked at the end of the Republic and the beginning of the empire and then very slowly began to decline, as the wars of easy conquest petered out. Such wars were the chief source of slaves, although piracy, kidnappings and abduction of foundlings, along with *verna*, the children of slaves born in the household, provided other major sources, as did trade with peoples beyond the empire.

THE GROWTH OF SLAVERY

Slavery had always existed in Rome as in almost every ancient society. The Twelve Tables of the Law of 451–450BC stipulated that Romans were only to be sold into slavery "across the Tiber" (outside Rome). A common form of early slavery was the *nexus*, in which a Roman citizen who had become indebted lost his freedom to his creditors. Debt bondage was abolished by the *Lex Poetelia* of 326BC.

Soon after, Rome began the series of wars of conquests that provided it for a time with seemingly inexhaustible supplies of unfree labour. About 11,000 Samnite war captives were reportedly enslaved after their final defeat in 290BC. But the fleets the Romans raised to fight the First Punic War in 260BC were rowed mostly by free men – usually citizens of the lower property classes – as were most later fleets of galleys. A perennial disadvantage of owning slaves was that they needed feeding all year round even when not working. War galleys, for example, spent more than half the year ashore.

In 167BC, the systematic destruction of the kingdom of the cities of Epirus (north-west Greece) reputedly brought 150,000 slaves as war captives to Rome, probably helping to raise the intellectual tone of the whole city. Less accomplished, and so cheaper, were the 65,000 Sardinian slaves put up for sale in 177BC. The slave markets must at times have faced gluts. Cato the Censor noted with disgust about this time that pretty slave boys were fetching higher prices in the slave market than sturdy ploughmen, reflecting supply and demand. In the 1st century BC, Strabo estimated that the great port at Delos in the Cyclades was capable of handling 10,000 slaves a day (although this was a maximum, not a norm). Strabo also noted that slaves were one of Britain's main exports. Gallic chieftains reputedly sold a slave for a single amphora of Italian wine. Slaves were among the main booty of Caesar's Gallic wars (58–51BC) soon afterwards.

Below: A slave bringing in food for a banquet, from a mosaic from Roman Carthage of the 3rd century AD. The more attractive or intelligent slave could hope for such domestic service. Those lacking such charms often ended up in the mines or on farms.

ASPECTS OF SLAVERY

Above: The mines of Las Medulas in Spain where many slaves were worked to premature deaths.

By the end of the Republic, owning a slave or two was as common even for quite ordinary Romans as owning a car is today, and scarcely more reprehensible. Often such slaves would do domestic duties or work on the farm or in the family business alongside free hired labourers, and they could be hard to tell apart from poor citizens. In contrast, great nobles could have hundreds of slaves around them in their houses and possibly thousands more working their *latifundiae* (great estates).

THE WORK OF SLAVES

Slaves performed many different tasks in the Roman world and so did not form a single economic or social class. Their jobs and their social status differed greatly, ranging from the highly educated Greeks whose intellectual powers were appreciated by Roman nobles who exploited them as secretaries, librarians, tutors or clerks – Epictetus the philosopher being the outstanding example – via attractive young girls and boys who were sexually exploited, to those at the very bottom of the servile scale. These last, lacking beauty, intelligence or any other notable qualities, could find themselves condemned to crushing work on the land or in the mines.

Left: A slave being freed, showing his progress from prostrate subjection to shaking his ex-master's hand.

Many farm and mining slaves were appallingly treated. Pliny the Younger talks of chain-gangs of agricultural slaves who had "speaking" iron collars forged around their necks. These collars, as uncomfortable as they were demeaning, requested the finder to return the slave to its rightful owner like a dog. Even worse were conditions in the mines where slaves worked alongside criminals. Although tiny quantities of coal were mined in Roman Britain, these were for the most part metal mines. Some of the largest and most profitable mines were imperial property. The copper mines in Cyprus and gold, silver and lead mines in Spain were huge. The biggest industrial undertakings in the whole empire, they employed many thousands of slaves who were worked to early deaths underground.

Elsewhere, in the fertile province of Africa for example, even large estates seem to have been worked mostly by free tenant farmers. In much of the empire free seasonal labour supplemented slaves at busy times like the harvest. Slavery therefore, while part of Roman culture, was not always fundamental to agriculture but it was to quarries and mines.

REVOLT AND REBELLION

Unsurprisingly, slaves sometimes revolted. In Sicily, where huge *latifundiae* worked by slaves were established early on, slave revolts in 135–132BC and again in 104–100BC threatened Roman control of the island.

In the second revolt, a Greek-speaking slave calling himself Antiochus briefly established control over almost all Sicily. Spartacus' gladiators' revolt of 73–71BC attracted many other slaves far closer to Rome. In the troubled 3rd century AD, much of central Gaul was for years in the hands of the *Bagaudae* (literally, brigands), who even set up their own courts.

Household slaves very seldom turned on their masters. The case of the senator Larcius Macedo, who was attacked by his domestic slaves *c.* 100AD, was shocking to his contemporaries precisely because it was so exceptional.

MANUMISSION

Something which impressed Greek visitors to Rome was the ceremony of *manumission*, in which Roman slave owners gave particularly favoured slaves their freedom. This often formed part of the owner's will.

With freedom normally came admission for the newly liberated to Roman citizenship. However, as *manumission* was granted through *paterpotestas*, the power of the head of the family, freedmen were normally considered bound to their former owners by ties of gratitude, taking their names and joining their patron's *clientalia*, network of retainers. Obviously, *manumission* was less significant for a small builder or blacksmith who only manumitted one or two exhausted slaves in his will, than for a noble who grandly freed many slaves. The promise of manumission must have helped to encourage good behaviour among slaves.

Although there were no famous abolitionists of slavery in the ancient world, the Greek philosopher Aristotle (384–322BC) did not consider slaves inherently inferior to free citizens and both the Stoics and Epicureans considered slaves capable of philosophy. For Christians, even the most degraded of slaves had immortal souls, an important part of their religion's early appeal, but richer Christians owned slaves like everyone else.

Every slave owner retained power of life and death over his human property, although more humane emperors tried to mitigate abuses of this power. Augustus saved the life of a slave boy whose irascible master, Vedius Pollio, had wanted to feed him to the lampreys for breaking a precious glass; and Claudius banned the

practice of masters reclaiming sick slaves left to die on the island in the Tiber, saying that if slaves recovered their health they also recovered their liberty. Domitian forbade the castration of slave boys for sexual purposes (although slaves still had no defence against their owners' sexual demands) and Hadrian stopped slave owners handing their slaves over to the gladiatorial schools as a punishment and made executing slaves dependent on the approval of the prefect of the *Vigiles* (night watchmen).

Slavery, if waning in importance, as an institution, survived both the gradual conversion of the empire to Christianity in the 4th century AD and the end of the West Roman empire in the 5th century AD.

Above: Relief from the theatre of Sabratha, showing a scene of a slave rebuked by his master, c. AD180.

Above: Claudius, an emperor who tried to limit the mistreatment of slaves.

BUSINESS AND COMMERCE

Like most aristocracies, the Roman nobility liked to advertise the fact that they could enjoy a life of leisure as well as their riches. In the later empire, senators were excluded from politics and the army although many still had their large estates to run. *Otium cum dignitate* (cultured, dignified leisure) was always their motto.

HARD WORK

Earlier, the senatorial order had been closely involved in public affairs during both the Republic and Principate. This is well illustrated by the careers of two men who lived near the empire's apogee: Pliny the Younger, who died *c.* AD112, probably in office as proconsul of Bithynia, after a career as a soldier, lawyer and a consul; and Sextus Julius Frontinus, who died at the age of 70 in AD100 while still the highly effective *curator aquarum* (controller of Rome's water supply) after a career as a consul, soldier and imperial administrator. Conscientious emperors – and most emperors were conscientious if not brilliant rulers – were often also grossly overworked.

At the other end of the social scale, the poorest among the free laboured until exhausted for a pittance. The supposedly pampered populace of Rome, although given *panem et circuses* (free bread and circuses), had to find other means to pay Rome's notoriously high rents. Many did odd labouring jobs, among which portering the huge quantities of food the capital demanded must have been one of the most important, along with working on construction. However, most Romans tried to divide their day clearly into *negotium* (literally: "not leisure", or business) and *otium* (leisure) – the latter having the real appeal.

Although winters in Rome can be chilly and wet, life for men was lived in the open as much as possible or at least in the shelter of porticoes, principally those surrounding the Forum Romanum, and the adjacent imperial fora. The Forum Romanum, at the heart of Roman public life, was also initially the site of the food markets, but these were moved out closer to the Tiber to the Forum Boarium (Cattle Market) and Forum Holitorium (Vegetable Market). This segregation of the messier aspects of commercial life from the ceremonial and social happened in other cities, such as Pompeii and Pozzuoli, and Lepcis Magna and Timgad in Africa, for Romans wanted to make each Forum a splendidly adorned centre of civic pride. In the Forum Romanum male citizens, supposedly all dressed in togas, would meet to discuss matters and renew their ties of mutual obligation. Women remained at home.

THE WORKING DAY

Business of many kinds, of which commercial business in the modern sense was only a part, occupied the first part of the day. This began early, often at first light. Although the Romans had numerous

Above: A Roman sundial from Utica in Africa. The Romans, who lacked mechanical clocks, relied on sundials, hourglasses and waterclocks to tell the time.

Below: A Roman relief depicting a vendor of pillows, furniture coverings and textiles. Many poorer Romans found underpaid work in such small-scale service industries.

public holidays, they did not have a specific day of the week as a day of rest as Sunday is today for many of us. However, the hours of their day, delimited chiefly by sundials, varied according to the time of year, both the hours and the day being far longer in summer. The Romans relied on sundials and water clocks copied from the Hellenistic world. Men working in particular trades, most of which had their own guilds, went out to work. The building trade was one of the most important in Rome up to the 3rd century AD, but there were also guilds of butchers, fishmongers and bakers, all of which held regular dinners.

In the morning every patron, who might be a powerful noble but who might also be considerably lower down the social and political ladder, would meet some of his *clientalia*, his retainers or supporters. Almost every citizen in Rome was tied by bonds of *obsequium*, mutual obligation, from the poorest man without work to great nobles. Only the emperor had no one above him. Clients were expected to vote for their patrons in return for the occasional gift, which often included daily *sportula* (small gifts of free food), as well as more substantial occasional gifts such

as a new toga for appearing in public, support in legal or social problems and financial aid at times. Later, after elections of magistrates were abolished in AD 14, clients were still expected to accompany their patron on his rounds through the city, perform little tasks for him and add to his general glory. Juvenal attacked the way each morning Rome's streets filled with clients hurrying to pay their respects in the *domus* (house) of their patron.

Above: The Forum Romanum in the 4th century AD, seen from the area of the House of the Vestal Virgins.

Below: A bas relief of the 2nd century AD showing a butcher hacking meat in his shop in Ostia. Many Romans were small shop-keepers.

LEISURE AND HOLIDAYS

Above: Gambling in bars and other public places was a common Roman pastime. These dice players are from a north African mosaic of the 3rd century AD.

Below: A wealthy Roman woman going to the baths accompanied by her servants, from a mosaic at Piazza Armerina, Sicily, of the 4th century AD. Women usually had different bathing times to those of men.

By midday, most Romans would have been up for six hours or more and would have hoped to have accomplished their *negotium* (business) – on days when business could be conducted at all. There were numerous *dies nefasti*, days of ill omen when judgements could not be made and when public assemblies could not be held.

DAYS OF ILL OMEN

On the many such inauspicious days the Romans celebrated religious rites such as the *Ludi Apollinares* dating from 208BC which ran from 6–13 July, or the *Ludi Victoriae Caesaris* which commemorated Caesar's military conquest of Gaul from 20–30 July.

The purpose of these displays was not to encourage mass idleness and drain the public coffers but to celebrate the power of the Roman people and honour the appropriate gods. The latter included deified former emperors. By the reign of Claudius (AD41–54) 159 days a year were *dies nefasti*. He and subsequent wise emperors such as Vespasian tried to reduce the number. Marcus Aurelius restored the business year to 230 days.

LEISURED AFTERNOONS

Even on *dies fasti* (when judgements could be made), the Forum emptied of citizens conducting business as the afternoon wore on. Most drifted off in search of entertainment in the warmest part of the day. One important event for the poorer citizens – who formed the majority of Rome's inhabitants – was the monthly distribution of the *annona*, the grain ration, which was handed out at the Porticus Minucia. By AD200 this came in the form of baked bread and was later supplemented by wine, oil and pork.

Far more spectacular were the gladiatorial games, the races at the circus and performances at the theatre which diverted the Roman people. As these huge public structures could contain much of the city's population – the Circus Maximus could seat about 300,000 people, the Colosseum and the Theatre of Pompey about 50,000 people each – this was truly mass entertainment.

The other enormous draw was the public baths. There were 170 in Rome by 33BC and 856 by AD400, but by the 4th century AD the small establishments had long been eclipsed by the 11 huge imperial baths, the *thermae*, that were some of the grandest Roman buildings. Starting relatively modestly with the Baths of Agrippa of 25BC, these assumed majestic form with the Baths of Trajan, which opened in AD109. The even larger *thermae* that followed in the next two centuries – the Baths of Caracalla, Diocletian and Constantine – expanded the same concept, which was copied in the provinces.

Lavishly designed and decorated, these complexes combined the functions of gyms, health centres, swimming pools, libraries, restaurants, meeting places and bordellos. Romans in cities around the empire would spend leisurely afternoon hours exercising in the *palaestra*, bathing in the *caldarium*, *tepidarium* and *frigidarium* (respectively the hot, warm and cold baths), swimming in the open-air *natatio* (swimming pool), walking in the gardens, relaxing, and enjoying relationships of varying degrees of intimacy with other bathers. Some women joined men at the baths. But as there were designated hours for women, it was probably only women of ill-repute who bathed with the men. When early Christians fulminated against the amount of time wasted sinfully at the baths, they were attacking less physical cleanliness – although Christian ascetics frowned upon washing, preferring to mortify their dirty flesh – than this openly sybaritic aspect of Roman life.

SHOPS AND BARS

Almost all of Rome's *tabernae* (shops) were small and specialized. They consisted of one room, often at the ground level of an *insula* (apartment block), with a wooden or masonry counter across the entrance that was closed off at night by shutters. They normally had a mezzanine floor above. Most *tabernae* lined the narrow streets. Bakers would have grain storage space, mills and baking ovens at the back of the shop. One shop in Ostia has murals of its goods behind the counter, such as grapes and olives. Another depicted on a terracotta plaque shows a poultry shop with baskets of eggs on the counter. A few jewellers and shops selling luxury goods remained in the Forum Romanum. Domitian tried to clear the streets of the clutter of shops, with limited success. However, complexes of shops were developed early at Terracina, and Livy mentions an early specialized food market near the Forum Romanum. Much the most splendid complex of markets and offices was Trajan's Market, rising above Trajan's Forum. This is thought to have offered covered shopping inside one of Rome's most remarkable buildings.

Rome and other cities also had plenty of bars where men could drop in for a quick drink or a snack. Some were tiny,

little more than holes in the wall, but others, such as that found in the House of Amphitrite in Herculaneum, had seating with *amphorae* stacked in wooden wall racks. Romans liked to gamble as well as drink in such bars, while snacking on olives, bread, seafood and sausages. There were also modest restaurants, such as that found in the Via di Diana in Ostia. This had shelves and counters lined with second-hand marble and simple tables.

Above: A tavern in the Via dell'Abbondanza in Pompeii, with amphorae *stacked behind the bar.*

Below: Interior of a tavern at Ostia, 1st century AD. Most taverns were just for drinking but this one had a table and bench and may have served snacks or even full meals.

DINNER PARTIES

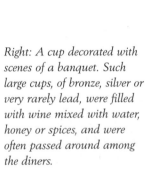

Above: A young servant girl, probably a slave, carrying a dish of food, from a fresco in the Villa of the Mysteries, Pompeii c. 60BC.

Towards evening, after their lengthy baths, Romans headed home for the meal that was usually the social highlight of the day: *cena*, dinner. This was eaten around the eighth hour in winter or ninth hour in summer, which is about 4–6 p.m. in modern terms, for the Roman day varied according to the season. Originally there had been three daily meals but by the late Republic the first two, *ientaculum* and *prandium*, seem to have become little more than snacks, eaten without formality or even a table. The *cena* was the great meal of the day, sometimes the occasion of excessive gourmandizing but more usually of modest meals, to which the Romans came bathed, in clean clothes if they had them.

THE DINING ROOM

All Romans who could afford it liked to dine reclining on *triclinia* (couches which ran on three sides of a table), set around a table, which gave the *triclinium* (dining room) its name. Covered with cushions and mattresses, these couches were sometimes built into the walls to save space. Others could be elaborately decorated and gilded. By the 2nd century BC women ate reclining alongside men. Only children and favoured slaves sat on stools or chairs at the end of the *triclinium*, a position which was considered undignified. Cato the Younger, one of Caesar's staunchest opponents, vowed never to eat reclining as long as Caesar's tyranny lasted, an extreme of self-denial more admired than imitated. (Cato committed suicide.) Some dining rooms were windowless, lit by oil lamps, but decorated with fine murals and mosaics. However, in country villas, *triclinia* could take advantage of the view seen through colonnades.

The couches were arranged around a table, one side of which was left free for service. The most honoured couch was opposite the empty side of the table and on each couch the most privileged position was that by the *fulcrum* or head of the couch. A *nomenclator* (usher) announced the guests and showed them their place on the couch, after they had removed their shoes. If more than nine people were to dine, other *triclinia* had to be brought in, twelve places being the usual maximum.

Right: A cup decorated with scenes of a banquet. Such large cups, of bronze, silver or very rarely lead, were filled with wine mixed with water, honey or spices, and were often passed around among the diners.

EATING AND DRINKING

M*instratores* (waiters) now brought in dishes and bowls. Diners had knives, toothpicks and several spoons, but as the Romans did not have forks, they ate mainly with their hands. They washed their hands frequently throughout the meal from bowls brought round by slaves. Every guest had his or her own napkin but some brought their own napkins with them which they filled with *apophoreta* (titbits) to take home. This was considered perfectly acceptable.

A grand *cena* could be formidable, an occasion for ostentatious display by the rich. Seven courses were not uncommon: a *gustatio* or hors d'oeuvre, three entrées, two roasts and a dessert. Juvenal *c.* AD120 described, "Huge lobsters garnished with asparagus…mullet from Corsica… goose's liver, a capon as big as a house, a piping hot boar…truffles and delicious mushrooms". Such descriptions might seem wildly exaggerated if not reiterated by the Greek historian Herodian 100 years later and by Macrobius, governor of Africa, in AD410. Juvenal also attacked hosts who kept the best dishes and wines for themselves and important guests, while giving "black meal" to the less important.

The Romans drank correspondingly. A first libation started the meal. *Mulsus* (honeyed wine) followed the first course and slaves went round refilling the *cratera* (mixing bowl), for wine was diluted with water. The proportion of water to wine could be low but generally it was somewhere in the region of 4:1.

After dinner there might be *acommissatio*, a drinking match in which diners had to empty their cups in one go. Dancers, clowns and striptease provided entertainment at some dinner parties, which could sometimes turn into orgies. Belching after such meals was perfectly acceptable and the emperor Claudius, who loved his food, considered an edict authorizing other emissions. But only the greediest diners vomited up their meal into pots held by slaves or on to the fine mosaic floors.

Only the length of such dinners tempered such excess, for they could go on for hours. Nero and his short-lived successor Vitellius, a noted gourmand, often stayed eating and drinking until after midnight, which was thought gross. Juvenal attacked those who "went to bed with the rise of Lucifer, the morning star, at an hour when our generals in the past would be moving their standards and camp".

Against such gourmandizing should be set the frugality of both Plinys. Pliny the Elder rose from the table when it was still light in summer and after only the first

hour of night in the winter, while his nephew praised "elegant but frugal meals". He accepted a dinner invitation once from Catilius Severus on the condition that "You treat me frugally and our table abounds only with philosophical conversation". Much more typical of most Roman meals than Neronian banquets was the dinner organized by the Funeral College in Rome for its members in AD133 at which each guest was given simply a loaf of bread, four sardines and an *amphora* of wine.

Above: A banquet in Carthage, depicted on a mosaic of the 4th century AD. The diners appear to be sitting up, perhaps to view the performers.

Below: This banquet scene from Ancona in eastern Italy shows the classic pattern of diners reclining on triclinia arranged around three sides of a table, the fourth side being left free for servants.

FOOD FOR RICH AND POOR

Above: Bread being sold at a bakery in Pompeii, a fresco of the 1st century AD. Note the flattened, circular shape of the baker's loaves.

Two things stand out about Roman attitudes towards food in general. The first is that they were almost omnivorous. "If it moves or grows, cook it and eat it" could have been their motto, for they lacked religious or sentimental dietary taboos (except against cannibalism, and they did not eat dogs or cats). A large type of dormouse was specially bred for eating and most song birds were considered fair game, or were bred in captivity. This catholic approach led to dishes of great variety and increasing complexity and richness on the tables of the rich in Rome and other great cities.

The other salient point is that meat was expensive and most people ate a simple diet, based on cereals, olive oil and vegetables with quite a lot of wine, and modest amounts of meat – principally pork, seldom beef or chicken – and seafood. Slaves and paupers ate often rancid cereals as a gruel or porridge and suffered chronic malnutrition, as modern analysis of skeletons at Pompeii has shown.

THE CHANGING DIET OF ROME

The early Roman diet was simple, based on cereals, olive oil and locally grown vegetables. Later orators used to praise the ancient frugality of Curius Dentatus, who "gathered his scanty vegetables and cooked them himself in his little stove". This moderation did not long survive Rome's rise to wealth and power.

From 200BC on, Rome could no longer be supplied locally and soon foreign wars led to imports of entirely new foods. Lucullus, the great late Republican general, for example, introduced the cherry to Rome from Asia Minor. However, most of the bulk of the food sucked into Rome remained the essential supplies of wheat, which came from Egypt, Africa and Sicily, and olive oil which came from Africa and Spain.

There were many other dishes but, as the Romans had no refrigeration, most perishable foods tended to be produced and eaten locally. Martial's *Epigrams* list

Right: From 200BC on, Rome began to import food, metals, textiles and other goods from a growing range of countries around the Mediterranean both for their luxuries and as staple necessities.

the many foods available for those who could afford them at the end of the 1st century AD. Pork came from Gaul, cured meats from Spain, spices from Asia, wines and fruits – including apples, pears, figs, grapes, melons and plums – from vineyards and orchards in Italy, along with asparagus (a favourite of Augustus), olives, beans, lentils, radishes, peas, pumpkins, lettuce and cabbages.

Seafood in all its variety was much prized in an empire centred on the sea. Red mullet and shellfish, especially lobster, were delicacies, but oysters were not a luxury and were transported inland along the roads, even in Britain, to be eaten by travellers. From the edges of the Sahara in Africa came pomegranates and dates, and fresh game came from the woods of Italy. Most dishes were cooked in sauces flavoured with spices from the East such as pepper. Perhaps the most characteristic Roman flavouring was *garum*. This was made from fish guts, salted and placed in tanks in the sun until they had gained sufficient potency to be used to flavour dishes – a process that could take four to six weeks.

By the 1st century AD Roman cuisine in all its sometimes overwhelming intricacy is revealed – albeit in caricatured form – in the great banquet that Trimalchio gave in the *Satyricon*, where the chef could create "'a fish out of a sow's belly, a wood pigeon out of bacon, a turtledove out of ham'". Dormice

"sprinkled with honey and poppy seed" made an amazing hors d'oeuvre and a boar stuffed with live thrushes that flew out as it was being carved made an eye-catching main roast. Although such absurdly complex courses must have been rare, Roman cooks delighted in concocting dishes that were unusual. However, as the still-life murals of bread, fruit and game from Pompeii suggest, most families would normally have eaten far more simply. Sausages, meat pies and cubes of roasted meat were popular, along with fruits both fresh and dried and buns filled with both savoury and sweet things. Honey was the universal sweetener.

WHAT THE ROMANS LACKED

Ancient Romans did not have citrus fruits such as oranges or grapefruit, nor rice, sugar, apricots, coffee, pheasant or peaches, all of which were introduced by the Arabs to Europe during the Middle Ages. They did not have tomatoes, potatoes, corn, peanuts, guinea fowl, red and green (bell) peppers, chocolate and turkey, which came to Europe from Central or North America in the 16th century.

The Romans did not drink tea, which was still a Chinese secret, and they scarcely ate butter, for it apparently seldom occurred to them to store surplus milk in this way. In fact, they did not eat much in the way of dairy products apart from cheese. Their diet approximated to the modern ideal of the Mediterranean diet.

Above: A still life showing fruit, nuts and a water jug from the House of the Stags at Herculaneum, 1st century AD. This fresco illustrates what the well-to-do Roman mainly ate better than some more elaborate written menus.

Below: Seafood of many types was much-prized by the Romans, both rich and also the poor if they lived near the sea. Lobster and mullet were thought delicacies. The Mediterranean in those unpolluted days still teemed with abundant marine life.

WINE AND VINEYARDS

Wine played a hugely important role in Roman life, for they had no tea, chocolate or coffee, nor soft drinks nor spirits. They hardly drank beer from the middle Republic on – they knew of it but considered it fit mainly for Germans, although beer was drunk by Roman soldiers on Hadrian's Wall. Romans drank wine, an estimated 100 million litres a year in Rome alone at its peak, most of which came from outside central Italy. For the undernourished majority, wine was an important food, a source of minerals, vitamins (including, we now know, vital anti-oxidants) and sugars. Slaves drank water with a little thin wine.

Above: The Romans had over 50 distinct varieties of grapes, but most of their wine was red.

ROMAN VITICULTURE

The Greeks had long grown wine in southern Italy, from where viticulture spread north to central Italy. Etruria was thought to produce some of Rome's best wines, such as Graviscanum, Caeres or Tiburtinum, but the especially renowned Falernian wine came from just north of Naples. Most famous vineyards were not far from the coast, as sea transport was so much cheaper than land transport. Greek wine was also highly regarded by the Romans, although it may not have tasted like Greek wines today. Spain later became another major wine exporter. Wine transported long distances in pinewood barrels may have acquired a resinous tang like modern retsina, but the Romans do not seem to have objected as they added various flavourings to their wine when they mixed them.

As trade around the empire boomed in the three centuries after 100BC, wine-growing spread to new regions. The Greek cities of southern Gaul, especially Marseilles, had always grown wine and under the Romans viticulture reached northern Gaul. In AD71 Pliny the Elder noted that vineyards already existed around Bordeaux but he knew little about their wines and they remained obscure. The warmer and drier Rhône valley was more promising territory for a viticulture based on Mediterranean methods and grape varieties. Trier, surrounded by sun-trapping vineyards hanging from the steep slopes above the river Moselle, may have produced wine as early as the 2nd century AD. However, evidence of its flourishing vineyards comes only from the second half of the 4th century AD, in a

Left: Pressing grapes in a winery from St Romain en Gal, France, c. AD200. Vine-growing was introduced into southern France by the Greeks.

famous poem by the imperial tutor, governor and poet Ausonius, supported by archaeological evidence in the form of wine presses in the Moselle valley at Piesport. The Moselle flowing past Trier, the Western empire's capital at the time, reminded Ausonius of his native Bordeaux, where vineyards lined the river Garonne. He described wealthy villas with their smoking chimneys, boatmen exchanging jocular insults with men working among the vines, fish playing in the river and, in a famous passage, the hills mirrored in the Moselle's waters.

What colour paints the river shallows, when Hesperus has brought the shades of evening.
The Moselle is dyed with the green of her hills; their tops quiver
In the ripples, vine leaves tremble from afar
And the grape clusters swell even in the clear stream.

The most informative Roman author on viticultural matters was Lucius Junius Columella in the 1st century AD. In *De re Rustica* (*About Rural Matters*) he wrote about many aspects of farming beside vineyards, but he did discuss different grape varieties and how to balance quantity against quality. He listed more than 50 grape varieties and praised a native Italian variety called the Amminean.

The Romans sometimes used to trail vines along elms and other trees such as poplars for support, and it has been suggested that the traditional English elm (now almost extinct) was first imported into Britain by Romans for such purposes.

Bacchus, the wine god, was an important deity to the Romans and libations, the pouring out of wine in honour of a god, were a common sacramental use of wine. The last of a particularly good wine was sometimes thrown on the floor

Right: Although the Romans drank wine regularly, being seen drunk in public as in this Hellenistic statue of an old woman was considered a disgraceful condition and was not the norm.

as an offering to the gods. Later, as the empire slowly became Christian, the frequent use of wine in the Eucharist again encouraged the spread of viticulture into northern Europe, for wine remained expensive to transport long distances until Bordeaux began shipping its wines north in the 12th century.

VINTAGES AND WINE STORAGE

Although the Romans may not have had completely airtight corks (they used lead as an extra sealant) they did develop glass bottles besides traditional pottery *amphorae* for better wines. These were marked with a distinguishing *pittacium* (label) stating their vintage. The Romans apparently kept certain of their finest wines for a remarkably long time. Horace when in his middle-age wrote of drinking a vintage older than himself, and the most famous vintage, that dating from the consulate of Opimius in 121BC, was reputedly kept for 125 years. However, most Roman wines were drunk young when they were sharp, even rough, and strong. The Romans never drank their wine neat, but diluted it usually with drinking water, sometimes with seawater, or they would sweeten the wine with honey. Roman wines at times could possibly have tasted a little like sangria.

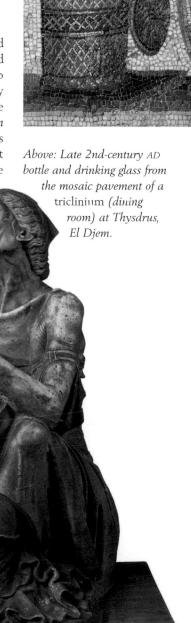

Above: Late 2nd-century AD bottle and drinking glass from the mosaic pavement of a triclinium (dining room) at Thysdrus, El Djem.

ROME THE GREAT CONSUMER

One of the chief concerns of those governing Rome, from the later Republic until the end of the ancient city in the 6th century AD, was supplying it with essential foods. Other large cities imported grain, but Rome's demands eclipsed all others.

WHEAT, WINE AND OIL

Since Clodius started the free distribution to male citizens over the age of ten of five *modii* per month of grain (880lbs/400kg per person of grain annually) in 58BC, rulers who failed to provide the *annona* (dole) faced riots. The emperor Claudius (AD41–54) was pelted with stale crusts by a hungry crowd after a poor harvest and storms delayed the grain fleets.

Claudius' response was to build a giant artificial harbour north of Ostia at Portus, which Trajan improved with an inland basin 60 years later. Grain, mainly wheat, and olive oil were the staples of the Roman diet, but olive oil also lit the city's countless oil lamps and was lavishly used for personal hygiene, in place of soap. Wine was almost the only drink available.

Wheat, wine and oil were therefore needed in unprecedented quantities – about 400,000 tons per year of foodstuffs, of which 240,000 tons were wheat. (Meat, seafood, fruit and vegetables, supplementary to these dietary basics, are less easily estimated, although early in the 3rd century AD Septimius Severus added oil, and in AD275 Aurelian pork and wine, to the *annona*, but by then the city's population was beginning to fall.)

The great mound rising beside the Tiber in Rome known as Monte Testaccio is made of pieces of broken *amphorae* (earthenware jars). Rising 112ft (34m), it has a circumference of 3,200ft (1km) and contains fragments of at least 53 million *amphorae*. The majority once held olive oil shipped from Spain in the years AD140–250. Africa was another large source of oil. Most *amphorae* came in a variety of standardized sizes. They were designed to be neatly stacked in ships' holds. They were usually broken up after being emptied because their interiors absorbed oil which went rancid, although a few were later used to lighten architectural vaults.

About 1,000 shiploads of wheat were needed for Rome each year, as the average merchant ship carried about 240 tons. Inclusion of the shipping needed for the estimated 100 million litres (22 million gallons) of wine and 20 million litres (4 million gallons) of oil would boost this total to at least 1,700 ships a year arriving at Rome's ports – excluding those lost.

Most ships arrived in the sailing season, which lasted 100–120 days a year. The Romans never developed state-controlled fleets but relied on private contractors, whom they encouraged in various ways. After the bread riots Claudius offered anyone who used a ship holding at least 10,000 *modii* (70 tons) to supply Rome, privileges ranging from citizenship for non-citizens to exemptions from various taxes.

Above: The symbols of grain merchants in a mosaic set in the street leading to the market in Ostia, Rome's great harbour town, c. AD100.

Below: Amphorae (earthenware jars) for transporting and storing oil and wine came in a variety of shapes and sizes, but under the empire their shapes were increasingly standardized. These amphorae *come from a sunken ship.*

Emperors from Augustus on appointed officials such as the *praefectus annonae* (wheat dole prefect), who soon acquired assistants. By AD200, the *sub-praefectus annonae* (wheat dole subprefect), was paid 100,000 sesterces, a large salary reflecting his importance. However, grain supplies always remained precariously dependent on the caprices of harvests and of storms at sea. A serious grain shortage in AD190 caused riots which the emperor Commodus only defused by having Cleander, his favourite minister, executed as a scapegoat.

HAULAGE AND STORAGE

When the food reached Rome's ports of Pozzuoli, Ostia or Portus it had to be unloaded, dragged up the river and stored. Grain and oil had to be rowed or hauled the 20 miles (32km) up the Tiber from the port in smaller boats or barges in a journey that took two to three days.

Four types of boat were used: the *scaphae*, *lintres* and *lenunculi*, all rowing boats, and the *codicariae*, specialized boats used to transport goods from Ostia and Portus up river to Rome. These had oars and lowerable masts but were often rowed or hauled, less often by slaves than by free but poor casual labourers. Although they had to be hauled upstream, they could be rowed or sailed downstream. The Romans did not use horses for haulage, as they never developed suitable horse collars. The boat haulers, known as *helciarii*, used to chant rhythmically as they trudged along pulling their heavy vessels up stream towards the city. They even had their own guild. Upon arrival in Rome, the grain, oil and wine were stored in *horrea*, specially built warehouses by the Tiber such as those below the Aventine Hill in the region called Marmorata (so-called because this is where the marble coming into Rome was unloaded).

Some *horrea* were immense: the Horrea Galbana, for example, had 140 rooms on the ground floor alone and covered about 5 acres (2ha). These multistorey warehouses were massively built, with walls at least 2ft (60cm) thick. They had small external windows and massive doors to preserve their valuable contents from thieves. Inside they had large internal windows, both between rooms and opening on to courtyards, to provide plentiful ventilation to keep the grain dry. For the same reason they normally had raised floors. The floors also stopped rodent activity and provided circulation of air to prevent the spontaneous combustion of over-heated grain. Much grain was lost to rodents nonetheless.

Above: Free labourers or slaves haul a barge full of wine barrels up a river, probably the Rhône, since the relief is from Avignon. The Romans could not use horses for such work as they did not have the right type of horsecollar.

Below: Many warehouses were monumental structures boasting fine architectural features, such as this grand gateway of the Horrea Epagathania in Ostia, whose pediment and pillars are worthy of a public building.

TUNICS AND TOGAS

Below: This Roman magistrate from Asia Minor in the 5th century AD wears similar clothes to those worn 500 years before.

It is striking how little fashions changed from the late Republic to the end of the Western empire 600 years later. A senator from Cicero's day might have looked rather oddly dressed four centuries later but he would not have seemed to be wearing fancy dress. The same could not be said today. The very slowly changing nature of Roman fashion, however, is more typical of most societies around the world than the increasingly rapid sartorial changes of recent centuries. Clothes generally denoted status in the Roman world and, while definitions of social status changed gradually, fashions were never dictated by designers, nor did individuals dress solely according to their own whims. Although the odd dandy like Caesar wore his toga with particularly wide sleeves, the Romans were generally rather puritanical about what citizens should wear, adhering to a simplicity that can be called classical.

TYPES OF FABRIC

The basic Roman garment for all classes was the *tunicum*, a simple tunic made of wool or, less commonly, linen. Cotton was rare for a long time and silk was always a luxury item imported from furthest Asia. Although the use of silk increased steadily, for a long time it was thought utterly effeminate for men. (Caligula caused a scandal by appearing once in gaudy silk robes.) However, under the Principate it became increasingly common for richer women. Finally, in the grandiose courts of the later empire (after AD284) most courtiers wore elaborate silk robes. Wool, undyed for

Above: A Roman wearing a pallium *(cloak) over his tunic from Sicily, 4th century AD. Only richer citizens could afford a* pallium.

poor people and white for richer citizens, remained the commonest material, however. The *tunicum* was made of two pieces of cloth sewn together, usually untailored so that the surplus produced short sleeves, with a belt around the waist. Slaves, labourers and the very poor wore almost nothing else, but richer citizens often wore a *pallium* or Greek-style cloak over their longer *tunicum*. It is possible that some Romans wore a *licium*, a loin cloth, as underwear.

Formal dress for male Roman citizens consisted of the toga, a large semicircular piece of woollen cloth about 9ft (2.7m) long worn draped over one shoulder to leave the other bare and almost reaching the ankles. Exactly how this was put on has been tentatively reconstructed. A toga was certainly a cumbersome, heavy garment, which citizens liked to discard as soon as possible but which emperors repeatedly tried to make citizens wear in public as late as the reign of Commodus

(AD180–92). In the evenings a *synthesis*, a comfortable compromise between a toga and a tunic, was often worn for dining on a couch. Senators were distinguished from ordinary citizens by the *laticlava*, a broad purple stripe running down their tunics, while equestrians had a narrower stripe, the *angusticlava*. Emperors wore the most purple, so "being raised to the purple" came to mean becoming emperor.

Hooded cloaks, *paenulae*, could be worn over the tunic or toga in bad weather but hats were generally unknown apart from straw hats worn informally against the sun. In bad weather part of the toga could be pulled over the head for protection, as it was for priestly roles. Trousers were known to the Romans but were long considered barbarous garments – worn by Persians and Germans – and were only adopted partially at the end of the empire, in a sign for conservatives of general decay. Clerical dress in the Catholic and Episcopalian or Lutheran churches, with its long, superimposed robes, still perpetuates old Roman dress. In the later empire, heavy military-style belts were worn by bureaucrats as well as soldiers, revealing the general militarization of Roman government.

WOMEN'S WEAR

Roman women also wore long loose tunics. These, called *stolae*, were often in bright colours and of fine material, such as good linen, cotton or silk. Underneath they often wore a *strophium*, a leather band that served as a simple bra. Over their *stola* went a rectangular woollen mantle, the *palla*, which was draped over the left shoulder, across the back and under the right arm. Prostitutes and convicted adulteresses wore female togas, the former often wearing transparent silks.

Women's dress also seems to have changed remarkably little over the centuries, although brooches – buttons were unknown to the Romans – became progressively more elaborate, as did jewellery generally.

FOOTWEAR

The basic Roman footwear was the sandal in varying shapes. The *solea* was a form of basic sandal of a type still worn by some Catholic monks, with the sole attached to the instep by straps. *Crepidae* were sandals secured by a strap passing through eyelets, while *calcei* were leather half boots with crossed laces. In the army soldiers wore *caligae*, hobnailed boots that laced up round the ankle. (*Caligula*, Little Boots, was the nickname of the emperor Gaius, who grew up in the camp of his father Germanicus.) The Romans increasingly wore *fasciae*, a form of puttee, around the feet and lower legs, in northern parts of the empire and in winter. Women wore either sandals or soft leather shoes, but high heels were unknown. Socks were sometimes worn.

Right: A pair of leather sandals from Egypt of the 3rd century AD. Sandals were the standard footwear across areas around the Mediterranean.

Above: As these women conversing on a mural from Pompeii c. AD70 show, Roman women wore long, loose brightly-coloured stolae (tunics) of linen, cotton or silk. Their fashions changed only very slowly over the centuries.

HAIRSTYLES AND COSMETICS

Above: The curly beard and hair of the 2nd century AD as sported by Lucius Verus.

Below: Women's hairstyles became very elaborate, then reverted to simpler styles with hair tied back and a middle parting, as in this Egyptian mummy portrait of the 4th century AD.

Although Roman clothing changed very slowly, hairstyles and fashions in beards underwent remarkable developments that perhaps reveal something about wider changes in Roman society itself.

BEARDED OR CLEAN-SHAVEN?

In the early Republic, according to tradition – such as the story about the Gauls pulling at the beards of elderly senators during the sack of Rome in 390BC – and in surviving portraits such as the so-called "Brutus", men had beards and short hair. The Romans always remained short-haired but by *c.* 150BC most Roman men were clean-shaven, possibly following Hellenistic styles. Fashion dictated that they remained so until after the death of Trajan in AD117. (A few soldiers had earlier had clipped beards and moustaches.)

Shaving was not, however, an easy or pain-free task for Romans, as they lacked both soap (for working up a lather) and high-quality steel for a clean shave. It was difficult and unusual even to try to shave oneself. Important Romans used to have barbers come to shave them in their houses and some, like Augustus, carried on their daily business at the same time. Ordinary Romans visited regularly but not always daily the *tonsor* (barber).

The barber's shop, the *tonstrina*, opened on to the street and was the place where men came to exchange news and gossip. Here they had their hair cut and their faces shaved, by a *novacula*, a blunt iron razor, by a form of poultice called *dropax*, made of several types of wax that depilated rather than shaved, or by *forcipes aduncae*, tweezers. The whole process was long and painful. Skilled barbers could make a lot of money; the unskilled made a painful mess of their customers' faces.

When Hadrian, either because he had a scar on his face that he wished to hide or because of his love of all things Greek, began wearing a beard after AD117, the fashion quickly spread and soon almost all Roman men sported beards. In the 4th century AD fashion changed again. Constantine always appears in his portraits clean-shaven, as do his sons. Julian, in emotive reaction against his Christian precursors, wore a beard like a Greek philosopher. Although Julian's successors were mostly clean-shaven, by the 6th century AD most men were bearded again.

While beards came and went, male hairstyles – with the flamboyant exception of Nero and some of his courtiers, who adopted *bouffant* big hair copying that of charioteers – remained short and generally plain until the 2nd century AD. They then became steadily more elaborate. Hadrian is shown with a head of curly hair and soon men adopted hairdos of really elaborate complexity. Lucius Verus, the idle co-emperor of Marcus Aurelius, had a tremendous head of curly hair, but so had the ascetic Marcus and the militaristic Septimius Severus, emperors who followed rather than set the style. Their intricate curls reflect the barbers' skills. The latter used combs or a *calamistrum*, a heated curling iron, and even dyed some customers' hair. In the catastrophe-ridden 3rd century AD, men's hair became short and plain again, as Gallienus' and Diocletian's respectively austere and grim busts attest.

WOMEN'S COIFFURE

Hairstyles for women in the Republic were simple, with the hair drawn back from a central parting and gathered in a chignon at the nape of the neck. Under Augustus, women's hair was often braided and with Messalina, Claudius' notoriously unfaithful wife, high-piled hairstyles appeared. Under the Flavian emperors and Trajan (AD69–117) female hair became extremely complicated, with great masses of curls piled high on the head. Trajan's sister Marciana and his niece Matilda both dressed their hair in diadems, "high as towers", the product of long hours spent with their *ornatrix*, or hairdresser.

Imperious Roman women of the nobility were prone to lash out at any hairdresser who failed to please them – many were slaves – at least according to the poet Martial, who tells of "Lalage avenging with the mirror in which she had seen it [an unfortunate hairdo] and Plecusa falls, hit because of those unruly locks of hair". Juvenal mocked women whose "numerous tiers and storeys piled upon one another on the head" made them look taller than they really were. Later hairstyles were less elaborate. Wigs were occasionally used to disguise baldness.

COSMETICS

In addition to her work as a hairdresser, an *ornatrix* also took care of wealthier women's makeup. Often lead-based – the Romans were not aware of the dangers of

lead – the cosmetics were stored in glass phials or flagons and alabaster vases. Creams, perfumes and unguents were extensively used. Red for the lips and cheeks was made from ochre, a lichen-like plant called *ficus* or from molluscs. Eyeliner was made from soot or powders of antimony, which was also used to thicken the eyebrows. Mirrors, an essential part of the daily toilette, were made of highly polished metal, for true mirrors of reflecting glass were unknown. Ovid, ever aware of the erotic side of life, advised women to bolt the door of their chamber when making themselves up for "[your beauty] lies stored in a hundred caskets". Women also adorned themselves with elaborate jewellery, including *armillae* (bracelets), *catellae* (trinkets) and *periscelides* (ankle circlets).

Above: A woman pouring perfume into a flask from the Villa Farnesina, c. AD10.

Below: A casket containing a wealthy Roman woman's toilette items from Cumae.

EROTIC LOVE

Above: Tombstone showing a brothel-keeper and customer. Prostitution was accepted and regulated in Rome.

Below: An erotic fresco from Pompeii. Many Romans enjoyed often fine erotic art such as this in private.

The Roman reputation for widespread sexual debauchery is hardly merited. It derives more from Suetonius' racy portraits of the first 12 Caesars, reinforced by Hollywood films and discoveries of "shocking" pictures at Pompeii, than from the reality of life for most people in the Roman world, who seldom had the opportunity for sexual depravity. Most of them worked hard, married young and remained reasonably faithful. If there were no lethal sexually transmitted diseases to discourage promiscuity, there were no contraceptives to facilitate it either. Prostitution existed, was recognized but not revered (unlike in Babylon or parts of Syria), and was regulated. Prostitutes wore distinctive toga-style dresses.

However, if unworried by Christian fears of eternal damnation for extramarital sex, the Romans were very concerned with the maintenance of public dignity and social stability, both of which were based on the conventional family unit. Monogamy within marriage was always the ideal and female "virtue" (chastity) was much praised in the legends of early Rome. Lucretia, a noble Roman virgin killed herself rather than give in to the advances of the Etruscan tyrant Tarquinius. (Tarquinius was soon after expelled from Rome.) However, as with most pagan religions, minor fertility gods around the empire were honoured by sometimes ithyphallic statues, while statues of major deities, often half-naked, adorned public places. These can give ancient cities an unwarranted air of eroticism to modern eyes.

SEXUAL MORALITY

Heterosexual romance and love were the main themes of many novels, plays and poetry, from the numerous plays of Plautus in the 2nd century BC to Longus' romantic novel *Daphnis and Chloe* 300 years later. Here the naivity of the peasant lovers is mocked. Apuleius, writing *The Golden Ass* at about the same time, caters to a more sophisticated audience, but he attributes bad faith and perversity to characters with Greek names.

In the late Republic there had been a marked loosening of sexual restrictions, at least among upper class Romans. Augustus tried to control this. The *Lex Julia* made adultery a criminal offence and he banished his own daughter, grand-daughter and the poet Ovid for sexual immorality. Augustus himself, however, had mistresses. Women, making use of their new freedoms, could choose or reject lovers, but women's own voices are seldom heard. That of Messalina, Claudius' notoriously promiscuous wife, is exceptional. Lesbianism presumably existed but escaped record because writers were men.

HOMOSEXUALITY

The Romans had no specific word for male homosexuality, for they seldom thought in terms of predetermined sexual orientation but rather about public behaviour. While the Romans never idealized homosexuality as some upper-class Greeks had, they did not demonize it either, as Christians later did. Homosexuality was, however, often considered a Greek habit and, as with most things Greek, it seems to have become more widespread in the later Republic. Augustus typically tried to discourage it by legislation in his attempt to boost the birth rate among citizens. Petronius' *Satyricon* involved the adventures of characters – bisexuals of singular cynicism – with Greek names in the still Greek cities of southern Italy. However, Roman poets such as Tibullus and Horace also revealed homosexual sentiments.

There remained a strong sexist bias in Roman attitudes to homosexuality: men who took the passive or female role in such relations were despised and risked losing their citizenship – hence the force of stories circulated by his political enemies that Julius Caesar, when young, had been King Nicomedes of Bithynia's boyfriend. (Caesar later became a noted womanizer.) Emperors like Nero who allowed themselves to be penetrated – according to Suetonius Nero appeared dressed as the bride at his own mock-wedding – forfeited public respect. Public decorum was the key.

When the popular Titus became emperor in AD79, he put aside his harem of catamites along with his much-loved Jewish mistress the princess Berenice. (The latter was thought unacceptable because she was an exotic royal foreigner rather than because of any Roman anti-semitism.) Trajan took a harem of boys with him on campaign but, as he was even more popular than Titus, this was accepted, at least outside Rome. By contrast, Hadrian's prolonged mourning for his boyfriend Antinous, who drowned in the Nile, struck many as excessive and

undignified for an emperor. Emperors such as Caligula in the 1st century AD and Elagabalus in the 3rd century AD behaved so outrageously in public – Elagabalus reputedly prostituted himself – that they were soon assassinated.

From the 3rd century AD on, attitudes towards sex began to change. If Christians were the only real ascetics – Origen castrated himself to avoid the temptations of a beautiful young female pupil – non-Christians too began to become more obviously restrained in their behaviour. Herodian's novel *The Ethiopian Story* of the 3rd century AD praises the fidelity of its two engaged young lovers so strongly that Christians later claimed him as a covert co-religionist, which he probably was not. However Neoplatonism, the dominant philosophy in the later empire, tended to regard the flesh as something to be transcended, an attitude dating back to Plato which now became increasingly common. On this point at least pagan and Christian could meet.

Above: An erotic scene from a bedroom in the huge villa at Piazza Armerina, Sicily, c. AD320, shows that Roman enjoyment of carnal pleasure persisted into the later empire.

Below: The emperor Hadrian erected huge numbers of statues of Antinous, his beautiful young lover who drowned in the Nile. This one is in Lepcis Magna, Libya.

FUNERALS AND THE AFTERLIFE

Above: The Mausoleum of Augustus in Rome, completed 28BC, housed the funerary urns of members of the imperial family and was once topped by cypress trees, a custom going back to the Etruscans.

The pagan Romans never had a consistent or united view about what happened to them after death. Beliefs varied greatly, from the uncompromising materialism of Lucretius, the poetic adherent of Epicurus who believed that we simply become again our constituent atoms, to the far more common belief that some aspect of an individual might survive death, but probably not in a very agreeable way. Only with the Roman world's gradual conversion to Christianity in the 4th and 5th centuries AD did fixed beliefs in heaven and hell emerge.

THE ROMAN AFTERLIFE

Before then, people generally took what seemed most attractive – or least incredible – from what has been called the "inherited conglomerate" of myths, legends and beliefs that was constantly added to over the centuries but never reformed or subtracted from. The original Roman mixture of Etruscan and Greek ideas, in which the first was initially the most significant, was later enriched by new religions such as the cults of Bacchus, Isis and Mithras, which promised their adherents salvation. There were as well as the secretive, mystical sects such as the Pythagoreans and Orphics, who apparently believed in metempsychosis (reincarnation as animals or even plants).

For most people in the Roman world, however, the afterlife was a gloomy place of shadows and sometimes of torment, hardly more cheerful than the Christian or Muslim ideas of hell, which they may well have influenced. (The early Jews had had little belief in life after death.) In Book VI of Virgil's *The Aeneid*, which soon became Rome's national epic, Aeneas visits Hades, the underworld, and there talks to the shade of his father Anchises, for he was a notably filial son. This is an obvious reference to Odysseus' not dissimilar experience in Homer's *Odyssey*, and apposite as Roman ideas of the underworld were influenced by the Greeks. However, the Roman view of Hades was perhaps even gloomier, following Etruscan beliefs.

According to the composite Graeco-Roman story, Hades, the shadowy underworld, was governed by Pluto, sometimes called Orcus, the god of wealth as well as death. The souls of the dead were carried off by *genii*, spirits, who could be good or evil. This kingdom had several entrances through caves on Earth, but to reach it the dead had to pass Cerberus, the many-headed hound who guarded its gates. They then crossed the River Styx by paying Charon, the boatman, an obol, who became identified with Charun, a sinister Etruscan god of the dead. Sometimes Rhadamynthus and Minos, legendary kings of Crete, would then judge the souls of the dead, most of whom were left in a fearful limbo. Only a few heroes or deified emperors were thought to escape to the Elysian fields. Another infernal deity was Dis Pater, whom the Romans feared and seldom worshipped openly.

Such dismal views of the afterworld frightened many ordinary people. Writers like Lucretius, Cicero and Seneca, all infused with different aspects of Greek

Below: A women's funerary choir performing a ritual dance from a tomb in Ruvo of the 5th century BC. Greek beliefs and customs deeply influenced Rome's in this field as in many others.

philosophy, tried in vain to reassure them. However, most Romans regarded life on Earth as the important thing, not as a mere trial before eternal life in heaven, as Christians were meant to do.

TOMB TYPES

One of the laws of the famous Twelve Tables of 451BC forbade burial within the sacred *pomerium* (city boundary) so, as Rome grew, burial sites were pushed outward by the expansion of the city. Tombs and burials were traditionally located along the roads out of the city, at least for the wealthy, from the Forum Romanum and the Esquiline Hill to the Campus Martius, an early favourite location between the Servian Wall and the Tiber. Here Augustus built a mausoleum for his own family, but this area too was rapidly built over. Soon cemeteries began to line the roads leading out of Rome, especially the Via Appia to the south, where many fine tombs still stand.

Augustus' Mausoleum, started in 28BC, is typical in revealing marked Etruscan influences although the Greeks and Persians had also had *tumuli*: circular masonry drums topped by conical earth mounds, on which trees were often planted. Hadrian's great mausoleum across the Tiber, built *c.* AD135 to house

his own and the Antonine dynasty's remains, now the Castel Sant'Angelo, perpetuates something of the same tradition but with stronger Greek influences. An alternative type of tomb, probably derived from Hellenistic Syria, consisted of several superimposed columnar structures with either a pyramidal or a conical roof. Diocletian built an octagonal mausoleum for his body in his retirement palace at Split, while his successor Galerius erected an equally grand monument to himself. Built at Thessalonica a few years later in *c.* AD311, it is now a church.

Below: Funeral relief of a woman from Rome, dating from the 2nd century AD but with a Greek inscription, indicating that the woman was Greek in origin and thereby demonstrating the cosmopolitan nature of Rome's population.

Above: Funerary banqueting scene on the urn of Julia Eleutherides (a Greek surname but Roman first name), from the 2nd century AD.

Below: Funerary relief showing mourners bearing the catafalque of a body in procession from Rome, 1st century AD. A banquet normally followed the cremation or burial.

One of the most eye-catching of all tombs in Rome and still almost intact, is the "Pyramid of Cestius". Erected south of the city *c.* 20BC, near the later Porta Ostiensis and housing the remains of an important Roman noble, it recalls in its form the brief passion for Egyptiana that followed the annexation of that kingdom to the empire in 30BC. However, few later nobles outside the imperial family built on such a large scale. Probably the most unusual imperial tomb is Trajan's. The ashes of this popular emperor, who died in Tarsus in AD117 after the failure of his Parthian campaign, were placed inside his great column in the heart of Rome. A special senatorial decree overrode the ancient laws to permit the interment.

OTHER TOMBS

Not all tombs were grandiose dynastic statements, for many ordinary inhabitants both of the capital and other cities wanted to perpetuate their names, partly as a protest against the anonymity of metropolitan life, partly because, with such

doubts about immortality, they wanted to be remembered after their deaths. Both interiors and exteriors were richly decorated, to impress the living and provide a fitting *domus aeterna* (eternal home) for the dead. The Romans often buried grave goods to accompany the dead, with elaborate furnishings suggesting an almost Egyptian belief in the deceased's continued existence. A fine example of such decorations comes from the painted stucco vaulting of the Mausoleum of the Anicii of the 2nd century AD.

A flamboyant but non-aristocratic tomb has been preserved at the Porta Maggiore in the Aurelianic Wall. This is the Tomb of Eurysaces, a wealthy baker and freedman of the late 1st century BC. The circular openings in the tomb probably emulate baker's ovens. The tomb of the Haterii, a family of rich builders, is another fine example of a resplendent non-aristocratic tomb.

Poorer citizens might subscribe to a burial club that would arrange a decent funeral for them, while all but the very poorest had their graves marked by *amphorae* buried in the ground up to their necks. Many survive in the Isola Sacra cemetery near Ostia. The inscriptions on some tombs can be humorous: "Here in my tomb I drain my cup more greedily, because here I must sleep and here must stay for ever". However, more often they are simply poignant: "May the passer-by who has seen these flowers and read this epitaph say to himself: 'This flower is Flavia's body'".

FUNERAL RITES

A funeral began with the laying out of the corpse for seven days so that friends and relatives could pay their last respects. There followed a funeral procession to the burial place where there was usually a funerary banquet, like a wake. The family would return regularly to the tomb during their mourning period, the first time only eight days later. They would continue to have commemorative picnics for long after. If the funeral was that of an

important person, the procession might wend its way to the Forum Romanum, where a funeral oration would be given. Originally these were reserved for men only, but by the 1st century AD exceptional women were also honoured in this way. Occasionally, as with the speech Mark Antony gave at Caesar's funeral, such speeches had political significance.

Cremation on a pyre in public was the usual form of disposing of bodies for most Romans up to *c.* AD 100, when fashions began to change for reasons that are not entirely clear. The change seems to have begun among the upper classes – although the emperors themselves long continued the custom of cremation – and then spread down through the social hierarchy. Whether this can be connected with the slow changes in other attitudes is unknown. It certainly encouraged some splendid sarcophagi, but the mythological scenes carved on them seldom suggest any very powerful belief in an afterlife. Typical scenes show cavorting Tritons and Nereids, mermen and sea nymphs, as on a sarcophagus in the Louvre. Battle scenes were also very popular, usually showing the sack of Troy or some other well-known legend, but few suggest any specific religious belief.

Christian attitudes towards tombs and burial were very different. As they confidently expected the resurrection of the body, cremation was always out of the question. Bodies were buried, sometimes in Rome's catacombs by both pagans and Christians, especially the latter, for Christians often wanted to keep a low profile even when not trying to avoid persecution. There the Greek word for fish, *ichthys*, served as an acrostic for the words "Jesus Christ, God's Son [and] Saviour". When Constantine made Christianity the imperially favoured cult, Christian art and iconography developed. The finest surviving early such tomb is the Mausoleum of Santa Constanza, a circular building whose interior is graced by delightful paintings of birds and flowers with no obvious religious connotations.

THE CULT OF THE ANCESTORS

Despite being in the underworld, the dead were strongly believed to haunt the living and therefore needed to be appeased – hence the origins of the gladiatorial games and their name *munera* (offerings). As the Christian writer Tertullian scathingly noted in *The Shows c.* AD 200, "Men believed that the souls of the dead were propitiated by human blood". (Tertullian also disapproved of those tombs that invited the passing to drink to the deceased's memory.) *Mos maiorum*, the customs of our ancestors, always had a strong appeal to the Romans as an ideal, for Roman piety and dynastic pride were both connected with honouring the dead. The family death masks were kept prominently in the *domus*, normally in the atrium, and taken out and paraded through the streets on special occasions.

Above: Hadrian giving the funeral oration of his wife Sabina in the Forum Romanum, 2nd century AD.

Below: Vault of Santa Constanza, Rome, the Mausoleum of Constantine's daughter Constantia.

INDEX

ACKNOWLEDGEMENTS

l = left, r= right, t = top,
m = middle, b = bottom.

Ancient Art and Architecture Collection:
40, 101t, 107, 144b, 166t, 168t, 169b, 172t, 178b, 185b, 189t, 202t, 216t, 352b, 353b, 377b.

The Art Archive:
14c, 16l, 16r, 37b, 48t, 49, 53t, 55b, 56t, 59, 62–3, 70t, 74t, 76b, 77t, 79b, 80t, 82, 83, 86, 89, 91b, 179b, 228t;

/Archaeological Mus. Naples/Dagli Orti 337b, 358b, 359t, 385t, 395b, 427t, 427b, 435t, 443t, 469t, 470t, 471t, 474b, 484t, 485t, 491t, 493b, 494b, 496b;
/Dagli Orti 22t, 24t, 34b, 45b, 46b, 99b, 100t, 104t, 105b, 106, 107t, 108t, 111t, 116b, 117, 118t, 119t, 120t, 127, 132–3, 134–5, 141t, 142, 143b, 145b, 149, 155t, 163b, 171t, 172b, 186t, 188t, 191b, 199t, 200t, 201, 211b, 212, 213b, 220–1, 224, 228b, 229, 231, 233, 235t, 237b, 242, 243b, 244t, 245, 247t, 248t, 252t, 256b, 272tl, 274t, 287b, 290b, 299b, 301b, 320l, 320r, 321t, 322t, 342b, 346t, 349t, 349b, 349b, 360b, 361t, 367b, 371b, 372t, 374t, 374b, 375t, 403b, 411b, 424b, 431b, 439b, 457b, 458t, 473b, 480b, 481t, 482t, 488t, 490tr, 495t, 496t;
/Album J. Enrique Molina 266–7, 299t;
/Archaeological Museum Alexandria/Dagli Orti 452t;
/Archaeological Museum Cherchel Algeria/Dagli Orti 464b, 465t;
/Archaeological Museum Florence/Dagli Orti 400b;
/Archaeological Museum Istanbul/Dagli Orti 350t, 490bl, 492t;
/Archaeological Museum Madrid/Dagli Orti 263m, 440b;
/Archaeological Museum Merida, Spain/Dagli Orti 439t;
/Archaeological Museum Ostia/Dagli Orti 425b, 456b, 460, 481b;
/Archaeological Museum Sfax/Dagli Orti 438t;
/Archaeological Museum Sousse, Tunisia/Dagli Orti 383t;
/Bardo Museum Tunis/Dagli Orti 259t, 363t, 419t, 421t, 444tr, 461t, 480t, 483t, 487t;
/Biblioteca Nazionale Marciana Venice/Dagli Orti 391t;
/Bibliothèque des Arts Décoratifs Paris/Dagli Orti 264–5, 378–9, 454b, 479t;
/The Bodleian Library 170, 173b, 241t;
/Cathedral Museum Ferrara/Dagli Orti 421b;
/Cathedral Treasury Aachen/Dagli Orti 404t;
/Diozesanmuseum Trier/Dagli Orti 369;
/Ephesus Museum Turkey/Dagli Orti 370t;
/Galleria Borghese Rome/Dagli Orti 432–3;
/Harper Collins Publishers 272b;
/Historical Picture Archive 269t;

/Musée des Antiquités St Germain en Laye/Dagli Orti 464t, 486b;
/Musée de la Civilisation Gallo-Romaine Lyons/Dagli Orti 441t;
/Musée de Cluny Paris/Dagli Orti 491b;
/Musée Granet Aix-en-Provence /Dagli Orti 416br;
/Musée du Louvre Paris/Dagli Orti 386t, 426t, 434t, 445b, 465b, 468t, 475b, 492b;
/Musée d'Orsay Paris/Dagli Orti 458b;
/Museo Capitolino Rome/Dagli Orti 305b, 426b, 430t, 497b, 499t;
/Museo della Civita Romana Rome/Dagli Orti 304b, 306t, 428b, 440t, 442t, 445tr, 457t, 461b, 462t, 472t, 474t, 475t, 476b, 483b, 494t, 498t, 498b;
/Museo Concordiese Portogruaro/Dagli Orti 456t;
/Museo Nazionale Ravenna/Dagli Orti 463b;
/Museo Nazionale Terme Rome/Dagli Orti 388t, 412t, 438b, 441b, 469b, 493t;
/Museo Nazionale Romano Rome 429b;
/Museo Opitergino Oderzo Treviso/Dagli Orti 434b;
/Museo Prenestino Palestrina 23t, 152b, 154;
/Museo di Roma Rome/Dagli Orti 292–3;
/National Archaeological Museum Athens/Dagli Orti 444b;
/National Archaeological Museum Chieti 141b;
/National Museum Bucharest 146–7;
/National Mus. Damascus Syria/Dagli Orti 416l;

/Private Collection/Eileen Tweedy 314;
/Provinciaal Museum G.M. Kam Nijmegen Netherlands/ Dagli Orti 396b;
/Santa Costanza Rome/Dagli Orti 259b, 499b;
/Nicolas Sapieha 341t;
/Villa of the Mysteries Pompeii/Dagli Orti 414–15, 424t.

Bridgeman Art Library:
16c, 33b, 37t, 50b, 57t, 61, 66t, 73, 79t, 124b, 126b, 130b, 131b, 179t, 187b, 196t, 234, 246t, 247b, 258t, 272tr, 275b, 279t, 303b, 326t, 364t, 380–1, 383b, 385b, 386b, 390tl, 393b, 395t, 405b, 423b;
/Index 207;
/Lauros Giraudon 190, 228t.

Colchester Museums: 157.

Corbis: 12t, 77b, 87, 88b, 92t, 261m, 297t, 315b, 410b;
/Alinari Archives 271t, 279b, 303t, 408b, 435b, 436t;
/Paul Almasy 75t, 194t, 270b, 375b;
/Roger Antrobus 452b;
/Araldo de Luca 318t, 321b, 329b, 338b, 361b, 389, 390b, 396tl, 397t, 400t, 401b, 407t, 409tl, 409br, 413t, 413b, 417br, 422, 428t, 443b, 471b, 478b, 487b;

/Archivo Iconografico, S.A. 17c, 28b, 54b, 71b, 112t, 113t, 118b, 121, 124t, 129b, 148b, 150, 155b, 168b, 203, 210, 239, 249, 281b, 316b, 323t, 366b, 406b, 436b, 437b, 479b, 482b, 489t; /Arte & Imagini srl 113b; /David Ball 347t; /Dave Bartruff 29t, 408t; /Nathan Benn 218b; /Yann Arthus-Bertrand 119b, 308t; /Bettmann 53b, 57b, 129t, 175b, 194b, 226t, 312b, 350b, 473t; /James P. Blair 12b; /Jonathan Blair 92b; /Tony Brown/Eye Ubiquitous 310t; /Burstein Collection 50t; /Michael Busselle 208b; /Christie's Images 14r, 18–19; /Elio Ciol 430b; /Stephanie Colasanti 366t; /Dean Conger 123, 213t; /Gérard Degeorge 411t; /Robert Estall 69b, 159, 160t; /Macduff Everton 116t, 343t, 344, 345b; /Werner Forman 338t, 402t, 407b, 410t, 497t; /Origlia Franco/Corbis Sygma 417t; /Freelance Consulting Service 311t; /Franz-Marc Frei 48b, 466–7; /Christel Gerstenberg 446–7; /Shai Ginott 219t; /Paul Hardy 323b; /Jason Hawkes 131t, 196b; /John & Dallas Heaton 33t; /Lindsay Hebberd 206b; /Chris Hellier 392b; /John Heseltine 26b; /Chris Hellier 253; /John Heseltine 291b, 315t, 449b; /Historical Picture Archive 216b; /Angelo Hornak 275t, 286b;

/John Howard Cordaiy Photo Library Ltd 240t; /Hulton – Deutsch 43b; /Hanan Isachar 125, 160b, 371t; /Andrea Jemolo 268b, 296b; /Mimmo Jodice 110t, 256t, 326b, 327t, 336b, 337t, 340t, 341b, 346b, 347b, 356t, 358t, 382t, 387t, 396tr, 398–9, 403t, 404b, 418t, 418b, 420t, 420b, 442b, 462b, 485b; /Wolfgang Kaehler 373; /Richard Klune 368b; /Bob Krist 195; /Paul H. Kuiper 180t; /David Lees 281t, 388b; /Charles and Josette Lenars 148t, 152t, 153, 171b, 184, 218t, 219b, 419b, 431t; /Massimo Listri 328b, 387b, 406t; /Araldo de Luca 20–1, 72t, 74b, 126t, 137, 143t, 144t, 156, 164–5, 178t, 182–3, 189b, 192; /Ludovic Maisant 302t; /Lawrence Manning 257b; /Dennis Marsico 278b; /Francis G. Mayer 14l, 17l, 67t, 222; /Michael Nicholson 58t, 161t, 282–3, 367t, 372b, 453t; /North Carolina Museum of Art 31t; /X. Noticias 476t; /Richard T Nowitz 58b, 188b, 286t; /Dagli Orti 15l, 56b; /Polypix Eye Ubiquitous 241b; /Enzo and Paolo Ragazzini 451b; /Vittoriano Rastelli 161b, 277br; /Carmen Redondo 39t, 273b, 276t, 332b, 333t; /Roger Ressmeyer 262m, 354–5, 356t; /Reuters 376t, 397b; /Benjamin Rondel 377t; /Bill Ross 277t; /Hans Georg Roth 285t; /Kevin Schafer 376b;

/Scheufler Collection 24b; /M.L. Sinibaldi 274b; /Grant Smith 145t; /Roman Soumar 177t; /Philip Spruyt 393t; /Stapleton Collection 78, 351t, 451t; /Mark L. Stephenson 313b; /Vince Streano 240b, 284b; /Liba Taylor 517t; /Gustavo Tomsich 27b, 271b; /Ruggero Vanni 39b, 76t, 102–3, 139t, 176b, 230, 244b, 252b, 310b, 318t, 368t, 402b; /Vanni Archive 101b, 110b, 176t, 236b, 238t, 309t, 313t, 317b, 339b, 351b, 357b, 360t, 382b, 394b, 489b; /Sandro Vannini 52t, 199b, 260m, 260r, 362b, 401t, 448t, 472b; /Patrick Ward 120b, 130t, 177b, 204–5; /K.M. Westermann 215t; /Nik Wheeler 114–15, 169t, 352t; /Wild Country 198; /Peter M Wilson 251b, 276b; /Roger Wood 11, 13b, 93, 95t, 98b, 136, 175t, 215b, 223t, 225, 238b, 304t, 309b, 336t, 345tl, 362t, 364b, 365b, 384b, 392t, 425t, 437t, 477t, 495b; /Adam Woolfitt 105t, 162, 180b, 200b, 237t, 243t; /Michael S. Yamashita 258b, 280t, 305t, 394t;

Dr Jon Coulston:
139b.

Dr Hazel Dodge:
28t, 185t.

Mary Evans Picture Library:
15c, 17r, 27t, 41, 140, 197b, 246b; /Edwin Wallace: 454t.

Getty Images/Bridgeman:
29b.

Robert Harding Picture Library:
23b.

www.miniatures.de <http://www.miniatures.de>: 158, 209.

Photo Scala, Florence:
10, 13t, 15r, 22b, 25, 26t, 30, 32, 34t, 35, 36, 38, 42–3, 44, 45t, 46t, 47t, 51b, 52b, 54t, 55t, 60, 67, 68, 69t, 70b, 71t, 72b, 75b, 80b, 81, 84–5, 88t, 90, 91t, 94, 95b, 96, 97, 99t, 100b, 104b, 108b, 109b, 111b, 112b, 122, 128, 138, 163t, 166b, 167, 173t, 174, 202b, 204t, 208t, 211t, 217, 223b, 226b, 232, 235b, 248b, 250, 251t; /© 1990 268tl, 269b, 289, 301t, 306b, 311b, 316t, 319t, 322b, 345tr, 349t, 363b, 412b, 423t, 459, 488b; /© 1999 263l, 280b; /© 1990 Fondo Edifici di Culto – Min. dell'Interno 300t; /© 1990/courtesy of the Ministero Beni e Att. Culturali 261l, 270t, 273t, 294b, 298b, 312t, 324–5, 328t, 330t, 330b, 331t, 331b, 332t, 342t, 343t, 391b, 405t, 448b; /© 2003/Fotografica Foglia 334–5, 450; /© 2003 Luciano Romano 340b; /© 2003/HIP 353t; /© 1998 470b.

512

Anness Publishing Limited, Algores Way, Wisbech
Cambridgeshire, PE13 2TQ

@ Anness Publishing Ltd 2024

Publisher: Joanna Lorenz
Editorial Director: Helen Sudell
Editor: Joy Wotton
Designer: Nigel Partridge
Illustrations and maps: Vanessa Card and Peter Bull Art Studio
Production Controller: Ben Worley

ISBN: 978-1-7821-4339-0

5 7 9 10 8 6

p1. A Roman garrison on the River Nile, from a late 1st-century BC mosaic.
pp. 2-3. View of the Colosseum in Rome.
p4. *Top*: Fresco Painting of the Arrival of Io in Egypt.
p4. *Bottom*: The Temple of Bel in Palmyra, AD32.
p5. *Top*: A 19th-century engraving of the Forum Romanum.
p5. *Bottom*: A wild beast fight.

Above: The imperial guard, from the base of the Obelisk of the 4th-century AD emperor Theodosius I, Constantinople (Istanbul).

Above: The Arch of Trajan at Timgad dominates the ruins of the colony for veterans founded by the emperor Trajan.